SAMS
Teach Yourself

Macromedia®
Studio MX 2004

John Ray

SAMS *800 East 96th Street, Indianapolis, Indiana, 46240 USA*

Sams Teach Yourself Macromedia® Studio MX 2004 All in One

International Standard Book Number: 0-672-32595-0

Library of Congress Catalog Card Number: 200309924

Printed in the United States of America

First Printing: March 2004

07   06   05   04   4   3   2   1

Trademarks

Warning and Disclaimer

Bulk Sales

Sams Publishing offers excellent discounts on this book when ordered in quantity for bulk purchases or special sales. For more information, please contact

> **U.S. Corporate and Government Sales**
> 1-800-382-3419
> corpsales@pearsontechgroup.com

For sales outside of the United States, please contact:

> **International Sales**
> 1-317-428-3341
> international@pearsontechgroup.com

Acquisitions Editor
Betsy Brown

Development Editor
Damon Jordan

Managing Editor
Charlotte Clapp

Project Editor
Sheila Schroeder

Indexer
Erika Millen

Proofreader
Linda Seifert

Technical Editor
Anne Groves

Publishing Coordinator
Vanessa Evans

Designer
Gary Adair

Page Layout
Kelly Maish

Contents at a Glance

Contents at a Glance

Table of Contents

xiv | Sams Teach Yourself Macromedia Studio MX 2004 All in One

Lead Author

John Ray is an award winning developer and technology consultant with more than 16 years of programming and administration experience. He has worked on projects for the FCC, The Ohio State University, Xerox, and the State of Florida, as well as serving as IT director for a Columbus, Ohio-based design and application development company. He has written or contributed to more than 11 titles currently in print, including *Mac OS X Panther Unleashed* and *Sams Teach Yourself Mac OS X Panther All in One*.

Contributing Authors

Betsy Bruce works at MediaPro, Inc., in the Seattle area, where she specializes in creating eLearing applications using Dreamweaver, Authorware, and Flash. She was lead developer on a project with the Cobalt Group, where her team won the 2003 Macromedia Innovation in eLearning award. She is a Macromedia certified trainer for Dreamweaver, CourseBuilder for Dreamweaver, Flash, and Authorware. Betsy received a bachelor's degree from the University of Iowa and is in the process of earning a master's in educational technology from San Diego State University. She is frequently a speaker at conferences on creating eLearning and using Dreamweaver. She is also the author of *eLearning with Dreamweaver MX: Creating Online Learning Applications* from New Riders Publishing. Born and raised in Iowa, Besty now lives on the West Coast. Her Web site is located at www.betsybruce.com.

Phillip Kerman is an independent programmer, teacher, and writer who specializes in Macromedia projects. Phillip has transistioned his expertise from Authorware to Director and, now, to Flash. Over the past decade, he has had to adapt to a total of 20 version upgrades—Flash MX 2004 being the most significant of them all! In addition to retooling and building his own skills, Phillip finds teaching the biggest challenge. He has trained and made presentations around the world, in such exotic locations as Reykjavik, Iceland; Melbourne, Australia; Amsterdam, Holland; and

McAlester, Oklahoma. His writing has appeared in *Macworld*, on the Macromedia DevNet Web site and *Developer Resource Kit* CD-ROM, and in his self-published *The Phillip Newsletter* (www.phillipkerman.com/newsletter). He is also the author of *Flash MX 2004 for Rich Internet Applications* and *ActionScripting in Flash MX* from New Riders Publishing.

Jackson West lives in the San Francisco Bay Area, where he consults on Web programming, graphics, and multimedia applications. He has spent time at a number of top software companies including Microsoft, Macromedia, and Sonic Solutions. He has written for CNET, McGraw-Hill, and Sams Publishing. He is always looking for ways to be cheaper and faster. You can visit Jackson on the Web at www.jacksonwest.com.

Dedication

This book is dedicated to memory.

Acknowledgments

Thanks to all the fine people at Sams: Betsy Brown, Damon Jordan, and Sheila Schroeder. Thanks also to Anne Groves for technical editing. Keeping track of hundreds of files, TOC changes, and finding the imaginatorative words I've made up is a Herculean task that they undertake with ease. Special thanks to all the authors involved in this project—it is their work that makes this a truly great guide.

We Want to Hear from You!

As the reader of this book, *you* are our most important critic and commentator. We value your opinion and want to know what we're doing right, what we could do better, what areas you'd like to see us publish in, and any other words of wisdom you're willing to pass our way.

You can email or write me directly to let me know what you did or didn't like about this book—as well as what we can do to make our books stronger.

Please note that I cannot help you with technical problems related to the topic of this book, and that due to the high volume of mail I receive, I might not be able to reply to every message.

When you write, please be sure to include this book's title and author as well as your name and phone or email address. I will carefully review your comments and share them with the author and editors who worked on the book.

E-mail: graphics@samspublishing.com

Mail: Mark Taber
Associate Publisher
Sams Publishing
800 East 96th Street
Indianapolis, IN 46240 USA

Reader Services

For more information about this book or others from Sams Publishing, visit our Web site at www.samspublishing.com. Type the ISBN (excluding hyphens) or the title of the book in the Search box to find the book you're looking for.

Introduction

Welcome to *Sams Teach Yourself Macromedia Studio MX 2004 All in One*. This book is designed to give you a fast and easy start with Macromedia's cutting edge Web, animation, and design tools. Macromedia's Studio MX 2004 bundle brings together the leading Web design tool, Dreamweaver MX 2004; the leading online and CD-ROM animation tool, Flash MX 2004; and the excellent bitmap and vector graphics software, Fireworks MX 2004 and FreeHand MX 2004. Together, these tools can create a smooth workflow for professional print or Web design, taking into account all aspects of the design and production process. If you haven't yet explored the Studio MX 2004 tools, here's what you'll find:

Dreamweaver MX 2004—Dreamweaver MX is arguably the most intuitive and easy-to-use Web design application to date. Using a fully WYSIWYG environment, Dreamweaver allows you to plan, design, and implement a Web site, be it 1 or 1,000 pages. Best of all, the HTML code written by Dreamweaver is easy to understand and is optimized to make your pages load as quickly as possible.

Fireworks MX 2004—Whereas Dreamweaver MX focuses on the design and layout facets of a Web site, Fireworks can be used for creating and manipulating the graphics you'll use on your pages. Everything from fine-tuned image optimization to creating rollover graphics can be handled in Fireworks. Not interested in Web graphics? Fireworks MX is also a great drawing and photo manipulation program!

Flash MX 2004—Flash is the undisputed champion of online and CD-ROM interactive animation. Flash MX provides the tools you need to create your own animated graphics and films from scratch. Unlike movies for your DVD player, Flash animation is very compressed and scalable, making it a viable solution for creating dynamic Web content, even on slow connections.

FreeHand MX—Rounding out the Macromedia Studio MX 2004 suite is FreeHand MX. FreeHand provides professional-grade illustration tools that can be used in Dreamweaver or Flash or manipulated in Fireworks. FreeHand's tools range from simple pens and pencils to 3D extrusion functions.

Other books you might have seen provide a basic reference to these applications, but we take you through the topics one by one and give you the steps you need to successfully use the product. We've also designed the book to let you start where to want, with the topics that interest you the most. There are, however, a few concepts you should be familiar with when getting started with Studio MX:

Panels—Panels are separate sections of the Studio MX workspace that provide control over various functions, such as selecting colors or organizing files.

Panel groups—Panels are arranged into panel groups. A group is a collection of related panels you can switch between by clicking tabs at the top of the group. For example, the Studio MX products include a Color Mixer panel and a Tint panel for finding the colors you want to use, and these panels are grouped in a Colors panel group.

Properties Inspector—A special panel in all the Studio tools is the Properties Inspector. When an object (a graphic, text, a table, an animation, and so on) is selected in your document, the Properties Inspector changes to show the special settings for that object. This enables you to perform complex editing operations without going to the menu bar or opening additional windows.

Menus—Finally, the Studio MX menu system shares several common menus: View controls how your document appears onscreen, with rulers, grids, and so on. The Insert menu adds objects to your document, and the Modify menu provides functions for manipulating the object that is currently selected in your document.

We start each product with an introduction to the interface elements; knowing these simple concepts will let you become comfortable with moving from one application to another. Chapter 1, "Understanding the Dreamweaver and Macromedia Studio Interface," covers these topics in depth and is a recommended read regardless of which application you're going to use first.

That said, we've got a lot of ground to cover, so let's get started using Macromedia Studio MX 2004!

PART I
Dreamweaver

CHAPTER 1

Understanding the Dreamweaver and Macromedia Studio Interface

I'm sure you are itching to begin creating dazzling and fun Web sites, the type that you'll show off to your friends, family members, and co-workers. Or maybe you've been assigned the task of creating a Web site in Dreamweaver for your job. First, however, you need to understand the Dreamweaver interface and the numerous functions that are going to help you be successful as a Web developer. Understanding the basic Macromedia user interface enables you to understand the instructions in the rest of this book and throughout the Macromedia 2004 Suite.

Even if you don't want to start with Dreamweaver MX, reviewing this chapter serves as a good primer for the rest of the Macromedia Studio products. Specifically, pay close attention to the section "Panels and Inspectors" as we won't be explaining this topic in the same amount of detail for the other Studio products.

By the Way

Acquainting Yourself with Dreamweaver

Dreamweaver is a complete Web development environment—an HTML (Hypertext Markup Language) editor, an authoring tool, a dynamic Web page development tool, and a Web site management tool, all rolled into one. Web pages are created using HTML, but you can do many things without ever laying your eyes on any HTML. If you want to produce professional-quality Web pages, including scripting, Dreamweaver makes it easy to do so.

HTML is the language of Web pages. It consists mainly of paired tags contained in angle brackets (<>). The tags surround objects on a Web page, such as text, or stand on their own. For instance, the HTML code to make text bold looks like this: `<b>bold text</b>`; these bold tags are an example of paired tags. The ending tag of paired tag always begins with a forward slash. Other tags, such as the tag used to insert an image into a Web page, are single tags: `<img src="smile.gif">`.

Dreamweaver is a WYSIWYG (what you see is what you get) Web page editor that is extremely powerful while also being easy to use. You can create new Web sites by using Dreamweaver, and you can import and edit existing Web sites. Dreamweaver will not change or rearrange your code. One of Dreamweaver's most popular features has always been that it leaves existing sites intact; the folks at Macromedia, the company that creates Dreamweaver, call this feature **Roundtrip HTML**.

Dreamweaver is also an authoring tool. What do I mean by *authoring tool*? **Authoring tools** enable you to create a complete application that includes interactivity. Dreamweaver can be used as simply an HTML editor, and it can also be used to create multimedia applications. You can author an experience for your viewers.

Dreamweaver MX 2004 can create dynamic Web pages. **Dynamic Web pages** are created using server-side scripting and require that you understand server technologies and other advanced topics. Although these topics are outside the scope of this book, they should not necessarily be outside the scope of *your* interests. This book teaches you how to create regular Web pages that do not depend on server-side scripting or any special server features to create. You'll need to understand the material in this book before you move on to dynamic Web pages.

Exploring the Dreamweaver Work Area

When you first open Dreamweaver in Windows, you are given the opportunity to choose either the Designer workspace or the HomeSite/Coder-Style workspace, as shown in Figure 1.1. I suggest that you pick the Designer workspace; all the figures and examples in this book refer to that workspace configuration. The HomeSite/Coder-Style workspace is designed for Web developers who write HTML by hand. The Macintosh version of Dreamweaver gives you the Designer workspace.

If you select the HomeSite/Coder-Style workspace and then want to change to the Designer workspace, you can do so in the Dreamweaver Preferences dialog box. To open the Preferences dialog box, select Edit, Preferences in Windows (Dreamweaver, Preferences on the Mac). Select the General category and click the Change Workspace button. You'll again see the Workspace Setup dialog box, and you can use it to change your workspace configuration. You'll explore many other Dreamweaver preferences throughout this book.

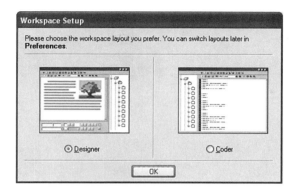

FIGURE 1.1
You can change the workspace by selecting either the Designer or the HomeSite/Coder-Style workspace in the Workspace Setup dialog box.

The Start Page

Dreamweaver initially displays a box with a green bar across the top, called the Start page. The Start page lists common Dreamweaver tasks, such as Open a Recent Item, Create New, and Create from Samples. At the bottom of the Start page are links to the Dreamweaver Quick Tour and the Dreamweaver Tutorial. Clicking the image of the Dreamweaver box takes you to the Macromedia Web site for up-to-date information on Dreamweaver, including tips and special offers. Whenever you don't have Web pages open in Dreamweaver, you will see the Start page displayed.

The Start page appears in an important part of Dreamweaver called the Document window. The **Document window** displays a Web page approximately as it will appear in a Web browser. The Document window is bordered on the right by **panels**, as shown in Figure 1.2. These panels contain the commands you use to modify and organize Web pages and Web page elements. The Document window, the panels, and other elements, which you'll explore in a few minutes, are grouped together into an integrated interface if you are working in the Windows operating system.

When you open Dreamweaver MX 2004 for Macintosh, you also see the Document window displaying the Start page, as shown in Figure 1.3. The Macintosh version of Dreamweaver MX 2004 has panels that float on top of the Document window. The floating panels, launched from the Window menu, can be moved to any location on the desktop. The Mac and Windows versions of Dreamweaver look slightly different from each other but have the same features and functionality.

Insert bar   Document window   Document toolbar   Panel group

FIGURE 1.2
The Dreamweaver workspace contains the Document window along with integrated panels.

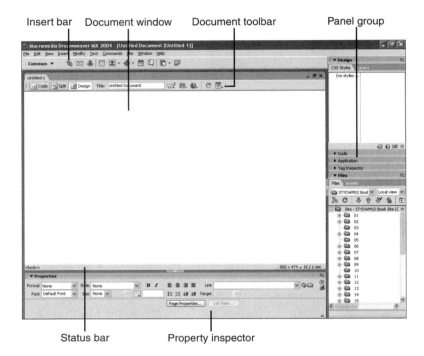

Status bar   Property inspector

Insert bar

FIGURE 1.3
The Macintosh workspace includes the Document window with panels that float on top.

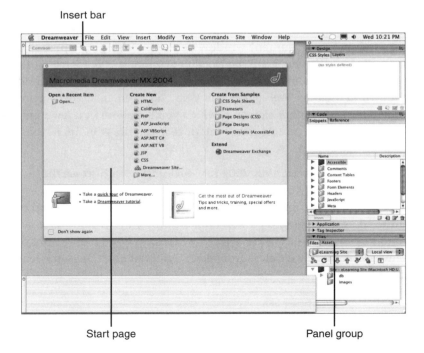

Start page   Panel group

The Menu Bar

Some people prefer using menu commands (I like keyboard shortcuts) and some people prefer clicking icons. For the menu crowd, this section describes the organization of Dreamweaver's menus. The File and Edit menus (see Figure 1.4) are standard in most programs. The File menu contains commands for opening, closing, saving, importing, and exporting files. The Edit menu contains the Cut, Copy, and Paste commands, along with the Find and Replace command and the Preferences command. Many elements of the Dreamweaver user interface and its operation can be configured with the Preferences command.

FIGURE 1.4
The File and Edit menus contain commands that are common to many applications, plus a few Dreamweaver-specific ones.

The View menu controls what you are seeing onscreen. In Dreamweaver MX, it turns on and off your view of the head content; invisible elements; layer, table, and frame borders; the status bar; and image maps. You can tell whether you are currently viewing one of these elements if a check mark is shown beside it. The View menu also has commands to turn on the ruler and grid, play plug-ins, and show a tracing image. It's okay if you don't understand what these commands enable you to do—you'll learn more about them in later chapters.

The Insert menu is roughly equivalent to the Insert bar or Tool panel because you can insert all the available items (objects, tools, and so on). If you prefer to click icons, use the Insert bar, but if you prefer to see the names of the objects you insert in your Web pages, use the Insert menu. The Modify menu enables you to modify properties of the currently selected object.

The Text menu gives you access to multiple ways of fine-tuning the appearance of the text in a Web page. Most important to those of you who are questionable spellers, the Text menu contains the Check Spelling command. The Text menu mirrors many of the properties available in the Properties Inspector when text is selected. You can use this menu to indent text, create a list, and modify font properties, as you will explore in the next chapter. The Commands menu offers useful commands such as Clean Up HTML and Clean Up Word HTML. You can also use this menu to record and play an animation or format and sort a table. And you can set up a color scheme and automatically jump out to Macromedia Fireworks to optimize an image.

The Site menu presents the commands that have to do with an entire Web site. You will explore Dreamweaver Web site management in Chapter 3, "Planning and Defining Your Project," and Chapter 18, "Uploading Your Dreamweaver Project." The Window menu opens all the Dreamweaver panels and inspectors. There's also a list of all the open files at the bottom of this menu.

You'll learn about the help system in a couple minutes. Along with providing links to the HTML-based help files, the Help menu, contains commands to register your Dreamweaver software online. Selecting the About Dreamweaver command is useful if you need to find out which version of Dreamweaver you are running or your serial number.

The Insert Bar

The **Insert bar** is directly beneath the menu bar in Windows and is a floating panel on the Mac. It contains buttons for inserting Web page elements, such as images, tables, forms, and hyperlinks. You can either click or drag a button's icon to insert that object into a Web page. All the objects in the Insert bar are also accessible from the Insert menu.

The Insert bar has a drop-down menu on its left that enables you to choose from the seven different categories of objects available: Common, Layout, Forms, Text, HTML, Application, and Favorites. To display the object buttons of a certain category, drop down the menu and then select the category. By default, the Common category is displayed, but if you are working on forms, you might want to display the Forms category, or if you are laying out the structure of a page, you might want to display the Layout category.

Some of the objects in the Insert bar are drop-down menus that organize a group of related objects. For instance, in the Common category, the Images object drops down a menu displaying Image, Placeholder Image, Rollover Image, Fireworks HTML, Navigation Bar, Draw Rectangle Hotspot, Draw Oval Hotspot, and Draw Polygon Hotspot. All these objects have to do with images, so they are grouped together in a single drop-down menu in the Insert bar.

The Insert bar is displayed in Menu mode by default, but you can display the Insert bar in Tabs mode by selecting the last command in the drop-down menu, the Show as Tabs command, as shown in Figure 1.5. Selecting the Show as Tabs command displays the Insert bar categories as tabs across the top of the Insert bar, as shown in Figure 1.6. To return the Insert bar to Menu mode, select the Show as Menu command in the Insert bar drop-down menu.

FIGURE 1.5
The Insert bar drop-down menu displays a list of the categories and the Show as Tabs command, which enables you to display a tabbed Insert bar.

Table 1.1 lists all the objects, with descriptions, that are available in the Insert bar. The table briefly describes each of the objects in the Insert bar except those found in the Application tab because those objects are used strictly for creating dynamic Web pages. The objects in the Layout tab are always found at the bottom of the floating Insert bar on the Mac. While you read through this table, familiarize yourself with the types of objects and content you can add to a Web page in Dreamweaver.

FIGURE 1.6
In Tabs mode, the
Insert bar cate-
gories appear as
tabs across the top
of the bar.

TABLE 1.1   Insert Bar Objects

Icon	Icon Name	Description
Common Category		
	Hyperlink	Inserts a hyperlink, including the text and the link location.
	Email Link	Adds a hyperlink that launches an empty email message to a specific email address when clicked.
	Named Anchor	Places a named anchor at the insertion point. **Named anchors** are used to create hyperlinks within a file.
	Table	Creates a table at the insertion point.
	Image	Places an image at the insertion point. (In the Images drop-down menu.)
	Image Placeholder	Inserts a placeholder for an image. (In the Images drop-down menu.)
	Rollover Image	Prompts you for two images: the regular image and the image that appears when the user puts his or her cursor over the image. (In the Images drop-down menu.)
	Fireworks HTML	Places HTML that has been exported from Macromedia Fireworks at the insertion point. (In the Images drop-down menu.)

TABLE 1.1 Continued

Icon	Icon Name	Description
Common Category		
	Navigation Bar	Inserts a set of button images to be used for navigating throughout the Web site. (In the Images drop-down menu.)
	Draw Rectangle Hotspot	Allows you to draw a rectangle over a specific region of an image and link it to a specific URL. (In the Images drop-down menu.)
	Draw Oval Hotspot	Allows you to draw an oval over a specific region of an image and link it to a specific URL. (In the Images drop-down menu.)
	Draw Polygon Hotspot	Allows you to draw a polygon over a specific region of an image and link it to a specific URL. (In the Images drop-down menu.)
	Flash	Places a Macromedia Flash movie at the insertion point. (In the Media drop-down menu.)
	Flash Button	Places one of the available prefabricated Macromedia Flash buttons at the insertion point. (In the Media drop-down menu.)
	Flash Text	Places an editable Flash Text object at the insertion point and creates a Flash file. (In the Media drop-down menu.)
	Shockwave	Places a **Shockwave movie** (that is, a Macromedia Director movie prepared for the Web) at the insertion point. (In the Media drop-down menu.)
	Applet	Places a Java applet at the insertion point. (In the Media drop-down menu.)
	Param	Inserts a tag that enables you to enter parameters and their values to pass to an applet or an ActiveX control. (In the Media drop-down menu.)
	ActiveX	Places an ActiveX control at the insertion point. (In the Media drop-down menu.)
	Plugin	Places any file requiring a browser plug-in at the insertion point. (In the Media drop-down menu.)
	Date	Inserts the current date at the insertion point.

TABLE 1.1   Continued

Icon	Icon Name	Description
Common Category		
	Comment	Inserts a comment at the insertion point.
	Make Template	Creates a Dreamweaver template from the current Web page. (In the Templates drop-down menu.)
	Make Nested Template	Creates a nested Dreamweaver template from the current template. (In the Templates drop-down menu.)
	Editable Region	Adds an editable region to a template. (In the Templates drop-down menu.)
	Optional Region	Adds an optional region to a template; this region can be set to either show or hide. (In the Templates drop-down menu.)
	Repeating Region	Adds a repeating region to a template. (In the Templates drop-down menu.)
	Editable Optional Region	Adds an editable optional region to a template. (In the Templates drop-down menu.)
	Repeating Table	Adds a repeating table to a template and defines which cells can be edited. (In the Templates drop-down menu.)
	Tag Chooser	Enables you to choose a tag to insert from a hierarchical menu of all available tags.
Layout Category		
	Table	Creates a table at the insertion point. (Also in the Common category.)
	Insert Div Tag	Adds a `<div>` tag, the tag that Dreamweaver uses to create layers.
	Draw Layer	Draws a layer container in a Web page.
Standard	Standard Mode	Turns on Dreamweaver's Standard mode, at the same time turning off either Expanded Tables mode or Layout mode.
Expanded	Expanded Tables Mode	Turns on Dreamweaver's Expanded Tables mode, temporarily adding cell padding and borders to all tables.
Layout	Layout Mode	Turns on Dreamweaver's Layout mode, enabling you to draw tables and table cells.

TABLE 1.1 Continued

Icon	Icon Name	Description
Layout Category		
	Layout Table	Draws a table while you're in Layout view.
	Draw Layout Cell	Draws a table cell while you're in Layout view.
	Insert Row Above	Adds a row above the currently selected row of a table.
	Insert Row Below	Adds a row beneath the currently selected row of a table.
	Insert Column to the Left	Adds a column to the left of the currently selected column in a table.
	Insert Column to the Right	Adds a column to the right of a currently selected column in a table.
	Left Frame	Creates a frame to the left of the current frame. (In the Frames drop-down menu.)
	Right Frame	Creates a frame to the right of the current frame. (In the Frames drop-down menu.)
	Top Frame	Creates a frame above the current frame. (In the Frames drop-down menu.)
	Bottom Frame	Creates a frame below the current frame. (In the Frames drop-down menu.)
	Bottom and Nested Left Frame	Creates a frame to the left of the current frame and then adds a frame below. (In the Frames drop-down menu.)
	Bottom and Nested Right Frame	Creates a frame to the right of the current frame and then adds a frame below. (In the Frames drop-down menu.)
	Left and Nested Bottom Frame	Creates a frame below the current frame and then adds a frame to the left. (In the Frames drop-down menu.)
	Right and Nested Bottom Frame	Creates a frame below the current frame and then adds a frame to the right. (In the Frames drop-down menu.)
	Top and Bottom Frame	Creates a frame below the current frame and then adds a frame above. (In the Frames drop-down menu.)

TABLE 1.1 Continued

Icon	Icon Name	Description
Layout Category		
	Left and Nested Top Frame	Creates a frame above the current frame and then adds a frame to the left. (In the Frames drop-down menu.)
	Right and Nested Top Frame	Creates a frame above the current frame and then adds a frame to the right. (In the Frames drop-down menu.)
	Top and Nested Left Frame	Creates a frame to the left of the current frame and then adds a frame above. (In the Frames drop-down menu.)
	Top and Nested Right Frame	Creates a frame to the right of the current frame and then adds a frame above. (In the Frames drop-down menu.)
	Tabular Data	Creates at the insertion point a table that is populated with data from a chosen file. (In the Frames drop-down menu.)
Forms Category		
	Form	Places a form at the insertion point.
	Text Field	Inserts a text field.
	Hidden Field	Inserts a hidden field.
	Textarea	Inserts a textarea, which is a multiline text field.
	Check Box	Inserts a check box.
	Radio Button	Inserts a radio button.
	Radio Group	Inserts a group of related radio buttons.
	List/Menu	Inserts a list or a drop-down menu.
	Jump Menu	Creates a jump menu that allows users to select a Web site from a menu and go to that site.
	Image Field	Inserts an image field, which enables an image to act as a button.

TABLE 1.1   Continued

Icon	Icon Name	Description
Forms Category		
	File Field	Inserts a file field, which enables the user to upload a file.
	Button	Inserts a button.
	Label	Assigns a label to a form element, enabling browsers for people with visual impairments to access extra information about the form elements nested within the label.
	Fieldset	Groups related form fields together to make the form accessible to browsers for people with visual impairments. Fieldset wraps around a group of form elements and appears to sighted people as a box drawn around the group, with the fieldset title at the top.
Text Category		
	Font Tag Editor	Opens the Font Tag Editor to set up the attributes of a font tag.
	Bold	Makes the selected text bold by using the b tag. This tag has been dropped from recent versions of HTML. The approved tag for bold text is the strong tag.
	Italic	Makes the selected text italic. This tag has been dropped from recent versions of HTML. The approved tag for italic text is the emphasis tag.
	Strong	Makes the selected text bold by using the approved strong tag.
	Emphasis	Makes the selected text italic by using the approved emphasis tag.
	Paragraph	Makes the selected text into a paragraph.
	Block Quote	Makes the selected text into a block quote, indented from the right and the left by using the blockquote tag.
	Preformatted Text	Makes the selected text preformatted (using the pre tag, displaying the text in a monospaced font and with the ability to enter spaces).

TABLE 1.1 Continued

Icon	Icon Name	Description
Text Category		
h1	Heading 1	Makes the selected text a heading size 1 (largest) by using the h1 tag.
h2	Heading 2	Makes the selected text a heading size 2 by using the h2 tag.
h3	Heading 3	Makes the selected text a heading size 3 by using the h3 tag.
ul	Unordered List	Makes the selected text into an unordered (bulleted) list.
ol	Ordered List	Makes the selected text into an ordered (numbered) list.
li	List Item	Makes the selected text into a list item (by using the li tag), a single item in an ordered or unordered list.
dl	Definition List	Creates a definition list. A **definition list** consists of definition terms and definition descriptions.
dt	Definition Term	Creates a definition term within a definition list.
dd	Definition Description	Creates a definition description within a definition list.
abbr.	Abbreviation	Wraps the abbr tag around text, adding a full-text definition to an abbreviation. This aids search engines in indexing a Web page properly.
W3C	Acronym	Wraps the acronym tag around text, adding a full-text definition to an acronym. This aids search engines in indexing a Web page properly.
BR	Line Break	Places a line break, the br tag, at the insertion point. (In the Characters drop-down menu.)
"	Left Quote	Inserts the special character for a left quote. (In the Characters drop-down menu.)
"	Right Quote	Inserts the special character for a right quote. (In the Characters drop-down menu.)
—	Em-Dash	Inserts the special character for an em dash (—). (In the Characters drop-down menu.)

TABLE 1.1 Continued

Icon	Icon Name	Description
Text Category		
£	Pound	Inserts the special character for the pound currency symbol. (In the Characters drop-down menu.)
€	Euro	Inserts the special character for the euro currency symbol. (In the Characters drop-down menu.)
¥	Yen	Inserts the special character for the yen currency symbol. (In the Characters drop-down menu.)
©	Copyright	Inserts the special character for the copyright symbol. (In the Characters drop-down menu.)
®	Registered Trademark	Inserts the special character for the registered trademark symbol. (In the Characters drop-down menu.)
TM	Trademark	Inserts the special character for the trademark symbol. (In the Characters drop-down menu.)
	Other Characters	Opens a menu that displays many additional special characters. (In the Characters drop-down menu.)
HTML Category		
	Horizontal Rule	Inserts a horizontal rule, a simple divider line across the page.
	Meta	Inserts a `meta` tag into the head section of a Web page. This object can insert a `name meta` tag, aiding search engines, or an `http-equiv meta` tag that can redirect the user to a different URL or give additional information about the Web page, such as assigning parental control information to a page. (In the Head drop-down menu.)
	Keywords	Inserts a `keywords` meta tag into the head section, adding keywords to the Web page to help search engines properly index it. (In the Head drop-down menu.)
	Description	Inserts a `description` meta tag into the head section, adding a description to the Web page helping search engines properly index it. (In the Head drop-down menu.)

TABLE 1.1　Continued

Icon	Icon Name	Description
HTML Category		
	Refresh	Inserts a `refresh` meta tag into the head section. This tag sets the number of seconds before the page will automatically jump to another Web page or reload itself. (In the Head drop-down menu.)
	Base	Inserts a `base` tag into the head section. This enables you to set a base URL or a base target window affecting all the paths on the Web page. (In the Head drop-down menu.)
	Link	Inserts the address of an external file, usually a script or style sheet file. (In the Head drop-down menu.)
	Table Tag	Inserts a `table` tag (in Code view only). (In the Tables drop-down menu.)
	Table Row	Inserts a `tr` tag (in Code view only). (In the Tables drop-down menu.)
	Table Header	Inserts a `th` tag (in Code view only). (In the Tables drop-down menu.)
	Table Data	Inserts a `td` tag (in Code view only). (In the Tables drop-down menu.)
	Table Caption	Inserts a `caption` tag (in Code view only). (In the Tables drop-down menu.)
	Frameset	Inserts a `frameset` tag (in Code view only). (In the Frames drop-down menu.)
	Frame	Inserts a `frame` tag (in Code view only). (In the Frames drop-down menu.)
	Floating Frame	Inserts an `iframe` tag (in Code view only). (In the Frames drop-down menu.)
	No Frames	Inserts a `noframes` tag to surround HTML code for browsers that cannot display frames (in Code view only). (In the Frames drop-down menu.)
	Script	Inserts scripted code at the insertion point. (In the Script drop-down menu.)

TABLE 1.1 Continued

Icon	Icon Name	Description
HTML Category		
	No Script	Inserts the `noscript` tag surrounding HTML code that will be displayed by browsers that do not support scripts. (In the Script drop-down menu.)
	Server-Side Include	Places a file that simulates a server-side include at the insertion point. (In the Script drop-down menu.)

The Favorites category enables you to add objects that you use frequently to a single Insert bar category. By the end of this book you will have a better idea of the types of objects you'll want to place in the Favorites category to help you work more quickly in Dreamweaver. These are your personal favorites, the objects that you use most often, collected in one handy Insert bar category.

The Document Window

By default the Document window is maximized and its title and filename appear at the very top of the screen. You'll explore saving a file, giving it a filename, and giving it a title in Chapter 2, "Creating a Basic Web Page with Text." The Document window is the part of the Dreamweaver interface that you will be using most often in your work. The Document toolbar appears at the top of the Document window.

The Document Toolbar

The Document toolbar, shown in Figure 1.7, gives you quick access to important commands. The three buttons on the left of the Document toolbar enable you to toggle between Code view, Design view, and a split view with both Code view and Design view visible. I probably use Design view 90% of the time and divide the other 10% of my Dreamweaver time between Code view and the split view. The split view showing both Design and Code views is useful when you're learning HTML because it enables you to see the tags that Dreamweaver adds while you create a Web page.

The text box in the Document toolbar is where you give a Web page a title (the default title—Untitled Document—isn't very interesting!). This Web page title appears in the user's browser title bar when the user views the page. It is also saved in the browser's Favorites or Bookmarks list as the name of the URL, so it needs to be meaningful.

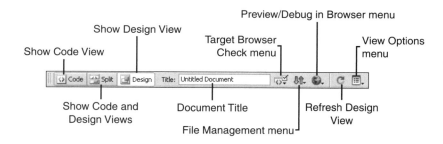

FIGURE 1.7
The Document
toolbar contains
commands you
commonly apply to
Web pages when
editing in
Dreamweaver.

There are four drop-down menus on the toolbar: the Target Browser Check menu, the File Management menu, the Preview/Debug in Browser menu, and the View Options menu. The Target Browser Check menu enables you to check that your Web page works correctly in various browsers. The File Management menu lists commands such as those for getting files to and from a Web server. The Preview/Debug in Browser menu gives you quick access to the list of browsers you'll use to preview Web pages. The Refresh Design View button refreshes Design view when you are editing the code (in Code view or the split screen view) so that you can instantly see the changes you make to the code.

By the Way

Where's My Document Toolbar?

If the Document toolbar isn't visible in your Document window, select View, Toolbar, Document.

The View Options menu changes, depending on whether you have Design or Code view open. While you're in Design view, this menu displays commands that are also in Dreamweaver's View menu, such as those for viewing head content or the rulers. While you're in Code view, the View Options menu contains commands that affect the way the code is displayed, such as Word Wrap and Line Numbers.

The Status Bar

The Dreamweaver Document windowhas a status bar along the bottom of the page. It contains the tag selector, the Window Size drop-down menu, and download statistics, as shown in Figure 1.8. These convenient tools are just some of the nice touches that Dreamweaver offers to help you have a productive and fun experience designing for the Web.

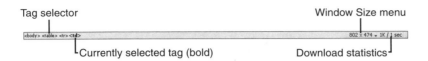

Tag selector

Window Size menu

`<body> <table> <tr> <td>`   802 x 474 ▾ 1K / 1 sec

Currently selected tag (bold)

Download statistics

FIGURE 1.8
The status bar contains tools that help you get information about a Web page.

The tag selector in the lower-left corner of the Document window provides easy access to the HTML tags that are involved in any object on the screen. If, for example, the cursor is located in a table cell, the tag selector enables selection of any of the HTML tags that control that object. The tag that is currently selected is shown in bold in the tag selector. The tags to the left of the selected tag are the tags that are wrapped around the selected tag.

The Tag Selector Is Your Friend

The tag selector will be important later, when you start using behaviors in Chapter 14, "Inserting Scripted Functionality by Using Behaviors," and Chapter 15, "Adding Advanced Behaviors: The Drag Layer Behavior." You apply behaviors to specific tags, and sometimes the tags are difficult to select, especially the <body> tag, which contains the entire Web page content. The tag selector makes it very easy to select the entire body of a Web page by clicking the <body> tag.

Did you Know?

The Window Size drop-down menu helps you re-create a target screen resolution by resizing the Document window. You will always want to make sure that your design looks good at a low (800×600) or high screen resolution. You can use the Window Size drop-down menu (see Figure 1.9) to quickly resize the Document window to view the approximate amount of screen real estate you will have at a certain resolution. The Window Size drop-down menu works only when you do not have the Document window maximized.

Notice the sizes available in the Window Size menu:

▶ The dimensions listed on the right (in parentheses) represent the screen resolutions.

▶ The numbers listed on the left are the estimated browser window dimensions. They are smaller than the screen resolutions because the browser interface (buttons and menus, for instance) takes up space. For example, when the viewer's monitor is set to 640×480, the viewable area is only 536×196 pixels.

Maximize button

FIGURE 1.9
The Window Size menu resizes the screen, approximating how the page will look at different screen resolutions.

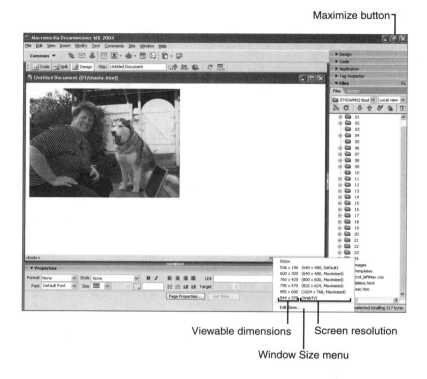

Viewable dimensions   Screen resolution

Window Size menu

Define Special Window Sizes

Create your own custom settings for the Window Size menu by selecting the last choice in the Window Size pop-up menu, the Edit Sizes command. This command takes you to the Status Bar category in the Dreamweaver Preferences dialog box, where you can add your custom window size. For instance, do you want to create a Web page that is readable on your wireless phone? My phone has the capability to view 120×160 pixels, so I could create a custom size to create a Web page for my phone.

Because bandwidth is often an issue when you're developing for the Web, it's nice to know the estimated file size and download time of a Web page. The estimated download time shown in the status bar is based on the modem setting in the Status Bar category in the Dreamweaver Preferences dialog box. The default modem setting is 28.8Kbps; you might want to change this setting to 56Kbps or whatever the bandwidth speed is for the targeted viewer of your Web page. (Most people in the United States browse the Web at a speed of at least 56Kbps.)

Dreamweaver takes into account images and other assets contained in the Web page when calculating the file size and download time.

Panels and Inspectors

You set properties of objects, display panels, and add functionality to Web page through Dreamweaver's panels and inspectors. Most commands in Dreamweaver are available in several places, usually as menu commands and as panel commands. Dreamweaver's panels are grouped into tabbed panel groups beside the Document window (Windows) or floating on top (Mac).

You can open every panel from the Window menu and by default Dreamweaver has all the important panels and the Properties Inspector open. If a panel or inspector is open, its command has a check mark beside it in the Window menu. To close a panel or an inspector, deselect the command in the Window menu. The panel doesn't actually go away, but the panel group's expander arrow turns and the panel group collapses so that you don't see it anymore. Command names in the Window menu may be slightly different from the names of the panels or inspectors they launch. For instance, you open the Properties Inspector using the Properties command and the Insert bar using the Insert command.

Panels and Panel Groups

You can expand or collapse a panel group or an inspector by clicking the expander arrow to the left of the panel title, as shown in Figure 1.10. Immediately to the left of the expander arrow is the gripper. You can undock a panel group or inspector by selecting its gripper and dragging the panel group away from where it is docked. To dock a panel group or inspector, select its gripper and drag-and-drop above or below the other panel groups or the Document window. When it is docked, you'll see an outline around the panel group. Because the Macintosh version of Dreamweaver has floating panels, you can move them wherever you want anytime!

In the Windows integrated user interface, resize the width of all the panel groups by dragging the bar that separates the panel groups and the Document window. To resize the height of an individual panel group, move your cursor to the edge of the panel until it turns into a double-arrow cursor and drag the edges of the panel to the desired height. Windows users can use the Collapse button, shown in Figure 1.11, within the bars that separate the Document window from the panel groups and the Properties Inspector to toggle expanding and collapsing those two areas. Mac users can change the size of floating panel groups by dragging the borders of the group to the desired width and height.

Gripper

Expander arrow

FIGURE 1.10
Expand and col-
lapse panel groups
using the expander
arrow.

Collapse button

FIGURE 1.11
The Collapse but-
tons collapse and
expand the panel
group area and the
Properties
Inspector area so
that you have more
room for the
Document
window.

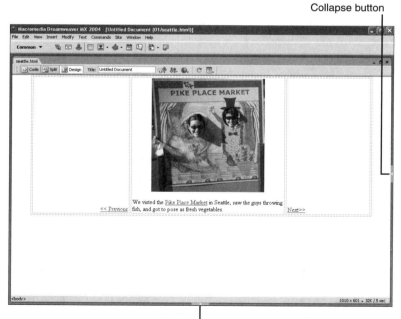

Collapse button

Advanced Panel Maintenance

You can completely close a panel group, removing it from display on the screen, by selecting the Close Panel Group command in the panel drop-down menu located in the upper right of each panel group. There's also a command listed in this menu that enables you to group a panel with a different panel group: Select the Group With command to select a different panel group.

The Properties Inspector

The Properties Inspector displays all the properties of the currently selected object. The Properties Inspector is like a chameleon that changes depending on the environment; it looks different and displays appropriate properties for whichever object is selected. For example, when text is selected onscreen, the Properties Inspector presents text properties, as shown in Figure 1.12.

Selected text

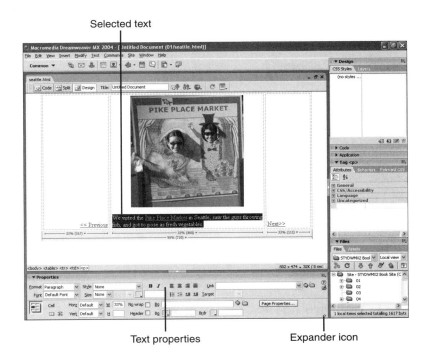

Text properties   Expander icon

FIGURE 1.12
The Properties Inspector displays text properties when text is selected.

You can expand the Properties Inspector by using the Expander icon so that you have access to every available property. You do this by selecting the expander arrow in the lower-right corner of the Properties Inspector.

Context Menus

There are multiple ways to access and modify object properties in the Macromedia Studio. I'm sure you'll find your favorite ways very quickly. Context menus are one of the choices available. These menus pop up when you right-click (Control+click on the Mac) an object in the Document window. The contents of the menu are dependent on which object you clicked. For instance, Figure 1.13 shows the context menu that pops up when you right-click a table.

FIGURE 1.13
The context menu for tables gives you quick access to many table commands.

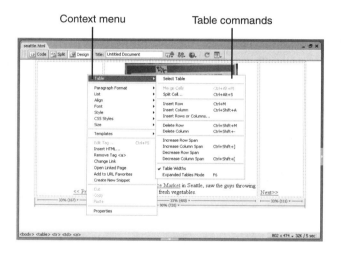

Getting Help

You select Help, Using Dreamweaver (or use the standard help shortcut key, F1) to launch the Dreamweaver help files. The left side of the help page contains the Contents, Index, Search, and Favorites tabs. The right side of the page is where the help content files appear. The Next and Previous arrow buttons enable you to page through all the help topics.

Did you Know?

Using Help to Learn About Dreamweaver

While you are getting familiar with Dreamweaver, you might want to use the arrow buttons in the upper- and lower-right corners of the help content area to navigate through the topics. The topics are grouped, so you might get more information on your current topic on the next page. If you keep clicking either of these arrows, eventually you will go on to another topic.

In Windows, the Contents tab displays the table of contents. The table of contents is organized in subject categories. Selecting one of the categories expands the list, with subtopics under that category. The Index button shows an alphabetical index of all topics in the help system. Select the Search tab to enter a topic you want to search for. Create your own list of favorite help topics by selecting the Favorites tab and clicking the Add button at the bottom to add the current topic.

Dreamweaver help on the Mac looks slightly different from Windows help; it displays in the Macintosh Help Viewer. Click on the Index or Table of Contents links at the top of the left panel to toggle between the two display modes.

One of the easiest ways to get help on your current task is to launch context-sensitive help. When you have an object selected (and you can see its properties in the Properties Inspector), click the Help icon in the Properties Inspector to go directly to information about that object.

Summary

In this chapter, you have learned about the Dreamweaver Document window and other elements of the Dreamweaver user interface, such as the Insert bar, menus, the status bar, and panels. You have explored expanding and docking panel groups. You have seen the commands available in Dreamweaver's menus and Insert bar. You have been introduced to the Properties Inspector and have learned how to get help on Dreamweaver topics.

CHAPTER 2

Creating a Basic Web Page with Text

The most common elements in a Web page are text and images, so in this chapter we'll start with text. You'll get started creating Web pages with Dreamweaver by becoming familiar with adding text and setting text properties.

Creating a New Page

To create a new Web page, select File, New. The New Document dialog box appears, enabling you to select the type of document you want to create. This dialog box is organized into a Category column and a column that lists the pages in the selected category. Select the Basic Page category, and then select HTML as the Basic Page type, as shown in Figure 2.1. Click the Create button. A new document is created, and you can add text, images, and other objects to it.

Entering and Centering Text

You can simply type into the Document window to enter text into a Web page. Type some text as a title at the top of the page, press the Enter key, and type a couple sentences. To align your title in the center of the page, follow these steps:

1. Open the Properties Inspector.

2. Select the title text.

3. Click the Align Center icon (see Figure 2.2) in the Properties Inspector.

Alternatively, with the text selected, select Text, Alignment, Center. The Text menu contains all the text formatting commands that you will use in this chapter.

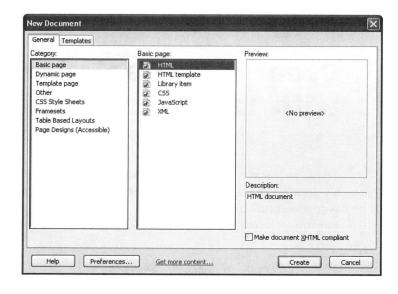

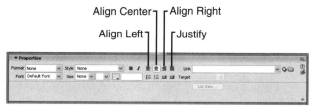

Applying Text Formatting

You apply standard HTML formatting to text by using the Format drop-down
menu in the Properties Inspector. There are four basic formatting options here:

- ▶ **None**—This option removes any formatting styles currently applied to the
  selection.

- ▶ **Paragraph**—This option applies paragraph tags (<p></p>) to the selection.
  This adds two carriage returns after the selection.

- ▶ **Heading 1 through Heading 6**—These options apply heading tags to the
  selection. Heading 1 is the largest heading, and Heading 6 is the smallest.
  Applying a heading tag makes everything on the line that heading size.

- ▶ **Preformatted**—This option displays text in a fixed-width, or monospaced,
  font—on most systems, 10-point Courier. The text resembles typewriter text.

Select the top line in your Web page and apply Heading 1 formatting. Try applying all the different formats to see what they look like.

Understanding Paragraph and Break Tags

It's important to understand the difference between paragraph (<p>) and break (<br>) tags. Paragraph tags surround a block of text, placing two carriage returns after the block. Think of the paragraph tags as creating a container for the block of text. You create a new paragraph by pressing the Enter or Return key.

The break tag inserts a single carriage return into text. You can insert a break into a Web page by using the keyboard shortcut Shift+Enter or selecting the Line Break object from the Characters drop-down menu in the Text category of the Insert bar. The break tag does not create a container as the paragraph tags do. Formatting such as the Heading 1 text applied to a block of text applies to all the text within the container.

It's important to understand the difference between paragraph and break tags. Pressing Shift+Enter twice, inserting two line breaks, instead of pressing Enter to create a paragraph looks identical to paragraph text. However, because you haven't created a paragraph container, any formatting applied to the paragraph gets applied to the entire container. This will become more important as you begin formatting portions of Web pages in different waysv.

Changing Text Size

You change text size by selecting one of the size settings in the Properties Inspector Size drop-down menu shown in Figure 2.3. The default text size is medium. If you select one of the numbers at the top of the list (or enter your own number), the Units drop-down menu becomes active so that you can select the unit type. Point and pixel are the most common unit types. You can also select one of the relative sizes (xx-small, medium, large, and so on). These text size settings enable the text to appear relative to the size settings that the user configures in his or her browser, and this is particularly useful for users who have vision impairment.

Use Pixels Instead of Points

I prefer to standardize by using pixels as my measurement unit of choice. Pixels seem to be the most predictable in various browsers and on various platforms. If you develop on Windows or on a Mac and it's important that your fonts look similar on the other operating system, use pixels as your unit of measure for fonts.

Did you Know?

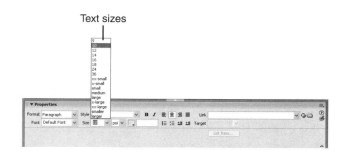

Text sizes

FIGURE 2.3
The Size drop-down menu in the Properties Inspector enables you to set the size of the selected text.

Selecting a Font

To apply a font, select some text and then select the Font drop-down menu in the Properties Inspector.

The fonts in the Font drop-down menu are defined in groups. Specifying a group instead of an individual font increases the odds that your viewers will have at least one of the fonts in the group. The browser will attempt to display text with the first font listed, but if that font isn't available, the browser will continue through the list. Dreamweaver has predefined groups to choose from, and you can also create your own groups.

Remember, just because you can see the font and it looks great on your machine doesn't mean that everyone has that font. If a font isn't available, the browser will use the default font—usually Times New Roman—instead. The fonts that are in the predefined font combinations in Dreamweaver are commonly available fonts in Windows and on the Macintosh.

Selecting a Text Color: Using the Color Picker

In a number of areas in Dreamweaver, you can change the color of an object or text. In HTML, colors are specified by using a hexadecimal numbering system, but if you don't know the hexadecimal translation of the color you'd like to use, you can use Dreamweaver's color picker. Change the text color to practice using the Dreamweaver color picker by first clicking the color box to the right of the Size drop-down menu in the Properties Inspector, as shown in Figure 2.4.

You can experiment with picking a color by using the color picker in a number of ways:

▶ Pick one of the available colors by clicking it with the eyedropper. You are in Eyedropper mode when the Eyedropper button is depressed in the color picker. Five panels are available: Color cubes, Continuous tone, Windows OS, Mac OS, and Grayscale.

▶ Use the eyedropper to pick up any color onscreen by simply clicking the eye-dropper on it. You can pick up any color on the screen, not just colors in Dreamweaver. Try selecting a color from one of the icons in the Insert bar.

▶ Select the System Color Picker button to create a custom color. This opens the system color picker, where you can either pick one of the basic colors or click anywhere in the color spectrum to mix your own color. Click the Add to Custom Colors button and then click the OK button to use the color.

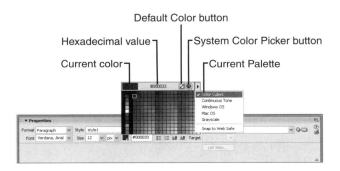

FIGURE 2.4
Select a color box to choose a color from the currently selected palette or create a custom color to use.

You can also type the color information directly into the color text box in the Properties Inspector:

▶ Colors are represented in HTML by three hexadecimal numbers preceded by the pound (#) sign. For instance, the RGB (red, green, blue) value for light blue is represented as #0099FF, where the value for R is 00, the value for G is 99, and the value of B is FF. If you know the hexadecimal value for a color, you can simply type it in.

▶ Most browsers display standard color names in addition to hexadecimal values. For instance, you could type in **red** instead of **#FF0000**.

To clear the current color without picking another color, click the Default Color button in the color picker.

Web-Safe Colors

The Dreamweaver **Web-safe palette** (also known as a *browser-safe palette*) is made up of 212 colors that work on both Windows and Macintosh operating systems displaying 256 colors. Choosing custom colors that are not part of the panel may have an undesirable appearance in older browsers. Most newer computers automatically display more than 256 colors (either thousands or millions of colors), so some Web professionals argue that the Web-safe palette is no longer necessary. But if your Web pages will potentially be viewed on older computers, you should be conservative and design your Web pages by using the Web-safe palette.

Watch Out!

Are You Locked Into Web Safe?

If you enter a color and Dreamweaver doesn't take the value, the color you entered isn't part of the Web-safe palette. If the Snap to Web Safe setting is selected in the color picker, Dreamweaver won't let you pick a non-Web-safe color. You'll need to turn off the Snap to Web Safe setting before Dreamweaver will allow you to use the color.

Using Dreamweaver's CSS Styles

Dreamweaver uses Cascading Style Sheets (CSS) to set point size and other text properties. CSS is covered in depth in Chapter 13, "Formatting Web Pages by Using Cascading Style Sheets." Using the CSS text specifications is the approved way of applying fonts, font sizes, and colors. Note that older browsers—pre-1997 browsers older than Internet Explorer 4 or Netscape Navigator 4—don't support CSS.

Goodbye, `<font>` Tag

The older method of formatting text is to use the `<font>` tag. This tag has been deprecated by the W3C, the Web standards organization. **Deprecated** means that the W3C is removing it from the approved tag list and eventually it may not be supported by browsers. Dreamweaver MX 2004 does not insert any `<font>` tags into your code.

When you apply text formatting in Dreamweaver, a CSS style is created in the code. This style defines the appearance of the text. You can see the style definition that Dreamweaver creates by looking at the CSS Styles panel, shown in Figure 2.5. Dreamweaver gives the style a default name, and you can edit that name by selecting the style in the CSS Styles panel and then selecting the Rename command from the menu in the upper-right corner of the panel.

FIGURE 2.5
The CSS Styles panel displays the CSS formatting that you've created in the Property inspector.

Instead of redefining the same formatting over and over, you can simply apply an existing CSS style to any text that you want to have the same font and font size. Select the CSS style from the Style drop-down menu in the Properties Inspector to apply it to the selected text. You'll learn how to edit the style definition in Chapter 13.

No Guarantees in Web Site Design

There is really no way to guarantee that a Web page will look the same on a viewer's computer as it does on your computer. Browser preferences enable the user to override font settings, size settings, background colors, and hyperlink colors. Don't depend on the page fonts and colors to be exact. If it makes you feel better, though, keep in mind that most users don't change the browser defaults.

Creating Lists and Indenting Text

By using Dreamweaver, you can implement bulleted lists, called *unordered lists* in HTML, and numbered lists, called *ordered lists* in HTML. The Unordered List and Ordered List buttons appear in the Properties Inspector when you have text selected.

First, create an unordered list by following these steps:

1. Type three items, pressing the Enter (or Return) key after each item so that each is on its own line.

2. Drag the cursor over all three items to select them.

3. Click the Unordered List button in the Properties Inspector, as shown in Figure 2.6.

Unordered List   Outdent

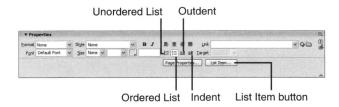

Ordered List   Indent   List Item button

FIGURE 2.6
The Properties Inspector has buttons to create ordered and unordered lists. You can select the Indent and Outdent buttons to nest lists or to indent and outdent text.

Now each line is preceded by a bullet. Next, add another list that is nested in the first list:

1. Place the insertion point after the last item.
2. Press the Enter key to make a new line. The new line should be preceded by a bullet.
3. Type three items, as you did in the previous list.
4. Drag the cursor over these new items and select the Indent button in the Properties Inspector.

Now the second list is nested within the third item of the first list. You can tell because it is indented and preceded by a different style of bullet. Use the Outdent button to place the nested list back in line with the main list.

Did you Know?

Customize Your Bullets and Numbers

You can change the bullet or number style by clicking the List Item button in the Properties Inspector (refer to Figure 2.6) when your cursor is located within the list. Oddly, the List Item button does not appear if you have the entire list selected. Pick the bullet style (either bullet or square) for an unordered list or pick a number style for an ordered list. You can also start the number count at a number other than one by entering the initial number in the Start Count box.

To turn the nested unordered list into an ordered list, select the three items again and click the Ordered List button in the Properties Inspector. To bring the nested list back in line with the main list, select the Outdent button.

With regular text, you use the Indent and Outdent buttons to modify the margins of a block of text. In HTML there is no easy way to tab or indent text, so Dreamweaver uses the `<blockquote>` tag to indent. This tag actually indents both the left and right sides of the text, so it may look strange if you indent multiple times.

Pasting Text from a File

Often, you need to transfer text that exists as a word processing document into a Web page. You can easily copy text from another application, such as Microsoft Word or even the spreadsheet application Microsoft Excel, and paste it into Dreamweaver. Dreamweaver can paste text two different ways: with and without formatting.

To copy and paste text from a word processing program or another program, follow these steps:

1. Open a document.

2. Select at least a couple paragraphs so that you can check for formatting retention in Dreamweaver.

3. Copy the text by selecting Edit, Copy or using the keyboard command (Ctrl+C for Windows or Command-C on the Mac).

4. Go to Dreamweaver and place the insertion point where you want to paste the text.

5. Select Edit, Paste or use the keyboard shortcut (Ctrl+V in Windows or Command-V on a Mac). The text is pasted into Dreamweaver, and it retains its formatting, including fonts, paragraphs, color, and other attributes.

Dreamweaver creates CSS styles that define the formatting of the pasted test. When you want to paste text into Dreamweaver without formatting, select Edit, Paste Text. This simply pastes the text characters without the formatting from the original document.

Adding a Separator to a Page: The Horizontal Rule

A graphical item that has been around since the Web stone age (a few years ago) is the horizontal rule. That little divider line is still useful. The horizontal rule creates a shaded line that divides a Web page into sections. Note that you can't place anything else on the same line with a horizontal rule.

Add a horizontal rule to your Web page by selecting the Horizontal Rule object from the HTML category of the Insert bar. Of course, if you're a menu kind of person, you can do this by selecting Insert, HTML, Horizontal Rule. In Figure 2.7, the Properties Inspector presents the properties of a horizontal rule. You can set width and height values in either pixels or percentages of the screen. You can also set the alignment and turn shading on and off.

FIGURE 2.7
Horizontal rule properties appear in the Properties Inspector when the rule is selected.

Many objects in HTML have width and height values either in absolute pixel values or as a percentage of the size of the container they are in. If a horizontal rule in the body of a Web page is set to a percentage value and the user changes the size of the browser window, the horizontal rule will resize to the new window size. If the horizontal rule is set to an absolute pixel size, it will not resize, and the user will see horizontal scrollbars if the horizontal rule is wider than the screen.

Setting Page Properties

So far in this chapter, you've created headings, paragraphs, and lists. You've also set text properties—properties that are applied to a specific block of text. You can also set global page properties, such as the default font and font size for all the text on the page. In addition, you can set the page title in the page properties. You can access the Page Properties dialog box in three ways:

- ▶ Select Modify, Page Properties.
- ▶ Click the Page Properties button in the Properties Inspector when it is visible.
- ▶ Right-click (Control+click on the Mac) an empty part of the Document window and select Page Properties from the context menu.

Adding a Page Title

The title of your Web page appears in the title bar of both Dreamweaver and the browser. This same page title is also saved to a user's browser Bookmarks or Favorites list when he or she saves the address of your site; therefore, you should make it meaningful and memorable.

To add a title to a document, follow these steps:

1. Select Modify, Page Properties and then type a descriptive title in the title box at the top of the Page Properties dialog box.

2. Click the Apply button. If you click the Apply button, you apply the changes you've made to the Web page and the Page Properties dialog box remains open and ready for your next page edits. If you click OK, the changes are applied but the dialog box closes.

There are various alphabets in the world, and using the Encoding command is how you tell a Web browser which one you are using for your Web page. By default, Dreamweaver lists the Western European encoding type used in the United States and Europe. If you create a page using another alphabet, you need to change the Encoding setting. You can change Dreamweaver's default encoding type in the New Document category in Dreamweaver's Preferences dialog box.

Setting Page Appearance

You use the settings in the Appearance category of the Page Properties dialog box to set the text font, size, and color, along with several other settings, for the entire Web page. The text on a page is black by default. You can change the default text color by using the color picker to select a different color. The settings you make here apply to all the text on the page.

Setting the Default Page Font, Size, and Color

Select the Appearance category in the Page Properties dialog box by clicking the category name on the left side of the dialog box. You can select the default font for the entire page along with the default text size and color. This setting will be overridden by any local text setting, such as the settings you applied to a paragraph earlier in this chapter.

To set the default font properties, follow these steps:

1. In the Page Properties dialog box, select the font family you want from the Page Font drop-down menu. You can also set the default text to be bold, italic, or both.

2. Select the font size in the Size drop-down menu. If you select a numeric font size, you also need to select a unit type, such as points or pixels.

3. Select a font color by using the Text Color color picker.

The default text settings will be overridden by any other styles that you place on the text. As before, Dreamweaver creates a CSS style that affects all the text on the page.

Setting the Background Color and Background Image

You can set the background color of an entire page in the Appearance category of the Page Properties dialog box. For example, if you'd like to set the Web page background color to white, you can enter the hexadecimal color code (**#FFFFFF**) into the Background Color text box, type **white** into the box, or use the color picker. Of course, you can pick any color that you want as the background color, but make sure that the combination of the background color and the text color doesn't make your Web page difficult to read. If you apply a dark background color, you need to use a light text color for contrast so that the viewer can read the text.

You can also set a background image for a Web page. This image is tiled both vertically and horizontally on the page. In order for the Web page background to really look nice, you should find or create an image especially designed as a Web page background. You can find these specially designed background images on the Web or in image galleries that you purchase. A background image should never interfere with the readability of a page.

Setting the Page Margins

Margins set the amount of space between the contents of the Web page and the edges of the browser window. You set the margins for a page in the Page Properties dialog box. The default setting for page margins is 15 pixels from the top and 10 pixels from the left in Internet Explorer and 20 pixels from the top and 8 pixels from the left in Netscape. Sometimes you might want to change the margins by entering a value into all the margin boxes, as shown in Figure 2.8. There are four settings for page margins: Left Margin, Top Margin, Right Margin, and Bottom Margin.

FIGURE 2.8
You set the default text properties, the page background color and image, and the page margins in the Appearance category in the Page Properties dialog box.

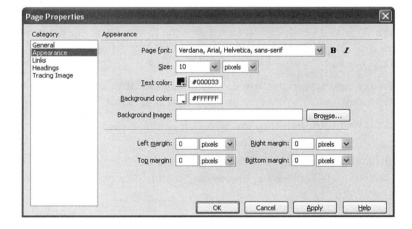

Custom Hyperlink Colors

By the Way

You can set custom colors for hyperlinks in the Links category of the Page Properties dialog box. We'll cover creating hyperlinks in Chapter 4, "Setting Lots O' Links: Hyperlinks, URLs, Anchors, and Mailto Links," and you'll have a chance to experiment with changing the link colors in the Page Properties dialog box.

Setting Heading Properties

In the Heading category of the Page Properties dialog box, you can set a default font for all six of the sizes of headings. You can also set a unique font size and color for each of the heading sizes. Dreamweaver creates a CSS style that enables this functionality to affect every heading on your Web page.

Saving Your Work and Previewing in a Browser

Even though Dreamweaver is a WYSIWYG tool, you need to see how your page really looks in particular browsers. It's a good idea to save your work before you preview it. Saving your work lets Dreamweaver set the paths to linked files, such as images, correctly. We'll explore the concept of linked files and paths further in Chapter 3, "Planning and Defining Your Project."

Macromedia says you can define up to 20 browsers for previewing. Good luck finding 20 browsers! I generally have the following browsers installed for testing: Microsoft Internet Explorer, Netscape, and sometimes Opera on my Windows machine and Internet Explorer, Netscape, Safari, and sometimes Opera on my Mac. You have to have these programs installed on your computer before you can use them to preview your Web pages. All the browsers mentioned have free versions and are available to download over the Internet.

First, set up a browser as follows:

1. Select File, Preview in Browser, Edit Browser List command. Dreamweaver's Preferences dialog box opens to the Preview in Browser category. Dreamweaver may have already located a browser and entered it here during the installation process, so the list may not be empty. My Windows installation of Dreamweaver always finds Internet Explorer and places it in this list for me.

2. Click the plus button to add a browser.

3. Leave the Name text box empty for now; Dreamweaver will automatically pick up the name of the browser.

4. Click the Browse button next to the Application text box and navigate to the browser program. For computers running Windows, the default installation location for most browsers is in the `Program Files` directory. For the Mac, look in your `Applications` folder.

5. Click either the Primary Browser check box or the Secondary Browser check box. This determines which keyboard shortcut you use to launch the browser. The keyboard shortcut for one primary browser is F12, and the shortcut for one secondary browser is Ctrl+F12.

6. Repeat steps 2–5 until all browsers have been added. Click the OK button when you are done.

Below the browser list is a single check box option that controls whether you directly view your Web page in the browser or whether you want Dreamweaver to create a temporary file to display in the browser. When the box is checked, you won't need to save your Web page prior to previewing in a browser because Dreamweaver will create a temporary file for you to display in the browser. If you uncheck this box, you will need to save your Web page prior to previewing it in the browser. I prefer to uncheck this box and know that I'm viewing the actual Web page instead of a temporary file. Even after you've saved your page in Dreamweaver and previewed it in the browser, you can still undo changes that you made prior to saving the page.

Select File, Preview in Browser or select Preview in Browser on the Document toolbar to view the current Web page. Select the browser you want to use from the menu. If the browser is already open, you might have to switch to the application to see your page. If the browser isn't already open, Dreamweaver will open it and load the requested page so you can preview it.

Dreamweaver MX 2004 actually checks each page you open in Dreamweaver for potential browser errors. The Check Browser menu on the Document toolbar displays whether you have any browser check errors in the target browsers selected. By default, Dreamweaver checks your page for errors in Internet Explorer 5 and Netscape 4. Modify the browsers and version in the Target Browsers dialog box by selecting Check Browser, Settings.

Congratulations! You've created your first Web page in Dreamweaver and learned a lot about formatting the page and text on the page. Many of the tasks described in this chapter will become habit to you with every Web page you create, and you will be able to quickly move through the steps you've practiced in this chapter.

Summary

In this chapter, you have learned how to enter and import text into a Web page. You have set text properties, including headings, fonts, lists, and alignment. You've been introduced to CSS, the language of presentation on the Web. You have used a horizontal rule to separate the page into sections and previewed your work in a browser.

CHAPTER 3

Planning and Defining Your Project

You use Dreamweaver's Files panel to plan, create, and manage projects. You might have created only a single Web page so far, but eventually you'll have lots of files: HTML files, image files, and maybe other types of files. It's important that you define your Web site so that Dreamweaver knows how to set links properly. Defining a new site should always be your first step when you start working on a new project.

Defining a New Web Site

Every Web site has a root directory. The **root** of a Web site is the main directory that contains files and other directories. When you define a Web site, Dreamweaver considers that directory and all the files within it to be the entire "universe" of that particular Web site. If you attempt to insert an image from outside this universe, Dreamweaver will prompt you to save the file inside the Web site.

Dreamweaver isn't overly controlling, though! The program needs to define the internal realm of your Web site so that it knows how to reference other files. For instance, if an image is located in an images directory within the site, Dreamweaver knows how to properly reference the image within a Web page. If, however, the image is somewhere outside the defined site, Dreamweaver may not be able to reference it properly, and you might end up with bad links in your Web site. You'll learn more about how Dreamweaver links to files in Chapter 4, "Setting Lots O' Links: Hyperlinks, URLs, Anchors, and Mailto Links."

You need to define a new Web site for every project you create. Even when projects are related, you might decide to break them down into smaller sites so that the number of files isn't unwieldy in a single site. For instance, I create e-learning applications, courses that people can take over the Web. When I'm working on a project, I often break individual lessons of a course into separate defined sites. When I need to work on Lesson 1, I open that site, and when I need Lesson 2, I open it. You can have only a single site open in Dreamweaver at one time.

Make sure that the Files panel is visible in Dreamweaver. After you've defined a Web site, you'll see a list of the files in the Web site displayed in the Files panel. Prior to defining your first site, you'll simply see either the Windows Desktop or the Macintosh Finder in the Files panel. If you don't have any site defined yet, click the Manage Sites link at the top of the Files panel to open the Manage Sites dialog box. If you already have sites defined in Dreamweaver, you'll see a list of them in the drop-down menu at the top of the Files panel. You can open the Manage Sites dialog box from the command at the bottom of this list.

You use the Files panel to open individual Web pages in Dreamweaver to work on. The file structure of a Web site is displayed in the Files panel, and you double-click Web pages in this panel to open them to edit them in Dreamweaver. Although it's best to always define a Web site, if you are just making a quick change to a single Web page, it'll be quicker for you to open the file without going to the effort to define a site. You open a single Web page by using File, Open.

The Manage Sites dialog box, shown in Figure 3.1, is where you can create, edit, duplicate, remove, export, and import Dreamweaver site definitions. The title says it all: This is where you manage your Web sites! To begin, click the New button in the Manage Sites dialog box and choose Site. The Site Definition dialog box appears.

FIGURE 3.1
The Manage Sites dialog box lists all the Web sites you have defined and enables you to manage them.

The Site Definition dialog box is where you name your site and point Dreamweaver to where the files are stored on your computer. You can define a site even if you don't have any files; you simply define the site in an empty directory that is ready to hold all the Web pages you create. The Site Definition dialog box, shown in Figure 3.2, has two tabs at the top: Basic and Advanced. You'll begin by using the settings on the Basic tab, so make sure that tab is selected. The Basic tab contains the Site Definition wizard, which walks you through the site definition. You can always go back and change or update your site if you need to.

Basic tab

Advanced tab   Sections

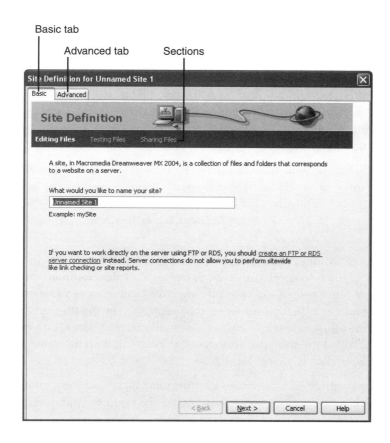

FIGURE 3.2
The Basic tab of
the Site Definition
dialog box walks
you through setting
up a site definition.

The Site Definition wizard has three main sections, shown as the section names at
the top of the wizard:

▶ **Editing Files**—This section helps you set up the local directory where you'll
  work on the Web site. You tell the wizard whether your site uses server-side
  technologies. None of the sites or Web pages in this book use these technologies, which connect Web pages, servers, and often databases.

▶ **Testing Files**—This section is needed only for sites that use server-side technologies.

▶ **Sharing Files**—This section enables you to tell Dreamweaver how you want
  to transfer files to a server or another central location to share. You'll
  explore this functionality in Chapter 18, "Uploading Your Dreamweaver
  Project."

Using the Site Definition Wizard

In the Site Definition wizard, give your site a name. This name is used only inside Dreamweaver, so you can use spaces and characters in it if you want. The site name should be meaningful—it should identify the purpose of the Web site when you drop down the Site menu to change sites. My Dreamweaver has about 30 to 40 sites defined at times, so clear names help me quickly find the site I want to edit. Click the Next button.

The next page of the wizard, Editing Files, Part 2, enables you to specify whether you will be using server-side scripting to create dynamic Web pages. Your Web pages in this book will be regular HTML pages, so you should select the top radio button that says No, I Do Not Want to Use a Server Technology. Click the Next button.

The next page, Editing Files, Part 3, helps you specify where the files in your site are located. The site that you are creating here is your **development site** not the final site that other people will view over the Web. You will need to move the files in your development site up to a server for people to view the files over the Web (the subject of Chapter 18). The Web site located on a Web server and available to the public is called the **live site**. I always work on an up-to-date copy of a Web site that is located on my local hard drive.

You can store your development files in three places: on your local machine, on a network drive, or on a server somewhere. Select the top radio button to elect to store the development files on your local machine. If you are working in a networked environment (at your office, for instance), you could use either of the other two choices.

As shown in Figure 3.3, the text box at the bottom of the dialog box asks you to enter the location of the site directory. Click the folder icon to the right of the text box to navigate to the directory. Use an existing directory on your hard drive or create a new directory for your site. Click the Next button.

By the Way

Name Your Files Properly to Avoid Problems

Spaces, punctuation, and special characters in file and directory names may cause problems. You can use underscores instead of spaces in names. All files should be named using a combination of letters, numbers, and underscores. If you are planning on adding scripting (using Dreamweaver behaviors, covered in Chapter 14, "Inserting Scripted Functionality by Using Behaviors"), you shouldn't name any files, including image files, beginning with a number.

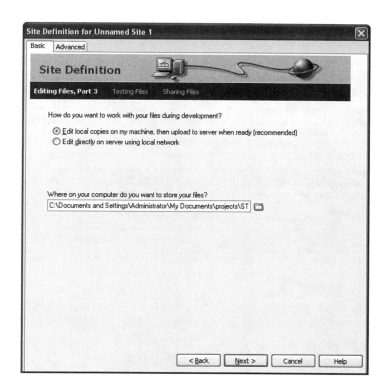

FIGURE 3.3
You enter the directory that will house your development files.

Servers May Be Case-Sensitive

Filenames are case-sensitive on some servers. Servers running the various flavors of the Unix operating system enable you to create files named `mydog.gif`, `Mydog.gif`, and `MYDOG.gif` all in the same directory because the capitalization differs. Microsoft servers are not case-sensitive.

Watch Out!

The next section in the Site Definition wizard enables you to configure how you share files. You can set up a central location where members of your team can share files. Or you can set up a location on a public Web server where you share your Web site with the world. You'll learn how to configure this section and transfer files in Chapter 18. For now, simply drop down the top menu and select None. Click the Next button.

The last page of the wizard displays a summary of your site, as shown in Figure 3.4. You can come back to this wizard at any time to change your site definition by selecting the Edit Sites command from the Site menu (either the one in the Files panel or the one in the Document window). Click the Done button.

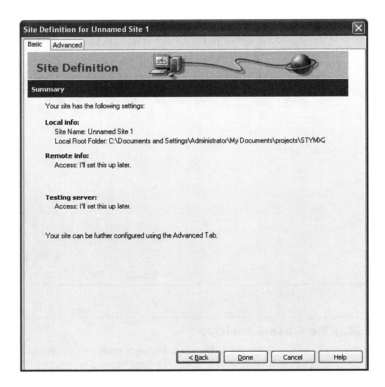

After you click the Done button, Dreamweaver displays a message, telling you that it will now create the initial site cache. When you click OK, a progress bar appears (and disappears very quickly if you have nothing in your site yet). The initial site cache is created each time you create a new site. The **site cache** is used to store information about the links in your site so that they can be quickly updated if they change. Dreamweaver continues to update the cache as you work.

Using the Files Panel

You select the site you'd like to work on in the Files panel, which is shown in Figure 3.5. This is where you open Web pages to edit in Dreamweaver. The Site drop-down menu gives you quick access to all your defined sites. It also gives you another way to launch the Manage Sites dialog box.

Site drop-down menu

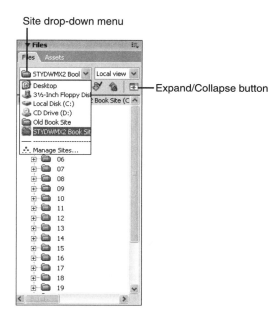

Expand/Collapse button

FIGURE 3.5
The Files panel enables you to change sites and open Web pages.

Using the Expanded Files Panel

To get a bigger view of a site and get access to more functionality, select the Expand/Collapse button in the Files panel to open the Expanded Files panel. The Expanded Files panel, shown in Figure 3.6, is a larger representation of the Files panel and has two panes: Local Files (on the right, by default) and Remote Site (on the left), which you will set up in Chapter 18. Because you have not yet defined a remote site, you should not have any files in the Remote Site pane at this point.

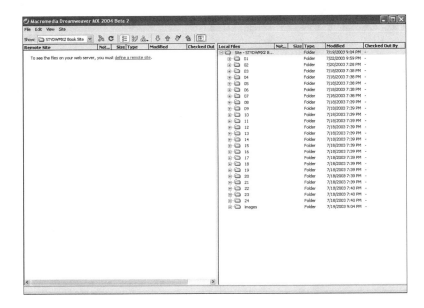

Creating New Files in the Files Panel

You can create new files and new folders right in the Dreamweaver Files panel. Right-click (Control+click on the Mac) in the Files panel to open the Files panel menu. This context menu has two commands of interest at the top: New File and New Folder. You'll use those commands to create files and folders (also called *directories*) in the Files panel.

The Web sites you create will need directories, and probably every site will have an images directory for all the images in the site. Create an images directory by using the New Folder command. An untitled folder is added to your site. Give this folder the name images. You need to be careful about what is selected when you select the New Folder command so that you do not nest the folder within another folder. To add a folder at the site root, select the top line, which begins with the word *Site*.

Now try adding a new file to your site. Right-click (or Control+click) on the root folder, the top line in the Files panel, which lists the name of the site, and select the New File command. A new untitled Web page is created in the Web site. Title the Web page **index.htm**, which is one of the popular default page names for many servers. Using the **default page name** enables the user to find your page more easily by just entering a basic Web page address without the specific page appended. Another common default page name is index.html. Both the .htm and the .html file extensions are acceptable. The .htm file extension became popular because the older versions of Microsoft Windows could only handle three-character file extensions; this is no longer a limitation in newer versions of Windows. After you add the new folder and a new file, the site should look as shown in Figure 3.7.

FIGURE 3.7
You can add files and folders in Dreamweaver's Files panel.

Editing a Site Definition

So far in this chapter, you have used the Basic tab in the Site Definition dialog box to initially define a Web site. Now let's explore the Advanced tab and use it to edit site settings. Open the Manage Sites dialog box again by selecting Manage Sites from the Site drop-down menu. Select the site you just created and then click the Edit button. The Site Definition dialog box opens again. Click the Advanced tab at the top of the dialog box. As shown in Figure 3.8, this is another view of the information that you entered into the wizard.

A Quick Way to Edit Site Definitions

A fast way to open the Site Definition dialog box is to simply double-click the name of the site in the Files panel's Site drop-down menu.

Did you Know?

FIGURE 3.8
The Advanced tab contains all the site properties.

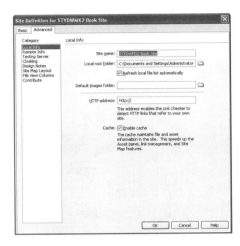

The left side of the Site Definition dialog box shows categories, and the right side lists the selected category's properties. Select the Local Info category and then select the folder icon next to the Default Images Folder text box. Navigate to the images folder you just created. Now Dreamweaver knows where you'll keep your images for the site. Click the OK button to save your changes. Click the Done button to close the Edit Sites dialog box.

You'll learn about other advanced options later in this book. In Chapter 18, you'll set up the Remote Info category in order to upload your files to a remote Web site.

Considering Site Organization

There are many opinions about the proper way to organize a Web site. Some people like to compartmentalize all the files into directories and subdirectories. Some people like to have a very shallow structure, with many files in a single directory. As you get more experienced at Web development, you'll find your ideal organization. It's nice to exchange ideas with other Web developers or hobbyists so that you can learn from the successes and failures of others and they can learn from yours.

I try to logically break up sections of Web sites into separate directories. If your Web site has obvious divisions (departments, lessons, products, and so on), you can create directories to hold the Web pages in each of the sections. You'll be surprised at how even a small Web site becomes quickly unmanageable when all the files are dumped into one directory.

Most Web sites use many image files. If you have different sections in your Web site, do you want to have separate images directories in each section? It might be a good way to organize your site. Then again, if images are used across multiple sections, it might make the images hard to find. Make sure that your organizational logic isn't going to break down as you add files to your site.

Luckily, if you do have to rearrange assets, Dreamweaver will update any links for you. When you move a file, Dreamweaver asks you if you want to search and update links to that file. That's what the site cache is created for. However, it is still best to make wise design decisions at the beginning of a big project.

Summary

In this chapter, you have learned how to define a Web site and determine its root. You have learned how to quickly add files and folders to a site. You have learned how to use the Files panel and expand it into the Expanded Files panel. And you have explored ideas about how to organize a site.

CHAPTER 4

Setting Lots O' Links: Hyperlinks, URLs, Anchors, and Mailto Links

Clicking a **hyperlink** allows the viewer to jump to another Web page, jump to another section of the current Web page, or launch an email message. A Web site is made up of a group of Web pages, and hyperlinks enable viewers to navigate from page to page. Hyperlinks, in the simplest form, are the familiar underlined and colored text that you click. You can also make an image a hyperlink.

A Web address is called a **uniform resource locator (URL)**. You can link many types of files over the Web, but only a few file types will actually be displayed in a browser. A browser can display the supported image formats, HTML, player applications (such as Flash), and a few other specialized types of files. If a link leads to a file that the browser can't display (a .zip file, for example), the browser will usually ask you whether you'd like to save the file to your hard drive.

Exploring Relative and Absolute Paths

Whenever you create a hyperlink to another Web page or place an external file (such as an image file) in a Web page, you need to enter a path to the file. Dreamweaver helps make sure that these paths are correct, but it's important that you understand the difference between the two main types of paths: absolute paths and document-relative paths. An **absolute path** is the full URL (more about URLs in a few minutes) to a file. A **document-relative path** points to the location of a file in relationship to the page being viewed.

The link to the Macromedia Dreamweaver Support Center shown in Figure 4.1 is an absolute path. It contains the entire path to a file on the Internet. Because you have no control over this site, linking to it means that you need to check to see that the link remains valid. If the site moves in the future, you will need to update the link.

FIGURE 4.1
Entering an
absolute path links
to a specific Web
page.

A hyperlink with an absolute path

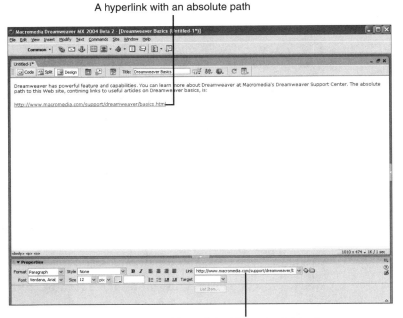

A hyperlink with an absolute path

A URL consists of up to five sections, as shown in Figure 4.2:

▶ **Protocol**—The first part of the URL is the protocol. It is http for Web pages
to indicate Hypertext Transfer Protocol (HTTP). Sometimes you might want
to link to a file on an FTP (File Transfer Protocol—another method of com-
municating over the Internet to move files to and from a server) server,
using ftp as the protocol instead of http.

▶ **Domain**—The second part of the address is the domain. This is the Web
server where the Web page is located; for example, in Figure 4.2, the
domain is www.betsybruce.com. A colon and two forward slashes (://) separate the protocol and the domain.

▶ **Port**—An optional third part of a URL is the port. The default port for a Web
server is port 80. When you enter http as the protocol, port 80 is implied
and doesn't usually need to be included. You might need to enter port information when entering addresses to specialized Web applications that listen
on a different port than port 80.

▶ **Path and filename**—The fourth part of the address is the path and file-name. The path includes all directories and the filename. Most Web pages end in .htm or .html. Other common file endings are .cgi, for Common Gateway Interface, .asp, for Active Server Pages, .jsp, for JavaServer Pages, .aspx, for ASP.NET files, .php, for PHP pages, and .cfm, for ColdFusion Markup Language.

▶ **Query string**—The filenames might be followed by an optional fifth part of a URL—a query string. A query string is added to a URL to send data to a script to be processed. We'll explore query strings in Chapter 17, "Sending and Reacting to Form Data."

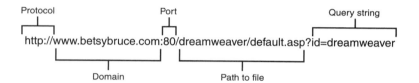

FIGURE 4.2
A URL consists of multiple sections. Every URL must contain a protocol, a domain name, and the complete path to a file.

You might see a URL that does not have a filename referenced at the end, such as http://www.macromedia.com/support/dreamweaver/. This type of address works because the Web server looks for a default page in the directory. Most Web servers have a default page name that doesn't need to be explicitly entered at the end of the URL. Usually the default page name is default.htm, default.html, index.htm, or index.html. On some servers, any of these names will work. This functionality can be configured in Web server software.

Default pages in the root of a site are often referred to as *home pages*. To create a home page for a Web site, ask your Webmaster or Web hosting service for the default page name for your Web server. If you don't have a default page on your Web site and a visitor doesn't enter a filename at the end of the URL, he or she might see all the contents of your directories instead of a Web page. Or the user might get an error message!

You usually do not need to enter the protocol into the browser's address box to go to a Web page. Most browsers assume that you want to use HTTP. However, if you are surfing to an FTP file, you need to enter ftp as the protocol at the beginning of the URL. Even though browsers assume HTTP, you still need to preface absolute links entered into Dreamweaver with http://.

Within your own Web site, you use document-relative paths so that you can move your site anywhere and your links will still work. While developing in Dreamweaver, you will create a Web site on your local hard drive and then eventually move the site to a Web server. Document-relative paths will work the same in both locations.

It's important to use document-relative paths instead of absolute paths in your Web site. If you have an absolute path to a file on your local drive, the link will look like the following:

```
file:///C¦/My Documents/first_page.html
```

This file, `first_page.html`, is on the `C:` drive in a directory called `My Documents`. If you preview this page in your browser, it works fine for you. So, what's the problem? The reason it works fine is that you have that page available on your hard drive, but other people don't have access to your hard drive and will not be able to access the page.

Document-relative paths don't require a complete URL. The path to the linked file is expressed relative to the current document. You use this type of path when inserting images into a Web page. You also use a document-relative path when creating a hyperlink to a Web page within your Web site.

By the Way

Links Work with Other Files, Too

You don't have to limit your links to Web pages. You can link to movies, word processing files (.doc files, for instance), PDF files, or audio files. The URLs work the same no matter what the content is.

The following are some examples of document-relative paths:

▶ When linking to a file that is in the same directory as your current file, you enter only the filename as the path. For instance, if the file `mktg.htm` in Figure 4.3 has a link to `sales.htm`, the path would simply be the filename because both files are in the same directory.

▶ To link to a file that is in a directory nested within the directory where the current file is located, you enter the directory name and the filename as a path. For instance, if the file `products.htm` in Figure 4.3 has a link to the file `rx5000.htm` in the products directory, the path is `products/rx5000.htm`.

▶ When linking to a file in a directory above the current directory (called the *parent directory*), you enter `../` plus the filename as a path. The `../` means go up to the next parent directory. For instance, if the file `sales.htm` in Figure 4.3 has a link to the file `products.htm` in the site root, the path is `../products.htm`.

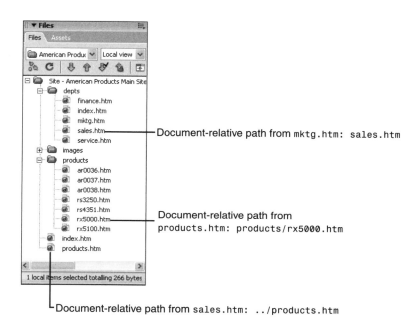

FIGURE 4.3
Document-relative paths depend on the relative position of the files in the directory structure.

Document-relative path from `mktg.htm`: `sales.htm`

Document-relative path from `products.htm`: `products/rx5000.htm`

Document-relative path from `sales.htm`: `../products.htm`

Before it saves your Web page, Dreamweaver inserts all links as absolute links. It does this because it cannot calculate a relative link until the file is saved. After the file has been saved, Dreamweaver can tell where your document is relative to all linked files and will change the links to document-relative addresses. Accidentally using absolute paths is an easy mistake to make. Dreamweaver looks out for you, however, and attempts to correct these problems for you.

There is a third type of path, called **site root-relative**. In a site root-relative link, the path is relative to the root of the entire Web site. The *root* of the Web site is defined as a certain directory of a Web site, usually where the site's home page is located. Site root-relative linking is used in professional environments where many different sections of the Web site need to access a common group of files, such as a corporate logo or common button images.

Site root-relative paths are not the best choice for beginners to Web development work. The main difficulty is that you can preview pages that have site root-relative links only if they are loaded on a Web server. Therefore, if you use these links, you won't be able to preview your work in a browser without loading it onto the server. Stay away from site root-relative paths until you are more experienced.

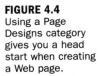

Be Careful with Your Slashes

A site root-relative path is preceded with a forward slash (/). An example of a site root-relative path is

```
/depts/products.html
```

Be careful not to enter a path this way by accident when typing in an address.

Adding a Hyperlink Within a Web Site

In this section you'll create several new Web pages and save them to your Web site. You'll need several so that you can practice linking to them, so create a couple now. You can use these pages to practice linking by using document-relative paths.

Create a new page that links to an existing page:

1. Select File, New to open the New Document dialog box.

2. Select the Page Designs category in the New Document dialog box, as shown in Figure 4.4. These designs come with Dreamweaver and are a great starting place for your Web page development. Select Image: Picture and Description Vertical from the Page Designs list. Make sure to create a document (instead of a template) by selecting the Document radio button. Click the Create button.

FIGURE 4.4
Using a Page Designs category gives you a head start when creating a Web page.

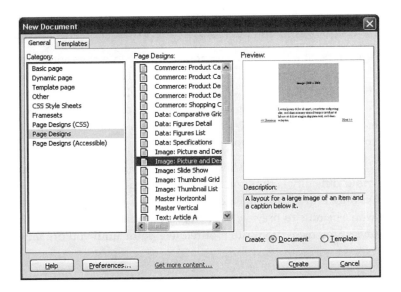

3. You now have a Web page with an image placeholder and some placeholder text. Save this document in the root of your site.

4. Repeat steps 1–3 to create several Web pages.

5. Select and replace the placeholder text, the text beginning with "Lorum ipsum," on one of the Web pages with some text of your own. You'll learn how to replace the placeholder image in Chapter 6, "Displaying Images on a Page."

6. Select the <<Previous link on the Web page.

7. Select the Browse icon (which looks like a folder) next to the Link drop-down menu in the Properties Inspector. Navigate to the directory where the index.htm file is located. Select the filename and click the Select button. Dreamweaver enters a relative URL into the Link drop-down menu, as shown in Figure 4.5.

Hyperlink

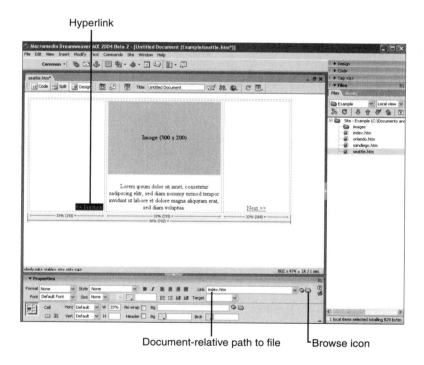

Document-relative path to file   Browse icon

FIGURE 4.5
In the Dreamweaver Document window, you select text that you want to become a hyperlink.

The selected text appears as an underlined blue hyperlink in the Dreamweaver Document window. Preview the Web page in the browser and click your link. You should jump to another page!

Setting Link Color Preferences

You set the link colors in the Page Properties dialog box just as you set the default text color in Chapter 2, "Creating a Basic Web Page with Text." Open the Page Properties dialog box and select the Links category. You set the link font and font size for all the links on the page at the top of the dialog box. There are four different options you can set here:

- ▶ **Link Color**—The default color of all the links on the page.
- ▶ **Visited Links**—The color of a link after it has been visited by the browser.
- ▶ **Rollover Links**—The color of a link when the cursor is over the link.
- ▶ **Active Links**—The color of the link when the user is actively clicking the link (while the mouse button is down).

Use the color picker to add a link color, visited link color, rollover link color, and active link color. When you apply the changes to your Web page, you should see all your links in the link color. When the viewer's browser has visited one of your links, the link will appear in the visited link color. The viewer sees the active link color while the mouse is actively clicking the link. The link colors are defined for the entire page, so all your links will be the color you specify.

Dreamweaver sets the link colors by using CSS styles. You can also turn off the hyperlink underline by setting the Underline style. There are four different choices here: Always Underline, Never Underline, Show Underline Only on Rollover, and Hide Underline on Rollover. Many usability experts advise against removing the underline because it makes links in the page more difficult to identify. Not using underline sure looks nice, though!

Organizing a Long Page by Using Named Anchors

Have you ever visited a Web page where you click a link, and it takes you to another part of the same Web page? That type of Web page is created with *named anchors*. You use named anchors because sometimes it's less confusing to jump within the same Web page than to jump to another Web page.

To create a long page with named anchors, first add a named anchor to the location on the page where the user will jump. Then create a hyperlink that is linked to the named anchor. You can start creating a named anchor with a page that has multiple sections, such as the one shown in Figure 4.6. To create the page for this example, follow these steps:

1. Create a new Web page by selecting File, New. This time create an HTML page (under the Basic Page category). Save your page.

2. Place the insertion point where the named anchor will be located. This is the area of the page where the user will jump when he or she clicks the link to the named anchor.

3. Select Insert, Named Anchor or select Named Anchor in the Common panel of the Insert bar. The Named Anchor dialog box, shown in Figure 4.7, appears.

4. Name the anchor and then click OK.

Menu items link to named anchors further down the page

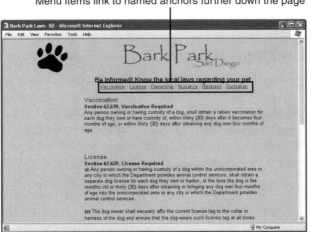

FIGURE 4.6
A Web site can have multiple sections, with a menu at the top of the page linking to the sections.

FIGURE 4.7
After you select the Named Anchor command, give the anchor a name in the Named Anchor dialog box.

Understanding Invisible Objects

You might get a message saying that you will not see a named anchor because it is invisible. Or you might have a small yellow symbol appear in the Document window. The small yellow symbol is an invisible element. An invisible element with an anchor on it will appear at the location where you inserted the named anchor; it is the visual representation of a named anchor.

Some objects that you insert into a Web page aren't designed to be viewable. Because Dreamweaver is a WYSIWYG design tool, Macromedia had to design a way for you to view objects that are invisible on the Web page. So, how can you see invisible objects, such as named anchors and forms, on the page? You choose View, Invisible Elements.

When Invisible Elements is turned on Dreamweaver displays the invisible elements such as the markers that represent named anchors (they look like little anchors on a gold shield). You can select the markers and view or edit the properties for the objects that they represent in the Properties Inspector.

Linking to a Named Anchor

You've created a named anchor, but that really isn't very useful unless you link something to it. Add a text link at the top of the page. It may not be obvious that your Web page is jumping to the named anchor location unless you have enough content to scroll in the browser, so add some extra text or simply some blank space so that you can see the jumping effect when you test your page in the browser. To link to the new named anchor, follow these steps:

1. Select the text that will link to the named anchor.

2. Enter the name of the named anchor, preceded by a pound sign (for example, #vaccination) in the Link box, as shown in Figure 4.8.

You can also link to a named anchor in another file. To do so, you simply append the name of the named anchor to the filename, as demonstrated in the following:

```
http://www.barkpark.org/laws.html#vaccinations
```

Named anchor

FIGURE 4.8
You enter the name of a named anchor, preceded by a pound sign, to create a link to it.

Link to a named anchor

Using the Point-to-File Icon

There's a little tool that you might have noticed on the Properties Inspector: the Point-to-File icon. This icon enables you to create links visually. You can drag the **Point-to-File icon**, shown in Figure 4.9, to a named anchor or a file located in the Files panel.

When the Point-to-File icon is dragged over a named anchor, the name of the anchor appears in the Link box of the Properties Inspector. To select the named anchor, simply release the mouse button while the Point-to-File icon is over the named anchor. Using this icon is a nice way to link to objects or files without having to know or type in the filenames. You can also use the Point-to-File icon to link to files listed in your Files panel by dragging the icon over to the panel and highlighting a particular file.

FIGURE 4.9
Drag the
Point-to-File icon to
a named anchor.
While the icon is
over the anchor, its
name appears in
the Link box.

Drag cursor to the named anchor

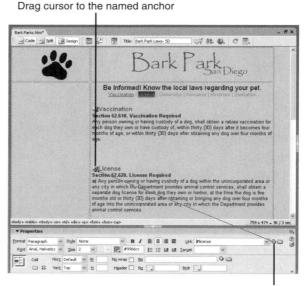

Point-to-File icon

Adding a Mailto Link

It's nice to put a link in a Web page to allow a viewer to send email. This type of link is called a **mailto link**. The Dreamweaver Email Link object helps you implement a mailto link. The user must have an email application set up to work with the browser in order for these links to work.

To create a mailto link, select some text to be the link. Click the Email Link object (in the Common panel of the Insert bar), and the Email Link dialog box appears. Enter the email address and click OK. The text looks like a hyperlink, but instead of linking to another page, it opens a preaddressed email message.

Watch
Out!

Spammers Love Mailto Links

Spammers troll the Internet for mailto links. If you use mailto links in your Web pages, expect to get a lot of **spam**, or junk email, sent to the email address used in the mailto links.

An **email link** is a hyperlink like any other except that it opens the user's default email application, such as Outlook or Eudora, with an email address already entered. Most users have a default email client, so these links are an easy and quick way for the user to send email. The email application has to be properly configured, with a server specified to send email, for the email to actually be sent.

Summary

In this chapter, you have learned the difference between absolute and relative addresses. You have created links to external Web sites and relative links to pages within a Web site. You have learned how to insert a named anchor and then link to it, and you have created a mailto link to allow a viewer to launch an email message directly from a Web page.

CHAPTER 5

Viewing and Modifying HTML

Even though Dreamweaver handles HTML behind the scenes, you might occasionally want to look at it. Dreamweaver also makes the transition easier for those stoic HTML hand-coders who are making a move to a visual HTML development tool such as Dreamweaver. You won't be sorry! I'm a very competent HTML hand-coder, but I can get my work done much quicker by using Dreamweaver.

Dreamweaver offers several ways to access HTML code. During this chapter, you will explore the HTML editing capabilities of Dreamweaver. You'll use Dreamweaver's capability to clean up the code produced when saving a Word document as HTML. If you don't already know HTML, you'll find that viewing HTML that Dreamweaver creates is a great way to learn.

Exploring Code View

The Dreamweaver Document window enables you to view a Web page in either Design view or Code view. You can see Design and Code views at the same time by selecting the Show Code and Design Views button in the toolbar. When you do this, it's easy to pop back and forth between the views with just a click of a button.

Did you Know?

Toggle the Panels Off

If you are using a floating panel version of Dreamweaver (as Mac users do), the panels continue to float over the code in Code view. You can toggle all the panels on and off by pressing the F4 key.

Create a new HTML page in Dreamweaver. Then click the Code View button in the toolbar to view the page's HTML code, as shown in Figure 5.1. The first line in the code is the **document type declaration**, which uses the doctype tag. It tells a validator which version of HTML the page uses. Dreamweaver adds this line automatically, so you shouldn't have to worry about it. After the document type declaration, the entire Web page is enclosed in HTML tags.

Head   Document type declaration

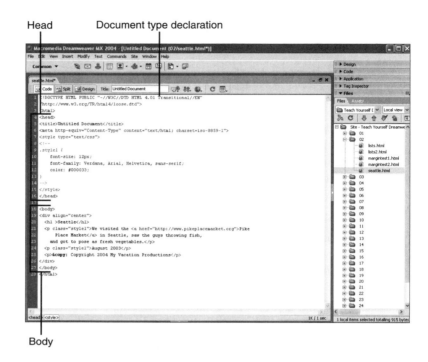

FIGURE 5.1
Code view displays
the code of a Web
page. This is a
basic HTML page
that Dreamweaver
creates without any
content.

Body

Dreamweaver creates Web pages by adding HTML tags (and other types of tags,
such as ASP.NET or XML, when you get more advanced). When you select an
object from Dreamweaver's Insert bar, Dreamweaver inserts the appropriate tag
or tags into your Web pages. Tags have properties called **attributes** that
Dreamweaver uses to fine-tune the way the object displays on the page. For
instance, an image tag (<img>) has the src (source) attribute, which sets the files
that the image tag displays. Most image tags also have height and width attributes that tell the browser the size of the image. These are just a few of the many
attributes of an image tag. Here is an example of an image tag with standard
attributes:

```
<img src="market.jpg" height="156" width="124">
```

Exploring the Head and Body of a Web Page

There are two main sections to a Web page: the head and the body. You'll see
these sections in the code. The head is surrounded by head tags, and the body is
surrounded by body tags. All the content visible in a Web page is in the body. The
head of the document contains code that supports the Web page. In the head of

the document, Dreamweaver automatically adds the `<title>` tag because the document title is part of the head. Right beneath the title, Dreamweaver inserts a meta tag, like this:

```
<meta http-equiv="Content-Type" content="text/html; charset=iso-8859-1">
```

This meta tag specifies the character set that the browser should use to display the page. The preceding example specifies the Latin character set for Western European languages. You can set the default character set for a Web page in the New Document category of Dreamweaver's Preferences dialog box. You can also set the font that Dreamweaver uses while you are working in Dreamweaver; you do this in the Fonts category of the Preferences dialog box.

Dreamweaver places other content into the head of the page as you author. The head is where most JavaScript and other scripting code, CSS definitions, and other code resides. You usually do not have to worry too much about editing the head of a document. While in Design mode, if you'd like to see a visual representation of the head content, select View, Head Content. You then see icons at the top of the Document window representing the elements in the head. When you select one of the icons, its properties appear in the Properties Inspector, as shown in Figure 5.2.

Head content

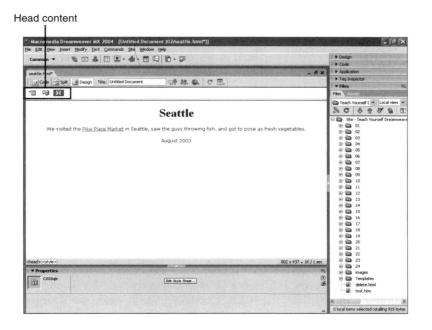

FIGURE 5.2
The elements in the head are represented by icons when you view the head content.

You display both Design view and Code view by selecting the middle button, the lengthily named Code and Design Views button. Place your cursor over the divider to modify the window size. Type some text into the Design view pane. The text is inserted into the body of the document. If you select an object in the Document window, the code for that object will be selected in Code view. This is a quick way to get to the code of a selected object. If your Web page is large, there might be a lot of HTML to go through, and it might not be easy to find the code that you are looking for. Try displaying only Design view. Highlight a single word that you typed. When you select Code view, Dreamweaver highlights that word.

Did you Know?

Inspecting Code

If you'd prefer to see the code in a window on top of the Document window, use the Code Inspector instead of Code view. You launch the Code Inspector by selecting Window, Code Inspector.

Discovering Code View Options

When you are in Code view, the View Options menu, shown in Figure 5.3, enables you to change the way the code is displayed. These commands are also available in View, Code View Options.

FIGURE 5.3
The View Options menu enables you to configure how code is displayed.

The following options are available in the View Options menu:

▶ **Word Wrap**—Wraps the lines of code so that you can view it all without scrolling horizontally. This setting does not change the code; it simply displays it differently.

▶ **Line Numbers**—Displays line numbers in the left margin.

▶ **Highlight Invalid HTML**—Turns on highlighting of invalid code that Dreamweaver doesn't understand.

▶ **Syntax Coloring**—Colors the code so that elements are easier to discern. You set the colors in the Code Coloring category of the Dreamweaver Preferences dialog box.

▶ **Auto Indent**—Makes the code automatically indent based on the settings in the Code Format category of the Preferences dialog box.

JavaScript Error? Check the Line Number

If you receive a JavaScript error when previewing a Web page in a browser, the error often displays the number of the code line that is causing the problem. You can view the code in Code view with the line numbers displayed to troubleshoot the error.

Did you Know?

If you make changes to the code in Code view, Dreamweaver doesn't display the changes in the Document window until you click the Refresh button in the toolbar. If you select View Options, Highlight Invalid Code, Dreamweaver highlights all invalid tags in bright yellow in both the Code Inspector and the Document window, as shown in Figure 5.4. When you select a highlighted tag, the Properties Inspector calls the tag invalid. It might give a reason why the tag is invalid and offer some direction on how to deal with it.

FIGURE 5.4
Invalid tags appear highlighted, and the Properties Inspector may offer insight into what to do about the problem.

Explanation

Invalid tag (it has no closing tag)

Viewing and Editing HTML Tags by Using the Quick Tag Editor

Using Dreamweaver's Quick Tag Editor is the quickest and easiest way to look at a single HTML tag and edit it. There are different ways you can access the Quick Tag Editor:

▶ Click the Quick Tag Editor icon on the Properties Inspector, as shown in Figure 5.5.

FIGURE 5.5
Click the Quick Tag Editor icon to view and edit the tag of the object that is currently selected.

Quick Tag Editor icon

▶ Right-click (Control+click on the Mac) any object and select the Edit Tag Code command from the context menu, as shown in Figure 5.6.

FIGURE 5.6
Using the Edit Tag Code command in the context menu launches the Quick Tag Editor.

▶ Select Modify, Quick Tag Editor.

▶ Right-click (Control+click on the Mac) a tag in the tag selector and select the Edit Tag command, as shown in Figure 5.7.

When you select the Quick Tag Editor icon in the Properties Inspector, the tag pops up beside the Quick Tag Editor icon. When you open the Quick Tag Editor from the context menu or Modify menu, the tag pops up directly above the object in the Document window.

FIGURE 5.7
Using the Edit Tag command in the tag selector launches the Quick Tag Editor.

The Quick Tag Editor has three modes:

▶ **Insert HTML**—This mode enables you to insert HTML in the Web page.

▶ **Edit Tag**—This mode enables you to edit the existing contents of a tag.

▶ **Wrap Tag**—This mode wraps another HTML tag around the selected tag.

When the Quick Tag Editor opens, you can toggle between the three modes by pressing Ctrl+T (Command-T on the Macintosh). The following sections explore each of the three modes.

Using the Insert HTML Mode

The Quick Tag Editor's Insert HTML mode, shows a pair of empty tag angle brackets with the insertion point between them. You can either enter text into the brackets, select from the tag drop-down menu, or both. Dreamweaver adds the closing tag automatically. The Quick Tag Editor starts in this mode when you do not have an object selected.

Using the Edit Tag Mode

The Quick Tag Editor's Edit Tag mode enables you to edit the HTML of an existing tag and the tag's contents. To add attributes of the selected tag, place the

80 | Chapter 5

insertion point at the end of the tag contents in the Quick Tag Editor and add a space. The tag drop-down menu appears, as shown in Figure 5.8, with attributes appropriate for the tag.

FIGURE 5.8

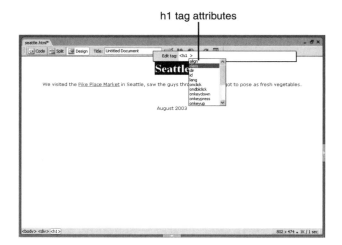

FIGURE 5.8
The tag drop-down menu presents attributes appropriate for the current tag. It appears automatically after the delay that is set in the Preferences dialog box.

When the Quick Tag Editor is open, you can use a keyboard shortcut to move up and down through the tag hierarchy. The Ctrl+Shift+< key combination (⌘-Shift-< on the Macintosh) selects the parent tag of the currently selected tag. As you press this key combination, the contents of the Quick Tag Editor change and the tag selector does, too. Use Ctrl+Shift+> (⌘-Shift-> on the Macintosh) to move down through the tag hierarchy. You can also use the Select Parent Tag and Select Child commands from the Edit menu.

Using the Wrap Tag Mode

The Quick Tag Editor's Wrap Tag mode, shown in Figure 5.9, enables you to wrap HTML around the current selection. For instance, when you have text selected, you can wrap a hyperlink (`<a href></a>`) or text formatting (`<h1></h1>`) around the text. Dreamweaver adds the opening tag before the selection and the closing tag after the selection. You can right-click (Control+click on the Mac) on the selection and select the Wrap Tag command. To add an attribute to the tag, press the spacebar to get the tag menu to drop down; you can pick the attribute you want from this list of attributes.

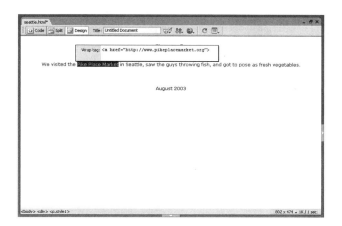

FIGURE 5.9
The Wrap Tag mode wraps an HTML tag around the current selection.

Setting Code Preferences

There are a number of preferences you can set for HTML. The four categories in Dreamweaver preferences that apply to HTML—Code Coloring, Code Format, Code Hints, and Code Rewriting—help control the way Dreamweaver creates and displays the code in your Web pages. If you are used to hand-coding your pages a certain way, don't complain about the way Dreamweaver formats it—change it!

Setting Code Color Preferences

The tags in Code view display code colored according to the settings in the Dreamweaver Preferences dialog box. You must have syntax coloring turned on in the View Options menu in order to see colored code. Select the Code Coloring category in the Preferences dialog box. You select which type of code you'd like to edit here. Also, this category enables you to set the background color for Code view. Either enter a color in hexadecimal format or use the color picker to select a color.

Select the HTML document type from the list and click the Edit Coloring Scheme button. The left side of the dialog box enables you to select a tag and then individually set a color for it on the right. To change a tag color, select a type of tag (HTML Image Tags are selected in Figure 5.10)and select a new text color or background color. You can also make the text bold, italic, or underlined.

FIGURE 5.10
You set the tag colors displayed in Code view in the Dreamweaver Preferences dialog box.

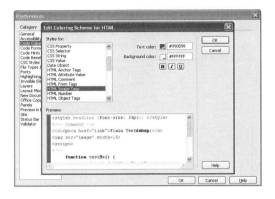

Setting Code Format Preferences

In the Code Format category of the Dreamweaver Preferences dialog box, shown in Figure 5.11, you set how Dreamweaver will create code. Dreamweaver indents code to make it easier to read. You can change the size of the indent in the Preferences dialog box. You can also select whether Dreamweaver should indent the code for tables and frames.

FIGURE 5.11
The Code Format category of the Dreamweaver Preferences dialog box enables you to set indentation, wrapping, and tag case.

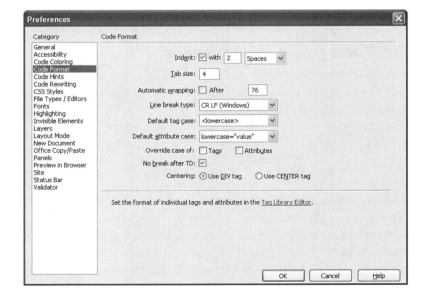

Apply Dreamweaver Formatting to Any Page
The Code Format category options apply only to new documents created in Dreamweaver. However, you can select Commands, Apply Source Formatting to apply the same formatting to an existing Web page.

Did you Know?

If automatic wrapping is selected, Dreamweaver will wrap a line that exceeds the column width entered in the After field in the Code Format category. Some lines may end up a little longer than that number because Dreamweaver does not wrap lines that will affect the appearance of the Web page. You can also set the type of line break that Dreamweaver uses. This can affect the way your code looks in different operating systems.

Because many W3C standards specify lowercase tags, it's a good idea to always use lowercase tags and lowercase attributes. By default, Dreamweaver uses lowercase for tags, the Default Tag Case setting, and attributes, the Default Attribute Case setting. In limited cases, you might want to override the case for tags or attributes. For instance, if you do not want Dreamweaver to change the tag or attribute case in an existing document, check the Override Case of Tags check box and the Override Case of Attributes check box, and Dreamweaver will leave the tag or attribute case as it exists.

The last setting is whether Dreamweaver will use center tags to center objects or div tags (`<div align="center"></div>`). Because the center tag has been deprecated in recent versions of the HTML specification, you should leave this setting at the default setting, Use DIV Tag.

Setting Code Hints Preferences

As you saw earlier this chapter, in the Quick Tag Editor examples, Dreamweaver drops down the **tag menu** displaying tag attributes for you to pick from. This is called a *code hint* in Dreamweaver. You can set which code hints Dreamweaver displays in the Code Hints category of the Preferences dialog box. Checking the Enable Auto Tag Completion setting makes Dreamweaver add a closing tag when you type the opening tag into Code view. You can also set the time delay for the tag menu by dragging the time slider bar at the top of the Code Hints dialog box.

Setting Code Rewriting Preferences

The code rewriting preferences set what changes Dreamweaver makes when it opens a Web page. Dreamweaver automatically fixes certain code problems, but only if you want it to. If you turn off the Rewrite Code options in the Code Rewriting category, Dreamweaver will still display invalid code that you can fix yourself if you need to.

Checking the Fix Invalidly Nested and Unclosed Tags check box tells Dreamweaver to rewrite tags that are invalidly nested. For instance, if you check this check box, Dreamweaver will rewrite `<b><i>hello</b></i>` as `<b><i>hello</i></b>`. Dreamweaver also inserts missing closing tags, quotation marks, or closing angle brackets when this setting is checked. When you select the Remove Extra Closing Tags check box, Dreamweaver will remove any stray closing tags that are left in the Web page.

Cleaning Up HTML Created with Microsoft Word

It's very convenient while working in Word to save a document as a Web page. Word does a great job of creating a Web page that looks very similar to the Word document and you can open and edit the HTML file in Word. The problem is that Word requires a lot of extra code to edit the Web page in Word. If you do not need to display a Web page in Word and you'd like to put it on the Web, you can use Dreamweaver to clean up the extra code.

To save a Word document as a Web page, in Word you select File, Save as Web Page. Word prompts you to name the document and adds the .htm file extension. The resulting page has a lot of extra code; Dreamweaver knows which code is extraneous and can delete that code. It's fun to take note of the number of lines of code in the file before you run the Clean Up Word HTML command. To do this, select Commands, Clean Up Word HTML.

Dreamweaver should automatically detect which version of Word created the HTML file from tags that Word adds to the file. You can also choose the version manually by using the Clean Up HTML From drop-down menu in the Clean Up Word HTML dialog box. The Clean Up Word HTML dialog box has two tabs—Basic and Detailed. The Basic tab has the following options:

▶ **Remove All Word Specific Markup**—Removes all the unnecessary Extensible Markup Language (XML), meta tags, and link tags from the head section; it also removes all Word XML markup, all conditional tags, all empty paragraphs, and all margins. You can select each of these options individually by using the settings on the Detailed tab.

► **Clean Up CSS**—Removes the extra CSS styles from the document. The styles removed are inline CSS styles, style attributes that begin with mso, non-CSS style declarations, CSS styles in table rows and cells, and unused styles. You can select these options individually by using the Detailed tab.

► **Clean Up <font> Tags**—Removes <font> tags.

► **Fix Invalidly Nested Tags**—Fixes the tags, particularly font markup tags, that are in an incorrect place.

► **Set Background Color**—Enables you to specify the background color of the Web page. Dreamweaver's default is white, #FFFFFF.

► **Apply Source Formatting**—Applies the code formatting options that are set in the Code Format category in the Preferences dialog box.

► **Show Log on Completion**—Displays a dialog box with a summary of the changes that Dreamweaver made to the Web page.

After you select the options from either the Basic or the Detailed tabs, click OK. Dreamweaver then cleans up the Web page. Your selected options will appear the next time you select the Clean Up Word HTML command. Make sure you look at how lean the code becomes! Now your file is optimized for display on the Web. Make sure you look in Code view and see how many lines of code were removed from the original.

Summary

In this chapter, you have learned how to use the Quick Tag Editor and Code view. You have learned how to set preferences for HTML tag colors, formatting, and rewriting. You have also learned how to use the Clean Up Word HTML command.

CHAPTER 6

Displaying Images on a Page

As Internet bandwidth increases, so does the opportunity to add images to Web pages. However, much of the emphasis in Web page creation remains on optimizing image file sizes so that they are as small as possible. Images offer a powerful way to send a message. One drawing or photograph can communicate a huge amount of information.

Adding an Image to a Page

Images are separate files that appear within a Web page. Because Dreamweaver is a WYSIWYG program, it enables you to see Web page images right in the Dreamweaver Document window. Images are not actually part of the HTML; they remain separate files that the browser inserts when you view the Web page.

Open the page that you created in Chapter 2, "Creating a Basic Web Page with Text." Delete the placeholder image. To insert an image into the Web page, follow these steps:

1. Place the cursor where you want to insert the image. You will see the insertion point blinking.

2. Select the Image command from the Insert bar (or the Insert menu).

3. Click the Browse icon (which looks like a folder) in the Properties Inspector to navigate to the directory where the image file resides. The Select Image Source dialog box appears.

4. Select an image file (see Figure 6.1). A thumbnail image is visible on the right side of the dialog box if the Preview Images check box is selected. Notice the file size, the dimensions of the image, and the download time located beneath the thumbnail. You set the target connection speed (14.4Kbps, 28.8Kbps, 33.6Kbps, 56Kbps, 64Kbps, 128Kbps, or 1500Kbps) that Dreamweaver uses to calculate these times in the Status Bar category of the Dreamweaver Preferences dialog box.

   When you locate the correct image, click OK.

FIGURE 6.1
The Select Image
Source dialog box
enables you to pre-
view an image
before you select it.

Thumbnail

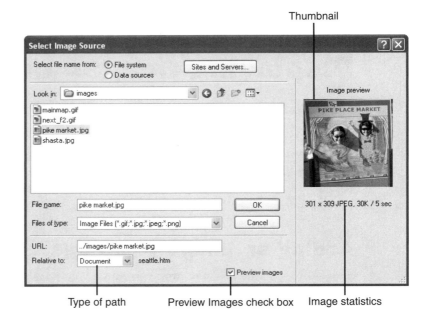

FIGURE 6.1
The Select Image
Source dialog box
enables you to pre-
view an image
before you select it.

Type of path   Preview Images check box   Image statistics

By the Way

Would You Like to Copy the File?

If you select an image from outside your currently selected Web site, Dreamweaver asks you if you would like to copy the image to the current site. If you've added a default images folder in your site definition, Dreamweaver automatically copies the image into that directory if you agree. Otherwise, Dreamweaver asks you where you'd like to copy the image. This is an easy way to add images to your site.

As shown in Figure 6.2, the image is now visible within the Web page. When the image is selected, the Properties Inspector displays the properties of the image. The Src (source) box displays the path to the image file. Notice that Dreamweaver automatically fills in the dimensions (width and height) of the image. Having the dimensions helps the browser load the image faster. The default unit of measure for width and height is pixels.

By the Way

Image Name Is Important for Rollover Images

Adding a name for an image will become more important later in this chapter, when you explore rollover images. Each rollover image must have a unique name that you add in the Properties Inspector. The JavaScript that facilitates the rollover requires that each image have a name.

Resizing handles

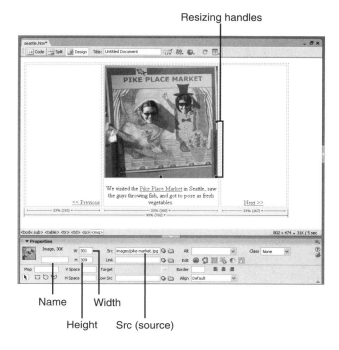

Name   Width
Height   Src (source)

FIGURE 6.2
The Properties
Inspector shows
the image's width,
height, and other
properties.

Don't Resize Images in Dreamweaver

You shouldn't resize an image in Dreamweaver. It's better to resize an image in a graphics program, such as Macromedia Fireworks or Adobe Photoshop. These programs optimize the file size, whereas Dreamweaver simply stretches or shrinks the image. However, if you accidentally resize an image in Dreamweaver, it's easy to return to the actual dimensions of the image. When the image dimensions have been modified, a small Refresh icon appears next to the width and height boxes in the Properties Inspector. Select this button to correct the image dimensions.

Watch Out!

Aligning an Image with Text

The Align drop-down menu in the Properties Inspector controls how objects that are located beside an image align with it. Align is very different from the text alignment settings you used in Chapter 2. You use the text alignment settings to align an image in the center or the left or the right of the screen. You use the Align drop-down menu to affect how *other* objects align with an image. In Figure 6.3, for instance, the image is aligned to the right of the text because Right is selected in the Align drop-down menu.

FIGURE 6.3
You can change
how an image
aligns with adjacent
objects in the Align
drop-down menu.

Image to the right of the text

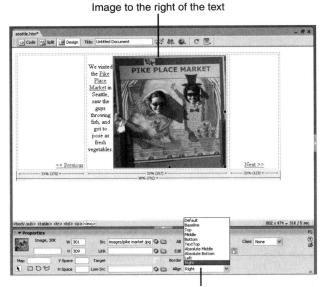

Alignment with other objects

Change the Align setting of the image so that all the text appears to the left, beside the image. To do this, select Right from the Align drop-down menu in the Properties Inspector. Why select Right? The image will be on the right. Remember that the Align options apply to the image but affect other elements within its vicinity. The alignment choices are described in Table 6.1.

TABLE 6.1 **Image Alignment Options in the Properties Inspector**

Align Option	Description
Default	Baseline-aligns the image, but this depends on the browser.
Baseline	Aligns the bottom of the image with the bottom of the element.
Top	Aligns the image with the highest element. Additional lines of text wrap beneath the image.
Middle	Aligns the baseline of the text with the middle of the image. Additional lines of text wrap beneath the image.
Bottom	Aligns the baseline of the text at the bottom of the image.
TextTop	Aligns the image with the highest text (not the highest element, as with the Top option). Additional lines of text wrap beneath the image.

TABLE 6.1 Continued

Align Option	Description
Absolute Middle	Aligns the middle of the image with the middle of the text beside it.
Absolute Bottom	Aligns the bottom of the highest element with the bottom of the image.
Left	Aligns the image to the left of other elements.
Right	Aligns the image to the right of other elements.

To increase the distance between the image and other page elements, set the V Space and H Space. V stands for vertical and H stands for horizontal. To add space to the right and left of an image, put a value in the H Space text box, as shown in Figure 6.4. Horizontal space is added to both the right and the left of the image. Vertical space is added to both the top and the bottom of the image.

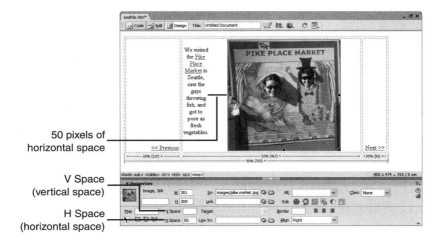

50 pixels of horizontal space

V Space (vertical space)

H Space (horizontal space)

FIGURE 6.4
Put a value in the H Space text box to increase the space to the right and the left of the image. Put a value in the V Space text box to increase the space above and below the image.

Adding Alternative Text

Believe it or not, some people who may surf to your Web pages are still using text-only browsers, such as Lynx. Others are stuck behind a very slow modem or Internet connection and have the images turned off in their browsers. Others are visually impaired and have text-to-speech (TTS) browsers that read the contents of Web pages. For all these viewers, you should add alternative text to your images.

You enter alternative text, called *alt text*, in the Alt drop-down menu in the Properties Inspector, as shown in Figure 6.5. Make the text descriptive of the image that it represents. Don't enter something such as "a picture." A better choice would be "Pike Place Market in Seattle." In some browsers, the Alt text also pops up like a ToolTip when the viewer puts the cursor over an image.

FIGURE 6.5
Alt text is useful for viewers who don't have images in their browsers or are visually impaired.

Alt (alternative) text

TTS browsers used by people who are visually impaired read the alt text description of an image to the user. When an image does not have the `Alt` attribute set, a TTS browser says the word *image*; listening to the browser say *image* over and over isn't very enjoyable! Some images on a Web page are purely ornamental and do not add information to the page—a divider line, for instance. Select `<empty>` from the Alt drop-down menu in the Properties Inspector to add alt text with no content; this makes text-to-speech browsers skip the image.

Did you Know?

> **Missing Alt Text Reporting**
> You can run a Missing Alt Text report by selecting Site, Reports. This report shows you all the images that are missing alt text.

Creating a Linked Image

The Link property appears in the Properties Inspector when you have text or an image selected. Linked images are common on the Web. When the user clicks a linked image, the browser loads the linked Web page. With an image selected, you can add a hyperlink in a couple ways:

▶ Type a URL into the Link box in the Properties Inspector.

▶ Browse for the linked page by selecting the Browse icon beside the Link box.

▶ Use the Point-to-File icon to link to a file. The Point-to-File icon enables you to simply drag the file over to the Files panel to create a link.

To enter a known URL as an image link, select an image on your Web page and make sure the Properties Inspector is open. Enter a URL in the Link box underneath the Src box.

Notice that when you enter a URL in the Link box, the Border property automatically changes to 0. This is so that you do not have the hyperlink highlight as a border around the image. If you prefer to have a highlighted border, set the border to a value greater than 0. You can also set a border for an image that isn't linked to anything. The border will then appear as a black box around the image.

After you save the Web page, preview it in a browser. When you click the image that has the hyperlink, your browser should go to the hyperlinked page.

Exploring Image Flavors: GIF, JPEG, and PNG

All browsers support the two standard image formats: GIF (pronounced either "gif" or "jif") and JPEG (pronounced "j-peg"). There is also a newer format, the portable network graphics (PNG—pronounced "ping") format. Here's a little more information about these three formats:

- ▶ **GIF**—This format is best for images that have blocks of continuous color, usually drawings.

- ▶ **JPEG**—This format is best for photographic images and images that do not have blocks of continuous color—for example, images that contain color gradients.

- ▶ **PNG**—This format is a replacement for the GIF format. It supports alpha channels that are useful for transparency. Although PNG is not as popular as the other two formats, its popularity is growing. This is the Macromedia Fireworks native file format.

Did you Know?

Optimize Your Images

Image optimization software programs can help you decide which image format is the most efficient to use for a particular image. These programs also help you reduce the number of colors in an image and improve other factors that reduce file size and download time.

You can select Command, Optimize Image in Fireworks when you have an image selected. This opens the image file in Fireworks, discussed starting in Chapter 20, "Getting to Know the Fireworks MX 2004 Interface."

The File Types/Editors category in the Preferences dialog box allows you to associate file extensions with different external programs. For example, you can associate the .jpg, .gif, and .png file extensions with Fireworks. When an image is selected in Dreamweaver, you can click the Edit button to open the image file in Fireworks. You make your edits and save the file. To associate an editor with a file extension, select a file extension in the File Types/Editors category, click the plus button, and browse to the image editor program.

While you're in an external image editor, you might want to create a low-resolution version of an image to link to from the Low Src box in the Properties Inspector. This image will appear during the initial loading of the Web page and then will turn into the higher-resolution version of the image. This functionality evolved to help speed up download times. Usually the low-resolution image is grayscale or a smaller version of a color image.

Editing Images Within Dreamweaver

Although you will probably want to become somewhat familiar with a graphics tool to create and optimize images to put in your Web sites, Dreamweaver has a few basic image editing capabilities to explore:

- ▶ **Edit**—Opens the selected image in Fireworks for editing (of course, you need to have Macromedia Fireworks or another image-editing program defined in the Preferences dialog box for this command to work).

- ▶ **Optimize**—Opens the selected image in the Fireworks optimization window.

- ▶ **Crop**—Lets you trim off unwanted portions of the image and saves the smaller file. This command works within Dreamweaver, enabling you to save the cropped image.

- ▶ **Resample**—This command becomes active after you've resized an image in Dreamweaver. It optimizes an image by adding or removing pixels in the image. This command works within Dreamweaver.

- ▶ **Brightness and Contrast**—Changes the brightness and contrast of an image to correct an image that is too bright or too dark. This command works within Dreamweaver.

- ▶ **Sharpen**—Sharpens a blurry image. This command works within Dreamweaver.

You can access all these image editing commands from the Properties Inspector when you have an image selected, as shown in Figure 6.6. Make sure you have a backup copy of any images you modify because Dreamweaver changes the actual image file.

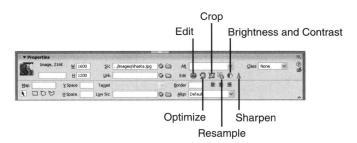

Crop

Edit   Brightness and Contrast

Optimize   Sharpen

Resample

FIGURE 6.6
Dreamweaver has image-editing commands that enable you to jump out to an image-editing program or edit an image directly in Dreamweaver.

Creating a Rollover Image

Dreamweaver makes it easy to implement rollover images by using the Rollover Image object. A **rollover image** is an image that swaps to another image when the viewer's cursor is over it. You need two image files with exactly the same dimensions in order to create a rollover.

To create a rollover image, follow these steps:

1. Place the insertion point where you want the rollover image to appear.

2. Select the Rollover Image object from the Insert bar or select Insert, Interactive Images, Rollover Image. The Insert Rollover Image dialog box appears.

3. Type a name for the image in the Image Name text field.

4. Select both the original image file and the rollover image file by clicking the Browse buttons next to those options and selecting the image files.

5. Check the Preload Rollover Image check box if you'd like the rollover image downloaded into the viewer's browser cache. With a preloaded image, there is less chance that the viewer will have to wait for the rollover image to download when he or she moves the cursor over the image.

6. Add a link to the rollover image by clicking the Browse button next to When Clicked, Go to URL or type in the external URL or named anchor.

7. The Insert Rollover Image dialog box should look as shown in Figure 6.7. Click the OK button.

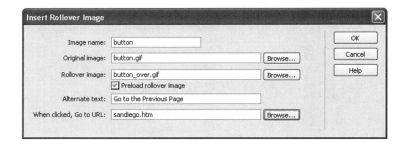

Flash Buttons and Text

Besides your standard run-of-the-mill graphics, Dreamweaver MX also makes it possible to include special Flash buttons and text in your document. While most heavy-duty Flash manipulation will take place in Flash MX, discussed starting in Chapter 31, "Understanding the Flash Interface," the Dreamweaver Flash buttons and text feature is worth a look.

Creating Flash Text

Dreamweaver has the capability to create special Text objects—Flash movies with text—directly in Dreamweaver. You do not need to have Flash installed on your computer to have this functionality. You can create Flash text and Flash buttons (you'll try this in a few minutes) right in Dreamweaver.

The Flash Text object enables you to create and insert a Flash movie consisting of text into your Web page. Inserting Flash text has the following advantages:

▶ You can use any font available on your computer. The viewer does not need to have the font installed on his or her computer.

▶ Flash text uses vector graphics, creating a very small file size—much smaller than if you created an image.

To insert a Flash Text object into a Web page, follow these steps:

1. Save your Web page. Select the Flash Text object from the Media menu of the Insert bar or the Insert menu. The Insert Flash Text dialog box appears (see Figure 6.8).

2. Select the font, size, style (bold or italic), and alignment. Select the color, which is the initial color of the text, and the rollover color, which is the color the user will see when he or she places the cursor over the text.

Enter text   Text characteristics

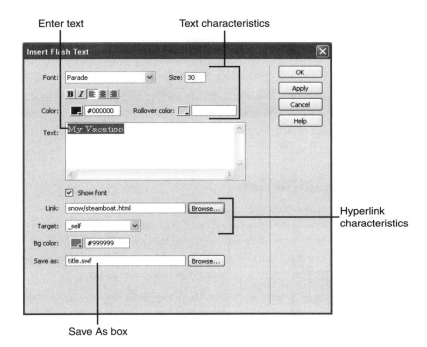

FIGURE 6.8
Set up the Flash Text object with a custom font, rollover color, and a background color.

Save As box

3. Type in the Text box the text that you want to appear. Make sure the Show Font check box is selected so that you can see what the font you have selected looks like.

4. Enter a URL in the Link text box or click the Browse button to browse to a Web page or enter a URL.

5. Optionally, use the Target text box to target a window for the link. You will learn more about this capability when you learn more about frames in Chapter 11, "Understanding and Building Frames and Framesets."

6. Select a background color from the Bg Color drop-down list. It's important to add a background color to the Flash movie if your Web page has a background color. Flash movies are not transparent, so if the background of your Web page is not white, the Flash movie will stand out as a white box. Simply use the eyedropper from the color picker and click your Web page behind the Insert Flash Text dialog box. Otherwise, your Flash text will be in a white box.

7. Enter a name for the Flash movie in the Save As box. Dreamweaver creates a separate Flash movie, with this name, for your Flash text.

8. Click OK. The text appears in the Dreamweaver Document window.

You can edit a Flash text movie after you have inserted it into a Web page by clicking the Edit button in the Properties Inspector when the movie is selected in the Document window. You can view the changes you make without closing the Insert Flash Text dialog box by selecting the Apply button.

In the Document window, you can resize Flash text by either dragging the resizing handles or entering new values for W (width) and H (height) in the Properties Inspector. Click the Reset Size button to return to the original dimensions of the movie.

Creating a Flash Button

Dreamweaver comes with a number of templates for creating Flash buttons right in Dreamweaver. As with the Flash Text object you just created, you can have Dreamweaver create Flash button movies automatically. Flash buttons use custom fonts and many have animations when the user places his or her mouse over the button. To insert a Flash button into a Web page, follow these steps:

1. Save your Web page. Select the Insert Flash Button object from the Media tab of the Insert bar or select Insert, Media, Insert Flash Button. The Insert Flash Button dialog box appears.

2. Select a button style from the Style list. A preview of the button appears in the Sample window at the top of the dialog box. You can click the preview to see what the down state of the button looks like and to see any animation effects that the button has.

3. Add text for the button in the Button Text field. Only buttons that already have the default "Button Text" text in the Sample window will display this text. You cannot add text to buttons that do not already display text.

4. Set the font and font size for the button text in the Font drop-down menu and Size text box. You can choose any font that's installed on your computer.

5. Enter a URL for a hyperlink and a target, if necessary, in the Link and Target text boxes, respectively. As when you create Flash text, you need to be careful about document-relative addressing. It's best to save the Flash movie in the same directory as the linked Web page.

6. Add a background color from the Bg Color drop-down list. This color appears around the button, not within the button art. Again, be sure to complete this step if you have a background color on your Web page so that there isn't any white surrounding your button.

7. Click OK. The button appears in the Dreamweaver Document window.

You can edit the Flash button as you did the Flash text. Both the button and the text movies are saved as Flash .swf files and can be edited in Flash. Some buttons can be used as groups. For instance, a number of e-commerce buttons are available to create purchasing and checkout applications.

Summary

In this chapter, you have learned how to insert an image into a Web page and how to set a link, low-resolution source, vertical space and horizontal space, and alt text. You have learned how to change the size of an image border and edit the image by using an external editor. You have learned how to align an image on a page and align it in relationship to other elements beside it. You have also created a rollover image and explored the built-in Flash features of Dreamweaver MX.

CHAPTER 7

Creating Image Maps and Navigation Bars

In Chapter 6, "Displaying Images on a Page," you inserted an image into a Web page and created a rollover image. In this chapter, you'll expand on that knowledge, creating an image map and a navigation bar. These are more complicated uses of images.

Adding Links to a Graphic by Using Image Maps

An **image map** is an image that has regions, called *hotspots*, defined as hyperlinks. When a viewer clicks a hotspot, it acts just like any other hyperlink. Instead of adding one hyperlink to an entire image, you can define a number of hotspots on different portions of an image. You can even create hotspots in different shapes.

Image maps are useful for presenting graphical menus that the viewer can click to select regions of a single image. For instance, you could create an image out of a picture of North America. You could draw hotspots around the different countries in North America. When the viewer clicked a country's hotspot, he or she could jump to a Web page with information on that country.

Dreamweaver creates **client-side** image maps, meaning that the Web page holds all the defined coordinates and hyperlinks. The other type of image map, a **server-side** image map, depends on a program that runs on a Web server to interpret coordinates and hyperlinks. Client-side image maps react more quickly than server-side image maps to user input because they don't have to contact the server for information.

Creating an Image Map

When an image is selected, you see four image map tools in the lower corner of the expanded Properties Inspector. These four tools are used to define image map hotspots. The arrow is the Pointer Hotspot tool, which is used to select or move the hotspots. There are three image map hotspot tools: One tool draws rectangles, one draws circles, and one draws polygons.

To create an image map, follow these steps:

1. Insert an image into a Web page. The image must be selected for the image map tools to appear in the Properties Inspector.

2. Give the map a name in the Map Name text box, as shown in Figure 7.1. The name needs to be unique from other map names in the page.

Map Name text box

FIGURE 7.1
Give an image map a name and use the hotspot tools to draw hotspots within an image map.

Hotspot tools

Pointer Hotspot tool

3. Select one of the hotspot tools. You'll spend the next minutes exploring each of the hotspot tools in depth.

4. With a newly drawn hotspot selected, type a URL in the Link box, or click the Browse icon to browse to a local Web page. You can also link a hotspot to a named anchor by entering a pound sign followed by the anchor name.

5. Enter alternative text for the hotspot in the Alt text box. As discussed in Chapter 6, some browsers display this text as a ToolTip.

6. Optionally, select a window target from the Target drop-down menu in the Properties Inspector. Target windows will be covered a little later in this chapter, in the section "Targeting a Link to Open in a New Browser Window," where you will open a new browser window by using the Target drop-down menu selections. Most of the time, you probably won't select a target.

You set all the image properties for an image map just as you would an ordinary image. You can set the vertical space, horizontal space, alt text, border, and alignment. If you copy and paste the image map into another Web page, all the image map properties come along, too.

Adding a Rectangular Hotspot to an Image Map

To add a rectangular hotspot to your image map, first select the Rectangle Hotspot tool. Click and drag the crosshair cursor to make a rectangle the dimensions of the hotspot you want to create. When you release the mouse, a highlighted box appears over the image, as in Figure 7.2. With the hotspot selected, enter a URL into the Link box in the Properties Inspector.

Rectangular hotspot

FIGURE 7.2
Create a rectangle and link it to a URL. Now it's a hotspot!

Rectangle Hotspot tool

To move or adjust the size of the hotspot, you need to first select the Pointer Hotspot tool. You can't use the other hotspot tools to adjust the hotspot, or you will end up creating another hotspot. Click the hotspot with the Pointer Hotspot tool and either move the hotspot to another location or resize the hotspot by using the resizing handles.

In the Web page HTML, the rectangular hotspot is defined by two sets of x and y coordinates. The upper-left corner of the rectangle is recorded as the first two coordinates in the code and the lower-right corner of the rectangle is recorded as the last two coordinates. The coordinates are in pixels, and they are relative to the image, not to the Web page. The HTML code for a rectangular area looks like this:

```
<area shape="rect" coords="127,143,251,291" href="services.htm">
```

In this example, the upper-left corner of the rectangle is 127 pixels from the left of the image and 143 pixels from the top of the image. The bottom-right corner of the rectangle is 251 pixels from the left of the image and 291 pixels from the top. It's nice to have a visual representation in Dreamweaver and not have to figure this out yourself, isn't it?

Adding a Circular Hotspot to an Image Map

A circular area might better define some areas in your image map than a rectangular one. You create a circular hotspot just as you create a rectangular one. Select the Circle Hotspot tool and then click and drag to create the hotspot. Notice that the hotspot is always a perfect circle and not an ellipse. Reposition or resize the hotspot by using the Pointer Hotspot tool.

You can understand why you can have only a circle and not an ellipse when you see how the circular hotspot coordinates are defined. A circle is defined by three values: The circle's radius and the x and y values that define the circle's center. The HTML code defining a circular area looks like this:

```
<area shape="circle" coords="138,186,77" href="about.htm">
```

Adding an Irregular Hotspot to an Image Map

Sometimes the area you'd like to turn into a hotspot just isn't circular or rectangular. The Polygon Hotspot tool enables you to create any shape you want to define an irregular hotspot.

You use the Polygon Hotspot tool a little differently than you use the Circle or Rectangle Hotspot tools. First, select the Polygon Hotspot tool from the Properties Inspector. Instead of clicking and dragging to create a shape, click once for every point in the polygon, as shown in Figure 7.3. You should move around the area you want to define as a hotspot in either a clockwise or counterclockwise manner; clicking randomly may create an odd polygon. When you are finished creating the points of the polygon, select the Pointer Hotspot tool to complete the polygon. You select the Pointer Hotspot tool in order to deselect the Polygon Hotspot tool so that you don't accidentally add stray points on the screen. Or you can double-click when you are finished drawing the polygon.

Polygon hotspot

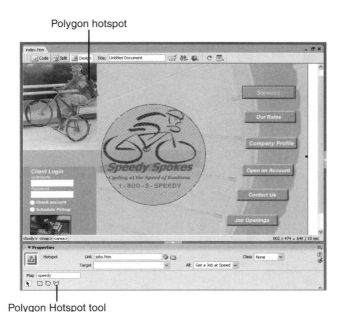

Polygon Hotspot tool

FIGURE 7.3
To create an irregu-
lar hotspot with the
Polygon Hotspot
tool, click once for
every point and
double-click to fin-
ish.

A polygon is defined by as many x and y coordinates, each representing one of
the corner points, as you need to define the hotspot shape. The HTML code for a
sample polygon hotspot looks like this:

```
<area shape="poly"
coords="85,14,32,33,29,116,130,99,137,130,140,70,156,66,198,84" href="jobs.htm">
```

The polygon defined in this HTML is made up of eight points, so there are eight
pairs of x and y coordinates.

Aligning Hotspots

Dreamweaver has built-in alignment tools that you can use to align the hotspots
in an image map. First, you need to select the hotspots you want to align. To
select all the hotspots in an image map, use the keyboard shortcut Ctrl+A in
Windows or Command-A on the Macintosh. Or you can hold down Shift as you
click hotspots to add them to the selection. You can tell when hotspots are selected
because you can see the resizing handles.

Sometimes it is difficult to finely align hotspots with your mouse. You can use the
arrow keys to move a hotspot or multiple hotspots one pixel at a time. The Align
submenu under the Modify menu contains commands to align hotspots, as

shown in Figure 7.4. You can align multiple hotspots on the left, right, top, or bottom. You can make multiple hotspots the same height by using the Make Same Height command or the same width by using the Make Same Width command.

FIGURE 7.4
The Modify menu's Align submenu has commands for aligning hotspots.

Hotspots can overlap each other. Whichever hotspot is on top (usually the one created first) will be the link triggered by clicking on the overlapping area. You can change the stacking order of hotspots by using the commands located in the Arrange submenu of the Modify menu. You might want to create overlapping hotspots on purpose as part of the design of an image map. For instance, you might use a circular hotspot over part of a rectangular hotspot. Alternatively, the overlapping might simply be a consequence of the limited shapes you have available to define the hotspots.

It's difficult to tell which hotspot is on top of another hotspot. If you've recently created the image map, you know which hotspot was created first and is therefore on top. You can manipulate the stacking order of the hotspots by selecting Modify, Arrange, Bring to Front or Send to Back. If a hotspot overlaps another and needs to be on top, select the Bring to Front command.

Targeting a Link to Open in a New Browser Window

When a hyperlink is selected, the Properties Inspector has a drop-down box called Target. Frames use the target attribute to load a page into a defined frame.

Frames are covered in Chapter 11, "Understanding and Building Frames and Framesets."

There are four reserved target names that you can use with any link. Three of the four reserved target names—*parent, self, and top*— are used mainly with frames. But the _blank reserved target name is useful when you want to leave the current browser window open and have the link open a new browser window with the linked Web page in it. To use it, select _blank from the Target drop-down menu when one of the hotspots is selected. Preview your Web page in the browser and select that link. Now the original window, containing your image map, is open, and so is a new window, with the linked file in it.

Opening a new window is useful when you want to keep your original Web page open but allow the user to jump to other Web pages. When the user closes the new window, the window containing your site will still be open. It's nice to warn the users about this so that they will not get confused. You can add text to a link that opens a new window a message that says something like "link opens new window" or "close new window to return." In Chapter 14, "Inserting Scripted Functionality by Using Behaviors," you'll learn how to use a Dreamweaver behavior to open a new window. Using JavaScript enables you to set the window size.

Creating a Navigation Bar with Rollover Images and Links

What if you wanted to create a bunch of rollover images as a navigation bar? And what if you wanted each of them to have a down button state, too? You could create all these buttons individually, or you could use the Dreamweaver Insert Navigation Bar dialog box to create all the buttons at once.

You simulate a button by swapping images that are the same size but look slightly different. Each image represents a **button state**. The default button state is up. The down state appears when the user clicks the mouse on the button; the down state image usually modifies the up state image so that it looks pressed down. The over state appears when the user passes his or her mouse over the button. The navigation bar can also add an over when down state, which appears when the user rolls the mouse over the button when it is already in the down state. You must add an up state image to a navigation bar, but all the other button states are optional.

To create a navigation bar, follow these steps:

1. Select the Navigation Bar object from the Object panel or select Insert, Image Objects, Navigation Bar). The Insert Navigation Bar dialog box appears.

2. An initial, unnamed button element is visible. Change the element name to the name of your first button. (If you simply go the next step, Dreamweaver will automatically give your button the same name as the name of the image file.)

3. Browse to load a button up image, a button over image, and a button down image. You can also enter an over while down image, which is a rollover image for the down state of a button. All these images must be the same size.

4. Enter a hyperlink in the When Clicked, Go to URL box. Type in a URL or browse to a Web page. The targeting drop-down menu next to the URL box enables you to target a specific frame. You'll explore targeting and frames in Chapter 11.

5. Check the Preload Images check box if you want the images to be automatically preloaded. Check the Show "Down Image" Initially check box if you want the button to appear pressed in at first.

6. Add additional buttons by clicking the plus button and repeating steps 2–5. Rearrange the order of the buttons by using the arrow buttons at the top of the Insert Navigation Bar dialog box. To delete a button, click the minus button.

7. At the bottom of the Insert Navigation Bar dialog box, choose to insert the navigation bar either horizontally or vertically into the Web page. Select the Use Tables check box if you'd like the navigation bar to be created in a table. (Chapter 10, "Designing Page Layout by Using Tables," explains how to use tables for layout.) The table layout occurs here for you automatically.

8. The Insert Navigation Bar dialog box should look as shown in Figure 7.5 after you have added several elements. When you are finished adding buttons, click OK.

To test the buttons, save your file and preview it in a browser. If you've made a mistake, don't fret! You can edit the navigation bar by selecting the Navigation Bar object again.

Add or remove elements

Reorder elements

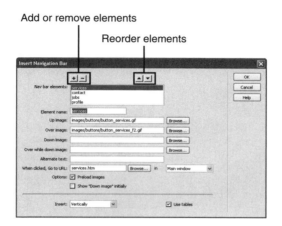

FIGURE 7.5
Each element in a navigation bar consists of multiple images linked to a URL. The navigation bar can be situated vertically or horizontally.

One Navigation Bar per Customer

You can have only one navigation bar per Web page.

By the Way

Make Button State Images the Same Size

Rollover and button images require that the up, over, and down images be all the same size. Otherwise, the over and down images will stretch to the size of the original up image and will be distorted.

Watch Out!

Summary

In this chapter, you have learned how to create a client-side image map that includes rectangular, circular, and polygonal shapes. You have learned how to use targeting to open a new browser window. You have also created a navigation bar with various button states.

CHAPTER 8

Managing Assets by Using the Assets Panel

After you have designed your Web page, you will populate it with page elements. The elements that make up your individual Web pages are likely to come from various sources and will be different types of objects. You might include Flash movies, images created in Fireworks, various colors, links, clip art, and photographs in your Web pages.

You need to gather and organize these page elements before you start to create a Web page. Dreamweaver MX 2004's Assets panel enables you to organize the elements of a Web site to quickly access and reuse items. The Assets panel can help you become more efficient and better organized!

What Are Assets?

Web pages are not just made out of text and code. You use images, movies, colors, and URLs to present information in Web pages. These Web page elements are called **assets**.

The Assets panel organizes these elements, enabling you to quickly find an image or a color that you want to use. You can preview assets in the Assets panel. You can also create a list of favorite assets—ones that you use often.

The Library and Templates panels are part of the Assets panel. These panels are covered in the next two chapters.

Managing Assets in the Assets Panel

Dreamweaver automatically catalogs the assets for an entire site. When you open the Assets panel, you can select one of the category buttons from along the left side of the panel to display a list of all the assets of that type in your site. The Assets panel includes the following categories:

- ▶ Images
- ▶ Colors
- ▶ URLs
- ▶ Flash Movies
- ▶ Shockwave Movies
- ▶ Movies
- ▶ Scripts
- ▶ Templates
- ▶ Library

You can browse an asset category to preview the assets until you find the one you want. The Assets panel enables you to quickly add a selected asset to your current page. Later this chapter you'll learn how to set some assets as favorites so that you can find them even more quickly.

Assets are specific to the current site that you are working in. Often you'll use certain page elements in multiple Web sites that you are working in. You can copy your assets to another Web site defined in Dreamweaver to use in that Web site.

Listing Assets in a Site

When you open the Assets panel, Dreamweaver goes through the cache and automatically catalogs all the assets within your current site. It places the assets into the correct categories by examining the file extensions of the files in the Web site. The Assets panel lists only the assets that are in the currently selected site. When you change sites, you might have a message box appear briefly while the Assets panel is being updated.

You can view all the assets in a category by selecting a category button along the left side of the Assets panel. Each of the categories except the Library and Templates categories has two radio buttons at the top of the panel, as shown in Figure 8.1, enabling you to select whether you want to see all the assets of that type or just your favorites. You'll learn how to create a favorite asset in a few minutes.

After you add an asset to your site, you might need to click the Refresh button to see it listed in the Assets panel. You can refresh the list of assets anytime.

Images

Colors

URLs

Flash Movies

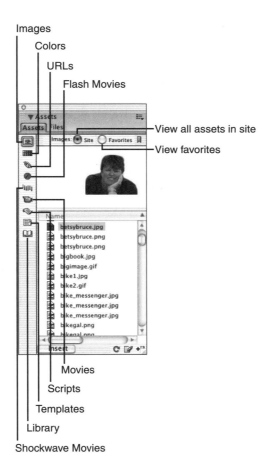

View all assets in site

View favorites

FIGURE 8.1
The Assets panel
has buttons for the
different categories
along the left side
and radio buttons
at the top to select
whether to view all
the assets or just
your favorites.

Movies

Scripts

Templates

Library

Shockwave Movies

Previewing Assets

When you select a category in the Assets panel, the first asset in the list of that
category is selected in the lower half of the panel, and a preview of that asset
appears in the upper half. You can preview assets by selecting them in the list. A
preview of the asset selected in the list appears in the upper half of the Assets
panel.

By default, the items listed in the Assets panel are sorted alphabetically. You can
sort the items by any of the available column headings by clicking a column
heading. For instance, if you want to sort your image assets by file size, you click
the column heading File Size.

Sometimes you might want to locate the original asset file in the Site Manager window. In Dreamweaver you can open the Site Manager window with the asset file highlighted: In Windows you right-click on an asset item (in Mac you Control+click) and then select the Locate in Site command from the context menu. This works only on assets that are individual files, such as movies or images, and not on assets that are elements of Web pages, such as URLs or colors.

Exploring Image Assets

The Images category of the Assets panel displays all the images in your defined Web site (refer to Figure 8.1). Dreamweaver catalogs images in GIF, JPG, or PNG format. Dreamweaver displays a preview of the selected image in the top half of the Assets panel.

Exploring Color Assets

The Colors category of the Assets panel, as shown in Figure 8.2, displays all the colors used in the defined Web site. The colors are catalogs, and they are displayed in hexadecimal format. Dreamweaver displays a preview of the selected color, along with both its hexadecimal and RGB (red, green, blue) definition, in the top half of the Assets panel. Beside the color name, Dreamweaver displays whether the color is part of the Web-safe palette.

FIGURE 8.2
The Colors category shows the hexadecimal and RGB definition of the colors in the Web site.

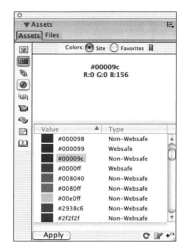

By the Way

Is the Color Web-Safe?

You explored the Dreamweaver palettes when you learned about the color picker in Chapter 2, "Creating a Basic Web Page with Text." One of the available palettes is the Web-safe palette, which contains the 216 colors that work on all browsers on both the Windows and Mac platforms. The Assets panel tells you whether the colors listed in the Colors category are within those 216 colors by marking them as Websafe or Non-Websafe in the Type column.

Exploring Link Assets

The URLs category of the Assets panel holds all the hyperlinks contained in the currently defined Web site (refer to Figure 10.2). This category lists all URLs in the site, including FTP, mailto, JavaScript, HTTP (Web), and HTTPS (secure Web).

Exploring Movie Assets

There are three different movie asset categories: Flash Movies, Shockwave Movies, and Movies. The Movies category catalogs movie types other than Flash or Shockwave movies, such as QuickTime or MPEG movies. There is a Play/Stop button in the upper-right corner of the preview window that enables you to play the movie in the preview window.

Exploring Script Assets

The Scripts category is where you will see some of the scripts you create with Dreamweaver. (You'll learn more about scripts in Chapter 14, "Inserting Scripted Functionality by Using Behaviors.") The Scripts category of the Assets panel catalogs all the *external* script files in your Web site, as shown in Figure 8.3. External script files end with the .js extension. These script files contain JavaScript functions that you can call from your Web pages. The preview window shows the actual code in the script.

You reference an external script in the head section of your Web page. If you call a function that is contained in an external script, you need to link the external script file to your Web page by dragging it from the Scripts category of the Assets panel into the Head Content section of the Dreamweaver Document window (which you open by selecting View, Head Content), as shown in Figure 8.4.

FIGURE 8.3
All the external
script files are
shown in the
Scripts category of
the Assets panel.

FIGURE 8.4
Drag an external
script from the
Scripts category of
the Assets panel
into the Head
Content section of
a Web page.

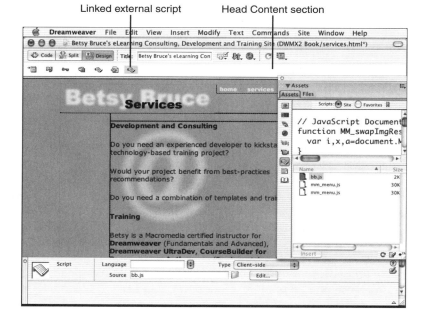

Adding Assets to a Web Page

Use the Assets panel to add assets to a Web page. To add an asset to your Web
page, follow these steps:

1. Select the category.

2. Find the asset you want to add by scrolling through the list for the name or viewing the preview in the preview window.

3. Place the insertion point in your Web page where you want the asset to be located.

4. Click the Insert button and the asset is inserted into your Web page.

You can also use assets from the Assets panel to affect other objects on a Web page. For instance, you can apply a color asset to some text on your Web page as follows:

1. Select some text on the page.

2. Drag a color from the Assets panel by picking up the name in either the preview window or the category list.

3. Drop the color on the selected text.

Instead of dragging and dropping, you can simply select the text and the color and then click the Apply button to apply the color to the text.

Jump Assets Alphabetically

To quickly jump to a section in the assets list, click within the assets list and then type the first letter of the name of the item you are looking for. You will jump to the first item that begins with that letter.

Did you Know?

Creating Favorite Assets

There are often assetsyour Web site that you use repeatedly. You can assign these assets to the favorites list so that they are easy to pick out of the Assets panel. The favorites list is displayed when the Favorites radio button is selected at the top of the Assets panel.

To create a favorite asset, select the asset in the Assets panel and then select the Add to Favorites button. When you select the Favorites radio button, the favorite assets that you just added should be listed, as shown in Figure 8.5. You can give a favorite a different name by right-clicking it, selecting the Edit Nickname command, and typing a name that is easy to remember.

FIGURE 8.5
You can list only
your favorite assets
in a certain Assets
panel category
instead of all the
assets in the site.

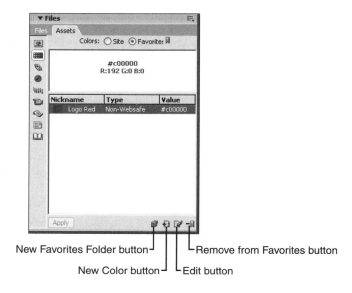

New Favorites Folder button ─┘   └─ Remove from Favorites button

New Color button ─┘ └─ Edit button

By the
Way

No Templates or Library Favorites

Favorites are not available for the Templates and Library categories of the Assets
panel.

You can organize your favorites into groups by creating new folders within the
favorites list. The New Favorites Folder button (shown in Figure 8.5) enables you
to create a folder within the favorites list. After you create a folder, drag and drop
items into the folder. Figure 8.6 shows favorite items organized into folders.
Expand the folder to view the contents by selecting the + button next to the folder
name. Collapse the folder view by selecting the − button next to the folder name.

Remove items from the favorites list by selecting the Remove from Favorites button. The item is removed only from the favorites list and is not deleted from the
Web site. You can also delete an item from the list by right-clicking the item and
selecting the Remove from Favorites command from the context menu.

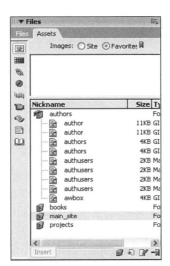

FIGURE 8.6
Organize your
favorite assets by
creating folders in
the favorites list.

Creating New Assets in the Assets Panel

You can use the Assets panel to help design your Web site. Dreamweaver enables you to create new assets in certain asset categories. You can add a new color, URL, template, or library item. Chapter 19, "Creating and Applying a Template," describes how to create new library items and templates.

When you begin creating a Web site, you can organize your development effort with the help of the Assets panel. Organize your image assets into favorites so that commonly used images are easy to find. Define commonly used links and colors so that they can be quickly applied to Web pages.

The Assets panel catalogs the assets that already exist in your site. When you are in the favorites list, you can also create new URLs and colors to use in your site. These new assets are then available, even though they haven't yet been used in your Web site.

To create a new color or link asset, follow these steps:

    1. Select the Favorites radio button at the top of the Assets panel. Select either the Colors category or the URLs category.

2. Right-click to launch a context menu and select the New Color or New URL command. Either the color picker appears or the Add URL dialog box appears.

3. Pick a color from the color picker or fill in the URL and nickname in the Add URL dialog box.

Copying Assets to Another Site

The Assets panel displays the assets of the current site. Sometimes you might want to share assets among different Web sites defined in Dreamweaver. You can copy a single asset, a group of assets, or a favorites group to another site.

To copy a single asset to another site, simply right-click (Control+click on the Mac) the item name and select the Copy to Site command. Select the defined site you want to copy the asset to. Dreamweaver copies the exact folder structure and the file for an image or movie asset.

To copy a group of assets to another defined site, select multiple asset items by holding down Shift while clicking (or Control+clicking on a Mac) on the item names. Right-click (or Control+click on a Mac) the group and select the Copy to Site command from the context menu. All the assets are then copied to the other site. You can also copy a group of favorites to another site by following these steps.

Summary

In this chapter, you have learned how to use assets from the Assets panel. You have learned how to sort, add, and organize assets. You have explored the various types of assets and learned how to create favorites. You have also learned how to copy assets from site to site.

CHAPTER 9

Displaying Data with Tables

Tables not only provide the ability to logically present data in columns and rows, but they also enable Web page designers to control where objects appear on the page. This chapter introduces you to creating tables. In Chapter 10, "Designing Page Layout by Using Tables," you'll explore controlling page layout with tables.

Using tables can be a powerful way to organize and display data. You use tables in HTML just as you use them in a word processing application. Tables consist of rows, columns, and cells. Dreamweaver presents many ways to format tables the way you would like them to appear to your viewer.

Creating a Table for Data

Let's begin exploring tables by adding to your Web page a table that will hold some data. Examples of this type of table are a phone list of people in your company or class at school, an ocean tide table with times and tide levels, and a recipe with amounts and ingredients. This type of table usually has a border around the cells, although it doesn't have to. Generally, tables used for page layout purposes, explored in the next chapter, have the table borders turned off.

Adding a Table to a Web Page

Dreamweaver has two modes, enabling you to create tables in two different ways. When Dreamweaver is in Standard mode, you insert a table by using the Table object and set the number of rows and columns in the Table dialog box. In Layout mode, you can draw tables and table cells by using the cursor. You set which mode you are in by clicking one of the buttons in the Layout category of the Insert bar or by selecting View, Table Mode. For this chapter, make sure you are in Standard mode and not Layout mode. You should not see a colored bar with the title "Layout mode" across the top of the Document window. You'll use Layout mode in Chapter 10.

To insert a table into your Web page, follow these steps:

1. Place the insertion point in your Web page where you want the table to be inserted.

2. Select the Table icon in the Insert bar or choose Insert, Table. The Table dialog box appears, as shown in Figure 9.1.

FIGURE 9.1
The Table dialog box allows you to set the initial values of the table. You can always edit these values in the Properties Inspector later.

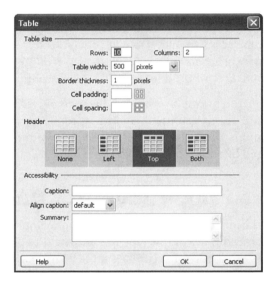

3. Accept the default values or enter your own values into the Rows and Columns text boxes. You can also select the width of the table and the border size in this dialog box. You'll learn about all these parameters later in this chapter.

4. When you're done setting values in this dialog box, click OK.

Tables (`<table>` and `</table>`) are made up of table rows (`<tr>` and `</tr>`) that contain table cells (`<td>` and `</td>`). In HTML, tables are structured by their rows; you do not need to define columns, and there isn't a tag in HTML that creates columns. In the rest of this chapter and the next chapter you will modify the attributes of tables, table rows, and table cells. There are also header tags (`<th>` and `</th>`) that you can optionally use to create header cells; the text in header cells appears bold and centered.

When you select a table or when the insertion point is within a table, Dreamweaver displays the width of the table and the width of each of the columns in the **table header**, which appears either above or below the table. The table header, shown in Figure 9.2, is visible only in Dreamweaver and doesn't appear in the Web browser. To turn off the display of the table header in Dreamweaver, select View, Visual Aids, Table Widths.

Rows   Columns   Table header

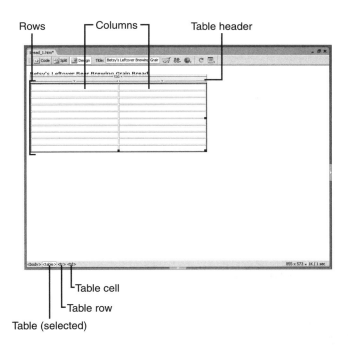

Table cell
Table row
Table (selected)

FIGURE 9.2
Dreamweaver displays the table header above a table.

Selecting Table Elements

You can select an entire table in a couple ways. I think the easiest way to select the table is to click the little arrow in the table header to open the table header menu, shown in Figure 9.3. Choose the Select Table command from the table header menu to select the table. You can also use the tag selector in Dreamweaver's status bar by clicking the table tag to select a table. Click inside one of the cells in your table. The status bar displays the tag hierarchy, including the table tag.

To select a cell, simply click inside it. To select an entire row, position your cursor slightly to the left of the table row until the cursor turns into a solid black arrow. Click while the cursor is the solid black arrow to select the row. Use the same procedure, positioning your cursor slightly above the column, to select an entire column. Or use the Select Column command from the column header menu.

FIGURE 9.3
The table header menu contains commands, including the Select Table command.

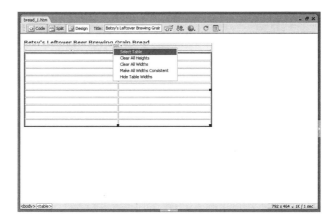

You can select a group of cells by dragging the cursor across them. Another way to select a group of cells is to first select one cell and then hold down Shift while you click another cell. All the cells between the two cells are then selected. To select cells individually, hold down Ctrl while you click (or Command+click on the Mac) a cell to add it to the selection.

Watch Out!

Drag Over Cells Carefully

When a table is empty, it's easy to drag the cursor across the group of cells you want to select. Start dragging while your cursor is inside the first cell. When the cells contain assets, however, it's too easy to accidentally move objects from their cells when you use this procedure.

The Properties Inspector shows different attributes, depending on what you currently have selected. There are two basic ways that the Properties Inspector appears while you're working with tables:

▶ When an entire table is selected, the Properties Inspector looks as shown in Figure 9.4, displaying properties of the entire table.

FIGURE 9.4
The Properties Inspector displays properties that apply to the entire table when the entire table is selected.

▶ When an individual cell, entire row, or entire column is selected, the Properties Inspector looks as shown in Figure 9.5, displaying properties that affect the selected cells.

FIGURE 9.5
The Properties Inspector displays properties of selected cells when an individual cell, entire row, or entire column is selected.

Setting Cell Padding and Cell Spacing

Let's start over by adding a new table. Again, click the Table icon in the Common category of the Insert bar. In the Table dialog box, set the number of rows and columns you'd like the table to have (you can always change this later). Set the table width to either a pixel or percentage value. Set the border thickness also.

The next settings in the Table dialog box are for **cell padding** and the **cell spacing** (see Figure 9.6):

▶ **Cell Padding**—This is where you set the amount of space between an object contained in a cell and the border of the cell. It's the padding that sits between the contents of the cell and the cell border.

▶ **Cell Spacing**—This is where you set the amount of space between two cells. This setting controls the amount of space between cells.

The Table dialog box displays illustrations next to each of these settings, highlighting the area of the cell that the setting affects.

Adding Header Cells to a Table

As mentioned earlier, contents of header cells appear bold and centered. You can select which table cells in a table should be header cells by selecting one of the choices in the Table dialog box. I usually think of header cells as the top cells in table columns. But you can add header cells along the left edge of a table as headers for each row or have headers for the rows and columns, too.

FIGURE 9.6
Set the Cell
Padding and the
Cell Spacing set-
tings in the Table
dialog box.

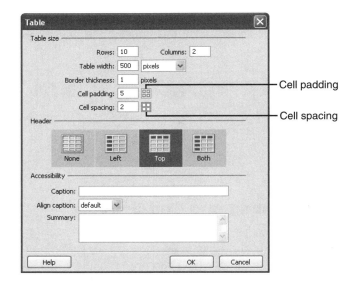

Making a Table Accessible to People with Disabilities

Users who are visually impaired and using text-to-speech synthesizer software to read your Web page will have the most trouble reading large tables full of data. These users will greatly appreciate your small effort to design a table that is easier for them to navigate and extract data from. Dreamweaver has made this easy for you by placing the accessibility settings at the bottom of the Table dialog box.

You can add a caption for a table that appears in the browser and is visible to everyone. You can set the alignment for the caption so that it appears either above or below or to the left or right of the table. You should always add a summary for your table. The summary is read only by text-to-speech browsers and helps the user evaluate whether to progress through the table data or skip the information.

Modifying a Table and Adding Content

When you have your table structure determined, you can start adding text or images to the table. You can also fine-tune the structure as you work in Dreamweaver by using the Properties Inspector and selecting table cells or entire tables. Later in this chapter you'll use some of the built-in table color schemes that are available in Dreamweaver.

Adding and Sorting Data

To enter data, you click in a table cell, type, and then tab to the next cell. You can press Shift+Tab to move backward through the table cells. When you reach the rightmost cell in the bottom row, pressing Tab creates a new row. Add data to your table until you have enough data to make it interesting to sort.

By the Way

> ### Creating New Table Rows
>
> When you press the Tab key to create a new table row, Dreamweaver gives the new row the attributes of the previous row. This might be what you want. But if you use Tab to create a new row from a header cell row, your row will be more header cells!

Dreamweaver makes it easy to sort the data in your table by using Commands, Sort Table. To sort a table by using the Sort Table command, follow these steps:

1. Select the table and then select Commands, Sort Table. The Sort Table dialog box appears. It contains a number of drop-down menus to help you sort the table.

2. Select the column to sort in the Sort By drop-down menu.

3. Select whether you want to sort the column alphabetically or numerically in the Order drop-down menu.

4. Select whether you want to sort in ascending or descending order in the drop-down list directly to the right of the Order drop-down menu.

5. Below this first set of sorting options you can set up a secondary search, if necessary. If you do this, Dreamweaver will first sort by the primary column and will then sort by the secondary column.

6. If the first row of the table is a header row, leave the Sort Includes the First Row box unchecked. If you don't have header cells, you should include the first row in the sort.

7. The Keep All Row Colors the Same After the Sort Has Been Completed check box allows you to keep table row attributes with the row after the sort. If you have formatted your table in a certain way, you should check this box so your formatting isn't lost.

8. Click OK to start the sort.

Adding and Removing Rows and Columns

To remove a row or column from a table, use the context menu that pops up when you right-click (Control+click on the Mac) a table cell. Right-click

(Control+click on the Mac) a table cell and select the Table submenu; another menu appears, with a number of commands to add and remove rows, columns, or both. Select one of these commands to make a change to the table.

Use the icons in the Layout category of the Insert bar to add rows either above or below the current row or to add columns to the left or the right of the current column. You can also add or remove rows and columns by editing the table properties in the Properties Inspector. Adjust the number of rows and columns in the Properties Inspector with an entire table selected to add or remove groups of cells.

Modifying the Number of Rows and Columns

When you use the Properties Inspector to adjust the number of rows and columns, Dreamweaver inserts a new column to the far right of the table. It inserts a new row at the bottom of the table. If you remove columns or rows in the Properties Inspector, the columns are removed from the right side and the rows are removed from the bottom. You lose any data that is in the removed columns or rows.

Changing Column Width and Row Height

You can change column width and row height by dragging the cell borders or by entering values in the Properties Inspector. If you prefer to "eyeball" the size, position the cursor over a cell border until the cursor turns into the double-line cursor. Drag the double-line cursor to change the column width or row height.

Use the W (width) and H (height) boxes in the Properties Inspector to give exact values to widths and heights. Values are expressed in either pixel or percentage values. As with the horizontal rule you created in Chapter 2, "Creating a Basic Web Page with Text," a percentage value will change your table size as the size of the browser window changes, whereas a pixel value will always display the table at a constant size.

Resizing a Table and Changing Border Colors

Just as you can change the size of cells, rows, and columns, you can change the size of an entire table. With the entire table selected, drag the resizing handles to make the table a different size. If you have not given width and height values to cells, rows, and columns, the cells will distribute themselves proportionally when the entire table size is changed. Or use the W and H boxes in the Properties Inspector, with the entire table selected, to give the table either pixel or percentage size values.

To clear all the width and height values from a table, select the table header menu when the table is selected in the Document window. This menu contains commands to clear the cell heights and clear the cell widths. It also contains commands to convert all the values to pixel values or to convert all the values to percentage values. These commands are handy if you set table attributes to pixel values and want to change them to percentage values or vice versa. Buttons for these commands are available in the lower half of the Properties Inspector when the table is selected, as shown in Figure 9.7.

Convert buttons
Clear buttons

FIGURE 9.7
When an entire table is selected, the Properties Inspector has buttons available to clear the row height and the column width. There are also buttons available to convert dimension values to pixels or percentage.

Using a Dreamweaver Preset Table Format

Dreamweaver contains a number of preset table formats that you can apply to a table. The format affects the colors, alignment, and border size of the table. Instead of applying colors and alignment to each cell, row, or column, you can use the Format Table command to quickly format an entire table.

To apply one of the preset formats to a table, follow these steps:

1. Select the table.

2. Select Commands, Format Table. The Format Table dialog box appears (see Figure 9.8). Dreamweaver doesn't allow you to add formatting to tables that have captions, so if you added a caption, first delete it by selecting it, clicking the <caption> tag in the tag selector, and pressing the Delete key.

3. Select a format from the scrolling menu in the upper-left corner of the Format Table dialog box. The little demonstration table in the dialog box shows a preview of the format's appearance.

4. Click the Apply button to apply the format to your table. Change the format until you are satisfied and then click the OK button.

FIGURE 9.8
The Format Table dialog box contains the commands to format all the cells, rows, and columns in a table.

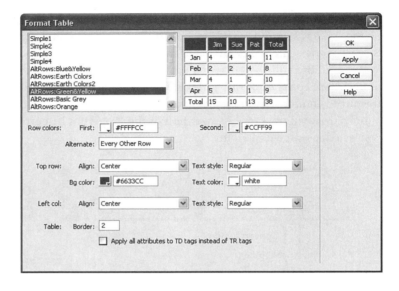

The Apply All Attributes to TD tags Instead of TR Tags check box at the bottom of the Format Table dialog box enables you to apply the formatting to table cells instead of table rows. Because there are usually more cells than rows, applying the formatting to all the cells results in more HTML code in your Web page. The HTML code applied to the cells, however, takes precedence over the code applied to rows.

You can use the Format Table command even if you use a custom color scheme for your Web page. Select one of the formats available but enter custom hexadecimal numbers for specific colors into the boxes for the first and second row colors. You can also use a custom text color and add a background color for the header row.

Exporting Data from a Table

You can export table data from an HTML table. You can then import the data into a spreadsheet, a database, or another application that has the capability to process delimited data; that is, data separated by a delimiter. A **delimiter** is the character used between the individual data fields. Commonly used delimiters are tabs, spaces, commas, semicolons, and colons. When you are exporting a data file, you need to pick a delimiter that does not appear in the data.

To export table data from Dreamweaver, follow these steps:

1. Select a table or place your cursor in any cell of a table.

2. Select File, Export, Export Table. The Export Table dialog box appears.

3. Select the data delimiter from the Delimiter drop-down menu.

4. Select the line break style from the Line Breaks drop-down menu. The line break style is dependent on the operating system, so select the operating system that will be running when the data file is imported. For example, if you are sending the data file to someone who will be running a spreadsheet on a Macintosh computer, select Macintosh.

5. Click the Export button and save the file.

Importing Table Data

If you already have data in a spreadsheet or database, why retype it or paste it into Dreamweaver? You can import data exported from spreadsheet or database applications into Dreamweaver by using the Import Tabular Data command. Most spreadsheets and database applications can export data into a text file that Dreamweaver can import. You need to know what character is used in the data file as a delimiter before you can successfully import data into Dreamweaver.

Did you Know?

Exported Files from Excel

Microsoft Excel, a commonly used spreadsheet application, imports and exports files with the file extension `.csv` as comma delimited and files with the file extension `.prn` as space delimited.

To import table data to Dreamweaver, follow these steps:

1. Place the insertion point in the Document window where you want the table located.

2. Select the Tabular Data object from the Common tab of the Insert bar or select Insert, Table, Tabular Data. The Import Tabular Data dialog box appears.

3. Select the Browse icon (which looks like a folder) to browse to the table data file to import it into Dreamweaver.

4. Dreamweaver attempts to automatically select the delimiter, or you can select the field delimiter manually from the Delimiter drop-down menu. If the delimiter isn't one of the four common delimiters listed, select Other from the Delimited drop-down menu and enter the delimiter.

5. In the boxes beside Table Width, select whether the new table should fit to the data or be a certain pixel or percentage value.

6. Enter values in the Cell Padding and Cell Spacing text boxes, if necessary. Remember, you can always change these values by editing the table later.

7. Select from the Format Top Row drop-down menu a value for the format of the first (header) row. You need to know whether the data file has column headings that will appear as header cells in your HTML table.

8. Enter a value for the table border size.

9. Click OK to import the table data.

Summary

In this chapter, you have learned how to add a table to a Web page. You have also learned how to add and remove table cells and rows and how to set the column width and row height of a table. You have entered data into a table and then sorted the data by using the Sort Table command. You have learned how to import data into a Dreamweaver table and how to export table data for an external application to use.

CHAPTER 10

Designing Page Layout by Using Tables

In Chapter 9, "Displaying Data with Tables," you explored some of the properties of tables and table cells. You used tables in Web pages in the same way you might use tables in a spreadsheet or a word processing application—to present data in an organized way. In this chapter, you will apply more properties and new commands, using tables to aid Web page layout.

Tables give Web developers the ability to make page elements appear in a specific place onscreen. Dreamweaver enables you to work in Layout mode so that you can draw table elements directly onto the Document window. This makes it easy to create tables for page layout.

Using Layout Mode

Traditionally, designing tables for page layout has been a complicated task. Making changes or creating the perfect number of cells has required Web developers to **merge**, **split**, and **span** (you'll learn more about these terms later in the chapter) various rows and columns to get pages to look the way they want them to. Dreamweaver includes Layout mode, which enables you to easily draw, move, and edit table cells.

To turn on Layout mode, select the Layout Mode button on the Layout mode tab of the Insert bar, shown in Figure 10.1. When you turn on Layout mode, the two layout buttons on the Insert bar become active. One of these buttons, Layout Table, draws a layout table; the other, Draw Layout Cell, draws an individual layout cell (a table cell). A **layout table** looks just like a regular HTML table in the Web browser, but it looks slightly different in Dreamweaver. In Dreamweaver, you can manipulate layout tables and layout table cells by dragging and dropping them into position on the page.

Layout Table button

Expanded Tables   Draw Layout
Mode button   Cell button

FIGURE 10.1
You select the
Layout Mode button
in the Layout tab of
the Insert bar. You
can go back and
forth between the
Layout and
Standard modes.

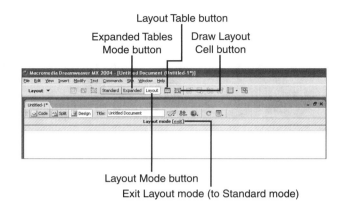

Layout Mode button

Exit Layout mode (to Standard mode)

Adding a Layout Table and Layout Cells

Dreamweaver's Layout mode enables you to draw onto the Document window a
design that will appear in table cells. You create areas for content, menus, and
other elements of a Web page by selecting the Draw Layout Cell command and
drawing cells for each page element. This is a different way of creating a table
than you used in Chapter 9. Using Layout mode isn't appropriate for tabular data
types of tables.

Did you
Know?

Choose a Screen Resolution for Your Design

Design for a specific screen resolution by first selecting a resolution from the
Window Size drop-down menu in Dreamweaver's status bar.

To create a page layout, follow these steps:

1. Select the Layout Mode button in the Layout category of the Insert bar.

2. Select the Draw Layout Cell button in the Insert bar.

3. Draw cells in the Document window for page elements, as shown in
   Figure 10.2. A layout table is automatically created to hold the layout cells.

4. When you place your cursor over the edges of a layout table cell that isn't
   currently selected, the outline of the cell changes from blue to red. When the
   cell is red, click the cell to select it. A selected cell appears as a darker solid
   blue, with resizing handles visible. Move cells by selecting and dragging
   them.

Layout table   Layout cells

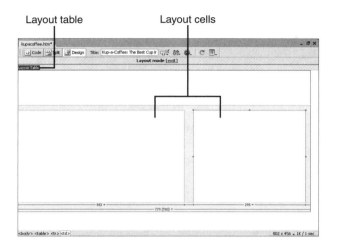

FIGURE 10.2
In Layout mode, you can draw table cells in the Document window. The cells are contained within a layout table.

5. Resize cells by dragging the resizing handles at the corners and sides of the cells.

6. Resize the table that contains the cells by dragging the resizing handles at the corners and sides of the table.

Draw Multiple Layout Cells

To create multiple layout cells without having to click the Draw Layout Cell button every time, select the Draw Layout Cell button, hold down the Ctrl key in Windows or the Command key on the Mac, and then draw a layout cell. As long as you hold down the Ctrl or Command key, you can continue drawing layout cells.

Did you Know?

To quickly select a cell to edit its properties, hold down Ctrl and click (Command+click on the Mac) within the cell. As shown in Figure 12.3, the Properties Inspector presents the Width, Height, Bg (background color), Horz (horizontal alignment) and Vert (vertical alignment), and No Wrap properties. These properties are exactly the same table cell properties that you learned about in the last chapter. There's one additional property, Autostretch, which is unique to layout tables.

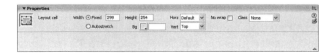

FIGURE 10.3
In Layout mode, the Properties Inspector displays layout cell properties.

Stretching Content to Fit the Page

Autostretch enables a column to stretch to fill all the available space in the browser window. No matter what size the browser window is, the table will span the entire window. When you turn on Autostretch for a specific cell, all the cells in that column will be stretched. This setting is particularly useful for cells that contain the main content of the page. The menus can stay the same width, but the content can stretch to take up all the available space. Or you can place a stretched cell on the right side of a table and stretch the background colors over the width of the screen, no matter what the user's resolution.

Expanded Tables Mode Shows Table Borders

Sometimes it's difficult to see the edges of tables when they don't have a border. You can turn on the Expanded Tables mode, using the button directly to the left of the Layout Mode button in the Insert bar, to display borders within Dreamweaver. This doesn't actually add borders to the Web page. It simply displays borders in Dreamweaver so that the table is easier to see.

Dreamweaver will automatically add spacer images to table cells to make sure they remain the size that you intend in all browsers. The spacer image trick is an old trick used by Web developers to ensure that table cells don't collapse when viewed in certain browsers. A transparent 1-pixel GIF is stretched to a specific width. This image is not visible in the browser. The GIF maintains the width of all the cells that are *not* in the autostretched column. If you do not add a spacer image, any columns without an image to hold their size may collapse.

To turn on Autostretch, follow these steps:

1. Select a cell by holding Ctrl while clicking the cell.

2. Select the Autostretch radio button in the Properties Inspector. The Choose Spacer Image dialog box appears.

3. In the Choose Spacer Image dialog box, you have three choices:

   ▶ **Create a Spacer Image File**—When you select this option, Dreamweaver creates an invisible 1-pixel GIF image, adds it to the top cell of each column, and stretches it to the column width. Dreamweaver asks you where you'd like to store the spacer.gif image that Dreamweaver creates.

   ▶ **Use an Existing Spacer Image File**—If you've already created a spacer image, select this option. Dreamweaver asks you to navigate to where the image is stored.

▶ **Don't Use Spacer Images for Autostretch Tables**—If you select this option, Dreamweaver warns you that your cells may collapse and not maintain the widths that you have set.

You can also apply the Autostretch command for an entire column by selecting the column header menu, shown in Figure 10.4. Each column heading displays the width of the column, in pixels. You can also simply add a spacer image to the column or remove it by selecting the appropriate commands from this menu. When a column has a spacer image added, the line at the top of the column appears thicker. When a column is set to Autostretch, a squiggly line appears instead of the column width.

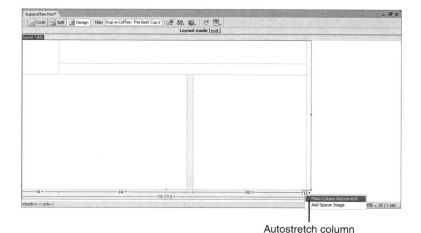

Autostretch column

FIGURE 10.4
Use the column header menu for a layout table column to turn on Autostretch for a table column.

You can set a spacer image for a site in the Dreamweaver Preferences dialog box. After you have set a spacer image for the site, Dreamweaver no longer prompts you to create or choose a spacer image; the image is simply added. Create or select a spacer image for an entire site by opening the Layout Mode category of the Dreamweaver Preferences dialog box. Note that you can also use this category to change the colors in which layout objects appear in Dreamweaver and whether spacer images are automatically inserted.

The Spacer Images Are in the Bottom Row

Dreamweaver adds an additional row at the bottom of your table for the spacer images. Do not remove this row.

Watch
Out!

Editing a Table in Standard Mode

After you've designed your layout in Layout mode, you need to add content to the table. You can also edit your layout table and add content in Standard mode by changing the attributes of the table and its cells. You also need to set the alignment of the contents of the cells. The following settings are available only when you are in Standard mode. You can either click the Standard Mode button in the Layout category of the Insert bar or click the [exit] link in the Layout mode bar at the top of the Document window.

Merging and Splitting Table Cells

You might want some rows or columns in your table to have fewer cells than other rows. For example, you might want the top row of a table to have a title that is centered over all the columns. How do you accomplish that?

You can increase or decrease the column span and row span by either **splitting** or **merging** cells. To merge an entire row so that it appears as one cell, select the row and click the Merge button in the Property Inspector or right-click (Control+click on the Mac) anywhere on the row and select the Merge Cells command from the Table submenu of the context menu. Now the content of the entire row can be positioned over all the columns.

Use the Split Cell command to add additional rows or columns to a cell. The Split button is beside the Merge button in the Properties Inspector. Select the Split button or right-click (Control+click on the Mac) in the cell and select the Split Cell command from the Table submenu of the context menu, and the Split Cell dialog box appears, as shown in Figure 10.5. Enter the number of rows or columns you would like the cell to be split into and click OK. Now a single cell is split into multiple cells.

FIGURE 10.5
The Split Cell dialog box enables you to split a single cell into multiple columns or rows.

Aligning Table Cell Contents

You can align the contents of a cell or a group of cells vertically—from top to bottom. The Vert drop-down menu sets the vertical alignment for the contents of an individual cell or a group of cells. When setting the vertical alignment, you have the following options:

- ► **Default**—This is usually the same as middle alignment of the cell contents.
- ► **Top**—This aligns the cell contents at the top of the cell.
- ► **Middle**—This aligns the cell contents in the middle of the cell.
- ► **Bottom**—This aligns the cell contents at the bottom of the cell.
- ► **Baseline**—This is applied to multiple cells in a row, aligning the bottom of the objects across all cells. For instance, if you have very large text in the first cell and small text in the second cell, the bottom of each line of text will be aligned with baseline vertical alignment.

Align the contents of a cell or a group of cells horizontally—from left to right—with the Horz drop-down menu. When setting the horizontal alignment, you have the following options:

- ► **Default**—This is usually the same as left for cell content and center for header cell content.
- ► **Left**—This aligns the cell contents on the left of the cell.
- ► **Center**—This aligns the cell contents in the center of the cell.
- ► **Right**—This aligns the cell contents on the right of the cell.

Adding Color to a Table

There are several places you can add color to a table:

- ► A background color for a table cell or group of cells
- ► A background color for the entire table
- ► A border color for a table cell or group of cells
- ► A border color for the entire table

Figure 10.6 shows where the different color settings are located in the Properties Inspector. Cell properties always have priority over the same properties in the table. For instance, if you applied blue as the table background color and then applied red to an individual cell, the one cell would be red and all the other cells would be blue. Set the table background and table border in the Properties Inspector. The Brdr Color setting determines the border color of the entire table.

FIGURE 10.6
Adding colors in the Properties Inspector controls the table border and table background color attributes.

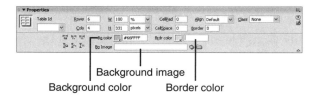

Background image

Background color   Border color

You can add a background image to a table cell or an entire table. Enter the URL for a background image in the box labeled Bg Image in the Properties Inspector. You can enter a pixel value in the Border text box to see a border; however, you don't usually add borders to a layout table. If you add a border color and don't see the border, you might have the border size set to zero. Set the cell background and cell border colors in the Properties Inspector with a cell or group of cells selected.

Nesting a Table Within a Table

Placing a table within a table cell creates a **nested** table. The dimensions of the table cell limit the nested table's width and height. To nest a table, place the insertion point inside a table cell and insert a new table (or draw a table when in Layout mode). Drawing a layout table by using the Draw Layout Table tool enables you to draw a table over an existing cell, as shown in Figure 10.7. The nested table will snap to the size of its parent cell.

Nested table

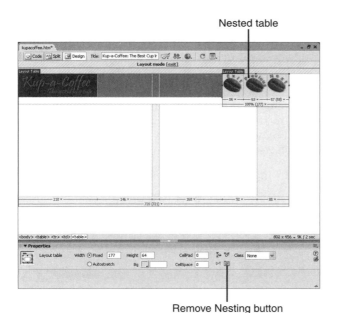

FIGURE 10.7
A nested table in
Layout mode snaps
to the size of its
parent cell.

Remove Nesting button

Using a Tracing Image to Transfer a Design to a Web Page

A tracing image is useful when you are creating a page design and you have an image showing all the completed page elements. You can use this image as a **tracing image**. Instead of estimating where the elements go onscreen, you can display a tracing image and lay the individual image and text elements over the tracing image perfectly. A tracing image makes it easy to align objects.

Load a tracing image into Dreamweaver in the Page Properties dialog box. The tracing image is visible only in Dreamweaver and is never visible in the browser. A tracing image covers any background color or background image. The background color or background image will still be visible in the browser.

Using a tracing image is very helpful when you are implementing a complicated design that has been created by a graphic artist. Usually page elements, such as buttons, titles, and logos, are sliced up in an image-editing program. The graphic artist (or you!) can export an image of the complete design (called *flattened* in graphic terms because all the visible image layers are merged into a single layer) to use in Dreamweaver as a tracing image.

To load a tracing image into Dreamweaver, follow these steps:

1. Open the Page Properties dialog box (by selecting Modify, Page Properties) and select the Tracing Image category. Click the Browse button beside the Tracing Image box to select the image that is a complete visual representation of your Web page.

2. Browse to the tracing image file. It needs to be a GIF, JPEG, or PNG.

3. Drag the Transparency slider to set how opaque (solid) or transparent the tracing image will be, as shown in Figure 10.8.

Tracing image

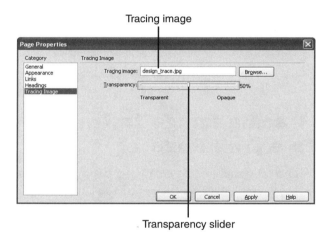

FIGURE 10.8
You can load a tracing image into the Page Properties dialog box. Set the transparency with the slider.

Transparency slider

4. Click OK. Your tracing image appears in the background of the Document window, with the transparency setting you specified.

5. Draw the design that you see in the tracing image. You also need to look in the Assets panel to see how the images in the design have been sliced up.

Did you Know?

View the Entire Tracing Image

If you use a tracing image with 0-pixel margins for the page, you will lose the 10 pixels at the top of the screen when you are in Layout mode. The Layout mode banner across the top blocks some of the tracing image. You can turn off the 10 pixels of the Layout mode banner by selecting View, Visual Aids, Hide All.

Turning a Table into a Group of Layers

In Chapter 12, "Using Dynamic HTML and Layers," you will use layers to position objects on a Web page. **Layers** allow absolute placement of objects on the page. Whereas tables are also relative to the content on the page, layers can position content at any position on the page. Using layers is another effective way to position content on the screen, and Dreamweaver can convert a table into a group of layers.

To convert a table into a group of layers, follow these steps:

1. Select the table and make sure you're in Standard mode. The Convert Tables to Layers command is unavailable while you are in Layout mode.

2. Select Modify, Convert, Convert Tables to Layers. (Did you notice that there's also a command to convert layers to a table?) The Convert Tables to Layers dialog box appears.

3. Accept the defaults and click OK. (You'll explore the properties controlled by the check boxes in the Convert Tables to Layers dialog box in the next chapter.)

The Layers panel lists all the layers that Dreamweaver created from the table.

Summary

In this chapter, you have learned how to use Layout mode to draw cells and tables to create a page layout. You have used the column and row spanning properties to merge and split individual cells and groups of cells. You have also learned how to align the contents of cells both vertically and horizontally. You have learned how to apply colors to an entire table, table cells, and table borders, and you have learned how to convert a table into a group of layers.

CHAPTER 11

Understanding and Building Frames and Framesets

Love 'em or hate 'em, many people seem to have strong opinions about frames. Creating a Web page with frames enables you to contain multiple Web pages in a single browser window. The user can select a link in one frame that loads content into another existing frame, enabling the user to stay in the same browser window.

Using frames can be an excellent way to present information on your Web site, but frames can also be a navigational nightmare for your users. Take care to make sure that your frames are carefully created so that the user can navigate to links that you provide in your site without being perpetually caught in your frames.

Creating a Frameset

Frames consist of individual Web pages—one for each frame—held together by a Web page that contains the frameset. The **frameset** defines the size and position of the individual frames. You can either load an existing Web page into a frame or create a new Web page. The frameset is like the "glue" that holds all the frames together. The frameset Web page isn't visible to the user; the user sees only the content held in the frames defined by the frameset.

Figure 11.1 shows an example of Dreamweaver's Top and Nested Left style of frameset. There is one Web page called banner.html that is displayed across the top of the framed page. The lower part of the page, below the banner, is split into two frames: the table of contents page on the left, made up of links, and the main display area on the right. The links in the left table of contents frame load content into the main display area. The banner and the table of contents remain constant, while different Web pages are loaded into the main display area.

FIGURE 11.1
This Web page contains three frames: one at the top, one in the lower left that contains the table of contents, and one in the lower right that displays different Web pages when the links in the table of contents are selected.

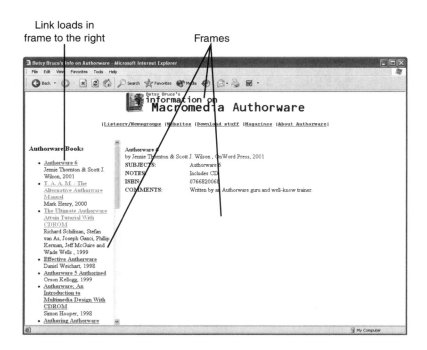

When you are creating real projects, you'll probably use the prebuilt framesets that come with Dreamweaver. There are a variety of configurations available; you access them by clicking the icons in the Frames menu of the Layout category in the Insert bar (or by selecting Insert, HTML, Frames). In this chapter you'll begin by creating a set of frames in a frameset by hand. This will familiarize you with how frames work, how they are named, and how they are saved.

When you are working with frames, using the Save command becomes more complicated than it usually is. Are you saving the Web page in a frame, or are you saving the frameset? While you are working with frames, Dreamweaver activates the Save Frameset and the Save Frameset As commands in the File menu. You can also use the Save All command to save all the frame content and the frameset, too. There is also an additional Open command, the Open in Frame command, which appears in the File menu when you are working with frames. You can open an existing Web page in a frame by using this command.

There are three methods of creating frames:

▶ View the frame borders (by selecting View, Visual Aids, Frame Borders) and then drag the borders to divide the page into frames.

- ▶ Use the commands under the Frameset submenu in Dreamweaver's Modify menu. You might need to use these menu commands when the frame configuration you want to create is not possible by dragging borders.

- ▶ Use the prebuilt frame configurations that are available in the Frames menu of the Layout category in the Insert bar.

Viewing Frame Borders

You need to view the frame borders before you can drag them to create frames. Select View, Visual Aids, Frame Borders. You see a set of borders surrounding the page. These borders are visual aids within Dreamweaver and don't represent how the finished page will look in the browser. While you are working with your Web pages, you can move these borders to resize your design. When you are ready to turn them off, simply select View, Visual Aids, Frame Borders again to toggle the setting off.

Splitting a Page into Frames

To create frames, drag the frame borders. Create two frames, top and bottom, in an empty Web page by dragging the top frame border down, as shown in Figure 11.2. You now have three Web pages: the page in the top frame, the page in the bottom frame, and the Web page with the frameset. When viewers enter the URL of the frameset page, the browser automatically loads the individual pages that belong in each frame.

Frame borders

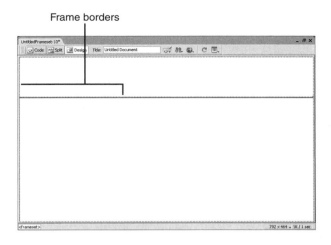

FIGURE 11.2
When you view the frame borders, you can simply drag one of the borders to create frames and a frameset.

> **Get Rid of a Frame**
>
> If you change your mind about a frame, just drag the border off the edge of the page, and it will be deleted.

Naming Frames

Naming and keeping track of frames can be confusing. Type the word **banner** into the top frame's Web page. With the cursor in the top frame, save the Web page as `banner.htm` after selecting File, Save Frame. When you are first working with frames, it's least confusing to save each frame individually. Repeat this procedure with the bottom frame: Type the word **main** in the frame and save it as `main.htm`. Your frames will look as shown in Figure 11.3.

FIGURE 11.3
This Web page is divided into two frames named `banner.htm` and `main.htm`.

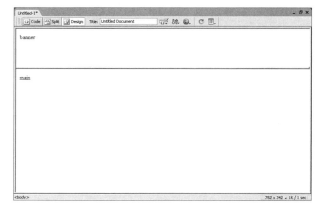

When the Frame Borders command is not checked under the Visual Aids submenu of the View menu, the Web page appears as it will in the browser. Later in this chapter, you will change the actual border sizes and other attributes of frames. It will be helpful to turn off the frame borders to approximate how the frames will look in the browser. Turn off the frame borders in the Visual Aids submenu of the View menu to see what your Web page looks like without them and then turn the borders on again.

Now you will divide the bottom frame into two frames. If you drag the left frame border, you will end up with four frames—two on the top and two on the bottom. Instead, split the bottom frame into two frames by using the commands in the Frameset submenu under the Modify menu. To do this, follow these steps:

1. With the cursor in the bottom frame, select Modify, Frameset, Split Frame Right. This places the existing frame on the right and adds a new frame on the left. Or, you can drag the left frame border while holding down the Ctrl key (the Command key on the Mac).

2. Type **table of contents** into the Web page within the new frame.

3. Save the Web page contained in the new table of contents frame. Remember to place your cursor in the frame and then select File, Save Frame. You can name this Web page `toc.htm`.

You have created three frames and saved the Web pages that they contain. It's sometimes difficult to select the frameset. The easiest way is to place your cursor over one of the frame borders and click. You can tell you have the frameset selected when you see the frameset tag in the tag selector. Save the frameset Web page by selecting File, Save Frameset. You can name the frameset `index.htm`. The URL of the frameset is the only address the viewer will need to view all the Web pages.

While you have the frameset selected, give the Web page a title in the toolbar. Only the title of the frameset, never any of the individual framed Web page titles, appears in the title bar of the browser. Because the titles of the individual frames do not appear in the browser's title bar, it isn't necessary to give a frame a title. However, it's always good practice to give Web pages titles, and if you ever reference the Web page outside the frames, you will be assured that each page already has a title.

If you haven't already saved the Web pages in the frames and the frameset Web page, Dreamweaver will prompt you to save before you preview in the browser. The first time you save, it's less confusing to individually save the Web pages contained in each frame and the frameset Web page than to save all the files at once when Dreamweaver prompts you. Dreamweaver will prompt you to save the files every time you preview the frames.

Using the Frames Panel

The Frames panel (which you open by selecting Window, Frames), shown in Figure 11.4, enables you to select individual frames and set frame attributes. Notice that the Frames panel visually represents the configuration of the frames in a Web page. Select a frame by clicking the frame's representation in the Frames panel. You can also select a frame by holding down Alt while clicking (Shift+clicking on the Macintosh) inside the frame in the Document window.

FIGURE 11.4
You select frames
in the Frames
panel. This panel
visually represents
the frame configu-
ration in the current
Web page.

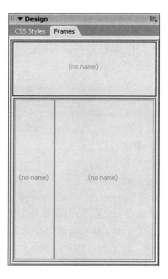

When you click the representation of a frame in the Frames panel, the properties
for that frame are available in the Properties Inspector, as shown in Figure 11.5.
The Properties Inspector is where you set up the frame's scrolling and border
attributes. You'll explore those in a few minutes. This is also where you give each
frame a unique name.

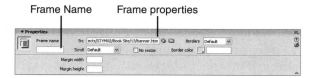

FIGURE 11.5
The Properties
Inspector presents
frame attributes,
such as Frame
Name, when an
individual frame is
selected.

It's important that each frame have a name. This is not the filename that you
gave each frame a few minutes ago; this is an actual name for a frame. The
frame name is used to target the frame, making a Web page load into the frame
when a link is clicked in another frame. Click on each frame in the Frames panel
and type a name in the Frame Name box in the Properties Inspector. You can
name the top frame banner, the left frame toc (for table of contents), and the
right frame main.

By the Way

Name Your Frames Correctly

Frame names should not contain punctuation, such as periods, hyphens, or spaces. You can, however, use underscores in frame names. Also, you should not use the reserved names top, parent, self, and blank.

Nesting Frames

You can nest one frameset inside another frameset to have **nested frames**. Actually, that is what you just did! When you split the bottom frame into two frames, Dreamweaver created a frameset defining the bottom two frames. The original frameset now consists of a frame on top of the nested frameset. You nest framesets by nesting one frameset tag within another, within a single frameset Web page.

Click one of the lower frames in the Frames panel and look at the tag selector. You should see a frame inside a frameset inside another frameset, as shown in Figure 11.6. Click the top frame in the Frames panel. The tag selector shows the frame is in one frameset. The bottom two frames are in a nested frameset.

Nested frameset tag

Frame tag

FIGURE 11.6
The tag selector shows that the currently selected frame is contained in a frameset nested within another frameset.

Dreamweaver creates an additional frameset because framesets can contain either rows or columns but not both. The first frameset you created has two rows. The second frameset you created has two columns.

Using Existing Web Pages with Frames

So far in this chapter, you have created new Web pages in all your frames. However, you might want to load a Web page that you created prior to setting up your frameset into a frame. To load an existing Web page into a frame, follow these steps:

1. In the Frames panel, click a frame.

2. In the Properties Inspector, select the Browse icon next to the Src text box and browse to an existing Web page. Or type an absolute URL into the Src box. You should see the Web page displayed if it is on a local drive. If you have referenced a URL to a Web page on the Internet, Dreamweaver will display a message saying that the frame contains a remote file and listing the URL.

Open an Existing Web Page in a Frame

You can open an existing Web page in a frame where the cursor is located by selecting File, Open in Frame.

Setting Frame and Frameset Attributes

There are separate attributes for the individual frames and the frameset that holds them together. Some of the attributes overlap (borders, for instance), so you must be careful what attributes you are setting and where you are setting them. You should experiment with frameset designs that come with Dreamweaver to quickly try different attributes.

Setting the Scrolling and Resize Attributes

Each frame has its own scrolling attributes displayed in the Properties Inspector when a frame is selected in the Frames panel. There are four settings in the Scroll drop-down menu of the Properties Inspector.

► **Yes**—This setting turns scrollbars on, whether the content requires them. Both vertical and horizontal scrollbars may appear, depending on the browser.

► **No**—This setting turns scrollbars off, whether the content requires them. If viewers cannot see all the content in the frame, they have no way to scroll to see it.

► **Auto**—This setting turns the scrollbars on if the content of the frame is larger than what is visible in the browser window. If all the content is visible, the scrollbars are off. This setting turns on only the necessary scrollbars, horizontal or vertical, and is usually a better choice than the Yes setting.

► **Default**—For most browsers, this setting is the same as Auto.

Select the No Resize check box in the Properties Inspector if you do not want the user to be able to resize your frames. Checking this check box keeps the user from resizing the frame size in the browser window. Allowing users to resize the frames can sometimes help them maintain the readability of your Web page, but it also might ruin your page design. If a frame-based Web page is well designed, taking into account how the page will look at various monitor resolutions, users shouldn't have to resize the frames.

Setting Borders

The default look for frame borders is a gray shaded border between the frames. You might not want your frame-based Web page to be so obviously "framed." While you're surfing the Web, it's sometimes difficult to identify Web sites that use frames because they have turned off the frame borders or colored them to blend with the site design.

In the Properties Inspector, you can turn borders on and off, set the border color, and change the border width. Border attributes are a little tricky because some of them are set in the frame, some are set in the frameset, and some can be set in both places. Setting properties in an individual frame overrides the same properties set in the frameset. If you set attributes for frames but they don't seem to work, check to make sure you have set the attributes in all the framesets; you might be working with a nested frame that is affected by *two* sets of frameset attributes.

Set the border width in the frameset. The easiest way to select the frameset and display the frameset attributes in the Properties Inspector is to select the frameset tag in the tag selector. The tag selector displays the frameset tag when a frame within the frameset is selected. You can also click the frame borders to select the frameset, as you did earlier in this chapter. Remember that nested frames may be in more than one frameset.

Select a frame in the Frames panel and click the frameset tag farthest to the left. The frameset properties enable you to change border width and color. Give the border a width value and select a color from the Border Color box. You should see these changes immediately in the Dreamweaver Document window.

To turn off the frame borders, make sure the frameset is selected and then select No from the Borders drop-down menu. You will need to turn the border off in all the framesets in the page. If the borders in the individual frames are set to Yes, they will override the frameset settings, and borders will be visible. To turn off a border, all the adjacent frames must have borders turned off, too. If you do not want borders to appear, you should also make sure there is not a border color assigned.

Setting the Frame Size

You can simply drag the frame borders in Dreamweaver to resize a frame. If you want finer control over the size of a frame, you can set frame sizes in the Properties Inspector while the frameset is selected, as shown in Figure 11.7. You can select the rows or columns in the frameset by clicking the small representation in the Properties Inspector. Often, the first frame has an **absolute** value (either pixel or percentage), whereas the second frame is defined as relative. When a frame is defined as **relative**, it takes up the remaining space either horizontally or vertically.

Selected frame

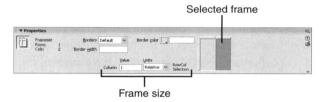

Frame size

FIGURE 11.7
A frame size value can be set to relative so that the frame takes up the remaining space in the browser window.

Creating an Alternative to Frames

Some people with disabilities, such as the visually impaired, may use software that does not easily interpret content in frames. To respect viewers who cannot view frames, you should use the NoFrames Content command.

Select Modify, Frameset, Edit NoFrames Content. Note that a gray bar that says NoFrames Content appears across the top of the Document window. You can simply type in a disclaimer or, better yet, you can provide a non-frames version of the Web page. Turn off the NoFrames Content command by deselecting it in the Frameset submenu of the Modify menu.

Dreamweaver automatically prompts you to add the title attribute for the frame tag if you have enabled frames accessibility prompting in the Dreamweaver Preferences dialog box. To turn on this feature, open the Preferences dialog box (by selecting Edit, Preferences), select the Accessibility category, and select the Frames check box. You can also turn on automatic prompting for the accessibility attributes of form objects, media, and images. When you turn on the frames' accessibility prompting, Dreamweaver asks you to give each frame a title that will be read by text-to-speech browsers.

Using Frames Objects

The quickest way to create frames in Dreamweaver is to use the prebuilt frames objects that are available in the Frames menu in the Layout category of the Insert bar. The Insert bar has several common frame configurations that can quickly get you going with a set of frames. If you are not quite sure what each of the configurations looks like, look at the Framesets category in the New Document dialog box, shown in Figure 11.8. This lists the same prebuilt frames objects as the Insert bar. There is a preview of the frames object's structure on the right side of the dialog box.

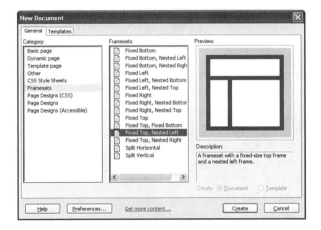

FIGURE 11.8
The Framesets category in the New Document dialog box enables you to preview what the frames will look like.

If one of these prebuilt configurations fits the way you want your frames to look, you'll have a head start by using the frames objects. You can fine-tune the frame settings by using the same methods you've used so far in this chapter.

With a new Web page open, add a frames object by either clicking an icon from the Frames menu in the Layout category of the Insert bar or selecting Insert, HTML, Frames. The framesets in these frames templates all have the borders turned off. The individual frames are already named, but you need to select and save each file as you did earlier in this chapter. Be careful not to preview the Web page before you save, or you will get caught in a series of confusing prompts to save Web pages when you have no idea which page you are saving!

Targeting Linked Pages to Open in a Specific Frame

One of the most exciting features of frames is their capability to load content in one frame after a user clicks a link in another frame. The frameset is the parent, and the frames or framesets it contains are its children. Understanding these concepts helps you understand **targeting**. You can load a Web page into a frame or window by targeting it. You add the target attribute to a hyperlink to send the linked content into a specific window or frame.

There are four reserved target names:

- ▶ **_top**—*This* opens a linked Web page in the entire browser window.

- ▶ **_self**—This opens a linked Web page in the same window or frame that contains the link. This is the default setting.

- ▶ **_parent**—This opens a linked Web page in the parent frameset. If the parent frameset is not nested, the linked page will fill the entire browser window.

- ▶ **_blank**—This opens a linked Web page in a new browser window.

The Target drop-down menu in the Properties Inspector lists all the reserved target names, plus the names of any of the frames you created that are currently open in the Document window, as shown in Figure 11.9. Creating a hyperlink and selecting a frame name from the Target drop-down menu will cause the linked page to load in that window. If no target is entered, the linked page will load in the frame that contains the link.

List of available frames to target

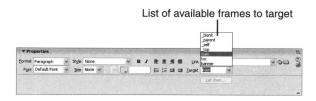

Use the original group of frames that you created at the beginning of this chapter to target a hyperlink, as follows:

1. Create a hyperlink in the frame named toc. Add a link to an existing Web page or to an external URL.

2. Select main from the Target drop-down menu. This loads the hyperlink into the selected frame.

3. Use the Save All command (by selecting File, Save All).

4. Preview the frames in the browser. Click the link, and the Web page should load in the other frame.

Set the Target for an Entire Page

If you are going to be targeting the same frame for all the links in a Web page, add the base tag to the head of the Web page, specifying the target once for all the links. While the insertion point is in the frame with the links, select Insert, HTML, Head Tags, Base and select a target name from the Target drop-down menu. You can leave the Href text box blank. Now you can leave off the target attribute for each individual hyperlink because the base target of the page is set.

Did you
Know?

Using the Go to URL Behavior to Load Frames

The Go to URL behavior has the capability to target frames, and using it is an easy way to get content to load into two frames at once. For instance, you might want to change both the table of contents and the main content frames when the user clicks a hyperlink in the banner frame. The user may select a different section of the content that has a different table of contents and main content Web pages. Because a hyperlink can change the contents in only one frame, you have to use the Go to URL behavior. To use the Go to URL behavior, follow these steps:

1. Add a hyperlink in the banner frame at the top of the page.

2. Type `javascript:;` into the Link box in the Properties Inspector to create a null link.

3. Open the Behaviors panel (by selecting Window, Behaviors); make sure you don't open the Server Behaviors panel—that is a different panel. With the hyperlink selected, click the + button in the Behaviors panel and select Go to URL.

4. The Go to URL dialog box opens. Select the frame named toc from the Open In list box. Enter a URL in the URL box and press the Tab key to record your changes.

5. Notice that there is an asterisk by the frame named toc. That means that there is a URL entered for this frame (you entered it in step 4). Add another URL to a different frame by first selecting the frame named main and then entering a URL in the URL box. Now both frames will load new URLs when the link is clicked. Click OK to save the behavior settings.

6. Save the frames and preview the page in a browser. Click the link in the top frame. Both lower frames should have the new URLs load.

Summary

In this chapter, you have learned how to create, name, and save frames and framesets. You have learned how to change the border, scrollbar, and resizing attributes. You have learned how to target content to a specific frame or browser window, and you have learned how to load two frames at once by using behaviors.

CHAPTER 12

Using Dynamic HTML and Layers

Dynamic HTML (DHTML) provides you with the flexibility to lay out your Web pages and make them interactive. Dreamweaver's layers provide a way to control where objects are placed on the page. You can place items precisely where you want them, without having to create elaborate tables. Layers are the more modern way to position content on a Web page. I use them extensively in the sites I create.

What Is DHTML?

DHTML enables you to create an interactive experience for the Web page user. DHTML isn't an official term; it's a term used by Web developers to reference a collection of technologies used together to produce a more interactive Web page. The three main components of DHTML are layers, Cascading Style Sheets (CSS; see Chapter 13, "Formatting Web Pages by Using Cascading Style Sheets"), and JavaScript (see Chapter 14, "Inserting Scripted Functionality by Using Behaviors," and Chapter 15, "Adding Advanced Behaviors: the Drag Layer Behavior").

DHTML is an extension of HTML that gives Web page developers greater control over page layout and positioning. DHTML also allows greater interactivity without depending on interaction with a server. When people talk about DHTML, they usually mean the combination of HTML 4—as defined by the W3C Web standards organization—and CSS. These elements work together through a scripting language, usually JavaScript.

Here's a short list of the types of things you can accomplish using DHTML:

- ▶ Add to your page images that are hidden from view that will appear when the user clicks a button or a hotspot.
- ▶ Create pop-up menus.
- ▶ Enable the user to drag and drop an object around the screen at will.

▶ Cause text to change color or size when the user rolls her mouse over it.

▶ Repetitively load text into an area of the screen as feedback to the user. For instance, if the user clicks the wrong answer in a quiz, you can give feedback and then replace that feedback when the user gets the answer right.

In this chapter, you'll experiment with **layers**, the containers that enable you to position items on the screen wherever you want.

Adding a Layer

Layers are containers that you'll use to position content on a Web page. The term *layers* is a Dreamweaver term, and if you speak with other Web developers who aren't using Dreamweaver (what's wrong with them?!), they won't know what you mean. Those who haven't been initiated into the wonders of Dreamweaver may call layers "divs," referring to the tag that is used to implement layers. The <div> tag is the most common tag to use to create layers in cross-browser development. The <div> tag is used to logically divide a Web page into sections.

Layers have two very interesting attributes:

▶ **Visibility**—This property enables you to hide all the content in a layer and then trigger its appearance when the user performs an action on the screen. For instance, you can simulate a click on a menu in a software program. The layer holding the menu image is initially hidden. When the user clicks on a menu title on the screen, a script changes the visibility of the menu layer from hidden to visible.

▶ **Z-index**—This property controls the *stacking order* of all the layers on the page. You can stack layers on top of one another (overlapping) and control which one is on top. This gives you the power to create complicated designs.

You can create a layer in Dreamweaver in two different ways:

▶ The simplest way is to select the Draw Layer object from the Layout category of the Insert bar and drag the crosshair cursor on your page to approximately the desired layer size, as shown in Figure 12.1.

▶ Select Insert, Layout Objects, Layer to insert a layer.

Drag handle   Layer   Image inside layer

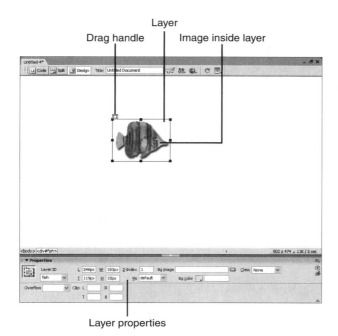

FIGURE 12.1
Selecting the Draw Layer object from the Insert bar enables you to draw a layer by dragging the crosshair cursor.

Layer properties

Draw Layer Doesn't Work in Layout Mode

If the Layer object is grayed out in the Insert bar, you are currently in Layout mode. Make sure that the Layout Mode button in the Layout category of the Insert bar isn't depressed and that you are in Standard mode.

By the Way

The Layers category in the Dreamweaver Preferences dialog box is where you set the default layer values. You can set the default visibility, width, height, background color, and background image. If you have a standard layer size that you use often, you might want to set that size as the default in the Preferences dialog box. You can also enable nesting by checking the Nesting check box.

Check the Add Resize Fix When Inserting Layer check box to have Dreamweaver automatically insert the Netscape layer fix behavior whenever you insert a layer into a Web page. On any page that includes layers and will be viewed in Netscape 4, insert the Netscape layer fix automatically by turning on this preference or manually by selecting Command, Add/Remove Netscape Layer Fix. This behavior resolves problems that happen when the user resizes a page that contains layers in Netscape 4. Dreamweaver inserts JavaScript into the page that solves the problem.

Use the Layer Fix Only If Necessary

Don't insert the Netscape layer fix unless it is absolutely necessary. The fix causes the page to reload and might be distracting to Netscape 4 users. Test your page by opening it in a small Netscape 4 window and then maximize the window. Do your layers stay small? If so, you need to apply the Netscape layer fix.

You'll notice the resizing handles on each border of your layer. You can drag these handles to make a layer bigger or smaller. You can also set the width and height of the layer in the Properties Inspector. The W and H properties in the Properties Inspector are the width and height of the layer. The default measurement unit is pixels.

It's a good idea to always name your layers. When you start adding behaviors, names will help you identify specific layers. You can specify a name in the Layer ID box in the Properties Inspector, as shown in Figure 12.2.

Layer name

FIGURE 12.2
Change the layer name in the Layer ID box of the Properties Inspector. It's important to give layers meaningful names.

No Punctuation in Layer Names

Don't use spaces or punctuation in layer names. If you later apply a behavior to the layer, sometimes JavaScript isn't happy with spaces or punctuation in a layer name. If you want to name your layer with multiple words, you can use capitalization or underscores to make the name readable. For instance, `CestLaVieBakery` and `Green_Grocer` are possible layer names.

You can also name Dreamweaver layers in the Layers panel. Double-click the name in the Layers panel Name column until it becomes editable and then type in a new name, as shown in Figure 12.3. Notice that when you select a layer in the Layers panel, the layer is selected in the Document window also.

Visibility

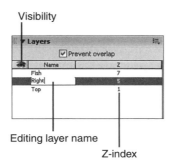

Editing layer name

Z-index

FIGURE 12.3
You can edit the
name of a layer in
the Layers panel
by double-clicking
the name and
changing it.

Setting Layer Positioning

A layer has a drag handle in the upper-left corner. You can reposition a layer by picking it up and moving it with this handle. To select multiple layers, hold down the Shift key while clicking layers to add them to the selection. You can also use the arrow keys on your keyboard to move a selected layer.

Get in the habit of moving layers by picking up the drag handle. It's very easy to accidentally move items contained in a layer instead of moving the layer itself. If you become accustomed to using the handle, you won't make that mistake. If you can't use the layer drag handle because the layer is at the very top of the Document window, select it in the Layers panel and use the arrow keys to move the layer. Or enter positioning values in the Properties Inspector.

Use the Layers panel to select one or many layers. The Layers panel enables you not only to select layers, but also to see and set some layer characteristics. You'll learn about the two characteristics that you can set—the z-index and the visibility—in a few minutes. Notice that you can select a check box at the top of the Layers panel to prevent layers from overlapping. If you notice that you cannot place your layers on top of one another, this check box is probably selected.

The main reason you would want to prevent overlaps is if you were going to eventually convert the layers into a table; a table cannot have overlapping elements. In chapter 10, you learned how to export a layout table as layers by using the Tables to Layers command (by selecting Modify, Convert, Convert Tables to Layers). You can also use the Layers to Table command (by selecting Modify, Convert, Convert Layers to Table) to turn the layers in your page into a layout table.

You can use the drag handle to drag a layer anywhere on the screen, or you can use the Properties Inspector to set the exact positioning of a layer. The L and T properties stand for the left, the offset from the left edge of the page, and top, the offset from the top edge of the page. These positions are relative to the entire browser window. You can move a layer either by dragging it (with its selection handle) or by positioning it exactly by entering values in the L (left) and T (top) boxes.

Adding a Background Color and Background Image

A layer can have a background color, as shown in Figure 12.4. You can use the color picker or type in a color in the standard HTML hexadecimal format, preceded by a #. Make sure you leave the Bg Color option blank if you want your layer to be transparent. If your page background is white and you make your layer background white, it will seem as if it's transparent until you position it over something else!

FIGURE 12.4
A layer can have a background color just as a table cell can. Enter a background color in the Properties Inspector.

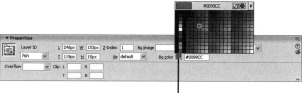

Layer background color

You can also place a background image in a layer. The image will repeat multiple times (called *tiling*) within the layer if the layer is larger than the image. Any objects or text that you put within the layer will be on top of the background image. Select the Browse icon (the folder) beside the Bg Image box in the Properties Inspector and navigate to the background image file. Figure 12.5 shows the Properties Inspector when a layer that contains a background image is selected.

Exploring Layer Stacking Order

Not only can you position layers in exact places on the page, you can also allow layers to overlap one another. So, which layer is on top? The stacking order decides which layer is on top of other layers. The **z-index** value, in turn, determines the stacking order. The z-index can be either a negative or a positive number.

Image tiled in layer

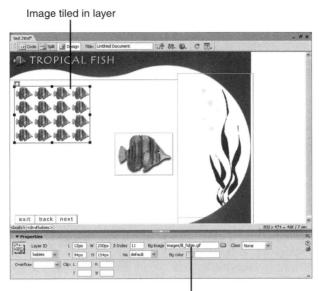

FIGURE 12.5
A background image will tile within a layer if the image is smaller than the layer.

Layer background image

The layer with the highest z-index is the one on the top. The term *z-index* comes from the coordinate system that you used back in geometry class—remember x and y coordinates? Well, the z-index is the third coordinate that is necessary to describe three-dimensional space. Imagine an arrow coming out of the paper or screen toward you and another going back into the screen or paper. That is the z-index.

Dreamweaver prefers to give each layer a unique z-index value. In HTML, you can legally have multiple layers that have the same z-index. Remember, though: If you reorder the layers, Dreamweaver will renumber each with a unique z-index, so why waste your time?

You can set the z-index in the Z-index box in the Properties Inspector, as shown in Figure 12.6. The Layers panel also displays the z-index to the right of the layer name. The Layers panel displays the layers according to z-index value, the top being the highest z-index and the bottom being the lowest. You can easily rearrange the stacking order by selecting the layer name in the Layers panel and then dragging and dropping it somewhere else.

FIGURE 12.6
The z-index value
represents the
stacking order of
layers. You can set
the z-index (as
either a positive or
negative value) in
the Properties
Inspector.

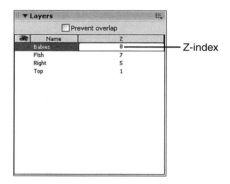

Aligning Layers and Using the Grid

The Dreamweaver grid commands are found under View, Grid. You can show the grid, snap to the grid, and adjust the grid settings. After you show the grid by selecting the Show Grid command, you see the grid lines in the Design window. You can turn off the grid by deselecting this same command. You can also turn the grid on and off from the View Options menu in the Dreamweaver toolbar.

The grid is especially useful if you have elements in your site that must be lined up and are similar in size. You can require layers to snap to the grid by selecting the Snap To command. You can also configure the gap between the grid lines.

Open the Grid Settings dialog box, by selecting the View, Grid, Grid Settings. If you need the grid to have larger or smaller increments, you can adjust its value in the Spacing box. You can also change the snapping increment. The grid can be displayed with either solid lines or dots. The dots are nice because they are lighter and less invasive on your page design. You can also select a grid color by using the color picker.

Changing Layer Visibility

Layers have a visibility attribute that can be set to Visible, Hidden, Inherit, or Default. The Vis drop-down menu is in the middle of the Properties Inspector when a layer is selected. These are the visibility settings:

▶ **Visible**—A layer set to Visible will appear on the Web page upon loading.

▶ **Hidden**—A layer set to Hidden will not appear on the Web page. You can later make the layer visible by using the Show-Hide Layer behavior.

▶ **Inherit**—A layer set to Inherit will have the same visibility as its parent. You'll learn more about nesting and parent layers in a few minutes. If the parent is set to Hidden and a layer is nested within that parent and set to Inherit, it will also be hidden.

▶ **Default**—The Default setting is actually the same as Inherit in most browsers.

It's obvious why you might want layers to be visible, but why might you want them to be hidden? So that you can display them later, after something has happened! You'll learn about using the Show-Hide Layers behavior in Chapter 14.

The Layers panel represents visibility with a picture of an eye. The eye beside a layer is open when the layer is set to Visible. It's closed when the layer is set to Hidden. The Inherit setting does not have an eye representation. The eye is a toggle that moves through the Default, Visible, and Hidden settings and then goes back to Default.

You can set the visibility characteristics of all the layers by selecting the eye icon in the header of the Layers panel.

Don't Accidentally Click the Eye Icon Column Header

Be careful when clicking the eye icon column setting for your top layer. It's easy to accidentally click the header instead and set all the eyes in the column.

Watch Out!

Nesting Layers

You can create a layer within another layer; the new layer is nested within its parent layer. When you move the parent layer, the new child layer moves with it. The child layer also inherits its parent's visibility attributes.

To create a nested layer, you place the cursor inside the parent layer and choose Insert, Layer. You draw a nested layer by using the Draw Layer object to draw inside an existing layer while holding down the Ctrl key (the Command key on the Mac). Also, you can place an existing layer within another layer by picking it up in the Layers panel while holding down the Ctrl key in Windows or the Command key on the Mac and then dropping it into another layer. The nested layer will appear indented in the Layers panel, as shown in Figure 12.7.

The easiest way to un-nest a layer if you make a mistake or change your mind is to pick it up in the Layers panel and drop it somewhere else in the list of layers, as shown in Figure 12.8.

Nested layers

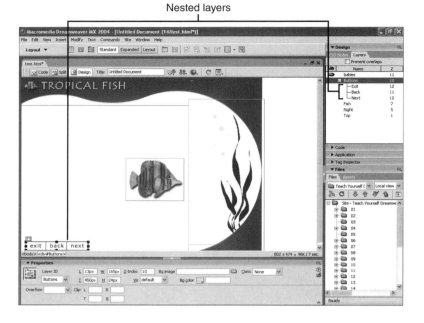

FIGURE 12.7
A layer nested within another layer appears indented in the Layers panel.

FIGURE 12.8
Pick up a nested layer and move it to another position within the Layers panel to un-nest it.

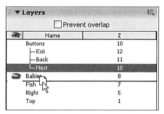

Did you Know?

Can't Draw? Check Prevent Overlaps

If Dreamweaver doesn't seem to be allowing you to draw a nested layer by holding down the Ctrl key, you probably have the Prevent Overlaps check box selected at the top of the Layers panel.

Watch Out!

Where Did the Layers Go?

Did your layer disappear from the screen when you un-nested it? When a layer is nested, its position is relative to its parent. When you un-nest the layer, its position is then relative to the page. The layer coordinates might cause the layer to be off the screen. To fix this problem, select the layer in the Layers panel and give it Left and Top attributes that place it back on the screen.

Summary

In this chapter, you have learned how to insert a layer into a Web page. You have learned how to change the layer's size, position, background color, and name. You have explored setting the stacking order, or z-index, of layers and setting layer visibility. You have also become familiar with the `<div>` tag.

CHAPTER 13

Formatting Web Pages by Using Cascading Style Sheets

The Cascading Style Sheets (CSS) standard enables you to apply a property or group of properties to an object by applying a style to that object. You define and apply styles in Dreamweaver's CSS Styles panel or in the Page Properties dialog box, as you did in Chapter 2, "Creating a Basic Web Page with Text." When thinking about styles, you usually think of creating and applying styles to text, which certainly is possible. However, styles can also be used for positioning objects, creating borders, and lots more.

The trend in Web standards is toward separating the presentation of a Web page, the way the page is displayed visually, from the content, the words and images that make up the page. Dreamweaver MX 2004 has been completely reengineered to rely on CSS; the CSS styles control the presentation of the HTML content. Separating the content from the presentation paves the way to supporting various operating systems, browsers, and devices such as personal digital devices (PDAs) and even toasters (you never know!).

There are three different CSS style types, and in this chapter, you will learn how to create styles that use all three: You will create a class, redefine an HTML tag, and use another type of style called a *CSS selector*.

Creating and Applying a Class

The CSS Styles panel lists classes that have been defined and are ready to apply to objects on your Web page. You define a class style by creating a new style and defining it in Dreamweaver. The Dreamweaver Style Definition dialog box has panels that list numerous style settings. First, you create a class and apply it to text. Then you can define the font, font size, and font color.

To create a class, follow these steps:

1. Click the New CSS Style button from the CSS Styles panel, shown in Figure 13.1. You can also select New from the menu in the upper-right corner of the CSS Styles panel or you can select Text, CSS Styles, New.

Class

FIGURE 13.1
You create a new
style with the New
CSS Style button.

New CSS Style button

2. The New CSS Style dialog box appears, as shown in Figure 13.2. Select the radio button beside Class (Can Apply to Any Tag).

Class name

FIGURE 13.2
You select which of
the three types of
styles you are
defining in the New
CSS Style dialog
box.

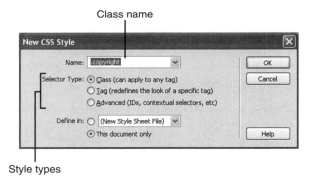

Style types

3. Enter a name for the style in the Name box at the top of the New CSS Style dialog box. A custom style name must begin with a period. Dreamweaver will enter the period for you if you forget to enter it.

Did you **Know?**

Naming Classes
Don't use spaces or punctuation in style names, and don't begin a style name with a number.

4. Select the radio button beside This Document Only in the Define In section. This places the style definition at the top of the current Web page, in the head of the Web page. If you forget this step, Dreamweaver will prompt you to save the style as an external style sheet. We'll discuss external style sheets later in this chapter.

5. The CSS Style Definition dialog box appears, as shown in Figure 13.3. The box opens with the Type category selected. In the Type category, select a font and font size from the appropriate drop-down menus. Also, select a font color by using the color picker.

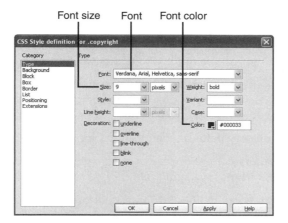

FIGURE 13.3
The CSS Style Definition dialog box is where you set up the attributes of a style.

6. Select OK to save the style. The CSS Styles panel lists the new class.

You select a block of text to apply your style to by dragging the cursor across it. You can also select a layer, a table cell, or any other object in the Web page and apply the style. All the text in the layer, table cell, or other object will then appear as defined by the style. Apply the class to an object by first selecting the object and then selecting the class from the Style drop-down menu in the Properties Inspector. Notice that the style names are displayed in their respective fonts and font styles in the Style drop-down menu.

Apply Styles to the Correct Tag

Some style attributes will work only when applied to certain tags. For instance, a style called bigcell with the cell padding values set in the Box category of the CSS Style Definition dialog box will not have any effect on text because padding is not an attribute of text. Applying this style to an appropriate object, such as a table cell, will have an effect.

Did you Know?

> **Remove a Style**
>
> If you accidentally apply a style to an object, you can remove it by selecting None in the Style drop-down menu in the Properties Inspector.

Exploring Style Settings

The CSS Style Definition dialog box has eight categories with numerous settings you can use to define a style. As you are defining a style, select the panels to gain access to the settings for each category. Any settings that you do not need to set should be left alone. The following categories are available:

▶ **Type**—This category defines type attributes, such as font and font size. These style settings can be applied to text or to objects that contain text.

▶ **Background**—This category defines background attributes, such as color and image. These style settings can be applied to objects, such as layers and tables, where you can set a background.

▶ **Block**—This category defines type attributes for paragraphs.

▶ **Box**—This category defines attributes, such as margin size, that are applied to box objects, such as layers and tables.

▶ **Border**—This category defines attributes that are applied to objects that have borders, such as layers and tables.

▶ **List**—This category defines list attributes, such as bullet type.

▶ **Positioning**—This category defines layer attributes, such as visibility and z-index.

▶ **Extensions**—This category defines miscellaneous attributes that are either future enhancements or for Internet Explorer only.

Table 13.1 lists the style settings available in the various categories of the CSS Style Definition dialog box.

TABLE 13.1 Style Settings in the CSS Style Definition Dialog Box

Setting	Description
Type Category	
Font	Sets the font family.
Size	Sets the font size and unit of measurement.
Style	Specifies the font as normal, italic, or oblique.

TABLE 13.1   Continued

Setting	Description
Type Category	
Line Height	Sets the height of the line of text and the unit of measurement. This setting is traditionally called *leading*. It is added before the line.
Decoration	Adds an underline, an overline, or a line through the text. You can set the text decoration to blink, or remove the decoration by choosing None.
Weight	Adds an amount of boldface to text. Regular bold is equal to 700.
Variant	Sets the small caps variant on text.
Case	Capitalizes the first letter of each word or sets all the text to lowercase or uppercase.
Color	Sets the text color.
Background Category	
Background Color	Sets a background color for an object.
Background Image	Sets a background image for an object.
Repeat	Controls how the background image is repeated. No Repeat displays the image only once, Repeat tiles the image horizontally and vertically, Repeat-x tiles the image only horizontally, and Repeat-y tiles the image only vertically.
Attachment	Sets whether the background image scrolls with the content or is fixed in its original position.
Horizontal Position	Specifies the initial horizontal position of the background image.
Vertical Position	Specifies the initial vertical position of the background image.
Block Category	
Word Spacing	Adds space around words. Negative values reduce the space between words.
Letter Spacing	Adds space between letters. Negative values reduce the space between letters.
Vertical Alignment	Sets the alignment of the object relative to objects around it (for example, the Alignment settings discussed in Chapter 6, "Displaying Images on a Page").
Text Align	Aligns text within an object. Choices are left, right, center, and justify.
Text Indent	Sets how far the first line is indented. Negative values set outdent.

TABLE 13.1   Continued

Setting	Description
Block Category	
Whitespace	Sets how whitespace will appear in an object. Normal collapses whitespace, Pre displays all the whitespace, and Nowrap sets the text to wrap only when a tag is encountered.
Display	Sets how and if an element is displayed. The None setting, for instance, hides the item on the page, the Block setting displays the element with a line break before and after, and the Inline settings displays the element with no line breaks.
Box Category	
Width	Sets the width of an object.
Height	Sets the height of an object.
Float	Sets whether text will float to the right or the left of the object. The None setting enables an object to appear where it is actually embedded in the code.
Clear	Clears floating so that objects (such as text) do not float around another object.
Padding	Sets the amount of space between the object and its border (or margin).
Margin	Sets the amount of space between the border of an object and other objects.
Border Category	
Style	Sets the style appearance of the borders. The choices are Dotted, Dashed, Solid, Double, Groove, Ridge, Inset, Outset, and None (for no border).
Width	Sets the border thickness. You can set the widths of the top, right, bottom, and left borders separately.
Color	Sets the border color. You can set the colors of the top, right, bottom, and left borders separately.
List Category	
Type	Sets the appearance of the bullets. The choices are Disc, Circle, Square, Decimal, Lower-roman, Upper-roman, Lower-alpha, Upper-alpha, and None.
Bullet Image	Sets a custom image for bullets.
Position	Sets whether the list content wraps to the indent (Outside) or to the margin (Inside).

TABLE 13.1   Continued

Setting	Description
Positioning Category	
Type	Sets how an element is positioned relative to the page. The choices are Relative (at the coordinates relative to its position on the page), Absolute (at the exact coordinates), and Static (at its place in the document flow).
Width	Sets the width of a layer.
Height	Sets the height of a layer.
Visibility	Sets the layer's visibility. The choices are Inherit, Visible, and Hidden.
Z-Index	Sets the layer's z-index (that is, stacking order).
Overflow	Sets what happens when the layer's contents exceed its size. The choices are Visible, Hidden, Scroll, and Auto.
Placement	Sets the left, top, width, and height attributes for a layer.
Clip	Sets the top, bottom, left, and right clipping attributes for a layer. *Clipping* defines how much of an element is visible.
Extensions Category	
Page Break	Forces a page break during printing, either before or after the object. This style is not widely supported, but may be in the future. Be careful with this property; use it only when you absolutely need to control where the page breaks for printing.
Cursor	Changes the cursor when it is placed over the object. Supported only in Internet Explorer 4.0 or later and Netscape 6 or later.
Filter	Applies special effects, including page transitions, opacity, and blurs, to objects. Supported only in Internet Explorer 4.0 or later. See msdn.microsoft.com/workshop/Author/filter/filters.asp for more information.

Redefining an HTML Tag

You can redefine HTML tags by using CSS styles. You apply these styles by applying the HTML tags as you normally would. For instance, you apply the <h3> tag by selecting Heading 3 from the Format drop-down menu in the Properties Inspector. Text formatted with the <h3> tag by default appears in a large italic font, slightly indented from the left margin, with one or two blank lines above and below. After you redefine the <h3> tag, any text with that tag applied to it will immediately appear with the new style formatting.

Type some text in the Dreamweaver Document window and apply Heading 3, the <h3> tag, to it. Do this so that you can see what the text looks like before you redefine the <h3> tag. Create a new style by clicking the New CSS Style button in the CSS Styles panel. The New CSS Style dialog box appears. Select the radio button beside Tag (Redefines the Look of a Specific Tag) and then select h3 from the Tag drop-down menu in the dialog box that appears.

By default, the <h3> tag makes objects left justified. To use styles to center the h3 text, select the Block category. Select Center from the Text Align drop-down menu, and click the OK button. Immediately after you click OK, the h3 text in your Web page should jump to center alignment. You can also apply a font in the Type category if you'd like.

Styles are defined in the <head> section of the Web page. Dreamweaver automatically records the styles you create in the CSS Styles panel into the <head> of the document. An example of the code for the h3 style looks like this:

```
h3 {
    font-family: Verdana, Arial, Helvetica, sans-serif;
    font-size: 13px;
    color: #6600FF;
    text-align: center;
}
```

If you look at the code inside the <head> section of a Web page, you'll see paired <style> tags surrounding the style definitions in the code. Nested within the style tags are paired comment tags (the <!-- and the closing -->). The comment tags are added so that older browsers simply ignore the styles and don't cause errors. The style definition contains the tag name, in this case, h3, followed by paired curly brackets containing the property name and the property value. Notice that a colon separates the property name and property value.

The CSS Styles panel also enables you to preview the style definition. The style name appears in the left column, and the style's definition appears in the right column, as shown in Figure 13.4. The CSS Styles panel displays all the styles applicable to the current Web page, including redefined HTML tags.

Style names   Style definitions

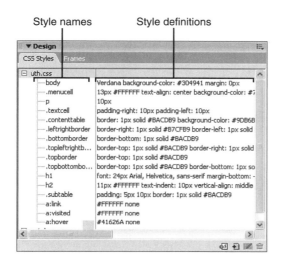

FIGURE 13.4
The CSS Styles panel enables you to view the style definition code.

Positioning a Layer by Using a Style

So far in this chapter, you've applied styles to text. When dealing with layers, it's useful to position objects on the page by using styles. If you need to position layers in a consistent place on the screen, it's an excellent idea to define a style for those layers. The other advantage to using styles is that if you'd like to move all the layers at once, you can simply edit the style definition.

To define a positioning style for a layer, follow these steps:

1. Create and name a new class, as you did earlier in this chapter.

2. Select the Positioning category in the CSS Style Definition dialog box. Notice that the properties in this category are properties that you used in Chapter 12, "Using Dynamic HTML and Layers," when you created layers.

3. Select Absolute in the Type drop-down list at the top of the dialog box. Set the Left, Top, Width, and Height drop-down lists.

4. Click the OK button to save your style.

Create a layer in your Web page. When you draw or insert a layer in your Web page, its positioning and other attributes are defined using an inline style, so layers already have CSS styles defined within them. First, you'll apply the new positioning style, and then you'll need to remove the existing inline style because it overrides the other style. Give this layer the name events.

You'll use a new method to apply this style to the layer. Select the layer and then right-click on `<div#events>` in the tag selector. Select the Set Class command in the tag selector menu, and select the new style you just created from the list. Next, delete the L (left), T (top), W (width), and H (height) layer properties, and the layer should hop to the position you defined in the style.

Did you Know?

Moving a Layer Overrides a Style

If you accidentally move the layer, you will override the style's top, left, width, and height attributes. To return the layer to its style-defined position, select the layer and remove the values in the Top, Left, Width, and Height boxes in the Properties Inspector. The layer should return to the location and size defined in the style. Also, you can always use the Undo command by selecting Edit, Undo.

Did you Know?

Style Can Create Layers

Instead of creating a layer first, you can simply apply a style you just created to a block of text in your Web page. The style will create a layer container around the text and position it according to the style settings.

Creating Advanced CSS Styles

The third type of style is advanced styles. This type of style can redefine a group of HTML tags instead of just one. For instance, you could use an advanced style to define what a specific heading tag looks like only within a table cell by entering the table cell tag, td, and then the paragraph tag, p. To do this, you enter all the tag names in the Selector box, as shown in Figure 13.5, and then define the style. The tags need to be in the correct hierarchical order, so if you create a style with a `<p>` tag nested within a `<td>` tag, `<td>` must come before `<p>` in the style selector.

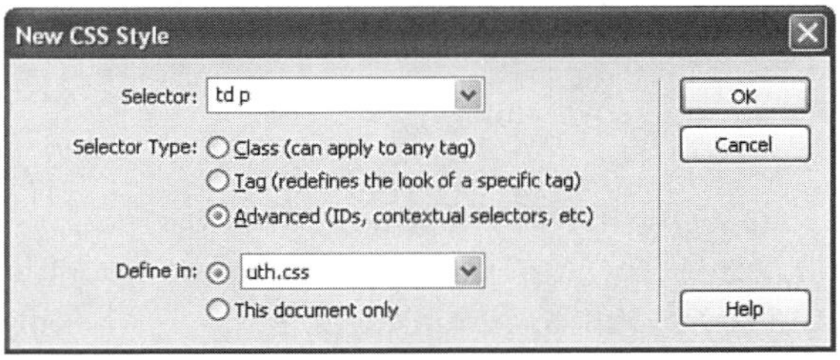

FIGURE 13.5
You can define attributes for a sequence of tags by using advanced styles in the New CSS Style dialog box.

Link Selector Styles

If you drop down the Selector menu instead of typing tags into the box, you will see a list of the selectors. These are the same CSS styles that you modified in the Page Properties dialog box in Chapter 2 when you changed the link attributes.

Did you
Know?

Creating an External Style Sheet

Adding styles to a single Web page is nice, but wouldn't it be great to apply the same styles to a number of Web pages? External style sheets allow you to do this. Instead of defining styles in the head of a Web page, you define all the styles in one text file. External style sheets end with the .css filename extension. When you update a style in an external style sheet, the changes apply to every page that is linked to that style sheet.

To create an external style sheet, follow these steps:

1. Create a new style and then select the top radio button in the Define In section of the New CSS Style dialog box. Select (New Style Sheet File) from the drop-down menu beside the radio button. Click the OK button.

2. The Save Style Sheet File As dialog box opens. Browse to the directory where you want to save your external style sheet. Enter a filename, and make sure it has the .css file extension. Click OK.

3. The CSS Style Definition dialog box opens. Notice that the title bar says that you are defining this style in the external style sheet that you just created. Create and save your style as you did earlier in this chapter.

When you create an external style sheet, Dreamweaver creates a new file and places the style definitions in it. Dreamweaver also references the external style sheet in the head of your Web page. To add additional styles to the external style sheet, select the name of the external style sheet from the Define In drop-down menu when you are defining a new style, as shown in Figure 13.6.

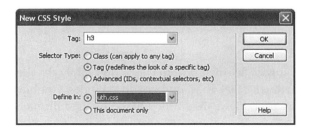

FIGURE 13.6
Select an external style sheet from the Define In drop-down menu to create a new style in the external style sheet.

Editing Styles

After you create styles, you may need to edit them. You can edit styles that are both internal to a Web page and contained in an external style sheet. Styles are listed as in the current document (the <head> section of the document) or in the external style sheet, as shown in Figure 15.14. Select any of the styles in the CSS Styles panel and click the Edit Style button to open the CSS Style Definition dialog box. Edit the style and save your changes.

FIGURE 13.7
You can easily edit CSS styles by using the Edit Style button in the CSS Styles panel.

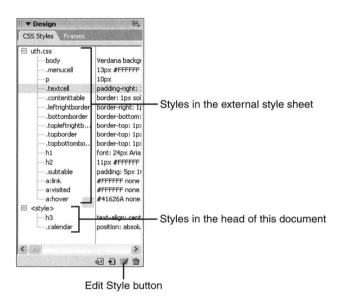

Styles in the external style sheet

Styles in the head of this document

Edit Style button

Export Internal Styles

If you already created some styles in a Web page and then decide to use an external style sheet, select File, Export, Export CSS Styles to export the styles defined in the Web page into an external .css file. Link to the .css file using the Attach to Style Sheet button at the bottom of the CSS Styles panel.

Summary

In this chapter, you have learned how to create and apply the three types of CSS styles: classes, redefined HTML tags, and advanced styles. You have also made an external style sheet that allows the same styles to be used throughout an entire Web site.

CHAPTER 14

Inserting Scripted Functionality by Using Behaviors

Dreamweaver behaviors add interactivity to Web pages. Interactivity usually requires coding in JavaScript, but Dreamweaver adds all the JavaScript for you, so you don't have to understand scripting to use behaviors. Behaviors enable you to make something happen when the user clicks the mouse, loads a Web page, or moves the cursor. You used your first behavior, the Go to URL behavior, in Chapter 11, "Understanding and Building Frames and Framesets."

Because some JavaScript doesn't work with older browsers, Dreamweaver enables you to choose browser versions. When you target 4.0 or higher versions of Internet Explorer or Netscape, you have access to many more behaviors than if you target 3.0 browsers. Dreamweaver also enables you to select Netscape and Internet Explorer because these browsers sometimes capture different event triggers. Dreamweaver behaviors are written to work in the major browsers.

What Is a Dreamweaver Behavior?

When you add a behavior to a Web page, Dreamweaver inserts JavaScript functions and function calls, enabling users to interact with the Web page or make something happen. I like to think of a **function** as a little code machine—you send it some information, it processes it, and it sends you a result or makes something happen. A **function call** is the code added to an object that triggers the function and sends it any information it needs to do its job. For instance, a popular Dreamweaver behavior is the Swap Image behavior that you used in Chapter 6, "Displaying Images on a Page." When you insert this behavior, Dreamweaver writes a function, called `MM_swapImage()`, in the head of the HTML document. The code in that function doesn't get called until some event on the page triggers it; the `MM_swapImage()` function is usually triggered by the `onMouseOver` event—the event fired when the cursor is placed over whatever object the function is attached to.

A **behavior** is an action that is triggered by an event, or you could look at it this way:

event + action = behavior

Actions are the type of JavaScript code that Dreamweaver inserts into a Web page. **Events** are triggers that are captured by the browser. Table 14.1 lists examples of common browser events. Different browsers may capture different events. Also, different objects capture different events. This is just a small sampling of the events that are available, but luckily, most of the events are named so that the functionality is fairly obvious. The onDblClick event, for instance, is similar to the onClick event, except that the user clicks twice instead of once.

TABLE 14.1   Common Browser Events

Event	Description
onMouseOver	Triggered when the user places the cursor over an object. This event is often captured from images or hyperlinks.
onMouseDown	Triggered when the user presses the mouse button. This event is often captured from images or hyperlinks.
onMouseUp	Triggered when the user releases the mouse button. This event is often captured from images or hyperlinks.
onClick	Triggered when the user presses and releases, or clicks, the mouse button. This event is often captured from images or hyperlinks.
onLoad	Triggered when the object or Web page finishes loading. This event is often captured from the body of a Web page and occasionally used with images.
onUnload	Triggered when the Web page is "unloaded" from the browser—when the user goes to a new URL or the browser is closed. This event is usually captured from the body of a Web page and is often responsible for triggering those annoying pop-up windows that seem impossible to close.
onChange	Triggered after a user has made and committed a change to a form object, usually a text field, textarea, drop-down menu, or list. The user commits to the change by leaving the form object, usually by putting the focus elsewhere on the Web page.
onSelect	Triggered when a user selects text within a form object, usually a text field or textarea.

TABLE 14.1   Continued

Event	Description
onSubmit	Triggered when the user submits a form by using a submit button or an image button.
onBlur	Triggered when an object loses **focus**, or becomes inactive. This event is often captured from the body of a Web page, when the user switches to a different Web page, or from form objects, such as a text field or a check box.
onFocus	Triggered when an object receives focus, or becomes active. This event is often captured from the body of a Web page, when the user switches to a different Web page, or from form objects, such as a text field or a check box.

To learn more about individual events, use the Dreamweaver Reference panel (by selecting Window, Reference), shown in Figure 14.1. There are several reference books built right into Dreamweaver. To find the events, select JavaScript Reference from the Book drop-down menu and select an event name from the Object menu. The Reference panel displays a description of the event, including which browsers support the event (in the upper-right corner) and typical targets for the event.

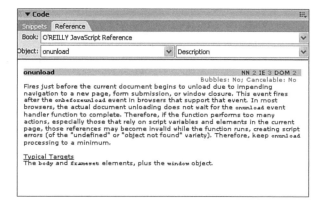

FIGURE 14.1
The Reference panel displays the JavaScript reference that includes descriptions of events.

Dreamweaver comes with many powerful behaviors. Table 14.2 lists the behaviors that are preinstalled in Dreamweaver.

TABLE 14.2   Dreamweaver Behaviors

Behavior	Description
Call JavaScript	Specifies custom JavaScript code. You use this behavior when you want to add custom JavaScript code to Dreamweaver.
Change Property	Changes an object's properties. This behavior enables you to change properties of layers, such as the background color or the size, form objects, and images.
Check Browser	Determines what browser the user has. This is useful when you are have authored content specific to various browser versions. This behavior can redirect the user to different Web pages based on which browser he is using.
Check Plugin	Determines whether the user has a particular plug-in installed. You usually trigger this behavior by using the onLoad event of the body tag.
Control Shockwave or Flash	Controls Shockwave or Flash movies. Can be set to Play, Stop, Rewind, or Go to Frame.
Drag Layer	Makes a layer draggable and defines a target to drag it to. You'll explore this behavior in Chapter 15, "Adding Advanced Behaviors: The Drag Layer Behavior."
Go to URL	Loads a URL into the browser. This behavior also enables you to load several new URLs into frames as described in Chapter 11.
Hide Pop-up Menu	Hides a Dreamweaver pop-up menu (described later in this table, with the Show Pop-up Menu behavior).
Jump Menu	Edits a jump menu. You'll create a jump menu in Chapter 16, "Creating a Form and Using It to Collect Data." This is a menu that enables users to jump to various URLs.
Jump Menu Go	Adds a custom jump menu's Go button. This button is used to trigger going to the newly selected URL.
Open Browser Window	Opens a new browser window. This behavior is often used to open additional windows containing extra information.
Play Sound	Plays a sound file.
Popup Message	Pops up a JavaScript alert box with text. This box contains an OK button that the user clicks to close the message.
Preload Images	Preloads images into the browser cache in the background. This behavior is often included with the Swap Image behavior. The image to be swapped will be loaded into the cache so that it appears quickly.

TABLE 14.2 Continued

Behavior	Description
Set Nav Bar Image	Changes the image in a navigation bar. You created a navigation bar in Chapter 7, "Creating Image Maps and Navigation Bars." This behavior enables you to set a button state.
Set Text of Frame	Puts text (or HTML) into a frame.
Set Text of Layer	Puts text (or HTML) into a layer.
Set Text of Status Bar	Puts text into the browser's status bar.
Set Text of Text Field	Puts text into a text field in a form.
Show Pop-up Menu	Shows a Dreamweaver pop-up menu with links. This menu uses CSS to present a complex menu. You use this behavior to set the color, position, text, and other attributes of the menu.
Show-Hide Layers	Shows or hides a layer or group of layers. This behavior changes the layer visibility attribute.
Swap Image	Swaps the image source for another image source.
Swap Image Restore	Restores a previous image swap.
Validate Form	Validates the data in a form, enabling you to check whether the user can entered information into certain text fields and validating whether it is the correct type of information. You'll use this behavior in Chapter 17, "Sending and Reacting to Form Data."

You attach behaviors to objects in a Web page. When you attach a behavior, Dreamweaver opens the appropriate behavior dialog box. After you've set up the behavior characteristics in the dialog box, you select the event to trigger the behavior. Dreamweaver inserts the necessary JavaScript into the head of the Web page. Code is also added to the object's tag to capture the event and call the JavaScript.

> When you add a behavior to an object, Dreamweaver adds an attribute to the HTML tag, enabling the tag to respond to the event. The attribute includes a function call to the appropriate function inserted by the behavior. For instance, the code for an image tag with a Show-Hide Layers behavior attached would look like this:
>
> ```
> <img src="button_up.gif" width="80" height="35"
> ➥onClick="MM_showHideLayers('Layer1','','hide')">
> ```
>
> When the user clicks this image, the layer named Layer1 will become hidden.

By the Way

You need to attach behaviors to appropriate objects. Dreamweaver won't let you attach behaviors that aren't appropriate for the object selected; inappropriate behaviors are grayed out. You can tell which object you have selected because it is displayed in the title bar of the Tag panel group, as shown in Figure 14.2. This is the panel group where you find the Behaviors panel.

Currently selected tag

FIGURE 14.2
The tag of the object that is currently selected is displayed in the title bar of the Tag panel group.

Watch Out!

The Behaviors panel is not the same as the Server Behaviors panel. The Server Behaviors panel works with sites that use server-side scripting, such as ASP, ASP.NET, JSP, PHP, and ColdFusion. The Behaviors panel uses JavaScript, which is client-side scripting (and does not rely on a server).

You can attach multiple behaviors to an object. One event can trigger several actions. In Figure 14.3, you can see that the onClick event triggers a number of actions. The actions happen in the order in which they are listed. You can change the order in which the actions occur by moving the actions with the up and down arrow buttons on the Behaviors panel.

The biggest difference between the various browsers is the events that they support. When you use behaviors, you need to be aware of which browsers you are going to support. If it's crucial that you support every browser available—on a government Web site, for instance—then you will be very limited in the events available to you.

Events   Actions

FIGURE 14.3
One event—for
example, the
onClick event
shown here—can
trigger multiple
actions, and you
can have multiple
behaviors attached
to a single object in
a Web page.

Dreamweaver enables you to set the browser events that it presents in the
Behaviors panel. The Show Events For drop-down menu, shown in Figure 14.4,
enables you to target specific browsers and browser versions. Depending on the
selection in this menu, different events will be available. You access the Show
Events For drop-down menu by clicking the + button in the Behaviors panel.

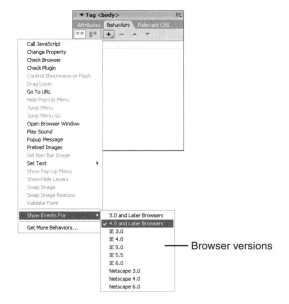

Browser versions

FIGURE 14.4
The Show Events
For submenu
enables you to
choose browsers
and browser ver-
sions. Only the
actions and events
that work with the
browser and ver-
sion you choose
will be available.

Did you
Know?

Which Events Setting Is Best?

You will have access to the largest number of events by choosing IE 6.0 and the fewest number of events choosing 3.0 and Later Browsers. The IE 4.0 and Netscape 4.0 events offer a good compromise between a useful number of events and compatibility with almost all browsers, so you'll generally want to choose the 4.0 and Later Browsers setting.

Watch
Out!

What Happens When the Event Isn't Supported?

If you select an event that does not work in a certain browser, users using that browser will either have nothing happen or will receive a JavaScript error.

Showing and Hiding Layers

Now you're ready to add your first behavior. The Show-Hide Layers behavior has a name that pretty much says it all: You can use it to show or hide a layer on the Web page. You don't usually apply a behavior to the object that it affects, so you'll need to have another object on the page that triggers the behavior. For instance, Dreamweaver won't allow you to attach the Show-Hide Layers behavior to the layer you want to hide. You need to add to your page an image or a hyperlink that captures the user's click and hides the layer. Dreamweaver is also smart enough to not display the Show-Hide Layers behavior in the Behaviors drop-down menu if you don't actually have any layers in the Web page, so you'll need to add a layer to the page before you add the behavior.

Selecting a Behavior

You will now use the Show-Hide Layers behavior to create a layer that your behavior will affect. It's important to name your layers when using the Show-Hide Layers behavior. The Show-Hide Layers dialog box displays all the layers on the page by name, so it helps for the layers to have meaningful names. Type some text in the layer, insert an image into it, or give it a background color.

To add a Show-Hide Layers behavior to a hyperlink, follow these steps:

1. Create a layer and set its visibility attribute to hidden. You learned about the visibility attribute in Chapter 12, "Using Dynamic HTML and Layers."

2. Add text or an image somewhere on the Web page. This text or image will be turned into a hyperlink; clicking it will trigger the Show-Hide Layers behavior to show the layer. Add a null hyperlink to the text or image by

first selecting it and then typing **javascript:;** (a null link) in the link box of the Properties Inspector.

3. Open the Behaviors panel and click somewhere within the newly created hyperlink. Make sure that <a> (the anchor tag) is visible in the title bar of the Tag panel group. This means that you are applying the behavior to the <a> tag, the tag that implements hyperlinks.

4. Click the + button in the Behaviors panel. Select the Show-Hide Layers behavior. The Show-Hide Layers dialog box appears.

5. The Show-Hide Layers dialog box, shown in Figure 14.5, lists all the layers in the page. There are three buttons: Show, Hide, and Default. Highlight the correct layer and click the Show button. The word *show* then appears in parentheses next to the layer name.

FIGURE 14.5
The Show-Hide Layers dialog box lists all the layers and enables you to change their visibility attributes.

The functions of the Show and Hide buttons in the Show-Hide Layers dialog box are obvious. You click the Show button to make a layer visible, and you click the Hide button to make a layer hidden. When a layer is set to Show, clicking the Show button again turns show off (the same goes for the other buttons). The Default button restores a layer to default visibility (which is usually visible).

6. Click the OK button to save your changes.

Selecting the Action That Triggers a Behavior

At this point, you have selected the action, but you also have to select the other half of the behavior: the event. The Behaviors panel lists the Show-Hide Layers behavior under the Action column and defaults to the onClick event. You could use the onClick event to trigger showing the layer, but that's too easy! Try using the onMouseUp event instead:

1. Drop down the Events menu by clicking the arrow button. You need to select the event for this button to be available.

2. Select onMouseUp in the event drop-down menu. Now the user letting up the mouse button will trigger the Show-Hide Layers behavior.

Now that you have set up the action (Show-Hide Layers) and the event (onMouseUp), you can test your work in the browser. First you have to make sure the layer you have set to show with the behavior is hidden (if you didn't do this earlier). Preview the Web page in the browser. Click the hyperlink, and your layer should appear!

By default, Dreamweaver displays in the Behaviors panel only events that have actions associated with them and are complete behaviors. You can set the Behaviors panel to display all the events available by clicking the Show All Events button, shown in Figure 14.6. What events are displayed depends on the object selected on the Web page and the browser(s) selected in the Show Events For drop-down menu. If any of the events have actions associated with them, you will see them displayed in the Actions column. If you want to display only events that have actions attached, click the Show Set Events button.

Show Set Events button
Show All Events button

FIGURE 14.6
You can display all available events by clicking the Show All Events button in the Behaviors panel.

Opening a New Window

Use the Open Browser Window behavior to open a new browser window and display a URL. This time you will capture the user clicking an image to trigger the action. When the user clicks the image, the onClick event will fire. This then triggers the Open Browser Window behavior that will open a new browser window.

You can open a browser window at a specific size and with specific browser attributes. Browser attributes, listed in Table 14.3, control whether the browser window has controls that enable the user to navigate out of the window. You set up the browser attributes in the Open Browser Window dialog box.

TABLE 14.3   Browser Properties for the Open Browser Window Behavior

Attribute	Description
URL	Sets the URL of the page that will be opened in the new window.
Width	Controls the width (in pixels) of the window.
Height	Controls the height (in pixels) of the window.
Navigation Toolbar	Contains the Back, Next, and other navigation buttons for moving to different URLs.
Location Toolbar	Displays the current URL.
Status Bar	Displays the status bar (the bar located at the bottom of the browser). The status bar displays the loading status of a Web page as well as the URL of a moused-over link.
Menu Bar	Contains all the standard browser menus.
Scrollbars as Needed	Enables the user to scroll the browser window.
Resize Handles	Enables the user to resize the browser window.
Window Name	Specifies the optional window name. This name can be used to control the window with JavaScript, so spaces and punctuation cannot be used in the name.

To have a new browser window open when the user clicks an image, follow these steps:

1. Save the Web page. The Open Browser Window behavior needs the Web page to be saved so that it knows how to build the URL that it will load in the new browser window.

2. Insert an image into this Web page. Select the image, and make sure the correct tag shows in the title bar of the Tag panel group (the <img> tag).

3. Click the + button in the Behaviors panel. Select the Open Browser Window behavior, and the Open Browser Window dialog box appears.

4. Fill in a URL that will load in the new window. You can use a Web page that you created previously or load an external Web page from any Web site.

5. Set the width and height of the window. Check the browser attributes (listed in Table 14.3) that you want the new browser window to have. Optionally, give the window a name.

6. The Open Browser Window dialog box should look something like the one shown in Figure 14.7. Click the OK button.

FIGURE 14.7
The Open Browser
Window dialog box
enables you to turn
on or off various
attributes of brows-
er windows.

7. In the Behaviors panel, select the onClick event from the Events drop-down menu if it wasn't selected by default.

Preview the Web page you created in a browser. When you click the image, your new window should appear. To edit a behavior, simply select the object where the behavior is applied. The behavior will appear in the Behaviors panel. Double-click the behavior to reopen the Open Browser Window dialog box and edit the settings. You can edit the event by simply selecting a different event in the Events drop-down menu. Delete a behavior by selecting it and clicking the - button in the Behaviors panel.

Popping Up a Message

Next, you'll add an additional behavior, a pop-up message, to the same object you used to open a browser window. The Popup Message behavior displays a JavaScript alert box with a message.

To add the Popup Message behavior, follow these steps:

1. Select the object where you applied the behavior in the preceding section. You should see the Open Browser Window behavior listed in the Behaviors panel. Make sure the appropriate tag appears in the title bar of the Tag panel group.

2. Click the + button and select the Popup Message behavior.

3. The Popup Message dialog box includes a text box where you type your message. Click OK after typing the message.

4. Select the onClick event as you did in the Open Browser Window dialog box earlier.

Preview your Web page in the browser. Does it work ideally? It would probably be better if the message popped up and then the user went to the new window after he or she clicked the OK button in the message box. You can change the order of behaviors that are triggered by the same event.

To change the order of the behaviors, follow these steps:

1. Select the object where the behaviors are applied. You should see both behaviors listed in the Behaviors panel.

2. Select the Popup Message behavior. Click the up arrow button to move the Popup Message behavior above the Open Browser Window behavior.

Preview your Web page in the browser. Now the pop-up message appears first. After you click the OK button on the pop-up message, the new browser window should appear.

Adding a Message in the Status Bar

You can insert behaviors that write to various objects: frames, layers, text entry fields, and the browser status bar. To use the Set Text of Status Bar behavior, follow these steps:

1. Select an object on a Web page to trigger the behavior. You can add this behavior to the same object you've used earlier in this chapter or you can add a null link to an object on any Web page.

2. Click the + button in the Behaviors panel. Choose the Set Text of Status Bar behavior from the Set Text submenu—the menu that appears when you place your mouse over Set Text in the Behaviors drop-down menu. The Set Text of Status Bar dialog box appears.

3. Enter some text to display in the status bar. Click OK.

4. Select an event from the Event drop-down menu in the Behaviors panel.

Preview the Web page in your browser. After the new window appears, the text you entered appears in the status bar at the bottom of the browser window.

Summary

In this chapter, you have learned that a Dreamweaver behavior consists of an event that triggers an action. You have used the Show-Hide Layers behavior, the Open Browser Window behavior, the Popup Message behavior, and the Set Text in Status Bar behavior. You have captured events from a hyperlink and an image. And you have used the onMouseUp and onClick events as triggers for Dreamweaver actions.

CHAPTER 15

Adding Advanced Behaviors: The Drag Layer Behavior

In this chapter, you will apply a more advanced Dreamweaver behavior: the Drag Layer behavior. The Drag Layer behavior enables you to create layers that the user can drag around the browser window. You can even constrain the area within which the layer can be dragged. This capability is useful for creating sliders, puzzles, dialog boxes, and other interactions.

You can use the Drag Layer behavior to let users interact with objects on your Web page. For instance, you might have a layer that contains a map legend. You could make that layer draggable so that the user could move it out of the way if it happened to be blocking part of the map. Or you could create a blank face and let people drag different noses, ears, eyes, and so on, onto the face.

Using the Tag Selector to Select the Body Tag

During this chapter, you'll use a more complicated Dreamweaver behavior than you've used in previous chapters. To get started, set up a Web page to use the Drag Layer behavior by first creating four layers that will be dragged. Then create a layer that will be the target. These layers can have anything in them, including text, images, and even other layers. Give each of these layers a meaningful name. The layers should look something like Figure 15.1. If you don't have any images handy, simply give the layers various background colors.

The Drag Layer behavior enables a layer to be dragged. You need to turn on this behavior before the layer can be dragged. This behavior can be triggered when the Web page loads by capturing the <body> tag's onLoad event. You select the <body> tag in Dreamweaver's tag selector. You should see <body> in the title of the Tag panel group.

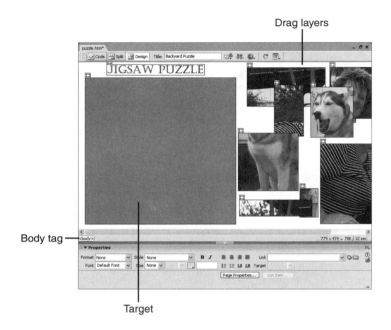

FIGURE 15.1
The user will drag layers onto the target layer to complete an interaction.

Drag layers

Body tag

Target

Constraining the Movement of a Layer

After you've created your drag and target layers and given them all names, you're ready to apply the Drag Layer behavior. To use the Drag Layer behavior, follow these steps:

1. Select the <body> tag from the tag selector in the Dreamweaver status bar.

2. Click the + button in the Behaviors panel and select Drag Layer. The Drag Layer dialog box appears, as shown in Figure 15.2.

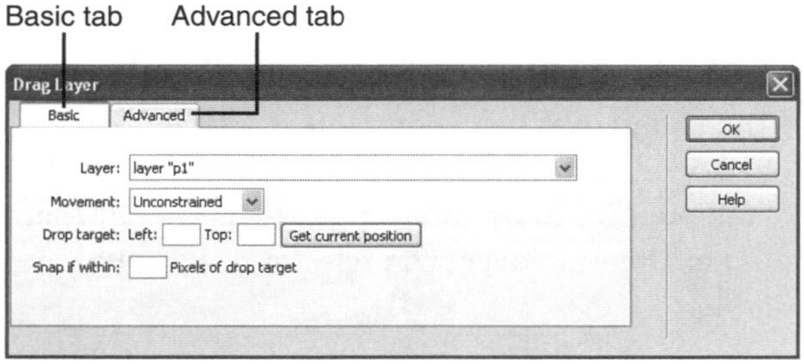

Basic tab   Advanced tab

FIGURE 15.2
The Drag Layer dialog box has a Basic tab and an Advanced tab.

3. Select from the Layer drop-down menu the name of a layer to be dragged.

4. Optionally, select Constrained from the Movement drop-down menu. Four boxes appear for you to enter the pixel values for coordinates of an area. To constrain movement to only vertical, enter values for Up and Down but enter 0 for Right and Left. To constrain movement to only horizontal, enter values for Left and Right but enter 0 for Up and Down. To define a rectangular area, enter values in all the boxes. Values are all relative to the original position of the layer. The Drag Layer dialog box should look as shown in Figure 15.3. This layer is constrained to move 20 pixels up, 300 pixels down, 400 pixels to the left, and 20 pixels to the right from its original position.

Constrained movement properties

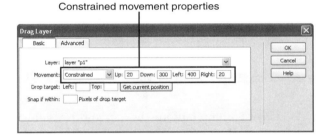

FIGURE 15.3
When you select Constrained from the Movement drop-down menu, four new boxes appear. Enter pixel values to define the constrained movement area.

Working with L and T Layer Attributes

An easy way to figure out which values to enter in the Movement boxes is to calculate them ahead of time. You can use Dreamweaver and a little math to decide on the numbers before you start to apply the Drag Layer behavior. Write down the original L (left) and T (top) values for the layer. Move the layer to the edges of the constraining area and write down those L and T values. Figure out the difference and enter those values into the Movement boxes when you set up the Drag Layer behavior. To return your layer to its original position, enter the original L and T values into the Properties Inspector.

Did you Know?

---

5. Click OK to save your changes.

6. Make sure that the onLoad event is listed in the Behaviors panel next to the Drag Layer action. This means the Drag Layer behavior is triggered when the Web page loads.

Check to see that the Drag Layer behavior is working the way you want it to by previewing the Web page in a browser. The correct layer should be draggable, and other layers shouldn't be draggable yet. The drag area should be constrained the way you want it. You will go back and edit the behavior in a few minutes.

Capturing the Drop Target Location

You could calculate or guess at the exact target location, which might work some of the time. But the easiest way to capture the perfect target location is to take advantage of the Drag Layer behavior's built-in Get Current Position button. This button will capture the position of the layer and fill in the coordinates for you. To capture the drop target location, first make sure the Prevent Layer Overlaps check box in the Layers panel is not selected. Then follow these steps:

1. Line up the layer that you set previously in the Drag Layer behavior in its final position on the target. Remember that you can use the arrow keys on the keyboard to move the layer 1 pixel at a time for fine-tuning.

2. Select the <body> tag from the tag selector.

3. Double-click the Drag Layer behavior you just set up in the Behaviors panel to edit it.

4. Click the Get Current Position button. The Left and Top values fill in automatically, as shown in Figure 15.4. The Snap If Within box automatically defaults to 50 pixels.

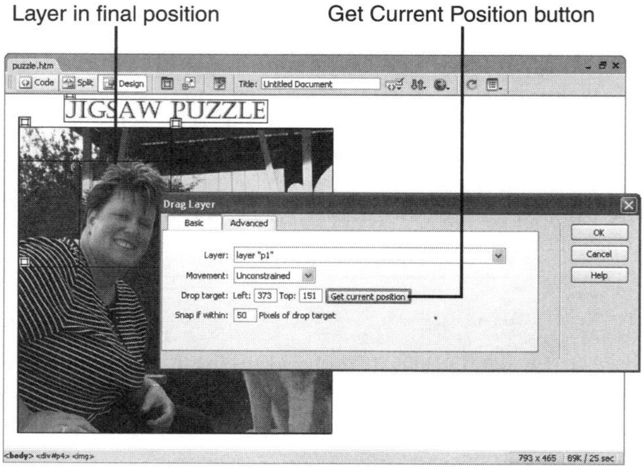

Layer in final position   Get Current Position button

FIGURE 15.4
The Get Current Position button automatically fills in the coordinates with the current position of the layer selected in the Drag Layer dialog box.

5. Accept the default Snap If Within value or change it. This value sets how close the user must drop the layer in order for it to snap, and it depends

upon the size of your target area. Make sure this value isn't so small that it's difficult for the user to position the layer or so big that the user doesn't need to be accurate.

6. Click OK.

7. Put the layer back in its original position. Then preview the page in a browser.

The Target Is Optional

You can use the Drag Layer behavior without a target layer if the interaction you are creating doesn't require the user to drop the layers on a target.

By the Way

Applying Advanced Attributes of the Drag Layer Behavior

At this point, you have a functioning interaction with a Drag Layer behavior and a target. The layer will snap when dropped within a certain distance of the target center. This interaction might work great for some situations, but in other situations you might want to use some of the advanced attributes of the Drag Layer dialog box, as shown in Figure 15.5.

FIGURE 15.5
The Advanced tab in the Drag Layer dialog box enables you to add advanced attributes, including JavaScript.

The Advanced tab in the Drag Layer dialog box enables you to define a specific area of the layer as a handle for dragging. This enables you to have finer control over what part of the layer the user actually clicks to drag the layer, and it can make the interaction more realistic. For instance, if you have an image of a file drawer that the user can drag open, you could limit the user to dragging the drawer handle instead of the entire drawer.

> **Coordinates Are Relative to the Layer**
>
> The coordinates for defining the dragging area within a layer are relative to the upper-left corner of the drag layer.

Another advanced attribute is the capability to control where the layer is positioned relative to other layers while dragging. You can set the layer to be on top of all other layers, regardless of its z-index value, while it is dragging. Its original z-index value can then be restored when it is dropped, or it can remain on top.

The capability to call JavaScript both while a layer is being dragged and after the layer has been dropped offers many powerful options. In a few minutes you'll experiment with adding some simple JavaScript into the Call JavaScript text boxes. Knowledge of JavaScript isn't required because these settings are purely optional.

To add advanced attributes to the Drag Layer behavior, follow these steps:

1. Open the Drag Layer dialog box to edit the existing behavior by double-clicking the behavior name in the Behaviors panel. Select the Advanced tab.

2. By default, Entire Layer is set in the Drag Handle drop-down menu. Optionally, if you want the user to be able to click only a specific portion of the layer to drag it, select the Area Within Layer command from the Drag Handle drop-down menu. Enter the left, top, width, and height coordinates. These coordinates positions are relative to the layer.

3. Make sure the check box beside Bring Layer to Front is checked so the layer will be on top of all others during dragging.

4. Select Restore Z-index or Leave on Top from the drop-down menu after the While Dragging check box. This will either put the layer back to its original z-index value after it has been on top while dragging or leave it on top.

Next, you'll place some simple JavaScript in the two boxes that will accept JavaScript on the Advanced tab in the Drag Layer dialog box. You can set the value of the browser status bar by giving a value to the `window.status` object. First, you set `window.status` to Dragging… while the user is dragging the layer. Then you set `window.status` to Dropped when the user has dropped the layer on the target. To enter JavaScript in the Drag Layer dialog box, follow these steps:

1. Carefully type this JavaScript code into the Call JavaScript box:

    ```
    window.status = 'Dragging...'
    ```

Be sure to use single quotes, not double quotes. In the code, this entire statement will be enclosed in double quotes, so you need to use single quotes
within the Call JavaScript box so that you don't interfere with the code
around this JavaScript.

2. Carefully type this JavaScript code into the When Dropped: Call JavaScript
box:

```
window.status = 'Dropped!'
```

Again, be sure to use single quotes, not double quotes.

3. Check the Only If Snapped check box, if the JavaScript should execute only
if the user drops the layer on the target. Leave the Only If Snapped check
box unchecked if the JavaScript should execute when the user drops the
drag layer.

4. Click OK.

5. Save your Web page and preview it in a browser. Notice the text changing
in the status bar? The status bar is a fun place to display extra information
about what's going on in the browser. However, you shouldn't place important information here because the user may not notice it.

The Call JavaScript Behavior

The Call JavaScript behavior works similarly to entering JavaScript in the Drag Layer
behavior, as you have just done. The Call JavaScript behavior dialog box opens a single line on which you can write a JavaScript statement, as you just did.

By the Way

You can, of course, continue to reopen the Drag Layer behavior and refine the
coordinates or change settings. You'll need to repeat the process of adding the
Drag Layer behavior for each layer that the user will be able to drag.

Selecting a Body Tag Event

When the Drag Layer behavior works the way you want it to, you need to add an
event to trigger the Drag Layer action. If you apply the behavior to the body tag,
it might have defaulted to the onLoad event. If the onLoad event is not already
selected, select it from the Event drop-down menu in the Behaviors panel.

You can trigger the Drag Layer behavior from other objects' events, too. For
instance, you might require the user to click something to show the layer that he
or she will drag. You could place the Drag Layer behavior under the Show-Hide
Layers behavior so that when the layer is visible, it is also draggable.

Summary

In this chapter, you have learned how to apply a behavior to the <body> tag. You have learned how to configure the Drag Layer behavior to create a drag-and-drop interaction. You have also set up advanced attributes of the Drag Layer behavior and selected an event to trigger the behavior.

CHAPTER 16

Creating a Form and Using It to Collect Data

In this chapter, you will create a form to collect user input. Dreamweaver gives you easy access to a number of different form elements, including text boxes, radio buttons, check boxes, lists, drop-down menus, and buttons to capture user choices. We'll cover how to submit form data in Chapter 17, "Sending and Reacting to Form Data."

With forms, you can collect information, such as comments or orders, and interact with your users. In your form, you can ask for your user's name and email address, have the user sign a guestbook, or have the user provide feedback on your Web site. You can send this information back to the Web server if you'd like. Dreamweaver enables you to validate information so that you know it's in the correct format.

Creating a Form

A **form** is a container for other objects, as well as an invisible element. When you add a form to a Web page, Dreamweaver represents it as a red, dashed-line box if you have Form Delimiter checked in the Invisible Elements category in the Preferences dialog box. Make sure you have this option selected so you can see the outline of each form.

While you're creating a form, it might be helpful to have the Forms category selected in the Insert bar, as shown in Figure 16.1. The first step in creating a form is to insert a Form object into your Web page to hold all the Form objects that will collect user input.

To add a form, follow these steps:

1. Create a new Web page and place the insertion point where you want to insert the form.

2. Select Insert, Form, Form or select the Form object in the Forms category of the Insert bar.

3. A message box may appear telling you that you will not be able to see the form unless you view the invisible elements. Click OK and then, if necessary, select View, Visual Aids, Invisible Elements.

4. A red, dashed-line box appears on the page, as shown in Figure 16.2. It represents the form.

FIGURE 16.1
The Forms category in the Insert bar presents all the Form objects that you insert into your Web page to collect user input.

Form delimiter

FIGURE 16.2
A form appears as a red, dashed-line box (a form delimiter) when invisible elements are turned on.

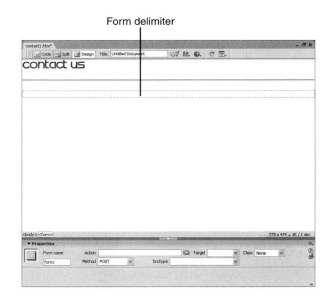

You can format the area within a form by using tables, horizontal rules, text, and other items that would normally be in a Web page. The only information that will be submitted, however, are the names of the form elements and the data the user enters into the form. The text and formatting objects you place within the form will not be submitted.

To select a form, click the edge of the form delimiter. The Properties Inspector shows the three properties you can enter for a form:

▶ **Form Name**—This property is necessary if you plan to apply any behaviors (or your own custom scripts) to a form. It's a good idea to always name your forms. Dreamweaver puts a default form name in for you.

▶ **Action**—This property is a URL that points to an application, usually a script, on the server that will process the form data. You'll explore more about the form action in Chapter 17.

▶ **Method**—This property tells the application on the server how the data should be processed. Again, you'll explore this in Chapter 17.

Give your form a name, as shown in Figure 16.3. Because you'll explore the Action and Method properties in the next chapter, you can just leave them blank for now. To select a form, click the form delimiter; the `<form>` tag appears in the tag selector. Place your cursor inside the form to insert objects into it.

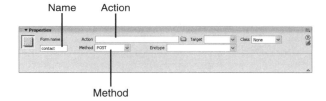

Name   Action

Method

FIGURE 16.3
The Properties Inspector shows the three attributes available to be set for a Form object.

Adding Text Fields to Forms

Text fields, as shown in Figure 16.4, are commonly used in forms. Single-line text fields enable you to type in a name, an address, a phone number, or other short pieces of text information. Text fields can also have multiple lines, suitable for comments or lengthy pieces of information. The example in Figure 16.4 was produced using one of the page designs available by selecting the Table Based Layouts category when creating a new page. This design is called UI:Send Email B.

Now you'll continue creating your own form from scratch. Create a group of text fields designed to collect the user's first and last names, email address, and comments. Begin by inserting a single-line text field into your Web page to collect the user's first name:

1. Make sure the insertion point is within the form.

2. Select the Text Field object from the Forms category of the Insert bar, or select Insert, Form, Text Field. A text field appears in the form, as shown in Figure 16.5.

FIGURE 16.4
A group of text fields, a textarea, and a submit button are used to collect user information on an order form that is submitted to the server and then processed.

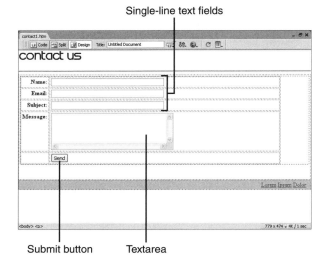

Single-line text fields

Submit button   Textarea

FIGURE 16.5
A text field is inserted within a form so that a script or an application on the server can collect the data that a user enters in the field on the Web page.

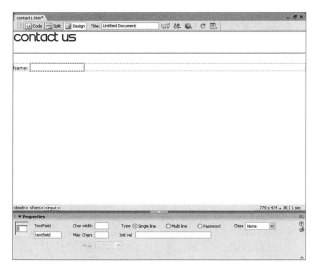

Did you
Know?

Dreamweaver Asks to Insert a Form When You've Already Inserted One

If you get a dialog box asking you to insert a form tag but you thought that you had already inserted one, the insertion point is not placed properly within the form. In this case, it's easiest to click No in the dialog box, delete the newly created object, and try again. If you are just beginning to create a form and forget to insert a form object first, click Yes in the dialog box. Dreamweaver will insert a form around the form element you have just created.

3. To add another text field directly to the right of the first one, place the insertion point after the text field and insert another text field for the email address.

4. Place the insertion point after the second text field you created. Press the Enter key to add a new paragraph within the form before you insert the text field. Add another single-line text field for the subject. The form should look as shown in Figure 16.6.

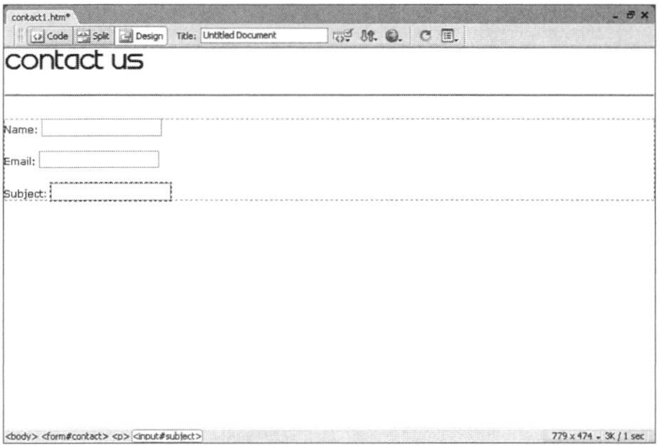

FIGURE 16.6
This form contains three text fields that you will use to collect the user's first name, email address, and subject.

Applying Text Field Attributes

When you have a text field selected, the Properties Inspector presents the text field attributes, as shown in Figure 16.6. Dreamweaver fills in a unique default name. Rename all the text fields in your form with meaningful and unique names; possible names would be firstname, email, and subject. As with other Dreamweaver objects, it is a good idea not to use spaces and punctuation in the names. Some scripts and applications are not designed to deal with form element names that contain spaces and punctuation.

You can set both the size of the text field and the number of characters a user can enter into it. There are two different width settings for a text field:

▶ **Char Width**—You use this setting to set the size of the text field and the number of characters that are visible in the field. If there are more characters in the text field than the width setting can accommodate, they will be submitted but simply won't be visible unless you scroll.

▶ **Max Chars**—You use this setting to limit the number of characters a user can enter into the text field. The user will not be able to enter more characters than the value of Max Chars. Setting Max Chars might be useful when you know the absolute length of the data the user should enter, such as a Social Security number, and do not want the user to enter additional characters.

You can set three different types of text fields in the Properties Inspector:

▶ **Single Line**—These text fields are useful for collecting small, discrete words, names, or phrases from the user.

▶ **Multi Line**—This type of text field presents an area with multiple lines that enables the user to enter larger blocks of text. This is the same as the Textarea object, which is available in the Forms category of the Insert bar.

▶ **Password**—These text fields are special single-line fields that mask what the user types into the field, using asterisks or bullets to shield the data from other people. This doesn't, however, encrypt the data that is submitted.

You can select any styles in the Class drop-down list to apply a CSS style to the text field. You learned about CSS styles in Chapter 13, "Formatting Web Pages by Using Cascading Style Sheets." You can set the font, background color, and other attributes of a text field by using CSS styles.

The first three fields in your form should remain single-line text fields. Add a fourth field—a message field—by creating a new paragraph and inserting a Textarea object from the Insert bar. This object is exactly like the text field object, but it has the Multi Line property already applied.

The Textarea object includes a property that enables you to enter the height of the object (the number of lines in the textarea). Enter a value into the Num Lines property to set the height. There is no Max Chars setting for a textarea; you can control only the number of lines that are visible on the screen.

Change Char Width to Change the Size

You can't resize text fields by clicking and dragging their borders. You can change the size only by changing the Char Width property in the Properties Inspector.

The Wrap property is another property that is unique to textarea objects. The default setting is for the text in a textarea to wrap around to a new line when the user reaches the end of a line. You can turn wrapping off by choosing the Off command from the Wrap drop-down menu. There are two additional wrap settings: Physical and Virtual. With Physical set, the lines of text can wrap at the end of the box if you place a hard return (that is, a CRLF character) there.

Virtual enables the lines of text to wrap at the end of the box, but no character is inserted.

You can add some text that appears in the text field when the user views the form. This could be instructions on what to enter into the field or a default value that the user could change if he or she wanted to. Enter text into the Init Val box in the Properties Inspector, so that text will be present when the user initially loads the form.

Dreamweaver includes some form elements, along with other items, in the Snippets panel. You drag snippets from the panel and drop them on your Web pages. A useful snippet for your form might be Text Field Autoclear; this snippet places a text field containing default text into a form. When the user clicks the text field, the default text automatically disappears.

Adding Radio Buttons and Check Boxes to Forms

Radio buttons are another type of form element that you can use to collect user input. Radio buttons are grouped so that the user can select only one button of the group at a time; when the user selects a different member of the group, the previously selected button is deselected. In order for radio buttons to be grouped, they all must have the same name.

To create a group of radio buttons, follow these steps:

1. Place the insertion point within a form where the radio buttons will be located.

2. Select the Radio Group object from the Forms category of the Insert bar or select Insert, Form, Radio Group.

3. Enter the name of the radio button group into the Name box of the Radio Group dialog box.

4. Enter a label name in the Label column and enter the value of the radio button when it is checked (called the *checked value*) in the Value column, as shown in Figure 16.7. The label is simply text that appears next to the button; it is not part of the form. Use the + and – buttons to add or remove radio buttons. At the bottom of the dialog box, select whether you'd like the buttons to be placed in a table or separated by line breaks. Click OK to save your settings.

FIGURE 16.7
Add a radio button group. Each button has a label and a value.

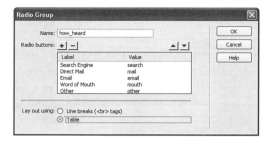

5. When you select an individual radio button, its properties are displayed in the Properties Inspector. Choose whether the button will be checked or unchecked when the user first loads the form by selecting either the Checked or Unchecked options, which are located beside Initial State.

Check boxes collect user input when the user either checks or unchecks them. They differ from radio buttons because they are not grouped; instead, they act independently. Radio buttons enable the user to select a single option, whereas check boxes enable the user to select any options that apply.

To add a check box to your form, follow these steps:

1. Place the insertion point within a form where the check box will be located.

2. Select the Checkbox object from the Insert bar or select the Insert, Form, Check Box.

3. Enter a name for the check box into the box in the far left of the Properties Inspector.

4. Enter a checked value into the Checked Value box. If you do not specify a checked value, the value "on" is sent for the check box when the form is submitted. If there is an entry for the Checked Value setting, that value will be sent instead of simply "on."

5. Choose whether the initial state of the check box will be checked or unchecked in the Initial State setting.

6. Type a text label beside the check box.

Adding Lists and Menus to Forms

Some form objects work better than others in certain situations (for example, selecting 1 of the 50 states for a U.S. address). If you allowed the user to enter a state in a text field, you might get some users entering the full name, like Washington, other users entering the correct postal abbreviation, like WA, and other users entering anything in between. Allowing the user to select from a drop-down menu helps you collect consistent data. In Dreamweaver, you add drop-down menus by using the List/Menu object.

The List/Menu object inserts a list of values. You create the List/Menu object as either a list, displaying a set number of lines, or a menu, a drop-down menu displaying all the list values. Figure 16.8 shows a list and a menu in a form displayed in a browser.

Menu   List

FIGURE 16.8
Lists display a certain number of values. A menu drops down when the user clicks it, allowing the user to select a value.

To create a list, follow these steps:

1. Place the insertion point within the form where the list will be located.

2. Select the List/Menu object from the Insert bar or select Insert, Form, List/Menu.

3. Enter the name of the list into the box in the far left of the Property inspector.

4. After you select the List radio button, the Height and Allow Multiple attributes become active.

5. In the Height box, type the number of list items that you want to be visible at one time. If there are more list items than can be shown, scrollbars will automatically appear.

6. Check the Allow Multiple check box if you want to allow the user to select multiple values in the list. You might want to add instructions that tell the user that he or she can select multiple entries by using the Ctrl key (or the Command key on the Macintosh) and clicking multiple selections.

7. Set up the list values by selecting the List Values button. The List Values dialog box appears, as shown in Figure 16.9.

FIGURE 16.9
Select the + button in the List Values dialog box to add an item to the list.

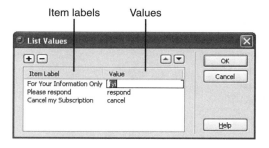

8. Enter an item label and a value for each item in the list. The item label is what the user will see and select. The value is what will be sent back to a script on the server for processing. They can be the same, if appropriate. To add an item, click the + sign, enter the item label, tab to the Value field, and enter a value. You can tab forward and use Shift+Tab to go back if you want. Use the – button to delete entries, and use the arrow buttons to rearrange entries. When you are at the end of the list, pressing Tab creates a new item label and value pair.

9. Click OK in the List Values dialog box.

10. Select an item from the Initially Selected box if one of the items should be selected by default. Otherwise, the first item will appear.

11. Add a label beside the list.

Whereas a list can show a number of lines, a menu shows only one line until the user drops down the menu by clicking. Menus use less space than lists because a menu can drop down over other objects on the page when clicked, but it shrinks to only one line when it is inactive. You create a menu exactly the same way you create a list, except that you don't set the height and you cannot allow the user to select multiple entries. You can turn a list into a drop-down menu by selecting the Menu option as the type.

For a quick and easy way to add standard menus, such as menus for years, numbers, or months, use the Snippets panel. The Forms section of the Snippets panel contains prebuilt menus and form elements that you can simply drag and drop onto your Web page.

Adding Push Buttons and Image Buttons to Forms

There are four different types of buttons that you can add to forms:

- ▶ **Submit**—This type of button sends the data the user has entered into a form to a script or an application on the server. The submit button triggers the action that you've set in the form's Action box in the Properties Inspector.

- ▶ **Reset**—This type of button erases all the data the user has entered in the form. It also reloads any initial values.

- ▶ **None**—This type of generic button has no automatic function. You can add functionality to a generic button by applying a behavior to it.

- ▶ **Image**—This type of button acts like a submit button. All the data in the form is submitted, and the coordinates of where the user clicked are sent, too.

The first three buttons are push buttons that you create by inserting Dreamweaver's Button object. They differ in the way they are configured in the Properties Inspector. The fourth button, the image button, is inserted using the Image Field object.

Adding Submit and Reset Buttons to Forms

In this section you'll add submit and reset buttons to your form. Usually, the submit button is on the left and the reset button is to the right of the submit button. To add a button to the form, follow these steps:

1. Position the insertion point and then select the Button object from the Insert bar or selecting Insert, Form, Button.

2. Select Submit Form as the action for this button.

3. Add another button to the right of the submit button.

4. Select Reset Form as the action for this button. The buttons should look like the buttons in Figure 16.10.

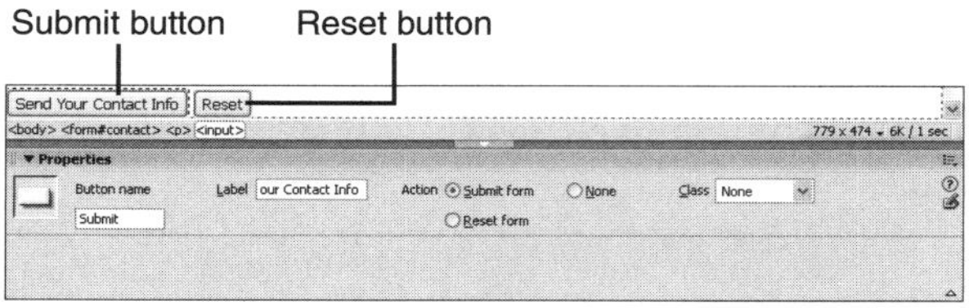

FIGURE 16.10
The submit button
is usually placed on
the left of the reset
button. You need
one submit button
per form if you are
sending this form
to a script or to an
application on a
server.

You can accept the default names that Dreamweaver gives the submit and reset buttons or you can give them new names. You can change the label of either button; a button does not need to say Submit to function as a submit button. Each form must have a submit button to send the form data. The reset button is optional. You should have only one submit button per form with multiple text fields.

Adding Image Buttons to Forms

You can replace a submit button with an image button. When the user clicks the image, the form contents are submitted, and the coordinates of the location where the user clicked the image button are sent, too. You could capture and process the coordinate information if you wanted to.

To add an image field to a form, first make sure the insertion point is inside the form. Add an image field by selecting the Image Field object from the Insert bar or selecting Insert, Form, Image Field. The Select Image Source dialog box appears, enabling you to navigate and select a standard Web image file. The Properties Inspector displays the name, width, height, source, alt text, and alignment attributes for the field. You set these attributes as you would for any image.

Adding Generic Buttons to Forms

Add a generic button by selecting the Button object from the Insert bar or selecting Insert, Form, Button. Name the button, give it a label, and select None as the action. Now you can apply to this button a behavior that can be triggered by a button click.

Deleting a Form

Sometimes it is difficult to delete a form from the page. The easiest way to delete a form is to right-click (or Command+click on the Mac) the form delimiter to view the context menu. Then choose the Remove Tag <form> command. If the Remove Tag command does not say <form>, you have the wrong object selected. You could, of course, always select the <form> tag in the tag selector to delete the form.

Did you Know?

Creating a Jump Menu to Navigate to Different URLs

A **jump menu** is a list of links that allows the viewer to jump to other Web sites or different Web pages within the current site. Dreamweaver's Jump Menu object makes it easy to set up this type of jump menu. You can create a jump menu of email links, images, or any objects that can be displayed in a browser. The Jump Menu object uses JavaScript to redirect the browser.

Dreamweaver's Jump Menu object inserts a drop-down menu similar to the one you created a few minutes ago along with the JavaScript code contained in the Jump Menu behavior. You set up the list values in a special dialog box. The item labels appear in the drop-down menu, and the values contain the URLs to the Web pages where the user will jump.

To create a jump menu, follow these steps:

1. Place the insertion point on the page where you want the jump menu to appear. You don't need to insert a form because the Jump Menu object will do that for you.

2. Either select the Jump Menu object from the Insert bar or select Insert, Form, Jump Menu. The Insert Jump Menu dialog box appears, as shown in Figure 16.11.

3. Type an item label for the first item in the jump menu in the Text box. The first item label is highlighted when you first open the Insert Jump Menu dialog box.

4. Enter a URL that will be launched when the item is selected. You can either type it in or use the Browse button to navigate to a local file.

5. Click the + button to add another item.

6. Repeat steps 3–5 until you have entered all the items for the jump menu.

7. Select a target for the links in the Open URLs In drop-down menu. You will have target options only if your current Web page is part of a frameset that is open in Dreamweaver.

8. Give the menu a unique name in the Menu Name box.

9. Select the appropriate Options check boxes. Click the Insert Go Button After Menu check box if you would like to have a button with the label Go that the user can press to jump. Even if the button is present, the user will still automatically go to the link after he or she has chosen it. The Go button enables the user to launch the first link without having to first launch another link. This is caused by form-processing idiosyncrasies. Select the Select First Item After URL Change check box if you want the first item to be reselected after each jump selection.

10. When you are done making selections in the Insert Jump Menu dialog box, click OK. The jump menu within a form is inserted into your Web page.

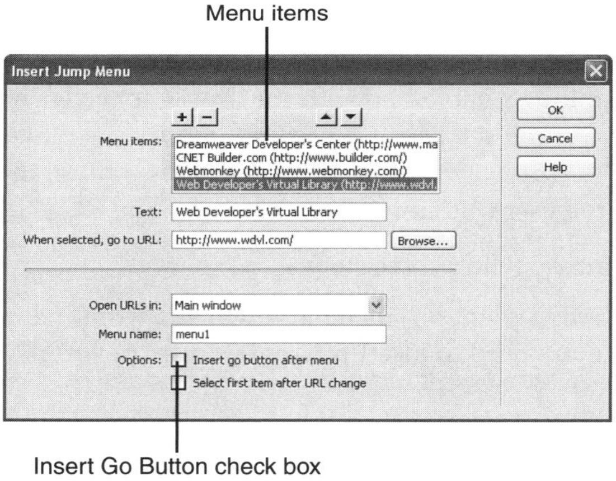

FIGURE 16.11
The Insert Jump Menu dialog box enables you to create a drop-down menu where the user can select an item to link to.

Menu items

Insert Go Button check box

Add an Initial Value

A common way to create a jump menu is to have the first item be the text Choose One... and do not give it a link. Because you never want the user to select this item, the inability to select the first item in the drop-down menu won't be a problem. Then select the check box that makes the first item always selected after you have jumped somewhere so that the Choose One... selection reappears.

You can edit the jump menu by editing the Jump Menu behavior. Select the List/Menu object that the Jump Menu command creates and double-click the

Jump Menu behavior in the Behaviors panel. Add or remove list items by using the + and – buttons. Rearrange the list by using the up and down arrow buttons. You can turn on or off the Select First Item After URL Change setting.

You cannot add a Go button by editing the Jump Menu behavior. You can add one manually, though. Create a generic button by inserting a button into the form, giving it the label Go, and setting its action to None. Apply the Jump Menu Go behavior to the button triggered by the onClick event. Select the jump menu name from the drop-down menu.

Summary

In this chapter, you have learned how to insert and configure a form. You have learned how to add text fields, radio buttons, check boxes, lists, and menus to the form. You have learned how to add submit and reset buttons to the form and create a generic button. You have learned how to use Dreamweaver's Jump Menu object to create a menu that consists of a bunch of URLs that the user can jump to.

CHAPTER 17

Sending and Reacting to Form Data

In Chapter 16, "Creating a Form and Using It to Collect Data," you learned how to create a form. In this chapter, you'll decide what to do with the data that the user enters into your form. You will need to send the data to a script on the server for processing. The script on the server can store data in a database, send it to an email address, send results back to the browser, or process it any way you want (depending on your scripting abilities!).

Some of the types of information you might want to receive in a form can include orders, feedback, comments, guest book entries, polls, and even uploaded files. Creating the form and inserting form elements is usually the easy part. The difficult part is installing and configuring the scripts that will process the data.

Validating a Form's Data by Using the Validate Form Behavior

Before you receive and process information from a form, you need to make sure the information is complete and in the right format. Dreamweaver has a Validate Form behavior that will force the user to enter data into a field, determine whether an email address has been entered, and make sure the user enters numbers correctly.

The Validate Form behavior requires the user to enter the form data correctly before she can submit the data to a script or an application on the server. You can validate the form in two ways:

▶ Attach the Validate Form behavior to the submit button to validate the entire form when the submit button is clicked. The onClick event triggers the behavior.

▶ Attach the Validate Form behavior to individual text fields so that the data entered is validated after the user leaves the field. The onChange event triggers the behavior when the user's focus leaves the field.

You must have a form with form objects in your Web page before the Validate Form behavior is active in the + drop-down menu of the Behaviors panel. To validate a form, follow these steps:

1. Create a new form that has various text fields or open the form you created in Chapter 16.

2. Select the submit button or a text field in the form.

3. Open the Behaviors panel. Click the + button and select the Validate Form behavior.

4. The Validate Form dialog box appears. A list of all the text fields appears in the dialog box.

5. If you have selected the submit button and are validating the entire form, set up validation settings for every text field that requires them. If you are validating an individual text field, set up the validation settings for that field.

6. Check the Required check box if an entry in the field must be filled in by the user.

7. Choose from among the four settings in the Accept category:

   ▶ **Anything**—Select this setting if the user needs to enter data into the field but that data can be in any format. For instance, if you are asking for a phone number, you do not want to limit the user to entering only numbers because phone numbers are often formatted with other characters.

   ▶ **Number**—Select this setting if the user needs to enter data that is numeric.

   ▶ **Email Address**—Select this setting if the user needs to enter an email address. This setting checks for an @ symbol.

   ▶ **Number From**—Select this setting to check for a number within a range of specific numbers. Fill in both the low and high ends of the range.

8. Notice that your settings appear in parentheses beside the name of the text field in the Named Fields list (shown in Figure 17.1). If you've attached the Validate Form behavior to a submit button, you will probably want to validate multiple text fields. Repeat steps 5–7 if you are validating more than one text field. If you've attached the behavior to a text field, you will validate the contents of that field only.

Required value   Field settings

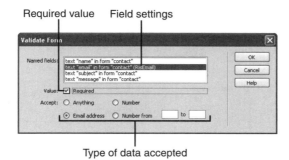

Type of data accepted

FIGURE 17.1
The validation settings appear in parentheses in the Named Fields list in the Validate Form dialog box.

9. When you are finished making changes in the Validate Form dialog box, click OK. Select the onClick event if the Validate Form behavior is attached to the submit button. Select the onChange event if the behavior is attached to an individual text field.

When the Validate Form behavior is triggered, the behavior will check the data in the field or fields against the settings you have entered. You should make sure that the labels and instructions for your form clearly tell the user what type of data to enter and which fields are required. You should give the user the information to fill out the form properly so that she doesn't get frustrated with error messages.

If the user enters incorrect data, the message box shown in Figure 17.2 appears. This message tells the user that errors have occurred, lists the text fields' names, and explains why the data was rejected. This is another place where a meaningful name for a Dreamweaver object is important. If you are validating a form, it is a good idea to name a text field the same name as the label beside the field so that the user can easily locate and change the field data.

FIGURE 17.2
After a form that
has errors is vali-
dated, the user
sees this message,
indicating which
fields have either
been omitted or
filled out incorrectly.

Receiving Information from a Form

The standard way to process a form is to have an application on the server that
parses the data and performs an action on it. **Parsing** data is the act of dividing
and interpreting the name–value pairs that are sent to the server.

Each name–value pair contains the name of the form element entered in
Dreamweaver and the value that the user has entered or selected for that field. A
text field will have a name–value pair that contains the name of the text field
and the value that was entered into the text field. A radio button group will send
a name–value pair with the name of the radio button group and the value of the
button that was selected when the user submitted the form. A list or a drop-down
menu will send the name of the object and any items the user selected.

The name–value pairs are sent to a server via an **HTTP request** from the Web
browser. The request is passed by the Web server software to the application server that handles the scripting language specified in the request. For instance, if the
script is written in ColdFusion Markup Language (CFML), the ColdFusion application server handles the request. Depending on what is written in the script, the
application server may request data from a database or send a request to an
email server to send a specific email message. There are many ways scripts can be
processed on the server. The application server usually returns some sort of output, usually HTML, that is sent by the Web server back to the browser. This all
takes place in milliseconds!

A popular way of processing forms on a server is by using a CGI script. Usually these scripts are written in Perl or other programming languages. Later in this chapter, you will learn other ways of processing forms, with Active Server Pages (ASP), ASP.NET, JavaServer Pages (JSP), Hypertext Preprocessor (PHP), and CFML— proprietary processing systems that are powerful in creating Web applications.

Luckily, there are a number of places on the Web to download CGI scripts that are already written. Because programming CGI scripts is beyond the scope of this book, the examples in this chapter use an existing script that processes form data and sends it to a specific email address.

Get Free Scripts on the Web

The Web is an incredibly generous place, and you can download all sorts of free scripts to use. If you don't know how to program CGI scripts and you are willing to process your forms generically, you'll find a number of great scripts available from Matt's Script Archive (www.scriptarchive.com) and Freescripts (www.freescripts.com).

Did you Know?

CGI stands for **Common Gateway Interface**, and it is the definition of the standard method of communication between a script and the Web server. The CGI script resides in a specific directory on the Web server. It is common for access to this directory to be limited to Webmasters for security reasons. You can contact your Webmaster and ask whether a script is already available on your server to do what you want to do or whether the Webmaster will install one for you. You may have a directory within your own Web directory that can hold CGI scripts. Often this directory is called cgi-bin or has cgi in the directory name.

You should double-check that your hosting service, if you are using one, supports CGI scripts. Sometimes you can use only the scripts that the service has available; check that a form mail script is available. Carefully review the features of the type of account you are signing up for and ask questions, if necessary.

Enter the URL to the CGI script in the Action text box in the Properties Inspector. The URL needs to be an absolute URL; it should not be relative, even if the script resides in a directory relative to your Web site. The documentation for the script will tell you whether the script expects the form name–value pairs to be submitted via either the GET or the POST method.

The GET and POST methods differ in the following ways:

▶ The GET method appends form data to the URL, a URL that can be saved as a bookmark in the browser. Data submitted via this method is limited to

1KB, you can't upload files, and sensitive data is displayed in the address field of the browser after submission.

▶ The POST method packages and sends the data invisibly to the user; the output doesn't appear in the URL. There are no limitations to the amount of data that can be sent, and the POST method allows uploading of files with forms.

Using the FormMail Script

Download Matt's FormMail script from www.worldwidemart.com/scripts to use with the rest of this chapter. This script sends the contents of a form to an email address. The script can be configured a number of different ways. If you are going to test the script, you need to install the script first. The script comes with a readme file that describes all the functions and parameters you can set in the script. The process to set up and call the FormMail script is similar to what you will do to submit a form to any CGI script.

To use the FormMail script, you must add to your form hidden fields containing parameters that tell the script what to do. If you open the FormMail script in a text editor, such as Notepad, you'll see instructions at the top of the file. The scripted processes are also contained in the file, so be careful what you change.

There are two variables that you need to configure at the top of the FormMail script before it is loaded onto the server:

▶ **$mailprog**—This variable needs to point to the Unix server's sendmail program. Leave it set at the default; if it doesn't work, your Webmaster can give you the path. You do not need this variable if you are running the Windows NT version of the script. If your hosting company provided the FormMail script for you, it has probably modified this variable for you. A common path to the sendmail program is usr/lib/sendmail; you'll have to read your hosting service's documentation or contact the service to determine what address you need to use.

▶ **@referers**—This variable contains the domains (usually one) that are allowed access to the script. This setting keeps unauthorized domains from using the script and the resources on your server. My domain is www.betsybruce.com, so that's what I would enter into this variable. This prevents people with forms in domains other than mine from using my script to process their forms.

Adding a Hidden Field to a Form

Hidden fields are sent along with all the other form fields. The users cannot change the contents of these fields, nor can they see the fields unless they view your HTML source. You should create hidden fields for the recipient of the emailed form data, the subject that appears in the email subject field, and the URL to which the user is redirected after filling out the form. You can explore many other settings on your own.

Make sure that your form has the URL to the FormMail script on the server set the Action text box in the Properties Inspector. The FormMail script can accept either the GET method or the POST method for submitting the data. I suggest the POST method because it is more common and because you do not risk exceeding the amount of data that the GET method can handle.

To add hidden fields to your form, follow these steps:

1. Place the insertion point anywhere inside your form. It does not matter where the hidden fields are located.

2. Select the Hidden Field object from the Insert bar or select Insert, Form, Hidden Field.

3. Dreamweaver displays the Hidden Field symbol in your Web page, as shown in Figure 17.3. You must have Invisible Elements checked (select View, Visual Aids, Invisible Elements); also, the Invisible Elements category in the Dreamweaver Preferences dialog box must have Hidden Form Fields checked.

4. Enter **recipient** in the text box on the left side of the Properties Inspector and your email address as the value, as shown in Figure 19.4. These name–value pairs are documented in the script documentation.

5. Optionally, add another hidden field to the form and enter the name **redirect**. Enter as the value of the field a URL that the user will be redirected to after submitting the form.

There are a number of optional form fields you can add to the FormMail script. See the documentation to read about them. When the user submits the form, the name–value pairs are sent to the email address specified in the hidden field named recipient. This is the simplest processing possible for a form. Other scripts can save data to databases, validate and process credit card information, and perform all sorts of other complex actions.

FIGURE 17.3
The Hidden Field symbol appears when you insert a hidden field into a form. The Properties Inspector shows a hidden field name–value pair.

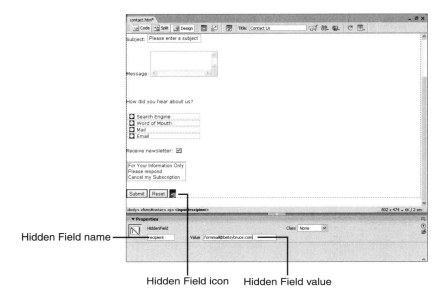

Hidden Field name

Hidden Field icon   Hidden Field value

Exploring Submission Security

When your users submit form information, it travels in packets across the Internet, along with millions of other packets. **Packets** are electronic bundles of information that carry data to the server. These packets of information can be intercepted and read by people who understand how to intercept and reassemble data taken from the Web. Even though this is not a common occurrence, you still should take steps to assure your users that sensitive data is secure.

Again, this is a Web server issue. The Web server on which your site is located must have secure sockets enabled. Many ISPs offer this service. Ask your Webmaster whether you have access to secure Web pages.

A user accesses a secure URL exactly as he or she would a regular URL. The only difference is that the protocol portion of the URL changes from http to https. The user must have a browser that is capable of accessing secure pages. The browser displays a Lock icon in the status bar, as shown in Figure 17.4, when it is in secure mode.

You need to worry about secure submissions only when the user enters sensitive information, such as credit card numbers or other financial data. For polls, guest books, or feedback forms, you don't need to shield the information from potential thieves. Customers will expect you to protect only their sensitive data.

Secure HTTP protocol

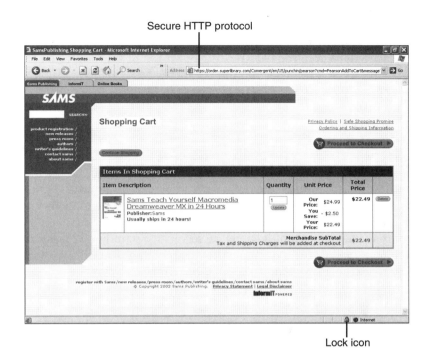

FIGURE 17.4
The browser dis-
plays a Lock icon
in the status bar
when the page is
served via secure
sockets.

Lock icon

You need a server certificate to add security to your form submissions. A **certificate** is an electronic document that verifies that you are who you say you are.
You might be able to use your Web host's certificate, or you might need to purchase your own. One of the major certificate vendors is VeriSign, and you can
learn more about certificates at VeriSign's Web site: www.verisign.com.

Uploading a File from a Form

You might need to add a **file field** that enables users to upload files. You can collect images, homework assignments, or any types of files that you might need to
have sent to you with a file field object. The user selects the Browse button to
select a file from his or her local drive. When the user presses the Submit button,
the file is sent to the server.

A file field has attributes similar to those of a text field, which you used in the
previous chapter. You can set the size of the file field by putting a value in the
Char Width box in the Properties Inspector. You can also set the Max Chars
attribute and the Init Val attribute in the Properties Inspector. You need to give
the file field a unique name.

The important question you need to answer before you use a file field is, does your server allow anonymous file uploads? You also need to select multipart/form-data from the Enctype drop-down list for the <form> tag so that the file is encoded correctly. Also, you should use the POST method to submit your form; the GET method does not work with file fields.

Preparing a Page to Interact with ASP, ASP.NET, JSP, PHP, or CFML

Besides using CGI scripts, there are other ways to process forms and create dynamic Web applications. Like CGI scripting, these technologies interact with the Web server to process Web page information. Dreamweaver enables you to create dynamic Web pages that incorporate server-side scripting. When you create a new Web page, you create a dynamic page by selecting the Dynamic Page category in the New Document dialog box, as shown in Figure 17.5.

FIGURE 17.5
You can create ASP, ASP.NET, JSP, PHP, and CFML pages with Dreamweaver 4.

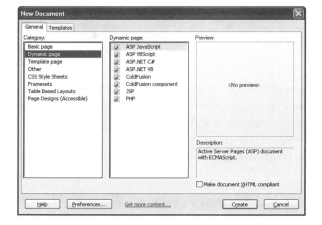

Dreamweaver supports these five major server-side scripting languages:

▶ **ASP**—Microsoft's ASP combines client-side scripting with processing on the server to create dynamic Web pages. The capability to process ASP comes with Microsoft's Internet Information Server (IIS) 4+, which runs on Windows NT. (You can add the capability to process ASP to IIS 3.) There are third-party applications, such as ChiliSoft, that interpret ASP on Unix servers.

▶ **ASP.NET**—Microsoft's ASP.NET, released in 2002, is a server-side application platform that will eventually replace ASP. To run ASP.NET on your server, you need Microsoft IIS 5.0 or later, running on Windows 2000, Windows XP, or Windows Server 2003. You also need the .NET Framework Redistributable installed (available from `msdn.microsoft.com/net` and included automatically in Windows Server 2003).

▶ **JSP**—JSP is a Java-based way to dynamically process Web pages. JSP scripts interact with a JSP-enabled server. The popular Apache Web server and the free Tomcat JSP application server are available. For Microsoft IIS, Macromedia JRun is a popular JSP application server.

▶ **PHP**—PHP is a free, open-source server-side scripting language that sends dynamic Web pages to the user after interpreting PHP code. PHP is the open-source movement's answer to ASP.

▶ **CFML**—Macromedia's ColdFusion server interprets CFML to create dynamic Web pages. The ColdFusion server application can run on many different operating systems. CFML is slightly different from the other scripting languages described here because it is a tag-based language, like HTML.

All these scripting languages accomplish the same thing: enabling a client-side Web page to interact with the server by accessing data, sending an email message, or processing input in some way. They all have advantages and disadvantages, and each uses a different syntax to add code to Web pages.

Intrigued? Want to Learn More?

Sams Teach Yourself Macromedia Dreamweaver MX 2004 in 21 Days by John Ray takes off where this book leaves off, introducing you to dynamic Web sites and scripting.

Did you
Know?

You can embed ASP, ASP.NET, JSP, PHP, and CFML into your Web pages, and Dreamweaver will represent the code with special icons, as shown in Figure 17.6. When you define your site as one containing dynamic pages, your page will look slightly different from this. In a dynamic site, Dreamweaver displays a representation of the code; you can display actual data from the database by viewing the Web page in Live Data view.

To edit the ASP, ASP.NET, JSP, PHP, or CFML code, select the representative icon on your Web page. The Properties Inspector appears. Click the Edit button to display the Edit Contents dialog box. You can edit your code directly in this dialog box.

ASP Script icon

FIGURE 17.6
Special icons, in
this case an ASP
Script icon, appear
when you're viewing
invisibles that rep-
resent code.

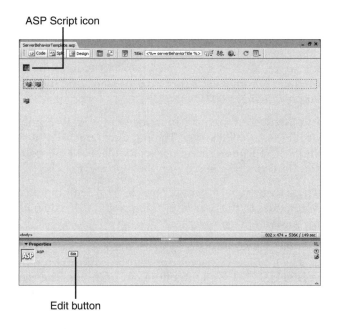

FIGURE 17.6
Special icons, in
this case an ASP
Script icon, appear
when you're viewing
invisibles that rep-
resent code.

Edit button

You can use ASP, ASP.NET, JSP, PHP, or CFML scripts contained in an external
script file to process a form. Such a script will act like the CGI script that you used
earlier this chapter. You reference the script's URL as the form's action in the
Properties Inspector. Again, the script's directory must have the proper permission
set in order for the script to execute. Figure 17.7 shows a form submitting its contents to an ASP script.

FIGURE 17.7
You enter the URL
of an ASP script if
the script will
process your form
when the user sub-
mits it.

When you define your site as a dynamic site, you can author dynamic Web pages
in Dreamweaver MX 2004. Dreamweaver MX 2004 enables you to easily hook up
your Web content to databases. You can visually add ASP, ASP.NET, JSP, or CFML
components. Dreamweaver generates the code for you behind the scenes and displays the dynamic elements. You can even see how your Web page will look with
real data from the database right within Dreamweaver.

Summary

In this chapter, you have learned how CGI scripts work and how form data is submitted to them. You have learned how to use the Validate Form behavior to validate the data that the user enters into your form. You have inserted into a form hidden fields that contain a name–value pair. You have set the action for a form and learned the difference between the GET and POST methods for submitting data. You have learned about secure transactions. You have learned how to edit and call ASP, ASP.NET, PHP, JSP, and CFML code.

CHAPTER 18

Uploading Your Dreamweaver Project

Finished Web sites reside on a Web server where many people access the Web pages. While you are working on your Web sites, you will want to move them onto the server for testing. At the end of the project, you'll need to move your Web pages to a public server so that other people can look at them. There are different ways to move the files onto a server and different methods for ensuring that the version of the files is correct and not accidentally overwritten.

Enabling Server Connection

When you define a Web site in Dreamweaver, you define a local site that exactly mirrors the final, public Web site. **Mirroring** means that the local site contains an exact copy of the files on the final site. Dreamweaver calls your final site the **remote site**. You work on the files in your local site and then upload them to the remote site by using Dreamweaver's file transfer commands.

When working in Dreamweaver, you don't need FTP transfer software or any other software in order to move your files onto the remote server. This capability is built right in to Dreamweaver! It's more convenient to set up your remote site and transfer files while working in Dreamweaver than to jump out to another application.

Adding Your Remote Site

You define a remote site by editing the Web site definition (which you get to by selecting Site, Manage Sites). Select a site and click the Edit button to launch the Site Definition dialog box for the selected Web site. In the Basic tab, click the Next button until you reach the Sharing Files section of the Site Definition Wizard, as shown in Figure 18.1.

FIGURE 18.1
You set up the remote site definition in the Sharing Files section of the Site Definition Wizard.

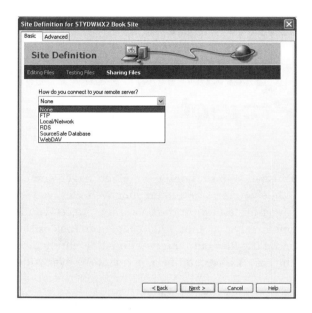

You can choose five transfer methods from the drop-down menu:

- ▶ FTP
- ▶ Local/Network
- ▶ RDS
- ▶ SourceSafe Database
- ▶ WebDAV

The transfer method you select depends on where your remote site is located. The site may be on your company's intranet, and if so, you can transfer the local site up to the remote site by using a LAN, or Local/Network, connection. The site may be at your ISP, the folks who provide you with an Internet dial-up service or a Web hosting service. In this case, you will probably connect to its servers by using FTP. SourceSafe, RDS, and WebDAV connections are less common than the others but are sometimes used in professional Web development environments.

Setting FTP Information

You should select FTP access, as shown in Figure 18.2, if you need to transfer files over the Web to a remote server. The server could be physically located in your building, or it could be on the other side of the world. You need to enter the name of the FTP server into the text box What Is the Hostname or FTP Address of Your Web Server? Often this is in the following format: `ftp.domain.com`.

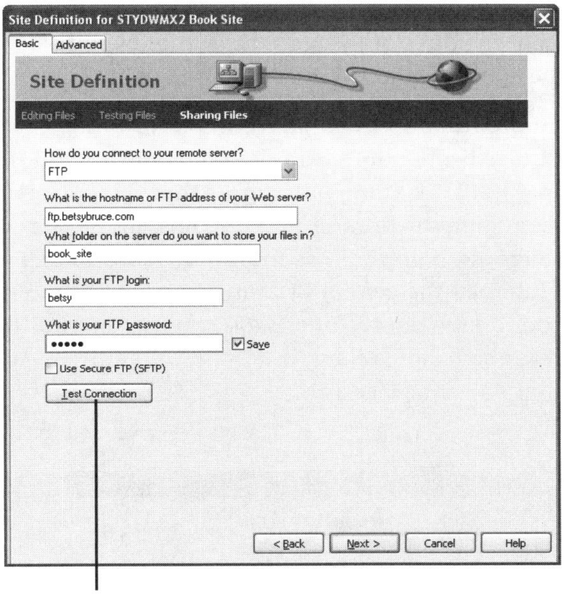

FIGURE 18.2
You need to set the FTP information, including the server address.

Test connection

Enter the correct directory in the text box What Folder on the Server Do You Want to Store Your Files In? You might need to get the path for this directory from your Web or network administrator. If you are unsure what the root directory is on the remote site, try leaving the What Is the Hostname or FTP Address of Your Web Server? box blank. The FTP server might put you in the correct directory because your account may be configured that way.

You need a login and a password to access the FTP server. The standard anonymous login, often used to download files over the Internet, will probably not work to upload files to a Web site. You need to log in as a user who has access and permission to get and put files in the directories that will house your Web site. Dreamweaver saves your password by default. If other people have access to Dreamweaver on your computer and you don't want them to access your FTP account, deselect the Save check box.

Click the Test Connection button to make sure that you've entered everything correctly and are successfully connecting to the FTP server. You can troubleshoot FTP connection problems by first closing the Site Definition dialog box and then selecting Window, Results and clicking the FTP Log tab. The FTP log lists the reason you didn't connect successfully. For instance, if the log states that the password was incorrect or the directory you are targeting doesn't exist, you can change these in the Site Definition Wizard and try again.

If you are behind a firewall or using a proxy server, you might have difficulties with FTP. Consult the network administrator about which settings you need to choose when setting up FTP. If you go through a firewall to access the Internet, you may need to configure the firewall port and host in the Site category of the Dreamweaver Preferences dialog box, as shown in Figure 18.3. If you have a slow connection to the Internet, the default FTP timeout might be too short, causing your FTP connection to time out too often. You can increase this time in the Site category of the Preferences dialog box.

FIGURE 18.3
Configure firewall settings in the Dreamweaver Preferences dialog box if you have problems connecting to an FTP server behind a firewall.

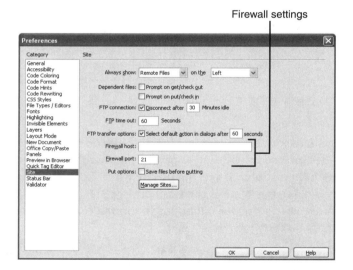

Setting LAN Information

You should select Local/Network in the Site Definition Wizard, if the server is on a computer that you can connect to directly by using a network. If you can access files on the server the same way you access your hard drive, moving files to and from it with ease, you have LAN access. You need to know the correct Web-accessible directory; your Web administrator should be able to give you that information.

Set up LAN access to the remote server by entering the path to the remote directory. Use the Browse icon to browse to the directory or type in the path. Checking the Refresh Remote File List Automatically may slow down Dreamweaver's performance a bit, but you will always have an up-to-date reflection of the remote site.

Setting RDS Access

You use the RDS setting only if your remote site is on a ColdFusion server. ColdFusion is one of the server-side scripting languages that Dreamweaver MX 2004 supports. As when you select FTP, you enter a hostname (the server address), a username, and a password to connect to this type of remote site.

Setting Source/Version-Control Application Information

You can connect directly from Dreamweaver to servers by using source- and version-control applications. If you are not in a professional environment that uses source-management software, you can skip this section or read it and file it away for later. Dreamweaver supports direct integration with Microsoft Visual SourceSafe, a popular version-control product. You can also exchange files with any source-control program that supports the WebDAV protocol.

Set up a Visual SourceSafe database as your remote site by selecting the SourceSafe Database choice in the Site Definition Wizard. Set up the SourceSafe database by clicking the Settings button. The Open SourceSafe Database dialog box appears. Enter the database path, project, username, and password in this dialog. You can get this information from your Visual SourceSafe administrator.

WebDAV

Another standard is WebDAV (sometimes just called DAV); the version-control information for WebDAV is set up similarly to a SourceSafe database. **WebDAV** stands for World Wide Web Distributed Authoring and Versioning, and it is a group of standards governing Web collaboration that is an extension to HTTP. It's predicted that WebDAV access will eventually replace FTP access by extending HTTP to enable users to not only read from the Web but also to write to the Web.

Select WebDAV from the drop-down menu in the Site Definition Wizard, and then click the Settings button. The settings, shown in Figure 18.4, look different from the SourceSafe settings because you access this type of version-control application over the Web via a URL.

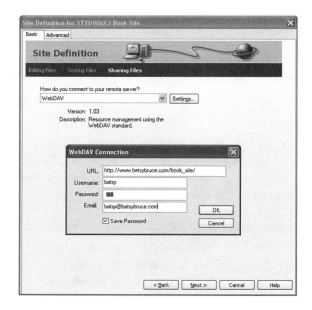

Using the Remote Site Advanced Tab

Click the Advanced tab of the Site Definition dialog box to see a different view of your remote site's settings. The Remote Info category, shown in Figure 18.5, displays the login information, along with firewall and other settings. You can click back and forth between the Basic and Advanced tabs if you like.

You can close the Site Definition dialog box by clicking OK to save your settings. Next you'll try connecting to the remote server and transferring your files.

Did you Know?

Passive FTP

If you are having problems connecting to the server when using FTP (you'll receive a message from Dreamweaver), you might want to select Use Passive FTP on the Advanced tab of the Site Definition dialog box. This often solves transfer problems, especially when you are transferring files from behind a firewall.

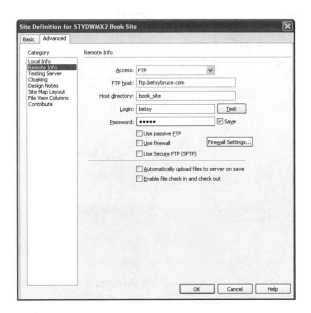

FIGURE 18.5
The Advanced tab shows all the remote site's settings.

Moving a Site onto a Remote Server

If your server is located on a LAN, you normally connect to the server when you log on to your computer, and you stay connected all day. If you access the remote server over the Internet by using FTP, you connect while getting and putting files onto the server, and then you disconnect. Even if you don't disconnect on your end, your connection will most likely time out on the server if you have been inactive for a period, and you will need to reconnect.

The Files panel contains buttons, as shown in Figure 18.6, that enable you to transfer files to and from the remote site. You can transfer files to your local site by selecting the Get button, and you can transfer files to the remote site by selecting the Put button. Later this chapter, you'll learn about using the Synchronize command, which is a better way to transfer files. The Synchronize command detects whether a local file (or remote file) is newer and transfers it only if necessary, thus saving transfer time.

FIGURE 18.6
The buttons at the top of the Files panel help you transfer files between the local and remote sites.

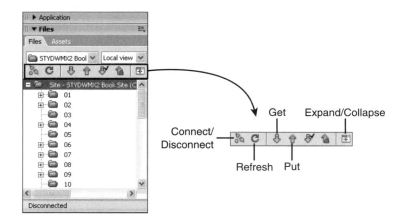

These are the buttons at the top of the Files panel:

▶ **Connect/Disconnect**—This button establishes a connection to an FTP server. The button has a little green light that is lit when you are connected to the FTP server. This button is always lit when you have LAN access to your remote site.

▶ **Refresh**—This button manually refreshes the list of files in the Files panel.

▶ **Get**—This button retrieves files from the remote site and moves them to your local site.

▶ **Put**—This button places files from your local site onto the remote site.

Click the Expand/Collapse button on the far right of the Files panel to expand the panel, as shown in Figure 18.7. The expanded Files panel not only shows the local site, as does the Files panel, but it also shows the remote site. A list of the files on the remote site appears when you are connected. When you want to collapse the expanded Files panel, click the Expand/Collapse button again.

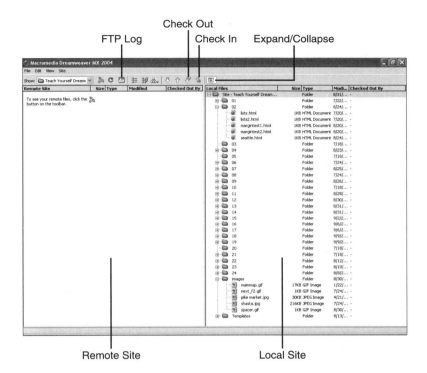

FIGURE 18.7
Use the
Expand/Collapse
button to expand
the Files panel.

Understanding Dreamweaver's Web Site Management Capabilities

You use the Check In/Check Out tools in Dreamweaver to make sure that only one person is working on a file at a time. When you have a file checked out, no one else can check out that file until you check it back in, just like when you have a DVD or video checked out from the video store. Dreamweaver marks the file as checked out by you so that your collaborators know who to bug if they also need to make changes to the file!

When you check out a file from the remote site, Dreamweaver retrieves a copy of that file from the remote server to ensure that you have the most up-to-date version of the file in your local site. When Dreamweaver gets the file, it overwrites the file that exists on your local drive. The checked-out file appears to

Dreamweaver users with your name beside it on the remote server, signaling to your collaborators that you have checked it out. The file has a green check mark beside it in your local site, showing that you currently have that file checked out.

Enabling Check In/Check Out

After you define the remote site in the Site Definition Wizard and click Next, Dreamweaver asks if you'd like to enable Check In/Check Out. Because you over-write files when you transfer them from the local site to the remote site, you need to be careful. You can use Check In/Check Out functionality so that you do not overwrite files that others have recently edited and uploaded to the remote site.

When you turn on Check In/Check Out on the Advanced tab of the Site Definition dialog box, options appear that enable you to configure this feature. You choose whether you'd like to check out a file when you open a file in your local site that isn't currently checked out. I suggest you choose to view it as a read-only copy because then you can look at a file without checking it out; if you then need to edit it, you can quickly check it out.

Enter a name and an email address so that others accessing the remote site can see who has the file checked out. They'll be able to click your name and send you an email message about the file you have checked out.

Transferring Files

When you check in a file to the remote site, Dreamweaver transfers the file back to the remote server to make it available for others to work on or view. The file will no longer appear to other Dreamweaver users with your name beside it.

Check In/Check Out is designed to help you manage a collaborative environ-ment. The Check Out procedure forces you to download the most recent version of the file. While you have the file checked out, others cannot work on it. After you check the file back in, you can open the file but cannot save any changes because Dreamweaver marks it as read-only.

Don't Leave Without Checking Your Files In!

Remember to check files back in when you are finished with them! Don't go on vaca-tion with a bunch of files checked out if you want your co-workers to happily wel-come you back when you return.

Dreamweaver enables you to circumvent some of the Check In/Check Out safe-guards. You can, for instance, override somebody else's checked-out file and check it out yourself. You can also turn off the read-only attribute of a file and edit it without checking it out. However, why would you want to do any of these things? Dreamweaver's Check In/Check Out process is fine for a small environment where you don't expect mischief. If you need tighter security and version control, however, you should use one of the products on the market, such as Microsoft Visual SourceSafe, that enable very tight control.

Did you Know?

Everyone Needs to Use Check In/Check Out

Your project will work more smoothly if everyone who is collaborating on the project turns on the Check In/Check Out functionality for the site. Otherwise, it's too easy to overwrite a file that someone else has updated. Check In/Check Out works only if everyone on the team uses Dreamweaver and enables the Check In/Check Out functionality.

You can still use Get and Put when you have Check In/Check Out enabled. The Get command will move a file from the remote server and overwrite the local file. The file will be read-only on your local machine because you won't have it checked out. If you try to put a file that someone has checked out onto the remote server, Dreamweaver warns you that changes to the remote copy of the file may be lost if you go ahead and transfer the file. You can choose to do the action anyway or cancel the action.

Did you Know?

The Synchronize Command

To get only the files that are more recent than the files on the local site onto the remote site, you use the Synchronize command.

To get or put files, first make sure the correct site is selected in the Site drop-down menu of the Files panel or the Site window. If you access your site via FTP, click the Connect button. If you are already connected or are accessing the files on a LAN, skip this step.

To get or check out files, follow these steps:

1. Select the files you want to transfer to your local site. You can also select an entire folder to transfer all of its contents.

2. Click the Get command, or click the Check Out command if you have Check In/Check Out enabled for this site.

3. Dreamweaver may display a dialog box, asking if you would also like to download dependent files. **Dependent files** are images and other assets that are linked to the files you are transferring. You can disable this dialog box by checking the Don't Ask Me Again check box. I prefer to transfer the asset files manually instead of having Dreamweaver do it automatically.

To put or check in files, follow these steps:

1. Select the files you want to transfer to the remote site.

2. Click the Put command, or click the Check In command if you have Check In/Check Out enabled for this site. If you transfer a file that is currently open, Dreamweaver will prompt you to save the file before you put it on the remote site.

3. Dreamweaver may display a dialog box, asking if you would also like to upload dependent files. You can disable this dialog box by checking the Don't Ask Me Again check box.

Importing an Existing Web Site

When a Web site already exists at a remote site, you need to define the Web site in Dreamweaver, connect to the remote site, and download all the files in the site to work on it. Remember, you can edit only files that are located on your own machine. You can download and edit an existing site even if it wasn't created with Dreamweaver.

Downloading a site for the first time might take some time, depending on how you are accessing the site and what your network connection speed is. After you initially download all the files, however, you should need only to download any files that change.

To import an existing Web site, all you need to do is mirror the existing site on your local drive. There is no conversion process, and the files will remain unchanged in Dreamweaver. To import an existing Web site, follow these steps:

1. Set up both your local and remote info in the Site Definition dialog box.

2. Get all the files on the remote site by selecting the top entry in the remote site of the Files panel. Selecting the top entry, the root folder, selects the entire site. If you select a file, you get only that file instead of the entire site.

3. Click the Get button to transfer all the files on the remote site to your local site.

You can also import and export a site definition, either to share with others or to back up your site definition. To do this, select the Export command from the Site menu in the Files panel. You can choose to either back up your site definition, saving your login, password, and local path information, or share the site definition with other users, without the personal information. Dreamweaver saves the file with the `.ste` extension. Select the Import command from the Site menu in the Files panel to import the site definition contained in the `.ste` file.

Summary

In this chapter, you have learned how to connect to a remote site and transfer files. You have learned how to use the Advanced tab of the Site Definition dialog box and how to set up FTP, local/network, Visual SourceSafe, and WebDAV connections. You have also learned how to use Dreamweaver's internal version-control feature, Check In/Check Out.

CHAPTER 19

Creating and Applying a Template

You create templates to provide a foundation for consistent, controlled Web pages. **Templates** contain objects that you mark as editable; the rest of the template is locked. When you update an original template, the changes you make to it will update throughout your site.

Creating a Template

You can create a template, save it to the Template category of the Assets panel, and then use it to create a new Web page within a Web site. Anyone working on the same Web site can use the template, and you can use templates created by others.

You need to define a Web site before Dreamweaver can insert a template. Dreamweaver creates a directory called `Templates` in the root of your Web site where it stores the original template files. Dreamweaver keeps the code of a template in a file in the `Templates` directory and inserts a copy of the code when you insert a template in a Web page.

The Difference Between Templates and Library Items

A template differs from a library item in that a template is an entire Web page, not just a portion of one.

By the Way

Using the Templates Category of the Assets Panel

To create and apply templates, open the Templates category of the Assets panel, as shown in Figure 19.1. The Templates category shows all the templates that exist in the current Web site. Each Web site that you create can have a different set of templates.

Download Templates from the Web

Does the Templates category of the Assets panel look bare? Copy one or more of the sites available in the `Templates` directory from the Dreamweaver CD-ROM to your hard drive and set it up as a site in the Files panel. These templates are also available for download from the Macromedia Web site, at `www.macromedia.com/software/dreamweaver/download/templates`.

FIGURE 19.1
The Templates category of the Assets panel displays all the templates in the current Web site.

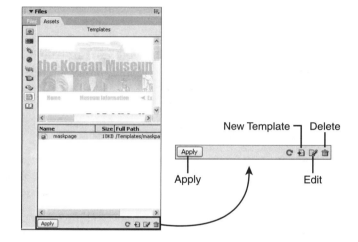

The Templates category of the Assets panel is divided into two halves. The top half displays the contents of the template, and the bottom half lists the names of the templates in the Web site. The buttons at the bottom of the panel include the following:

- ▶ **Apply**—You click this button to apply the currently selected template to the Web page.

- ▶ **New Template**—You click this button to create a new, blank template.

- ▶ **Edit**—You click this button to open the template in its own Dreamweaver Document window for editing.

- ▶ **Delete**—You click this button to remove the template from the `Templates` directory. This doesn't affect any instances of the templates except that the deleted template can no longer be updated throughout the site.

Creating a Template

There are two ways to create templates:

▶ **From an existing Web page**—When you decide to create a template out of a Web page, you can save the page as a template.

▶ **From scratch, as a new, empty template**—You can create a new template, open it, and then add objects to the template just as though it were a regular Web page.

When you apply a template to a Web page, a copy of all the content that the template contains is inserted into the page. You no longer need to have the original template present in order for the Web page to display. When you upload your Web page onto a remote Web site, you do not need to upload the Templates directory. You might want to upload the template onto your server so that others can use the templates, too. You should keep the directory in case you want to make changes to templates throughout your Web site.

Did you Know?

Cloaking Affects Templates

Use Dreamweaver's Cloaking feature to prevent the Templates directory from being synchronized or uploaded when you are transferring files. You enable Cloaking in the Site menu and then right-click (Control+click on the Mac) the Templates directory and select Cloaking, Cloak. The folder will appear in the site with a red line through it.

Creating a Template from an Existing Web Page

To create a template from an existing Web page, follow these steps:

1. Select File, Save As Template.

2. The Save As Template dialog box appears. Enter a meaningful name for the template. Click the Save button to save the template to the Templates directory.

3. A dialog box may appear, asking if you'd like to update links. Click the Yes button to agree. This tells Dreamweaver to make sure the document-relative links are correct when the template is saved to the Templates directory. If you plan on having all the linked objects, usually images, editable in the template, you do not need to worry about the path being correct for the linked objects.

By the Way

Template Files

Dreamweaver creates an individual file for each template. The file extension for templates is `.dwt`. In the `Templates` directory of your Web site, you will see one `.dwt` file for each template you have in your Web site.

Creating a Template from Scratch

To create a new, empty template and then add objects to it, follow these steps:

1. Click the New Template button at the bottom of the Templates category of the Assets panel. Dreamweaver creates a new blank template, as shown in Figure 19.2. A message appears in the top half of the Templates category of the Assets panel, telling you how to add content to the blank template.

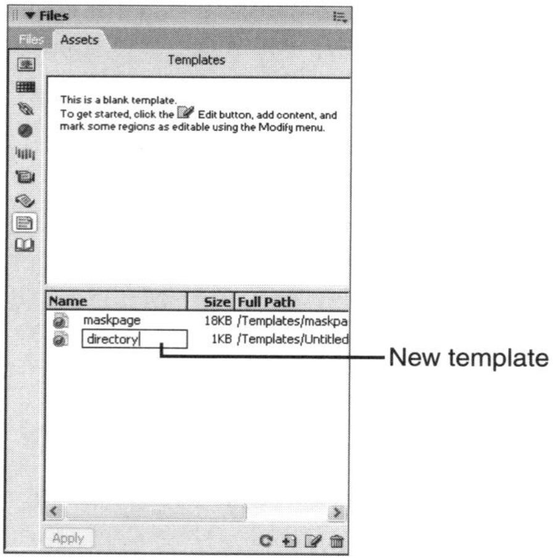

FIGURE 19.2
A message appears in the Templates category after you create a new blank template. The message tells you how to add content to the new template.

New template

2. Give the template a name. For example, create a template for displaying your CD or book collection and call it `CD` or `book`.

3. Double-click the template in the Templates category of the Assets panel. Dreamweaver opens the template in a separate Document window. You can tell that you have a template open because Dreamweaver displays `<<Template>>` along with the name of the template in the title bar.

4. Insert objects into the template's Document window just as you would with any Web page.

5. Close the Document window and save the template. Your changes will be reflected in the Templates category of the Assets panel. Don't worry right now about the message you receive about your template not having any editable regions. You'll add some editable regions in a few minutes.

The Templates category of the Assets panel has a pop-up menu that contains useful commands. Different commands are available, depending on what is currently selected.

Making an Existing Region Editable

Before you apply a template to a Web page, you need to mark regions of the template as **editable**. By default, all regions in the template are locked. Mark a region as editable if you will need to change, add, or update the content of this region in the pages you will create based on this template.

You should leave locked all regions that do not need to be changed. If you need to make changes to a locked region, you can change the original template file and update all the Web pages that are linked to that template. The commands for manipulating editable regions are located in the Templates submenu of the Modify menu.

Placeholder Images

Use a placeholder image in your template to represent an image. You add a placeholder image to the page by selecting Insert, Image Objects, Image Placeholder.

Did you Know?

To make an existing region editable, follow these steps:

1. Open a template and select the region that needs to be editable.

2. Select Insert, Template Objects, Editable Region. The New Editable Region dialog box appears, as shown in Figure 19.3.

3. Give the region a meaningful name.

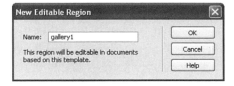

FIGURE 19.3
Name the new editable region in the New Editable Region dialog box.

After you create an editable region, the name of the region is listed at the bottom of the Templates submenu of the Modify menu while you are working on the template. Select one of the region names in the menu to highlight that region in the Document window. Dreamweaver also automatically creates editable regions for the title of the document (called `doctitle`) and an empty region in the head of the document that is available for JavaScript code.

Dreamweaver gives you the ability to create editable regions on various objects in a template. For instance, you can make a layer editable. You can move the layer or change any of its properties after you apply the template to a Web page. Or you can leave the layer locked and create an editable region within the layer. Then you can't move the layer or change the layer properties when you've applied the template, but you can put content within the layer.

By the Way

Import XML into Templates

You can import or export the editable regions of a Dreamweaver template as XML. To do so, use the commands under the Import and Export submenus of the File menu. This is a useful way to automate importing objects, especially text, into templates. The difficult part of this is creating the XML files, files marked up with custom tags, in the first place. If you already have a source of XML files that need to go into Web pages, you should consider importing them into Dreamweaver templates.

Dreamweaver highlights editable regions so that they are easy to pick out in the Document window. The highlights are visible in Dreamweaver but not in the browser. To see highlights, select View, Invisible Elements. Set the highlight color in the Highlighting category in the Dreamweaver Preferences dialog box. The editable regions are highlighted only while you are editing the original template file. Just the opposite is true in a Web page with a template applied: The locked regions are highlighted.

Making a New Editable Region

You can create an optional editable region in a template. To do so, select Insert, Template Objects, Optional Region. Then name the new region in the New Optional Region dialog box that appears. An optional editable region enables the Web page author to decide whether content is needed in this region on the Web page. If the region isn't necessary, the author can turn it off. An editable region appears with a rectangle around it and a tab showing its name, as shown in Figure 19.4.

Editable region   Optional region   Placeholder image

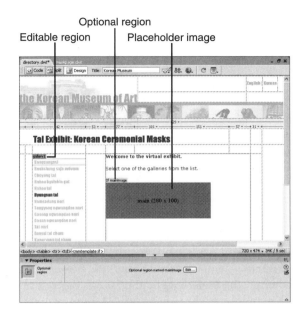

FIGURE 19.4
After you insert a new editable region into a template, it appears as a high-lighted rectangular outline.

You Can't Place an Editable Region Within an Editable Region

If Dreamweaver displays the message that the selection is already a part of an editable region, you need to move the selection. Examine the tag selector and look for the tag <mmtemplate:editable> or <mmtemplate:if>. If you see one of these tags, you need to modify your selection until that tag is no longer part of the selection.

Did you
Know?

Inserting an optional region enables you to turn the region on or off in the page. It doesn't, however, enable you to edit the region if you decide to leave it turned on. You must click inside the optional region within your template and nest an editable region inside it in order to edit the content in a Web page that is based on the template.

To lock a region that has previously been marked as editable, select Modify, Templates, Remove Template Markup while your cursor is within the region you'd like to remove the template markup from. If you have entered information into previously editable regions in Web pages, you will lose that information after you lock the region and update the Web pages.

Creating a Web Page from a Template

You can apply a template in three different ways:

▶ Simply drag the template from the Templates category of the Assets panel and drop it onto a new Web page.

▶ Select a template in the Templates category of the Assets panel and click the Apply button.

▶ Select the New command and choose the Templates tab. Select the site that contains the template from the Templates For list box and select the template you want to use for your page from the Site list box on the right. This creates a new Web page based on the template.

Web pages based on templates allow you to edit content only in the editable regions. You can see these editable regions highlighted in the Document window (you need to have Invisible Elements turned on in the View menu and Highlighting turned on in the Preferences dialog box). The rest of the Web page will be blocked from editing. Simply remove any placeholder text or images within the editable region and add the final content to create a new Web page.

When you create a Web page based on a template with optional regions (either optional or optional editable), you need to set whether the optional content is turned on or off. Use Modify, Template Properties to open the Template Properties dialog box, as shown in Figure 19.5, to either turn on or turn off the optional region. The Template Properties command is available only when you are working on a page based on a Dreamweaver template; it isn't available while actually editing a template file.

FIGURE 19.5
Turn an optional region on or off in the Template Properties dialog box.

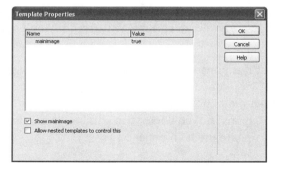

Making Changes to a Template and Updating Pages

You edit a template by opening the template to add or change its contents. You can open the template from the Templates category of the Assets panel, or you can open it from the Site Manager. Edits to locked objects are applied to all the Web pages that use the template. Edits to editable objects have no effect on Web pages that use the template.

After you edit and save a template, Dreamweaver asks you whether you want to update files. Select the files you want to update in the Update Template Files dialog box and then click Update to automatically update the linked files. The Update Pages dialog box displays statistics on how many files were examined, updated, and not able to be updated. Check the Show Log check box to see these statistics. Click the Close button to close the Update Pages dialog box.

You can also manually update files linked to templates. To do so, right-click the template in the Templates category of the Assets panel and select either the Update Current Page command, to update the current Web page, or the Update Site command, to update the entire Web site. The Update Current Page command acts immediately, and no dialog box appears. When you issue the Update Site command, the Update Pages dialog box appears, as shown in Figure 19.6. Click the Start button to update all the linked templates in the Web site.

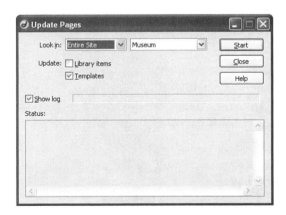

FIGURE 19.6
Update all the Web pages that are based on templates (and library items, too) in a site.

Using Behaviors and Styles in Templates

You can use behaviors and styles in templates. Styles and JavaScript will be applied to a Web page based on the template. For you to be able to edit styles and behaviors in a Web page, objects they are applied to must be editable. Select an object that has a style or behavior and edit the style or behavior in the CSS Styles panel or the Behaviors panel.

Summary

In this chapter, you have learned how to create templates, both from existing content and from scratch. You have learned how to use the Templates category of the Assets panel to manage templates, and you have learned how to open and edit templates. You have learned how to make regions of a template editable regions and optional regions. You have learned how Dreamweaver automatically updates all the linked templates in a Web site and how you can launch that process manually.

This marks the conclusion of our look at Dreamweaver MX 2004, and the start of Fireworks MX. Now that you have webpage design down, it's time to look at getting your pages' visual elements ready and optimized for the web.

PART II
Fireworks

CHAPTER 20

Getting to Know the Fireworks MX 2004 Interface

As with the other Studio MX 2004 tools, Fireworks sports a clean streamlined interface that eliminates many of the inconsistencies in previous versions.

In this chapter, you take a tour through the new interface. This material will help you get off the ground in Fireworks by introducing the tools and menus you will have at your disposal. Experienced Fireworks users might want to skip ahead to the next chapter to start working with images immediately.

Getting Started with Fireworks MX 2004

This section gets you started by introducing you to the Fireworks MX 2004 interface and showing you how to open an image so you can begin working. The commands shown work in both the Microsoft Windows XP edition of Fireworks MX 2004 and the Macintosh OS X edition, as well previous versions of both operating systems. Keyboard shortcuts are shown for both editions of Fireworks MX 2004.

Opening Fireworks MX 2004 for the First Time

To begin using Fireworks, select Start from the Windows Desktop or press the Applications button on your keyboard. Move your mouse pointer over (mouseover) All Programs, then Macromedia, and finally Macromedia Fireworks MX 2004. The first time Fireworks loads, the screen looks similar to Figure 20.1.

> If you are using Macintosh OS X, navigate to your Applications folder by selecting Applications from the Go menu in the Finder or by pressing Shift+Command+A. Open the Macromedia Fireworks MX 2004 folder and double-click Fireworks MX 2004 to run Fireworks.

By the Way

The Welcome screen in the middle lets you start one of the tutorials (Graphic Design, Web Design, or Using Fireworks with Other Applications), take a tour of the

Fireworks interface, open recent documents, create new documents, or extend the Fireworks environment with the components from Fireworks Exchange. If you haven't purchased the software yet, you'll also see a link to purchase a license for your trial copy.

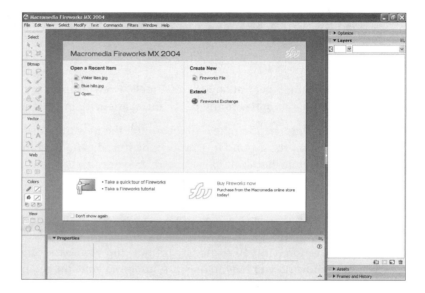

If you haven't already taken a look at the tutorials or tour, now may be a good time. Otherwise, you can get started exploring the workspace right now! We'll be using menus for executing commands, panels for working with documents and objects, and a work area for document windows.

By the Way

The welcome screen stays open behind the Fireworks workspace unless you keep it from appearing by clicking the Don't Show Again check box.

On the top of the workspace is the Menu. Below and to the left is the Tools panel, and to the right of the Tools panel is a work area. Further right are the docked panel groups. The Layers panel, by default, is fully expanded. Below the docked panels is the Properties panel, also known as the Properties Inspector. The Properties Inspector is common to many of the Studio MX 2004 applications; its options change depending on what you're working on. Right now you haven't started working yet, so it is blank. We'll cover the Properties Inspector in more detail in a few moments.

The Menu includes the File, Edit, View, Select, Modify, Text, Commands, Filters, Window, and Help menus. We'll go over each one in more detail. For now, open an image file from your hard drive. Click File, Open from the drop-down menu or use the keyboard shortcut Ctrl+O. The Open dialog box appears and opens to your My Pictures folder. If you are using Macintosh OS X, the file opens to your Pictures folder.

Double-click the Sample Pictures folder that came with Windows to open it. If you're a Macintosh OS X user, you can find an image in the Desktop Pictures folder under the Library folder on your startup drive. We recommend Snowy Hills from the Nature folder for Macintosh OS X users and Blue Hills for Windows XP users. Select an image by clicking it, and then click Open or press Return. The photo appears in your workspace, as shown in Figure 20.2.

FIGURE 20.2
Now you're ready to start working on the photo of your choice.

File Menu

The File menu contains the basic file operation commands you're already familiar with, such as Open, Open Recent, Close, Save, Save As, Page Setup, Print, and Quit. The File menu is also where you'll go to import and export graphics, update or preview HTML, and batch process a number of files automatically. (On Mac OS X, Quit can be found under the Fireworks application menu.)

Edit Menu

The Edit menu is where you'll find the Cut, Copy, and Paste commands as well as a number of special graphics functions, such as Duplicate, Paste Attributes, and Crop. The Find and Replace function is common to word-processing programs, but Fireworks lets you use Find and Replace for graphics as well as text. This is also where you can make changes to your preferences or add and change Fireworks' keyboard shortcuts. (On Mac OS X, preferences and keyboard shortcuts can be found under the Fireworks menu.)

View Menu

The View options include controls such as Zoom In, Zoom Out, Magnification, and Fit to Window. Other options let you set up rulers, a grid, or guides and allow you to show and hide Fireworks interface elements, such as edges, panels, and the status bar.

Select Menu

With the Select menu options, you can modify what's selected in several ways. The Select All command selects all the pixels in a bitmap or all the elements on the Canvas. Feather Selection enables you to create a gradual transition around your selection. Marquee options give you the ultimate control over complex selections, which you can then save using Save Bitmap Selection.

Modify Menu

Modify includes many of the most common image operations. You can resize the Canvas, transform (scale, rotate, and so on) an object, arrange it in front of or behind other objects, group them, and then use Flatten Selection to create a single bitmap image from a number of objects.

Did you Know?

Common commands from the File and Modify menus can be added as toolbars to the Fireworks workspace with the Toolbars option under the Window menu.

Text Menu

The Text menu options include the familiar Font, Size, Style, and Align attributes. Fireworks lets you edit text directly in the image. You can even check your text with Check Spelling without having to leave Fireworks!

Commands Menu

The Commands menu enables you to manage saved commands, manage extensions, and run scripts. A number of commands come with Fireworks, including the data-driven Graphics Wizard and Web commands such as Create Shared Palette. You can download Macromedia extensions or create your own custom scripts and add them to the Commands menu quickly and easily. The Command editor works virtually identically across the Macromedia product suite, so we'll leave it to you to explore its use in Fireworks.

Filters Menu

Filters are graphics tools that enable you to make complex changes to an image or selection, such as blur, sharpen, or adjust color. Eye Candy and Alien Skin have included some of their more creative filters, and more filters can be added if you run out of interesting effects.

Window Menu

The Window menu allows you to access a panel quickly if it has been closed. You can also cascade or tile images to make them easier to find and work with or select an image file to bring it to the front.

Help Menu

The Help menu is there whenever you need it. You can begin one of the tutorials by opening the Welcome screen, browse the Using Fireworks PDF, visit the Support Center, or interact with other Fireworks users in the Macromedia Online Forums.

Finding Your Tools

In Fireworks MX 2004, tools are grouped according to what they are used for—Select, Bitmap, Vector, Web, Colors, and View. Clicking a tool icon selects that tool. Related tools can be found by clicking and holding on a tool if a dark gray triangle appears in the lower-right of the icon. If you get confused, hold your mouse over a tool icon for a ToolTip that names the tool and shows you the keyboard shortcut.

If you are an experienced graphic designer, this section should lead you right to the tools you need to get started working on your own. If you are a new user, some of these terms and tools might seem strange and useless. Don't despair! You will learn to use all of them in due time. For now, it's adequate to acquaint yourself with the names of the tools and be able to find them on the Tools panel.

Select Tools

The Select tools are used to choose objects on the canvas to work with, including bitmap, vector, text, and group objects. They are shown in Figure 20.3.

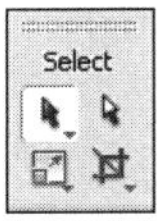

FIGURE 20.3
The Select group includes the pointer, subselection, free transform, and crop tools, in that order.

Pointer and Select Behind

The pointer tool is used to select objects on the Canvas, whereas the select behind tool is used to select an object arranged behind another object. Press V or the number 0 to select the tool and toggle between the pointer and select behind tools.

Subselection

The subselection tool is used with groups and paths to choose only part of an object. Press A or 1 to choose the subselection tool.

Scale, Skew, and Distort

The Scale tool is used to change the size or aspect ratio of an object. The Skew tool can shift two sides of an object diagonally, and the Distort tool stretches any corner of an object. Select an object and press Q one or more times to select the Scale, Skew, or Distort tool.

Crop, Export Area

The Crop tool enables you to choose an area of the Canvas to preserve and then discards the rest. The Export Area tool allows you to export any portion of the Canvas quickly. Toggle between the Crop and Export Area tools by pressing C.

Bitmap Tools

The Bitmap tools, shown in Figure 20.4, are used for creating or editing bitmap objects.

FIGURE 20.4
The Fireworks MX 2004 Bitmap tools enable you to modify bitmap images.

Marquee and Oval Marquee

The Marquee tool selects a rectangular group of pixels in a bitmap object. The Oval Marquee tool selects an oval or round group of pixels in a bitmap. To toggle between the Marquee tool and the Oval Marquee tool, press M.

Lasso and Polygon Lasso

The Lasso tool enables you to select any group of pixels by drawing a shape around the pixels you would like to select. The Polygon Lasso is similar, except that instead of drawing a single line, you select only points that are connected by straight lines. To cycle through the Lasso and Polygon Lasso tools, press L.

Magic Wand

The Magic Wand tool selects surrounding pixels with color values similar to the original pixel you selected. This is good for selecting areas of solid or shaded color. To use the Magic Wand tool, press W.

Brush

The Brush is used for painting pixels. All sorts of interesting digital painting effects are possible with the Brush. To start using the Brush tool, press B. If the Pencil tool is selected, press B again.

Pencil

The Pencil is similar to the Brush, except that it is more often used for editing individual pixels than for broad strokes. To use the Pencil tool, press B. If the Brush tool is selected, press B again.

Eraser

The Eraser tool is used to remove portions of the bitmap. You can switch to the Eraser tool by pressing E.

Blur, Sharpen, Dodge, Burn, and Smudge

These tools are for fine photo retouching. The Blur tool blurs an area of the bitmap, and the Sharpen tool does the opposite. Dodge makes a portion of the bitmap lighter, whereas Burn makes it darker. The Smudge tool is used to smudge pixels together like a finger smudging a wet painting. Press R to cycle through these tools.

Rubber Stamp

The Rubber Stamp tool can copy one area of pixels to another. It can remove facial blemishes, repair dusty or scratched images, and do all sorts of other neat things. To select the Rubber Stamp tool, press S.

Eyedropper

The Eyedropper tool is used to sample a color from the Canvas. Sampled colors can then be used in other parts of the image or added to the Swatch panel. Press I to select the Eyedropper tool.

Paint Bucket and Gradient

The Paint Bucket is used to fill an area of the bitmap with a new color. The Gradient tool is used to create a gradual transition between colors in a filled area. Press G to toggle between the Paint Bucket and Gradient tools.

Vector Tools

The Vector tools are used to create and edit vector objects, such as lines, shapes, and text. The Vector tool group is shown in Figure 20.5.

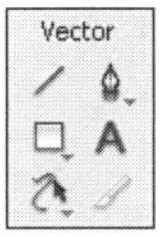

FIGURE 20.5
The Vector group includes the Path, Line, and Pen tools.

Line

The Line tool is used to create a straight path between two points. Press N to select it.

Pen, Vector Path, and Redraw Path

The Pen tool is used to create and edit precise paths. The Vector Path tool is used to draw a path freehand; it determines points and curves automatically. You can use Redraw Path to alter a portion of a vector path. Press P to cycle through these tools.

Rectangle, Ellipse, Polygon, and Many More

These tools create simple filled shapes. The Rectangle tool creates rectangles and squares, Ellipse creates circles and ovals, and Polygon creates a regular multisided shape. Press U to select a Vector shape tool. In addition to these simple shape tools, you can also choose from more complex objects such as doughnuts and pies. Getting hungry?

Text

The Text tool enables you to enter text directly on the Canvas. To start typing, press T and click an area of the Canvas.

Freeform Path, Reshape Path, and Path Scrubber

Freeform Path allows you to grab points and lines on the path to edit them by eye; you simply click and drag a point to change a section. Reshape Path is another method for altering an area of the path instead of a point or line segment. The Path Scrubber tool gives you access to speed and pressure settings for path strokes, allowing you to vary settings such as stroke width, color density, and edge softness as though you were working with a real brush. Cycle between these tools by pressing O.

Knife

The Knife tool slices a continuous path (like a line) into segments. It is available only when you have selected one or more ungrouped path objects. To select the Knife tool, press Y when you have a path object selected.

Web Tools

The Web tools, shown in Figure 20.6, are used for laying out HTML tables and adding interactivity to your graphics.

FIGURE 20.6
The Web group of tools includes the Slice tool for creating HTML table slices on the Web layer.

Rectangle, Circle, and Polygon Hotspot

These tools allow you to create links within an image or a slice. They create an image map that is exported as HTML. To cycle between the Hotspot tools, press J.

Slice and Polygon Slice

Fireworks creates HTML table layouts for your image from slices you draw with the Slice and Polygon Slice tools. Press K to begin slicing your image.

Hide and Show Slices and Hotspots

The last two Web tools enable you to quickly show or hide your slices and hotspots, making the transition from graphic design to Web design instantaneous. To toggle Slice and Hotspot visibility, press 2.

Color Tools

The Color tools, shown in Figure 20.7, can be used to select the colors for the bitmap painting tools or to change the stroke and fill settings for vector paths.

FIGURE 20.7
The stroke and fill colors can be set, reset, turned off, or swapped with the tools in the Color group.

Stroke Color

When drawing with the Brush, Pencil, or any of the Vector tools, you can specify a stroke color, which is the color of the line the path defines. Click the pencil to select Stroke color, and then click the triangle underneath the current color to bring up a standard palette or your custom swatches.

Fill Color

When using the Paint Bucket or drawing with any of the Vector tools, you must specify the color inside the shape in the Fill color palette. You can also change the Stroke and Fill colors with the Eyedropper.

Default Stroke and Fill

Resets the stroke and fill color defaults set in the Fireworks preferences (initially a black stroke and white fill). When a path object or group is selected, you can press D to change the strokes and fills back to the default. Click the button on the Tools panel to reset the stroke and fill when you have no objects selected.

No Stroke or Fill

Select the Stroke or Fill setting and click this button to turn off the stroke or fill color. This makes the stroke or fill disappear.

Swap Stroke and Fill Colors

This changes the stroke color to the fill color and vice versa. Press X to swap stroke and fill colors when one or more path objects are selected.

View Tools

The View controls allow you to maximize screen space or change the magnification and position of your canvas in the workspace. They are shown in Figure 20.8.

FIGURE 20.8
The View tools include the Screen Mode, Hand, and Zoom tools.

Standard Screen, Full Screen with Menus, and Full Screen Mode

These modes enable you to maximize your workspace. The default is Standard Screen, which displays the Canvas in its own window and displays the Menu at the top. Full Screen with Menus removes a good portion of the Canvas window, freeing up more space for working on the image. Full Screen mode removes everything but the panels for maximum workspace. Press F to cycle through the various modes.

Hand

The Hand tool is used to navigate an image that might be larger than the screen or Canvas window. By clicking and dragging, you can move the image around as though it were a slide under a microscope. Press H to select the Hand tool.

Zoom

The Zoom tool is pretty straightforward. Press Z to activate the Zoom tool. Then click an area of the Canvas to zoom in.

Working with View Tools

Okay, now that you have an image open in your workspace and an idea of where to find your tools, you can begin with some basic image-navigation techniques. As you work on an image, you'll often want to zoom in to work on a detail and then quickly zoom out to evaluate your work. This can all be done with the View tools and their equivalent keyboard shortcuts.

By the Way

> The Canvas in Fireworks is the where you will spend most of your time working. Each image file lies on a Canvas, but the Canvas does not carry any image information itself except for dimensions and a background color. Objects such as bitmap images, vector graphics, and text are arranged on the Canvas to create the final image, the same way you might create a collage from picture and text clippings.

Navigating the Canvas

With a document window open in the work area, select the Zoom tool from the Tools panel by clicking its magnifying glass icon. Move your cursor over the Canvas. The cursor changes to a magnifying glass with a plus sign in the middle. Click your mouse button to zoom in on your image. Now hold down Alt (Windows) or Option (Macintosh). The plus sign changes to a minus sign. While still holding down the Alt/Option key, click the Canvas again. Your image zooms out to its original view.

You can also zoom in and out by holding Ctrl (Option on the Mac) and pressing the minus (hyphen) key or the plus (equals) key. To quickly zoom to where the entire Canvas can be seen, press Ctrl (or Option) and the number 0. You can also access all these commands through the View menu. Adjust the magnification by clicking View, Magnification, 100%. As a shortcut, you can simply double-click the magnifying glass to return to a 100% magnification. This shows the image at its native, or original, resolution. Here you can see each individual pixel that goes into composing the image.

Zooming in on the Canvas can sometimes make large portions of the image invisible because they can't fit in the workspace. To view portions of an image that won't fit completely on your screen, use the Hand tool to move the image relative to the view window. To select the Hand tool, click it or press H. When you move the cursor over the Canvas, it becomes a hand icon. Now click and drag the hand to the left. You'll notice as you move the hand that the visible portion of the Canvas in the workspace changes.

Exploring the Various Screen Modes

Now that you're familiar with some of the tools and with all the View controls, go ahead and switch screen modes. This can be initially disorienting for a new user, but you should be well prepared to take the plunge. By learning the keyboard shortcuts and View controls, you can get rid of all the panels and use the whole screen for working with your image!

To switch screen modes, do the following:

1. Click the Full Screen with Menus Mode button under View on the Tools panel. Alternatively, you can press F to cycle to this setting (see Figure 20.9).

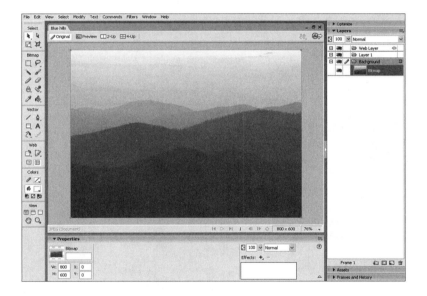

FIGURE 20.9
Full Screen with Menus Mode gives you more room to work.

2. Press the Tab key. Voilà! All your panels have disappeared. Don't worry—you still have the Menu up above (see Figure 20.10).

3. Press F to cycle to Full Screen Mode. Now you can work with an image on your entire screen (see Figure 20.11).

4. Press Z to activate the Zoom tool, and click the Canvas to zoom in. Do it one more time.

5. Press H to select the Hand tool. Click and drag the Canvas to inspect it in its entirety.

6. Press Ctrl+0 (Windows) or Command-0 (Macintosh) to zoom out and center the image so it fits the screen.

FIGURE 20.10
The Tab key toggles panels on and off, clearing out the clutter.

FIGURE 20.11
Full Screen Mode enables you to use the entire monitor you've paid for.

7. Press the Tab key to bring the panels back.

8. Press F to cycle back to Standard Screen Mode.

> To fit a particular area of the screen into the window, use the Zoom tool and click-drag a rectangular area of the Canvas. That area now fills the workspace.

Did you Know?

Now that you're familiar with the tools and comfortable with the View tools, you can move on to the rest of the panels you'll be using while you work.

Using the Properties Inspector

The Properties Inspector is the panel at the bottom of your workspace labeled Properties. It is *contextual*, which means the menu options change depending on in which context you're working. If a bitmap object is selected on the Canvas, the Properties Inspector enables you to view and change the settings for that bitmap object. If you select the Brush to paint on the Canvas, the Properties Inspector shows the Brush tool options. Whatever you're working with or working on, all the features and settings are only one click away. The Properties Inspector is shown in Figure 20.12.

FIGURE 20.12
The Properties Inspector is where you specify settings for tools and objects.

With the sample photo open in the workspace, select the Pointer tool (by pressing V or 0) from the Tool panel and click the image of rolling hills. It is surrounded by a thin border with square handles at the corners.

You'll also notice in Figure 20.12 that the Properties Inspector now shows a small thumbnail and is labeled `Bitmap` on the left. This is to let you know it is a bitmap object, and the thumbnail shows you the entire object (in case it's masked or obscured by other objects). On the bottom right of the Properties Inspector is an arrow. This toggles the Properties Inspector from simple to advanced options. If the arrow is pointing down, click it to reveal the entire Properties Inspector.

Below `Bitmap` is a form field where you can name the object. Naming objects can be useful when you are trying to keep track of many objects, for advanced techniques such as scripting, and just as a good habit. Below that are the dimensions and location of the image. W is the width of the image in pixels; H is the height; and X is the horizontal position of the bitmap object's upper-left corner.

The position is measured in pixels and is relative to the upper-left corner of the Canvas. Y is the vertical position. Positions on the Canvas are always measured from the upper-left corner, and negative X or Y values place the image off the Canvas to the left and above, respectively.

On the right of the Properties Inspector are the transparency settings for the object. 100% means completely opaque, whereas 0% means completely transparent. Various types of transparency renderings are available from the drop-down menu to the right. Below that the Properties Inspector lists the effects that have been applied to the object. These topics merit much more discussion, but we'll skip them for now. Knowing where to find them is all you need until you learn more about them in Chapter 22, "Editing Bitmap Graphics."

With the bitmap object selected, click the Brush tool icon or press B. The Properties Inspector now shows the Brush tool icon and name in the upper-left corner. To the right is the Brush settings, including the stroke color, brush size, brush style, edge softness, texture, and texture density. Click another tool and examine the changes in the Properties Inspector. This is a great way to get to know your tools.

Before you move on to the other panels, take a moment to examine the Canvas properties. Zoom out until a gray area is around the image. Now click the gray area with the Pointer tool selected. The Properties Inspector shows a thumbnail of your entire image, the filename, and the Canvas settings. You can now change the Canvas background color, Canvas size, image size, and compression preset.

Other Panels

Fireworks presents options to users with Macromedia panels, just as you've seen in the other Studio products. These panels can be rearranged and even saved in custom layouts using the drop-down menu in the upper-right corner of a panel group.

Let's take a look at the Fireworks MX 2004 panels. We'll go over each panel briefly and learn the keyboard shortcut so you can always find it quickly. All the panels can be opened individually from the Window menu:

- ▶ **Tools**—We've already gone over the Tools panel a little. To toggle the Tools panel on and off, press Ctrl+F2 (Windows) or Command-F2 (Macintosh).

▶ **Properties Inspector**—The Properties Inspector is also a panel. To show or hide the Properties Inspector, press Ctrl+F3 (Windows) or Command-F3 (Macintosh).

▶ **Optimize**—This panel contains compression and export settings. F6 (Windows and Macintosh).

▶ **Layers**—To help you manage your Canvas, the Layers panel contains many useful features. F2 (Windows and Macintosh).

▶ **Frames**—Frames are used in animations and other tasks. Shift+F2 (Windows and Macintosh).

▶ **History**—The History panel keeps track of everything you do so you can undo it or repeat it. Shift+F10 (Windows and Macintosh).

▶ **Auto Shapes**—These are complex images such as speech bubbles, tubes, and other fun things.

▶ **Styles**—Styles are custom stroke, fill, and effect settings you can use to quickly apply your signature look. Shift+F11 (Windows and Macintosh).

▶ **Library**—The Library is where you can organize symbols and graphics for easy access. F11 (Windows and Macintosh).

▶ **URL**—The URL panel lets you specify the location for a Hotspot or Button link. Alt+Shift+F10 (Windows) or Option-Shift-F10 (Macintosh).

▶ **Color Mixer**—The Color Mixer gives you complete control over choosing your colors. Shift+F9 (Windows and Macintosh).

▶ **Swatches**—Swatches are palettes of colors you can save and share with others. Ctrl+F9 (Windows) or Command-F9 (Macintosh).

▶ **Info**—The Info panel gives you statistics about cursor location and the color value of the pixel underneath. Alt+Shift+F12 (Windows) or Option-Shift-F12 (Macintosh).

▶ **Behaviors**—Behaviors are special interactive features used with button symbols and hotspots. Shift+F3 (Windows and Macintosh).

▶ **Find** —The Find panel lets you make quick changes to documents with no hassle. Ctrl+F (Windows) or Command-F (Macintosh).

▶ **Align**—The Align panel helps you align objects on the Canvas for a more professional look. You can assign your own keyboard shortcut to be used with this panel.

Looking for More Help?

If you ever need help, it's rarely more than a click away. Whether you are online or offline, you can always find a Fireworks Help resource handy. Before you continue, take a look at your options for finding out what you need to know.

To access Fireworks Help at any time, just press F1 (Windows) or Command-? (Macintosh). This opens the *Using Fireworks* documentation, shown in Figure 20.13. You can also open *Using Fireworks* from the Help menu. The Help menu is where you'll also find links to the Macromedia Fireworks Support Web site, with TechNotes and a searchable knowledge base. The Macromedia Online Forums are a great place to talk shop and swap files with other Macromedia Fireworks MX 2004 users.

FIGURE 20.13
The *Using Fireworks* guide is just a click away from the keyboard, Help menu, or Help buttons.

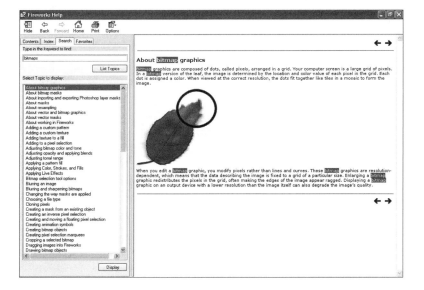

Help is also available for panels via the Help button, a question mark icon. This can often be found in the upper-right of a panel, and it takes you to the appropriate section of the *Using Fireworks* guide for whichever panel you're having trouble with. If you need help with a tool or an object, select it with the pointer and click the Help button in the Properties Inspector. This brings up help about that particular tool or type of object.

If you feel like you need some more hands-on experience with Fireworks before you begin working on the examples, you should take the time to go through at least the graphic design tutorial. You can come back to the Web design tutorial when you're more comfortable with some of the concepts behind good Web design, which are discussed later.

Summary

With a streamlined look and feel, the Fireworks MX 2004 interface is better than ever. So far, you should know how to use the menus, be familiar with some of the tools, know how to open and examine an image, and even be able to save your own custom layout to make your life less cluttered.

Although the design tools weren't covered in this chapter, you learned your way around, and in subsequent chapters it should be much easier to find what you need, which is generally half the problem. If some features of the Fireworks interface still seem confusing, don't worry. We'll examine elements in detail soon.

CHAPTER 21

Working with Bitmap Images

In this chapter you begin working with bitmap images, which are the foundation of computer graphics such as Web images and photographs. First you learn how to work with the Canvas, layers, and colors, and then you explore the bitmap drawing and painting tools. The next chapter introduces you to bitmap editing and advanced creative techniques.

What Is a Bitmap?

A *bitmap image* is a two-dimensional grid of units called *pixels*. The two dimensions are width and height. The resolution of a bitmap is measured in dots or points per inch (dpi or PPI). A higher dpi generally means a more detailed image. As you increase the magnification of a bitmap image using the Zoom tool, the individual pixels become larger and larger until you can see each individual area of color.

Bitmaps are limited in two ways: Extreme resizing can degrade image detail, and as image size or resolution is doubled, the file size increases fourfold. In particular, if an image is made very small, most of the detail will be lost. If a small image is made bigger, on the other hand, artifacts called *jaggies* occur. Such situations are improved somewhat by a resampling algorithm, but large changes still degrade the final image. And as color depth or pixel dimensions increase, file size begins to increase exponentially. A 24-bit scan at 300dpi of an 8 1/2"×11" drawing, for example, is over 24 megabytes (MB) if not compressed. Doubling the resolution to 600dpi quadruples the file size to nearly 100MB!

Changing the Canvas

On the Web images are rarely more than a few hundred pixels wide or tall, and by using GIF or JPEG compression, you can keep almost any image under 100 kilobytes (KB) without sacrificing too much detail. Using the Properties Inspector, you can easily and quickly resample a bitmap image or change the size of the Canvas to cut a bitmap down to size.

By the Way
Sometimes you will want to rotate both the image and the dimensions of the canvas. To do this, select Rotate 180, Rotate 90 CW, or Rotate 90 CCW from the Canvas submenu on the Modify menu. This rotates the Canvas and all the objects on it. If you want to make the Canvas smaller to fit just the objects that are visible, use Trim Canvas. If you want to make the Canvas larger to accommodate objects that might otherwise run off it, select Fit Canvas. You can also access the Image Size, Canvas Size, and Canvas Color options from the Modify menu.

Changing the Image and Canvas Size

If you want to resize the entire image in Fireworks, you use the Image Size command. You can also access the Image Size command from the Canvas commands on the Modify menu or the Properties Inspector as shown in Figure 21.1.

FIGURE 21.1
The Image Size dialog box changes the Canvas size and all the objects on the Canvas proportionately.

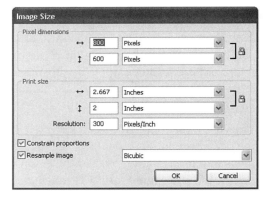

Because the image size has changed as the magnification has remained the same, the image appears smaller in the workspace. Press Ctrl+0 (Windows) or Command-0 (Macintosh) or select Fit All from the View menu to change the magnification to fit the Canvas within the workspace, if you'd like.

Now, suppose you want to add on to an image but the Canvas isn't large enough. To solve the problem and give yourself a larger working area, you need to resize the Canvas. With the Properties Inspector showing information for the Canvas, click the Canvas Size button to bring up the Canvas Size dialog box. When you change the Canvas's size, the size of objects on the Canvas do not change, meaning that bitmap objects are not resampled. The Canvas resize dialog box is shown in Figure 21.2.

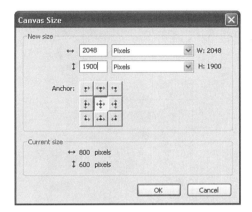

FIGURE 21.2
Altering the Canvas size does not affect the size of objects on the Canvas. The anchor specifies which point the changes reference. Anchoring a point and making the Canvas smaller removes pixels from the area opposite the anchor. Click OK or press Enter to accept the changes.

The new area of the Canvas appears as a grid of gray and white squares. This grid indicates complete transparency, which is the default Canvas color in Fireworks. You can change this color with the Canvas setting in the Properties Inspector. Try changing it to white by clicking the swatch to open the swatch palette and selecting white with the Eyedropper.

If you've expanded the Canvas beyond all your graphic objects and want to shrink it to fit them exactly, click the Fit Canvas button in the Properties Inspector.

Did you Know?

Using the Layers Panel

Fireworks, like many other graphics applications, uses layers to help you manage objects in an image. Layers are like transparent sheets; you can draw on individual sheets and then change how they're stacked, in order to change which elements are in the background and which are in the foreground. In this case, the Canvas is the surface on which you layer the sheets.

You can work with layers through the Layers panel (see Figure 21.3). Bitmap editing is considered destructive; when you change a pixel, any information that was previously there is lost. This is why it's important to back up your source images. By using layers and bitmap objects, you can break your bitmaps into discrete parts, so you can preserve and compare your editing decisions nondestructively.

At the top of the Layers panel, you'll see a small icon of a gray-and-white grid, which means transparency. The field next to this icon is the transparency setting for that layer: 100% means fully opaque, and 0% means fully transparent. You can quickly change the transparency of the layer with the drop-down menu immediately to the right of the opacity field.

FIGURE 21.3
The Layers panel is one of the most important tools when working with bitmaps.

Next to the transparency setting is the Blending Mode menu. Blending modes change how two layers or objects interact based on their color values. Several interesting effects are possible with blending modes, and these are discussed later in this chapter, in the section "Drawing and Painting."

Underneath the transparency and blending mode settings is the actual list of layers. The first, top layer is always the Web Layer in Fireworks. There can be only one Web Layer, and it cannot be duplicated, deleted, or renamed. The Web Layer is where you define your slices for HTML table layouts. Information in the Web Layer is not actually displayed in the image, and you cannot draw or place objects (other than slices) on the Web Layer.

Below the Web Layer are all your other layers; these layers are where you assemble your graphics and images. Each layer is a row in this table, and the topmost layer of the image appears above any layers below it. The arrangement of objects in a layer is also visible when the layer is expanded; objects, like layers, appear on top of objects arranged beneath them on the same layer. Next to each layer's name is a folder icon, and next to each object within a layer is a thumbnail of the object. To expand a layer, click the expand/collapse icon in the leftmost column of the layer row on the Layers panel. Figure 21.4 shows several layers in use.

Each row in the Layers panel also allows you to show the layer (second column, eyeball icon visible) or hide the layer (no icon). You can also hide objects within a layer. Simply click the eyeball icon to hide a layer. For a hidden layer, click the empty area next to the layer or object. Hidden layers and hidden objects are not exported with the image—this can be used to export many different versions of a document. The column next to the layer's name displays whether the layer is active, inactive, or locked. If a layer is active, a pencil appears in this column and the layer name appears on a blue background. To lock a layer and prevent changes to it, click this column; a padlock icon appears. To unlock a locked layer, click the padlock, and the lock icon disappears. To make a layer active, click its name in the Layers panel or select an object on that layer. A locked layer cannot be the active layer.

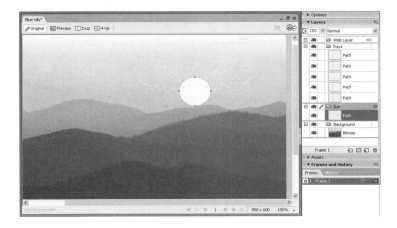

FIGURE 21.4
The Layers panel now contains several layers and objects.

Each layer and each object in a layer can have a name. This can be critical when organizing a detailed layout or when sharing your graphics with others. To rename a layer or an object, double-click its current name. You are presented with a dialog box where you can type a new name. You can also choose to share a layer across frames. This means the layer will be visible in all the frames of a document. The Web Layer is always shared across frames. If a layer is shared across frames, a filmstrip icon appears to the right of the layer name. (Frames are discussed in more detail later in the book.)

At the bottom-right corner of the Layers panel are the layer controls: New/Duplicate Layer, Add Mask, New Bitmap Image, and Delete Selection. The New/Duplicate Layer option creates either a blank new layer or a duplicate layer. To create a new layer, click the New/Duplicate Layer button. To duplicate a layer, select an existing layer, click and hold to drag it, and then release it over the New/Duplicate Layer button. The duplicate layer is created below the selected layer.

The Add Mask button enables you to mask a layer with a bitmap alpha channel. A mask reveals some parts of the image and hides others. A black mask hides everything; a white mask makes everything visible; and shades of gray allow for gradation in the mask. This technique is used mostly with bitmap layers because applying a mask to a layer flattens all the objects on that layer into a single masked image.

The New Bitmap Image button creates an empty (transparent) bitmap object of the same dimensions as the Canvas in the selected layer. This enables you to quickly employ a bitmap fill or begin drawing to a bitmap object on the Canvas. The Delete Selection button does just that. Select a layer or an object in the Layers panel and click the Delete Selection button to delete it. You can also drag and drop the selection on this button to delete it.

The Layers panel Options menu—the drop-down menu at the upper-right of the panel—also has some important layer functions, Flatten Selection and Merge Down. Flatten Selection takes all the objects or layers selected and creates a single bitmap image on a single layer, much like what happens when you export a Fireworks PNG. Merge Down is similar to Flatten Selection except that it merges all selected objects to a bitmap image residing below the bottommost object. If a bitmap object is not available, Merge Down is not available on the Options menu.

Choosing Colors and Managing Swatches

Another critical area of working with bitmap objects and the drawing tools is understanding how to work with the color mixer and swatches. The color mixer helps you select individual colors to use with the drawing tools. *Swatches* are a way of saving a group of individual colors that you will be using repeatedly. Remember that a bitmap image is simply a grid of pixels with different color values, and a palette is the group of color swatches used in the particular image. Understanding the concepts behind the color palette is very important.

Fireworks uses a 24-bit RGB palette. *RGB* stands for red, green, and blue. A 24-bit image is actually composed of three 8-bit grayscale images—one for each color. The three channels are combined to represent the colors onscreen. Your computer monitor is an RGB device; each point, or pixel, is composed of three phosphors—a red one, a green one, and a blue one (in the case of liquid crystal displays, each point is a group of charged crystals). This is the process of additive color. Generally, anyone browsing the Web will be viewing images (and their colors) in the additive color space.

The colors in the RGB color space, or *spectrum*, have names expressed in hexadecimal numbers, or *hex codes*, which are derived from a base 16 character set (the ten digits, 0–9, and the first six letters of the alphabet, A–F). Each color name consists of six characters. The hex code for absolute black is 000000; the hex code for white is FFFFFF; and the hex code for medium gray is 6C6C6C. If you've been using Dreamweaver MX, this is old hat for you. It's not important to know how to find a color with hex codes, but it is helpful to know that you can refer to colors by specific names when you want to ensure you're using the same colors as someone else.

Fireworks makes finding and organizing colors easy. The Mixer panel allows you to mix colors by changing their relative values of red, green, and blue (or gray, if you are working with a grayscale image). The Swatches panel lets you save individual colors so you can quickly find them later. The following sections describe the options for these two panels.

Color Mixer Panel

The Color Mixer panel, shown in Figure 21.5, enables you to mix colors numerically or by eye. The Color Mixer panel is always available from the Window menu. The first two settings are for the stroke and fill colors. The stroke color, denoted by the pencil icon, is the color applied to any pencil or brush strokes as well as to vector lines. The fill color can be applied with the paint bucket or as the fill color for a vector shape.

FIGURE 21.5
Use the Color Mixer panel to choose and manipulate colors.

Clicking the stroke or fill color swatch opens the Swatch menu, shown in Figure 21.6. The current swatch palette pops up (the default palette is the Web 216 palette). The white swatch with the diagonal red line indicates colorless transparency. To open the system color picker, click the color wheel icon at the upper-right of the pop-up swatch menu. The arrow at the upper-right lets you select different swatch layouts and palette sets. The stroke and fill swatches are also available on the Tools panel, in the Color section.

FIGURE 21.6
The Swatch menu
pops up when you
click a stroke or fill
color.

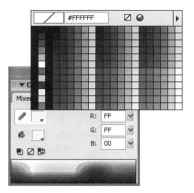

At the bottom of the mixer pane are Set Default Stroke/Fill Colors, which automatically sets the stroke to black and the fill to white; No Stroke or Fill, which makes the selected swatch transparent; and Swap Stroke and Fill Colors, which quickly changes the stroke color to the fill color and vice versa.

Below the stroke and fill controls is a color spectrum. The hue changes horizontally and the saturation changes vertically. You can use this tool to quickly select an approximate color from the full spectrum. To fine-tune this color, you can use the red, green, and blue pop-up sliders to add or subtract tones from the color. As you move the slider, a value changes in the field. You can also edit this value by selecting it and typing a new value. The range of values for each channel is 0–255.

If you need to know the hex code for a color or want to define a color with values other than RGB, use the Mixer panel Options menu (upper-right corner of the panel) to select RGB, Hexadecimal, CMY (not CMYK, but the equivalent of inverse RGB), HSB (hue, saturation, brightness), or Grayscale.

Swatches

The Swatches panel, shown in Figure 21.7, is pretty simple. Using the Mixer, select a color for the stroke or fill. Then open the Swatches panel. When you mouse over the gray area at the bottom of the Swatches panel, the cursor changes to the paint bucket. Click to add this color to your swatch palette. To select a color from the swatch palette, with the stroke or fill active, mouse over a swatch in the palette. The cursor changes to the Eyedropper. Click to change the stroke or fill to this color.

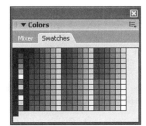

FIGURE 21.7
The Swatches panel shows your palette of selected colors.

The Swatches panel's Options menu also has tools to let you add, replace, save, and clear swatches in the palette. Swatches are saved in color table or ACT files. To save a palette, open the Swatches panel's Options menu by clicking the icon in the upper-right of the panel. Select Save Swatches, name the file, and select a folder on your hard disk in which to save it. To add colors, select Add Swatches and select an ACT file from your hard disk. Use Clear Swatches to clear all the swatches from the palette. Replace Swatches clears the current swatches and then adds new swatches from a color table file you select.

Drawing and Painting

The tools you'll use most often when drawing and painting in bitmap mode are the pencil, brush, and eraser. The paint bucket is also very useful, and it is discussed along with the color selection tools in Chapter 22, "Editing Bitmap Graphics." The pencil is used mostly for editing at the pixel level and for creating fine outlines for masks. The Brush tool is really a set of brushes; it can mimic an airbrush, watercolors, oils, acrylics—you name it. The Brush tool is used for creative bitmap work and retouching. The eraser removes color information from pixels, and the paint bucket fills an area of similarly colored pixels.

The most useful tool when working with bitmaps is undo. Undo has the power to immediately erase your mistakes and return your work to wherever you started. You can undo a drawing step by selecting Undo from the Edit menu or by pressing Ctrl+Z (Windows) or Command-Z (Macintosh). Fireworks saves multiple levels of undo in the History panel, allowing you to go back any number of steps to correct any mistakes.

Did you Know?

The settings and options for each tool are available in the Properties Inspector when the tool is selected. Before you start working, though, let's examine each tool's properties.

Pencil

The Pencil tool has only one stroke style—single pixel. To draw with the Pencil tool, select the tool and click an area of the Canvas (if a bitmap object has not been created on the active layer, a new one is created when the pencil or brush is used). Holding down the mouse button, drag the cursor over an area of the Canvas. Only the pixels directly underneath the cursor are changed to the pencil color (the default is black). Release the mouse button to stop drawing.

> To draw a straight line with the Pencil, hold down the Shift key while clicking and dragging vertically, horizontally, or diagonally. The Shift key constrains the mouse to 45° angles.

The properties for the Pencil tool include the stroke color (which is the same as the stroke color setting on the Tools or Mixer panel) and Anti-Aliased, Auto-erase, Preserve Transparency, Opacity, and Blending Mode settings. The Anti-Aliased option adds shaded pixels to curves and lines to make them look smoother. Auto-erase means that, if you click an existing pixel of the stroke color with the Pencil tool, it is erased instead of remaining unchanged. Preserve Transparency prevents you from editing areas of pixels that are transparent; you are allowed to draw over only existing pixels. Opacity is the transparency setting for the pencil stroke, and the Blending mode can change the interaction between the color being changed and the color being applied. The next section, about the Brush tool, explains blending modes.

Brush

The Brush tool is one of the most versatile tools in Fireworks. You can create any number of images and effects using the brush, from standard 1-pixel lines to air-brush and watercolor effects. To draw with the brush, simply select the brush, select the appropriate settings, and then click-drag a bitmap object (if no bitmap object exists on the active layer, one is created for you). Release the mouse button to finish your brush stroke. To restrict your brush to straight lines at 45° angles, hold down the Shift key while clicking and dragging.

> Another useful tool for drawing and painting, in any mode, is a tablet and stylus. You'll find that simple drawing tasks, such as signing your name, are almost impossible with a mouse, trackball, or touch pad. Small, inexpensive stylus tablets are available from Wacom and other manufacturers for both Macintosh and Windows machines with USB or serial adapters.

Several settings are available for the Brush tool. They are available in the Properties Inspector when the Brush tool is selected, as shown in Figure 21.8. The first row of options includes stroke color, stroke weight, and stroke style. Set the stroke color by clicking the swatch and selecting a color from the pop-up swatch palette (you can also set the stroke color in the Tools panel or Mixer panel). The stroke weight is the width or diameter, in pixels, of a square or round brush, respectively. A number of stroke style groups are available, including Pencil, Basic, Air Brush, Calligraphy, Charcoal, Crayon, Felt Tip, Oil, Random, Watercolor, and Unnatural. The Stroke Options setting lets you specify advanced stroke settings and save custom strokes to the stroke style menu.

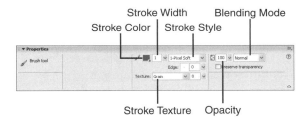

FIGURE 21.8
The Properties Inspector lets you fine-tune your tools, such as the Brush tool.

The next row lets you change some of the basic stroke style settings, including edge softness and texturing. Edge softness is the gradual feathering of the brush tip and is measured as a percentage from 0 to 100 of the total width of the brush tip. A value of 0 means the tip is uniformly colored; 100 means the tip begins to soften immediately from the center.

Textures can be applied to create all kinds of interesting effects. A texture can be created from any Fireworks PNG file by selecting Other from the Texture drop-down menu. A *texture* is a tiled image that fills any area covered by the brush. The mix of stroke color and texture is on a percentage scale, with 0 being no texture and 100 no color.

To the right of the brush stroke settings are the Opacity and Blending Mode settings. Opacity is the measurement of how opaque or transparent the stroke color or texture will appear. A value of 0 is transparent; 100 is opaque.

Blending modes are a powerful tool you can use with the brush as well as with other objects and layers. Blending modes change the way the applied blend color affects the base color to which it's applied. For instance, the Normal blend mode replaces the base color with the blend color, and the result is the blend color. The other blending modes are as follows:

▶ **Multiply**—Multiply adds the blend color to the base color, resulting in a darker combination of the two.

▶ **Screen**—Screen inverts the blend color before adding it to the base color, lightening the base color.

▶ **Darken**—Darken compares the blend color to the base color and chooses the darker of the two as the result.

▶ **Lighten**—Lighten is similar to Darken, but the result is the lighter of the base color or blend color.

▶ **Difference**—Difference subtracts the lighter color from the darker color. If the blend color is lighter than the base color, the blend color is subtracted from the base color.

▶ **Hue**—Hue changes the hue of the base color to the hue of the blend color, but saturation and brightness are not changed.

▶ **Saturation**—Saturation changes the saturation of the base color to the saturation of the blend color, but hue and brightness are not changed.

▶ **Color**—Color changes the base color hue and saturation to that of the blend color but does not change the brightness.

▶ **Luminosity**—Luminosity changes the brightness of the base color to that of the blend color but does not affect hue or saturation.

▶ **Invert**—Invert inverts the base color (like a color negative), regardless of the blend color.

▶ **Tint**—Tint adds neutral gray to the base color.

▶ **Erase**—Erase removes all color information from the base color.

Eraser

The Eraser tool is pretty straightforward: It removes pixels from a bitmap object. With the Eraser tool selected, you can change its settings in the Properties Inspector. These include Size, in pixels; Edge Softness, a percentage of size; Shape, either round or square; and Transparency, where the eraser transparency is inverted—100 means the eraser makes pixels completely transparent, and 0 means the eraser does not change the pixels. To draw with the eraser, click-drag an area of a bitmap object. Holding down Shift forces the cursor to travel in a straight line.

Summary

So far, you've explored the tip of the iceberg. You should be familiar with how bitmaps are stored and displayed as a grid of colored pixels, with the difference between destructive and nondestructive bitmap editing, and with using the bitmap drawing and painting tools. In the next chapter, you learn how the bitmap selection tools chop up existing graphics, which you can then start to change and rearrange.

CHAPTER 22

Editing Bitmap Graphics

In the previous chapter, "Working with Bitmap Images," you learned how to create bitmap objects and work with colors, layers, and the drawing and painting tools. This chapter focuses on editing existing images. With Fireworks, you can do all sorts of interesting things to photos and graphics that you can't do in the darkroom or on the drafting table.

Area Selection Tools

One of the keys to successful graphic design is the ability to focus on critical visual details. One of most common ways to cut down on visual clutter is to remove or sublimate the unimportant parts of an image. The area selection tools select an area of pixels in a bitmap to be cut or copied and also help define areas on the image that you want to edit while preventing other areas from being changed.

First, you need to learn about some of the critical tools and their options; then you can start using them on some real photos. These tools include the Pointer and Crop tools in the Select group and the Marquee, Lasso, and Magic Wand tools in the Bitmap group on the Tools panel, shown in Figure 22.1.

Pointer Tool

You'll be using the pointer much of the time, whether you are editing bitmaps, vectors, or slices. The pointer selects objects on the Canvas. The pointer does not have any settings in the Properties Inspector; instead, you use the pointer to select an object to bring up the object's settings in the Properties Inspector.

To select an object with the pointer, click the object in the Canvas. It becomes highlighted, as in Figure 22.2. The pointer selects an object only if it is arranged on an active layer and is visible. If the object you want to select is arranged behind a selectable object, you can use the Select Behind tool (press V or 0 to toggle between the Pointer and Select Behind tools). In the case of bitmaps with transparent areas, the pointer does not select a bitmap object if you click an area with no pixels. You must select a colored area to select the object.

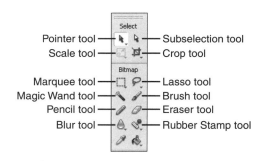

When the Pointer tool is selected, you can browse the objects on the Canvas by mousing over them. When the mouse is over a selectable object, the object is highlighted in red (default). Click to select an object when it is highlighted. The box changes to blue (default). The object is now selected, and its properties come up in the Properties Inspector.

When an object is selected with the Pointer tool, you can move the object by click-dragging the image to where you want it. You can also use the arrow keys on the keyboard to move the image one pixel at a time (left, right, up, or down). You also can position the object precisely by changing the X and Y position values in the Properties Inspector (below the object thumbnail). The values are relative to the upper-left corner of the canvas (0,0). Check out the change in properties from Figure 22.2 to Figure 22.3.

FIGURE 22.3
Width, height, and position can be changed numerically in the Properties Inspector.

You can also quickly resize and resample a bitmap by clicking and dragging the blue boxes at the corners. Holding down Shift while dragging forces the width and height attributes to change in proportion. This can also be done by changing the W and H dimension values in the Properties Inspector. Resizing is discussed in more detail later in this chapter in the section on transforming bitmaps.

Crop Tool

The Crop tool is useful for quickly editing images and the Canvas simultaneously. With the Crop tool, you click-drag to create a square area on the Canvas that you want to preserve, as in Figure 22.4. You can change the crop area by clicking the square handles at the corners and on the sides. You can also type the crop area width, height, and X,Y position in the Properties Inspector when the Crop tool is selected.

When you're done selecting your crop area, you can double-click within the crop area or select Crop Document from the Edit menu. The canvas is resized to the size of the crop area, removing all of the image that falls outside the selected area, as in Figure 22.5.

You can also select a bitmap object with the Pointer tool and then select Crop Selected Bitmap to set the crop area to the position and dimensions of the selected bitmap object.

Did you Know?

FIGURE 22.4
The crop bounding box can be adjusted with the handles on the sides and at the corners.

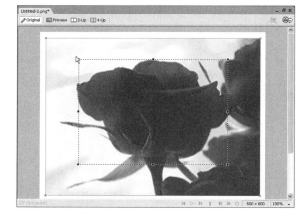

FIGURE 22.5
The image and Canvas have now been cropped to the same size.

Pressing C cycles between the Crop tool and the Export Area tool. With the Export Area tool, you choose an area of the Canvas the same way as you would with the Crop tool. Double-click within the area to bring up the Export Preview dialog box so you can quickly output the area as a graphics file.

Marquee Tools

The Marquee and Oval Marquee tools select rectangular and elliptical areas of pixels, respectively, in a bitmap object. You can toggle between them by pressing M. With the Marquee or Oval Marquee tool selected, click-drag to draw a rectangle or an ellipse over a bitmap object on the Canvas. Holding down Shift while dragging forces the marquee proportions to be equal, creating a square or circular selection, as in Figure 22.6.

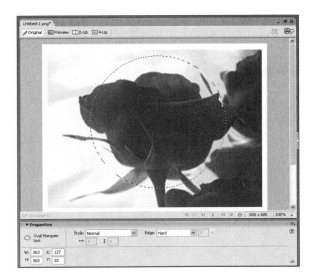

If you want to change the dimensions or position of a marquee, you can edit the width, height, and X and Y position values in the Properties Inspector. If you want to specify an aspect ratio or a fixed size for your selection before you draw it, set the marquee Style setting in the Properties Inspector to Fixed Ratio or Fixed Size; then set the desired width and height ratio or size in the fields below. Click-drag to create an area with a fixed ratio. If Fixed Size is selected, simply click the upper-left corner of the area you want to select—the marquee appears in that position at the specified dimensions.

A marquee selection edge can be set as Hard, Anti-aliased, or Feathered. Examples are shown in Figure 22.7. A hard edge means that pixels within the selection are selected and pixels beyond the selection are disregarded, with no gradation. Antialiasing creates a softer edge by creating a faint softness around the selection, especially in curved sections. Antialiased pixels contain gradual alpha values around the selection. To increase this gradual transition around the selection, select Feather and specify an amount in pixels. Setting Feather to 10 creates a 10-pixel transition around the selection, with pixels toward the outside gradually tending toward transparency.

Lasso Tools

The Lasso and Polygon Lasso tools are more flexible versions of the basic marquee tools and can be toggled using the L key. With the Lasso tool, you click-drag to draw a line around the pixels you want selected, as in Figure 22.8. With the

Polygon Lasso tool, you click points to define corners of a polygon; straight lines are created between the points. When you return to the point where you started, a small box appears with the lasso cursor to let you know you are about to close the shape and create the selection.

FIGURE 22.7
To the right of the original (shown with marquee) is a copy of the pixels within the marquee with the edge set to hard. Below the original is the antialiased version. To the left of that is a copy with the edge set to a 10-pixel feather.

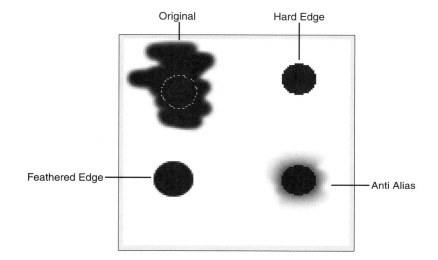

FIGURE 22.8
The lasso lets you create a freeform marquee around a group of pixels.

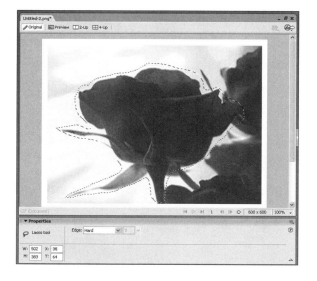

After you've created a lasso or polygon lasso selection, you can change the dimensions or position of the selected pixels on the Properties Inspector. This turns the selection into a new bitmap object with the specified width, height, and X and Y position values. To change the edge of the selection, select Hard, Anti-alias, or Feather to harden or soften the edges of the marquee.

Magic Wand Tool

The Magic Wand tool is as powerful as it sounds. Clicking a portion of a bitmap object with the Magic Wand tool selects a contiguous area of similarly colored pixels. This is often used to select large fields of color for removal from backgrounds (to restore transparency to a JPEG image, for example) or for selecting natural shapes in an image. A Magic Wand selection was made in Figure 22.9 by clicking one of the original colored pixels—that is, one that has not been affected by applying any feathering.

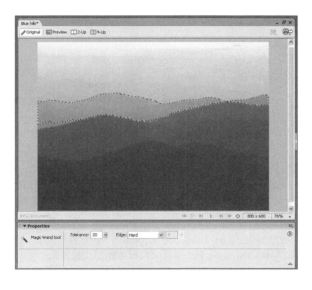

FIGURE 22.9
The Magic Wand with the tolerance set to 20 affects only pixels of a very similar color.

The settings for the Magic Wand include Tolerance and Edge softness. Tolerance is a measurement of just how similar colors need to be in order to be included in the selection. A value of 0 means that only pixels of the same color as the originally selected pixel will be selected. A value of 255 means the pixels can be of a different hue or shade and will still be selected.

When an area of pixels is selected, you can add to that area by holding down Shift and starting your additional selection on an unselected portion of the object. To remove an area of a selection, hold down Alt (Windows) or Option (Macintosh) and choose an already selected portion of the object. This works with any of the selection tools in the Bitmap group on the Tools panel.

Paint Bucket Tool

The paint bucket is kind of like a combination of the Brush and Magic Wand tools. The paint bucket either fills an area of pixels based on their similarity to the pixel you click or fills an area defined by a marquee selection. First, you should learn the Properties Inspector settings for the Paint Bucket tool, which are shown in Figure 22.10.

FIGURE 22.10
The paint bucket fills areas of pixels with colors or patterns.

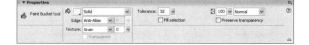

The settings are as follows:

- **Fill Color**—A solid fill color can be chosen from the pop-up swatch menu. If a Web dither, pattern, or gradient fill style is chosen, the Fill Color box displays the appropriate pop-up menu.

- **Fill Style**—This setting lets you choose between the different fill options. These include None, or transparent; Solid, which fills the area with a solid color; Web Dither, which uses up to four colors to create a dithered pattern; and Pattern, which tiles an existing PNG image as the fill. Below these are the various gradient fills.

- **Edge**—This setting is similar to the selection edge settings, allowing you to choose Hard, Anti-alias, or Feather, except that the setting applies to the edges of the filled area.

- **Texture**—This enables you to add a texture to the fill style. Clicking Transparent turns the texture into an alpha mask so the texture won't influence the color of the fill.

- **Tolerance**—Similar to the tolerance setting for the Magic Wand, the paint bucket tolerance setting enables you to specify how broad the definition of similarity to the selected pixel will be. A value of 0 means only pixels the same color as the original will be changed; a value of 100 means any pixel of a generally similar color will be changed.

▶ **Fill Selection**—Fill Selection overrides the tolerance setting, filling any pixel within an existing marquee selection.

▶ **Transparency**—This can be used to set the opacity of the fill. A setting of 0 means no pixels will be changed, whereas a setting of 100 means none of the original color will be visible through the fill.

▶ **Blending Mode**—These settings for the Paint Bucket tool are the same as the layer and object blending modes. These change how the fill color (blend color) interacts with the original colors (base color).

▶ **Preserve Transparency**—By checking the Preserve Transparency setting, the fill will not affect areas of the bitmap that are fully transparent—only pixels with existing color information will be saved.

Drawing and Painting with Selections

One of the important aspects of bitmap selections is how they affect the drawing and painting tools. When an area of a bitmap is selected, the Pencil, Brush, and Eraser tools affect only the selected area; areas outside the selection are not affected. If the marquee is feathered, the feathering also affects the drawing tool.

To work on the area that isn't selected, you can deselect the current selection. Otherwise, choose Select Inverse from the Select menu to select the pixels outside the current selection and deselect the current area.

Selection Options

In addition, several important selection options are available from the Select menu. Most are available only when an area of a bitmap object is selected. Superselect and Subselect are for working with groups of objects and are discussed in the next few chapters. The options are as follows:

▶ **Select All**—Select All can be used with the Pointer or Marquee tool. When the Pointer tool is chosen, Select All selects all the objects on active layers. To select all the pixels in a bitmap object, double-click the object with the Pointer tool to switch to the Marquee tool and choose Select All. You can press Ctrl+A (Windows) or Command-A (Macintosh) for Select All.

▶ **Deselect**—Deselect clears any object or marquee selections. Press Ctrl+D (Windows) or Command-D (Macintosh) to deselect any objects or pixels. This does not change the content of the selection in any way.

▶ **Select Similar**—Select Similar is like the Magic Wand tool but averages the chosen color from the current selection and then adds all similar colors in the object to the selection.

▶ **Select Inverse**—Select Inverse is an important tool. It selects all the pixels in the bitmap object that aren't selected and deselects the pixels in the current selection. For Select Inverse, press Ctrl+Shift+I (Windows) or Command-Shift-I (Macintosh).

▶ **Feather**—Feather changes the feathering around an existing marquee. After selecting Feather from the Select menu, you are prompted for a value in pixels, which determines the amount of feathering around the selection.

▶ **Expand Marquee**—Expand Marquee expands the area of the selection by the specified number of pixels.

▶ **Contract Marquee**—The inverse of Expand Marquee, this contracts the selection area by the specified number of pixels.

▶ **Border Marquee**—Border Marquee changes the selection into a new selection that borders on the original selection. The width of the border is specified in pixels.

▶ **Smooth Marquee**—Smooth Marquee removes any jagged edges from the shape of the selection by resampling the marquee. Smoothing a marquee eliminates excess pixels along the edges of a pixel selection. This is most useful if excess pixels appear along the border of a pixel selection when you have used the Magic Wand tool.

▶ **Save Selection**—Save Selection saves the current marquee selection with the bitmap object so you can come back to it later.

▶ **Restore Selection**—Restore Selection restores the selection saved with a bitmap object.

How to Filter Pixel Selections

Another important way to use selections is as a guide for applying filters from the Filters menu. Filters change the values of the pixels within the selection, based on the type of filter and the settings you specify. Filters can do all sorts of things, such as changing the colors, changing the focus, and creating interesting effects. Filters can also be applied as effects to bitmap objects, as is discussed later in this chapter. Filters are destructive because they change the original pixels. Effects are not, however, because they are rendered temporarily, preserving the original data.

To apply a filter to the pixels in a marquee or an object, simply select the filter from the Filters menu. A filter with additional settings has its name followed by an ellipsis. After a filter has been applied, the only way to recover the original data is to use Undo from the Edit menu or to replace the altered image with a copy of the original.

Adjusting Color

The color adjustment filters improve or change colors in an image or a selection. These are covered in more detail in the next chapter, "Working with Photos." They are as follows:

▶ **Auto Levels**—Auto Levels analyzes the data in the image and makes mathematical assumptions about the exposure to improve the image. This is not always effective.

▶ **Brightness/Contrast**—This quickly adjusts the brightness and contrast of the selected pixels.

▶ **Curves**—Curves gives you ultimate control over image exposure and color by allowing you to finely adjust the values of individual channels.

▶ **Hue/Saturation**—Hue and Saturation are used to adjust the color values for all the selected pixels and are used for correction and creative effects.

▶ **Invert**—Invert changes all the colors to their opposites, creating a negative image.

▶ **Levels**—Levels provides a histogram display of color values in the image and provides tools to quickly adjust the relative levels of channels in an image.

Blur

The blur filters act by blurring detail and high contrast in an image or a selection, giving an out-of-focus look. Blur and Blur More are actually just presets of the Gaussian Blur filter. These are as follows:

▶ **Blur**—Blur adjusts the colors of pixels to merge with the colors of the adjacent pixels, making the image softer. This filter is often used to sublimate high-contrast areas, such as dust, scratches, and creases, or as a focus effect.

▶ **Blur More**—Blur More blurs the image about three times as much as Blur does.

▶ **Gaussian Blur**—Gaussian Blur lets you change the radius of pixels that the evening of values affects, enabling you to control the amount of blur.

- ▶ **Motion Blur**—Motion Blur enables you to enter a distance and a directional angle to make your image appear to be "moving" in that direction.

- ▶ **Radial Blur**—Radial Blur creates a rotational blur effect within your selection, as if it were spinning.

- ▶ **Zoom Blur**—Zoom Blur adds a "zooming" effect to the image, as if captured through a camera rapidly zooming in .

Other

The filters in this group are special tools for using bitmaps as creative elements:

- ▶ **Convert to Alpha**—This filter converts the bitmap into a grayscale alpha map. Lighter areas are made more transparent; darker areas are made opaque black . This effect is often used to create a mask for another bitmap object.

- ▶ **Find Edges**—This filter creates an image in which solid areas are black and areas with high contrast, such as lines, are light, creating an effect similar to a pencil sketch. This can be useful when tracing a bitmap for use as a vector graphic.

Noise

The Noise filter adds random noise to the image. This can be used to help blend two dissimilar images or for artistic effect, such as creating television "fuzz."

Sharpen

These filters improve detail and focus in a blurry image and improve images after they've been resampled. Sharpen and Sharpen More are actually just presets of the Unsharp Mask filter:

- ▶ **Sharpen**—Sharpen is the opposite of Blur. It increases contrast between adjacent pixels, lending an image the appearance of more crisp focus.

- ▶ **Sharpen More**—Sharpen More applies an increased level of sharpening, approximately three times as much as Sharpen.

- ▶ **Unsharp Mask**—The Unsharp Mask filter is commonly used to increase the clarity of bitmaps used in print and on the Web because the digitization and output processes are very different from the original photographic processes. Unsharp Mask gives you very fine control over how the contrast between pixels interacts.

Eye Candy 4000 LE

These third-party filters are included for free with Fireworks as examples of additional filters you can purchase and add to Fireworks:

▶ **Bevel Boss**—This filter bevels the edges of an image as though they were cut with a router. You can adjust the bevel smoothness, lighting, width, and depth.

▶ **Marble**—Instead of working with your image, Marble replaces it as a type of fill. You can adjust the style of marbling in the dialog box.

▶ **Motion Trail**—This filter is useful when working with action images that seem frozen by a flash or high shutter speed and to suggest motion with limited frames in GIF animations. You can adjust the direction, length, taper, opacity, and color blending of the effect.

Alien Skin Splat LE

Alien Skin is another company that makes filter plug-ins for Fireworks and other applications. It has the following filter:

▶ **Edges**—The Edges filter adds interesting randomized borders to your selection. You can make the image look like a piece of torn paper or add a retro print look with graduated halftone dots.

> Fireworks accepts any third-party plug-in filters that are compatible with Adobe Photoshop 5.x, including those that came with Photoshop. To use these filters, copy them into the `Plug-Ins` folder in the Fireworks application folder.

By the Way

Selections and the Edit Menu

Now you know how to use selections to designate areas of an image for editing, but you can also use the selection with the Edit commands to repeat or delete pixels selected in a bitmap object:

▶ **Cut**—Cut removes the pixels in the selected area and copies them to the clipboard so you can paste them elsewhere. Press Ctrl+ X (Windows) or Command-Shift-X (Macintosh) to cut the current selection.

▶ **Copy**—Copy adds the selected pixels to the clipboard so you can paste them elsewhere. Press Ctrl+C (Windows) or Command-Shift-C (Macintosh) to copy the current selection while leaving the original intact.

▶ **Paste**—This pastes the pixels on the clipboard onto the Canvas as selected pixels (if working with a selection tool) or as a new bitmap object (if no bitmap object is currently selected). Press Ctrl+V (Windows) or Command-Shift-V (Macintosh) to paste the contents of the clipboard.

▶ **Clear**—This clears all color information from the selected pixels, rendering them transparent. If all the pixels in a bitmap object are cleared, the bitmap object is also deleted. To clear the pixels in a selection press Backspace (Windows) or Delete (Macintosh).

Working with Bitmaps As Objects

Working with pixel selections is very useful, but changes to pixels in a bitmap are destructive changes: They destroy the original information in the bitmap. To mitigate this dilemma, you can work with bitmaps as objects, allowing you to manage multiple elements and compose on the Canvas quickly and easily. Only when changes are made to the object's actual pixels is data destroyed.

To select a bitmap object, use the pointer to click the object on the Canvas or select it from the Layers panel (expand the layer to reveal objects on that layer). To create a new bitmap object from an existing one, select Duplicate or Clone from the Edit menu. Duplicate puts the new copy below and to the right of the original, whereas Clone creates the new copy in the same location. To create a bitmap object from a marquee selection, select Copy and Paste from the Edit menu. The contents appear within a new marquee in the same location as the original pixels.

Did you Know?

An easy way to make sure you always have an original copy of a bitmap object handy is to import the object to a backup layer and then paste a copy of the object onto the layer where you would like to work with it. Keep the backup layer locked and hidden, as in Figure 22.11. This way you always have an unaltered copy handy without having to reimport any graphics.

Transforming Bitmap Objects

You can transform a bitmap object with the Scale, Skew, and Distort tools, available on the Tools panel. You can also transform objects via the Transform commands in the Modify menu. Transformations to bitmap objects are destructive, so keep another copy handy.

FIGURE 22.11
A locked and hidden layer is a great place to keep copies of all your original bitmap objects.

Free Transform

Free Transform is not really a tool but rather a set of tools that enable you to transform objects freely with the mouse by eye. Press Q to cycle through the Free Transform tools, Scale, Skew, and Distort. For numeric information while using a Free Transform tool, make sure the Info panel is visible. The Info panel, which can be located via the Window menu, lets you know how far you've moved a handle or the angle of rotation, as well as the new dimensions of the image. The Free Transform mode and Info panel are shown in Figure 22.12.

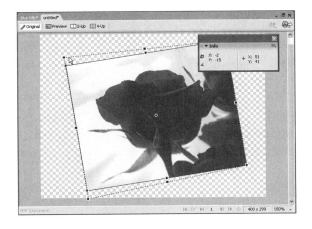

FIGURE 22.12
You can use the Free Transform tools to alter a bitmap object quickly. The Info panel provides real-time feedback on the size and angle of the transformed object.

Scale

When you are transforming the selected objects, a black box surrounds the objects. At each corner and on the sides of the black box are square handles. Click-drag a corner to adjust the scale of the object proportionally, and click a side to change either the width or height of the object.

Did you Know? You can transform multiple objects by using Shift+click with the Pointer tool and then selecting a Free Transform tool.

To move the image, click-drag within the bounding box. To rotate the object, click outside the box and drag the mouse around through the desired angle of rotation. To change the point around which the image rotates, click the circle in the center of the bounding box and drag it to where you want the new anchor point to be (it can be outside the bounding box, if necessary). Selecting Undo from the Edit menu removes any transformations and restores the original object. Double-clicking with the cursor applies your changes to the object.

Skew

The Skew tool enables you to change the relative angles of the bounding box to create perspective effects. Grabbing a handle on one of the sides moves that side parallel to the opposite side, changing the bounding box and the proportions of its contents from a rectangle to a parallelogram. Grabbing a handle on one of the corners moves each corner on that side an equal distance from the center, changing the bounding box into a trapezoid. You can also move and rotate the object as you would with the Scale tool.

Distort

The Distort tool lets you more fluidly change any aspect of the bounding box's angles or size. Clicking a handle on the side of the bounding box anchors the angle of the selected side and the opposite side; clicking a handle on the corner anchors the segments joining at the opposite corner. You can also move and rotate the object as you would with the Scale and Skew tools.

Numeric Transform

When you select Numeric Transform from the Transform commands in the Modify menu—or by pressing Ctrl+Shift+T (Windows) or Command-Shift-T

(Macintosh)—you are presented with a dialog box. At the top of the dialog box is a drop-down menu where you can select Scale, Resize, or Rotate. Scale changes the dimensions by percentage, Resize lets you specify a new size in pixels, and Rotate lets you specify an angle of rotation down to 1/10°. Selecting Scale Attributes applies to vector objects (it scales or rotates the fill, stroke, and effects, such as feathering, along with the path). Selecting Constrain Proportions maintains the original ratio between width and height.

Applying Effects to Bitmap Objects

You can add effects to bitmap objects with the Properties Inspector. Effects are available when an object is selected, as in Figure 22.13, and are nondestructive: After you've added an effect, you can remove it or change the settings, and the effect is recomputed from the original bitmap object data. You can add as many effects as you like in a specific order, which determines how they'll work together to create the final result. Effects also can be applied to vector objects, expanding the possibilities for working with vector art.

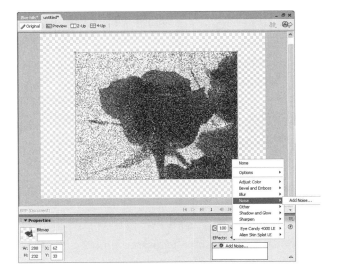

FIGURE 22.13
The Effects settings are available on the right side of the Properties Inspector when an object is selected with the Pointer tool.

The Effects menu includes all the filters in the Filters menu. Some effects aren't available as filters because they work only with object selections.

Options

These are some of the general effects options:

- ▶ **Save As Style**—This option saves all the current effects as a style in the Styles panel (part of the Assets Panel group). This enables you to apply all the same effect settings to other objects by selecting them and choosing the style from the Styles panel.

- ▶ **All On/Off**—This option toggles all the effects on or off simultaneously.

- ▶ **Locate Plug-ins**—With this option, you can browse your hard drive for third-party filter plug-ins.

Bevel and Emboss

Bevel and Emboss create a simple 3D effect around an object. Settings for each include width, in pixels; depth, a percentage; edge softness, on a scale of 1–10; and lighting angle, in degrees:

- ▶ **Inner Bevel**—This insets the bevel within the current bounds of an object. Options include the style of bevel curve (Flat, Smooth, Sloped, Frame 1 or 2, Ring, or Ruffle) and depth (Raised, Highlighted, Inset, or Inverted).

- ▶ **Inset Emboss**—This makes an object look as though it were stamped on a sheet of paper by adding shadows outside the bounds of the object. You can choose to turn the original image on or off.

- ▶ **Outer Bevel**—This is similar to Inner Bevel but adds the beveling outside the bounds of the image.

- ▶ **Raised Emboss**—This is similar to Inset Emboss but makes the object appear stamped from behind.

Shadow and Glow

Shadow and Glow add simple lighting effects to an object:

- ▶ **Drop Shadow**—This adds a shadow around an image as though it were floating above the canvas. Settings include Offset, or distance from the image bounds, in pixels; Opacity, a percentage; Color, from the pop-up swatch palette; Edge Softness from 0 to 30; Lighting Angle, in degrees; and a check box to let you knock out the original image.

- ▶ **Glow**—Glow adds a glow effect around the object. Settings include Width, in pixels; Opacity, a percentage; Color, from the pop-up swatch palette; Edge Softness from 0 to 30; and Offset, which creates a border between the image and glow border.

▶ **Inner Glow**—This is similar to Glow but insets the glow within the bounds of the object.

▶ **Inner Shadow**—This effect is similar to Drop Shadow but insets the shadow within the bounds of the object.

To apply an effect, simply select an object with the Pointer tool. In the Properties Inspector, click the plus sign icon next to Effects to bring up the menu of available effects. Select an effect and specify any settings in the dialog box (Effects that have additional settings are followed by an ellipsis). When an effect is applied, it appears in the list of effects below. Clicking the check mark next to the effect turns it off; clicking the red X turns it on. Double-click the effect name to change the settings, or click it and then click the minus symbol to remove it. Click-drag an effect up or down to change the order in which the effects are applied.

Summary

Now you should be comfortable editing bitmaps, at both the pixel and the object levels. A lot of bitmap editing is destructive, so care must be taken to preserve copies of original images. Use objects to separate individual bitmap elements and editing decisions and create copies of your layers before merging or flattening them.

The previous chapter and this one have focused on explaining the tools and how you can work with them, with tasks oriented toward understanding basic concepts. In the next chapter you'll look at how these techniques and others can be applied to a common type of bitmap image: a photograph.

CHAPTER 23

Working with Photos

Now that you're comfortable with the most common bitmap creation and editing tools, you will learn some techniques used by professionals when working with bitmap images. Remember that a bitmap image is a lot like a traditional photographic print. Many of the techniques that were used in the darkroom can now be done with Fireworks. These include color and contrast correction, correcting the exposure and detail in particular areas of the image, touching up dust and scratches, and getting creative with multiple exposures or interesting effects.

Color and Contrast Correction with Fireworks

Just because an image is digital does not mean it is well exposed or color accurate. If an image was taken with a digital camera, it almost certainly needs some sort of correction. If the image originated on photographic film, there are even more steps in the process that could affect the eventual color balance and contrast: the time, temperature, and chemicals used to develop the film; the exposure and development of the print; and the settings used when the film or print was scanned.

Cameras and scanners make predictable decisions about how an image should be exposed, but that doesn't mean they are always the correct ones. When shooting a subject that is backlit, the camera averages the very light areas with the very dark areas to determine the appropriate shutter speed and aperture. This means the dark areas are underexposed and the light areas are overexposed because the average is somewhere in the middle. The same goes for developing film; much of the process is done by a machine that uses similar methods to determine how an image should be developed and printed.

Of course, it is best to work with images that have already been color-corrected in the photographic or scanning process. With digital cameras, the image will not have gone through either process and thus will probably need to be color-corrected with graphics software, such as Fireworks. When scanning images, it is best to do as much color correction as possible with the scanner itself using the scanner's software. This is because the color correction is applied by the hardware while the image is being scanned, as opposed to being applied by filtering the digital data with software.

When working with color correction in Fireworks, it's important to remember that filters change the underlying bitmap data, whereas effects are rendered temporarily and can be removed or changed at any time. If you want to correct a portion of an object that has been selected with a marquee, you must use filters. Keep an unfiltered copy on a locked and hidden layer so you can refer to it to reapply the changes (you can also use the Save Selection command from the Select menu to save the marquee before filtering, so you can restore it later). Effects apply only to objects; they do not affect the original data, saving you the trouble of having to keep a backup. Effect settings and groups can also be saved as styles so they can be applied to several images, such as an entire roll of film that needs the same type of correction (for instance, daylight film shot indoors).

Evaluating Exposures

The same exposure rules apply whether an image is in color or in black and white. A well-exposed image contains a full range of tones, with detail—shadows and highlights—present at both extremes of the scale. The same holds true for digital images. If an image is overexposed, details are lost in the highlights. If it is underexposed, no detail will exist in the shadows.

The same goes for focus. If an image is photographed out of focus, there is very little you can do about it. No graphics program can magically restore a bad photograph! Fireworks is very good at tweaking a good exposure until it's just right, and it's good at creating effects you just can't achieve with a camera or in a darkroom. What Fireworks can't do is go back and take a better picture for you.

Tones and the Zone System

The information that immediately follows might not be of interest to all of you. However, understanding terminology and the way exposure is determined will certainly be of long-term value if you work with photographs.

Ansel Adams systematized the language of exposure when he created the Zone system. The Zone system is composed of 11 graduated levels, starting with 0 (pure black) and ending with X (pure white). It is usually written with Roman numerals (see Figure 23.1). Zone 0 and Zone X contain no detail; they are meant to represent the boundaries of the potential tonal range. A well-exposed image typically ranges from Zone I to Zone IX, the maximum tonal range that can contain detail. Of course, a bride in a white dress seated in a white gazebo might not contain any shadows darker than Zone III or IV, and an image of a dark subject at night might not have any highlights brighter than Zone VI or VII.

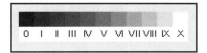

FIGURE 23.1
The Zone system breaks tones down into 11 regions from black to white.

The Zone system is used mainly when creating an exposure with a camera or an enlarger, but it can also be an important way to understand and describe any image with a full range of continuous tones. *Shadows* in an image range from Zone 0 to Zone III. *Midtones* are from Zones III to VII, and *highlights* are anything above Zone VII. The light meter or auto-exposure feature on a camera usually averages the entire frame and exposes it for Zone V, or medium gray. If the image is heavy with Zone III material, this overexposes the image, and details from Zones VIII and IX are pushed into Zone X. If it has more Zone VII material, the details in Zones II and III are lost. These same mistakes can be made when working with digital images; detail in shadows or highlights can be lost when a print is scanned or when the brightness is changed with filters or effects.

Understanding Contrast

Contrast in an image can also be described with the Zone system. An image that contains only Zone 0 and Zone X information is considered to have absolute contrast. This is used in lithography, where gradual tones are approximated with a dot screen or halftone. (The pages of this book are a good example; look at a screen shot graphic through a magnifying glass to see how a single black tone creates lighter gradations through lots of little dots of different sizes.) An image that contains information only between Zones IV and VI is considered very low contrast. There are no shadows or highlights in such an image. Everything is a muddy gray.

Contrast in an image is a lot like focus. It is easier to increase contrast than it is to reduce it without losing image information, just as it's easier to make a sharp image look blurry and out of focus than it is to make a blurry image look sharp and focused. Still, contrast can be increased, within limits. It's critical that the image contain a range of tones covering most of the Zone scale and that the image is not cut off at either end, which would indicate a loss of detail. You can accurately judge this by using the histogram that comes with the Levels effect.

Using Levels to Adjust the Brightness and Contrast of a Black-and-White Image

Open a black-and-white image in Fireworks. You could adjust the image with the Brightness/Contrast effect, but this method reduces total detail in an image. Making the image brighter moves the shadows toward middle gray, resulting in a loss of shadow detail. Making the image darker moves the highlights toward middle gray, which also reduces detail. With levels, though, you can adjust the shadow tones, midtones, and highlight tones without sacrificing details in the shadows or highlights. Here's how:

1. Select the bitmap object with the Pointer tool.

2. Click the Plus icon next to Effects on the Properties Inspector. Select Levels from the Adjust Color group. You are presented with the dialog box shown in Figure 23.2. The histogram is the bar graph in the middle of the dialog box. The x-axis represents the tonal range, from black on the left to white on the right. The y-axis represents the relative number of pixels present.

FIGURE 23.2
The Levels dialog box enables you to view the histogram, a great tool for evaluating the tonal quality of a digital image.

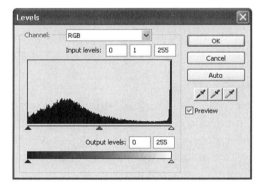

3. At the top is a drop-down menu that enables you to choose the channel you want to evaluate or adjust—Red, Green, Blue, or RGB (all three simultaneously). This image was photographed on color film and scanned as 24-bit color, but because the subject is black and white, the three colors come out pretty much the same (shades of gray or neutral tones are created by equal values of red, green, and blue). For this reason, you'll edit only the combined RGB values. For a full-color subject, you would edit each channel individually.

4. The sliders at the bottom represent the shadow boundary, midpoint, and highlight boundary. Click the black slider and move it to where the bar graph begins, or type **9** in the first Input Levels field. You know that no detail has been lost because no pixels exist below the shadow slider.

A histogram should be an unbroken mass of black that begins and ends between the two extremes of the x-axis. If the histogram is cut off at either end, you know detail has been lost in the shadows or highlights; there probably was information in those areas, but it has now been merged into Zone 0 or Zone X. If gaps exist in the histogram where no pixels are present for a given tone, details and tone continuity have been lost in the midtones. Gaps appear when an image has been compressed or filtered. Some gapping is okay, but heavy gapping means that posterization and noise are present and that a better original should be found.

Did you Know?

5. Now adjust the highlight slider either by clicking it and moving it to the end of the bar graph or by typing **233** in the last field to the left of Input Levels. This sets the brightest pixel in the image to white, just as the previous slider set the darkest pixel to black. No information has been lost because no pixels exist after this point on the graph.

6. Finally, adjust the midpoint slider, which is the gray slider between the shadow and highlight sliders. This adjusts the midpoint toward the shadows, providing more room for highlight detail and lightening some of the shadow detail.

7. You'll notice that the details become clearer and more noticeable because of the Levels adjustment, as in Figure 23.3, which shows both an original and the adjusted image.

FIGURE 23.3
By adjusting the contrast with the Levels effect, details have been brought out and the tonal accuracy across the image has been improved. The left image in this figure shows the newly adjusted photograph, with the original to the right of it.

Using Hue/Saturation and Color Fill

As an example, say that a blue color fringe was introduced in a photograph when you scanned it. You want it removed, and you want to add a nice sepia tone to the photograph to "antique" it. These tasks can be accomplished with additional color adjustments:

1. First, take all the color information out of the image to remove the blue cast and smudge. With the bitmap selected, choose the Hue/Saturation effect from the Adjust Color group.

2. With the Hue/Saturation dialog box open, drag the Saturation slider all the way to the left or type **-100** in the Saturation field, as in Figure 23.4.

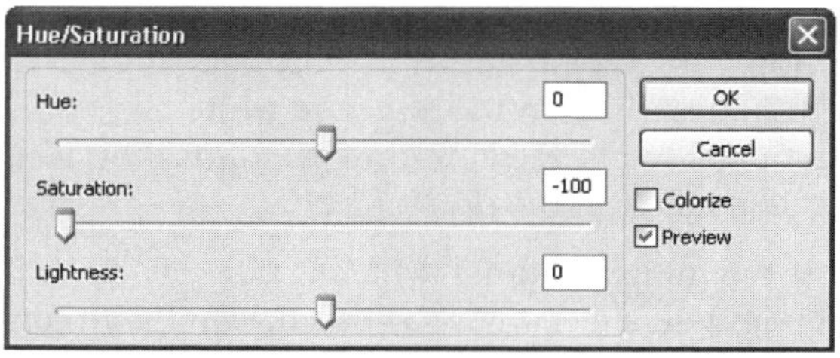

FIGURE 23.4
After the image is completely desaturated, it is converted into a grayscale, with only tone information and no color information.

3. Use the Color Fill effect in the Adjust Color group to add some color and flair to the image. You can give the black-and-white image a sepia tone effect. When you select the Color Fill effect, a small settings pane opens above the Properties Inspector, as in Figure 23.5.

4. Change the Blending mode to Color. Set the color to be blended to #FFCC99 by clicking the swatch and typing the hex code in the field at the top of the pop-up swatch panel. Change the opacity to 75% by typing in the field or using the slider.

FIGURE 23.5
The Color Fill effect enables you to fill an entire bitmap object with a color.

5. Now the image looks more like an antique. You can easily save this set of effects by selecting Save As Style from the Options group. You can apply this style by selecting an object and then selecting the custom style from the Style panel in the Assets panel group.

Color Correction Considerations

It's important to remember three things when adjusting the relative levels of color in an image: the color in the actual subject, how the color was captured, and how the color will be output. The color in the subject is determined by the color temperature of the light and the surface from which it is reflected into the lens of the camera. The capture color is determined by optics and film; color can be adjusted by a filter placed over the lens or a film coating designed to work with a specific color temperature (such as outdoor or daylight film). In the case of digital equipment, the captured color is determined by the camera's exposure settings, which affect how the CCDs behind the lens interpret colors reflected onto them. Finally, the colors are output to a subtractive medium, such as a printer, or to an additive medium, such as a television or computer monitor.

When you color-correct, you are usually trying to present an accurate representation of the original colors by changing how the capture colors are output. This can be very subjective, and in many cases you might not know what the actual colors in the subject were. It's also important that the output colors work with the other colors on the Web page, including those in other photographs. It might be more important to preserve a particular color balance throughout a number of photos than for each one to be corrected out of context with the others. If it looks good, do it.

Using Curves for Color Correction

The Curves effect is a powerful way to correct color imbalances in a photo. You'll use curves to ensure that the neutral tones are really neutral across the tonal range—in other words, that grays are really gray. For example, assume one of your images has a reddish cast. In that case, you would select the image, select the Adjust Color Curves effect, and then select the Red channel from the drop-down menu at the top of the dialog box, as shown in Figure 23.6.

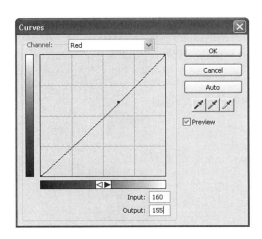

FIGURE 23.6
The Curves effect shows a graph with the input values on the y-axis and the output values on the x-axis.

Click to create a point, ensuring that it is near the middle of the line. Placing the point anywhere else results in strange and unwanted results. By adjusting this point, you can change how a pixel of the input value is output. Change the Input field at the bottom of the panel to 160; then change the Output field to 155. This means that pixels with a value of 150 Red are now changed to 145 Red. The curve means that input values higher and lower than the adjustment point are also adjusted toward the output value. Some red has been removed from the midtones.

Using the point you added to the curve, you can drag up and down to change the input and output values and, if the preview button is checked, view the results as you work. Click OK to add the effect.

Photo Retouching Techniques

Many tools can be used for fine photo retouching. *Retouching* is the process of editing out blemishes, such as dust, scratches, creases, light leaks, and any other small details that detract from the quality of the final image.

Taking Advantage of the Exposure and Focus Tools

Another way to correct an image's exposure and detail is with the Dodge, Burn, Blur, Sharpen, and Smudge tools. Located in the Tools panel, as shown in Figure 23.7, these tools are similar to the Brush tool except that instead of blending color in, they simply adjust the values of the pixels. Dodging and burning are done in the darkroom by using masks to reduce or increase the amount of light that hits the photosensitive emulsion on the paper. Blurring, smudging, and sharpening don't really have a darkroom equivalent; you can adjust the focus of the enlarger but only for the whole image, and when critical focus is reached, it certainly can't be exceeded (this holds true for digital images, as well). That's when the important part of your composition is sharp and has the correct degree of contrast.

FIGURE 23.7
Located in the Tools panel, the Exposure and Focus tools enable you to adjust the values of pixels in your image.

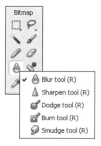

▶ **Dodge**—Dodge lightens the area under the cursor as you click-drag a bitmap object. This can be used to bring out details in the shadows or remove details from highlights. The Dodge tool settings in the Properties Inspector include Size, in pixels, from 1 to 100; Edge Softness, a percentage; Shape, either round or square; Range, which can include Shadows, Midtones, or Highlights; and Exposure, from 1 to 100. Exposure adjusts the intensity of the dodge.

▶ **Burn**—Burn is exactly the opposite of dodge; instead of lightening the area, it darkens the area. Burn and dodge change only the luminosity of the color, not its hue or saturation. The Burn tool options in the Properties Inspector are the same as those for the Dodge tool, except that Exposure adjusts the intensity of darkness.

Did you Know?

> While applying the Dodge or Burn tool effect, you can swap between dodge and burn quickly by pressing the Alt (or Option) key.

▶ **Blur**—The Blur tool is used to add blur to the any part of an image simply by clicking, instead of exclusively to an individual object or preselected area. Blur tool settings in the Properties Inspector include Size, in pixels, from 1 to 100; Edge Softness, a percentage; Shape, either round or square; and Intensity, or the level of blur to be applied. An intensity of 100 completely averages the values between two contiguous pixels, and an intensity of 1 slightly softens areas of high contrast.

▶ **Sharpen**—The Sharpen tool increases the contrast in a selected area, the opposite of the action performed by the Blur tool. Settings in the Properties Inspector are the same, except that the intensity setting applies to the level of contrast added instead of removed. A setting higher than 20 severely affects the quality of your image; sharpening should be applied lightly and carefully to prevent high-contrast noise from appearing.

Did you Know?

> You can use the marquee selection tools to constrain changes to an area of the bitmap. The Dodge and Burn tools will work only on pixels that are within the marquee. Feather the edge of the marquee to ensure that changes will blend more seamlessly into the image and that no unnaturally hard edges will be apparent.

Smudging, Cloning, and Sampling Pixels

Some Fireworks tools are obviously very powerful in design terms, but the value and applicability of others can initially be less obvious. The Smudging, Cloning, and Sampling Pixels options might well fall into this latter group:

▶ **Smudge**—The Smudge tool is in the same group as the Burn, Dodge, Blur, and Sharpen tools, but it doesn't really fit in. The Smudge tool acts like a finger in wet paint; colors are mixed under the tool and moved or wiped in the direction of the tool's movement. Smudge settings include the Size of the smudge area, in pixels, from 1 to 100; the Edge Softness, a percentage; Shape, either round or square; Use Entire Document, which works with all colors on all visible and active layers if checked and with only the active bitmap object if unchecked; Smudge Color, which applies the selected color to the beginning of the smudge; and Pressure, which determines the depth of the smudge. Low pressure barely blends and moves the colors, and high pressure completely blends the colors. Colors persist throughout the smudge stroke.

▶ **Rubber Stamp**—The Rubber Stamp tool is one of the most powerful tools in the Bitmap group on the Tools panel, and it is often used to retouch blemishes in a photograph by copying an unblemished area of the image over the blemished area. With the Rubber Stamp tool, you first click to select the area of pixels you want to use as the source, and then you select the destination for those pixels. If you click and drag, pixels are rubber-stamped relative to the original relationship between the source and destination cursors. To choose a new relationship, Alt+click (Windows) or Option+click (Macintosh) to reset the source pixels.

Options available for the Rubber Stamp tool on the Properties Inspector include Size, in pixels, from 1 to 100; Edge Softness, a percentage; Source Aligned, which if checked maintains the relationship between source and destination cursors, and if unchecked keeps the source cursor at the original location regardless of where the destination is clicked; Use Entire Document, which if checked rubber-stamps data from any visible element on the Canvas, and if unchecked works with only the active element; Opacity, a percentage; and the Blending mode.

▶ **Replace Color**—The Replace Color tool enables you to choose a "change" color and a "to" color in the Properties Inspector. This paintbrush-like tool then recolors any portions of the image from the "change" color to the "to" color, such as turning green areas into red. You can set a tolerance and strength for the tool to control how exactly it matches the chosen colors and how it replaces them, as well as a size and shape for the replace color tool.

▶ **Red Eye Removal**—The Red Eye Removal tool enables a photographer to quickly remove dreaded "red eye" from a photograph. After clicking the tool, "paint" across the portions of the photograph that exhibit red eye effects. The red areas have the red color information removed. Similar to the Replace Color tool and others, you can set a tolerance and strength if you find the tool is not working well on your images.

▶ **Eyedropper**—The Eyedropper tool is another incredibly useful tool because it allows you to sample a color value from one or more pixels. To use the eyedropper, select it from the Tools panel, select the stroke or fill color setting, and then click an area of the Canvas. The stroke or fill color changes to that of the selected pixel. You can also choose to sample a 3×3-pixel or 5×5-pixel average in the Properties Inspector; this takes the average color from an area that big (9 or 25 pixels, respectively) centered on the selected pixel.

Masking Bitmap Objects with Grayscale Images

Another way to edit a bitmap's appearance is through masks, which can be added to bitmap objects in the Layers panel. A *mask* is another bitmap image that's used to selectively show and hide areas of the bitmap it's masking. To add a mask, select the bitmap object in the Layers panel and click the Add Mask button. A new thumbnail appears to the right of the original bitmap thumbnail. The bitmap object on the Canvas has a diamond in the center when selected to let you know it is masked. Double-click the diamond to edit only the mask, not the bitmap itself, or click the mask's thumbnail in the Layers panel. To remove a mask, select Delete Mask from the Options menu in the Layers panel. You can also select Disable Mask if you want to keep the mask but don't want it displayed.

When you create a new mask, you are automatically in Mask Editing mode. The stroke and fill swatches change to grayscale. Masks are made up of a grayscale image. Therefore, the darker the area, the more it is hidden and the lighter the area, the more it is shown. Black areas become transparent, whereas white areas are unchanged. You can edit masks with any of the bitmap tools, or you can use Paste As Mask in the Edit menu to paste a bitmap object as a mask to the selected object. If a mask exists, you are asked whether you want to replace the current mask or add the information to the current mask. Any color information is automatically changed to grayscale.

Masks can be created and used in a number of ways. They are a great way to draw an accurate outline to isolate a subject from a bitmap. When layered over a color, masks can be used to enhance exposures or create great color fill effects.

Use Invert to quickly reverse the masked parts and the visible parts. Use Brightness to quickly show more or less of the entire bitmap, or use Contrast to increase or decrease the variation in the mask's depth. You must apply the effects or filters to a bitmap before it is copied and pasted as a mask.

Using a Mask

As explained already, masks show or hide specific parts of an image. A mask through the colors of the pixels, either dark or transparent, covers some but not all of the underlying image. Do the following:

1. In Fireworks create a new document and set the background to be transparent; then add a photographic image to work with. Show the Layers panel, if it is not already visible.

2. At the bottom of the Layers panel, click the Add Mask button. The blank mask appears next to the bitmap in the panel, as shown in Figure 23.8.

FIGURE 23.8
Add a blank mask to the bitmap.

3. As soon as it is created, the mask becomes the selected item. When you draw over the mask, the mask changes and reveals the underlying background (or any image behind the photograph on the canvas).

4. Select the Brush tool from the Bitmap area of the Tools panel.

5. Now draw it onto the Canvas. In Figure 23.9, the Brush tool was simply applied to remove the center of the flower. Note that the background shows through clearly where the brush was applied.

Specifying Areas in an Image to Apply Selective JPEG Compression

A great way to improve the output of a compressed photograph is by employing selective JPEG compression. This enables you to select one or more areas of the image and apply either more or less compression than what is applied to the unselected areas. With a portrait of a seated subject, for example, you could select the hands, torso, and face for light compression. Then you could compress the background more heavily, preserving more subject detail for the same file size than if the compression were applied equally.

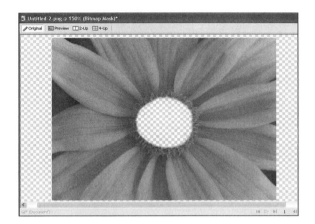

FIGURE 23.9
The background shows through the mask.

First, identify the area of an image that needs to retain maximum quality. You then choose the correct compression for different areas of the file, before selecting the most appropriate optimization settings in preparation for exporting. The area that is compressed separately, called a *selective JPEG*, can be as large as you want.

Next, you select areas that should be compressed less than other areas using the Lasso tool (maintaining a higher level of detail).

Select Settings from the Selective JPEG commands in the Modify menu. Check to Enable Selective Quality, as shown in Figure 23.10. You can leave the quality setting at the default for now. After selective quality is enabled, you can access it directly from the Optimize panel.

Now select Save Selection As JPEG Mask from the Selective JPEG commands in the Modify menu. The selection is covered by a semitransparent mask of the color specified in the Settings dialog box from the previous step.

Now expand the Optimize panel and select JPEG as the compression format. Set the Quality to 30—this is the quality for everything *except* the selection in the image. Set the Selective Quality to 90 and the Smoothing level to 2. Finally, click the Preview button above the Canvas to see the effect.

FIGURE 23.10
Enable selective
quality.

If you like what you see, select Export from the File menu to save the selectively compressed JPEG.

Summary

You should now be very familiar with all the bitmap editing tools and what they're used for. Don't be afraid to experiment! Play around with the tools or try out an idea you might have come up with while reading this book. There are an infinite variety of things you can do with bitmaps!

In the next chapter, you'll work mostly with vectors, but many of the same techniques that apply to vector objects in Fireworks apply to bitmap objects, as well, including grouping, gradient fills (very handy with masks), and masking bitmaps with a vector image instead of with a grayscale mask. If you've never worked with vectors before, you'll be delighted with how easy and intuitive it is with Fireworks, even for a dedicated pixel pusher!

CHAPTER 24

Working with Vector Paths

Fireworks is particularly well suited for working interchangeably with bitmaps and vector paths. Vector paths are derived from calculus, but they are a useful way to present visual information derived from mathematical functions, or algorithms, instead of using bitmaps or databases for the display. Because of this, vector graphics have many interesting properties. Vector lines and shapes can be resized again and again without a loss of quality. In this chapter, you begin working with the Fireworks Vector tool group on the Tools panel.

Drawing Points and Lines

When you draw with the vector tools, you're not actually editing pixels. Instead, the movements of the cursor are interpreted as points along a continuous path. For instance, when you draw with the brush (see the top object in Figure 24.1), a bitmap object is created and the color information of the individual pixels underneath the brush tip is changed to match the brush settings. But if you want to smooth out a bump or make the line a little shorter, you'll have to use another bitmap tool to change the color information of those pixels back to the original setting. You can also use Undo and completely redraw the line.

With a vector path, the line itself is all that matters. Instead of having to edit a bitmap to change the size or shape of the line, you can change the shape of the line simply by moving the points that define it. Furthermore, the stroke settings, such as width and color, can be changed at any time. Only when the vector is rendered through flattening or export does it become bitmap data and lose the path information. If the vector is saved in the Fireworks PNG source format, its appearance can be edited with the vector tools at any time. In Figure 24.2, both graphics were scaled down and then returned to their original proportions. The top sequence is the bitmap image, whereas the bottom sequence is the vector drawing. Scaling the bitmap down went smoothly, but scaling it back up ruined it.

FIGURE 24.1
Here you can see similar figures drawn with different tools. The top one was drawn with the brush. The bottom was drawn with the pen but with the same settings as the brush. Notice how the paths are highlighted individually for the vector drawing, whereas the bitmap is one distinct element.

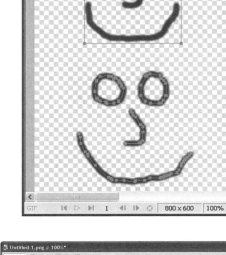

FIGURE 24.2
The vector stroke looks perfect even after two transformations have been applied.

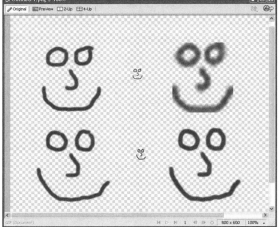

To create a path, you can use any of the drawing tools in the Vector group on the Tools panel. These include the Line, Pen, Vector Path, Rectangle, Rounded

Rectangle, Ellipse, and Polygon tools. You'll learn about the rest of the tools in the Vector group in the next chapter.

▶ **Line**—The Line tool is probably the simplest of the drawing tools. Press N to select the Line tool. Click and drag on the Canvas to create a line that starts where you click and ends where you release. At each end of the line, vector points are created, with the path joining them. Hold down Shift to constrain the line within 45° angles. You cannot create shapes with the Line tool, only single line segments. Only the stroke, opacity, and Blending mode settings are available in the Properties Inspector.

▶ **Pen**—The Pen tool is a very powerful tool because it is used for both creating and editing paths. Press P to select the Pen tool. It's important to watch the cursor when using the Pen tool; it switches to a different mode, depending on where you click. Click the plus sign under the Pen tool cursor to add a point, and click again to add a corner point. A line is then created between them. Click-drag to create a curve point to add a curve to the line segment. You'll learn about the other Pen tool features in the next section, "Editing Bézier Curves." Options for the Pen tool in the Properties Inspector include fill, stroke, opacity, and Blending mode.

▶ **Vector Path**—The Vector Path tool is similar to the Brush tool in the Bitmap group. Press P to cycle to the Vector Path tool. With the Vector Path tool, you can click-drag to draw a freeform line. The line, points, and curves in the path are automatically created after you release the mouse button. If the line ends where it began, a closed shape is created, which can then be filled. The Vector Path tool also allows you to employ pressure and angle settings if you are using a tablet and stylus. Options for the Vector Path tool include stroke, opacity, and Blending mode.

▶ **Redraw Vector Path**—The Redraw Vector Path tool is used to edit or extend an existing vector path. To use the tool, cycle to it by pressing P or select it from the Pen tool pop-up menu. After it's selected, draw the tool over the portion of the path you want to edit or extend. The portion of the path being replaced is highlight in red as you draw.

▶ **Rectangle**—The Rectangle tool creates a closed shape composed of four lines at 90° angles. To create a square, hold down Shift to constrain the proportions of the rectangle. Options for the Rectangle tool include fill, stroke, opacity, and Blending mode.

▶ **Ellipse**—This tool creates ovals and circles. Hold down Shift to constrain the proportions to a regular circle. Ellipse settings include fill, stroke, opacity, and Blending mode.

▶ **Polygon**—This tool creates regular multisided figures, from triangles (3 sides) to nearly circular, 25-sided figures. In the Properties Inspector you can set the type to polygon or star, select the number of sides (or points, if a star), and select the angle of the corners. Click the box to the right of the angle setting to have Fireworks set the angle automatically. Other settings include fill, stroke, opacity, and Blending mode.

By the Way

> There are eleven other shapes you can select in the same tool menu as the Rectangle, Ellipse, and Polygon tools, such as arrows, pies, and stars. Be sure to explore the possibilities of each object because they can save you a lot of time as opposed to generating the images yourself.

The selection tools and free transform tools work with paths in the same way that they work with bitmap objects. Like bitmaps, each path is an object in Fireworks. Moving the Pointer tool over a path reveals the points and line segments. Clicking with the pointer selects the path object, as in Figure 24.3. Selecting a path object brings up the Path settings in the Properties Inspector, including size, position, fill, stroke, opacity, and Blending mode.

FIGURE 24.3
An entire path object can be selected with the Pointer tool.

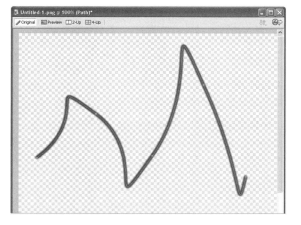

Another selection tool that's used with paths and grouped objects, which you'll read about later, is the Subselection tool, located next to the Pointer tool on the Tools panel. The Subselection tool enables you to select individual points in a path. Shift-click selects multiple points, which can then be moved with the cursor keys (Up, Down, Left, and Right) or by click-dragging a selected point with the Subselection tool (see Figure 24.4).

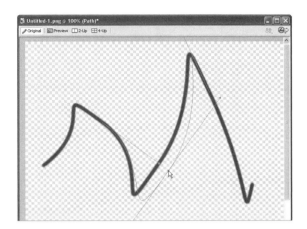

FIGURE 24.4
Use the Subselection tool to select a single point along the path or to select an object within a group of objects.

Using the free transform tools is an easy way to edit paths. The transformations change only the relationships between points, not curves or lines, which means an object can be endlessly transformed without the risk to quality inherent to transforming bitmaps. Select a path with the Pointer tool and then select one of the free transform tools to transform a path by eye. You can also transform paths numerically using the Numeric Transform command, which is located in the Transform submenu from the Modify menu. When using Numeric Transform, uncheck the Scale Attributes setting if you do not want to scale stroke widths and feathering along with the path itself.

The Crop tool, depending on your preference settings, can affect the Canvas as well as onscreen objects. If you you want to crop the Canvas so that paths outside the bounds of the cropped Canvas will remain in their positions relative to the original Canvas, open the Preferences dialog box and then select the Editing tab; make sure that Delete Objects when Cropping is *not* selected.

You can use the Export Area tool with paths just as you would with bitmaps— click and drag to create an area to export, double-click with the mouse, and specify optimization settings in the Export Preview dialog box. The vectors are exported as bitmap information in the appropriate format.

Editing Bézier Curves

Two types of points can define a path—corner points and curve points. Line segments between corner points remain straight, joining a corner point at an angle. Curve points allow you to create smooth mathematical curves from line segments. These are known as Bézier curves, named after Pierre Bézier, who came up with the equation to mathematically describe the shape of Renault auto bodies. Some examples are shown in Figure 24.5.

FIGURE 24.5
There are four paths here. The first is a straight line with two corner points. The next one has a curve point with a vector on the left and a corner point on the right. The third path has two curve points, each with a vector, and the last one is a fractured curve that doubles back on itself.

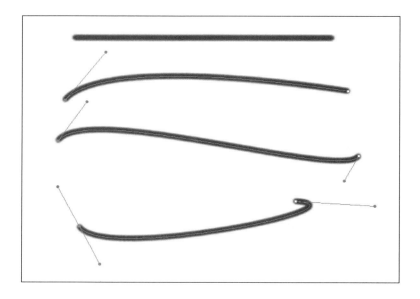

The simplest curved line segment is defined by four points—the *origin point*, *destination point*, *origin vector*, and *destination vector*. The origin and destination points are the points that make up the path. The curve of the line segment is defined by the angle and distance of the vector points from the origin and destination points. A line between two Bézier curve points can be made into a soft roll, a quarter circle, a cresting wave, or even a complete loop.

When you click with the Pen tool, you create a corner point. If you hold down the mouse button and drag away from the point, you'll notice that a straight line is created through the point and that the path begins to curve on either side. You are applying equal and opposite vector points on either side of the origin point. You can edit these vector points with the Subselection tool by selecting the origin point and then click-dragging the circles at the end of either vector. Moving the vector back to the origin point deletes the curve information, creating a corner point. To create a curve point, click a selected corner point and drag with the Pen tool to add vector handles.

You can also add and delete points with the Pen tool to change a line segment. With the Pen tool, mouse over a point that isn't selected. The cursor changes to show a minus sign under the Pen icon; click to delete this point. To add a new point, click with the Pen tool on a line segment. Then, click and drag to create a curve point. A new point is added, with or without vector handles.

Did you Know?

> You can do a lot with the Pen and Subselection tools. They are the core tools for path editing. With the Subselection tool, you can change the position of individual points and edit their vector handles. You can also delete points and the adjoining line segment with the Subselection tool—to open a closed shape, for instance. With the Pen tool, you can quickly and precisely edit paths by adjusting curves and removing points without removing the line segment and opening a closed shape. You can also use the Pen tool to close a shape by clicking either end of the line path.

Changing the Appearance of a Path Object

You can edit the stroke and fill styles in the Properties Inspector before or after drawing a path. These are the same settings used with the Brush and Paint Bucket tools in the Bitmap group. Object settings, such as opacity, Blending mode, and effects, can also be specified for path objects.

Fill settings apply to any path. If a path does not form a closed shape, an empty line segment is created between the endpoints of the path to define the fill boundary. Select the no-color swatch (white with a diagonal red line) if you don't want to use a fill. The fill color can also be set on the Tools panel or in the Color Mixer panel. All the settings are available in the Properties Inspector when a path object is selected. These include fill type, edge softness, and texture. Transparency can be applied to the texture by checking the Transparency box.

Stroke settings include stroke color, stroke type, edge softness, stroke width, and texture. These are the same as the settings for the bitmap Brush tool, and any number of styles can be chosen. If you don't want to use a stroke, select either the no-color swatch or the None stroke type.

The object settings apply to the entire object, including stroke and fill. You can set the opacity with the opacity slider. Blending modes work the same way that they would with the bitmap tools, except they can be changed at any time. You can also use any of the effects that you can use with the bitmap tools, and the effects change along with the path if the stroke and fill settings are changed, points are edited, or the object is transformed.

Arranging Path Objects with the Layers Panel

Similar to bitmap objects, path objects can be selected and arranged using the Layers panel. Objects further down in a layer are arranged behind the objects above them. You can change the opacity and Blending mode for all the paths on the layer by selecting the layer and changing the opacity and Blending mode settings in the Layers panel. These are applied in addition to any opacity or Blending mode settings already applied to individual paths (see Figure 24.6).

FIGURE 24.6
You can name and arrange paths using the Layers panel, just as you would with bitmap objects.

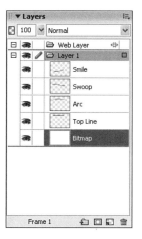

You can also use the Arrange commands in the Modify menu to change the stacking order of paths. Bring Forward (Ctrl+up arrow or Command-up arrow) moves the path above the next path on the layer. Send Backward (Ctrl+down arrow or Command-down arrow) moves it behind the path immediately behind it, whereas Bring to Front (Ctrl+up arrow or Command-Shift-up arrow) moves the path to the top of the layer. Send to Back (Ctrl+down arrow or Command-Shift-down arrow) makes it the last element in the layer.

You can also use the Layers panel to show or hide a path or change the path object's name. Click the Eyeball icon to the left of the object name to hide the path. Click again to show it. To change a path object's name, simply double-click the current name. You can type a new name in the field that appears; then press Return to apply the new name to the object.

Standard output formats, such as JPEG and GIF, do not support Fireworks paths. All paths are flattened into bitmaps before exporting. Be sure to always save an original Fireworks source PNG and back it up; you can't rely on your exported files if you want to continue working with the vector paths.

Watch Out!

Working with Groups of Paths

Another important method for organizing path objects is grouping. Paths that are grouped together are treated like a single path when changes are applied. To group paths, select multiple objects by holding down the Shift key and clicking them with the Pointer tool (you can also select multiple paths from the Layers panel using Shift and clicking the path objects). Select Group from the Modify menu or press Ctrl+G (Windows) or Command-G (Macintosh). The selection highlight changes to four handles around the elements in the group that form the group's bounding box (see Figure 24.7).

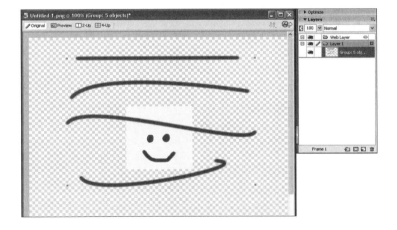

FIGURE 24.7
A group of objects can include vector and bitmap objects. The entire group can be quickly scaled with the handles at the corners. Notice that the new group object in the Layers panel has replaced the individual path objects.

Grouping works with any object, including bitmaps. When you group a number of objects, a new Group object appears on that layer in the Layers panel. Grouped objects cannot span more than one layer; if you select objects on more than one layer, they are grouped together in the same layer as the topmost selected object. To rename a group on the Layers panel, double-click the group name as you would a bitmap or path object. To ungroup the objects, press Ctrl+Shift+G (Windows) or Command-Shift-G (Macintosh) or select Ungroup from the Modify menu.

When path objects are grouped, you can change the settings for the entire group at once. For instance, changing the stroke settings in the Properties Inspector with a group selected applies the new settings to all the paths in the group. The same goes for fill, opacity, and Blending mode. When items are grouped, they are also transformed in their original proportions. Click the handles at any of the four corners of the group with the pointer to quickly resize a group. Hold down the Shift key to constrain the resized group to its original aspect ratio. You can also transform or add effects to a group object in the same way that you would with an individual bitmap or path object.

If you want to edit a part of a group without ungrouping it, you can use the Subselection tool to select an individual path or bitmap object within the group. This way you can change the stroke, fill, effect, or position of an element within a group without affecting other elements in the group. Conversely, you can create a group of groups so you can edit large numbers of objects very quickly. When a group containing other groups is ungrouped, the original groups are retained.

Summary

Hopefully, this has been a successful foray into the world of geometric art. Don't fret if the math is confusing. It's math—of course it's confusing. Just remember that you can draw with the Vector Path tool just as you would with the Brush tool in Bitmap mode, but the path is more flexible when you use the Vector Path tool. You can make changes quickly and easily, and the lines will always look clean and smooth—no noise or jaggies, even after scaling or other transformations. In the next chapter you'll work with the Fireworks text tools to introduce typography into your designs.

CHAPTER 25

Creating Text and Typographic Effects

One of the core elements of designing graphics for the Web is employing text. Because Web pages are limited by the fonts available on the user's system, rather than those on the author's system, only a small set of fonts is available for text on a Web page. But any font can be used when composing bitmap graphics. These can then be laid out on a Web page in addition to HTML-formatted text to create pages with typographic flair at minimal file sizes. This chapter introduces you to the text tools and capabilities of Fireworks MX 2004.

Using the Text Tool

Let's get started with text in Fireworks. To add text to a document, you can simply select the Text tool, specify the desired settings in the Properties Inspector, click an area of the canvas, and begin typing. It's that simple!

Creating Text Objects

Clicking the Canvas with the Text tool creates a text object, much like painting with the bitmap tools or drawing with a vector tool. And like bitmap or vector objects, text objects can be selected and rearranged on the Layers panel, grouped with other types of objects, transformed, and altered with effects. Similar to vector objects, text objects can be changed at any time until they're converted into bitmaps through merging, flattening, or exporting. A text object also can be converted into a vector object, which is discussed later in the book.

Selecting Text

The Text tool cursor enables you to select portions of a text object. With the Text tool, click the area of a text object where you would like to start the selection and then drag to the point where you want to end the selection. In this way you can select parts of a text passage and apply different settings to the text within the text object. You can also cut, copy, or paste over the selection using commands from the

Edit menu. To paste text within an object, click with the Text tool to place the text cursor where you want to paste the passage.

The Pointer and Subselection tools can also be used with text objects. Double-clicking a text object with the Pointer tool brings up the Text tool cursor, so you can edit the text content. Selecting a text object allows you to view the object settings and change them in the Properties Inspector. When an object is selected, you can also move it; scale it; or use the Edit commands to cut, copy, or paste it. If a text object is within a group, you can use the Subselection tool in the same way you would use the Pointer tool with an independent text object.

By the Way

> To open the original Fireworks editor (which operates more like a traditional word processor), Simply select a text object with the pointer or create one with the Text tool by clicking the Canvas. Now select Editor from the Text menu to open the classic Fireworks Text Editor dialog box that you're used to.

Importing Text from Other Applications

There are three ways to import text from other applications. You can copy text from one application on your system to the clipboard, switch to Fireworks, and then select Paste from the Edit menu. A new text object containing the text from the clipboard appears on the Canvas. If the clipboard also contains rich text information, such as the font, size, and style, that information is pasted, as well. Not all applications copy rich text information to the clipboard along with the text content, however. Figure 25.1 shows text pasted directly into Fireworks from Word.

FIGURE 25.1
Not only can you type directly into Fireworks, but you can also paste text from most well-known applications directly into the Fireworks document window.

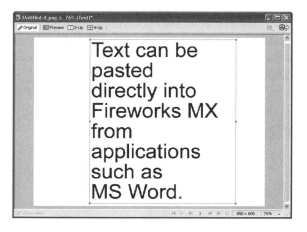

Another method is to use the Import command to import a standard text file (.txt) or a rich text format (.rtf) file. The text from the file appears as a new text object on the Canvas. If an RTF file is used, information such as font, size, and style is also applied. You can create RTF files with WordPad for Windows XP or TextEdit for Macintosh OS X.

Finally, when you open or import files from other graphics applications that support editable text (such as Photoshop [PSD], CorelDRAW [CDR], and Adobe Illustrator [AI]), you can select Preserve Editability as the text setting in the Import dialog box. Although this can sometimes change the appearance of the text (for instance, if the font specified is not available on your system), it does allow you to edit and reapply settings to the object. Select Preserve Appearance in the Import dialog box if you want to ensure that the text appears as it was intended.

Proofreading Text with Fireworks MX

All of us make mistakes, and there's nothing like a typo to draw attention away from an otherwise good design. Fireworks MX provides two great tools for editing and proofreading text—Find and Replace on the Edit menu and Check Spelling on the Text menu.

Find and Replace

Find and Replace is a powerful feature that isn't just for text. Press Ctrl+F (Windows) or Command-F (Macintosh) to open the Find and Replace panel. From this panel, you can choose to search the selection, the current frame, the entire document, the files in the Project log, or files you choose using the Open dialog box. You can search for text, fonts, colors, URLs, or colors that aren't Web safe.

If you're familiar with programming, you can use Regular Expressions, such as wildcards or a series of values. Regular Expressions enable you to match part of a word or words as part of the search process. As you'll see with Check Spelling, Find and Replace works only with text objects. Objects that have been flattened, merged, or converted to paths are ignored.

Check Spelling

You can check the spelling of any text in a Fireworks file by pressing Shift+F7. By default, this checks all spelling in the currently open document. This checks only text objects—if text has been flattened, merged, or converted to paths, it is ignored by the spell checker. It also checks text that has added effects, such as shadows or bevels, attached. Use Spelling Setup from the Text menu to select a dictionary, edit your custom dictionary, and specify other spell-checker settings.

Setting Properties for Text and Text Objects

After you've placed your text on the Canvas (and have you checked the spelling?), you can start applying formatting to the text. Remember that you can apply formatting to all the text in the object by selecting it with the Pointer tool. If you want to apply formatting to a portion of text within an object, use the Text tool to select a passage by click-dragging. Figure 25.2 shows the Properties Inspector with a text object selected. Also following is a list of the options available when working with text.

FIGURE 25.2
With a text object selected in the document window, the Properties Inspector offers many tools and features to format the text any way you want.

▶ **Font**—You can change the font for a selection by selecting a font from those listed in the Text menu. You can also type the name of a font in the Font field in the Properties Inspector or select a font from the pop-up menu.

▶ **Size**—Font size is measured in points. You can choose a point size from the sizes available under Size on the Text menu. You can also select Other to specify a font size numerically. When a text object or passage is selected, you can change the size using the Size field on the Properties Inspector by typing the new size in the field or by using the slider.

When you set a text size in points and then transform the text to be smaller or larger, the size setting remains the same. When you change the size setting of transformed text, it is resized in relation to its transformed size.

▶ **Style**—Styles for text include Bold, Italic, and Underline. To remove styles from a text object or passage, select Plain from the Styles available in the Text menu.

▶ **Alignment**—Alignment specifies how the text content is aligned within the text box. Left and Right align text to the left or right side of the bounding box, respectively. Center centers lines of text within the box, and Justified adjusts the space between characters to make each line of text align to both the left and right sides of the box. Stretched Alignment stretches each line to align it equally on both sides.

You can also align text vertically by selecting Top or Bottom alignment. You can also Center, Justify, or Stretch vertically. All these options are available under Align in the Text menu or from the Properties Inspector.

When you align text vertically, notice that the other alignment options change in the Properties Inspector. Instead of Left, Center, and Right, you now have Top, Center, and Bottom.

Did you Know?

▶ **Color**—Use the fill color to specify the color for a text object or passage selection. The color can be changed by using the Properties Inspector or from the fill color swatch on the Tools panel. You can also choose to add an outline to the font by changing the stroke color. You can select the stroke color from the Properties Inspector or from the stroke color swatch on the Tools panel.

▶ **Anti-aliasing**—Anti-aliasing can be applied to character edges. You can find the Anti-aliasing menu next to the stroke color setting. No anti-aliasing is best for font sizes below 10 points. Crisp applies a light anti-alias suitable for font sizes from 10 to 18 points, whereas Strong applies more anti-aliasing than Crisp but not as much as Smooth. Strong is generally used for font sizes between 18 and 36 points; Smooth is for anything larger than 36 points.

▶ **Opacity and Blending Mode**—As with any other object, you can set the opacity and blending mode for a text object. This affects how the object appears when layered over other objects.

▶ **Effects**—You can also add effects to a text object, just as you would add them to any other object. The advantage of using effects is that you can change or remove them at any time while retaining text editability. Using a filter command with a text object converts the text into a bitmap object.

▶ **Paragraph Settings**—Controls for modifying font and paragraph spacing and text kerning. These tools are discussed shortly.

Changing Text Flow with Text Blocks, Paragraph Settings, and Paths

After you've entered some text, you can change how the lines of text flow on the page in several ways. You can change the style and shape of the text block, change how lines are spaced and paragraphs indented, and even change the text to flow along a curved path or shape.

Text Blocks

When you select a text block with the Pointer tool (or a text block within a group with the Subselection tool), you'll notice that handles appear at the corners of the block and on two of its sides. Text object handles work differently from bitmap or vector object handles—they don't resize the content they contain. They specify the width of the text object, which affects how the lines wrap within the text object. As you change the handles on the sides, the text box grows taller or shorter, as more or fewer lines are necessary. Changing the handles on the bottom corners affects only the width of the block, but changing the handles on the top corners changes both the width and the point at which the text starts. If you choose a vertical alignment setting, the width handles become height handles to handle vertical text wrapping.

Paragraph Settings

You can adjust the spacing between characters, lines, and paragraphs using the paragraph settings for a text object in the Properties Inspector. The tools available are also explained here:

▶ **Kerning**—Kerning is the space between individual characters. A negative percentage in the kerning field on the Properties Inspector indicates that characters are closer together. To move them farther apart, set the kerning value to a positive percentage. Check the Auto-Kerning check box to turn on a font's native kerning. Turn off native kerning when you are working with small point sizes and when anti-aliasing is turned off.

When working within a text block, you can apply kerning between two characters by moving the cursor between them. You can apply kerning to a passage by selecting the passage with the Text tool. Use the pointer to select a text object and apply the same kerning to all characters. Press Ctrl+left arrow (Windows) or Command-left arrow (Macintosh) to decrease kerning by 1%; Ctrl+right arrow (Windows) or Command-right arrow (Macintosh) increases kerning by 1%. Holding down the Shift key with the preceding commands changes kerning in 10% increments.

▶ **Leading**—Leading is the distance between lines of text. It is measured either as a percentage of the character's point size or in pixels. Click the Leading Units menu on the Properties Inspector and select % for percentage or px for pixels. To select one or more lines for which to set the leading, select the passages of text where you want the leading change to start and finish. Leading affects the distance between all selected lines and the line immediately above the selected passage. Select a text object with the pointer to change the leading for the entire object. You can also use Ctrl+up arrow (Windows) or Command-up arrow (Macintosh) to increase leading by 1 unit. Press Ctrl+down arrow (Windows) or Command-down arrow (Macintosh) to decrease leading by 1 unit.

▶ **Horizontal Scale**—This changes the width of characters in the selected object or passage. Decreasing the percentage makes them skinnier; increasing it makes them wider. Any character width setting is applied before transformations, allowing you to use character width to affect text within the text block before scaling or transforming the text object.

▶ **Indents**—To indent text, use the Paragraph Indent field in the Properties Inspector to specify a number of pixels to indent text on the first line after a line break.

▶ **Spacing**—You can also set the spacing between line breaks by setting the distance from the preceding paragraph or the distance from the paragraph after the line break. This is measured in pixels.

Attaching Text to Paths

Another great effect you can use with text is to attach lines of text to a path. Text is normally placed along a straight line, but by attaching it to a path, you can make text flow along any kind of curve or angle.

You can use any type of path, either open or closed. If the path is a closed shape, you cannot use line breaks—only the first line flows around a shape. With an open path, line breaks and word wrapping work as though the path is the baseline and new lines repeat the same path.

To attach text to a path, simply select the text object with the Pointer tool and then Shift-click to select the path to which you want to attach the text. Select Attach to Path from the Text menu or press Ctrl+Shift+Y (Windows) or Command-Shift-Y (Macintosh), as shown in Figure 25.3.

To edit text after it's attached to the path, simply double-click with the pointer or insert a cursor with the Text tool. This text can also be spell-checked or searched with the Find and Replace option. To change the path, select Detach from Path on the Text menu, change the path, and then reattach the text to the new path.

FIGURE 25.3
Text can be attached to vector paths.

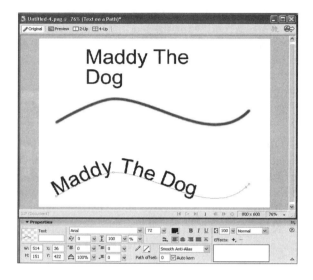

By the Way

When you attach text to a path, the stroke and fill settings for the path are saved but invisible. Stroke and fill settings in the Properties Inspector for the object now affect the text. When you detach the path, the path reappears with its original stroke and fill settings intact. In the Properties Inspector, when you select the object, you can also change by how many pixels the lines of text are offset from the path.

Orienting Text Along a Path

To change how the characters are oriented along the path, select an Orientation setting from the Text menu after you have attached the text to the path:

- ▶ **Rotate Around Path**—This rotates the characters to be parallel with the angle of the path underneath them.

- ▶ **Vertical**—This keeps characters along the path parallel to the horizontal axis. The path simply moves them up or down.

- ▶ **Skew Vertical**—As the angle of the path increases or decreases, the characters are skewed vertically by the same degree.

- ▶ **Skew Horizontal**—As the angle of the path increases or decreases, the characters are skewed horizontally by the same degree.

Summary

By now you should be comfortable working with text in Fireworks. Because of the typographic constraints of HTML, you'll find that for really distinctive text effects, you'll want to export text as GIF files. This gives you much more flexibility in applying fonts, colors, text flow, and effects.

CHAPTER 26

Using Creative Fills and Effects on Vectors and Text

This chapter covers some of the most complex tools available in Fireworks for creating and editing graphics and shows you how to apply the fundamentals you've learned earlier to create professional-quality graphics. For example, you'll learn how to work with gradient fills, such as using them to create incredible masking and transparency effects. You'll also learn how to create great custom brushes and textures. Finally, you'll discover how to use anti-aliasing and effects to create more realistic drawings.

Creative Fill Techniques

You can employ a number of tricks with fills to give your graphics a little extra snap. Simple filled shapes can make great design elements in a Web design. You can use gradients and patterns to add more visual flair. You can also use these techniques in purely creative work to add style and realism to vector drawings.

Working with Gradients

Gradients are a powerful graphics tool. A *gradient* is a fill that gradually shifts between two or more colors, as in Figure 26.1. Gradients use math to make accurate transitions that span a full range of possible tones. You won't have to worry too much about this because Fireworks MX makes applying and editing gradient fills easy.

To apply a gradient fill to a selected object, select Fill Options from the Fill category menu next to Fill Color on the Properties Inspector. You can select the type of gradient from the Styles menu at the top of the panel that appears. A number of gradients are available, ranging from Linear to Folds. Each style produces a different gradient effect. Experiment to find the ones you like. Linear, Radial, and Ellipse are the most common gradients used.

FIGURE 26.1
A linear gradient fill applied to a vector shape. Note the gradient-fill control handles across the middle—they determine the distance and direction of the transition.

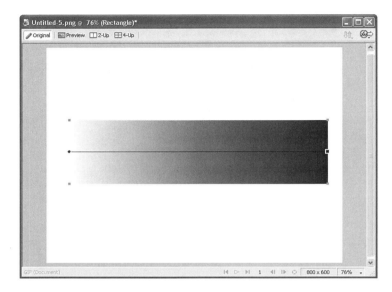

Below the gradient style is the color setting for the gradient. You can select a preset from the drop-down menu on the left, or you can click the Edit button to customize the colors and transparency settings for the gradient. When you click the Edit button, you are presented with the Gradient Editing menu, as shown in Figure 26.2. At the top are sliders for the alpha, or transparency, of the gradient. Below the gradient bar are the color sliders. Click a slider to change the opacity or color setting for that point on the gradient. Click anywhere along the gradient bar to add a new slider at that point. Click and drag a slider to change its position along the bar, or drag a slider off the end of the bar to delete it (note that there must always be at least two sliders, however). Select a preset to see how the preset gradient colors are achieved. Click the Fill Options panel to make the changes. You can return to this panel by clicking the fill color swatch whenever it's a gradient.

After you select a gradient style and colors, you can change how the gradient is applied relative to the object. Select a gradient-filled object with the Pointer tool; the gradient-fill handles appear with the object. The round handle is where the gradient starts (if linear) or where it is centered (if radial or elliptical). The square handle (or handles if an ellipse) defines the range and angle of the gradient. Click and drag a handle to move it. You can move either handle outside the area of the fill if you want the gradient to start or end outside the shape. The handles scale in proportion to the object when transformed.

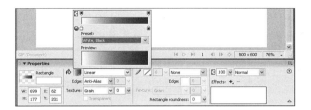

FIGURE 26.2
The Gradient Editor, available in the Fill Options menu, enables you to adjust transparency and color ranges for a gradient.

You can save a gradient fill as a style for later. Click the Add Effects button in the Properties Inspector and select Save As Style from the Options group. You can name the style in the field at the top. Make sure that Fill Type is selected among the Properties check boxes. Then click OK to save the new style. You can access it from the Styles panel, which is in the Assets panel group by default.

You can easily create gradient transparency effects for one or more objects by creating a rectangular path around the objects and giving it a grayscale gradient fill (the Black and White preset is very handy here). Use Cut or Copy to add the filled shape to the clipboard and then select the objects to be masked. Use Paste As Mask from the Edit menu to add the rectangular path with the gradient fill from the clipboard as a vector mask. Select the Mask thumbnail in the Layers panel and click the Grayscale Appearance button on the Properties Inspector. Darker areas of the gradient become more transparent, whereas lighter areas become more opaque. You can even edit the gradient fill handles for the mask object at any time by unlinking the mask and selecting the masking path with the Pointer tool to bring up the handles.

Did you Know?

Using Preset and Custom Patterns

Another way to distinguish filled areas is to use patterns. Fireworks comes with several custom patterns, but you can use any Fireworks PNG, GIF, JPEG, BMP, or TIFF image. To choose a patterned fill for an object, select the object with the pointer and select Fill Options after clicking the color swatch. Select Pattern from the Type menu at the top. Use the next menu to select one of the preset fills, or select Other to select an image file from your hard drive. The pattern Leaves is shown in Figure 26.3. When you select an image file for a pattern, it is added to your list of preset patterns.

When a pattern fill has been applied to an object, the pattern-fill handles appear when the object is selected with the Pointer tool. Moving the round handle changes where the tiling is centered relative to the object. The square handles can be moved to scale or skew the tiles in the pattern. Click and drag any of these handles to move them. Graphics used for patterns are always treated as bitmaps (even if they were vectors in a Fireworks PNG file) and are resampled if scaled with the pattern-fill handles.

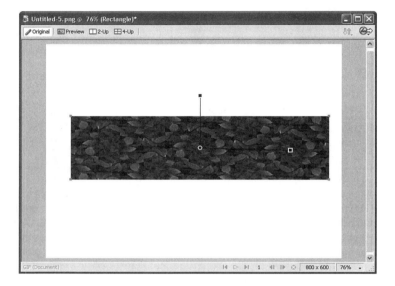

To change the pattern used in a pattern fill, simply select the fill color to bring up the Pattern Fill menu and preview. You can also use the Fill Options menu. You can save pattern fills as styles or apply them as masks in the same way you would for a gradient fill. Pattern and gradient fills can also be applied to bitmaps through the Paint Bucket tool. You can also combine gradients and patterns with textures for even more flexibility. You'll learn more about textures in the next section after this tip.

Did you Know?

You can also use patterns to mask a bitmap image. Simply select a vector object you would like to use as a mask and apply the bitmap you want to mask as a pattern. You can scale the bitmap relative to the path by using the pattern-fill handles. The bitmap pattern is transformed in proportion to the path when scaled, skewed, or distorted.

Advanced Stroke Options

If you want ultimate control over how the stroke on a path appears, you can use the Stroke Options and the Edit Stroke dialog box to specify every little detail.

These custom strokes can then be saved as a stroke style or as part of a style on the Styles panel. Custom strokes can be used for vector objects or for the Brush tool in the Bitmap group on the Tools panel.

To create a custom stroke, simply select a vector object, a drawing tool, or the Brush tool. On the Properties Inspector select Stroke Options from the Stroke category menu next to the stroke color swatch. From this menu, you can select the style, color, tip softness, stroke width, texture, and path orientation—inside, outside, or centered. You can also choose to place the fill over the stroke in places where they intersect. Click the Advanced button to bring up the Edit Stroke dialog box, shown in Figure 26.4.

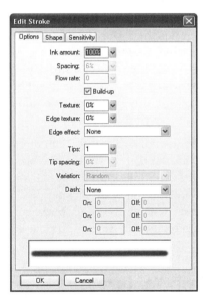

FIGURE 26.4
The Edit Stroke dialog box gives you the ultimate control over creating custom strokes to use with vector and bitmap drawing tools.

The Edit Stroke dialog box has three tabs. The Options tab has settings for Ink Amount, the density of the stroke color; Spacing between points of color applied by the tip; the Flow Rate, which increases the amount of ink applied over time; and Build-up, for adding density by scrubbing with the tip over a point. You can apply Texture to the stroke center or the stroke edge, and you can also try one of the Edge Effects to further stylize a line. For cross-hatching and other techniques, you can choose more than one tip. If more than one tip is selected, you can use the Variation menu to set the spacing relative to the stroke width and choose how the colors vary between each tip. A preview screen at the bottom lets you preview your changes.

By the Way

> You must select a preset stroke style as a starting point for your custom stroke. Some features, such as spacing and flow rate, are available only for certain stroke styles, such as the Air Brush tips.

Select the Shape tab to specify the shape of the stroke tip. Checking the Square box creates a square tip, and leaving it unchecked makes it round. You can set the size of the tip in pixels; the edge softness percentage; the aspect, or ratio, of width to height; and, finally, the angle at which the tip is held. For square tips or tips with an aspect less than 100%, you can set the angle of the tip for calligraphic effects.

The Sensitivity tab can be used in conjunction with a stylus and tablet to vary the stroke relative to the pressure or speed of the stylus. You can also vary a stroke property depending on its angle by assigning horizontal or vertical variation to a property. The Random function randomly changes the property as it's applied, regardless of pressure, speed, or angle. Select a stroke property from the menu at the top, and then select by which input variable it will be affected. You can vary any of the stroke properties with any input variable and combine variations to create interesting effects.

To save your custom stroke, click OK to exit the Edit Stroke dialog box and save your changes, and then click the custom stroke Save button (the document with a + icon) at the bottom left of the Stroke Options panel. You can also save the stroke as a style on the Properties panel by clicking the Add Effect button and selecting Save As Style from the Options group. Make sure that the Stroke Type check box is selected before giving it a name and clicking OK to save the new style.

Creating Your Own Textures

Textures are a lot like patterns except that they can be applied to strokes or fills and do not contain any color information. Textures are used to add brightness details to strokes and fills. A texture has been applied to the fill in Figure 26.5. Textures do not change the hue of the stroke or fill color; they only vary the brightness or alpha. To add a texture to a fill or stroke, select the texture from the Texture menu on the Properties Inspector or in the Fill or Stroke Options menu. Select a percentage of intensity for the texture. For fills, lighter areas of the texture can be made transparent by checking the box next to Transparent.

To create your own texture, simply select Other from the Texture menu. You can select a Fireworks PNG, GIF, JPEG, BMP, or TIFF file to use. Color information is ignored, and the image is tiled to fill the textured area. After you have chosen a custom texture, it is added to the texture menu for use at any time.

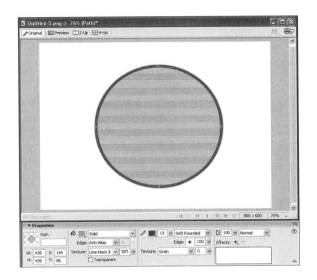

FIGURE 26.5
The preset texture Line-Horiz 3 has been added at the default 50% intensity. Notice how light and dark horizontal lines are imposed on the pattern fill.

Adding Effects to Vectors

Another way to stylize your vector graphics is to employ effects. Some effects are particularly well suited for vector graphics, such as the Bevel and Emboss effects and the Shadow and Glow effects. By using effects with your vector graphics, you can create the appearance of three dimensions through lighting, shadow, and focus. Effects can be applied to any object, including bitmaps, paths, text, and groups. To further expand the possibilities, effects can also be applied to objects that have been masked. Use Save As Style from the effects Options to save your effect decisions as a style on the Styles panel.

You can use the Gaussian Blur effect to blur a vector graphic, making it look out of focus. This is also a good way to create a diffuse shadow or highlight, and it is the basis of the shadow and glow effects. The object in Figure 26.6 has been blurred with Gaussian Blur. Gaussian Blur is also useful because it blurs the vector object in the same way it would a bitmap object—there is no distinction between the stroke and fill.

To add lighting effects to a vector object, use the Shadow and Glow effects. Using Drop Shadow makes the object appear lit from the front. A drop shadow has been added to the object in Figure 26.7. To cast a bigger shadow, change the offset.

Changing the color cast and intensity of the shadow alters the color and opacity, respectively. Change the angle of the shadow to match the angle of the light source. Use Knock Out to treat the shadow as a separate object and remove the original object from the effect output. Inner Shadow can be used to simulate shadows cast on the object by other objects. Glow and Inner Glow are useful for making an object appear to be a source of light, and they can be used to create shadow effects by choosing a dark glow color.

FIGURE 26.6
Gaussian Blur with a radius of 10 pixels has been applied. Note that the object and pattern fill handles are still available. If any aspect of the object is changed, the results of the effect change, too.

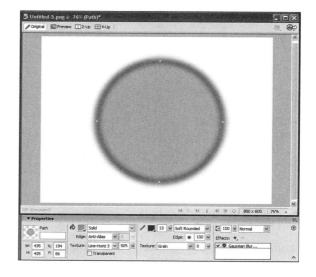

FIGURE 26.7
Drop Shadow has been used to add a shadow behind the object, making it appear to be above the Canvas and lit from the top left. You can change the depth and angle with the Drop Shadow effects at the bottom right of the screen shot.

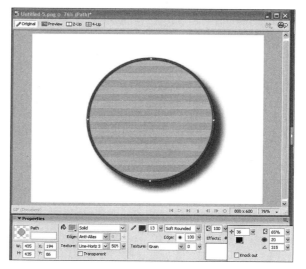

Use Bevel and Emboss to give 3D shading to an object. Raised and Inset Emboss make something appear as though it has been stamped onto a surface, such as a sheet of paper. Raised Emboss has been used on the graphic in Figure 26.8. You can set the width, or apparent depth, of the embossment, as well as the contrast, softness, and angle of the lighting. You also can choose whether to show or hide the object. Bevel can be used in the same way, except that it enables you to add color to the depth shading. Inset Bevel and Inset Emboss can be used to make the object appear to recede instead of protrude. This is often applied to buttons on a Web site to make them appear more like real push buttons.

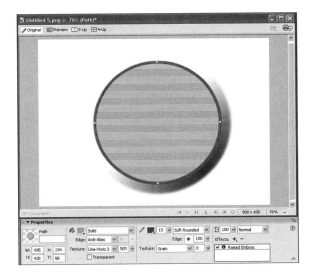

FIGURE 26.8
Using the Raised Emboss effect gives an object the appearance of being stamped or raised, like a seal on a document or a key on a keyboard.

Another great effect to use with vectors is the Motion Trail effect from Eye Candy. The Light version of this software ships with Fireworks and is available via the Filters menu. Change the Direction to suggest which way the object is moving, and change the Length and Taper to suggest distance and speed. Select Bleed Color from Edges to create a more abstract effect. Leave it deselected for a more realistic visual appearance.

Did you Know?

Summary

Phew! We've covered pretty much everything you can do with vector and bitmap graphics in Fireworks. By combining vector and bitmap tools, Fireworks MX makes working in either mode easy. Blending bitmaps and effects with vector graphics and masks enables you to explore a vast array of creative possibilities.

CHAPTER 27

Tools and Techniques for Design and Layout

Now that you're familiar with all the potential graphic elements in Fireworks—bitmap, path, and text objects—you can work on effective design and composition with a number of objects. The flexibility of paths makes creating a variety of graphics from just a few simple lines and shapes easy. You'll also learn how to use layout tools, such as rules, grids, and the Align panel, to make composition a breeze.

Reshaping, Altering, and Combining Paths

So far, we've looked at several ways to edit paths—stroke, fill, opacity, and effects settings in the Properties Inspector; position, rotation, and scaling with the Selection and Transform tools; and editing paths with the Pen and Knife tools. Fireworks MX also includes a number of other path tools to aid graphic design.

Freeform Path Editing

You can use three tools to edit the shape of a path by eye. These include the Redraw Path tool, Freeform tool, and Reshape Area tool in the Vector group on the Tools panel. These are useful for smoothing out freeform paths and making small adjustments by hand, such as changing the facial expressions on an animated character. Fireworks adjusts all the points and curves along the path for you.

Using the Redraw Path Tool

To use the Redraw Path tool, first select with the pointer the path to be edited; then press P to cycle through the Pen and Freeform path tools to the Redraw Path tool. When you mouse over the selected path, the selection outline changes color. Click where you would like to start redrawing and drag to create the new shape of the path. Returning the cursor to a point along the original path and releasing it changes the path to the new shape, as shown in Figure 27.1. Releasing it at a point off the original path causes the path to end at the release point, creating a line instead of a closed shape. The edited sections of the path automatically inherit the original path object properties. If no path is selected, the Redraw Path tool acts the same as the Vector Path tool and defaults to the most recent Vector Path object settings.

FIGURE 27.1
As you can see from this before-and-after figure, redrawing the path enables you to totally change the direction and shape of a path.

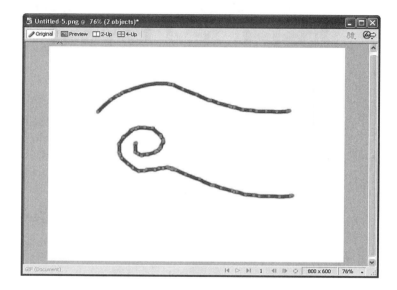

Pushing and Pulling Paths with the Freeform Path Tool

The Freeform Path tool lets you push and pull lines and shapes much like they were strings laid out on a table. Select a path to edit with the pointer, and then press O to select the Freeform Path tool. Mouse over a line segment along the path to bring up the Freeform pointer. Click-drag to edit the line segment; as you drag, the points and curves are changed for that line segment.

To make changes along a larger segment or the entire path, click with the Freeform Path tool on a blank area of the Canvas. A round, red cursor appears; drag the cursor along the path to push or pull the line when it comes into contact with the outer edge of the cursor. Press the left-arrow key while holding down the mouse key to make the Freeform tool area smaller. Or, you can press the right-arrow key to make it bigger. The size can also be set in the Properties Inspector along with pressure sensitivity (when used with a tablet stylus) and Preview (to see the changes as you're making them). In Figure 27.2 the path you just redrew has been edited with the Freeform Path tool.

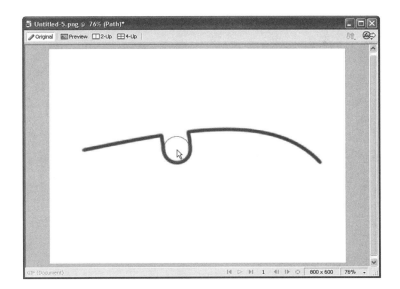

FIGURE 27.2
Use the Freeform
Path tool to click
and drag a line seg-
ment, nudging it
anywhere along the
path.

> To increase the size of the Freeform tool's tip while working, click the up or right
> arrow. To decrease it, use the down or left arrow.

Did you Know?

Massaging Shapes with the Reshape Area Tool

Grouped with the Freeform tool is the Reshape Area tool. Press the letter O to toggle between the Freeform tool and the Reshape Area tool. The Reshape Area tool
uses the inside of the circular cursor as its bounds, instead of using the outside of
the circle like the Freeform tool. Use the Reshape Area tool to bring curves within
the boundaries of the cursor. Click-drag with the mouse to bring up the cursor
and reshape an area of the path. Figure 27.3 shows a curve where the center has
been reshaped.

The Reshape Area tool has two settings: size and strength. These correspond to the
two circles of the cursor. The size, in pixels, is the outer limit of the cursor, whereas the strength, a percentage, is the amount of the area that's changed within the
boundary of the cursor. You can set the pressure feedback from a tablet stylus to
affect the size, strength, or both as you click and drag.

> If you want to change the size of the Reshape Area tool's tip while working, press 2
> on the numeric keypad to increase it; press 1 to decrease it.

Did you Know?

Adding or Subtracting Pressure Information with the Path Scrubber Tools

The Path Scrubber tools can add or subtract pressure information from a path drawn with either the Vector Path tool or the Pen tool. Fireworks has some pressure-sensitive stroke categories, such as Calligraphy, Charcoal, and Air Brush. If you use a digital drawing tablet, you can affect both the pressure and speed of these strokes, whereas using a mouse, you can adjust only the speed. The effect of the stroke is directly affected by the amount of pressure when applying a stroke. This works in the same way as the different appearances achieved when you use old-fashioned crayons: Press hard and fast, and the outcome is very different from slow, gentle strokes.

You can select the Path Scrubber tools only by clicking the tool group arrow below the Freeform tool or the Reshape Area tool. Additive adds pressure or speed; Subtractive reduces pressure or speed. Use the Properties Inspector to choose between changing the pressure, speed, or both and the rate at which pressure or speed is changed. With the additive or subtractive Path Scrubber selected, click-drag along a path to add or subtract pressure or speed.

To set how pressure and speed affect the stroke, you can bring up the Edit Stroke dialog box by selecting an object or a vector drawing tool, selecting Stroke options from the Stroke style in the Properties Inspector, and then clicking the Advanced button. At the top of the dialog box is the Sensitivity tab, where you can choose from among the different stroke properties that can be affected by the pressure, speed, and angle of the stroke. Click OK to save and apply the changes. From the stroke options box, click Save Custom Stroke to save your settings as a stroke style in the current stroke style group.

**Did you
Know?**

Combining Paths

By combining multiple paths, you can create any number of new shapes. To combine two or more paths, select them with the pointer and select a combination method from the Combine Paths commands in the Modify menu.

When you employ a path operation from the Modify menu, you lose any speed and pressure information for the stroke. This includes speed and pressure applied either from a tablet stylus or with the Path Scrubber tools.

**By the
Way**

Join and Split

Use the Join command to create a composite path from multiple paths. Any filled areas that overlap are removed. Layering a circular path over a larger square path and joining them adds the circular stroke inside the other path and removes the fill where the circle and square overlap, creating a transparent void in the larger path, as in Figure 27.4. Although Join creates a single path object, it does not create a shape that can be filled from disconnected paths. Use the Pen tool to join the ends of two or more paths to create a shape you can fill. Use Split to return joined paths to their original states as individual objects.

Union

Union creates a single shape from two or more paths. All selected path objects are turned into a single, contiguous shape around their outline, as shown in Figure 27.5, which shows before-and-after shots of a Union being created. This works only with overlapping paths. The stroke and fill attributes of the new path are applied from the path that's furthest back in the stacking order (closest to the bottom in the Layers panel).

FIGURE 27.4
A circle has been
added inside the
original path using
Join. Notice that
the selected object
in the Layers panel
is now a composite
path.

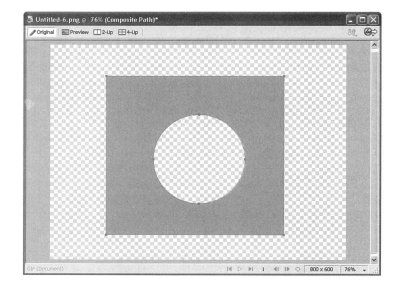

FIGURE 27.5
A Union takes mul-
tiple overlapping
paths and creates
a single path from
them. Here you can
see the before-and-
after effect of this.

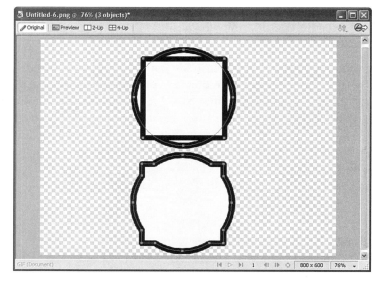

Intersect

Intersect creates a new shape from the common area between all selected paths.
For example, laying the corner of a rectangular path over the edge of a circular
path and selecting Intersect would create a new path in the shape of the area

where both paths meet. The result would be a three-sided object: a corner formed by two straight line segments, which are connected by an arc, as shown in the before-and-after shots in Figure 27.6. The stroke and fill properties are inherited from the path that's furthest back.

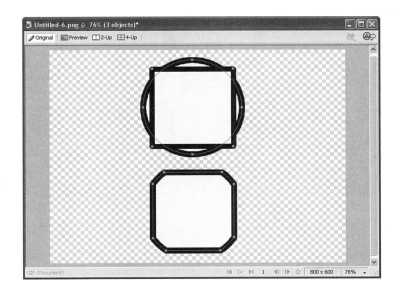

FIGURE 27.6
Intersecting paths result in the creation of a new shape. which comes from the overlapping area of the joined paths.

Punch

Punch is used to remove the area of a shape that's covered by another shape. A rectangle layered over a circle would punch out a section of the circle, as shown by the before-and-after shots in Figure 27.7. Selecting more than one object punches out any area in the bottom object covered by another path layered over it. The new shape retains the stroke and fill settings of the bottom object.

Crop

Use the Crop command to preserve areas of paths layered underneath the top-most path and remove areas of paths outside the topmost path—similar to the way the Crop tool works with the canvas. The object used as the cropping path disappears, and cropped paths beneath it retain the stroke and fill settings.

Altering Paths

Another way to change the shape and size of a path is by using the Alter Path commands in the Modify menu. You can also use this set of commands to change the edge setting for a path fill to make it hard, anti-aliased, or feathered.

FIGURE 27.7
Punching an area
removes the over-
lapped section of
the shape below.
Here you can see
that part of the cir-
cle is removed by
punching a square.

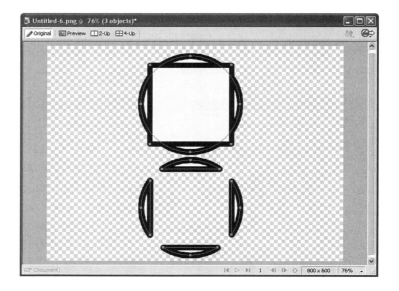

Simplify

Simplify removes unnecessary points from a path that would otherwise result in jagged paths or large vector graphics files. You can set the amount of simplification from 1 to 25. A setting of 1 removes the fewest points and best preserves the original shape of the path. Setting 25 removes the most points and can change the path so much that it would be no longer recognizable. Three levels of simplification are shown in Figure 27.8. You can always use Undo to discard changes.

Expand Stroke

Expanding the stroke of a path is useful for creating a fill in the same shape as the selected stroke. The fill is removed, but the selected stroke is retained on the inside as a composite path and a new, expanded stroke is created around it, with the original fill between. Expanding the stroke of a circular path creates a toroid, or doughnut, shape. Expand Stroke settings include the width, in pixels, between the original and expanded strokes. Other Expand Stroke settings determine the style of corners—miter, round, or beveled—and the miter limit, if mitered corners are chosen (the miter limit sets the ratio between the length of the corner and the width of the stroke). Furthermore, Expand Stroke settings establish how the line segments are end capped—butted, squared, or rounded. Figure 27.9 shows the same rectangle three times, with different stroke expansion options applied.

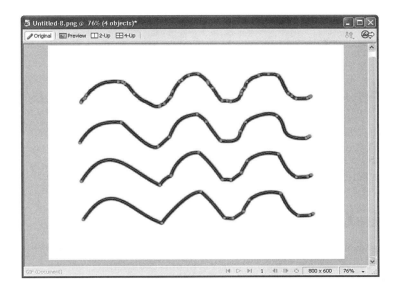

FIGURE 27.8
The object in the top has not been simplified. Below it is a copy that has been simplified by 5. The next object (lower left) has been simplified by 15, and the last by 25. Each has fewer points than the previous, which results in less visual similarity.

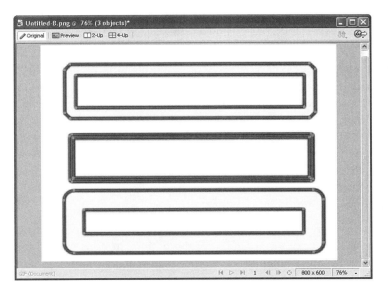

FIGURE 27.9
Expand the stroke of your path to create a composite path. Here you can see the same rectangle after the stroke has been expanded three different ways.

A *miter* is a joint made by beveling each of two surfaces to be joined, usually at a 45° angle, to form a corner, usually a 90° angle. The most obvious use of mitering is in the creation of picture frames.

Did you Know?

Inset Path

Inset Path can actually be used to expand or contract a selected path. The end result is to create a larger or smaller path object with the same fill and other settings as the original, while retaining the aspect ratio. You can select Inside to create a smaller path or Outside to create a larger path. When you inset a path, the stroke and fill settings and relationships are not changed. You can set corners to be miter, round, or beveled and set the miter limit, if miter corners are selected. Very interesting effects can be created when layering an outside inset path behind the original or an inside inset path on top. Use Clone or Duplicate to create a copy of the selected path and inset the copy to work with both.

Converting Text into Paths

Text objects are made up of many paths that define the characters in a font. When you convert a text object into a path, you are sacrificing control over the text content (the characters you typed or pasted) to gain control over the shapes of the characters in the selected font. This means the spell checker and the Find and Replace panel do not work with text objects that have been converted into path objects.

To convert a text object into a group of path objects, simply select a text object with the pointer and then select Convert to Paths from the Text menu or press Ctrl+Shift+P (Windows) or Command-Shift-P (Macintosh). The text object changes to a group object on the Canvas and in the Layers panel, as shown in Figure 27.10. Press Ctrl+Shift+G (Windows) or Command-Shift-G (Macintosh) to ungroup the object so you can select individual characters with the Pointer tool. Many text characters that contain voids, such as P, Q, and R, are composite paths. Use Split from the Combine commands on the Modify menu to break these paths apart, or use Join to restore them.

After you've converted text to a path, you can work with the paths through any of the tools in the Vector group or any of the path operations in the Modify menu. This technique is often used when designing logo graphics to lend more flexibility to how characters appear graphically. Remember to always keep an original copy of the text object on a locked or hidden layer, in case you need to change a character later.

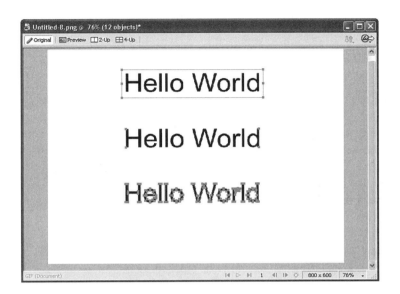

FIGURE 27.10
The first object is a text object; note the text object bounding box. The next is the same object converted to paths; converted text is initially grouped. Below that are the ungrouped paths. Each character is an individual path object.

Converting text into paths was a common operation for working with documents that were to be moved from one machine to another, to ensure font decisions were preserved. Fireworks MX caches a copy of all fonts used in a source PNG so the file can travel freely without your having to worry about which fonts are available on the system. You can still use this technique when exporting a Photoshop PSD or Adobe Illustrator file; any fonts in the exported document have to be available on the system for which the document is destined. Remember to keep a text object original in case the text needs to be changed!

Did you Know?

Using Paths As Masks

You've learned how to add bitmaps as masks to other bitmaps. You can also use path objects as masks in much the same way. A *mask* selectively shows or hides the object or group being masked. You can use path or text objects to mask bitmaps, paths, text, or groups. You can also use grayscale or alpha-channel bitmaps to mask paths, text, or groups just like you would mask a bitmap.

To use a path as a mask, draw or paste the path over the objects you would like to mask. Make sure the path you intend to mask with is the topmost object. Now use Shift+click to select the masking path and all the objects you want to mask with the Pointer tool. From the Mask commands on the Modify menu, select Group As Mask. In the topmost object, areas within the path outline (the area covered by the mask's fill) are visible, whereas areas outside it are not.

When an object is masked, the mask appears next to the object on the Layers panel. Vector masks are marked with a pen tip icon in the lower-right corner. Select the masked object and then select Disable Mask from the Mask commands in the Modify menu to remove the mask and restore the paths within the mask. Select Delete Mask to delete the mask and any paths in it. You can also use the Paste As Mask command in the Edit menu to add a mask. Simply copy the path you would like to use as a mask, select with the Pointer tool the objects you want to mask, and select Paste As Mask from the Edit menu (it's also available from the Mask commands in the Modify menu).

Did you Know?

There's one more way to apply a mask. Instead of copying an object and pasting it as a mask, you can copy the objects to be masked, select the objects with the Pointer tool to mask them, and either select Paste Inside from the Edit menu or press Ctrl+Shift+V (Windows) or Command-Shift-V (Macintosh). The objects in the clipboard are pasted within the outlines of the selected path object.

Click the mask icon in the Layers panel to bring up the mask setting in the Properties Inspector. You can choose to mask to the Path Outline (default) or use the grayscale appearance properties of the path's fill and stroke like you would with a bitmap mask. Darker areas hide more, and lighter areas reveal more. When Path Outline is selected, you can also choose the Show Fill and Stroke command. The fill and stroke settings for the masking path are available at the bottom of the Properties Inspector. The opacity, Blending mode, and effect settings affect the entire masked object as a group. Use the Subselection tool to select elements within a masked group to change their stroke, fill, opacity, Blending mode, or effect settings individually.

Using Rules, the Grid, and Alignment

After you begin adding elements to a design or layout, things can start to get pretty cluttered. Eventually, you are going to want everything neatly placed on the Canvas. This is where layout guides can come in handy.

Placing Guides with the Rulers

To begin placing vertical or horizontal guides, select Rulers from the View menu or press Ctrl+Alt+R (Windows) or Command-Option-R (Macintosh). This toggles the rulers in the workspace. The ruler units default to pixels. With the rulers visible, click the top ruler and drag it into the Canvas to place a horizontal guide. Click the left ruler and drag it over the canvas to place a vertical guide, as shown in Figure 27.11. Next, click the guide and drag it to reposition it. Double-click the guide to enter a numerical value for the position.

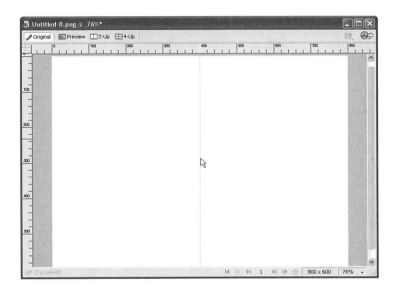

FIGURE 27.11
Use the rulers to place guides on the Canvas for help in aligning objects.

Select Show Guides from the Guides commands in the View menu to show or hide the guides. Select Lock Guides to lock the guides in their current positions. When Snap to Guides is checked, the cursor automatically positions itself along the guide while drawing or moving an object or point. Selecting Edit Guides lets you change the color of the guidelines and also lets you select Show, Snap to, or Lock Guides.

Ruler guides are different from slice guides, which are used to lay out slices on the Web layer. Ruler guides are used only for laying out artwork on the Canvas. Ruler guides are not objects and don't exist within a particular layer. They are never exported as part of an image.

By the Way

Laying Out and Drawing with the Grid

You can also use a grid in place of or in addition to rulers and guides. To show the grid, select Show Grid from the Grid commands in the View menu or press

Ctrl+Alt+G (Windows) or Command-Option-G (Macintosh). The grid appears on the Canvas. Select Snap to Grid to have the cursor snap to the nearest line on the grid when drawing or moving objects or points. Select Edit Grid to change how the grid is shown and laid out, as demonstrated in Figure 27.12. You can select the color of the grid and the sizing of the gridlines, and you can select Show or Snap to Grid.

FIGURE 27.12
You can customize your grid layout by changing color and sizing.

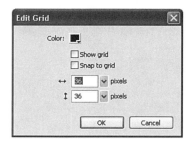

Aligning Objects with the Align Panel

Another way to ensure that two objects line up horizontally or vertically is to use the Align panel or the Align commands on the Modify menu. Aligning to the left aligns all selected objects to the leftmost point among them. Center Horizontal aligns them all down the middle, and Distribute Widths or Heights distributes the objects evenly between their current bounds.

Select Align from the Window menu to bring up the Align panel, where you can see icons representing how the alignment would look, as shown in Figure 27.13. With the Align panel, you can also click the To Canvas button to align objects on the sides or down the middle of the canvas. You can also choose to distribute objects, match the vertical or horizontal dimensions of the objects, or space the objects evenly. Clicking the Anchors button lets you align points selected with the Subselection tool within a path. You can also choose to align to the preceding control points of selected anchor points, the selected anchor and control points, or the succeeding control points of the selected anchor points.

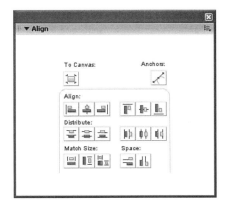

FIGURE 27.13
The Align panel can align a bunch of paths along the canvas edges, and so on.

Summary

Give yourself a hand; you should now have a firm grasp of the fundamentals of the Fireworks MX vector graphics tools. If you've worked with vector graphics before, you should now be able to find most of the tools you would ever need to work with Paths in Fireworks. And because you can also create and edit bitmaps in the same application, you will be able to save time that you otherwise would have spent switching from one application to another.

CHAPTER 28

Choosing Optimization Settings and Exporting Graphics

Where Fireworks really shines is in enabling you to export graphics into many formats quickly and easily, with fine control over every detail, including colors, transparency, and compression. Now that you've mastered the Fireworks graphics creation tools, let's discuss how your creations can be saved in formats other than the default Fireworks PNG files.

Working with Different Output Formats

Fireworks can export a number of different graphics formats, each with its own strengths and weaknesses. For instance, exporting as TIFF might create a file even bigger than the Fireworks source PNG. JPEG is particularly bad as a format for images with lots of text, such as a screenshot or button. The following is a list of file formats that can be optimized and exported with Fireworks:

GIF—GIF images are one of the most widely supported formats for computers and the Web. Images with a lot of text or line art and a limited palette work best as GIF images. GIF images have a palette of no more than 8 bits but can create very small files. GIF images can also contain a transparency mask.

Animated GIF—Animated GIF export creates files of the same format as regular GIF files, but they can contain multiple frames and display them at intervals to create moving images. Animated GIFs can become very large unless special steps are taken to optimize them.

JPEG—Another widely used format for the Web is JPEG, which is best for photos and other images with a full range of colors. With JPEG you can vary the level of compression by trading image detail for file size—the smaller the file size in bytes, the less detail the image will contain. This is considered a *lossy* compression method.

PNG—PNG export is for creating PNG graphics without Fireworks' special features. Most Web browsers and graphic applications do not support all of Fireworks' special PNG features but do support the more basic format features. The basic PNG format uses non-lossy compression like GIF but saves more detailed color and transparency information.

WBMP—The wireless bitmap format is used for creating graphics for tiny, monochrome displays common on wireless devices, such as cell phones and PDAs. These images are naturally very small because each pixel must be either black or white and the dimensions must be similarly restrained. Non-lossy compression, such as GIF compression, is employed to make the files even smaller.

TIFF—This format is often used in the print industry and for moving images between graphics applications. Many Web browsers do not support this format. TIFF files exported from Fireworks employ non-lossy compression and can contain the full RGB palette plus an 8-bit alpha channel.

By the Way

When your image-processing software, in order to reduce the file size, removes information that is more or less redundant to the human eye, this is known as *lossy compression*. The advantage of lossy compression is that it gives a high degree of compression, often 5–30 times. The disadvantage is that the quality of the image is reduced as the compression increases.

When you use a *non-lossy compression* format, all original information is saved in the image. The disadvantage is that the compression ratio is much lower, leading to larger file sizes.

In Chapter 23, "Working with Photos," we discussed selective JPEG compression, which enables you to choose areas of a photograph that can be highly compressed without losing visible detail.

PICT—Used almost exclusively on the Apple Macintosh platform, this format does not use compression; files can be made smaller only by restricting the palette or dimensions. PICT image files are rarely used in Web pages. They are used mostly in production as a backup or transfer format.

BMP—This is the basic image format for Microsoft Windows. Like PICT, it can use the full RGB palette but does not use compression—but this can also create large files. For this reason, this format is also less common on the Web.

Comparing Compression

Fireworks makes choosing between different compression formats easy. Open a bitmap file from your computer so you can see how different compression formats affect image quality and file size.

With the Canvas open in your workspace, find the buttons Original, Preview, 2-Up, and 4-Up above the Canvas and below the menus, as shown in Figure 28.1. These tabs let you switch between editing the original and previewing the export output. When you want to view or edit the source graphic, select the Original tab (default). To preview how the output file will appear when exported into a different format, click the Preview tab. The 2-Up and 4-Up tabs let you compare different types of compression at the same time.

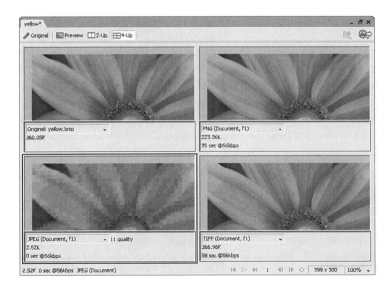

FIGURE 28.1
The view mode tabs include Original, Preview, 2-Up, and 4-Up.

To change the optimization settings, you can use the Optimize panel, as shown in Figure 28.2. Expand the Optimize panel in the dock by clicking the arrow next to its name. If the Optimize panel isn't visible, select Optimize from the Window menu or press F6.

At the top of the Optimize panel is a drop-down menu named Settings. This menu is where optimization presets are stored. The default setting is GIF WebSnap 128. If this isn't the current setting, select it now. Now change the setting to

JPEG—Smaller File. Click the 2-Up Preview tab; then notice how the image preview on the right changes. Also, underneath the two previews is the file size and an estimate of how long it will take to download over a 56Kbps modem.

FIGURE 28.2
The Optimize panel lets you fine-tune format settings.

To compare the current setting to the original images, select the 2-Up tab. The workspace splits into two—the left represents how the original document appears, and the right previews the optimized file. To compare the original to different compression options, select the 4-Up tab. The workspace splits into four windows, with the original image in the top left. Click a quadrant to change the optimization settings for that preview. This lets you preview several compression settings at once, with the original as a reference.

Advanced Compression Settings

Now take a closer look at the two most common compression formats you'll be using, GIF and JPEG. Because they approach file size compression completely differently from each other and also handle colors and other information differently, they should be used for distinct purposes. If you're ever confused as to which one to apply, use the Preview tabs in the workspace to compare and contrast.

GIF Compression

CompuServe created the GIF standard when 256 colors were all that most computers were capable of displaying. Over the years the format developed into the 89a version, which is still in use today. GIF was popular for line art and text scanning and early multimedia applications, but for photographic purposes it is limited. With photographs, the limited palette means dithering and posterization must be added to approximate the original color. This can be considered an artifact of the compression because it artificially compromises image detail.

Still, for the vast majority of uses on the Web, GIF is a fine tool for designers. GIF images are used for typographic effects, icons, buttons, and all sorts of elemental design graphics. Incredibly small GIFs, when tiled, can create interesting effects. The GIF format also supports multiframe, or animated, images.

To access the GIF format directly on the Optimize panel, simply select it from the drop-down menu at the top right, underneath the Settings menu, as shown in Figure 28.3.

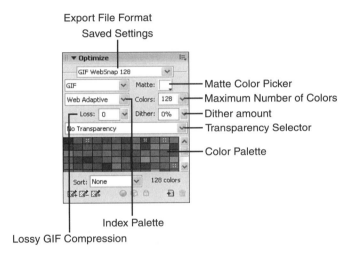

Export File Format
Saved Settings
Matte Color Picker
Maximum Number of Colors
Dither amount
Transparency Selector
Color Palette
Index Palette
Lossy GIF Compression

FIGURE 28.3
The GIF format forces you into an 8-bit palette but creates small files and gives you ultimate control.

Palette

The GIF palette is limited to 256 total colors, or 8 bits. However, the palette can consist of as few as 2 colors, or 1 bit. The following is a list of the palette settings and tools available on the Optimize panel with the GIF format. When the GIF format is chosen, the palette presets are available from the drop-down menu directly beneath the format menu. Many of these palette and optimization settings are also available for other 8-bit formats, including PNG, PICT, BMP, and TIFF:

> **Adaptive**—An adaptive palette chooses colors based on the colors in the original image, approximating similar colors to reduce the total number of colors. This means slight gradations flatten into a single color (posterize) and some important colors might be changed slightly.

> **WebSnap Adaptive**—This is similar to the adaptive setting except it favors colors within the Web-safe palette. This is important when you've chosen to use Web-safe colors but don't want to lose them to approximation by a regular adaptive palette.

Web 216—The Web 216, or Web-safe, palette consists of colors that can be assumed to look the same on both Macintosh and Windows systems. Because of gamma, however, colors generally appear darker on a Windows system and brighter on a Macintosh system. To preview the Web 216 palette at a different gamma setting, select Macintosh Gamma or Windows Gamma from the View menu.

Exact—This can be used only when the source graphic already contains an 8-bit palette, as do imported GIFs and some bitmap and TIFF images. This preserves the original palette colors.

Macintosh—This is the Macintosh system palette. These colors always appear correctly on Macintosh systems.

Windows—This is the Windows system palette. These colors always appear correctly on Windows systems.

Grayscale—The grayscale palette consists entirely of gray (neutral) colors. This removes any color information from the output but most reliably maintains subtle gradations of light and dark.

Black and White—Black and White is a 1-bit format that contains only two colors: black and white. This is typically used for line art and transparency masks.

Uniform—Uniform preserves the gradation of the palette itself, disregarding the original color information. The uniform palette is based on pixel values from the RGB Color Model.

Custom—Custom palettes can be imported from ACT palette files and other GIF images. This is especially useful because it means you can apply a pre-existing palette to new output, ensuring consistency throughout a project. After you select the custom setting, Fireworks prompts you with a dialog box to open the ACT or GIF file.

When you change the palette setting, the results are reflected in the palette view below. These swatches represent each of the colors that will be used in the final output. The following sections list a number of advanced controls for editing the palette.

Color Depth

To reduce the size of a GIF image quickly, use the Colors setting to reduce the number of colors. This setting determines the total number of colors available for the palette. This figure can be anywhere from 2 to 256. Halving the number of colors generally halves the size of the image. Of course, this makes fewer colors available to the image output and could compromise quality.

You can use dithering to approximate lost colors. Dithering arranges the available colors to simulate gradations in shading. It can compromise quality when used with anti-aliasing or transparency, and dithering can carry a penalty in output file size. Setting Dither to 0 forces no dithering, whereas setting it to 100 dithers any colors outside the palette. Loss can also be used to offset the size of a full-palette or dithered GIF but carries a penalty in detail similar to JPEG compression. A setting of 0 ensures pixel accuracy; 100 fully compromises detail for file size.

Transparency

GIF images support transparency. Transparent pixels allow any color information under them, such as a Web page background color or another image layered underneath, to show through. Use the Matte setting to choose the intended background color, if different from the Canvas background color. Directly above the palette is a drop-down menu that enables you to choose between No Transparency (the default), Index Transparency, and Alpha Transparency. GIFs support only Index Transparency—pixels are either on or off, so there can be no gradation to the transparency, which often conflicts with anti-alias shading (much more on this later in the book, but see the following tip for now). Alpha transparency enables transparency shading but is supported only by the PNG format. To pick a color for transparency, select the Select Transparent Color eyedropper at the bottom of the Optimize panel. To add more colors as transparent, select Add Color to Transparency; to remove them, select Remove Color from Transparency. Transparency appears in the palette as a swatch of gray-and-white grid.

Did you **Know?**

> *Aliasing* is the jagged edging of curved and diagonal lines in a bitmap image. Enlarging a bitmap image accentuates the effect of aliasing. *Anti-aliasing* is the process of smoothing out those edges and is often also referred to as *font smoothing*. Font-smoothing software anti-aliases onscreen type. Graphics software programs have options to anti-alias text and graphics.

Swatches

There are more tools for managing the different colors, or swatches, in the palette. Directly below the palette display is the Sort menu, which enables you to sort the colors by Luminance or Popularity. Luminance sorts from light to dark;

Popularity sorts pixels based on how often they appear in the output. Below this, and next to the transparency tools, are tools for managing individual swatches. Select a swatch and select Edit Color to select a new value from the system color picker. Select Snap to Web Safe to change the color to the nearest value in the Web 216 palette. The Lock color button enables you to lock the color value from further changes. To the right, Add Color and Delete Color let you add or remove specific colors.

A few options for optimizing GIFs are available only through the Optimize panel's Options menu. As shown in Figure 28.4, this menu is located in the upper-right corner of the Optimize panel.

FIGURE 28.4
The Optimize panel's Options menu offers more options for optimizing images, based on your current selection. Here you see the Options menu when GIF format is selected.

Interlaced

Interlacing enables the pixels in an image to be written in alternating order, so that as the image downloads, it can seem to appear full size more quickly. Every other line loads first, and these are all doubled to display an approximation of the original. Then the remaining lines are loaded in place of the doubles, clearing up the image to full detail. This is commonly used to make images appear more quickly when loading on Web pages because it carries only a small file-size penalty.

Remove Unused Colors

The default for GIF optimization, this allows you to trim down the palette quickly by removing any colors that aren't used in the output (generally because they aren't in the original, either). Remove Unused Colors does not affect locked colors in the palette. Turn this off if you want to work with a full palette and delete colors yourself.

Save Palette

This saves the palette as an ACT palette file for use with Fireworks or other applications. The Load Palette command can also be accessed from the Optimize panel menu, but this is identical to selecting a Custom palette from the palette settings in the panel itself.

JPEG Compression

Because of the limitations GIF poses to photographers, the Joint Photo Experts Group commissioned a standard that came to be known as JPEG. JPEG uses variable lossy compression, which trades quality for file size by approximating the original pixels with an algorithm. The more compression applied, the less original data available for the image, a fact which makes the image appear blurry. This blurriness is another artifact because the approximations won't always be correct, especially at high compression ratios.

JPEGs are now a standard for sharing detailed images in high resolutions. As with GIF images, the Optimize panel offers choices specific to JPEG images, as shown in Figure 28.5.

FIGURE 28.5
The JPEG format is deceptively simple but can offer incredible compression ratios with acceptable loss.

Matte

Use the matte color to change the background color if the image contains any transparency information. JPEG images do not support transparency. This does not affect the Canvas background color.

Quality

This is the setting for the level of lossy compression. A value of 100 is indistinguishable from the original, whereas 0 creates the absolutely smallest files. In terms of file size, the change is most noticeable between 100 and 80; a setting in this range dramatically decreases file size with a minimum of detail loss. A setting of 60 or below gives a very small file, but detail is noticeably compromised.

Selective Quality

One of the great features of the JPEG format is the capability to use selective compression. With this process, important details can be compressed at one level while background information is compressed at another. You learned about selective quality in Chapter 23.

Smoothing

JPEG compression breaks an image into a grid and then uses a mathematical algorithm to approximate the content of the grid. The more compression applied, the more noticeable the grid and the approximations become. To help alleviate the problem, smoothing can be applied to blur these artifacts. Smoothing is a compromise, however, because it does not improve image detail and can make images appear blurry or out of focus.

Two important JPEG settings are available from the drop-down menu in the upper-right corner of the Optimize panel. Progressive JPEG, which is similar to the GIF Interlaced setting, allows for faster image displays for the Web. Sharpen Color Edges can improve text and line art detail compressed in the JPEG format.

Saving Compression Presets

After you've worked with the Optimize panel and the preview window to examine the various qualities of GIF and JPEG compression, you might want to save them for use later. Saved setting presets are available in the Settings menu on the Optimize panel, so they're easy to find later, and as a file on your hard disk, so you can share them with others.

To save a custom setting, simply make your optimization choices and select Save Settings from the panel pop-up menu. You are then prompted for a name for your preset. Enter one and click OK to continue. The preset is now available in the Settings drop-down menu. To remove a setting from the menu, select it and then click the minus icon. You are asked to confirm the deletion. You can also save your custom preset with the Optimize panel drop-down menu by selecting Save Settings.

Another great tool available for GIF, JPEG, and PNG compression is Optimize to Size, which you can find in the Optimize panel's drop-down menu. You are prompted to enter a size in kilobytes, and the format settings are automatically changed to fit the image under that value.

Did you Know?

Exporting from Fireworks

Now it's time to export your image for use on the Web. You'll have to glance over some basic Web publishing and HTML page topics while you're getting started. You will also be introduced to the Export Preview dialog box, where you can fine-tune your optimization settings before exporting and finish a simple placeholder page for your Web site.

Exporting an Image As a Page for the Web

You have had a chance to look through the most commonly used optimization settings. Now you will take an image file and work through the process of exporting it for Web usage. Do the following:

1. Select Export Preview from the File menu or press Ctrl+Shift+X (Windows) or Command-Shift-X (Macintosh).

2. The Export Preview dialog box appears, as shown in Figure 28.6. On the left is where you specify format options, as well as file and animation settings, which are available as tabs in the upper left. On the right is the preview area, which gives you file size feedback, the Settings drop-down menu, and an area to preview the image output.

3. From the Format drop-down menu on the Options tab, make sure JPEG is selected and that the Quality setting is at 70.

4. Check the box to select Progressive to create a progressive JPEG. This should also help reduce the file size, which should be less than 30KB.

5. Check the box to select Sharpen Color Edges. Zoom in on the text and graphic with the magnifying glass to see how this affects text and line art—there should be a subtle improvement.

6. In the lower right are the dialog options. Export begins the process of exporting your graphics, whereas OK saves the current export settings and changes the Optimize panel settings to reflect your decisions. Cancel disregards any changes and returns to where you left off. Click Export to continue exporting your image.

FIGURE 28.6
The Export Preview
dialog box lets you
focus on the export
output settings.

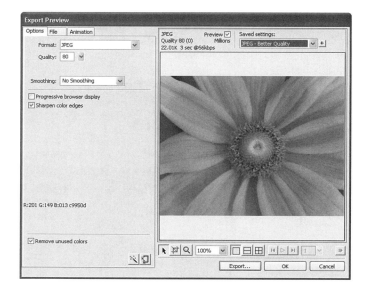

7. The Export dialog box is where you will save images for use on the Web and other applications. Navigate to an empty area on your drive and type **index**; this saves the image file as `index.jpg`.

8. From the Save As menu, select HTML and Images. This exports code generated automatically by Fireworks along with the image.

9. The HTML drop-down menu should now be active. Make sure Export to File is selected—this creates a file named `index.htm`. Copy to Clipboard copies the HTML source code to the clipboard for use in another application, such as a text editor.

By the Way

> On a Web server, the `index.htm` file is often the default file displayed when the parent directory is accessed. Your Web host or network administrator will tell you what your file needs to be called. Other common names are `index.html`, `default.htm`, and `default.html`.

10. Now you can click Save or press Return to export your image and Web page.

11. Launch your favorite browser and select Open from the File menu. Browse to the file `index.htm`. The Web page now opens in your browser and displays the image `index.jpg`.

Great! You've started a Web site. You're not quite qualified to start advertising your services as a Web designer, but you should easily be able to get any image into a format ready for the Web. We'll talk more about exporting HTML in the next chapter.

Summary

In this chapter we covered the basics of export formats and compression techniques, including available export file formats, GIF and JPEG optimization with the Optimize panel, previewing export output, and using Export to save your output to your hard drive along with a simple HTML file so you can post the image to the Web.

CHAPTER 29

Slicing Layouts

One of the most powerful strategies for designing Web pages is to quickly cut up an image into small parts to add links, save file size, and arrange graphics and animation on a page along with text. Using the Web Layer in Fireworks MX, you can create slice objects to partition your template layout into areas that are then exported into separate files. Slices can also be named, optimized individually, and then exported with HTML code for the Web and other applications.

What Are Slices, and Why Should I Use Them?

In the early days of the Web, the people who put many current standards in place didn't necessarily envision the explosion of color, sound, and movement that Web pages now use regularly. The basic language of Web pages—Hypertext Markup Language (HTML)—was designed specifically for academic documents. The early developers thought only scientists and professors would likely use the Web because it was largely intended as a research and communication tool.

When commercial interests began to hire graphic designers to create visually compelling Web pages, the designers had to work around the limitations of HTML as a design medium with what were sometimes inelegant solutions. The most important innovation was with HTML tables, which were originally meant for laying out rows and columns of statistics and data. Using tables, text and graphics could be laid out together with more control and file sizes could be kept minimal. Being able to hand-code, or *hack*, tables became a fundamental Web design skill. But coding these intricate tables and cropping all the graphics to fit were complicated and time-consuming—making small changes took almost as long as reworking the whole layout.

Fireworks came to the rescue with a system for cutting up source images and automatically computing the HTML code necessary for the table layout. A *slice* represents an area of the source image that will be exported as an individual file and laid out with other slices using an HTML table. Of course, slices can also be used for simply making multiple crops from a single image or cutting graphics up for use in Flash or

Director as individual symbols or cast members. Fireworks can export slices for use as a graphics library for a site in Dreamweaver MX, for instance. And because designers are beginning to move away from HTML, Fireworks can create layouts using Cascading Style Sheets (CSS) or XHTML, as well.

> According to the World Wide Web Consortium, which governs such matters, HTML will be phased out in favor of XML. It declares, "XHTML... is the next step in the evolution of the Internet." In other words, XHTML is the "bridge language" that will get us to XML. In theory, XHTML provides a markup language that doesn't force developers to re-create the same document for different browsers or different devices because the extensibility mechanism will eventually be able to sniff out the client and return the right information in the right form, whether the device is a high-resolution computer monitor or a four-line PDA.

Creating Slices on the Web Layer

To create a slice on the Web Layer, simply select the Slice tool by pressing K and click-drag to create a rectangular slice, as in Figure 29.1. Most slices are rectangular because bitmap image files and HTML table cells are also rectangular. A transparent green box with red outlines appears on the canvas. Lines also appear, running away from the top and bottom of the sliced image. Because of how tables work, slice guides are created, which ensures that when loading into a browser separately, the slice and the rest of the image come together accurately to form a complete image. You can arrange other slices along these guides or choose not to export areas that aren't actually part of a slice.

When a slice is created or selected, the Web Layer automatically becomes the active layer in the Layers panel. A slice is an object just like a bitmap, path, text, group, or symbol and can be copied or pasted, but it cannot be grouped or placed on any layer other than the Web Layer. Slices also apply to all frames—the Web Layer is always shared across frames. Slices on the Web Layer can be selected with the Pointer tool. To change the dimensions of a slice, click any of the square handles at the corners of the bounding box with the Pointer tool and drag to change the position of that corner.

While changing or creating slices, the cursor snaps to other slices or slice guides already on the Web Layer. This is important because overlapping slices do not display correctly when laid out using HTML tables. Use the Zoom tool to magnify slice borders to ensure that slices are correctly aligned before finally exporting. You can also use the slice guides, which are the lines that extend from the slice bounding boxes into areas of the document that aren't sliced.

FIGURE 29.1
The Slice tool can create a slice object on the Web Layer. Each slice object represents an HTML table cell and can contain either an image file or HTML code.

When working with graphics, you can lock or hide the slice layer to ensure you don't make any inadvertent changes to the image slicing. You can change the color of the slice guides and decide whether to show or hide them by selecting Edit Guides from the Guides commands on the View menu. For the same reason, it's also good to lock layers with graphics before working with the Web Layer. Slices and their settings can be saved with the document only by using the Save command from the File menu to create a Fireworks source PNG.

Sometimes you might need to create slices that aren't rectangular. You can press K to toggle between the Slice tool and the Polygon Slice tool. You can also select a vector path object on the Canvas and select Slice from the Insert commands on the Edit menu to convert it into a rectangular or polygon slice on the Web Layer. Polygon slices are exported as regular rectangular bitmaps with a polygon image map hotspot.

Did you Know?

Specifying Slice Properties

To change the settings for a slice selected with the Pointer tool, simply use the Properties Inspector panel, as shown in Figure 29.2. Slice settings include the slice name, dimensions, position, and type. The names are automatically appended with row and column designators. The slice name in the Properties Inspector is used to name the file when the area is exported. You can change the width, height, and X and Y positions by entering new values in the Properties Inspector. You can also change the color of the slice if it's interfering with the graphics layered below. Click the color swatch in the middle of the Properties Inspector to change the color of the slice.

FIGURE 29.2
Adjust the properties of the slice.

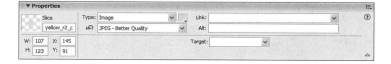

Other settings depend on the type of slice. A slice can be either an image slice or an HTML slice. An image slice area is exported as an image file and laid out on the page in a table cell. An HTML slice area adds a portion of HTML code, such as HTML tags or text.

When using the Reconstitute Table command on the File menu to import an existing Web page and graphics as a Fireworks source PNG, or when working with Dreamweaver MX, you can edit non-image portions of the HTML source within areas defined by an HTML slice. No graphics are exported in areas covered by an HTML slice.

Image slice settings include the compression preset to be used; a URL, or Web link, that's activated when a user clicks the image; a value for the Alt tag, which is used as an alternative text description for systems that don't display images; and a target attribute for the link to open the link in another frame or window. If you don't want to use a compression preset for the selected slice, change the optimization settings through the Optimize panel. Each slice can be optimized with different settings. To apply new settings to multiple slices simultaneously, use Shift+click with the Pointer tool to select more than one slice and then specify settings through the Optimize panel or select a preset from the Properties Inspector.

By the Way

It's important to use Alt tags to describe images whenever possible—especially if the image contains text, such as a title or link. Although only a small percentage of users use Web browsers or systems that don't display images, they are still part of a global audience. Many users with slow systems or Internet connections choose not to display images because of the slowdown. This is especially true of handheld wireless users, whose screens are small and have limited bandwidth. Alt tags also help search engines better categorize the content on your site, potentially increasing valuable traffic.

Exporting Image Slices

To export a template layout with slices on a Web layer with or without HTML code, use the Export command from the File menu. Select Images Only from the Save As Type menu if you don't need to export HTML code, or select HTML and Images if you want to export HTML along with the sliced images. When exporting HTML, you can click the Options button to bring up the HTML Setup dialog box.

You can choose to turn off slicing and export the entire document at the canvas optimization setting by selecting None from the Slices menu. Export Slices exports all slice objects. Slice Along Guides uses the layout guides placed with the rulers as the slicing scheme but does not export symbol properties like behaviors.

Options for image slicing include a check box to export Selected Slices Only, which exports only one or more slice objects selected with the Pointer tool. Include Areas Without Slices exports areas of the Canvas between the slice guides that aren't part of a slice object. If more than one frame exists, you can choose to export all the frames or the current frame only. If you are exporting HTML and images, you can save the images to a subfolder relative to the location of the HTML file. Click Browse to change the folder.

Importing Existing Sliced Pages into Fireworks

If you have an existing HTML Web page you've inherited but don't have the Fireworks or Dreamweaver file that created it, don't despair. Fireworks MX 2004 can open existing HTML files and their associated images and covert them into a new Fireworks PNG document.

To do this, make sure the images and HTML file are on your computer and loaded correctly in a Web browser. Next, select Reconstitute Table from the File menu, and select the HTML page. After a few seconds, the page appears laid out (without text) as it would appear in your browser. You can then edit and export the document as you would any other Fireworks PNG file.

The Reconstitute Table command rebuilds the Web page using all the tables in the HTML file. If you'd like to only use the first table, simply select Open from the File menu and select the HTML document. Only the first HTML table is then imported.

Summary

Whether or not you want to create your graphics in Fireworks, you can still use Fireworks to segment your layout into files for an HTML table layout using slices. With the tricks shown here, you can create Web pages that load quickly and that every user can access and navigate easily. In the next chapter you'll start adding interactivity, including links and button behaviors that respond to the user.

CHAPTER 30

Planning and Creating Animation for the Web

In this chapter you will begin working with animated graphics. You'll learn the tools you'll use to create animations in Fireworks MX. These tools include frames, symbols, and shared layers, which can be used to aid Web site design as well as to create motion graphics.

Creating and Organizing New Frames

When working with animations, you'll be using the Frames panel, which by default is grouped with the History panel. All images in Fireworks MX have at least one frame, which is all you need to create a static image. To add a frame, simply click the New/Duplicate Frame button at the bottom of the Frames panel, shown in Figure 30.1. This adds a frame after the last frame in the list. You can also use the Add Frames command in the Frames panel Options menu. You can choose to add one or more frames at the beginning, before the current frame, after the current frame, or at the end.

To select a frame, click the frame in the Frames panel. It becomes the active frame shown in the Canvas, and the frame row in the Frames panel is denoted by a dotted border. To select a group of contiguous frames use Shift+click. To select a group that is not contiguous, use Ctrl+Shift+click (Windows) or Command-click (Macintosh).

To duplicate one or more frames, select them and then click-drag the selected frames to the New/Duplicate Frame button on the Frames panel. Select one or more frames and click the Delete Frame button to delete the selected frames (if all the frames are selected, the first frame is not deleted).

> All frames in a document share the same Canvas. You cannot change the Canvas size for individual frames. For that, you must create a new document. Naturally, the frames also share all the other Canvas settings, including resolution and background color.
>
> **By the Way**

FIGURE 30.1
The Frames panel
is where you can
choose which
frames to view,
edit, add,
rearrange, or
delete.

If you would like to change the order of the frames, select one or more frames and then click-drag them to their new positions in the frame sequence. A black bar shows where the frames will be inserted. To step through frames or preview an animation, use the controls in the workspace below the Canvas. The first left arrow brings you to the first frame. The white right arrow plays the animation, and the next right arrow brings you to the end of the animation. The number of the current frame in the sequence is noted here. The next two arrows step one frame backward and forward, respectively.

While the animation is playing, the white arrow changes to a black stop button. It then automatically changes back when the animation is stopped.

Specifying Frame Names, Timing, and Looping

By default, frames are named in the order they appear in the sequence, beginning at 1. When you rearrange frames, the default names change to remain in numerical order. When you change the name of a frame, the custom name is not changed when the frame's position in the sequence is changed. To name a frame, double-click the current frame name listed in the Frames panel. A field appears in which you can type the new name. Press the Enter key to apply and save the new name.

By double-clicking the right column of a frame's row, you can change the duration of the frame in the sequence, as shown in Figure 30.2. Durations are specified in hundredths of a second. A value of 100 displays the frame for 1 second, whereas a value of 6000 displays the frame for 1 minute. To calculate the frames per second (fps), divide 100 by the desired frame rate. A rate of 5 fps means each frame's duration is 20/100 of a second. You can also disable a frame from export by unchecking the Include when Exporting box. A red X appears in the duration column, but the frame is not deleted or changed.

FIGURE 30.2
Specify the length of time each frame is held onscreen.

To specify sequence looping, click the Looping button at the bottom of the Frames panel. You can select No Looping if you do not want the animation to repeat. You can also specify a number of times to loop from 1 to 20. Forever loops the animation endlessly. The current number of loops is listed to the right of the button. You can also specify an exact number of loops using the Export Preview dialog box, which is discussed later in the chapter.

Working with Layers and Frames

Layers created for any frame are present for all frames in the document but might not contain graphics on individual frames. The content of the layers can change from frame to frame, but their names, settings, and stacking order in the Layers panel do not. You can share a layer to make its contents the same for all frames. To share a layer from any frame (the frame name is noted at the bottom of the Layers panel), double-click the layer name in the Layers panel and check the Share Across Frames box. The objects on the shared layer from the current active frame become available on that layer in all frames. A filmstrip icon with an arrow pointing left and right appears in the layer's row to denote a shared layer. The Web Layer is always shared—slice objects on the Web Layer cannot change from frame to frame.

Frames can also be a great tool for laying out Web pages. Template elements such as guides, symbols, buttons, and background graphics can be placed on a shared layer. New frames can be created for each page that uses the template, and text or graphics for each page can quickly be composed within the template. Guides and grids don't change from frame to frame, making it easy to align graphics and text from page to page. Comparing pages against each other becomes a snap!

Converting Objects into Symbols

An important feature of Fireworks is its capability to convert graphic objects into symbols. Any object in Fireworks can be converted into a bitmap, path, text, or group. Symbol objects are similar to groups but have special features, such as the capability to edit instances of the symbol individually or universally and to apply behaviors (such as button interaction or animation) to them. When one or more objects are converted into a symbol object, a new item is created in the Library panel, so you can simply drag and drop symbols from the Library onto the canvas.

There are three types of symbols—graphic symbols, animation symbols, and button symbols. In this chapter you'll use graphic and animation symbols to create some simple animations. You'll also use the familiar menus and the Layers, Frames, and Properties (Properties Inspector) panels to work with symbols.

To create a symbol from objects on the Canvas, select the objects with the Pointer tool and select Convert to Symbol from the Symbol commands on the Modify menu or press F8 (Windows and Macintosh). You can choose to create a symbol object of the Graphic, Animation, or Button type. To remove the objects from a symbol, select the symbol with the Pointer tool and select Break Apart from the Symbol commands on the Modify menu.

Inserting Motion Tweens

An easy way to animate an object across multiple frames is to use tweening. In traditional animation the artist drew the keyframes for character motion and interaction and the assistant drew the frames in between. These in-between frames ended up with the nickname *tweens*. Fireworks can act as your animation assistant by drawing all the necessary steps between two copies of a graphics symbol.

To tween one or more objects, select them with the pointer and use Convert to Symbol from the Symbol commands on the Modify menu or press F8. Name the symbol and select the graphic type. The objects are now a selected symbol on the Canvas. Use Duplicate from the Edit menu to create a copy of the symbol on the same layer. Click and drag with the pointer or use the Transform tools to move and modify the copy. You can also use tweening for copies with a different opacity, as shown in Figure 30.3.

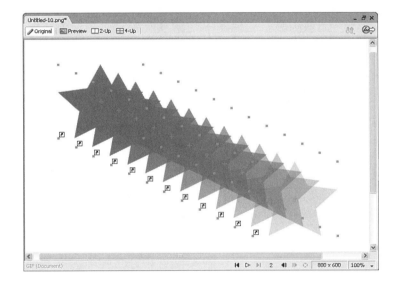

FIGURE 30.3
These are two copies of the same graphic symbol, but the one on the right has been transformed and its opacity has been halved.

Use Shift+click with the Pointer tool to select both copies of the symbol. Select Tween Instances from the Symbol commands on the Modify menu, or press Ctrl+Alt+Shift+T (Windows) or Command-Option-Shift-T (Macintosh). The Tween Instances dialog box opens; it has only two fields, as follows:

▶ **Steps**—Use this text field to input the number of steps of changes you want between the two objects. The greater the number of steps, the smoother the resulting animation will be. The more steps there are, the larger the file size, however.

▶ **Distribute to Frames**—Distributing across frames places all the tweened symbol instances on successive frames. The symbol instances are distributed based on their stacking order, starting at the bottom, with the topmost instance being last in the sequence.

New frames are created automatically if there are currently not enough for the number of steps indicated in your settings. Each symbol instance is also on the same layer throughout the frames. Unchecking the Distribute to Frames check box places all instances of the symbol on the same frame, as shown in Figure 30.4. You can distribute them later by selecting them with the pointer and then clicking the Distribute to Frames button on the Frames panel.

FIGURE 30.4
New instances of the symbol are created between the two copies, with scale, rotation, and opacity gradually adjusted for each step.

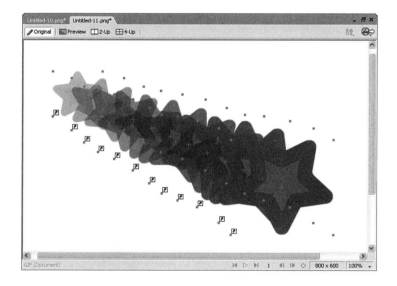

Did you Know?

Tweens are not used only with animation. They can also create exciting geometric effects within a static image, lending dynamic motion effects to backgrounds and borders. Using a path object, convert it into a symbol and place another copy of the new symbol object elsewhere on the Canvas. Use the Transform tools, opacity setting, or effects to change the copy. Select both symbols and use Tween Instances to create new instances between them. Choose a number of steps but don't distribute to frames. More steps means a smoother transition. A cool morphing effect is achieved as the symbol changes incrementally.

Viewing and Selecting Objects Across Frames

If you have a lot of objects distributed across a number of frames, it could take a long time to adjust each one individually. Imagine that you've tweened a pair of symbol instances and distributed them across frames so they appear to move from left to right across the bottom of the Canvas. If you now want them to move across the top of the Canvas, you don't want to have to move each step. You can use the Multi-Frame Editing option in the Frames panel to work with an object from more than one continuous frame.

To view objects from more than one frame, you can use *onion skins*, shown in Figure 30.5. Onion skins were used in traditional animation drawings when drawings were sketched on translucent paper and then layered to show their motion over time. The onion skins were often used by tweeners. The character artist could sketch the first and last drawings, and the tweener could layer these with blank sheets for each frame in between. In Fireworks objects on adjacent frames are shown on the Canvas semitransparently, although their actual opacity settings remain unchanged. The object on the currently active frame is fully opaque.

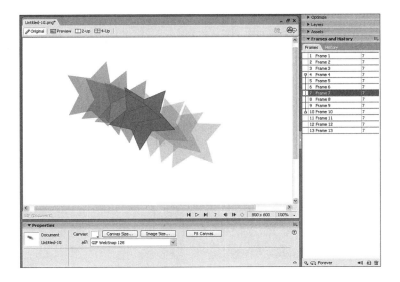

FIGURE 30.5
Objects within the onion skin range markers in the left column of the Frames panel are shown as semi-transparent. The opaque object is the object on the active frame.

The onion skin options can be easily accessed from the Frames panel by clicking the Onion Skinning button, located at the bottom left next to the GIF Animation Looping button. Click this button to select whether you want no onion skinning or whether you want to see only the next frame, the frames before and after, or all frames. Selecting Custom brings up the Onion Skinning dialog box, shown in Figure 30.6, where you can specify the number of frames you want to see before and after the selected frame, as well as the opacity at which each will be displayed.

FIGURE 30.6
Selecting Custom from the Onion Skinning button menu brings up the Onion Skinning settings dialog box.

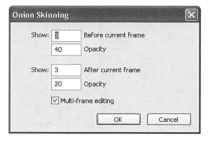

You can turn multiframe editing on or off with the check box on this dialog box or from the Onion Skinning button menu. Multiframe editing enables you to select objects displayed as onion skins and edit them, even if they aren't on the active frame. This means you can change properties for any object on any frame. You can use the pointer, Transform, Align, or the Properties Inspector to edit objects selected across frames. When multiframe editing is turned off, objects shown as onion skins cannot be selected or changed.

When onion skins are turned on, the frame range markers expand across onion-skinned frames in the left column of the frame rows on the Frames panel. Clicking a frame row with the mouse makes it the currently active frame, and the range markers adjust themselves in the sequence. If you click the left column of a frame row above the top marker, the top marker moves to include that frame. Clicking below the bottom marker displays a frame further along in the sequence, whereas clicking between the markers makes the range shorter. You can also adjust the frame range markers by typing values into the Show fields in the custom Onion Skinning dialog box.

To select an object visible on a frame other than the currently active frame, make sure the Multi-Frame Editing check box is checked. Select the Pointer tool and move it over the object. The object's handles become highlighted. Click to select it; the object's settings are now available in the Properties Inspector. To select other objects visible on the active frame or in another onion skin, simply hold down the Shift key and click the objects you want selected. You can use the pointer or the Properties Inspector to change their positions, opacities, or effects. Grouping objects moves all selected objects to the first frame between the onion-skin range markers.

Exporting an Animated GIF

There are two ways to export an animated GIF from Fireworks. The first is to set the document's optimization settings in the Optimize panel. From the Export File Format menu, select Animated GIF. You can choose the color palette settings just as you would for a regular GIF image, including matte background color, preset or custom palettes, and color depth. You can also set the amount of acceptable loss to reduce file size and the amount of dithering to approximate lost colors. Animated GIFs also support index transparency, just like regular GIFs. You can edit individual colors directly on the palette. The Remove Unused Colors setting can be found on the Optimize panel's Options menu, located at the top right of the panel.

You can preview the optimized GIF image using the Preview button at the top of the workspace window. Onion skins are disabled in the preview mode. You can use the animation controls at the bottom of the workspace to jump to the beginning or end, play the animation, or step through the frames. You can also click a frame in the Frames panel to jump to that frame. Use the Export Preview command on the File menu to bring up the Export Preview dialog box. You can optimize the palette and compression with the Options tab. Use the Animation tab to change the Animated GIF settings.

On the Animation tab each frame is listed in rows on the left (see Figure 30.7). The first column can be used to enable or disable frames to be exported. The next column shows a frame's name, disposal method, and delay. To change the delay for a frame, click the frame's row and enter a new value in the Frame Delay field above the frame listing. Any change is reflected in the Frames panel after you're done.

The disposal method (trash can icon) is used for optimizing a GIF's file size by specifying how frame information is repeated or changed. The four options are outlined here:

▶ **Unspecified**—This setting simply replaces the current frame with the next frame when the delay period is over.

- **None**—This setting shows both the current frame and the new frame.

- **Restore to Background**—This setting replaces unchanged areas with the Matte background color.

- **Restore to Previous**—This setting repeats unchanged areas from the last frame. You can also select the Auto Crop and Auto Difference check boxes on the Animations tab in the Export Preview dialog box if you want disposal method decisions to be made for you.

To change the disposal method, select the frame from the list and choose a method from the Disposal Method button menu. U stands for Unspecified (default), N stands for None (or Do Not Dispose), B stands for Restore to Background, and P stands for Restore to Previous.

FIGURE 30.7
The Animation tab in the Export Preview dialog box enables you to completely control the export settings for an animated GIF file.

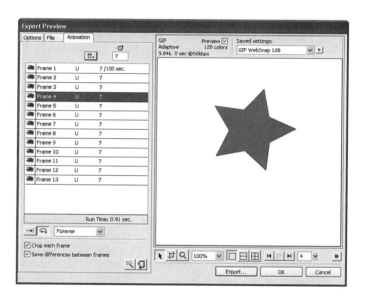

> **Watch Out!**
>
> Some early Netscape browsers (before 4.0) do not support the Restore to Background and Restore to Previous disposal methods correctly, so be careful when using these methods.

Exporting Individual Frames As Files

Another method for exporting animation is to export each frame as an individual file. The settings in the Optimize panel are applied to each frame in the document so you can export into any of the Fireworks export formats. Select the

Export command from the File menu, and then select Frames to Files from the Save As menu. After this option is selected, you can specify whether you want to trim images by checking the corresponding check box. If this box is selected, each frame is cropped to include the objects in that frame. If it is unchecked, the entire Canvas is exported for each frame. You can also export layers to files from the Save As Type menu. This exports each layer of the current frame into the format specified in the Optimize panel. You can use Trim to Images as you would when exporting frames.

Importing Animated GIFs

Another important feature in Fireworks is the ability to import and refine animated GIFs from previous projects. This feature can also be used to study the work done by other animators. You can save an animated GIF from the Web in the same way that you would any image visible in your Web browser. When you use the Open command to open an animated GIF file in Fireworks, the document opens with multiple frames. Each frame contains a bitmapped object that appears the same way the frame would appear in your browser. The exact palette from the GIF is automatically loaded in the Optimize panel, and Frame Delay settings are also preserved in the Frames panel. Use the Save command from the File menu to save the animated GIF as a Fireworks source PNG.

When you import an animated GIF into an existing document, it is placed on the current active layer and frame as an Animation symbol. If the animation has more frames than are available in the document, you are asked whether you want to add enough frames to complete the animation. Now you can add even more motion, rotation, scaling, or transparency to the animation by changing the settings from the Animation commands in the Modify menu. You can access the individual frames in the symbol either by using the Symbol Editor and double-clicking an instance that is present on the Canvas or by selecting the symbol in the Library panel, double-clicking to change the properties, and clicking the Edit button to bring up the Symbol Editor.

Summary

Now you should be familiar with all the tools available for animation with Fireworks MX. These include motion tweening, onion skinning, and multiframe editing. After you finish your animation, you can export it as an animated GIF image, a series of individual images in a static format, or a Flash SWF animation, which you'll learn more about starting in Chapter 33, "Importing Graphics into Flash."

PART III
Flash

CHAPTER 31

Understanding the Flash Interface

The Flash environment is deceptively simple. With it, you can get started drawing and animating right away. However, Flash might not act the way you expect it to.

To ensure that you get off on the right foot, it pays to first cover some basics, just as we have for the other applications in Studio MX. Experienced users and novices alike should understand the basics covered here.

Getting Your Bearings

The key to understanding Flash is always knowing where you are. You're given the power to edit everything: static graphics, animations, buttons, and more. At all times, you need to be conscious of what you're currently editing. It's easy to become disoriented about exactly which element you're working on. This section helps you get your bearings.

Let's take a quick tour of the Flash workspace:

- ▶ The Stage is the visual workspace. Any graphics placed in this area are visible to the user.

- ▶ The Tools panel contains all the many drawing tools in Flash, including those you can add later (by selecting Edit, Customize Tools Panel). The Flash tools are covered in depth in Chapter 32, "Drawing and Painting Original Art in Flash."

- ▶ The Timeline panel contains the sequence of images that make an animation. The Timeline can also include many layers of animations. This way, certain graphics can appear above or below others, and you can have several animations playing simultaneously.

The Stage

The large white rectangle in the center of Flash's workspace is called the Stage. Text, graphics, photos—anything the user sees—goes on the Stage (see Figure 31.1).

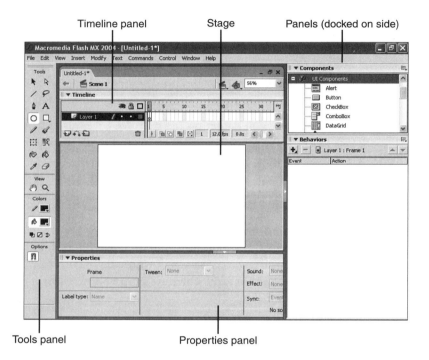

Timeline panel   Stage   Panels (docked on side)

Tools panel   Properties panel

Think of the Stage as the canvas on which a painter paints or the frame in which a photographer composes pictures. Sometimes you'll want a graphic to begin outside the Stage and then animate onto the Stage. Off the Stage is the gray area around the outside of the white area. You can see the "off Stage" area only when the View menu shows a check mark next to Work Area. (Selecting this option toggles between checked and unchecked.) The default setting (Work Area checked) is preferable because it means you can position graphics off the Stage. Realize, however, that any changes you make to the View menu affect only what you see. Changes here have no effect on what the user sees.

There's not too much to learn about the Stage—it's simply your visual workspace. However, two important concepts are worth covering now: Stage size and zoom level. By default, the Stage is a rectangle that is 550 pixels wide by 400 pixels tall.

Later in this chapter, in the "Document Properties" section, you'll see how to change the width and height of a movie. However, the specific dimensions in pixels are less important than the resulting shape of the Stage (called the *aspect ratio*). The pixel numbers are unimportant because, when you deliver a Flash movie to the Web, you can specify that Flash scale to any pixel dimension.

Aspect ratio is the ratio of height to width. Any square or rectangular viewing area has an aspect ratio. For example, television has a 3:4 aspect ratio—that is, no matter how big a standard TV screen is, it's always three units tall and four units wide. 35mm film has an aspect ratio of 2:3 (such as a 4"×6" print), and high-definition television (HDTV) uses a 16:9 ratio. Most computer screen resolutions have an aspect ratio of 3:4 (480×640, 600×800, and 768×1024). You can use any ratio you want in a Web page; just remember that the portion of the screen you don't use will be left blank. A "wide-screen" ratio (as wide as 1:3, like film) has a much different aesthetic effect than something with a square ratio (1:1).

To scale means to resize as necessary. A Flash movie retains its aspect ratio when it scales, instead of getting distorted. For example, you could specify that a Flash movie in a Web page scale to 100% of the user's browser window size. You could also scale a movie with the dimensions 100×100 to 400×400.

Not only can you deliver a Flash movie in any size (because Flash scales well), but while working in Flash, you can also zoom in on certain portions of the Stage to take a closer look without having any effect on the actual Stage size.

The Zoom control is located at the top right of the Stage above the Timeline. This control provides one way to change the current view setting. Other ways include selecting View, Magnification and using the Zoom tool (the magnifier button in the Tools panel).

If the entire Stage is not visible, you can view the other parts of the Stage in one of two ways: by using the standard window scrollbars on the right and bottom or by using the Hand tool. The Hand tool is best accessed by simply holding down the spacebar. Go ahead and hold down the spacebar; then click and drag. You're *panning* to other parts of the Stage without actually moving anything. It's important to understand that the Hand tool only changes your view port onto the whole Stage. The best thing about using the spacebar to select the Hand tool is that it's spring loaded—that is, the Hand tool is active only while you hold down the spacebar.

Several interesting tools are available from the View menu, including grids, guides, and snap settings. Select View, Grid, Show Grid. Behind all the graphics onstage, you see a grid (which the user won't see), as shown in Figure 31.2. For this example, click once on the eyeball at the top left of the Timeline to temporarily hide all the graphics (so you can more easily see the grid). You'll learn in the next chapter how the grid can help you line up graphics perfectly. Notice that after you select View, Grid, you can select Edit Grid to edit the color and spacing of the grid. Turn off the grid now by selecting View, Grid, Show Grid (so there's no check mark next to this menu item).

FIGURE 31.2
Turning on the grid helps you align objects.

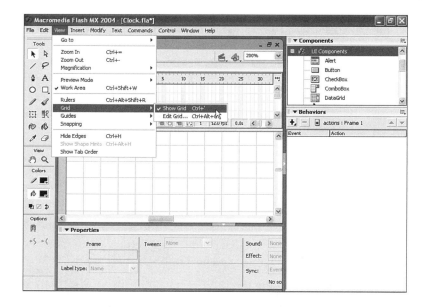

Guides are just like the grid, except you drag them into place where you want them. First, select View Rulers (so there's a check mark next to this item). Now you can click either ruler and drag toward the Stage to create and put into place a single guide, as shown in Figure 31.3. You make vertical guides by dragging from the left ruler, and you make horizontal guides by dragging from the top ruler. To remove the guides, drag them back to the ruler. As with the grid, you find the option to edit the guide settings—as well as a way to lock the guides in place—by selecting View, Guides, Edit Guides.

The Tools Panel

The Tools panel is the panel with which you will likely become most familiar. Any time you create or edit anything on the Stage, you need to have one tool selected from the Tools panel. Like many toolbars, the Tools panel is dockable.

The default location is locked to the left side of the Flash interface (or, on a Mac, floating on the left).

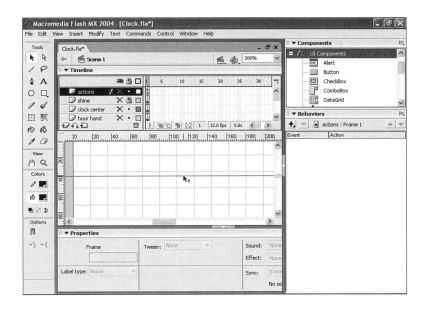

FIGURE 31.3
Guides are similar to the grid, but you can position the vertical and horizontal lines wherever you want them.

Although the Tools panel is used primarily to draw on the Stage, it's also used to edit what you've already drawn. As shown in Figure 31.4, the Tools panel is actually broken into several sections: Tools, View, Color, and Options.

FIGURE 31.4
The Tools panel has tools for drawing, editing, and viewing, plus options that vary, depending on the currently selected tool.

The Tools section enables you to create graphics and text (via the Line tool and Text tool), edit graphics (via the Eraser tool and Paint Bucket tool), and simply select graphics (via the Selection tool, Subselect tool, and Lasso tool). You'll learn about all these tools in the next chapter. The View section lets you change your view of the Stage. The Colors section gives you control over the color of objects drawn. Finally, the Options section is dedicated to additional modifiers for certain tools. Depending on which tool is selected, you might not see anything in the Options section.

You'll look at these tools in detail in the next few chapters. For now, play with these tools. Be sure you understand how to dock the toolbars and try to figure out each tool's purpose.

The Timeline

You'll look at the Timeline in depth when you start animating. Nevertheless, let's take a brief tour of the Timeline now. The Timeline contains the sequence of individual images that make up an animation. When the user watches your animation, he sees the images on Frame 1 followed by Frame 2, and so on. It's as if you took the actual film from a conventional movie and laid it horizontally across the screen, with the beginning on the left and the end toward the right.

Like many other windows, the Timeline can be undocked so it floats above everything else, as shown in Figure 31.5. Docking is just one more way to organize your workspace. If you want, you can dock the Timeline under the Stage—or nearly anywhere else you want. People who have the hardware to support two monitors have even greater flexibility in the way they organize their workspace. Personally, I like the default arrangement, with the Timeline above the Stage and the Tools panel to the left. I used this arrangement for most of the figures throughout this book. If you completely close the Timeline to make more space (which is possible only when it's floating), you can always get it back by selecting Window, Timeline.

When you start to create animations, the Timeline includes many visual clues to help you. For example, you can quickly see the length of an animation simply by looking at the Timeline. Also, Flash uses a few subtle icons and color codes in the Timeline; this way, you can see how the animation will play.

In addition to frames, the Timeline lets you have as many layers as you want in animations. As is the case with other drawing programs, objects drawn in one layer appear above or below objects in other layers. Each layer can contain a separate animation. This way, multiple animations can occur at the same time. By using layer names and special effects (such as masking), you can create complex animations. Figure 31.6 shows the Timeline and layers of a finished movie.

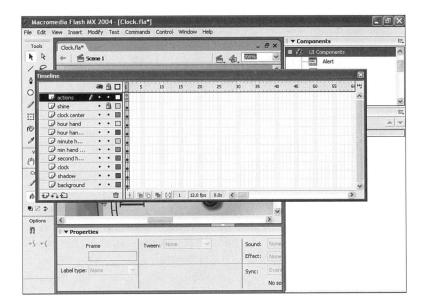

FIGURE 31.5
The Timeline (and other panels) can be picked up and moved like any floating window. It can also be docked back in its original location. This lets you customize your workspace.

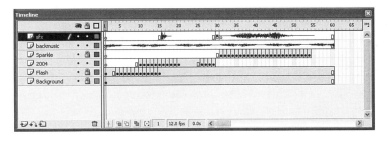

FIGURE 31.6
Most animations involve many layers. Each layer is independent of the others.

The Properties Panel

As in the other Studio 2004 applications, the Properties panel displays properties of the currently selected object so you can make adjustments. For example, when you select a block of text, the Properties panel lets you view and change the font face and size. When you select a filled shape, you can adjust the fill color of that shape.

If nothing is selected, you can still make changes to the Properties panel. Although this seems to have no effect, you're actually specifying what will happen the next time you create an object. For example, if you first select the Text tool and (before clicking to type) you make a change to the font in the Properties panel, you'll see that font change in text you create later.

Exploring Text Options

Flash 2004 has some really powerful text options. While in a new file, you can select the Text tool, click the Stage, and then type a few words. When you finish typing, you can click the Selection tool. From the Properties panel, you can select a different font, change the font size, change the color, and control the text in many common ways. By the way, the Format button on the Properties panel includes additional options related to margins.

The Library

The Library is the best storage facility for all the media elements used in a Flash file. Media placed in the Library can be used repeatedly within a file, and—regardless of how many times you use those media—it doesn't significantly add to the file size! For example, if you put a drawing of a cloud in the Library, you can then drag 100 copies of the cloud onto the Stage (making a whole sky full of clouds), but deep inside the Flash file, only one cloud exists. Using the Library is one way you can keep Flash movies small.

In practice, the Library is used in two basic ways: for editing and for maintaining (or accessing) the Library's contents. You might need to edit the contents of one Library item (called a *symbol*), and when you do, you are editing the contents of the Library. You might also need to access the Library to simply organize all the contents or to drag instances of the symbols into a movie. In such a case, you are maintaining the Library (as opposed to editing its contents).

A *symbol* is the name for anything—usually something visual, such as a graphic shape—you create and place in a file's Library. Although different types of symbols exist, the idea is that by creating a symbol, you're storing the graphic once in the Library. After it is in the Library, the symbol can be used several times throughout a movie without having a significant impact on file size.

An *instance* is one copy of a symbol used in a movie. Every time you drag a symbol from the Library, you create another instance. It's not a "copy" in the traditional sense of the word because there's only one master and each instance has negligible impact on file size. Think of the original negative of a photograph as the symbol and each print as another instance. You'll see that, like photographic prints, instances can vary widely (in their sizes, for example).

The Library behaves like any other panel. You can access it by selecting Window, Library or by pressing Ctrl+L.

Getting Around in Flash

As mentioned earlier, an important concept in Flash is to understand where you are at all times. If you think you're in the Library, editing the contents of a symbol, for example, you better hope you are really there. It can be confusing because, although it's always possible to figure out where you are in Flash, the clues are often subtle. The following sections look at how you can determine where you are by reading the subtle clues in the interface.

The Current Layer

One important concept is that you can be in only one layer at a time. That is, if you draw or paste graphics, they are added to the currently active layer. The current layer is the layer with the pencil icon, as shown in Figure 31.7. You can just single-click another layer to make it the active layer (notice that the pencil moves to the layer you click). The key here is to always pay attention to what layer you're currently editing. For example, if the current layer is locked, you won't be able to affect it at all.

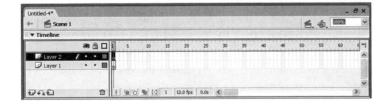

FIGURE 31.7
Not only is the current layer highlighted (in black), but it also has the pencil icon, indicating that this is the layer where anything that is drawn or pasted will go.

The Current Frame

In the Timeline, a red marker indicates which frame is currently being viewed (see Figure 31.8). This red current-frame marker can be in only one frame at a time—the frame you're currently editing. Initially, you'll find that you can't move the current-frame marker past Frame 1 unless your file has more frames. You'll have plenty of opportunity to do this later; for now, just realize that the red marker indicates the current frame. If it helps, imagine a time machine. You can visit any moment in time, but you can visit only one moment at a time.

FIGURE 31.8
The red current-frame marker (on Frame 11 here) can be in only one frame at a time. It's important to realize where this current-frame marker is located at all times.

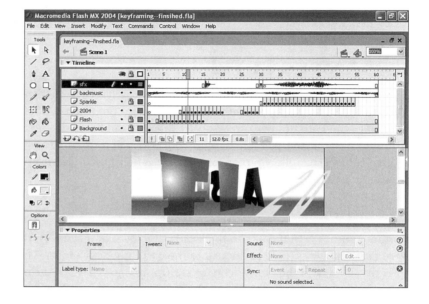

The Current Scene or Current Symbol

By far, the most difficult concept for new Flash users is that in Flash, there's more than one Timeline! A large or complicated movie can be broken into several scenes. You can think of scenes as chapters in a novel. Deep inside Flash, there's always just one long Timeline (just like a novel has one continuous story), but if you break a file into scenes, you can access the scenes individually. This is a nice feature because it means you can easily change the order or sequence of the scenes. It should be apparent that at all times you should know in which scene you're currently working. The name of the current scene is always listed above the Stage (and above the Timeline if it's docked) on what I refer to as the *edit bar*. The default name is Scene 1, and you should see this next to the icon for scenes—a movie "clapper" (see Figure 31.9).

Navigating Through the Interface

You've seen how the Flash interface gives you clues that tell you where you are at all times. But how did you get where you are in the first place? And how do you get out? Navigating through a Flash file is easy—and maybe that's why getting lost is so easy. Let's look at a few ways to get around.

Scene name and clapper icon

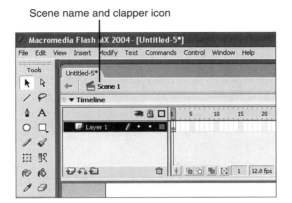

FIGURE 31.9
In the upper-left corner of the Stage, you usually see the name of the current scene. The clapper icon indicates that this is the name of a scene.

The edit bar contains the hierarchy of your current location, and it provides a means of navigation. You can click the edit bar. If, for example, you're inside a symbol within Scene 1, you should see Scene 1: *SymbolName*. If you simply click Scene 1, you are taken back to that scene (see Figure 31.10). Any time you see the edit bar, you can navigate back through the hierarchy. Remember that the edit bar provides information and that it's clickable.

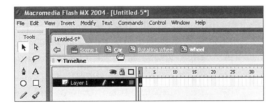

FIGURE 31.10
The edit bar provides more than just information. You can click the arrow or any name listed to jump back. Here, you can click Scene 1 to jump all the way back to the top.

Finally, you should notice two menus way off to the right of the edit bar: Edit Scene and Edit Symbol. From these two menus, you can jump to any scene or symbol in the current movie. Of course, if you have no symbols and just one scene, using these menus won't be very interesting. However, in big files, these menus provide a quick way for you to get around.

There are plenty more ways to get around in Flash, and you'll see them all in these chapters. For now, try to get comfortable moving around and be sure to notice all the clues Flash gives concerning where you are.

Document Properties

You need to specify a few far-reaching settings early in the creation of any movie. Most of these are found in the Document Properties dialog box, shown in Figure 31.11, which you access by selecting Modify, Document or double-clicking the bottom of the Timeline (where you see 12.0 fps). You should access the Document Properties dialog box now so you can experiment with a few of its settings. (Notice that most of the same settings appear in the Properties panel if you click the Stage or otherwise deselect all objects.)

FIGURE 31.11
The Document Properties dialog box provides many global settings that should be determined at the beginning of every project.

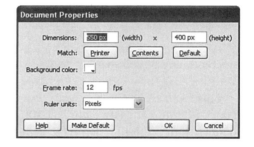

First of all, you need to ensure that Ruler Units is set to Pixels. This is the standard unit of measurement in multimedia and Web pages. It's important to set Ruler Units to Pixels because this affects several other dialog boxes (including the Info panel). Next to Background Color, you should see a white swatch that, when clicked, enables you to change the Stage color. This isn't actually as useful as you might think because at the time you publish a movie to the Web, you can specify any background color you want and it overrides this setting. Feel free to change Background Color any time you want. Maybe gray will be easier on your eyes, or black will make selecting white graphics easier. I often use a bright red background just so it's super clear while I'm editing. Do whatever you want—not only can you change this setting later, but it also affects only the Stage color while you're editing.

Two other Document Properties dialog box settings are important to establish early in any project: Frame Rate and Dimensions. Frame Rate specifies the rate—that is, how many frames per second—at which Flash *attempts* to play. I say *attempts* because some of your users might not have a computer fast enough to keep up, so Flash just can't display the specified number of frames in a second. Flash will not exceed the frame rate you specify, but it could get bogged down and not keep up. Dimensions are only important to the degree that they affect the aspect ratio of your Stage, as discussed earlier. You need to decide up front on the shape for your Stage (sorry, it can't be round). Do you want a wide-screen CinemaScope look, or do you want a square Stage? You might even want a vertical rectangle if, for instance, you were building a button bar to appear on the left side of a Web page. You need to consider this early on because the Stage shape influences how you position graphics and changing it later makes for a lot of repositioning.

People often confuse frame rate with speed, which is more of a visual effect. Animators can use tricks to make something appear to speed across the screen even while using a very low frame rate. For example, if you see a picture of a car on the left side of the screen and then a fraction of a second later, it's on the right side of the screen, that can tell your brain that the car is moving fast. However, such a trick requires only two frames—and at a frame rate of 4 fps, the second frame appears only a quarter second after the first! Frame rate—that is, how many chunks into which each second is broken—controls the visual resolution. Four frames per second can look "chunky"—each change occurs only four times per second. However, 30 fps (equivalent to the frame rate of TV) is such a fine increment that you're not likely to see the steps between discrete frames (although, of course, that's what's really happening). By the way, you can still move a car across the screen in a quarter of a second by using 60 fps—it would just involve 15 frames.

File Types

Clearly, the most common use for Flash is to create interactive animations for the Web. Sifting through all the different file types involved can be a little confusing. At a minimum, you need to understand three types: source (`.fla`) files, exported (`.swf`) files, and Hypertext Markup Language (`.htm` or `.html`) files.

Source (`.fla`) Files

One of the two main file types in Flash is the source Flash movie that you save while working. It uses the file extension `.fla` (often pronounced *fla*). You can open and edit any `.fla` file, provided that you own Flash. This is your source file. With the `.fla` file, you can always restore the other file types—but nothing can restore a `.fla` file (except, maybe, doing all the work over again).

When sharing files with other workers who need to edit the source file, you share the `.fla` file. Anyone who has Flash 2004 or Flash Professional 2004 (for either

Mac or Windows) can open and edit the `.fla` file you create. However, you can't put `.fla` files into a Web page for people to view—they're just files that contain your source content.

Exported (`.swf`) Files

When you're finished editing a source file and ready to distribute your creation, you simply export a `.swf` (pronounced *swif*) Flash Player file. A `.swf` file can be viewed by anyone who has an Internet browser and the Flash Player plug-in. The audience can't edit the `.swf`—they can only watch it.

The process for creating a new `.swf` file is simple. You open a `.fla` file; select File, Export Movie; and then specify the name and file location for the `.swf` file in the Export Movie dialog box. Although more details are involved, the important point to understand is that exporting involves creating a new file (the `.swf` file), but the `.fla` file remains untouched. It's similar to using Save As or Save a Copy As in some other software programs. Whatever you do, you should always keep a copy of your `.fla` file. You can always create more `.swf` files from it—or make edits and then create more `.swf` files.

Summary

We covered a lot of ground in this chapter without actually creating any finished work. Don't worry—you'll get your hands dirty in the next chapter. Besides, the information covered in this chapter should be useful throughout your Flash career.

In this chapter you were introduced to Flash's main workspace, including the Stage, Timeline, and Tools panel. You learned about interface clues and navigation tools that help you track your current location at all times. The edit bar at the top left always tells you where you are, and the two menus at the top right let you navigate to other scenes and symbols (provided you have some).

Finally, you learned about the file formats you'll likely create in Flash. It's important to take the time to understand all the files you create. You'll probably create many files, so it's also a good idea to keep your files and folders organized so you can track what's going on.

CHAPTER 32

Drawing and Painting Original Art in Flash

Believe it or not, Flash started life as drawing software. The creators of Flash intended to make a "more natural" drawing tool. Of course, Flash has evolved to become an animation tool and, now, even a rich application development platform. Because you'll be animating images, it's convenient that you can draw these images right inside Flash.

If you have little or no background creating graphics on a computer, you're in luck! Flash is so unique that the less you know, the better—just let your mind act like a sponge and soak up all the information. If you have experience with computer graphics, try to forget everything you know about drawing software and get ready to learn the "Flash way."

Drawing on the Stage

Everything your audience sees is drawn on the Stage. Sometimes, you'll want a graphic to start off the Stage and then animate into view. Drawing off the Stage requires that you have the work area selected with a check mark in the View menu. I recommend you leave this setting checked, but you should realize that the gray area around the outside of the Stage is considered "off the Stage" and does not appear in your finished movie. The Stage is the white rectangular area.

Tools

Your drawing tools should appear, by default, on the left side of the screen, as shown in Figure 32.1. If the tools aren't visible, you can access them by selecting Window, Tools.

The following sections look at how to draw with these tools. You'll learn about all of them in this chapter, although the really advanced techniques are covered throughout the Flash chapters. Keep in mind that whereas some tools (such as the Pencil and Brush tools) let you create artwork, others (such as the Arrow and Zoom tools) simply help you modify or view your artwork. In the following sections, you'll learn how to create and edit artwork.

FIGURE 32.1
Flash's drawing toolbar might look simple, but because most tools have additional options, there's more than meets the eye.

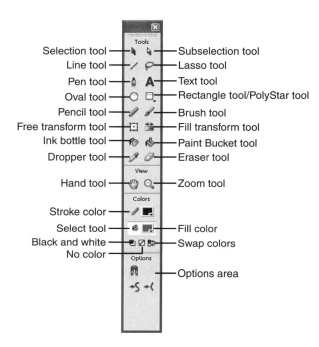

Selection tool — Subselection tool
Line tool — Lasso tool
Pen tool — Text tool
Oval tool — Rectangle tool/PolyStar tool
Pencil tool — Brush tool
Free transform tool — Fill transform tool
Ink bottle tool — Paint Bucket tool
Dropper tool — Eraser tool

Hand tool — Zoom tool

Stroke color
Select tool — Fill color
Black and white — Swap colors
No color

Options area

Viewing and Modification Tools

Both View tools—Hand and Zoom—have no effect on artwork. You simply use them to help see your artwork. The following example walks you through a scenario in which you use both tools.

Follow these steps:

1. Because you haven't drawn anything yet, you can use one of the sample files that ships with Flash. Open the sample file called `TraceBitmap.fla`. It should be listed under File, Open Recent. (If it is not, select File, Open and navigate to `C:\Program Files\Macromedia\Flash 2004\en\First Run\Samples\TraceBitmapPanel\TraceBitmap.fla` on the PC or `/Applications/Macromedia Flash MX 2004/First Run/Samples/TraceBitmapPanel/TraceBitmap.fla` on the Mac)

2. You can zoom in to critically inspect or change the artwork in the file. Click to select the Zoom tool (it's the one that looks like a magnifying glass).

Notice that, as with many other tools, when you select the Zoom tool, additional buttons appear in the Options section of the toolbar. You should see two more magnifying glasses appear in the Options area, as shown in Figure 32.2.

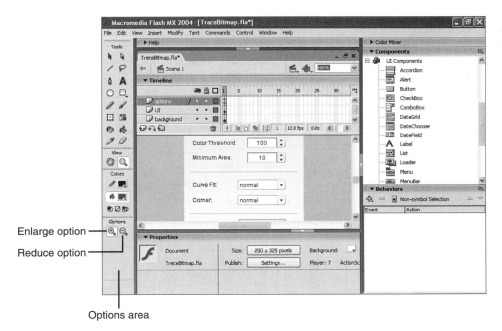

FIGURE 32.2
The Zoom tool has two options: Enlarge and Reduce.

Enlarge option

Reduce option

Options area

3. Make sure Enlarge is selected (the option with the plus sign) and then click one of the arrow buttons displayed on the Stage. Click the same arrow a few more times, and you keep zooming in.

4. While you're close up, chances are that most of the Stage is out of view. Of course, you can use the standard scrollbars on the left and bottom to change the portion of the (now very close-up) Stage. You can also do this by using the Hand tool: Select the Hand and then click and drag to change your view.

5. Now you can zoom out. Just select the Zoom tool and be sure to remember to select the Reduce option (the one with the minus sign). Click, and you zoom back out.

You used the Enlarge option of the Zoom tool by simply clicking the Stage. Another way to zoom is to click and drag. You see a rectangle as you drag, and when you let go, that rectangle defines the viewable portion of the Stage. In the sample file, you can click and drag with the Zoom tool and draw a small rectangle around a part of the image to zoom in on just that portion. You always see the current zoom level displayed in the drop-down list at the top right of the Stage (above the Timeline, if it's docked). If you click the Zoom control drop-down list, you can return to 100%. Another quick way to return to 100% is to double-click the Zoom tool (not the Enlarge or Reduce option, but the main Zoom tool's magnifier). For those enamoured with keyboard shortcuts, Ctrl+spacebar zooms and Alt+spacebar reduces. Mac users can simply substitute Command for Ctrl and Option for Alt to access the same shortcuts.

Speaking of quick techniques, both the Zoom and Hand tools have "spring-loaded" options. That means, for example, that while you're using another tool, you can press and hold down the spacebar to get the Hand tool. Then, when you let go of the spacebar, Flash springs back to the tool you had. Holding down Ctrl+spacebar gives you the Enlarge option of the Zoom tool, and holding down Ctrl+Shift+spacebar gives you the Reduce option. These spring-loaded features provide quick ways to temporarily select tools without actually going to the toolbar.

Creation Tools

Although the View tools prove very useful, they can't change a file. To create artwork in Flash, you have to add to an image, change something you've already drawn, or remove some or all of what you've drawn. In the following sections, you'll see how to add to your artwork. This naturally gives you something to change or remove later. Let's go through each tool individually and then analyze how they can all be used together.

Drawing Lines

Two tools are available for just drawing lines: the Line tool and the Pencil tool. (To be fair, the Oval and Rectangle tools draw lines, but they also draw fills, as you'll see in the "Painting Fills" section, later in this chapter.) Lines can be given a stroke color, stroke height, and stroke style, just as in Fireworks MX.

For example

1. Start a new file (by pressing Ctrl+N and selecting New Document). Lines can have different stroke attributes, so make sure the Properties panel is in a convenient place first. If your Properties panel isn't present, select Window, Properties. Then you can drag the Properties panel to a blank area of the screen, as shown in Figure 32.3.

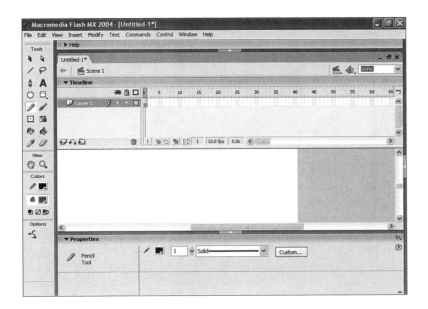

FIGURE 32.3
The Properties panel lets you set attributes of the lines you draw.

2. Select the Line tool, which draws straight lines. When your cursor is on the Stage, it changes to a crosshairs. Click and drag to create a line. You might notice a dark ring that sometimes appears while you drag. This is Flash's way of assisting you while drawing. In the case of the line, you'll find drawing perfectly horizontal and vertical lines to be easy when the Snap to Objects option is selected from the View menu.

3. First setting the stroke height or stroke color affects subsequent lines you draw. Select a different color in the square swatch on the Properties panel. Then change the stroke height, either by typing a number in the Stroke Height field or by clicking the arrow and dragging the slider. Then draw another line.

4. If you want to change the stroke attributes of a line you've already drawn, first select the Selection tool and then click once to select the line. While a line is selected, you can use the Properties panel to affect its attributes.

5. Select the Pencil tool. Notice that the Pencil tool has the option Pencil Mode. Click and hold the button that appears in the Options section to change the Pencil Mode setting, as shown in Figure 32.4.

6. The Straighten option attempts to straighten what you draw. Try drawing the letter S. It's likely to look jagged. Now try drawing the letter Z. It probably looks more like what you wanted.

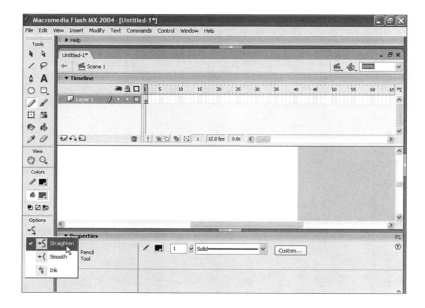

7. Select the Smooth option and try drawing an *S* and a *Z*. What happens to the *S* is nice, but the *Z* has curves where there weren't any before. The Smooth option can come in handy if you find that your hand-drawn images look too jagged.

8. Finally, the Ink Pencil Mode setting draws *almost* exactly what you draw. Flash adjusts what you draw to reduce the file size. The simple line Flash creates takes less data to describe and results in a smaller file that's faster to download.

The Properties panel affects lines drawn with the Pencil tool in the same way it affects those drawn with the Line tool. The one attribute in the Properties panel you haven't yet experimented with is the stroke style. The drop-down list shows a visual representation of each style. Solid (the default) is similar to Hairline, but Hairline effectively sets the stroke height to the lowest number possible.

When a line tool is selected, the Custom button on the Properties panel provides a way for you to create your own custom stroke styles. The dialog box that appears after you click the Custom button lets you control several attributes of your own custom line styles.

Painting Fills

In Flash, there can be only two components to any shape you draw: lines and fills. Some shapes are just lines (as you saw in the previous section), but some shapes are just fills (as you're about to see), and some shapes contain both. Fills and lines are different. A line has no thickness—only applied stroke attributes. A fill, on the other hand, has a left side, right side, top, and bottom. You can think of lines as the candy coating on an M&M and fills as the chocolate center (if that helps).

The two tools to create fills are the Brush tool and the Paint Bucket tool. Try this example to see how the tools function:

1. In a new file, use the Pencil tool to draw a few large circles. Make sure that at least one is totally closed, one is almost closed, and another is obviously not closed.

2. Select the Paint Bucket tool. Notice that the Options section has two buttons: Gap Size and Lock Fill.

3. If you click with the Paint Bucket tool in an empty part of the Stage, nothing happens. The Paint Bucket tool fills closed shapes with the selected fill color (the swatch next to the small paint bucket in the Colors section of the toolbox). It also changes the fill color of any fill already created. Change the Gap Size option to Close Large Gaps. Adjusting the Gap Size option should enable you to fill all your circles—even if they are not totally closed.

4. Select the Brush tool and quickly draw a line. Because you've used the Brush tool, it's really a fill (not a line), despite the fact that it might look like a line.

5. Now, select a new fill color by clicking and holding the color fill color swatch (from the Colors section of the Tools panel). Then select the Paint Bucket tool and fill the shape you just drew with the Brush tool. Not only can the Paint Bucket tool change the colors of the filled circles you've already filled, but it can also change the color of fills created with the Brush tool.

6. Now look at the Brush tool's Options area. The two drop-down lists that appear to be the same are actually quite different. The top one (Brush Size) controls the brush's tip size. On the other hand, the Brush Shape option controls the brush's tip shape. For example, you can have a calligraphy look with the angled tip, as shown in Figure 32.5. Lock Fill is covered later, but the other option, Brush Mode, is very interesting and is covered in step 7.

FIGURE 32.5
The Brush Shape
option affects the
style of a drawing.
Here's a calligraphy
effect using the
angled Brush
Shape option.

7. Figure 32.6 demonstrates each Brush Mode option. Try one now. Select the Paint Inside Brush Mode option to experiment with it. Either use the closed circles you drew earlier or draw a few more circles using the Pencil tool. Make sure you have the Brush tool selected (notice that the Brush Mode option remains where you last left it); then click and paint inside one of the circles. Try painting outside the lines. If you start painting inside the circle, the Paint Inside Brush Mode option prevents you from spilling any paint outside the shape! With Paint Inside selected, if you first click outside the shape, nothing happens.

FIGURE 32.6
The Brush tool has
several Brush
modes. In the Paint
Selection example,
I first selected the
windows. The Paint
Inside example
worked only when I
started painting
inside the house
graphic.

Let me recap just a few important points that are consistent for all the tools. First, certain tools have additional options that appear in the bottom section of the Tools panel. If you can't seem to find an option you've seen before, you might have to remember for which tool it was designed. This fact shouldn't be too frustrating because any attribute you need to change after drawing is usually found in the Properties panel (which you'll learn to leave open all the time).

Incidentally, Flash 2004 has added a Smoothing setting right into the Properties panel for the Brush tool. You can experiment and see Flash perform extra correction when the Smoothing setting is set high.

Drawing and Modifying Shapes Using Lines and Fills

When you use either the Oval tool or the Rectangle tool, you create a shape using both a line and a fill. These shapes have a fill and a stroke, with all the attributes set in the Properties panel. You can actually draw an oval or a rectangle that has no fill by changing the fill to no color (the red line with an arrow pointing to it).

Similarly, you can create a shape without a stroke by changing the stroke color to no color. These tools are pretty self-explanatory. The only Rectangle tool option to take note of is the Round Rectangle Radius setting. If this setting is selected before you draw, it makes all rectangles you draw have rounded corners.

There are two fundamental components to the shapes you create—lines (or *strokes*) and fills—and each has a different set of tools. The Oval tool and Rectangle tool can create both strokes and fills at the same time. To create a new fill or affect one that's onscreen, you use the Brush tool or Paint Bucket tool. You can create lines using the Pencil tool or the Line tool, and you can change their characteristics using the Ink Bottle tool. I find it easiest to remember that the Ink Bottle tool draws lines because it appears in the left column of tools—under the Line and Pencil tools. The Paint Bucket tool is under the Paint Brush tool.

The Pen tool is primarily used to draw lines, but anytime you use it to draw a closed shape, the shape is filled automatically.

By simply clicking with the Pen tool, you can add sharp anchor points on straight lines. The Pen tool can also draw curves. Instead of just clicking to create a point, you can click and drag to create a curve. The direction in which you drag creates what will become a tangent to your curve. The distance you drag determines how gradual or extreme the curve will be—this is a Bézier curve and is described fully in Chapter 24, "Working with Vector Paths." You'll just have to experience it to understand.

Creating Text

To create text, you simply select the Text tool, click, and start typing. You can modify the font, color, and style of what you've typed after you create it. Modifying your text after it's typed usually makes sense because only then will you be able to best judge how it looks.

Creating text in Flash has never been easier or more sophisticated. The following task walks you through a couple quick maneuvers.

For example, try the text tool by following these steps:

1. Select the Text tool, click the Stage, and then type **Hello**. This "click-and-type" technique expands the margin for the block of text to the exact width of whatever you type. The circle that appears at the upper-right corner of the text block indicates that the margin will automatically adjust in this way (see Figure 32.7).

FIGURE 32.7
Creating text is easy. The subtle circle that appears is used to set the margins.

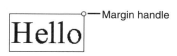

2. When you click and drag this circle (to adjust the width), it turns into a square to indicate that the margins are fixed. You can double-click the square margin control to restore the automatic margin adjustment (that is, to make it a circle again).

3. While editing the text block, you can set the margin. (Make sure the I-beam is blinking in the block; click inside the block of text, if necessary.) Grab the little circle at the upper-right corner of the text block and widen or narrow the block of text. The circle margin handle changes to a square, which indicates that, from now on, any text you paste or type into this block will wrap when it reaches this margin. Type a couple lines of text. You should see the text wrap even though you don't press the Enter key.

4. Now that you have some text in the block and have set the margins, it's time to modify some attributes of the text. Click the Selection tool to stop editing the text. Your text block should become selected. (If it isn't, just click it once, and a rectangle appears around it.)

5. With the block selected, observe the Properties panel to make modifications. For now, just modify the text's color, font, and font height, as shown in Figure 32.8. You'll find these options easy to understand and use. The font preview that flies out from the drop-down list is especially nice when you scroll through all your fonts.

6. Change the text style of just part of your text block to bold or italic by first selecting just the characters you want to change and then selecting Bold or Italic. Double-clicking the text block automatically selects the Text tool. You can select the characters as you would in any word processor (just click and drag). While some text is selected, use the Properties panel's settings to change just that text. If you want to change the font, the preview includes

the text you have selected. You can use this method to change the properties of individual characters within any block of text.

7. Choose the Selection tool and then select the block of text. Using the Properties panel, change the alignment to Center Justify. Explore the other settings, which control attributes such as the margin padding and line spacing, by clicking the Format button.

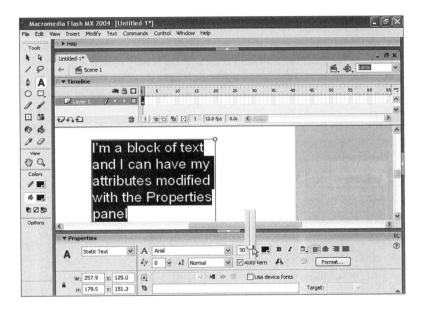

FIGURE 32.8
The Properties panel enables you to change text attributes such as font size and color.

Selecting and Transforming Objects

Now that you've seen how to create lines, fills, shapes (with both lines and fills), and text, it's time to explore how to modify them. The process is simple. You select the object you want to modify using the Selection tool and then you modify it. Selecting exactly what you want to modify is actually the most challenging part.

Selection Tools

The two basic selection tools are the Selection tool and Lasso tool. The Subselect tool (the white arrow) is for selecting and editing individual anchor points (in the same way the Pen tool created them). Again, if you read about Fireworks MX, this should be very familiar to you.

The Selection tool is used to select an object by clicking it once. The key to the Selection tool is that the cursor changes to tell you what will happen when you click, such as resizing, moving, and reshaping. You can try this tool by adding objects to your document and then moving the cursor around the perimeter of the objects.

Another way to select an object is to *marquee* it. With the Selection tool selected, click outside the object and drag until you've drawn an imaginary rectangle that surrounds it entirely. When you let go, the object becomes selected.

Sometimes the arrangement of other shapes onscreen makes the marquee technique difficult or impossible. Another tool you can use to do this is the Lasso tool. Select the Lasso tool and then click and drag around a shape to select it. The Polygon Mode option for the Lasso tool makes the tool act almost like the Pen tool. Select the Polygon Mode option, and click and let go. Then click and release in a new location to extend the selection. Continue to extend the selection and then double-click when you're done.

Finally, you can decide to select just a portion of a shape. Suppose you want to chop off the top of the circle. You can use either the Lasso tool or the marquee technique with the Selection tool to select the portion desired.

You use the Selection tool to employ the marquee technique. If you click and drag an object, it moves or bends. However, when you click the Stage where there are no objects, you see a rectangle appear while you drag (this is the marquee). You can draw that rectangle around other objects, and they will be selected when you let go. Using this marquee technique to select objects is often easier than clicking to select objects.

The Dropper Tool

One of the easiest ways to modify what you've drawn is to simply change the color. For example, the Paint Bucket tool can change a fill's color, and the Ink Bottle tool can change a stroke (its color and other attributes). This works fine when you make the effort to first select the fill color, for example, and then select the Paint Bucket tool and click a fill to change it. Sometimes, however, you want one fill to match the color of another. The Dropper tool lets you sample a color from an object that is already onscreen.

Transforming Scale, Rotation, Envelop, and Distortion

The Free Transform tool is your key to advanced modifications. Basically, you just have to select an object with the Free Transform tool active. Four options appear any time you use the Free Transform tool and have an object selected. You can also find these options by selecting Modify, Transform.

Here's an example:

1. Use the Rectangle tool to draw a square. Select the Free Transform tool and double-click the center of the square to select it entirely. (Interestingly, the Free Transform tool can perform many selection tasks.)

2. At this point, none of the four options should be selected (see Figure 32.9). This means you're in Free Transform mode, and if you have a steady hand, you can rotate, scale, or distort the shape.

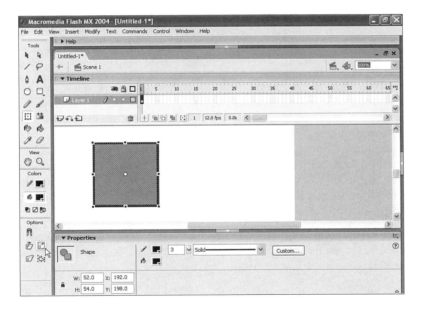

FIGURE 32.9
When an object is selected, you can select the Free Transform tool's Scale option.

3. Explore the possibilities by rolling your cursor over the square handles at the corners and sides of the shape—but don't click yet. Depending on where you move your mouse, the cursor changes to two versions of the Scale option, as well as Rotate and Skew (as in Figure 32.10). Actually, if you hold down Ctrl, the corners make the cursor change to the Distort option.

FIGURE 32.10
Depending on which handle you grab and which option is selected, you can use both Scale and Rotate to modify the shape in multiple ways.

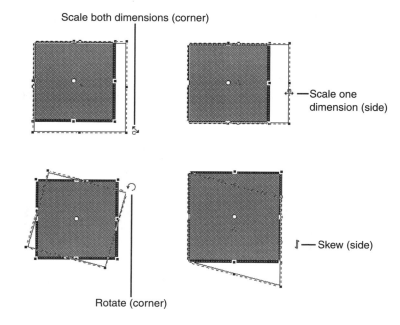

Scale both dimensions (corner)

Scale one dimension (side)

Rotate (corner)

Skew (side)

4. Free Transform mode can be really touchy, so let's go through the options individually. The selected object shows square handles in the corners and on the sides. Notice that the cursor changes when you roll over these handles. The corner handles let you scale both width and height equally and at the same time. The side handles let you change just width or just height. Click and drag a corner handle to change the scale. Notice that this version of Scale (compared to Scale in Free Transform mode) maintains your shape's proportions (horizontally and vertically). Now drag a side handle, and you change just the width.

5. Make sure the square is still selected and select the Rotate and Skew option. Now the corner handles rotate; side handles skew. Roll your cursor over the handles to see the cursor change.

6. Click and drag a corner handle and notice that you can rotate the square. Actually, if the default Snap to Objects option is selected (that is, if the magnet button is pressed in), the object snaps into place at 45° rotations.

7. Select the Distort option. Drag the shape by the handles on the corners to distort. It turns out that the Selection tool can create the same effect as Distort, but only when the shape itself has a corner to grab. Without this Distort option, making a distorted ellipse nearly would be nearly impossible.

Finally, try holding down the Shift key when you distort (by dragging a corner handle). This way, you can distort two sides evenly.

8. Finally, the wildest of transformation options is Envelop. To best understand this option, draw a new square, select the Free Transform tool, and click the Envelop option. When your shape is selected, you see many handles. Move the square handles to "influence" the shape. It's as though the shape tries to touch all the squares, even if they're pulled out to one side. The circle handles are like the tangents created when you draw using the Pen tool. They control the rate at which a shape bends to reach the square handles.

Smoothing and Straightening Shapes

After you draw a shape, you can at any time smooth or straighten what you've drawn. The Smooth and Straighten options are available when the Selection tool is selected. The process is quite simple: You select a shape and click either Smooth or Straighten. Clicking repeatedly continues to smooth or straighten whatever is selected.

Using Snap to Objects to Connect Shapes

By selecting View, Snapping, Snap to Objects (or clicking the magnet button in the main toolbar when the Arrow or Free Transform tool is active), you can draw perfectly round circles, perfectly horizontal or vertical lines, and much more. The visual clue that Snap to Objects is helping you is the dark ring that often appears next to your cursor while you drag. When you see that ring, you know Flash is trying to help you draw.

You might already know from using other software that holding the Shift key constrains your cursor similarly to Snap to Objects. But Snap to Objects can do much more. In addition to helping you draw perfect shapes, Snap to Objects also enables you to connect two shapes. It's much more than simply making two shapes touch—they actually become bonded. In Flash, unless two shapes have been snapped together, they might look connected when they actually aren't.

Summary

This chapter looked at practically every drawing tool in Flash. You have learned how to create lines, fills, combination shapes, and text. After you created some objects, you found ways to modify their color, shape, size, rotation, and location.

You even learned how to snap two shapes together. Even if you don't think you'll be creating artwork in Flash (maybe you're working with someone else who's the "artist" for your team), you should understand two important concepts: First, the simpler the shape, the smaller the file. Second, only shapes that are snapped together are truly connected. Of course, if you're going to create the artwork, thanks to what you've learned in this chapter you now know how to use the fundamental drawing capabilities in Flash.

CHAPTER 33

Importing Graphics into Flash

In the last two chapters, you've seen how you can create sophisticated custom graphics very quickly in Flash. Despite how powerful Flash's graphic creation tools are, eventually you might want to import graphics created elsewhere. Two good reasons for this are to use photographic images or use existing graphics (instead of re-creating them from scratch). You can certainly use these other graphics inside Flash—and that's what you're going to learn how to do here.

Reasons to Avoid Importing Graphics

Flash's capability to create nice vector graphics might be the best justification for this warning: Don't import graphics into Flash unless you have to! In this chapter, you'll learn how to import graphics—but that doesn't mean it's always a good idea. If there's one way to make your Flash movie download or play more slowly, it's importing graphics unnecessarily. You need to find ways to avoid importing graphics.

Wanting to import graphics is a natural tendency. If you show a graphics professional who's an expert with Illustrator or FreeHand how to draw in Flash, his first question will be how to bring his Illustrator or FreeHand files into Flash. In this chapter you'll learn the answer.

However, if you consider why a graphics professional would ask that in the first place, you expose a problem. People can do some amazing (and complicated) things with other drawing tools. Some of the ways graphics files get more complicated include use of gradients, intricate text, and lots of individual objects. Using such complicated graphics in Flash causes two problems. First, Flash can't always handle all the intricacies in a complicated file, so the task becomes difficult. Second, a complicated file downloads and plays more slowly than one that isn't complicated—so why would you want such a file in a Flash movie? The number-one consideration when deciding whether to import a graphic into Flash is whether a simpler version can be re-created in Flash or whether the graphic can at least be simplified before being imported into Flash.

Even so, you might still need to import graphics. Maybe you have a photograph (or another raster graphic) you want to use, or perhaps you have a simple existing vector graphic (such as a company logo) you don't want to redraw in Flash. We'll discuss raster graphics in the section "Using Bitmaps (Also Known As Raster Graphics)," later in this chapter, but first let's look at importing vector graphics.

Importing Vector Graphics

Sometimes you might have an existing vector graphic that you need to include in a Flash movie. Such a vector graphic is likely to be geometric—although not necessarily. Regardless of the exact form of the vector graphic, unless it's super complicated, you'll be able to import it into Flash.

Importing from a File

One way to incorporate other graphics into Flash is to import them from a file. It's as simple as selecting File, Import to open the Import menu and then pointing to the file you want. You see several file types listed, but that doesn't mean they all work equally well.

Although many file types are listed in the Import dialog box, only three vector formats are worth considering: FreeHand (`.FH11` through `.FH7`), Illustrator (`.ai`), and Flash Player (`.swf`). It used to be that the best option was FreeHand, but the support for Illustrator was expanded in Flash 2004—so all three of these formats appear to work equally well. Occasionally, complex data in FreeHand or Illustrator won't translate perfectly. Because of this limit, you might get the best results if you export a `.swf` (Flash Player) file from Illustrator or FreeHand. We'll discuss how this choice affects importing later in this chapter, in the section "Importing Flash Player Files" (because it limits some of your options).

Importing FreeHand MX and Illustrator Files

Several options are available when you import Illustrator or FreeHand documents into Flash. For example, you can turn pages into keyframes or scenes. Flash just needs to know how you want to handle pages. All the options are fairly easy to interpret and are selected when you import a file into Flash. (Also, you'll see the same set of options when importing Adobe Acrobat files—PDFs.)

Here are some tips to help you import drawings into Flash. First, if you use FreeHand, be sure to take advantage of FreeHand's symbols because they translate directly to Flash's symbols so that graphics can be recycled. Also, each object created in FreeHand should be separated into its own layer. Although you can easily put multiple objects on one layer, the file imports better if you create multiple layers.

You can create many text effects in FreeHand and Illustrator that don't translate to Flash. For example, text attached to paths doesn't remain editable when a file is imported into Flash. Also, because only FreeHand supports strokes on text, Flash ignores this effect. Fine adjustments to font sizes and kerning are possible in FreeHand and Illustrator, but they don't work as well in Flash, so font spacing often changes slightly when a file is imported into Flash. Sometimes text automatically converts to paths (which means it isn't editable when it gets into Flash). You'll learn about converting to outlines as a solution to some text problems later in this chapter, in the section "Maintaining Image Integrity." These are just some general tips. Creating the smallest, best-looking image that imports seamlessly into Flash might take some additional experimenting in either FreeHand or Illustrator.

Importing Flash Player Files

The most reliable option for importing vector graphics into Flash (besides, possibly, simply importing native FreeHand files) is to import Flash Player (.swf) files. Most graphics people don't think of .swf as an image file format, but it's certainly a standard. Of course, a .swf is not like a FreeHand file or an Illustrator file because it's not fully editable. When using newer versions of FreeHand and Illustrator (Illustrator 8 requires the free Macromedia Flash Writer plug-in), you can export your working files into the .swf format. They export amazingly well: The final files are smaller, and the image retains all the details and quality of the original.

The best process is to create a graphic in whatever program you prefer and then if that program doesn't export .swfs, open the file in a program that does (such as FreeHand, Illustrator, or Fireworks). Then simply export it as a .swf. You can then import it directly into a movie. Even if the graphics program you use doesn't support exporting .swf files, you can open the file in a tool that does and export a .swf from there. This means the graphics tool you select must export files in a format supported by the tool you use to export .swf files.

If you have trouble with the process of exporting .swf files from the graphics program and importing into Flash, you can try several remedies. First, you can investigate the export options in the graphics program. In Figure 33.1, you can see dialog boxes that appear when you export .swf files. You should notice some similarities between the options. Experimenting with these options is a good place to start.

In addition to exporting to .swf files, there are a few specific techniques you can try (covered in the section "Maintaining Image Integrity," later in this chapter). Ultimately, however, the solution sometimes involves making the graphic simpler—that is, reducing its complexity.

FIGURE 33.1
When exporting a .swf file from FreeHand or Illustrator, you're given one of these dialog boxes.

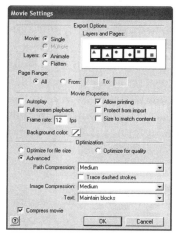

FreeHand MX
(via the Setup button when exporting)

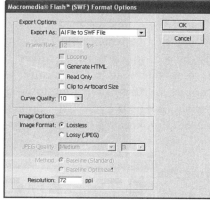

Illustrator 10

Although exporting a .swf for Flash to import is the safest bet, it means elements such as text are not editable inside Flash. Naturally, you could do the text layout in Flash—but that might not be ideal for your purposes. I guess the point is that .swf importing is the safest, but not always the most complete, option.

Maintaining Image Integrity

Despite how simple the export/import process might sound, it can be very frustrating when it doesn't work! I don't want to sound like a broken record, but the best way to maintain image quality is to create all your graphics inside Flash. When you must import an existing graphic or use a more advanced drawing tool, you can do several things to maintain image integrity. However, some of these tips are unnecessary when you're exporting .swf files from either Illustrator or FreeHand.

Font and text effects are usually the first things to go. Most drawing tools provide incredible font control, but Flash doesn't. The first consideration with text is whether the text must be editable within Flash. If you don't need to edit the text within Flash, you'll see the highest-quality results if the text is first converted to paths. You are given an option to do this automatically when exporting .swf files from FreeHand, and it doesn't affect the source FreeHand file—just the exported .swf. FreeHand's Convert to Paths feature is the same as Illustrator's Create Outlines and is equivalent to Flash's Break Apart option under the Modify menu. Of course, you'll never be able to edit the text after you use one of these options, so you should save a backup first. In addition, this can increase file size.

If you use gradients, you should consider using the Export .swf option. Using this option helps keep the file size down and performance speed up (rather than simply retaining quality). A simple gradient, for example, is likely to include a separate circle for each step. Imagine hundreds of concentric circles, each varying only slightly in color and size. You can see this effect when you pick up and move an imported graphic that has this characteristic, as in Figure 33.2. It's easy to see that such a gradient creates a larger file that plays relatively slowly—it's simply more complicated than it needs to be. When you export .swf files from Illustrator or FreeHand, the gradients are converted to Flash gradients.

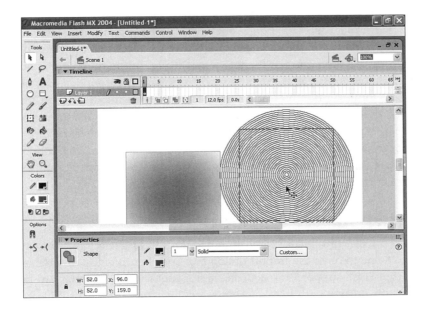

FIGURE 33.2
Often an imported graphic is much bigger than it needs to be. This seemingly innocuous gradient is actually many individual concentric circles.

Using Bitmaps (Also Known As Raster Graphics)

In this section you'll see how bitmap (raster) graphics can be used in Flash. Raster graphics have inherently unique characteristics that can't be created inside Flash. The only warning related to using this option is to ensure you really need raster graphics. The following are some uses that require raster graphics:

- ▶ A photograph. The only time to consider using a vector alternative to a photograph is when the picture is of a very geometric object. Otherwise, photographs should be raster graphics.

- ▶ A series of still images extracted from frames of a video.

- ▶ An image with special effects that can't be achieved by using a vector tool, such as clouds, fire, water, and other natural effects. (Of course, this is an invitation for a talented artist to re-create such an effect by using a vector tool.)

If you're unfamiliar with the difference between vector graphics and raster graphics, learning when one choice is better than the other can take some time. The file formats `.gif`, `.jpg`, `.png`, `.bmp`, and `.pct` are all raster graphics formats. However, just because a file was saved in one of these formats doesn't mean it was done appropriately. It's the nature of the image in the file that matters. If all you have is a `.gif`, for example, you need to first look at its contents to judge whether it's appropriate for raster graphics. Here's an easy way to decide: If you can trace or redraw the image in the file (with Flash's drawing toolbar, for instance), you're much better off redrawing it. If it's a photograph, you would never be able to trace it, so leave it as a raster graphic. If it's a picture of a plain box, maybe you could draw it and thus take advantage of all the benefits of vector graphics without even bothering with raster graphics.

Importing Raster Graphics

Importing a raster graphic is pretty simple to do. You just select File, Import, Import to Stage to open the Import dialog box and then point to any raster graphic that Flash supports: `.jpg`, `.png`, `.gif`, `.bmp`, or `.pct`. That's it. (In fact, Flash imports a few other esoteric formats—such as Photoshop version 2.5—but the five listed here are by far the most popular.)

However, importing not only places the graphic on the Stage but also puts a master bitmap item into the Library. If you import a raster graphic and then delete the object from the Stage, the master bitmap item will still be in the Library (which you can find by selecting Window, Library). It's called a bitmap item, and it has a little icon that looks like a picture of a tree (as shown in Figure 33.3).

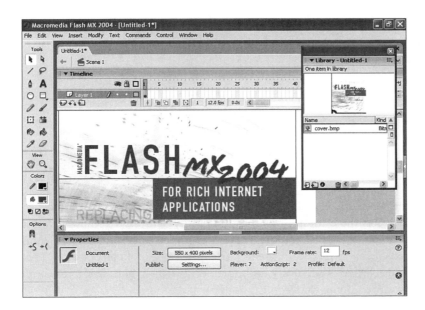

FIGURE 33.3
After you import a raster graphic, the bitmap item appears in your Library.

After a raster graphic is imported, you need to keep it in the Library. The bitmap icon that appears in the Library provides a way to specify how the image should be exported when you create a movie for the Web. If you leave it unchanged, your raster graphics export using the default settings. You can also specify special settings for just that image.

Adjusting Bitmap Properties

Flash imports all kinds of raster formats but only uses JPG, GIF, or PNG in an exported movie. In addition, any raster graphic is called a bitmap item when it is inside Flash's Library. This means that no matter what file type you import, you must use the Bitmap Properties dialog box to choose between JPEG (and its compression level) and lossless GIF/PNG for exporting. You can experiment with the Bitmap Properties dialog box and click the Test button after each change to see the effects on both image quality (in the little picture at the top left) and file size (in the text information at the bottom of the dialog box). Figure 33.4 shows an example. The process involves experimentation—making adjustments and viewing the corresponding results.

Image window

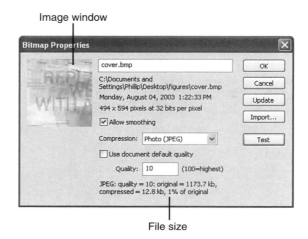

FIGURE 33.4
Selecting a low
JPEG compression
(10) and clicking
Test provides a pre-
view of the result-
ing image and its
file size.

File size

JPEG compression is usually the most efficient option. Unless you import a .png or .gif, Flash sets the bitmap properties to JPEG by default. It's slightly confusing because, if you import a .jpg file, Flash uses Imported JPEG Data by default. This option tells Flash to maintain the imported file's original compression. Leaving this option selected is generally desirable because it's a bad idea to recompress (which happens if you deselect this option).

Importing other popular formats, such as .bmp and .pct, also causes Flash to opt for JPEG compression by default. However, the Bitmap Properties dialog box displays a different option: Use Document Default Quality. Although this looks similar to the Use Imported JPEG Data option discussed earlier, it's a different option entirely. Leaving this option selected causes Flash to use a global setting to compress the file. The global settings are made when you publish the movie. These topics are discussed in more detail throughout the chapters in this part.

You can control which compression method is used on individual imported images by simply deselecting Use Document Default Quality (or deselecting Use Imported JPEG Data for that matter—but keep in mind the earlier caution about recompression). When this option is deselected, a field appears where you can type the JPEG compression level you desire. Instead of guessing which compression level is best, you can use the Bitmap Properties dialog box to experiment. A lower number results in a smaller file but also lowers the quality. If you click Test after each change, you see a drastic difference between 100 and 1. After you make each change, you can click the Test button to review the effect on file size and quality, as shown in Figure 33.5. You should experiment until you get the best compromise of image quality and file size.

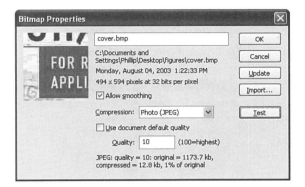

FIGURE 33.5
Setting the quality to 10 cuts this image size to less than 1/100 of its original, but the quality is visually affected.

The image portion shown in the image window at the top left of the Bitmap Properties dialog box shows exactly how the image will look when it is exported. You can zoom into this window by right-clicking, and then you can pan around to get a better view.

You get the ultimate quality by using the compression option Lossless (GIF/PNG). It is selected by default when you import .png and .gif files, but you can select it any other time you want to use it. When this option is selected, Flash leaves the image in its original state. This option always provides the best quality—but not without a price. File size is always highest when this option is selected. This is a suitable alternative if you're making a movie that doesn't need to download from the Web—maybe if you're just making a presentation you'll deliver on your hard drive or CD-ROM. Otherwise, you should use this option only on images you want to retain the best quality possible. If your imported image is a .gif that already has a small file size, selecting Lossless is perfectly suitable. And because even 100% JPEG compression causes some image degradation, the Lossless option is suitable for images that are particularly important. Finally, the only way Flash supports 32-bit graphics (that is, raster images with varying degrees of transparency) is through .png items you set to Lossless. That is to say, the fact that PNG is the only format that supports transparency is another perfectly legitimate reason to use PNG.

Converting a Bitmap to a Vector Graphic

Two common situations call for converting a bitmap into a vector graphic. The first is when you have a raster file that would be more suitable as a vector graphic (so you would like to take advantage of what vectors offer). The second is when you want to create a special effect, such as a posterized look or an outlined effect.

To do this, zoom in on a graphic so you can see what a bitmap looks like close up. It should look grainy, like the image in Figure 33.6. Obviously, this image wouldn't scale well, which is a characteristic of bitmaps.

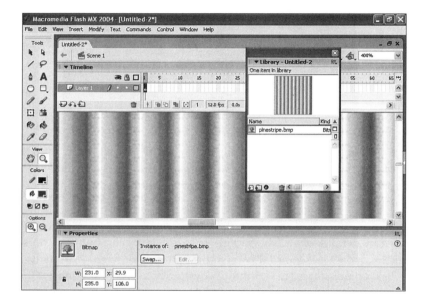

With the object selected, select Modify, Bitmap, Trace Bitmap. In the Trace Bitmap dialog box that appears, enter **1** in the Color Threshold field. This indicates how close two colors must be to be considered the same color. Minimum Area specifies how small the smallest vector shape can be. Set this at 10. Leave Curve Fit and Corner Threshold set to Normal. (You'll see how they work in a minute.) Click OK.

The graphic is now all vector shapes. The stripes on the edge might be bent, and you might see some weird artifacts on the top or bottom (which can be fixed). Even so, the graphic not only looks as good as the original, but it looks better—especially if you need to scale to a larger size.

With its nice, clear geometric shapes, the image I selected for the preceding task is particularly well suited to conversion to a vector graphic. Sometimes it's not easy for Flash to convert a graphic to a vector graphic because the image is too intricate. Other tools that are especially designed for these types of conversions, such as Adobe's Streamline, use more sophisticated processing methods. However, before you give up on this feature, you should experiment with the settings in the Trace Bitmap dialog box. The Help button provides details about each setting.

The Trace Bitmap dialog box has several interesting options:

▶ **Color Threshold**—When you're tracing an image, Flash tries to lump areas of the bitmap into single shapes. The Color Threshold option specifies how different two colors can be (in RGB values) and still be considered the same. If you set this option to a high number, you end up with fewer colors and fewer areas.

▶ **Minimum Area**—This option specifies the smallest area Flash will create. For a very detailed image, this number should be set rather low, unless you want a mosaic effect.

▶ **Curve Fit**—This option affects how closely straight and curved areas will be copied. Using the Very Smooth end of the Curve Fit scale is like having a very large pen with which to draw a shape in one quick movement. If you could use a fine pencil and as many strokes as needed, that would be like the other extreme, Pixels or Very Tight.

▶ **Corner Threshold**—This option determines whether corners are left alone or removed.

In addition to converting a bitmap to a vector graphic, you can "vectorize" a bitmap for an artistic effect. It just takes experimentation. Keep in mind that using Trace Bitmap sometimes results in an image that looks identical to the bitmap but with a larger file size. Consider this option only when the nature of the image is most suitable as a vector or when you want a special effect.

Bitmap Sequences

Although Flash supports video, sometimes all you need is a sequence of still images. This isn't "video" because it doesn't have any synchronized sound. It is a rather simple process of using video editing software to export a bitmap of each frame and then importing it into Flash. This solution is great when you don't need synchronized sound.

You might expect that it would take a long time to import one frame at a time. Luckily, Flash is smart when importing a series of graphics. If you have several images that contain sequential numbers in their filenames (pic_001.bmp, pic_002.bmp, and pic_003.bmp, for example) and that are in the same folder, you simply import the first image. Flash asks whether you intend to import the entire sequence (as in Figure 33.7). Flash then does the additional work to create a frame-by-frame animation. With a little planning (mainly involving naming the files correctly), you can import several images in one move.

FIGURE 33.7
Flash often recog-
nizes when you're
attempting to
import several
images in
sequence.

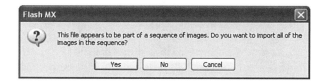

Summary

You should create all the graphics that you can right inside Flash. If this chapter taught you nothing else, remember that it's always better to create graphics in Flash than to try to import them from outside.

However, there are times when you want to import graphics, such as when you have an existing graphic that would be impossible or difficult to re-create in Flash or when a graphic requires a raster file type (usually a photograph). When you're certain you want to import, there are ways to do so. If you're importing a vector graphic, you'll do best if you use a graphics tool that can export .swf files.

A raster graphic is pretty easy to import. Flash has options for compressing on export. Also, you can change an imported bitmap into a true vector graphic.

CHAPTER 34

Applied Advanced Drawing Techniques

The last two chapters have covered basic drawing and graphic-importing skills. This chapter, you're going to concentrate on gaining fine control of the features involved with these skills.

You'll see the power and ease of drawing in Flash. Flash may not replace other drawing tools, such as Freehand, but it's definitely the most appropriate tool for creating the artwork you include in an animated Web site.

Colors and Gradients

Choosing colors in Flash is a matter of personal choice. Although you must take into account some technical considerations when publishing to the Web, generally you can use any color or color combination you want. In the following sections you'll learn how to create and save color swatches to easily create customized color palettes for movies. You'll also see how gradients can be created and used.

Creating Solid and Gradient Swatches

Up until now, anytime you wanted to color a line or fill, you selected the swatch of your choice from the Fill Color or Stroke controls in the Tools panel or Properties panel. Clicking the fill color exposes all the swatches that are currently available. By default, only 216 "Web-safe" colors are available.

Creating a custom color swatch involves two basic steps: using the Color Mixer panel to pick a color and then saving it as a swatch. This process is easy, but it's still worth stepping through carefully the first time. Let's try creating a custom color by using both the Color Mixer panel and the Swatches panel.

Here are the steps to follow:

1. Make sure both the Color Mixer panel and the Swatches panel are visible.

2. In the Color Mixer panel, click the color bar, shown in Figure 34.1, and drag as you move through all the colors. Although this choice of colors isn't infinite, there are many more than 216 variations.

Color bar

FIGURE 34.1
Selecting a color
from the Color
Mixer panel
requires that you
click the color bar.

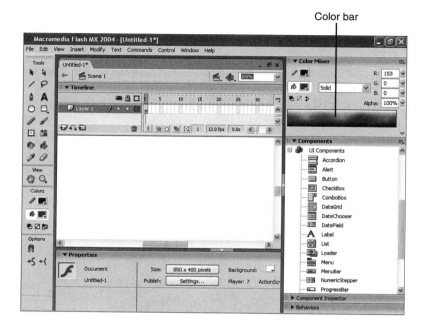

FIGURE 34.1
Selecting a color from the Color Mixer panel requires that you click the color bar.

3. You should notice as you move through the color bar that the numbers in the RGB fields (for red, green, and blue) change. Colors are mixed from 256 shades of the colors red, green, and blue, with numeric values 0 to 255. These numeric values can be particularly useful. For example, a company that wants its logo colors to remain consistent can provide specific RGB values.

4. Another way to select a color is to sample it from somewhere else, even from outside Flash. For example, to use the exact shade of beige used on the Macromedia Web site, point your Web browser to www.macromedia.com and resize the Flash application so that you can see both at the same time.

5. In the Mixer panel or Tools panel, click and hold the fill color. As you drag, move to the Web site in the background (see Figure 34.2). The current fill color changes to exactly the same color when you click.

6. Now that you've created a new color, you could use it immediately by selecting the Brush tool and trying it out. Instead of trying it now, save it as a swatch so you can easily select it later, without using the Color Mixer panel. In the Color Mixer panel's options menu select Add Swatch. This adds the current color to the bottom of the Swatches panel. Alternatively, you can add a swatch by enlarging the Swatches panel and then clicking underneath all the swatches.

7. Scroll to the last color in the Swatches panel to find the new color. You can also find the color any time you click to select a color for your fill color or stroke color.

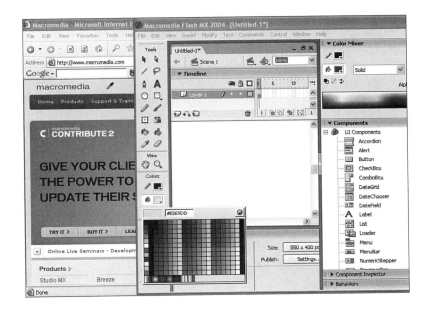

FIGURE 34.2
Sampling a color from outside Flash is possible. On the left side of the screen, a Web page is positioned for sampling.

You've seen a couple ways to select colors and one way to save a swatch. Naturally, there are additional methods. You might prefer to use a different color system instead of RGB. For example, you can use either HSB (for hue, saturation, brightness) or Hex (for hexadecimal), which refers to the way HTML uses six characters to describe any color. From the Color Mixer panel's options menu, you can select HSB. In order to set Hex values, you need to make sure the Color Mixer panel is fully expanded; to do this, you simply click the arrow at the bottom right of the panel if it's currently pointing down. You might also notice that for any color setting, there's an option for the percentage of alpha. The lower this percentage, the more transparent the color will be. Generally, though, you don't need to set the alpha when you're creating a color.

Even though the process you just learned for creating swatches is time-consuming at first, it can really help you down the line. For instance, although swatches are saved only with the current Flash file, after you've taken the time to create custom swatches, you can save them as a Flash Color Set file. From the Swatches panel's options menu, you select Save Colors. The file that you save can be used with other files or by other team members. To load colors that have been saved this way, you select Replace Colors from the Swatches panel's options menu. (Notice that the feature is called Replace, not Add—so it will replace any custom colors you've already created.)

Two other options can appear to be the same—Load Default Colors and Web 216. The default colors that ship with Flash are Web 216. However, if you want, you can first create some custom colors (or use Replace Colors) and then select Save as Default. Then, every new file you create will initialize with these colors. Web 216 will always take you back to the base colors that ship with Flash.

One other note about saving colors: The .act color table format is a standard file format. You can load these color tables into other programs, such as Photoshop. For that matter, Photoshop can save .act files, which can then, in turn, be loaded into Flash. The whole idea is to make consistent color control something you can share among files and team members.

No doubt you've noticed that the fill color can be a gradient. You'll see both radial and linear gradients in the default color swatches anytime you click to specify the fill color. Let's try creating a custom gradient.

Be sure that the Mixer is fully expanded and that the Swatches panel is present, then follow these steps:

1. Expand the Color Mixer panel and arrange the Swatches panel so that the two panels are not docked to each other.

2. Select Linear from the Fill Style drop-down list. Notice that the Color Mixer panel changes in several ways. The fill and stroke swatches change to a single swatch (called a color proxy), and a gradation appears with a little arrow at each end (see Figure 34.3).

3. Either arrow (indicating the end of a gradient range) can be edited. The one with a black triangle indicates that it's the one being edited currently. Click the one on the left, and the pointer head changes to black. Now edit this starting color by clicking to select a color of your choice in the Color Mixer panel's color bar, as shown in Figure 34.4. Be sure to move the brightness slider, or your color may remain black.

4. Select Radial Gradient from the Fill Style drop-down list, and you see the Color Mixer panel change again.

5. Click the pointer on the right side of the gradient and then select a bright blue color. Remember that simply clicking in the color bar only selects a hue; you probably need to raise the brightness (by clicking in the white-to-black vertical gradient). You should now have a radial blend that goes from yellow to blue.

6. To add more colors to the gradient, click underneath the gradient definition bar in the Color Mixer panel (the wide sample gradient). New pointers appear, and you can move them and edit their colors. To remove a color, drag the pointer down (not left or right).

7. To save this gradient in your Swatches panel, either select Add Swatch in the Color Mixer panel's options menu or just click in the Swatches panel to the right of the gradients that are already saved.

Now that you have a custom gradient, let's see how you can use it.

Color proxy

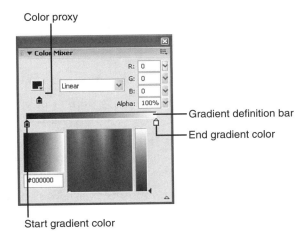

Gradient definition bar

End gradient color

Start gradient color

FIGURE 34.3
The Color Mixer panel changes when you make a gradation.

FIGURE 34.4
With the left side of the gradient selected, you can use the Color Mixer panel to change the color.

Using and Transforming Gradients

Whether you use the default gradients or create your own, there's more to using gradients than simply selecting one of your choice for the fill color. The Fill Transform tool gives you some powerful ways to edit the precise look of your fills.

The Fill Transform tool gives you handles that you can use to adjust the attributes of a gradation after it is used as a fill. The falloff rate, center point, rotation, and shape (for radial gradients) can all be adjusted. Also, when you create fills that use a gradation—such as when you use the Bucket tool—you have an option called Lock Fill. When Lock Fill is selected, a white-to-black linear gradation makes one transition (from white to black) through several shapes. If Lock Fill is not selected, each shape has its own gradation from white to black.

Using a Bitmap As a Fill

Let's take a look at a special feature—using a bitmap as a fill. Basically, any previously imported raster graphic can be used as a fill that will appear tiled in any shape in which it's used. The following steps walk you through creating this effect:

1. Import any raster graphic (`.gif`, `.bmp`, `.pct`, `.jpg`, or `.png`)

2. Delete the copy of the graphic from the Stage. (Don't worry; the graphic is safely in your Library.)

3. From the Color Mixer panel, select Bitmap from the Fill Style drop-down list. You see a thumbnail of the imported graphic. Click the thumbnail to select it.

4. A very small version of the graphic appears as the current fill color. Use the Brush tool and scribble some shapes on the Stage.

Use the Transform Fill option under the Paint Bucket tool to adjust the tiled bitmap's size, scale, and rotation.

Text Effects

Let's take a look at some fancy ways to use gradients and bitmaps as fills. You'll quickly find out, however, that gradients and bitmap fills apply only to fills—not to strokes and text. However, you can convert text to a fill. After the text is a fill, you can use all the techniques described in this chapter.

Converting text to a fill is quite simple. You just create a block of text and make sure the font, size, and style are set up correctly. Next, you select the block of text and then select Modify, Break Apart. After the text is broken apart, it can be treated as a fill. Be forewarned, however, that after the text is broken apart, you'll never be able to edit the words again!

Here are a few ideas to spark your creativity. One neat effect is to fill text with a gradation—either each character individually or, with Lock Fill, the entire word. It's also pretty cool to revisit the Transform Tool's distort and envelop options. A subtle perspective effect on text can be really powerful. Finally, you can try adding a stroke outline to text after it's broken apart. It's as if you're creating new typefaces with thick or custom stroke styles.

You've pretty much learned the basics of each of the default Flash tools, but there are even more tools hidden deep inside a new Flash 2004 feature. You can even add and remove tools in the Tools panel by choosing Edit, Customize Tools Panel.

Did you Know?

Isolating Objects

The most basic isolation technique is to make simple selections. By now, you know that to move a line, you must click once to select the line and then click again to drag it. You might have noticed that if a line has any corners (or kinks) in it, a single click on the line selects just the portion of the line you clicked. For example, if you draw a rectangle (with a stroke) and single click the stroke, only that side of the rectangle becomes selected. But when you double-click, you get the entire outline. This doesn't work with an oval because there are no kinks— you get the whole outline when you single-click. Similarly, clicking the fill once selects only the fill, but double-clicking selects both the fill and the outline.

If you think that's cool, just wait until you see some of the other ways you can select objects in Flash!

If You Can See It, You Can Select It

The first time I saw Flash demonstrated, the Macromedia representative presented it like a carnival barker, selling a device that "slices and dices." The most memorable and helpful thing he said was this: In Flash, if you can see it, you can select it. That's really true, and when you understand this concept, you'll find that selecting portions of drawings to modify them, move them, or delete them is easy.

To see this in action, draw an oval and then take the Brush tool and paint a thick fill (in a different color) across the center, as shown in Figure 34.5. Because you can see the left section of the circle, you can select it.

FIGURE 34.5
Anything you can
see, you can
select. When this
oval is bisected
with the Brush tool,
you can come back
later to easily
select any portion
you can visually
separate.

Using Levels

A concept that is related to "if you can see it, you can select it" is the fact that everything you draw is at the same level. Nothing is really on top of or behind anything else. If you select and move the fill brush stroke from Figure 34.5, you find that the oval is then missing its midsection—as if the Brush tool had burned a hole in the oval. To use Flash terminology, everything you paint or draw is on the *canvas level.* Notice that the word is *level,* not *layer.* Layers do let you stack graphics, but they're used primarily for independent animations. For now, you should understand these two points: The terminology is *levels* (not *layers*), and the seeming limitation that levels present can actually help you draw.

Up to this point, you've probably been frustrated by the fact that anything you draw "eats away" at everything else. However, you can creatively use the fact that everything resides in the canvas level to your advantage to create some complex shapes. In the following example, you'll try this out as you create a crescent moon.

Here are the steps to follow:

1. With the Oval tool selected and your stroke color set to a solid color, draw a perfect circle.

2. Select the Selection tool and double-click the fill of the circle to select the fill and the outline.

3. Select Edit, Copy or press Ctrl+C. Then select Edit, Paste in Place or press Ctrl+Shift+V.

4. While the duplicate is still selected, use the arrow keys on your keyboard to nudge it to the right. (Holding Shift as you press arrow keys moves the object in bigger steps.)

5. Deselect everything (by clicking a blank area on the Stage), and the shapes eat away at each other.

6. Now you can selectively click and delete the excessive portions—the fill and extra outline of the second circle—until a crescent shape remains on the Stage.

It's amazing how you can use a little bit of geometry theory to make all kinds of shapes.

Grouping Objects

Despite my promise that you can learn to love the way everything is on the canvas level, you'll eventually need to stack graphics without them effectively trashing each other. Imagine that you place a client's logo on top of another graphic, as shown in Figure 34.6. As long as you draw this three-circle logo second and position it in the right place on the first try, everything looks fine.

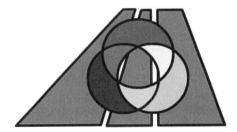

FIGURE 34.6
As soon as you try moving the circle logo, the shapes underneath are ruined.

If your clients are unlike mine, they will be satisfied with where you placed the logo the first time. However, it's likely that they'll want to move it around to see what it looks like in other locations. As you can see in Figure 34.7, this causes problems because it eats away at the other graphic.

Finally, images with complex layered graphics are next to impossible to create—given what you know so far. But that's just because you haven't learned the effects of grouping.

The Effects of Grouping

Grouping has two effects:

▶ It takes the grouped objects into a level of their own (above the canvas), allowing the group to be stacked above or below other groups without eating away at them.

▶ It locks the images together, allowing them to move, rotate, and scale as a group, while preventing individual colors and lines from being edited accidentally.

Let's take a look at both effects. First, you can try an example to see how the stacking effect works. Draw a rectangle and then draw an oval directly above it. Select both objects and group them together by selecting Modify, Group or pressing Ctrl+G. Draw another rectangle, select the rectangle fill and stroke (remember, Flash treats these as separate objects), and group it. Grouping something by itself is a way to make an object exhibit the properties of a group. Now you have a couple groups that can be placed in the same space without eating away at each other.

Notice, too, that the second group you created is "on top of" the other. Each group has an effective level in which it resides—you don't see "Level 1" and "Level 2" here, but these levels do exist. You can change the stacking order by selecting Modify, Arrange, Send to Back. If you have three or more groups, the rest of the Arrange menu makes sense. Move Ahead and Move Behind move the selected group one level at a time. Send to Back moves the group behind all other groups, and Bring to Front moves the group in front of all other groups.

The second effect of using groups is that the objects are locked together. If you move the grouped circle and square, it's pretty obvious that they stay together in the same relative location. Until you either ungroup or edit a group (which is covered in the next section), moving, scaling, and rotating affect the group as a whole. There is an exception to the rule that everything is in the canvas level until it's grouped. This exception involves text. Unless you break it apart, text isn't really a line or a fill. Therefore, text is an exception to the canvas level rule, as it remains above objects in the canvas level. When you break it apart and make it a fill, text acts as if it's grouped from the start.

Editing Groups

You can move, rotate, and scale individual groups with little effort. You can also change the stacking order of multiple groups by selecting Modify, Arrange and the appropriate menu options. But what if you want to change the fill color of an object in a group? Clicking with the Paint Bucket tool does nothing. If you want two objects within a group to be closer together, the only obvious way to make this happen is to first ungroup the objects (by selecting Modify, Ungroup), make the edit, and group the objects again. However, while these objects are ungrouped, they could easily eat away at other objects in the canvas level. The answer to this dilemma is to take a go inside the group. Try this out for yourself:

1. Make sure Snap to Objects is selected in the View menu. Draw a perfect square. Select the fill and stroke and then select Modify, Group or press Ctrl+G.

2. Rotate the square exactly 45 degrees.

3. Change the fill color swatch and draw a perfect circle.

4. Select the entire circle (by double-clicking its fill) and drag it by its center to snap it to the top corner of the square, as shown in Figure 34.8. Because the square is grouped, neither object will eat away at the other. Notice that the circle shape is stacked behind the square group. Remember that groups are automatically stacked at a higher level than the canvas level.

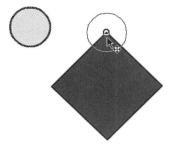

FIGURE 34.8
Selecting the circle and then dragging it by its center allows you to snap the circle to the corner of the square.

5. At this point, you need to make a fundamental change to the square. You don't want to ungroup it because it would then eat away at the circle. Instead, you can temporarily enter the group without affecting anything else. Simply double-click the square, and you are taken inside the square's group.

6. Notice that the darkened edit bar at the top of the Stage reads "Scene 1:Group". Also notice that the other contents of the Stage are dimmed

slightly. These are clues that you are inside the group. Anything you do here will affect only the square group's contents.

7. While you're in the group, deselect everything by single-clicking outside the shape. Then bend the two lower sides of the square inward to make a wing-like shape, as shown in Figure 34.9.

FIGURE 34.9
When you're inside the square's group, you can make fundamental changes to its shape.

8. Make any other changes to the square that you want to make, such as changing the fill or stroke color. When you're done, return to the main scene. You can return in three different ways. The most deliberate way is to simply click Scene 1 in the edit bar. There's also a small blue Go Back arrow button that you can click at the left of the edit bar. The other way is to double-click an empty part of the Stage. Save this file and leave it open— you'll be using it again.

The edit bar changing and the contents on the Stage dimming are critically important. These are your main clues that you're inside a group. For instance, if you start adding shapes and then return to the scene, the shapes you added to the group move and change with everything else in the group. There are certainly times when you need to add to a group, but it's important that you do so deliberately. Overlooking the edit bar change happens to be one of the most common mistakes made in Flash, so you need to pay close attention when you see it change.

One last thing about groups: There's no rule that you can't have groups within groups. In fact, it comes in handy quite often. You can take the square and circle from the previous example, select the entire circle, and group it. Then you can group the square and the circle groups. The interesting thing about such nested groups is that you can take a trip inside any level of the hierarchy. If you double-click the circle/square group, you get inside that group. If you double-click the square, you get inside that group. The entire hierarchy is displayed in the edit bar to help you avoid getting lost. Figure 34.10 shows an example of this.

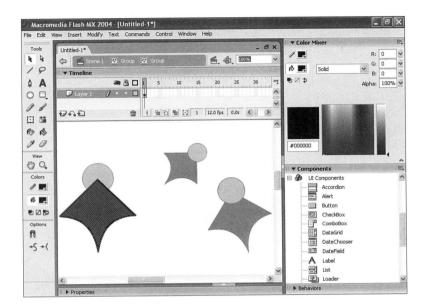

FIGURE 34.10
Both the circle and
the square are
grouped and then
grouped together
(and duplicated a
couple times). You
can double-click a
group. Double-click
again, and you can
edit a nested
group.

Summary

You've acquired a lot of skills in these past few Flash chapters. Refining those
skills and applying them to whatever challenges you encounter is just a matter of
practice. Of course, becoming a great artist involves more than technique—you
have to learn to see.

In this chapter, you created and used swatches and custom gradients. You saw
how fills—whether gradients or bitmaps—can be transformed with the Fill
Transform tool.

You also learned about the two main benefits of grouping shapes: It isolates
shapes from the other shapes so that they don't eat away at each other and it
allows you to stack the shapes. Finally, you learned that the fact that every
ungrouped object exists on the same level can actually help you draw some
unique shapes.

CHAPTER 35

Using the Library for Productivity

Flash's Library is so fundamental that creating a Flash movie *without* it is almost impossible. If you don't use the Library, it's fair to say that you're doing something wrong. Like the Library function in the rest of the Macromedia suite, using the Library as much as possible is your key to productivity and efficiency. It's a key to productivity because you can have "master" versions of graphics that, with one edit, reflect the change throughout a movie. It's a key to efficiency because graphics stored in the Library—despite how many times they're used in a movie—are stored and downloaded only once, in the Library. By far, the Library is the most important Flash feature to understand and use, so after this chapter, be sure to use the Library whenever you can.

The Concept of the Library

Symbols are what you put in the Library. Anything created in Flash (shapes, groups, other symbols, even animations) can be converted to a symbol and placed in the Library. There are several symbol types that you can choose from, and each has unique characteristics. In addition, the Library also contains several media types that can be imported into Flash (not created in Flash): bitmaps, audio, and digital video. However, symbols created in Flash are surely the Library items with which you'll become most familiar.

Instance is the term given to a symbol anytime it's used outside the Library. As you'll see, there's only one master of any symbol—the one that's in the Library. However, you can drag as many instances of a master symbol out of the Library as you like. Each instance is like a copy of the original. However, as you'll see in this chapter, instances aren't really copies because they don't add to the file size the way extra copies would.

Creating and Using Symbols

You can use two methods to create symbols: You can either convert a selected object to a symbol or make a symbol from scratch. Let's try using the Convert to Symbol route to begin:

1. In a new file, use the Oval tool to draw a circle. Select the Selection tool and make sure the circle is entirely selected (you can double-click the center, marquee the whole thing, or do a Select All).

2. Select Modify, Convert to Symbol (or press F8). Flash forces you to specify the name and default behavior for this symbol (as shown in Figure 35.1).

FIGURE 35.1
When you convert to a symbol, you must specify a name and behavior.

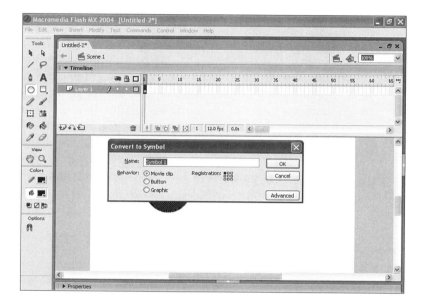

3. You should always name symbols logically. The default Symbol 1 might seem logical, but having 35 symbols all named in this manner can become unwieldy. (You'll learn more about naming symbols later in this chapter, in the section "Managing the Library by Using Names, Sorting, and Folders.") Name this one Circle. We'll look at all three types of default behavior eventually, but for now just consider Movie Clip the best choice when you're not sure which behavior is best. Button is useful only when you're creating buttons, and Graphic is primarily used for synchronization applications such as lip-synching. Leave Behavior set to the default, Movie Clip, and click OK.

4. Open your Library window by selecting Window, Library, and you should notice one symbol, Circle, in the Library. When you selected Convert to Symbol, you did two things in one move: You put your selected shape in the Library and you caused the object that remained on the Stage to become an instance of the symbol. If you drag more instances from the Library window (by single-clicking and dragging the picture of the circle from the Library

window onto the Stage), all those instances will be equivalent to the instance already on the Stage. (If you double-click by accident, you see Scene 1: Circle in your edit bar, indicating that you're editing the master version of the symbol. In this case, you can simply click Scene 1 to get back to the main Stage.)

5. After you've dragged a few instances of the Circle symbol onto the Stage, it might look like you have several copies of the master, but actually you have multiple instances of the master. You're about to make a change to the master version (in the Library), and you'll see that change in each instance on the Stage.

6. You have several ways to edit the contents of the master version of your Circle symbol. One way is to single-click it in your Library window and then from the options menu of the Library, choose Edit.

7. It might appear that nothing has happened, but behind the Library window, the screen has changed. The best indication is the edit bar (see Figure 35.2). In addition, you should see only one copy of your circle (the original) in the center of the Stage, which appears to have no borders. These clues tell you that you are currently inside the master version of the Circle symbol, about to edit it.

Edit bar

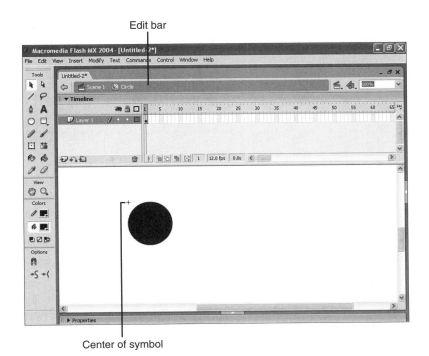

FIGURE 35.2
You know you're editing the contents of a symbol when you look at the edit bar.

Center of symbol

8. Now get out of the master version and reenter another way. Click Scene 1 from the edit bar, and you return to the main scene (with multiple instances of the Circle symbol). Enter the master version of the symbol by double-clicking an instance of it. You should see the edit bar change (which is always your best clue) and all the other instances dim slightly. In this case, you're doing what's called *Edit in Place*. This time you are editing the Circle symbol.

9. Take a "bite" out of the master graphic of the circle by using the marquee technique with the Selection tool (see Figure 35.3) and choosing Edit, clear. This is a drastic edit—not something subtle, such as changing the color.

FIGURE 35.3
The edits you make to this symbol will affect each instance.

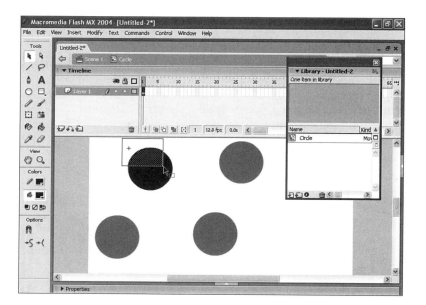

10. Go back to the main scene by clicking Scene 1 in the edit bar. Now all the instances of the Circle symbol have the same bite taken out of them! Any new instances of the symbol that you drag from the Library will have the same effect.

In the preceding steps, you converted a selection into a symbol. This left behind, on the Stage, an instance of the symbol you created. The other way to create a symbol is to simply decide that you want a new symbol and create it, as described in the following example. Neither method is better than the other, and both give you the same result.

Now let's try making a symbol by using the New Symbol feature. Follow these steps:

1. In the file that contains the Circle symbol (or a new file), make sure nothing is selected and choose Insert, New Symbol.

2. You see nearly the same Symbol Properties dialog box that you see when you use Convert to Symbol. In this case, name the new symbol Square and set the Behavior option to Movie Clip. This time when you click OK, you are taken inside the master version of the Square symbol (which is yet to be drawn), as shown in Figure 35.4. You should see the edit bar change accordingly. Think of it this way: Convert to Symbol puts your selection in the Library (end of story), whereas after you name the symbol, New Symbol takes you to the master version of the symbol so you can draw something—effectively saying, "Okay, you want a new symbol? Draw it."

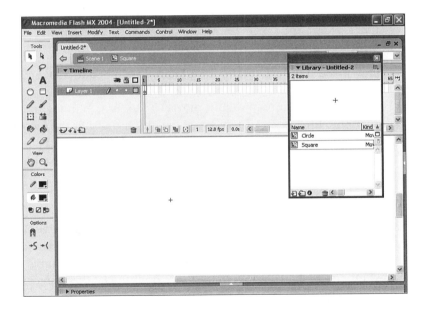

FIGURE 35.4
Selecting New Symbol takes you into a blank symbol so that you can draw its contents.

3. Now that you're in the master version of the Square symbol, you can draw the square. You'll probably want to draw it in the center of the Stage, indicated by the plus sign (shown in Figure 35.4). This becomes the reference point whenever you view the instance's location onscreen. But how do you get the square you draw in the center? Surely by now you've discovered the Paste in Place command from the Edit menu. It lets you paste anything in the same location from which you copied it, unlike the Paste command, which centers whatever you paste on the Stage. However, this time the

regular Paste function will be useful. Just cut and immediately paste your square. Presto! It's centered.

4. When you're done creating the Square symbol, go back to the main scene by either clicking Scene 1 in the edit bar or selecting Edit Scene, Scene 1. Where's the square? Well, New Symbol just creates a symbol and keeps it safe in the Library. Drag a couple instances out on the Stage by opening the Library and then dragging as many instances of the Square symbol onto the Stage as you like.

How Symbols Help You

You might already be thinking of some ways symbols can help you, but likely there are many more you haven't even imagined. Let's go over the two fundamental advantages of storing symbols in the Library: reducing the movie's file size and minimizing your work.

Reducing File Size

Believe it or not, if you have one graphic in a Library symbol and 100 instances of that symbol on the Stage, your file is no larger than if you have only 1 instance. Here's how it works: The graphic, movie clip, or button in the master symbol contributes to the file size. Therefore, if the graphic is 1KB, the master symbol adds 1KB; if the master symbol is 100KB, it adds 100KB. The size depends on what's in that symbol. No matter how many times a symbol is used, however, it's only stored once.

Minimizing Work

In addition to reducing file size, the Library can reduce the amount of work you do. For example, say you have a block of text (maybe a title) that's used in several places within a movie. If you first put the text in the Library, each time you need that text onscreen, you can drag an instance from the Library. Later, if you want to change the text, you can edit the master version in the Library and see the change in every instance. This advantage requires only that you invest a little bit of time and planning.

Using the Library

Although you've already used the Library to do several tasks, we haven't yet taken time to really explore all the details of the Library. Let's do that now so you're sure to take full advantage of the Library's offerings.

Getting Your Bearings

Using the Library can be very confusing if you don't pay attention to subtle clues. Before you select a tool from the drawing toolbar, you should ask yourself exactly where you are and what you are doing there.

Here are a few clues to help you get your bearings in the Library:

▶ The edit bar, the edit bar, the edit bar is the most important indicator and one to which you should pay attention at all times.

▶ Anytime you're in the Library, you see a plus sign in the center that indicates the default axis around which scaling occurs. You don't see this if you're editing the contents of a regular scene.

▶ In addition to the plus sign, while editing a symbol, you never see edges to the Stage because there isn't a Stage. When you drag instances onto the Stage, you need to place them within the Stage borders (if you want the users to see the objects). Symbols simply don't have a Stage—the point of reference of a symbol is its center.

▶ You can access the contents of a master symbol in several ways:

  ▶ First, from the Library window, you can select the symbol and then choose Edit in the Library's options menu. Alternatively, you can just double-click the symbol (double-clicking the symbol name lets you rename the symbol).

  ▶ Second, you can simply double-click any instance onscreen, and you are taken to the master symbol to edit. The difference in doing it this way as opposed to using the Library window is that while editing, you see the rest of your onscreen contents dimmed out but in position. You can also do this by right-clicking an instance and selecting Edit in Place.

  ▶ Third, you can access any symbol from the Edit Symbols menu. Recall the two buttons at the top right of the screen: The clapper button is the Edit Scene button, and the circle-square-triangle button (which looks like a graphic symbol's icon) is the Edit Symbols button (see Figure 35.5). The Edit Symbols menu provides a list of all the symbols in a movie. Also, the Edit Scene menu is an easy way to get back to a scene.

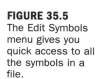

FIGURE 35.5
The Edit Symbols menu gives you quick access to all the symbols in a file.

Edit symbol

Edit scene

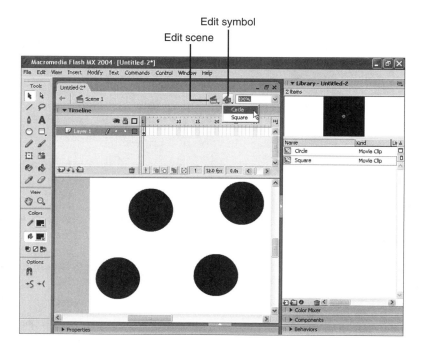

Managing the Library by Using Names, Sorting, and Folders

The Library is so great that you'll use it all the time. As the total number of symbols in the Library grows, you'll want to develop ways to keep them organized. You can manage the Library anyway you want, but this section looks at three ways in particular: naming, sorting, and using folders.

Because every symbol must have a name (and symbols are easy to rename), naming symbols consistently makes sense. How to best name symbols is subjective, but some standard practices are worth following. First, you should be clear and concise. If you have an image of a circle, you can call it Circle. There's no need to be cryptic and call it Cir. However, a name such as Red Circle with No Line might be a bit much. You should say what you have to, but nothing more.

The Library automatically sorts symbols alphabetically by name. If you widen the Library window, you can explore additional sorting options. (You can either resize the window by dragging a corner of it or click the Wide View button on the right side of the Library, as shown in Figure 35.6.) You should take a look at Figure 35.6

to familiarize yourself with the Library window. Note that you can sort by name, by kind (all the graphic symbols are listed separately from the button symbols, for example), by use count (meaning how many instances you've dragged from the Library), or by date modified.

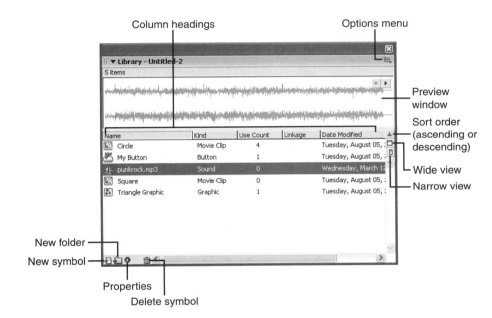

FIGURE 35.6
Several indicators and tools are built in to the Library.

The Library window has several useful features:

▶ The preview window gives you a thumbnail view and preview of any animation or audio.

▶ Column headings do more than just explain what's listed in the column. If you click a column heading, the Library is sorted by the attribute you select (Name, Date Modified, Use Count, or Kind).

▶ You can click the tiny arrow to toggle between ascending and descending alphabetical sorting.

▶ Clicking New Symbol has the same effect as selecting Insert, New Symbol.

▶ New Folder lets you create a new folder to hold several Library items.

▶ Clicking Properties gives you access to the same Symbol Properties dialog box that you see when you create a symbol.

- ▶ Wide View stretches the window for you. Narrow View changes the window to a narrower view.

- ▶ The Options menu provides all the options that are available. (Don't forget it's here!)

Finally, you can organize your Library by using folders. This is almost identical to using files and folders on your computer's hard drive, except that in the Library you have symbols and folders. Creating a folder is as simple as selecting New Folder in the Library's options menu or clicking the yellow New Folder button at the bottom of the Library. You can name the folder immediately after you create it, or you can name it later, the same way you rename symbols (by double-clicking the name or selecting Rename from the options menu). You can put symbols inside folders by simply dragging a symbol's icon (which appears to the left of its name) on top of the folder. You can open a folder (to reveal its contents) by double-clicking the folder's icon. You can even put folders inside folders.

Using Symbols from the Library

So far, the concept of dragging a symbol from the Library to create as many instances as you want has been pretty straightforward. It's powerful but easy to use. For a simple example, imagine that you made one symbol of a cloud. You could create many instances of the cloud symbol to make a cloudy sky. But you could do much more than that. Each instance on the Stage could be different from the next. One could be large and another one could be stretched out and darkened and so on.

Placing Instances of Symbols on the Stage

This discussion might seem like repeated material, but the concept and process are very specific. One master symbol in the Library can be dragged on the Stage as many times as you like. If you copy and paste an instance that is already on the Stage, you are simply creating an instance.

Modifying Instances of Symbols

Believe it or not, by simply dragging two instances of the same symbol onto the Stage, you create two instances with different properties—because they vary in position. In other words, each instance is in a different location on the Stage. Each instance can be made different in other ways, too. For example, you can transform the scale of any instance on the Stage—without adding to the file size in any significant way. You can rotate each instance separately, as well.

Using Color Styles

You might think that varying each instance's position, scale, and rotation provides for a lot of combinations—and it does. However, there's more. Each instance on the Stage can have a color style applied to it. Styles include tinting the color of an instance and changing an instance's alpha property (that is, its opacity). Similarly to how each instance can have a different location, each instance can have different color effects. To move an instance, though, you just pick it up and move it. To apply a style, you use the Properties panel.

To change an instance's color style, you simply make sure the Properties panel is visible and select the instance on the Stage. While the instance is selected, you can specify any style you want by selecting from the Color drop-down list.

Take a look at Figure 35.7 and the following list to familiarize yourself with these effects:

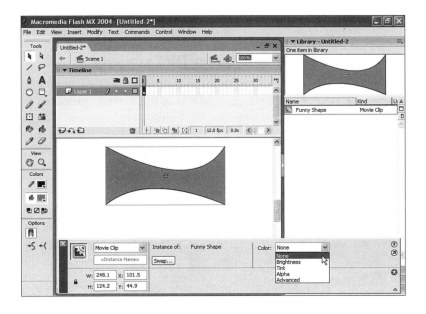

FIGURE 35.7
The Properties panel provides several ways to change an instance.

▶ **Brightness**—This effect allows you to add black or white to the instance. It is similar to turning the lights out or turning them way up.

▶ **Tint**—This effect is similar to brightness, but instead of causing the instance to be more white (or more black), it tints the instance any color you want.

▶ **Alpha**—This effect, which is the same as opacity, lets you specify how "see through" the instance will be.

▶ **Advanced**—This effect lets you combine tint and alpha.

One way to describe color is by specifying the three factors: hue, saturation, and brightness. If you want to explore these factors, you can change the Color Mixer panel's option arrow from RGB (red, green, blue) to HSB (hue, saturation, brightness). **Hue** is the base color. Moving from left to right in the Flash Color Mixer panel, you see the hue change from red to yellow to green to blue and to red again (with every shade of color in between). **Brightness** is how much white is included in a color. Imagine a paint store with a bunch of hues of paint. The store could mix in white paint to create other colors. In the Flash Color Mixer panel, the brightness is shown vertically—at the top, the colors are all white and at the bottom, they're all black. Finally, **saturation** is the amount of color. For example, if you were staining a wood fence, the more stain you used, the more saturated the color would become. In Flash you vary the saturation by changing the Tint Amount slider.

How Each Instance Behaves Differently

You've already seen how each instance on the Stage can be uniquely positioned, scaled, rotated, and colored. There's one more way in which instances can be different from one another: They can behave differently. Remember the Behavior option for creating a symbol? You have to decide among Graphic, Button, and Movie Clip. So far, I've suggested just using Movie Clip, which is the default. Later, we'll look at these other behaviors. For now, we'll discuss how the Behavior option relates to instances on the Stage.

When you create a symbol, you must select a behavior. Later on you'll learn about the differences between the behaviors, but for now they're not terribly important because you can change the behavior later. From the Library window, you can change any symbol's behavior via Properties, which you access by clicking the little blue i button, by selecting the Library's options menu, or by right-clicking the item and selecting Properties. The Symbol Properties dialog box reappears; it's almost identical to the dialog box you use when you create a symbol in the first place (this one, though, has an additional button labeled Edit, as shown in Figure 35.8, which takes you into the master symbol to edit it). Think of this setting as the default behavior. Any instance dragged out of the Library while the symbol is, say, set to Graphic starts out as a graphic. Changing the master symbol to another default behavior has no effect on instances already spawned. However, you can change the default behavior to affect new instances dragged from the Library.

FIGURE 35.8
The Symbol Properties dialog box lets you change the default behavior for a symbol.

Not only does a master symbol have a default behavior, but each instance onscreen also has its own behavior. You can use the Properties panel to see and change the behavior of any instance or instances already on the Stage. For example, you can use the Properties panel to see that the instances used in the last two tasks have the Movie Clip behavior. That's because the master symbol was created as a movie clip at the time. You can change the behavior of any onscreen instance by simply selecting it and changing the Behavior drop-down list in the Properties panel. You can actually control several instances at the same time by using this technique.

You can drag a symbol from the Library and create an instance anytime. You can even use instances of one symbol to create other symbols! Just build the symbol exactly as you normally would, but using instances of existing symbols.

Did you Know?

Summary

There's more to the Library than you might expect. In this chapter, you have learned the basics of managing the Library as well as some of the ramifications of using the Library. You can get shapes into the Library either by selecting New Symbol or by selecting Convert to Symbol. Remember that converting to a symbol leaves behind an instance of the symbol you just created.

When you have some symbols in the Library, you can use them anywhere in a movie. Instances of symbols don't significantly add to the file size. Plus, each instance can be modified in terms of position, rotation, scale, tint, brightness, and alpha. Therefore, you can recycle but change a single graphic. You also learned that you can use instances of symbols in the creation of other symbols. As you begin to understand the hierarchy of symbols, you'll be unstoppable.

CHAPTER 36

Understanding Animation

There's nothing like animation. It can inspire, educate, and entertain. It's memorable, too; no doubt when you hear the name *Disney*, images pop into your head immediately. You are on the verge of gaining the power to communicate with animation. Before we jump into animation, there are several concepts worth studying first. This chapter discusses animation in general and as applied to Flash to ensure that you understand exactly where you're headed. If your goal is clear, acquiring and applying the technical animation skills discussed in the next several chapters will be easier.

How Animation Works

Animation is made from individual images. Regardless of how motion is created in an animation, an animation is still a collection of fixed images. Suppose you see a car drive by. You see the car throughout the entire time it's within sight, but you are likely to blink. Your brain covers up the fact that you missed part of the action. When you watch a movie or television, the screen is blinking very fast—sometimes it shows an image, and other times it's black. The fact that the black moments are so short makes you *think* you're watching full motion.

The image projected onto the retina of your eyes remains even after the light stops. If you close your eyes, the last thing you saw remains imprinted for just an instant, and then it fades. This **persistence of vision** is why you don't notice the blank spots between frames of a movie, assuming that they are short enough.

Components of Animation

Now that you know a little bit about how animation works, we can discuss how it applies to Flash. As discussed in the following sections, several general animation terms have specific meanings in Flash. You need to understand both the general meanings and how the terms apply to Flash.

Frames and Frame Rate

As mentioned earlier in this chapter, animation is a series of still images. Each image is called a *frame*. In movies, frames are the individual pictures on the film itself. In Flash, frames are the little rectangular cells in the Timeline. They're numbered at the top of the Timeline, and every fifth frame is gray; the rest of the frames are white with a gray outline. The Timeline displays all the frames, but normally you can look at the contents of one frame at a time. (Later you'll use the Onion Skin option to view multiple frames.) The red current-frame marker can be in only one place at a time—the frame you're currently viewing. You don't draw into a frame on the Timeline—you draw onto the Stage. The current-frame marker indicates the frame whose contents are currently onscreen. Figure 36.1 shows the Timeline in its initial state. Until this movie's duration is extended, you can't move the red current-frame marker past 1, and only Frame 1 is enclosed by a solid white box with a hollow circle.

FIGURE 36.1
The Timeline, with its many cells, is initially only one frame long.

By default, a Timeline is initially one frame long. The current-frame marker is unmovable at that point because it can be placed only in a frame of an animation, and so far the animation has only one frame. Let's look at an animation that has more frames, but instead of building an animation, you can download

a sample from my Web site: `www.phillipkerman.com/teachyourself/`
`sourcefiles/keyframing.`

Download and open the `keyframing.fla` file so you can follow along. Now you
can click in the numbered area of the Timeline on Frame 15. The current-frame
marker moves to where you click; be sure to click in the numbered area toward
the top of the Timeline—not in the cells.

This example illustrates a few important concepts. First, if you click and drag the
current-frame marker in the number area above the frames all the way from
Frame 1 to Frame 60, you see a quick preview of the animation. This technique is
called *scrubbing.* The preview you're given is dependent on how fast you scrub.
Naturally, the *frame rate* is locked when the user watches an animation. If you
select Control, Play or just press Enter, you see this animation play at its correct
frame rate. To stop, you press Enter again. You should also notice the status area
near the bottom left of the Timeline. The three numbers are the current frame
number, the frame rate, and the current time elapsed (see Figure 36.2).

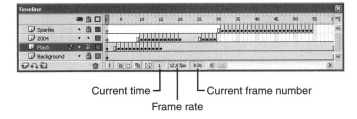

Current time ⏌
Frame rate
⏌ Current frame number

FIGURE 36.2
The status area in
the Timeline con-
tains three impor-
tant numbers
related to timing.

Frame rate is the rate at which frames are played back for the user, measured in
frames per second (fps). A frame rate of 30 fps means that 30 frames will be displayed every second. It is easy to confuse frame rate with speed, but they're not
necessarily the same. If an entire animation uses 10 frames at 10 fps, it might
look identical to the same movement using 20 frames if the frame rate is set to 20
fps. Both of these animations take 1 second to finish.

Speed isn't the reason you pick one rate over another. The issue is the capability
of the user's machine. The frame rate you specify should really be called "maximum frame rate." Your movie will never exceed this rate, but on a slow computer,
it might play more slowly.

The current frame number (on the left) indicates the location of the red current-
frame marker. It changes while you're playing or scrubbing, reflecting that you

can be in only one frame at a time. The frame rate (the middle number) normally indicates the frame rate for the movie that you last specified (by selecting Modify, Document and making a selection in the Document Properties dialog box). However, the number shown can be reduced if after you play the movie, Flash estimates that it can't actually keep up with the "requested" frame rate. It's not entirely accurate, but it does provide a good estimate.

Let's change the frame rate to something very high and see what happens. With the `keyframing.fla` sample file open, you can access the Document Properties dialog box by selecting Modify, Document. (You can also open this dialog box by pressing Ctrl+J, by double-clicking the frame rate number on the Timeline, or through the Properties panel, when nothing is selected, by pressing the button to the right of Size.) Change the frame rate to 120. Press Enter to play the movie and notice that as the red current-frame marker moves through the Timeline, the frame rate changes to show how fast Flash is actually playing. It wants to go 120 fps, but it may not be able to keep up. Now the status shows a more realistic frame rate, one that your computer can maintain. In reality, however, the frame rate shown here is not particularly accurate because it shows only how fast Flash plays during authoring—not in the actual exported movie. If you were to export this movie and play it in a browser, it would likely play slightly faster because the Flash authoring environment is not part of the picture.

Current time (the third number) indicates how long it takes to reach the frame you're viewing from the start of the movie. For example, how long it takes an animation to play 50 frames depends on the frame rate. At 24 fps, it should take about 2 seconds. At 12 fps, it should take about 4 seconds. The duration of the movie is based on the frame rate.

Frame Rate Versus the Number of Frames

The numbers in the status area are very important. When you design an animation, you should pick a frame rate and stick to it. When you change the frame rate, you're changing it for the entire movie. For example, say I have an animation of a character walking, running, jumping, and sitting still for a few seconds. If the portion where he's walking is too slow and I try to speed it up by increasing the frame rate, that portion might look better. But then the character will run extra fast, his sitting time will go by more quickly—everything will be faster! It's best to leave the frame rate alone and find another way to increase the speed.

There are ways to change the *effective speed*. Suppose you have an animation of an airplane moving across the sky. You need to decide the effective speed of the airplane according to the size of the airplane and how much sky you're showing. If you move the airplane all the way across the screen in 36 frames, you can't determine whether that's the right speed unless you consider the frame rate. At 12 fps, the airplane takes 3 seconds to move across the sky.

Effective speed is how fast something seems to move. **Actual speed**, in comparison, is absolute and can be measured. If an animation uses 12 frames (at 12 fps), the elapsed time of 1 second is the animation's actual speed. The viewer's psychological impression determines effective speed. Therefore, you can use illusions to increase or decrease an animation's effective speed. If a lot of action and changes occur in those 12 frames, it's effectively fast. If only one slight change occurs, the effective speed is slow.

If an airplane in the sky travels completely through my view in 3 seconds, the airplane is probably pretty close to me. If the plane is at 20,000 feet, it would take about 15 seconds (or longer) to move across the sky. If 3 seconds is too fast for the airplane in an animation, you can make it appear slower by slowing down the frame rate or by increasing the number of frames used in the Timeline. If you slow the frame rate to 2 fps, it will take 18 seconds for 36 frames, but the animation will be very jumpy (plus you're changing the rest of the animation). If you extend the animation to take 240 frames, the airplane takes 20 seconds to complete the motion. You'll learn how to do these things in the next few chapters, but for now, it's only important to understand the difference between frame rate and total frames.

Frame Rates of Different Types of Animation

To put the animation you're about to embark upon into perspective, let's compare some traditional animation media. In a motion picture, the frame rate at which the images appear is 24 fps. Even at this relatively slow rate, you don't notice the moments when the screen is black. Television plays at 30 fps.

In computer animation, the screen doesn't blink between frames, but you do have a choice about what frame rate to use. Technically, the user's monitor will flicker as much or as little as she has it set to flicker, but in any case, it will be much faster than an animation's frame rate. In computer animation, frame rate affects how frequently the onscreen graphic changes or, conversely, how long it pauses before advancing to the next frame. In practice, if you go much below Flash's default setting of 12 fps, your user will start to notice jumpiness, and if it's much higher than 36 fps, it may not perform well on all machines. Remember that traditional movies use 24 fps and look quite smooth.

It might seem that you should always crank up the frame rate as high as you can, which would address the problem of jumpiness. However, it's not that easy. First of all, more frames can mean that your movie has a bigger file size. Also, it often requires a computer that can display images quickly. If your user's machine can't keep up, it slows down the animation and makes it not only jumpy but slow.

Finally, creative animation techniques enable you to fool the user in ways other than relying on persistence of vision and a fast frame rate. You'll see examples throughout the Flash chapters, but for now, just remember that frame rate is important, but it isn't everything.

Keyframes and Blank Keyframes

A keyframe is simply a frame in which you establish exactly what should appear on the Stage at a particular point. A keyframe might include an image, or it might be blank. A blank keyframe is still a keyframe; it's just one in which nothing appears on the Stage.

In traditional film animation, every frame is a keyframe—that is, something new appears onscreen each frame. In Flash you can make every frame a keyframe, but you can also take some shortcuts. If the first keyframe occurs on Frame 1 and the next keyframe doesn't occur until Frame 10, there won't be any changes onscreen during Frames 2–9. The keyframe in Frame 1 establishes what will appear in Frame 1, and it doesn't change until the keyframe in Frame 10, which establishes what appears then. This is totally appropriate for something that doesn't need to change every fraction of a second.

Establishing a keyframe is simply a matter of clicking the cell in the Timeline exactly where you want a keyframe to occur. After you click a single cell in the Timeline, select Insert, Timeline, Keyframe (or, better yet, press F6). A couple things happen when you do this. Flash places a keyframe in that frame (indicated by either a solid or hollow circle), and it copies the Stage content from the previous keyframe. If at the previous keyframe you have nothing on the Stage, a blank keyframe is inserted. If at the previous keyframe you have something drawn on the Stage, that shape or symbol instance is copied onto the Stage at the new keyframe. This can be convenient because a keyframe gives you a chance to specify both when you want an onscreen change to occur and what the onscreen contents should change to. Often you want just a small change. Creating a keyframe enables you to start with a copy of the previous keyframe's content instead of redrawing it from scratch.

Whatever you draw in a keyframe continues to be displayed until the Timeline arrives at the next keyframe (blank or otherwise). If keyframes are placed one after another, the screen changes with every frame. If the frame rate is 10 fps, you see 10 keyframes in 1 second.

However, keyframes don't have to occur one after another. If you insert keyframes at alternating frames, changes appear five times per second (still at 10 fps). For any frames between keyframes, you see the content of the previous keyframe, either an image or a blank screen. Say you want a box to appear onscreen and remain still for 1 second before it moves. In one keyframe you draw a box, and then 10 frames later (1 second at 10 fps) you insert a new keyframe in which you can move the box to a new location.

Tweening

You can put whatever you want in keyframes. The space between two keyframes effectively "holds" the onscreen contents from the first keyframe. Alternatively, you can tell Flash to interpolate the change in a process called *tweening*. For example, suppose that in one keyframe there is an airplane on the left of the stage. The next keyframe shows the airplane on the right side of the stage. Flash can calculate how to move the first image to the second.

Tweening is the process of interpolating two keyframes. Tweening smoothes out a big change by breaking it into little steps. If a circle at the bottom of the screen jumps to the top of the screen 1 second later (at 10 fps), the change appears abrupt. If the two frames are tweened, you see the circle move a little bit (about 1/10 of the total distance) 10 times. The coarse movement is smoothed out with small changes in the in-between frames. Flash calculates these tweened or inter-polated frames so you don't have to do all the work.

Just so you can see what it looks like, check out the tweened frames in Figure 36.3. Tweening really is as simple as drawing two frames and making Flash tween the difference. You'll learn more about tweening starting in Chapter 39, "Using Timeline Effects and Commands." For now, you just need to realize that Flash will help you by doing some of the tedious work.

FIGURE 36.3
When you have two
keyframes separat-
ed by several
frames, you can tell
Flash how to get
from one to the
next.

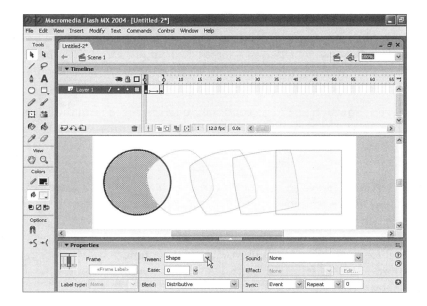

FIGURE 36.3
When you have two
keyframes separat-
ed by several
frames, you can tell
Flash how to get
from one to the
next.

Summary

Although you didn't actually create any animations this chapter, you did take a
good look at animation. The concepts discussed in this chapter, however, prepare
you for what comes next. In this chapter you learned about familiar media such
as television and film, including how persistence of vision gives the illusion of
animation work.

As a part of this discussion, you learned several important terms, including frame
rate, keyframes, and tweening. Frame rate is how fast Flash attempts to display
the contents of each frame in sequence. Keyframes are where you establish what
will be on the Stage at a particular time. Finally, tweening is Flash's way of filling
the spaces between keyframes. These three concepts (and many more) will
become almost second nature as you practice during the next few chapters.

CHAPTER 37

Creating Animation

It's finally time to animate! You've assembled the graphics that will be animated, and you learned about the basic components of an animation (frames, keyframes, frame rate, and tweening). Now you're ready to create your own animation.

Instead of starting with the two ways Flash can tween for you, you're going to begin by animating each step in an animation the old-fashioned way: frame-by-frame, *then* move on to tweening.

Understanding the Brute-Force Animation Technique

If you've ever made a flip-book, you already know how to make a frame-by-frame animation. Each page in a flip-book contains a slightly different image so that when you fan through all the pages, the image is animated. That's basically what you're going to do in this chapter. However, instead of drawing something different on each page of a book, you'll be drawing a different image in each keyframe of the Flash Timeline. Whether you draw each image on a page of the book or in a Flash keyframe, I call this the brute-*force technique* because it's manual and very involved.

In this chapter you will learn about features and techniques of Flash that make the animation process easier. However, frame-by-frame animation isn't a "feature" of Flash; it's a technique that you implement by using Flash's features. I mention this because I doubt you'll find "frame-by-frame" anywhere in the Flash manual or help files.

Enough talk! In the following example you'll make a quick animation, and then we can discuss what you've built.

Follow these steps:

1. Draw a stick man by using only lines (no fills) and make sure everything is snapped together, as in Figure 37.1.

FIGURE 37.1
In this stick man
drawn with lines,
lines are used
because they are
easier to modify
than shape fills.

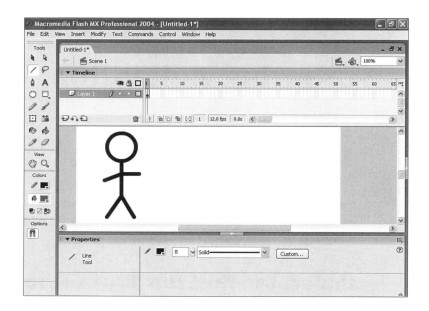

2. Single-click just to the right of the keyframe dot in Layer 1—that is, click in the second cell of Layer 1.

3. Select Insert, Timeline, Keyframe or press F6 to insert a keyframe in Frame 2 with a copy of the stick man graphic.

4. To make a slight change to the stick man in Frame 2, first make sure that you are editing Frame 2. You should see the red current-frame marker in Frame 2. If it's not there, click in Frame 2 of the Timeline.

5. Bend one leg of the stick man slightly and change the end point of the arm so it looks like it's swinging (as in Figure 37.2).

6. If you want to preview what you have so far, use the scrub technique. Grab the red current-frame marker and drag it back and forth. Okay, there's not much yet, but you can see the stick man beginning to take a step.

7. To create the third frame, click in Layer 1 right after Frame 2 and select Insert, Timeline, Keyframe to copy the contents of Frame 2 into the new keyframe in Frame 3.

8. Make a slight change to the stick man—bend the leg more and swing the arm more.

9. Continue to insert keyframes, one at a time. Make an edit to each new frame to keep the arms and legs moving, and then select Insert, Timeline, Keyframe again.

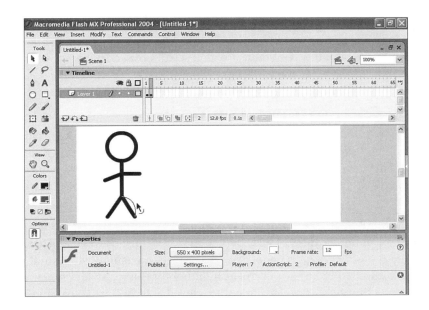

FIGURE 37.2
In the second keyframe, you bend the stick man's leg in preparation for taking a step.

Previewing an Animation by Using Test Movie

There are three ways to watch an entire animation: scrubbing, playing, and testing. Scrubbing the red current-frame marker is a good way to preview as you work. The only problem with scrubbing is that the speed isn't consistent—it is only as smooth as you scrub. To play an animation, you select Control, Play or use the Play option on the Controller toolbar or press Enter. However, as you'll see later (when creating buttons the user can click, special effects layers such as masks, and animating using movie clips), playing a movie doesn't always show you *exactly* what your viewers will see, so I strongly recommend that you avoid previewing by using Play. The best way to view an animation is by using selecting Control, Test Movie.

Test Movie exports a .swf file into the folder where your file is saved, names this file the same as your file but with a .swf extension, and then launches the Flash Player program so that you can view the results. You'll see how this works when you first save your source .fla file into a new, empty folder. After you use Test Movie, the folder will contain an additional .swf file.

You might have noticed that when you're testing a movie, the menus change. That's because you're actually running Flash Player, which is a different program than Flash. Also, the movie loops by default, which is something you'll learn about later, when you publish a movie to the Web. The easiest way to get back to your source while testing is to close the Flash Player program. The good news about Test Movie is that when you use it, you see almost exactly what your viewers will see!

Editing One Keyframe at a Time

The frame-by-frame animation technique is simple. You just put a keyframe on each frame. An entirely different image appears on each frame—sometimes drastically different, sometimes only slightly different. The beauty is that you can put anything you want in one keyframe because it doesn't matter what's in the other keyframes.

Although frame-by-frame animation is a simple concept, it can be a lot of work. Imagine conventional animation, in which an artist must draw each frame even when only a slight change is necessary. It's detailed, meticulous work and, unfortunately, it's not really any easier in Flash, although Flash provides functions such as Undo that help. You need to realize that this technique is for situations that require it—such as when you're working with something that has lots of details, such as an animation of someone walking. No other Flash animation technique gives you this level of control to change each frame.

Changing the Frame View Setting

Just because frame-by-frame animation is a lot of work doesn't mean you can't use a little help. One way to make the process a little easier is by changing the Frame View setting. In Figure 37.3 you can see the Frame View drop-down menu. If you select Preview, each keyframe in the Timeline is displayed as it appears on the Stage. Figure 37.3 shows the stick man animation with Frame View set to Preview. Preview lets you see all the frames of the animation without actually stepping through them. The Preview in Context setting draws the preview in the correct proportions (including blank whitespace), so the stick man would likely appear smaller.

The Frame View settings don't actually change an animation. For example, if you set Frame View to Large, it just makes the Timeline take up more space within Flash; the user will never notice the difference. Also, you can change the Frame View setting any time and change it back without changing the file.

Frame view button

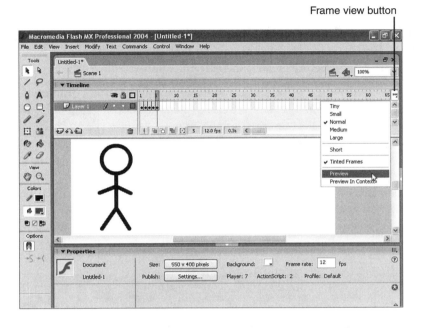

FIGURE 37.3
The Frame View drop-down menu is available to change the size and character of the Timeline. You can make each frame larger or include a visual preview of the contents of the Stage in each frame.

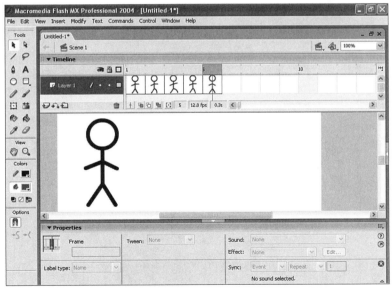

FIGURE 37.4
The stick man animation is shown with Frame View set to Preview so that an image of the onscreen contents appears in each frame of the Timeline.

Using the Onion Skin Tools

Probably the greatest helpers for frame-by-frame animations are Flash's Onion Skin tools. Flash's Onion Skin feature allows you to edit one keyframe while viewing as many frames before or after the current frame as you want.

To begin working with the Onion Skin tools, open the stick man animation file and click the leftmost Onion Skin button at the bottom of the Timeline (see Figure 37.5). Select Large by clicking the Frame View drop-down menu that is just to the right of the Timeline's frame numbers. With Onion Skin turned on, you can place the red current-frame marker on any frame you want and edit that frame, and then you see a dim view of the other frames in the animation. Which frames appear depends on where you position the Start Onion Skin and End Onion Skin markers. These markers can be difficult to grab when you try to move them; I often find myself accidentally grabbing the current-frame marker. It's easiest to grab the markers when Frame View is set to Large.

FIGURE 37.5
When Onion Skin is turned on (via the leftmost button), you can see the contents of adjacent frames.

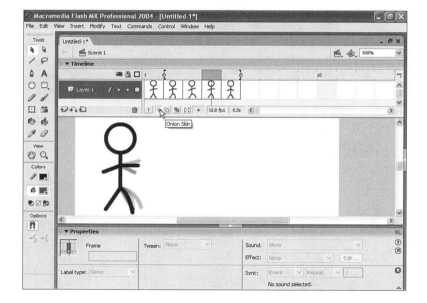

You would probably turn on Onion Skin while creating an animation (instead of after it's done). To practice, try re-creating the stick man animation—this time with the help of Onion Skin.

When you have several frames, experiment with changing both the Start and End Onion Skin markers. By default, the markers are set to Onion 2, meaning you can see two frames ahead and two behind. I rarely use the End Onion Skin marker at all—I just position it at the current-frame marker. I would rather see where I've been than where I'm headed. You can move the markers to several preset positions from the Modify Onion Markers drop-down menu (the rightmost Onion Skin button.

Modify Onion Markers has several preset options:

▶ **Always Show Markers**—This option leaves a faint version of the markers visible in the Timeline even after you turn off Onion Skin.

▶ **Anchor Onion**—This option locks the two markers where they are, no matter where the red current-frame marker is.

▶ **Onion 2**—This option sets the markers to two frames ahead and two frames behind.

▶ **Onion 5**—This option sets the markers to five frames ahead and five frames behind.

▶ **Onion All**—This option moves the Start Onion Skin Marker to Frame 1 and the End Onion Skin Marker to your last frame.

Before we finish with Onion Skin, let's look at two remaining features: Onion Skin Outlines and Edit Multiple Frames. You can choose either Onion Skin or Onion Skin Outlines, but not both. Onion Skin Outlines displays the other frames within the Onion markers as outlines instead of as dim images. Outlines can be helpful when the dim view makes images difficult to distinguish.

Edit Multiple Frames is quite interesting. In the previous example, you used onion skinning to see the contents of surrounding keyframes, but you were editing only one frame at a time—the current frame. You could move the stick man's leg close to the faded image in the previous frame without affecting the previous frame. Edit Multiple Frames lets you edit the contents of all the frames within the Start Onion Skin and End Onion Skin markers. Generally, Edit Multiple Frames is useful for editing a finished animation rather than for creating an animation because you would never know which you're editing. However, when you want to return to an animation and move the contents of every frame, Edit Multiple Frames is invaluable. In this situation, you just turn on Edit Multiple Frames, select Modify Onion Markers, Onion All, select everything on the Stage (or press Ctrl+A), and move everything anywhere you want.

Enhancing a Frame-by-Frame Animation

Frame-by-frame animation can be a ton of work. Even with helpers such as the Onion Skin tools, it still requires that you draw each frame by hand. But just because frame-by-frame animation *can* be a lot of work doesn't mean it has to be. For animation that has the same look as a feature animated movie, frame-by-frame animation is required, and it involves skill and patience. However, by using a few tricks, you can pull off the same effects with a fraction of the work.

The following sections look at a few tricks that are especially suited to frame-by-frame animation.

Incorporating Pauses

There's no rule that says you *must* put a keyframe in every frame. If your frame rate is left at the default 12 frames per second (fps) and every frame is a keyframe, the image changes 12 times per second. This might be unnecessary, and it becomes a lot of work when you consider the total number of frames you must draw. What if you don't always want the images to change every 1/12 second? Incorporating pauses is the answer—and it's very easy.

In the previous examples you inserted a keyframe in every frame, one after another. Remember that a keyframe is where you tell Flash that something new is appearing on the Stage. In addition, a keyframe says "this image should appear now, and it should remain until a new keyframe comes." To incorporate a pause, you just follow a keyframe with a non-keyframe frame. If you want a 1-second pause (and you're running at 12 fps), you just follow your keyframe with 12 frames.

There are two ways to create pauses, either as you're making an animation or after you've made one. To incorporate a pause while creating an animation, you either insert a keyframe (by pressing F6) or insert frames (by pressing F5 or selecting Insert, Timeline, Frame) farther down the Timeline than the next frame.

Creating a pause is slightly different when you want to edit an animation you've already created. To insert a pause (or increase one that already exists), you click the keyframe you want to pause and select Insert, Frame. This effectively pushes out everything that appears later in the Timeline.

In a practical sense, pauses can enhance an animation. A pause can become a visual element of an animation. Suppose the stick man walks all the way across the Stage, and you want him to walk back. In this case, you might want to include a pause when he's about to turn around. Later, you'll see how pauses can cause the audience to anticipate that a change is about to happen, which makes people pay closer attention.

Implying Motion

Two frames are all you really need for an animation. Suppose that the stick man begins on the left side of the Stage in Frame 1. The next frame is a keyframe, and he's all the way over on the right side. Show this "animation" to enough people, and you'll find some who swear that they actually saw him move across the screen. In the real world, there's no way to get from one place to another without traveling through all points between, but in animation, you don't have to draw every step.

To prove the two-frame theory, you can make a simple animation of the stick man kicking a soccer ball. Draw a stick man in Frame 1 with a ball near his foot. In Frame 10, insert a keyframe and move the ball off to the right. Extend the stick man's leg so that it looks like he just kicked the ball. It's pretty amazing, but it looks convincing. If you add just one more keyframe at Frame 4 and move the stick man's leg back a tad (as if he's about to kick), the animation looks great! Stick man stands (pause), he winds up (pause), and he kicks. Imagine how much more work it would take to draw all 10 frames.

Creating implied motion is a great skill. In a way, you're trying to fool the audience, but it's more than that. Unnecessary animation adds extra work and can actually detract from your core message. It's hard enough to tell a story with animation; the last thing you need is a distracting animation that's superfluous.

The Flicker Effect

How do you make something blink? You just need one keyframe with an image in it, followed by another keyframe with *nothing* in it (also known as a blank keyframe), followed by another keyframe with the original image in it. There are several ways to create this kind of blinking or flicker, the easiest is to add a keyframe, then select and remove the contents of the stage.

Creating a Motion Tween

Creating an animation frame-by-frame can be a lot of work because you have to draw every frame yourself. With *tweening*, Flash fills in the blank frames between two keyframes. Flash has two types of tweening: motion tweening and shape tweening. In the remainder of this chapter we'll cover motion tweening. Motion tweening animates clip properties such as location, scale, rotation, tint, and alpha. Shape tweening morphs one shape into another.

A basic motion tween is very easy to produce. Let's create one in the following example, and then we can analyze it:

1. In a new file, draw a circle on the Stage.

2. Select the entire circle and choose Modify, Convert to Symbol (or press F8). Name it `Circle`, leave the behavior set to the default Movie Clip, and click OK.

3. Click Frame 30 in the Timeline and select Insert, Timeline, Keyframe (or press F6).

4. Click on the keyframe in Frame 1; the red current-frame marker moves to Frame 1. Position the circle where you want it to appear at the beginning—in this case, to the left side of the Stage.

5. Click in the last keyframe (Frame 30) and notice that the red current-frame marker moves to Frame 30. Position the circle on the right side of the Stage.

6. Try scrubbing. The animation looks pretty abrupt. The circle stays on the left side for 29 frames and then jumps to the right side. To make the movement smoother, you can use tweening to have Flash take care of the in-between frames.

7. Set tweening in the beginning keyframe, in this case the first keyframe (in Frame 1). Select the keyframe in Frame 1 and then observe the Properties panel. When a frame is selected, the Properties panel contains a Tween drop-down list.

8. Select Motion from the Tween drop-down list. Leave all the default settings, as shown in Figure 37.6.

   That's it! Notice in Figure 37.7 that Flash has drawn an arrow with a blue background to represent the interpolated frames—those between two keyframes.

9. Select Control, Test Movie (or press Ctrl+Enter) to see what happens.

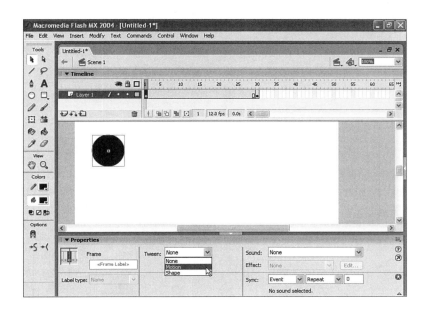

FIGURE 37.6
The Properties panel opens, with the first keyframe selected.

Interpolated frames

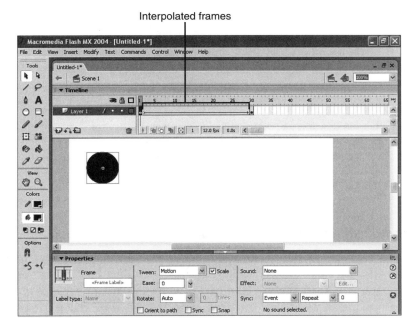

FIGURE 37.7
The Timeline includes an arrow on a blue background to indicate that Flash is tweening these frames.

Following the Rules of a Motion Tween

The previous example worked because the instructions carefully followed the rules of a motion tween:

▶ You can't have multiple objects in keyframes.

▶ The one object you do have must be a symbol.

Flash is very unforgiving when you don't follow these rules.

The good news is that Flash gives you several hints when you don't follow the rules for a motion tween. Sometimes you'll see an exclamation point button on the Properties panel (when you select the first frame of a tween that breaks one of these rules). When you click the exclamation point button, the message "Motion tweening will not occur on layers with ungrouped shapes or on layers with more than one group or symbol" appears. In other words, this message is saying, "You didn't follow the two rules." You don't even have to press a button to know something is wrong—the exclamation point is enough. In addition to this warning appearing, the resulting Timeline will often look different. A dashed line will appear as another indication that you broke the rule.

Watch Out!

Motion Tweens and Groups

You probably noticed when you pressed the exclamation point button that the warning implies that you can motion tween either a symbol or a group. Unfortunately, Flash gives you a break here, but I would still recommend that you follow the rule that you only motion tween symbols (and one symbol at a time). If you have a grouped shape in the first keyframe and then you insert a keyframe later in the Timeline, you can use motion tweening with no apparent harm. However, Flash turns your grouped shape into a symbol, calls it Tween 1, and pretends nothing happened. It's as if Flash does the thinking for you. Personally, I would rather be in control and create symbols intentionally when I'm about to do a motion tween.

Motion Tweening Techniques and Tips

You should feel proud of the circle you moved across the screen in the preceding example. Actually, Flash did the work—you just established the two keyframes. As you're about to see, Flash can tween any two keyframes, no matter how different they are from one another. Plus, there are some ways to make the process even easier for you.

Tweening More Than Position

Recall from Chapter 35, "Using the Library for Productivity," that you learned that each instance on the Stage can be different from all the others, even if you just have one master symbol in the Library. Instances can be positioned in different locations, scaled to different sizes, rotated differently, and have their color effects set differently. There are seven ways in which instances can be varied: position, scale, rotation, skew (which is a type of rotation), brightness, tint, and alpha. Flash can tween changes in all these properties.

Alpha Tweens Affect Performance

Although you can tween the Position, Scale, Rotation, and Alpha effects, it doesn't mean you have to. The Alpha effect forces your audience's computers to work a bit harder. The message you're trying to communicate might be overlooked when the user notices everything slowing down to a crawl. I don't want to suggest that you should never tween alpha, but it's the most processor-intensive effect available, and sometimes you can simulate the same effect in other ways. Consider tweening based on the Brightness color effect. If the background is white anyway, this is visually no different from using alpha, but it doesn't slow down the computer as much.

Watch Out!

A Motion Tween Shortcut

Because you'll likely use motion tweens a lot, there's a great shortcut to know. Just right-click your starting keyframe (on a Macintosh, use Control+click), and then select the option Create Motion Tween from the list that pops up.

Did you Know?

Staying Out of Flash's Territory

You are responsible for establishing keyframes. When you choose to tween, Flash is responsible for the frames between your keyframes. Consider this to be "no-man's-land," although Flash calls these frames *interpolated frames*. If you edit anything you see on the Stage while the red current-frame marker is between two keyframes, you might get some unexpected results.

To illustrate, suppose you have two keyframes and no tweening. Remember that keyframes establish when something should be on the Stage and where it will remain until another keyframe comes along. If you position the red current-frame marker anywhere in the middle and grab the object onscreen, you'll be editing the contents of the previous keyframe and thus influencing every frame from the first keyframe to the next. (You'll see a visual clue of this when you click an object on the Stage: The span in the Timeline that the first keyframe influences will turn black.)

Messing with no-man's-land is even stranger when you have a motion tween already established. If you position the red current-frame marker in the middle of a motion tween (as in Figure 37.8), it won't be apparent that you can even select the symbol on the Stage. If you click and drag it, you can move it. However, if you move a symbol in the middle of a motion tween, you add a keyframe. Flash is forfeiting control of that frame to you by giving you a keyframe. Adding a keyframe in the middle of a motion tween is sometimes useful, as you'll see later. Just realize that you're taking away Flash's control of a frame when you insert a keyframe (either by using Insert Keyframe or by grabbing the symbol and moving it).

FIGURE 37.8
The red current-frame marker is positioned over the interpolated frames of the tween.

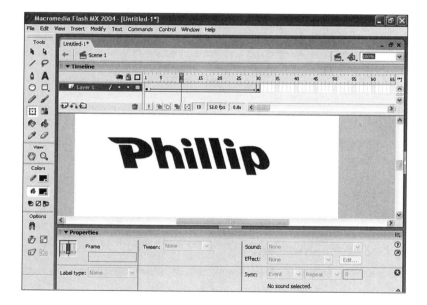

Knowing Where You Are

It's important to pay attention to the red current-frame marker as you edit keyframes for a motion tween. Consider the examples you've done so far this chapter. If you want the motion to go from the left to the right, your starting keyframe should have the symbol positioned on the left. If you accidentally leave the current-frame marker on the end frame and then move the symbol to the left, you're actually editing the end keyframe, and the object will move to the left—not to the right. Always be sure the red current-frame marker is in the right place before you edit the contents on the Stage.

Sticking to a Pattern

Hopefully you're beginning to see a pattern. To summarize, here's the basic pattern we've used so far:

1. Motion tween will tween only one object, and that object is a symbol. Make that object a symbol before creating the ending keyframe, or else the new keyframe will contain a shape, not a symbol.

2. After you've created your beginning and ending keyframes containing one instance each, you can adjust the position, scale, rotation, skew, brightness, tint, and alpha of either the beginning or end keyframe.

3. Keep an eye on the current-frame marker in your Timeline to be sure it's located in the keyframe you want to edit.

You'll refine your technique over time, but you should follow these basic steps during your entire Flash career.

Fine-Tuning a Motion Tween

Making a motion tween is pretty easy when you know how. Making it look good is another matter. There are a few basic techniques for fine-tuning a motion tween that will make the results more natural and believable.

Using Multiple Keyframes

Every motion tween involves just two keyframes. In the first, you tell Flash how to tween to the next keyframe. But suppose you want a symbol to move up and then back down. In this case, you need three keyframes: one in the initial location, another in the upper location, and a third in the end location. However, in this case you have only two tweens: one going up from the first keyframe to the second keyframe, and one going down from the second keyframe to the third keyframe. The process will be easier if you can sort things out this simply.

Often, you want the end of a motion tween to correspond exactly with the beginning (like a yo-yo moving down and then back to where it started). In the following example you can try this:

1. In a new file, draw a circle.

2. Select the circle and convert it to a symbol (by selecting Modify, Convert to Symbol or pressing F8). Call it Yo-Yo, leave the behavior set to the default Movie Clip, and click OK.

3. Position the yo-yo in its starting position, near the top of the screen.

4. Click Frame 10 in the Timeline and insert a keyframe (by selecting Insert, Timeline, Keyframe or pressing F6).

5. Before you move anything, click Frame 20 in the Timeline and insert another keyframe. At this point you should have three identical keyframes.

6. Position the red current-frame marker on Frame 10 and move the yo-yo down to the bottom of the Stage. (Clicking the keyframe in Frame 10 not only moves the current-frame marker but also selects all the contents of this frame that are on the Stage.)

7. Set motion tweening for Frame 1 (which specifies how to tween to Frame 10) and for Frame 10 (which specifies how to tween to Frame 20). To do this, you can use the right-click method if you want. To set tweening for two keyframes (Frames 1 and 10) at the same time, click the keyframe in Frame 1, hold Shift, and then click the keyframe in Frame 10. Then access the Properties panel and set tweening for both keyframes (see Figure 37.9). Select Motion.

FIGURE 37.9
The Properties panel affects every keyframe selected.

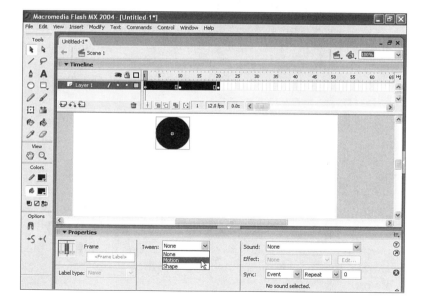

8. Select Control, Test Movie (or press Ctrl+Enter). Save the animation. (You'll add to it in a minute.)

Step back and consider what you just did. You made sure the first and last keyframes were identical before editing the middle keyframe. It's very common in animation to establish the ending keyframes first before editing the initial frames. You did it here so that the first and last keyframes contained the yo-yo in the same position.

Using Ease In and Ease Out

The only problem with letting the computer (or Flash) do tweening for you is that the result looks like a computer did it—it's almost too perfect. For example, the yo-yo from the preceding example moves down at the same rate as it moves up, and the entire animation plays at the same rate.

Flash has a way to address the fact that some kinds of motion accelerate while others decelerate: the Ease In and Ease Out effects. Because every tween is between only two keyframes, you only have to think of two keyframes at a time. *Easing in* (think "ease into animation") means that the motion starts off slow and speeds up at the end. *Easing out* is the opposite—the object starts by going fast and then slows down at the end of its motion.

You can see the effects of easing by opening the yo-yo animation you just created. Click the first keyframe and from the Properties panel set the Ease slider to –100 (by moving the slider down). Notice that the word "In" appears to the right of the slider. This causes the animation to start off slowly and then accelerate at the end. When you select Control, Test Movie, you'll see that the trip down should look pretty good.

For the second tween (between Frames 10 and 20), you want to ease out as it reaches the peak, so select the keyframe in Frame 10 and from the Properties panel set Ease to 100 (by moving the slider up). Then select Control, Test Movie again. The result is that the yo-yo slows down before it reaches the top, making it look more natural. You'll find other ways to make your animation believable, and this quick experiment should spark some ideas.

If you can have only one Ease setting per tween, what if you want one smooth tween to both ease in (at the beginning) and ease out (at the end)? It *is* possible— you just can't do it with only two keyframes. The solution involves three keyframes: one at the start, where you set the tweening to Ease In, one in the middle, with tweening set to Ease Out, and one at the end. To let Flash help you, first create a tween between the first and last frames and insert a keyframe in the middle. The following example explains how you do this:

1. In a new file, draw any shape and make it a symbol. Place the symbol somewhere on the left side of the Stage.

2. Click Frame 50 in the Timeline and insert a keyframe (by selecting Insert, Timeline, Keyframe or pressing F6).

3. While the red current-frame marker is in Frame 50, move the instance of the symbol to the right side of the Stage.

4. Go back to the keyframe in Frame 1 and create a motion tween (by right-clicking and selecting Create Motion Tween).

5. Test the movie (by selecting Control, Test Movie) and remember how it looks.

6. Place the red current-frame marker in the middle (Frame 25).

7. If you insert a keyframe in Frame 25 (where there's already a motion tween), not only will Flash copy the contents of the previous keyframe, but it will position the contents of the new keyframe in the appropriate mid-stream location. Go ahead and insert a keyframe in Frame 25 (by making sure you're at Frame 25 and pressing F6). Nothing moves. Just the keyframe appears, and the symbol is already in its tweened location. Test the movie again; it should be unchanged.

8. To see easing in action, in Frame 1, set the Properties panel Ease setting to Ease Out (set it to 100 to make it obvious). In Frame 25, set the Ease setting to Ease In (–100).

You used two interesting tricks in the preceding example. First, you needed three keyframes (or two tweened spans) to have two different easing settings. Second, you squeezed a keyframe into the middle of an existing tween. That way, the newly created keyframe was in the appropriate location—halfway between the two existing keyframes. This will happen to any property that is being tweened. If the symbol in Frame 1 were tinted blue and the symbol in Frame 50 were tinted red, the newly inserted keyframe would include an instance of the symbol with a tint somewhere between. In this example you just happened to be tweening only position.

This example had a different approach from the yo-yo example. In the yo-yo example you made identical keyframes at the beginning and the end and then repositioned the contents of the middle keyframe manually. In comparison, the preceding example involved establishing keyframes at the beginning and end (in different locations), letting Flash do a tween, and then doubling back to add a mid-keyframe based on Flash's tween. The fundamental result (three keyframes, two tweens) was the same, but the approach taken was different.

Rotating in a Motion Tween

If you manually rotate a symbol in one keyframe, Flash tweens the rotation appropriately. In addition, in a motion tween you can tell Flash to rotate a symbol a specific number of rotations. For example, you can use this option to make an animation of a wheel rotating. In the Properties panel when a keyframe set to motion tweening is selected, you can set the Rotate drop-down list to CW (for clockwise) or CCW (for counterclockwise). One rotation is usually plenty; any more will just cause the increments of rotation between frames to be greater. Also, notice that the default setting for Rotate is Automatic, meaning that Flash will tween rotation if you manually rotate the symbol in either keyframe. The None setting will leave a manually rotated symbol in its rotated position during the entire tween. Because perfectly round symbols are not interesting when rotated, if you want to try rotating the yo-yo, consider drawing a graphic off-center inside the master version of the yo-yo symbol.

Summary

Congratulations! You've learned the fundamental skills of frame-by-frame animation and motion tweening. While frame-by-frame animation gives you the ultimate in control, it's fun making Flash do all the work. Nevertheless, a few strategically placed keyframes (presented frame-by-frame) can often be just as effective as—or even more effective than—a computer-generated tween. The best animators think in keyframes. It's fine to employ Flash to come in and tween certain segments, but it's a skeleton of well-placed keyframes that makes a good animation.

CHAPTER 38

Using Shape Tween to Morph

There are several ways to keep a Flash movie small and running swiftly. Recycling symbols from the Library and using motion tweening are two of the best ways. Unfortunately, the shape tween, as you're about to learn, is one of the least efficient features in Flash because it causes file size will grow. However, shape tweening is pretty cool looking! There's no other way to get the "morph" effect in Flash. So when appropriate, it's perfectly acceptable to use shape tweens.

A **morph** is a kind of animation that naturally changes one shape to another. *Morph* is a general term, but it's the closest common term that describes how Flash's shape tween works.

Making a Shape Tween

Shape tweens are fun because they look really cool and they're easy to create. Compared to motion tweens, they look more dynamic because every attribute— including the shape—animates. Basically, all you do is draw a shape or shapes in two keyframes and set the tweening in the first keyframe to Shape. Let's create one in the following example, and then we can analyze it:

1. In a new file, draw a circle on the Stage. (Don't group anything and don't convert anything to a symbol.)

2. Insert a keyframe in Frame 30 (by clicking in the Timeline at Frame 30 and pressing F6 or selecting Insert, Timeline, Keyframe). This will be the end of the tween, and it will match the beginning.

3. Insert a keyframe in Frame 15. While the red current-frame marker is on Frame 15, put a little dimple into the circle: Use the Selection tool to first deselect the circle (click off the circle), and then bring the pointer close to the edge until the cursor changes to a curved-tail pointer. Click and drag toward the center of the circle to reshape it, as shown in Figure 38.1.

4. Set shape tweening for the two spans. To do this, click Frame 1, hold Shift, and then Click Frame 15. In the Properties panel, select Shape from the Tween drop-down list.

5. Select Control, Test Movie (or press Ctrl+Enter) to see what happens.

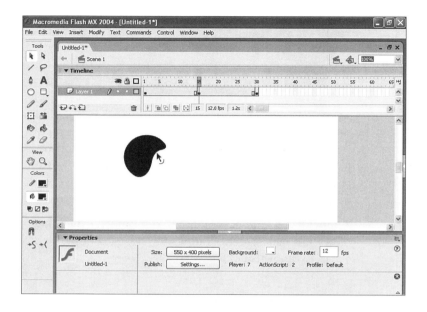

Following the Rules of a Shape Tween

Flash is unforgiving when you don't follow its rules. Luckily, the rules for a shape tween are very simple: no groups and no symbols. That's it! Remember these two things, and shape tweens will be easy.

Watch Out!

> ## Turning Text into a Shape
>
> Recall that text acts as if it is grouped from the beginning. This means that you can't use text in a shape tween unless you first break it apart (by selecting Modify, Break Apart). If text contains more than one character, you have to break apart twice—once to break the text into individual characters and another time to turn it into shapes. Remember, too, that after text becomes a shape, it's no longer editable!

Although there's no way around the no group, no symbol rules, you can still take advantage of some of the benefits of groups and symbols when using shape tweening. For example, groups are often necessary to isolate shapes while drawing. You can use groups all you want while designing a shape tween. You just have to remember, as a last step before tweening, to ungroup everything. The same is true with symbols from your Library. If you have an image in the Library you would like to use in a shape tween, you can—you just have to remember to break it apart before the shape tween will work. You can't really get around the rules, but you can break the rules temporarily while working.

Techniques and Tips

Just because the rules for a shape tween are simple doesn't mean that creating a good-looking shape tween is easy. There are several techniques to make the process easier and the results better.

Keep It Simple

If you ignore all other tips, keeping it simple is one you really should heed. There are very few rules for a shape tween—as long as you don't group anything or use symbols, it will work. However, when you have a million different shapes tweening to a million other shapes, the results will look random. The two symptoms that you aren't keeping it simple are unexpected results and the "checkerboard" effect you're about to see.

For example, consider these unexpected results. You imagined your name morphing gradually into a circle shape, but despite breaking apart the text, you got a garbled mess. Or you got the checkerboard effect in the tweened areas (as in Figure 38.2). These are signs that you're likely creating something too complicated for Flash. Actually, Flash is interpolating the in-between frames very accurately, but it can be very difficult to go from one extreme such as your name to something as simple as a circle. Flash will get you from here to there, but the trip might look pretty messy.

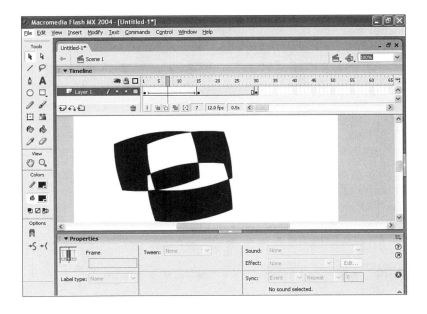

FIGURE 38.2
The checkerboard effect is the common result of an overly complex shape tween.

The solution is to keep it simple. The simpler the animation is, the better. You'll find that a simple animation will be easier to create and more like what you expect, and it will also probably result in a smaller file that plays better.

Don't Mix Lines and Fills

It's best to avoid tweening between shapes that don't have the same combination of fills and lines because the results are unpredictable. Tweening a straight line into a bent line usually works fine. But if you try to tween from a line to a filled shape, you might get unpredictable results. As an analogy, consider bending a wire. You could also start with clay and reshape it. But if you had to turn a wire into the shape of clay, it would be difficult or impossible. This analogy is similar to Flash tweening lines and fills. Flash can tween lines; Flash can tween fills; it can even tween a fill with a line. Flash has difficulty, however, when one keyframe has a line and the other has a fill or when one keyframe has both line and fill and the other only has one. Flash does what it can to interpolate the in-between frames when you mix them, but eventually something has to give; Flash can't perform miracles.

To avoid these problems, convert the lines to fills by using Modify, Shape, Convert Lines to Fills. Better yet, keep things simple by drawing in both keyframes of a tween just lines, just fills, or both.

Stay Out of Flash's Territory

When Flash is tweening a span of frames, it colors the tweened frames in the Timeline either blue (for motion tweening) or green (for shape tweening). These *interpolated* frames are what I call Flash's territory (see Figure 38.3). Generally, you should stay out of this area. For one thing, you can only draw into keyframes, so you can't draw into this territory. Also, in shape tweens, you can't even select objects when the red current-frame marker is in this territory. (However, you saw in the last chapter that with motion tweens you can actually grab and move symbols in interpolated frames, which adds keyframes.)

You can't do any harm to interpolated frames of shape tweens, but trying to edit them can be very frustrating. You can't draw into them, and you can't select objects. The best way to think of these frames is that they are Flash's territory—not yours. You are responsible for the keyframes, and Flash is responsible for the tweening.

Know When a Motion Tween Will Suffice

It's easy to fall in love with the shape tween. There's nothing like it. Feel free to use it when necessary. However, because shape tweens are inherently less efficient than motion tweens (the file sizes are larger and play more slowly), you should always choose motion tweening when you can. If you can get the same effect with either, you should always opt for motion tweening.

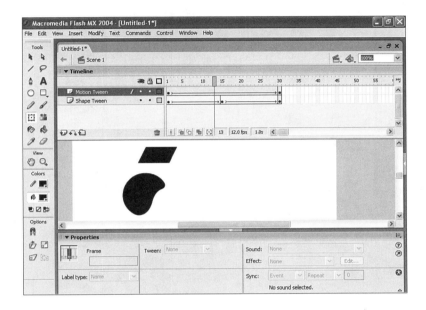

FIGURE 38.3
The interpolated frames (where Flash is responsible for doing the tweening) are green for a shape tween and blue for a motion tween.

Let's say you have a shape you want to tween from a blue circle to a red square. Only a shape tween will suffice because the actual shape is changing. However, if you just want to tween a blue circle into a red circle, you're much better off doing it as a motion tween. Draw a circle, convert it to a symbol, insert a keyframe later in the Timeline, use the Properties panel to set Color Effect to tint the circle instance in the second keyframe, and set Tween to Motion when you select the first keyframe. To do the same animation as a shape tween, you would draw a circle (don't convert it to a symbol), insert a keyframe later in the Timeline, fill the circle in the second keyframe with a new color (perhaps using the Bucket tool), and set shape tweening in the first keyframe. The result of each operation is the same, but the motion tween method is better because it gives you only one master version of the circle and therefore a smaller file size.

Sometimes it's obvious which type of tween is more appropriate. If something's just moving or changing color, a motion tween is appropriate, whereas significant changes to a shape require the shape tween. Sometimes, however, it's not so obvious. For example, you can drastically change a symbol's shape by using the Free Transform tool's Rotate, Scale, and (especially) Skew options. Notice in Figure 38.4

how several instances of the same symbol can be distorted significantly; a motion tween would suffice if you tweened any two of these symbols.

FIGURE 38.4
Multiple instances of the same box can be drastically distorted and still used in a motion tween. Notice the original box in the Library.

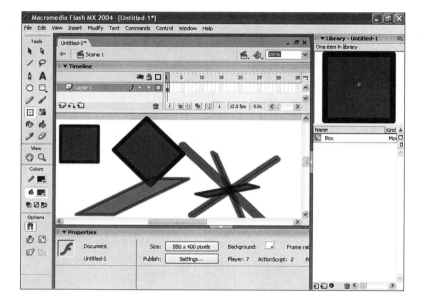

Although you should definitely lean toward motion tweening when you can, don't forget the keyframe techniques you learned in the last chapter. A few strategically designed keyframes can often be more effective than a drawn-out tween (of either type). It's what the user thinks she sees that matters—not what she actually sees.

Refining and Fine-Tuning a Shape Tween

Shape tweens don't always come out the way you expect. The tips we just covered are really more like rules and cautions. Even if you heed all the warnings, you still might have shape tweening results that are anything but what you expect. Flash has a feature especially for shape tweening that helps you tell Flash what you really want. It's called the Shape Hint feature, and it can make the difference between a shape tween that looks like a mess and one that looks like what you had in mind.

Using Shape Hints

A shape hint gives you a way to tell Flash exactly how to map one point in a shape to another point during the shape tween. You'll want to use shape hints when Flash doesn't create a shape tween that matches what you had in mind.

Points inside an image are **mapped** during any tween. The term *map* refers to how one point in the starting shape corresponds to a specific point in the ending shape. Consider how every point on a printed map corresponds to a real location. A point on the map can be mapped to a real location. When Flash motion tweens a box from small to large, one corner of the small box is mapped to the same corner in the large box. Every point is mapped. Mapping points in a shape tween is more complex, so there's a feature called Shape Hints that lets you control how Flash maps individual points. In the following example you'll step through how to use shape hints:

1. In a new file, draw a perfect square by using the Rectangle tool (just hold Shift while you drag).

2. In Frame 25 of the Timeline, insert a keyframe (by clicking in the Timeline at Frame 25 and then pressing F6 or selecting Insert, Timeline, Keyframe).

3. Change the shape in Frame 25 to a triangle. There are many ways to do this, including starting from scratch and using the Onion Skin tools to help line up the triangle with the square. You should make the triangle as similar as possible to the square by following the next steps.

4. In Frame 25, draw a vertical line that doesn't touch the square.

5. Select the Selection tool (make sure Snap to Objects is turned on under View, Options), click once on the line to select it, and click and hold in the center of the line. (Make sure you have the solid circle, indicating that you've grabbed the center; if you don't, try grabbing the line again.) Now drag the line so it snaps in the center of the horizontal top of the square.

6. Click off the line and grab the top-left corner of the square. Drag it until it snaps to this bisecting line. Do the same for the top-right corner of the square.

7. Select and delete the excess portions of the vertical line.

8. Select the first keyframe and use the Properties panel to set Tween to Shape. Scrub, and you see that the results are probably not what you expected. Now is your chance to use the Shape Hints feature.

9. Under the View menu, ensure that Show Shape Hints has a check mark (select it if not).

10. Place the red current-frame marker in Frame 1 and select Modify, Shape, Add Shape Hint (or press Ctrl+Shift+H).

11. Notice a little red circle with the letter *a* (a shape hint). Temporarily move the red current-frame marker to Frame 25 and notice that there's also an *a* shape hint in this frame.

12. Make sure you're back in Frame 1 and that Snap to Objects is turned on (by selecting View, Snapping, Snap to Objects). Use the Selection tool to drag the shape hint so that it snaps to the top-left corner of the square. (Notice in Figure 38.5 that it's still red, indicating that you haven't really mapped this point to an end point yet.)

FIGURE 38.5
Although you've added a shape hint in the first keyframe and even attached it to the shape, it's still colored red because you haven't added a shape hint for the ending keyframe.

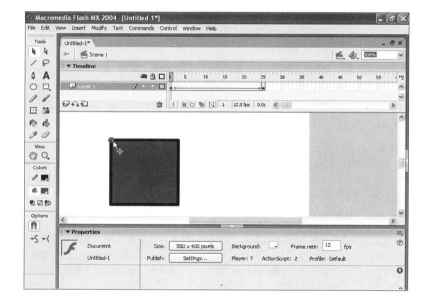

13. Go to Frame 25 and position Shape Hint *a* so that it snaps to the middle of the left side of the triangle. Notice that the shape hint turns green, indicating that it's been mapped. Also, when you return to Frame 1, the shape hint is colored yellow to indicate that it's been mapped.

14. Scrub to see the results so far. If it looks good, you don't need to add any more shape hints. (For this exercise, however, it will likely not look very good.)

15. In Frame 1, add another shape hint (by pressing Ctrl+Shift+H), and the new hint is automatically given the name *b*. Position it in the top-right corner of the square.

16. In Frame 25, map Shape Hint *b* to snap to the middle of the right side of the triangle (similarly to how Shape Hint *a* was mapped). See Figure 38.6.

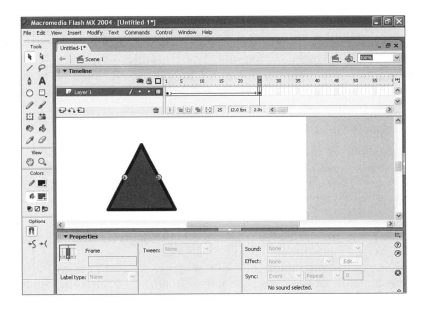

FIGURE 38.6
Shape Hint *b* is snapped to the middle of the right side of the triangle in the second keyframe.

17. At this point, the results should be much better than before you added any hints. Use Test Movie to see.

Understanding Shape Hints

The time-consuming part of the preceding example was creating the triangle to match the square perfectly (and that should have been a review). Adding the shape hints was fairly simple. Granted, I told you where to place the hints. However, figuring out logical positions for shape hints is usually pretty easy. Think of it this way: You're telling Flash "this point in the starting shape goes with that point in the ending shape."

You should notice that after you add one shape hint, you can see how the point under the hint in the first keyframe hurries to the corresponding point (under the hint) in the end keyframe. Carefully watch the points while you slowly scrub.

Less Is More

Don't use more Shape Hints than necessary. Don't add 10 shape hints to the first frame and then map them all. Rather, add one shape hint and map it, and then evaluate the results; one might be enough. Feel free to continue adding shape hints all day long, but realize that sometimes less work is necessary. There's no reason to add more hints than you really need.

A few more details about shape hints are worth understanding:

▶ You can't add shape hints unless you are currently in the first keyframe of a span with shape tweening already set. In other words, you have to have a shape tween already and be in the first frame in order to add a shape hint.

▶ You can use the menu selection View, Show Shape Hints to make the shape hints you have invisible (but they will still be used).

▶ Shape hints are recognized only after they've been mapped—that is, snapped to a point on the shape in both the first keyframe and the last keyframe. They change color after they are mapped. This means you still have to snap both the start and end hint, even if their default positions seem acceptable as is.

▶ You can remove one hint at a time by right-clicking (or using Control+click on a Macintosh). This only works for removing the hints in the first keyframe of an animation (although it also removes the second one at the same time). In addition, you can remove them all by selecting Modify, Shape, Remove All Hints.

▶ Shape hints can be used only with a pair of keyframes! Just as tweening occurs between only two keyframes at a time, a shape hint works between only two keyframes at a time. However, shape hints can't be used from one keyframe to a second and then to a third. In the previous example, you might want to add a third keyframe where the shape turns into a square again. If you want to use shape hints from one keyframe to another and then a third, you must have four keyframes. Use a shape hint from the first to the second and then use another from the third to the fourth.

Reasons to Avoid Shape Tweens

I suppose the best reason to avoid using shape tweens is that sometimes you don't need one. Shape tweens inherently create larger files (which means longer download times for your users). Consider what happens when you insert a keyframe. The contents of the previous keyframe are copied into the inserted keyframe. If you have a square shape in the first keyframe and insert a second keyframe, the result is two copies of the square. Even if you modify the second square by distorting it, you have two shapes.

Compare this to what happens in a motion tween if you have a symbol of a square in the first keyframe and insert a keyframe (copying the contents of the first keyframe). You have two copies of that symbol, but because it's in the Library, the Flash file really contains only one master version of the square. Before you even specify the type of tweening, the two keyframes (with shapes) for the shape tween have created a larger file. Add to this all the subtleties that are necessary for a complicated shape tween, and the result is that shape tweens are larger than motion tweens (often twice as large).

Shape tweens are also harder for the designer to maintain than motion tweens. If you have a bunch of shape hints, it's even harder. Because motion tweens use the Library extensively, with them, you benefit from all the productivity features of the Library. Don't use shape tweens unless you must.

Summary

Now that you understand shape tweens, you know both ways Flash can do tweening for you (shape and motion). You learned in this chapter that a shape tween is fundamentally unique in that it allows you to morph shapes. The only rules with shape tweens are that you can't have grouped shapes and you can't have symbols. This makes shape tweens easy to create, but some techniques are necessary to ensure that the results come out as expected.

CHAPTER 39

Using Timeline Effects and Commands

Now that you know all the ways to manually create animations (frame-by-frame and by using motion tweens and shape tweens), we can move on to automated features. Flash MX 2004 is extensible, meaning that other developers and companies can produce add-on products to help automate your workflow. In fact, in this chapter you'll see how to create the equivalent of a macro—called a **command** in Flash. We'll cover the two primary extensibility features: Timeline effects and commands.

Although there are several extensibility features in Flash, I decided to cover just Timeline effects and commands in this chapter. These two are particularly useful, and you can make your own commands very easily.

Timeline Effects

It seems fitting that only now that you have all the basics of animation under your belt, we are looking at the automated feature of Timeline effects. This is a brand-new feature in Flash MX 2004. I'll admit I was skeptical at first. How can you automate a creative process? Now I think of it like motion tweening: It should not be overused, but when appropriate—and in the right hands—it can be effective. In the following sections we'll first look at adding Timeline effects to your movies and then at how to make edits. Even more than motion tweening, Timeline effects have plenty of room for you to add personal flavor.

Using Timeline Effects

To produce a Timeline effect, start by selecting a shape, a symbol instance, or text. Then select Insert, Timeline Effects and choose an effect, as shown in Figure 39.1.

After you select a particular Timeline effect, you should see a dialog box full of options for the selected effect as well as an area where a preview plays, as shown in Figure 39.2. We'll walk through the options for a few such dialog boxes in the upcoming example. When you're done tweaking the settings, Flash creates the effect by physically populating your movie. You can even come back later and re-edit the effect, provided that you haven't manually changed it. Even though it looks like you're re-editing an effect, Flash actually just deletes your old effect and reproduces it with new settings (all behind-the-scenes).

FIGURE 39.1
You can add any Timeline effects by selecting an object and then accessing the Insert menu.

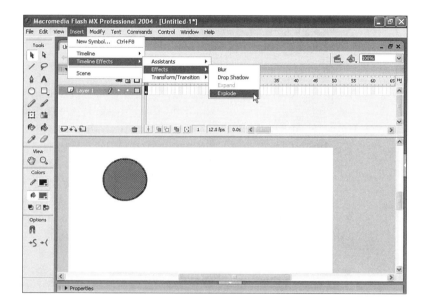

This is the process: Select an object, apply an effect, and optionally re-edit it. There are a few details to understand. First, you should remember to use the Insert, Timeline Effects menu, not the similarly named Modify, Timeline Effects menu. It makes sense: One is for inserting the effect, and the other is for modifying one already in place. Still, it's easy to forget.

Another important step is that after making any changes to the settings, you need to remember to click Update Preview in order to see the impact of your changes (see Figure 39.2). The reason Flash doesn't continually update automatically is because it has to create all the clips and nested Timelines even for the preview, and that can take time. If you're making several changes, there's no sense in updating the preview until after you've made a few changes.

Finally, a particularly fundamental limit of Timeline effects is that you can't apply them to objects that already have effects applied. That is, when you select a shape, a bitmap instance, or text and then insert a Timeline effect, your object gets converted to a Graphic symbol (with the effect inside). You can also insert

Timeline effects on movie clips, in which case you're left with a movie clip. However, you can't select an object that already has a Timeline effect inserted and then apply another one. Obviously, you don't have this limit when nesting your own symbol instances inside symbols. However, it is possible to take a Timeline effect that Flash created and nest it within another symbol. It's really not terribly confusing because you'll just see that all the Timeline effects are disabled when you're breaking this rule.

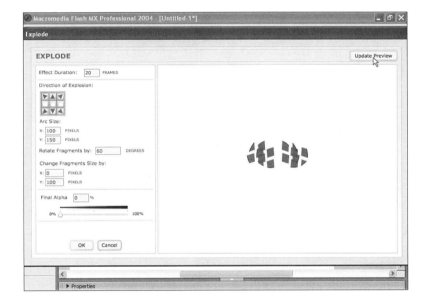

FIGURE 39.2
You need to remember to update previews in order to see the impact of changes you make to Timeline effect settings.

There are a few more "gotchas" that relate to editing effects that are in place. For now, though, you can jump right into producing an effect, in the following example, and then we can cover further details as they pop up:

1. In a new file, draw a square by using the Rectangle tool. There's no rule that your Timeline effects get applied to simple shapes, but when you're first exploring, it's easiest to see the effect when you start with a simple shape.

2. Double-click to select the entire shape and then select Insert, Timeline Effects, Effects, Blur. You'll see a blur settings dialog box and a default effect (based on your square), as shown in Figure 39.3. (You might consider dragging the dialog box halfway off the right side of your screen so you don't have to watch it loop.)

   Interestingly, this dialog box is built entirely as a Flash .swf.

FIGURE 39.3
You can see a preview of the Blur effect, which has several available settings.

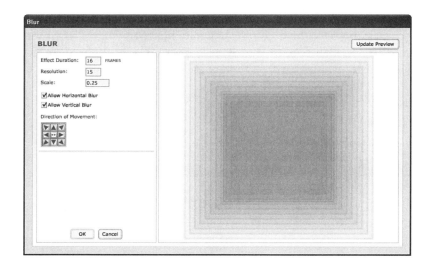

3. Experiment with the various settings in this dialog box. When you're done playing with the options, click OK.

4. Either scrub or select Control, Test Movie to see the results.

The preceding example was pretty easy, but there are several points worth noting. First, you should have experienced a noticeable delay every time you clicked Update Preview. That's because Flash converts your shape to a symbol and produces a multilayer animation. (You'll get to investigate what Flash created later.) The point is, it's a lot of work and takes a second or two to complete.

Also notice that because you started with a plain shape, the result is that you have a Graphic symbol on the Stage. That's because Timeline effects turn shapes into Graphic symbols. If you had started with a Movie Clip symbol, you'd be left with a movie clip. As you'll learn in Chapter 42, "Animating Using Movie Clip and Graphic Symbols," Graphic symbols need to reside in a Timeline with a matching number of frames in order to complete their nested animation. The main point here is that if you want to have a Graphic symbol in the end, you start with a shape. If you want a Movie Clip symbol, start with a movie clip.

Finally, notice that your library contains the Blur symbol (which is on the Stage now), plus an Effects folder that contains the symbol used inside the Blur symbol. Even Timeline effects are smart enough to use the Library wisely. You'll see in the next section that the Effects folder contains the assets used in effects, where-as the Blur symbol contains the actual animation.

Modifying and Editing Timeline Effects

After you have built a Timeline effect, there are three primary ways to edit it:

▶ Modify the nature or behavior of the effect by re-editing it.

▶ Change the graphic contents of the objects being animated.

▶ Break down the animation to its core elements so that you can edit any and all aspects of it. Note that this approach makes it impossible to re-edit by using the original effect's settings dialog box.

To simply modify the nature of a Timeline effect, first select the object and then select Modify, Timeline Effects, Edit Effect or click Edit in the Properties panel, as shown in Figure 39.4.

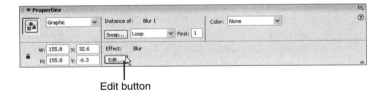

Edit button

FIGURE 39.4
The Properties panel includes the Edit button when you select an object with an effect applied.

When you select Modify, Timeline Effects, Edit Effect (or you click the Edit button in the Properties panel), you are taken right back to the effect's settings dialog box, the way you left it. You can make changes just as you did before (clicking Update Preview as necessary) and then save your changes. Not much work on your part.

Just realize that you won't be able to re-edit a Timeline effect this way if you manually edit its contents. In the following example you will walk through how to do this. Don't worry—Flash will give you a warning dialog box before you make any drastic edits.

The second way to edit a Timeline effect is to simply edit the graphic contents of the objects being animated. It's really easy; you just have to edit the right object. In the case of the Blur effect created in the preceding example, you'll find two symbols: Blur 1 and (inside the Effects folder) Symbol 1. Blur 1 should appear on the Stage, and if you attempt to edit it, you'll get the warning dialog box shown in Figure 39.5. However, the items inside the Effects folder (in this case, Symbol 1) contain whatever you had selected when you first created the Timeline effect. You can think of Insert, Timeline Effect as being like Insert, Convert to Symbol—except with Timeline effects, the object left on the Stage is a special off-limits symbol, and your selected object shows up inside the Effects folder.

FIGURE 39.5
This warning dialog box appears before you can edit the contents of a Timeline effect.

When a Timeline effect turns a single object into two symbols, it does so to be efficient. When you see the contents of a Timeline effect in the next example, you'll see that the off-limits symbol contains one or more instances of the symbol in the Effects folder. All this talk, and I just wanted to make one point: To edit the object being animated, simply edit the symbol inside the Effects folder. For example, from the previous example, open the Library and double-click Symbol 1 (inside the Effects folder) to edit it. Change the contents of the symbol by changing the shape or coloring it. Go back to test the movie or even re-edit the Timeline effect, and you'll see the new graphics.

Sometimes you need to *really* change a Timeline effect. Perhaps you need to change the speed of part of the effect without changing all of it. Although the effect's settings dialog box may have lots of options, there's always a chance you'll want to do more. The following example shows you how:

1. Either take the file you created in the first example in this chapter or redo the Blur Timeline effect in a new file.

2. Notice that even if you re-edit the Timeline effect, there are no options to start the effect in one tint and change the tint over time. (Some Timeline effects have color settings, but this one doesn't.) In order to make that effect, you'll have to do it by hand. Normally you can just double-click an instance on the Stage, but because this instance contains a Timeline effect, you have to right-click and then select Edit in Place.

3. Click OK on the warning dialog box that appears. You should be inside the Blur symbol, which will have 16 layers (or more, if you opted for more steps when creating the effect).

4. You'll learn more about layers in Chapter 41, "Using Layers in Animations," but for now you should edit the Color effect on the first keyframe of each layer. To make it easy to select objects, make all layers invisible by clicking the Show/Hide eye at the top of the Timeline (see Figure 39.6). This will make all layers invisible.

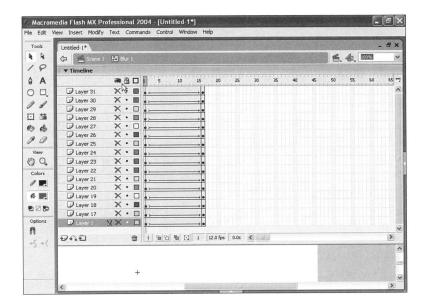

FIGURE 39.6
If you hide all layers, it will be easier to show one layer at a time for editing.

5. Reveal just the top layer by clicking the dot under the eye. Select the instance of your symbol on the Stage and then access the Properties panel. Click the Settings button to access the Advanced Color Settings dialog box. Type **255** into the top-right field to tint the object red. Click OK.

6. Repeat step 5 for all the other layers. That is, first hide the layer you just edited (by clicking the dot under the eye). Then show the next layer (by clicking the dot under the eye in the second layer). Then select an object, click Settings, type **255**, and click OK. If nothing else, doing this for all 16 layers will bring home the fact that Timeline effects are pretty sweet when you can use them as they are. Realize that all these layers were created programmatically.

7. When you're done, you can test the movie to see it blur, but this time the blur starts in red. You won't be able to make any more edits to this animation unless you do so by hand.

Although you've only worked with the Blur effect, you know the main possibilities for any Timeline effect. That is, you can create an effect, modify it, and even decompile it if you want. Looking at exactly how an effect is produced can be educational, so I recommend that you make a sample of each of the Timeline effects just so you can deconstruct how they're made.

The following tips will help you get the most out of Timeline effects:

▶ **Start small**—It's easiest to see how the various options affect an effect when you animate a simple object. For example, you might want to apply the Blur Timeline effect to a glowing clip of the sun that includes a nested animation. You should start by just exploring the options on a static image of the sun so that the nested effects don't distract you.

▶ **Work offline**—Timeline effects are "destructive" in that they actually edit your file. Luckily, there's always Undo. However, it's best to explore potential Timeline effects in a new file. Just copy the pieces you'll be animating into a new file. After everything is the way you want, you can come back to your real file to apply the Timeline effect.

▶ **Consider starting over**—Timeline effects are so easy to add that you might find it's sometimes easier to start over than to make a tweak to an existing file. In fact, Flash effectively starts over every time you make a change by removing the old effect and creating a new one. You can apply this same technique when an effect you've been editing gets overly cumbersome.

▶ **Explore the Timeline effects**—The best tip I can offer is to explore the Timeline effects at your leisure. Don't expect them to do everything. Like motion tweens, they're only appropriate for certain situations.

Commands

Flash MX 2004 has introduced a way to script the authoring environment: using commands. A command is almost like a macro from a word processing program. That is, any steps you perform in Flash by using your mouse and keyboard can be recorded and played back. In fact, Flash is recording every step you take in order for the Edit menu's Undo and Redo to work. What's new in Flash MX 2004 is that the code to re-create those steps is exposed through the JavaScript Flash (JSFL) language. It's like you can make a player-piano version of Flash that replays steps you've recorded. A command is simply a set of steps you save to play back any time.

How Commands Work

A command is simply a text file that contains JSFL code. As you'll see in the next example, you can easily create your own commands without needing to learn JSFL. You can also download and install commands that others have built from the Flash Exchange (just select Commands, Get More Commands). To make installing commands easier, be sure to download the free Extension Manager (available at www.macromedia.com/exchange/em_download/). All your installed commands appear in the Commands menu.

When you select a command, the recorded steps execute as they did when the command was recorded. Actually, some commands include the code to display a dialog box where you can set parameters to specify exactly how you want the command to perform. For example, if the command draws an outline around the Stage, it could include options for line thickness—provided that the developer who created the command includes such a feature.

In addition to triggering commands as just described, you can also select Commands, Run Command and then point to a text file that contains the commands JSFL. This is a quick way to test a command without actually installing it. Finally, JSFL code can appear in a Flash .swf file that you run as if it's a panel. Such .swf files get installed in the WindowSWF folder, which is inside the First Run folder adjacent to your installed version of Flash MX 2004.

Now you know the three ways to trigger commands (from the Commands menu, by using a JSFL text file, or by using a custom panel). But if you're going to make your own command, you need to first record the steps and then save them as a command. It's really easy to do this by using the History panel, as the following example shows:

1. In a new file, select Window, Other Panels, History. Keep an eye on the History panel while you perform the following steps.

2. Select the Rectangle tool and draw a rectangle in the upper-left corner of the Stage. Click the center of the rectangle and press Delete so you're left with just an outline.

3. Select the Text tool and create a block of static text inside the rectangle. Enter text such as your name.

4. Refine the layout on your text and rectangle.

5. When everything is in place the way you like, click to select and then drag rows in the History panel from the bottom up to where the rectangle was drawn.

6. Press the disk icon button at the bottom right of the History panel to save the command. You are prompted to give this command a name; call it My First Command.

7. Close this file without saving. Create a new file. Select Commands, My First Command.

You can't save some maneuvers into a command. For example, if you bend a line by using the Selection tool, you'll see that the corresponding row in the History panel has a red x. This simply means you can't save that step in a command (and you'll be prompted about that if you try saving it).

The History panel made the preceding example very easy. You can get a peek into the actual JSFL code if you change the View option in the History panel's options menu to Arguments in Panel or JavaScript in Panel. As you'll see in the next example, the History panel has an option to copy the JSFL to your Clipboard so you can paste it into a text editor and then make refinements. This way, you can make commands that are slightly more dynamic instead of doing exactly the same thing every time. For example:

1. In a new file, open the History panel.

2. Draw an asymmetric shape (anything other than a perfect square or circle) and then select what you've drawn. Immediately select Clear History from the History panel's options menu to effectively start recording (see Figure 39.7). Click Yes in the confirmation dialog box that appears.

3. Visually confirm that the shape is still selected and hold Shift+Alt while you click the shape and drag it to the right. This creates a duplicate of the shape.

4. With the duplicate still selected, choose Modify, Transform, Flip Horizontal.

5. Select all the steps in the History panel and press the Copy to Clipboard button next to the Save as Command button.

6. Open a text editor and press Ctrl+V to paste. The text that appears should look something like this:

```
fl.getDocumentDOM().duplicateSelection();
fl.getDocumentDOM().moveSelectionBy({x:124, y:0});
fl.getDocumentDOM().scaleSelection(-1, 1);
```

Most likely your version will have a different number in place of 124 (because I moved my shape by 124 pixels), but everything else should be identical. That number should be dynamic—that is, it should always move the duplicate 20 pixels to the right of the original.

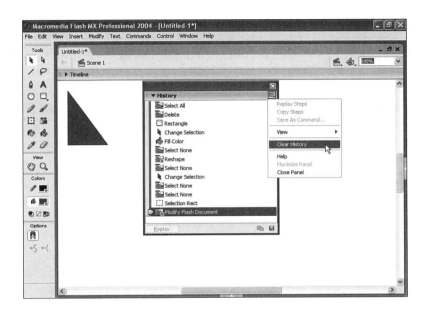

FIGURE 39.7
Clearing the History panel makes it easier to save only the necessary steps in a command.

Calculating a Dynamic Value

Instead of moving the selected duplicate by 124 pixels, let's move it over 20 pixels. However, just changing 124 to 20 won't work. For example, if the object is 100 pixels wide, moving it by 20 means it will overlap the original. When I said "move it over 20 pixels," what I really should have said was "move it over so that 20 pixels separate the two objects." Being more specific, I could say "move it over an amount equal to its width plus 20 pixels." In the case of a 100-pixel object, that is 120.

By the Way

7. The key part to the formula "width plus 20" is the width of the object. The width has to be dynamic because the selected object could be any width. Luckily, it doesn't take you very long to find how JSFL can use its `getElementProperty` action to calculate the width of a selected object. Edit your text file by adding a line above what you have and changing the 124 to `w+20`. The result should look like this:

```
var w=document.getElementProperty("width");
fl.getDocumentDOM().duplicateSelection();
fl.getDocumentDOM().moveSelectionBy({x:w+20, y:0});
fl.getDocumentDOM().scaleSelection(-1, 1);
```

The idea is that `w` will contain whatever the object's width is, and instead of 124, you use `w+20`, which results in the width plus 20.

8. Save the text file on you desktop and name it `another_command.jsfl`.

9. In a new file, draw any shape and select it. Then select Command, Run Command and point to the file another_command.jsfl. No matter what the width of the object, you'll always get a duplicate of it 20 pixels to the right.

Just because the preceding example was so much fun, the next example is much more practical. In the past, I often wished I could change the off-Stage color from gray to black (or really to any color). I ended up just drawing a shape for each of the four sides of the Stage—effectively drawing one large square with a rectangle the size of the Stage cut out of the middle. This is a perfect case for a real-world example that masks the off-stage area, as you'll see here:

1. In a new file, open the History panel and then draw a large rectangle.

2. Use the Selection tool to marquee a rectangle (that you'll remove shortly), as Figure 39.8 shows.

FIGURE 39.8
The command begins with the steps to clear a square shape from within a larger shape.

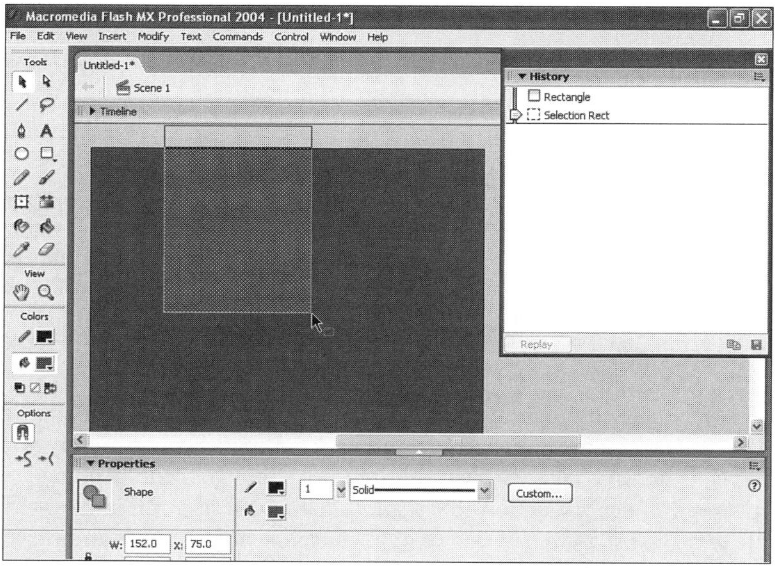

3. Delete the selected shape.

4. Select all the rows in the History panel and click the Copy to Clipboard button at the bottom right of the panel.

5. Open a text editor such as Notepad and paste. Your code should look something like this:

```
fl.getDocumentDOM().addNewRectangle({left:35, top:71, right:368.0,
bottom:404.0}, 0);
fl.getDocumentDOM().setSelectionRect(({left:82, top:50, right:229,
bottom:225}));
fl.getDocumentDOM().deleteSelection();
```

6. That code is fine, but you want to draw a rectangle that's bigger than the Stage, and you want to select a rectangle (to delete) that's the same size as the Stage. Modify the text file so that it reads as follows:

```
var w=fl.getDocumentDOM().width;
var h=fl.getDocumentDOM().height;
fl.getDocumentDOM().addNewRectangle({left:-500, top:-500, right:w+500,
bottom:h+500}, 0);
fl.getDocumentDOM().setSelectionRect({left:0, top:0, right:w, bottom:h});
fl.getDocumentDOM().deleteSelection();
```

The first two lines ascertain the width and the height of the stage. Then those variables are used in both the new rectangle (500 pixels bigger than the Stage) and the selection that gets deleted. The last three lines are simply dynamic versions of the code gathered in step 5.

Hopefully this section has shown you that commands are easy to create, only mildly difficult to modify, and very sophisticated. In fact, we haven't even touched the topic of displaying user interface (UI) dialog boxes when a command runs. That requires a language called XML to UI, which involves creating an XML text file to describe each UI dialog box. The coolest part about commands is that the best ones have yet to be created. Just try to think of any repetitive or mundane procedure you currently do manually inside Flash. Most likely it can be automated in a command.

Summary

Timeline effects and commands are the most visible extensibility features in Flash MX 2004. You can immediately see the results of a Timeline effect, and you can reduce manual labor by using commands.

In this chapter you have used, modified, and even deconstructed Timeline effects. The skills you have acquired here can help you with future Timeline effects that become available. Decompiling a Timeline effect you've inserted gives you a glimpse into more advanced animation techniques.

In the case of commands, you should have a good idea what's possible as well as how you can make your own. It's one thing to say that you'll see some cool commands once developers see the power in this feature. It's another thing entirely to make your own useful commands. You have gotten a good taste of both how to make simple commands as well as how to modify commands to make them more dynamic.

CHAPTER 40

Including Sound in Animations

Sound really makes a movie come alive, but the power of audio is subtle. People often don't even notice or remember the sounds you use. But create a movie without sound (or with bad sounds), and the audience notices right away. The effect of audio is often subconscious, and that's what makes it so powerful.

Regardless of why sound is useful, it's very important to use audio effectively because it's invariably the largest portion of an exported movie's file size. There's no reason to allow the audio to add more size than it has to. Unfortunately, there's no "Make the Audio Come Out Good" button. The choice between good audio and a small file size is more of a battle than a balancing act. It's simply a matter of understanding the technology, and that's the goal of this chapter.

Importing Sounds

Flash has great support for audio but no internal way to record or create sounds. You need to find an existing sound, have one provided for you, or use sound software to record or create your own. This simply means that in Flash, you can import sounds but you just can't create them.

Two basic steps are involved in getting audio into a Flash movie. First, you need to import the sound. Then, you need to decide where and how to use it. This is similar to importing raster graphics. When you import a sound, it's stored in the Library like an imported bitmap. But a sound is not quite a symbol. Rather, the item in the Library contains all the individual properties of the particular sound (just like bitmap properties).

Digging Up Sounds or Making Your Own

There are many sources for existing audio, such as clip media CDs. You might find, however, that rather than search existing sources, it's often easier to hire a professional musician or narrator to provide exactly what you need. This is also true for customized graphics or photographs versus clip art. Although in the short term hiring someone to create sound or art for you might mean a much bigger investment, it's often worth it. Consider that you're likely to get the perfect match for your message compared to something you find that's just "close enough" (but not quite right either). Also, you have direct contact with the artist, so you can resolve copyright issues at the start. Finally, by customizing your audio or graphics (and purchasing exclusive rights to its use), you won't risk another company using your art. Several potential problems arise when multiple parties use the same image or sound. Some other company's product or message could reflect poorly on yours, its Web site could be more popular than yours (making you look like a follower), or an image could become overused, making everyone's use look unoriginal and cliché.

Supported Formats

Flash can import digital audio in the following file formats:

- ► MP3
- ► WAV
- ► AIF (also called AIFF)
- ► AU

The only catch is that unless you have a newer version of QuickTime installed, when running Windows, you can't import AIF or AU, and on a Macintosh, you can't import WAV. Just download and install the free QuickTime player software from www.apple.com, however, and you'll be able to import audio in any of these four formats.

People often want to know which format is best. In general, it doesn't matter. You should simply start with the best quality sound possible. Between AIF and WAV, there's no inherent quality difference. A high-quality AIF file is the same as a high-quality WAV file. The AU format is nearly always compressed at a low quality, so you can all but forget that format. MP3 files always have some compression, so ultimately those files are not best. However, when MP3s are compressed very little, their quality remains high. There are two valid reasons to use MP3s:

- ► Your only source is an MP3 file.
- ► You believe the MP3 file you have has already been optimally compressed.

MP3s don't get any worse after you bring them into Flash, but they certainly can't get any better. What's more, some MP3s aren't very good to begin with. I recommend avoiding MP3s as source files unless they're all you have or you're totally satisfied with their current quality.

You'll learn more about digital audio later this chapter, in the section "Digital Audio Fundamentals." For now, it's enough to know that just four sound formats can be imported into Flash. What about songs on audio CDs? CD audio tracks aren't in WAV, AIF, AU, or MP3 format, so you can't use them directly. Luckily, however, most sound-editing software provides the ability to extract music from a CD and save it in WAV or AIF format. Of course, you should realize that significant copyright concerns arise when you use audio from a published CD.

It turns out you can use sound in your animation without necessarily worrying about all these details, as you'll see in the following example:

1. In a new file, select File, Import, Import to Stage, and then select an audio file to import. (In Windows, you'll likely find a few WAV files in the folder `C:\Windows\Media` or `My Documents\My Music`, or you can just search for `*.wav` and `*.mp3`; Macintosh users can use Find for Files of Type: Sound.) You can filter the files shown in the Import dialog box by setting the Files of Type drop-down list to All Sound Formats, as shown in Figure 40.1.

2. After you select an audio file and click OK in the Import dialog box, you probably won't see (or hear) anything different. However, the sound has been imported and now resides in the Library. Just open the Library window (by pressing Ctrl+L) to see it. Now that the movie contains the sound file, you can use the sound.

3. Although we're not covering how to "use" sounds in depth until the next section, it's very easy. Let's do it now. There are two basic ways to use the sound in a keyframe. One way is to drag the sound from the Library window onto the Stage. However, this method requires an available editable frame (both an unlocked layer marked as editable with pencil and the current-frame marker in a non-tweened frame). The other method requires you to select a keyframe (by clicking under 1 in the Timeline) and then in the Properties panel select the sound you imported from the drop-down list. This list will display all the sounds previously imported into the movie.

4. Test the movie, and you should hear the sound. (Of course, your computer speakers and sound card must be functioning.)

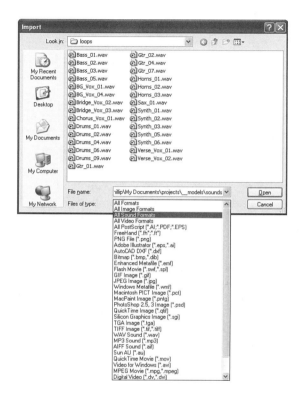

FIGURE 40.1
When importing audio (or any media type, for that matter), you can filter the types of files listed to include just sound formats.

Using Sounds

Now that you've imported sounds into a movie, you can explore how to make them play at the correct times. There's really only one place you can use sounds in Flash: in keyframes. (One exception is adding sounds dynamically by using the Sound object in the ActionScript language.) If you want a sound to play whenever the user places his or her cursor over a button, you still need to place the sound in a keyframe—it's just a keyframe in the button. Attaching sounds to a button is rather more complex, and we'll cover it in depth in Chapter 43, "Making Interactive Buttons."

Now that you know sounds go in keyframes, you need a way to put them there. When you select a keyframe, the Properties panel provides a way to control what sounds play when you reach the selected keyframe. Flash provides other clues for you to "see" where sounds have been placed. For example, if your Timeline is long enough, you'll see a waveform (a picture of a sound) for the sounds being used.

However, using the Properties panel is the best way to see which sounds have been added to which keyframes. But just like any other panel, the Properties panel displays only the sound used in the *selected* keyframe. Misreading this panel is very easy because it changes when you deselect keyframes. In Figure 40.2, the Properties panel shows that no sound is being used. When you look closely at the Timeline, you see that there's a waveform displayed but no keyframe selected. Therefore, it's necessary to look at the Properties panel *after* you've selected a particular keyframe.

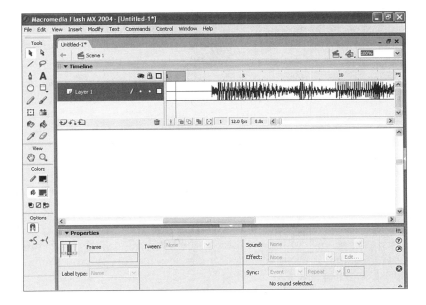

FIGURE 40.2
The Properties panel can be confusing. It only displays (or lets you specify) sounds when a keyframe is currently selected. Here, the keyframe isn't currently selected, so the Properties panel displays nothing.

Sync Settings

When you have the Properties panel reflecting sound for the intended keyframe, you can decide exactly how the sound should play. The most fundamental choice you need to make for each use of a sound is its Sync setting. This controls exactly how a particular instance of the sound will play—or, more specifically, the priority of the sound compared to the visual elements in the animation. Before you try out the Sync settings, see the following list and Figure 40.3 for an explanation of each:

▶ **Event**—This is the default setting and, generally, the best performance choice, especially for sound effects and other "incidental" sounds. When Event is chosen, sounds will start to play when the keyframe is reached and keep playing until they're done. Event sounds might not coincide with visual elements the same way on everyone's machine. Sounds don't play more slowly or quickly (that would make them sound funny), but a machine with slower graphics performance might take longer to display visual elements. Suppose you have a 1-second sound set to Event and your frame rate is 12 fps. You would expect that during the sound, 12 frames would be displayed, but a slow machine might display only 6 fps, in which case the sound would finish in 1 second, as you would expect, but after only six frames would have been displayed.

▶ **Start**—This setting is almost the same as Event, except that multiple instances of the same sound are prevented. With Event, a sound can be layered on top of itself, similar to singing a "round." Start, on the other hand, plays a sound if it's not already playing.

▶ **Stop**—This setting is kind of weird—it's for when you want a specified sound to stop playing. For example, if you import a sound called "background music" and by whatever means have it playing, when a keyframe is encountered that has the same sound (background music) set to Stop, just that sound will stop. Any other sounds already playing will continue. This is a bit strange because you use the Properties panel to specify the sound (just as when you want the sound to play), but you specify it as the particular sound you want to stop. Think of Stop as "stop this sound if it's playing."

▶ **Stream**—This setting causes the sound to remain perfectly synchronized with the Timeline. Because, again, you can't have sounds playing slowly if the user's machine can't draw frames quickly enough, with this setting, Flash will skip frames to keep up. Stream sounds start playing when the first frame is reached and continue to play as long as there is space in the Timeline. In other words, if your sound is 3 seconds long and you're playing at 12 fps, the Timeline has to be at least 36 frames; otherwise, part of the sound will never be reached. The benefit of this setting is that the synchronization will always be the same. If in this case you place a graphic in Frame 12, it will coincide perfectly with the first second of your sound. Just remember that when you're using Stream, you have to ensure that there are enough frames in the Timeline to accommodate the length of the sound. Finally, you preview Stream sounds as you scrub, thus making the process of synchronizing audio to images possible.

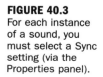

FIGURE 40.3
For each instance of a sound, you must select a Sync setting (via the Properties panel).

The decision as to which Sync setting to use isn't terribly difficult. Event should be used for any short incidental sounds—such as *rollover sounds*. Actually, I suggest Event for all sounds that don't require critical synchronization. Background music that just plays and loops doesn't need to be synchronized. Therefore, you should use Event for it. Start is a perfectly good alternative to Event because it's the same but prevents the same sound from layering on itself. For example, suppose you have a row of five buttons. If each button has the same rollover sound and the user quickly moves across all five, an Event sound will play once for each button. If the sounds are short enough, this is probably appropriate. However, if the sounds are quite long, they will become discordant. If you use the Start Sync setting, only one instance of the sound will play at a time, regardless of how fast the user moves his or her mouse. Event can be a better choice than Start when a little bit of overlap is okay. Consider a "ding" sound every time a ball bounces on the ground. If you choose Event, the ball can bounce a second time and even if the first sound isn't totally finished, it will play again. In any event, Start and Event are good for the majority of sounds you'll play.

Rollover is when the user places his or her cursor over a button, so a **rollover sound** is a sound that plays when the user rolls over a button. You'll learn about rollover effects for buttons in Chapter 43.

The Stop Sync setting is very powerful. It gives you a way to stop specific sounds. Using this method can be a little tricky because it stops only one sound per keyframe. When you learn about behaviors (in Chapter 44, "Using ActionScript and Behaviors to Create Nonlinear Movies"), you'll learn that you can insert the Stop All Sounds behavior to stop all sounds at once. Depending on the situation, this might be appropriate. If you're giving the user the ability to get several sounds going at once, you'll want to learn about Stop All Sounds. However, suppose you have one sound playing in the background, and when a tween starts, you want a special sound effect to play (and keep playing) until the tween ends. You can put the background sound in an early keyframe and then, in the first keyframe of the tween, place the sound effect and set its Sync setting to Event or Start. In the last frame of the tween, you can put the same sound effect but with the Stop Sync setting. This way, the sound effect will stop at the end of the tween, but the background sound will continue.

Finally, Stream is good for one thing: synchronizing graphics with sound. This is especially useful for character animation in which you want a character's lips to synchronize with its voice. When trying to synchronize sounds with images, you can use the scrub technique, and if you use Stream sounds, you can hear the sound as you scrub. Because Stream sounds effectively lock themselves to the

Timeline, you probably don't want to change the movie's frame rate. For example, a 3-second sound will take 36 frames at 12 fps. If you do some work and then change the frame rate to 24 fps, the same 3-second sound spans 72 frames! Flash automatically spreads the Stream sound out so that it takes 3 seconds when you change the frame rate, but Flash doesn't change your graphics, which now play in 1.5 seconds. See Figure 40.4 for a before-and-after example of changing the frame rate after an animation is built.

FIGURE 40.4
Here, the same animation and sound are shown with frame rates of 18 fps (top) and 6 fps (bottom). Notice that keyframes and tweening are not affected, but the sound needs to take more room when the Timeline is only advancing 6 fps (the audio can't expand or contract because that would sound funny).

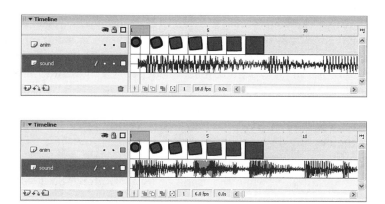

In spite of this issue, you should stick with a frame rate (which, really, isn't anything new—it comes up even if you don't use sounds). Stream sounds remain pretty appealing. However, you should realize that on slower-performing machines, frames will be skipped to make sure the sound stays synchronized. It's often more important that every frame of your animation appears even if it means the sounds may drift out of synchronization. My point is that you should use Stream only when the synchronization is critical (and you don't mind dropping frames). Otherwise, use Event or Start.

Effect Settings

The Properties panel provides some pretty fancy effects you can apply to a selected sound. In the drop-down list next to Effect are effects such as Fade In and Fade Out as well as Fade from Left to Right and Fade from Right to Left. In order to understand and customize these settings further, you can either select Custom from the list or click the Edit button on the Properties panel to access the Edit Envelope dialog box, which is shown in Figure 40.5.

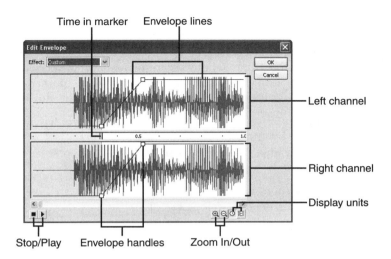

Time in marker   Envelope lines

Left channel

Right channel

Display units

Stop/Play   Envelope handles   Zoom In/Out

FIGURE 40.5
The Edit Envelope dialog box lets you select from prebuilt panning effects or create your own.

Here are additional details for the Effect settings:

▶ **Left Channel/Right Channel**—This option displays different wave forms if your original sound was stereo. Even if you use only mono sounds, you'll get the left and right channels so that you can still create panning effects. In the case of mono, the same sounds will come out of each speaker—you'll just be able to modify the volume of each.

▶ **Envelope lines**—These indicate the volume level at any particular time in the sound. When the line is at the top, the sound plays at full 100% volume. (Some audio tools are different because they use the middle to indicate 100% and anything higher to indicate amplified or boosted sound, but this is not the case in Flash.) If the envelope line is getting higher as you move to the right, the volume will increase.

▶ **Envelope handles**—These are like keyframes within sound. If you want the envelope lines (indicating volume) to change direction, you need to insert a handle. All you need to do is click anywhere on a line, and a handle will be inserted. No matter which channel you click, a matching handle is placed in the other channel. A handle in one channel must match the moment in time (left to right) of the handle in the other channel. However, the volume (height) can vary between the two.

▶ **Time In marker**—This marker lets you establish the starting point of a sound. You're effectively trimming the extra sound (or silence) at the beginning of the sound file. You're not telling the sound to start any later, but the sound you hear will begin wherever the Time In marker is placed.

▶ **Time Out marker**—This marker lets you trim extra sound off the end of a sound file. Often you'll have a moment of silence at the end of a sound file, and even if you don't hear anything, it still adds to the file size. You can get rid of it by moving the Time Out marker to the left. You won't actually destroy the source sound in your Library, but when you export the movie, the unused portions of the sound won't be used (so your file stays small).

▶ **Stop/Play**—This option lets you preview all the settings you've made. This is important because although the waveform can let you "see" a sound, you ultimately want to judge the effect of a sound with your ears.

▶ **Zoom In/Out**—This option lets you zoom out so the entire sound fits in the current window or zoom in for a close up to control precisely how you place the Time In/Out markers or envelope handles.

▶ **Display Units (Time or Frames)**—This option simply changes the units displayed (in the center portion) from time units (seconds) to frame units. Time is not as useful as Frames when you want to match sound to a particular frame (where something visual occurs). If the display shows a peak in the music at 1 second, you have to use frame rate to calculate exactly which frame that translates to. With the display set to Frames, Flash does the calculations for you.

Panning is an effect that makes sound seem to move from left to right or right to left. It's simply a trick in which the volume for one channel (left or right) is increased while the volume for the other channel is decreased. When combined with a graphic moving in the same direction, this technique can be very effective. Imagine, for example, a car moving across the screen at the same time the audio pans in the same direction.

Despite all the details in the Edit Envelope dialog box, you really only have two basic ways to use it: You can either use a preset effect or make your own. Actually, you can start with a preset (such as Fade In) and then make modifications to it, essentially making a custom effect based on a preset. Use the effects in any way you think appropriate. Listen to the effect after each change by clicking the Play button. Nothing you do here will affect the master sound in your Library. You can actually use the same sound several times throughout a movie, with different effects in each instance.

One of the most important things to remember is that the Time In and Time Out markers can save file size. Only the sounds and portions of sounds actually used will be exported when you publish a movie. Unused sounds in the Library and portions trimmed from the beginning or end of a sound will not be exported.

Trimming a few seconds off the end of a sound can mean many seconds (even minutes) saved in download time for your users. Also, changing the volume of a sound has no impact on file size, so setting the envelope lines to the lowest level makes no sense.

Loop Settings

The Properties panel has an option to either let you specify how many times a sound repeats or have the sound loop forever.

Some sounds loop better than others. Basically, a sound that loops well ends the same way it starts. There's an art to making sounds loop. Although importing a large song and using the Time In and Time Out markers to establish a nice looping sound is possible, it isn't easy. More likely, you'll have to find a sound already prepared by an audio engineer. A professionally prepared sound can loop so seamlessly that you can listen to it and not even notice it's looping; it will just sound like it's endless.

Creating Sounds That Loop

Creating loops and even songs built from many separate loops isn't all that difficult. Tools such as Sonic Foundry's Sound Forge and Acid Pro give you all the tools necessary to create and assemble loops. These are professional tools that go beyond the needs of average Flash users—but you'll probably be surprised how easily you can use them to create music. Like Flash, you can try Sound Forge and Acid Pro free (visit www.sonicfoundry.com).

By the Way

You'll get to explore looping sounds as well as other effects in the next example:

1. Download the file `keyframing.fla` from my Web site (`www.phillipkerman.com/teachyourself/sourcefiles/keyframing`). In Flash, open this file and then press Enter to watch the animation.

2. Open the Library for the `keyframing.fla` file by selecting Window, Library (or pressing Ctrl+L). We'll drag the sounds from this file into keyframes.

3. First you need to make a new layer just for the sounds by selecting Insert, Timeline, Layer. (Don't worry if Flash puts the new layer under all others—it doesn't really matter where it appears.) Name this layer Background Music.

4. Select the first frame of the Background Music layer and look at the Properties panel. From the Sound drop-down list, select Visor Hum Loop. To make this sound loop continuously, change the drop-down list from Repeat to Loop (see Figure 40.6).

FIGURE 40.6
Flash can loop a
sound indefinitely
with the Loop
setting.

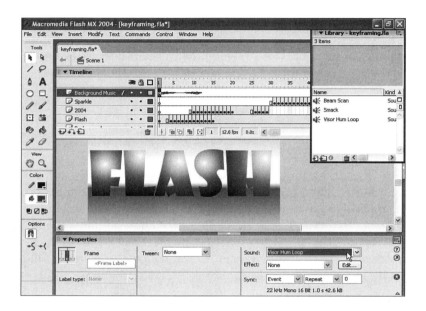

5. Select Control, Test Movie. The sound loops nicely, and it adds a bit of drama to the movie. In the following steps, add some incidental sound effects.

6. Select Insert, Timeline, Layer and name the layer Sound Effects. You're going to insert a sound effect right when the 2004 hits its lowest point, which happens at about Frame 17. In Frame 16 of Sound Effects, select Insert, Timeline, Keyframe (or press F6).

7. Select the keyframe you just inserted and from the Properties panel select Smack from the Sound drop-down list. Just leave the default settings (Event Sync and Repeat 0) because you don't want this sound to loop.

8. Select Control, Test Movie. The Smack effect is good, but the hum keeps humming throughout the whole movie.

9. To stop the hum, select Frame 30 of the Sound Effects layer and select Insert, Keyframe (or press F6). Make sure you're selecting just this keyframe, and then use the Properties panel to insert the Visor Hum Loop again, but this time select the Stop Sync setting to cause any instances of this sound to stop. (You can use Test Movie again to see and hear the results.)

10. Finally, add a sound effect for when the pink sparkle animates. At Frame 31 of the Sound Effects layer, select Insert, Keyframe (or press F6), select just this keyframe, and then insert the Beam Scan sound. Use Test Movie, and it

should be measurably better than the silent version. (By the way, these sounds only add about 3KB to the total file size!) One thing you can try is to remove the excess silence at the start of the Beam Scan sound. Just select Frame 31 in the Sound Effects layer and press Edit on the Properties panel. Then you can cut sound off the beginning by dragging the Time In marker in the Edit Envelope dialog box (refer to Figure 40.5).

Controlling Quality and File Size

Now that you know how to incorporate sound in a movie, it's time to talk about optimizing it for export. A direct relationship exists between quality and file size. If you want the best-quality sound, the file size will grow. Conversely, small file size means lower sound quality. This is just a fact. You ultimately need to make a decision about how to balance this tradeoff. Is a high-quality sound important enough to make your audience sit through an extended download time? Is a speedy download worth the sacrifice in quality? You should be very deliberate in your decision-making process to end up with the best compromise possible.

While exploring this topic further, we'll first cover some digital audio fundamentals, and then you'll learn how to apply this knowledge to Flash's compression settings.

Digital Audio Fundamentals

Digital sounds on a computer are not continuous. Similarly to how a fluorescent light or a computer monitor flickers, digital audio is a series of discrete bursts called *samples*. The frequency at which these samples occur is so fast that you think you're hearing a continuous sound.

Exactly how fast the samples are occurring is called the **frequency rate** (also sometimes called the **sampling rate**). Naturally, a higher frequency rate (many bursts per second) sounds better than a low rate. The frequency rate of all audio CDs, for example, is 44,100 Hertz, commonly referred to as 44 kiloHertz (KHz). Sound-editing software can convert a song to a lower rate, but it won't sound as good. Why not always use the highest-frequency rate possible? Simple. Each sample takes up disk space and adds to the file size. A sound with a frequency rate of 22,050Hz, for example, is *half* the size of one at 44,100Hz, and it may still sound good.

In addition to frequency rate, another important factor is **bit depth**. Similarly to how each pixel on a computer monitor can be one of 256 colors (when the color

546   Chapter 40

depth is 8 bit) or one of 16.7 million colors (when the color depth is 32 bit), each sample in an audio track can be one of many sound levels. (Think of these sound levels as "shades of sound.") A sound with an 8-bit depth means that for every sample, the sound can be one of 256 different levels. A 16-bit sound has the potential of being one of 65,536 different levels. The higher the bit depth, the better the sound quality. (By the way, audio CDs have 16-bit depth.)

Frequency rate and bit depth are independent of one another. One sound could have a high frequency rate (such as 44,100) but a low bit depth (maybe 8 bit). When you increase either factor (to improve quality), file size grows. To make matters worse, a stereo sound is always twice as large as the same sound in mono (because it contains information in two channels). Finally, the length of the sound affects file size directly: A longer sound is larger. There are ways to calculate the exact size impact of frequency rate and bit depth. The bottom line, however, is that audio takes up a lot of disk space. One minute of CD-quality sound, for example, takes about 9MB! The fact that pure CD-quality sound takes up so much space is why you want to find a better way.

One solution is compression. MP3 compression, for example, analyzes the sound file and finds ways to reduce the file size with minimal sacrifice to quality. By using MP3 compression, that same 9MB of CD-quality sound might get reduced to about 1MB! Just like how JPG compression reduces the file size by removing parts of the image you don't notice, MP3 compression uses a technique to remove the parts of a sound that you're not likely to miss. Exactly how it does this, I don't know. It's magic, I guess. However, Flash can perform MP3 compression based on the level to which you would like your sounds brought down (namely, the bit rate). The best-quality MP3 that Flash 5 supports is 160Kbps. A lower number means lower quality (but also means the amount of data per second is lower). One last note: When MP3 reaches 160Kbps (or whatever level you specify), it makes its own decisions regarding the balance between frequency rate and bit depth.

Export Settings

All this theory is interesting, but how do you apply it to your sounds? You have two places in Flash where you can specify quality settings: the Sound Properties dialog box, which is unique to each imported sound, and the Flash tab of the Publish Settings dialog box. The Sound Properties dialog box affects settings that are unique to the individual sound and the Publish Settings dialog box affects all sounds globally.

Global Publish Settings

To set the default sound format for every sound in a Flash movie, you select File, Publish Settings . Make sure that under the Formats tab you've checked Flash (.swf), and then click the Flash tab (see Figure 40.7). You see two different sound settings in this dialog box: Audio Stream and Audio Event. Audio Stream affects sound instances that use the Stream Sync setting, whereas Audio Event affects sounds that use the Event or Start Sync setting. If you click the Set button, you can see all the options available, as shown in Figure 40.8.

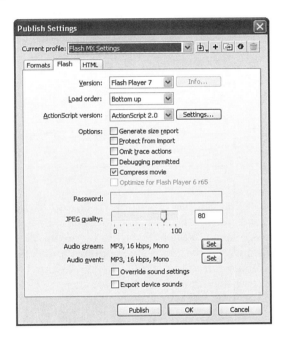

FIGURE 40.7
The Flash tab of the Publish Settings dialog box provides a way to set the default sound settings globally for an entire file.

There's a Set button next to both Stream and Event so you can set the compression for sounds used each way separately. There are five choices for sound compression. With the exception of when you use Raw (which is really no compression), you need to specify additional options for the compression you choose. For example, you can't just say "compress using MP3"—you have to specify how much MP3 compression. Because each option has its own unique characteristics, let's look at each in detail:

▶ **Disable**—This option is pretty simple: It tells Flash not to export any sounds. When you select Disable from the drop-down list, there are no other options to set.

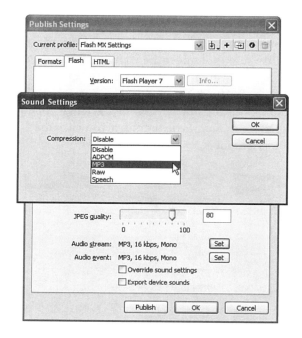

▶ **ADPCM**—This option is almost the same as Raw (discussed later in this list), except that it performs a little bit of compression. The options for Sample Rate and Convert Stereo to Mono have the same effects as discussed earlier, but the ADPCM bits specify the level of compression. A higher number means better quality but not as small a file. Pretty much the only reason to use this option rather than MP3 is when you have to deliver a movie to Flash Player 3.

▶ **MP3**—This option provides great compression. When exporting, always use the Quality setting Best because it won't affect the file size but will improve quality. However, while working, you might consider temporarily changing this to Fast because every time you test a movie (by using Test Movie), it will go quicker. The bit rate is simply how much data per second you're letting the MP3 file take. The higher the number, the better. In theory, a bit rate of 56Kbps will be maintainable on a 56Kbps modem, although reality is some-times different from theory because other factors can slow the download performance. You really just have to test this and keep lowering the bit rate until just before the sound becomes unacceptable. You can judge the result by testing the movie or, as you'll see in the next section, "Individual Export Settings," you can test each sound individually.

▶ **Speech Compression**—This setting is optimized for the human voice. In practice, however, you should always compare the quality/file size effects of speech compression to MP3 because the best choice varies case-by-case.

▶ **Raw**—This option leaves your sounds intact, although you do need to specify a sample rate (frequency rate). Also, if you select Convert Stereo to Mono, any stereo sounds will become half their original size. Raw is useful while you're testing because you won't have to sit through the time Flash takes to compress your sounds every time you use Test Movie. Just remember to set it back later, or your files will be huge.

Now you've learned how you can set the default sound settings for both Stream and Event sounds from the Publish Settings dialog box. Also note the Override Sound Settings check box. Checking this box causes the settings you apply here to be imposed on *all* sounds in the movie, regardless of their individual export settings. You're about to see how to specify sound settings individually per sound. Override Sound Settings can be useful when you want to publish a single copy for a special purpose. Say you want a copy to demonstrate from your hard drive—download time isn't an issue, so you could make all the sounds play at their highest quality (Raw).

Individual Export Settings

In addition to a movie's globally specified sound settings, each sound item in the Library can have its own individual settings, which apply to every instance of that sound. Just double-click a sound in the Library (or select Options, Properties), and you see the Sound Properties dialog box, as shown in Figure 40.9.

This dialog box is similar to the Bitmap Properties dialog box you've seen before. In the same way that individual imported bitmaps can have their own sets of compression settings, so, too, can imported audio. The choice of settings is practically identical to the settings in the Publish Settings dialog box. However, in this dialog box, for each change you make, you're given details of the effect on file size and quality. Down at the bottom of the dialog box you can see how much the file compresses for each change. If you click the Test button, not only does Flash perform the compression you specified, but the sound starts playing and you can hear how it sounds. (This is similar to the Test button for bitmaps, although with bitmaps you judge the visual effect.) This gives you all the information you need to decide what settings to use. You can listen to the sound while assessing the effect on file size.

FIGURE 40.9
The Sound Properties dialog box provides individual control of exactly how a sound will be exported, regardless of the default publish settings.

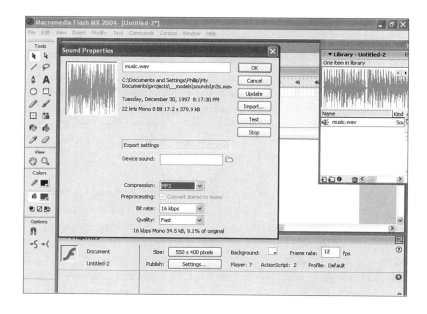

The Sound Properties dialog box has a couple other items you should note. If you select the Default option, Flash uses whatever settings you specify in the Publish Settings dialog box. Also, you have the same ability to replace sounds as you do for replacing bitmaps. For instance, if you've edited a sound in a sound editor and you want to import the replacement sound, just click the Update button. (If the file has moved, you are asked to point to the new location.) In addition, if you want to replace a sound (without taking the trouble of reassigning every keyframe where you've already used the sound), just click Import and select the new file when prompted.

Summary

Flash supports audio elegantly. Including audio in a movie is a simple process of importing the sound and then deciding in which keyframe you want the audio to play. Many options are available on *how* the audio plays—for example, whether it plays and finishes naturally (the Event Sync setting) or whether you want it to lock itself to the Timeline so images remain synchronized no matter what (the Stream Sync setting). You can also use sophisticated envelope controls for each instance of a sound used.

Because the effect on file size is the biggest "cost" of using audio, Flash provides a variety of compression technologies and settings to individually or globally specify the kind of compression to use. I'm sure you'll find MP3 or Speech to be the best quality, when considering file size, for almost any sound you want to use, but other alternatives do exist. If nothing else, I hope this chapter has made you more deliberate and restrained about adding audio to your movies. Don't get me wrong—the power of audio is great. Just try not to abuse this power; your slow-connection users will thank you.

CHAPTER 41

Using Layers in Animations

The most interesting thing about layers in Flash is the fact that most people think they're for visual layering. This is understandable because almost every graphics editing tool has layers for just this purpose: to layer graphics on top of or below other graphics. Despite the fact that layers in Flash have a similar effect, that's not their real value. Rather, each layer is a concurrent Timeline where an animation can play. This hour you'll learn how layers primarily help you animate and, to a lesser degree, let you control visual layering.

How Layers Work

If you're familiar with Photoshop, Fireworks, or almost any other graphics editing tool, you are already familiar with using layers as a visual tool to control stacking order. In Flash, layers provide the same visual effect. But you have already learned that graphics can be stacked if they are first grouped or turned into symbols—so why do we need layers?

The True Purpose of Layers

In Flash, multiple layers are really multiple Timelines—and that's their value. The images contained in layers are stacked above or below other layers, but their primary purpose is to provide you with separate Timelines in which you can control animations independently.

You might recall from Chapter 37, "Creating Animation," that the rule for motion tweens is that you can animate only one thing per layer (and that *thing* has to be an instance of a symbol). Suppose you want two circles, with one appearing to race past the other. It's simple; just use two layers. In the following example you'll try something simple to get started with layers.

Here you'll make two circles move across the screen. One will appear to move faster than the other:

1. In a new file, draw a circle, select it, and convert it to a symbol (by pressing F8). Name it Circle, leave the behavior set to the default Movie Clip, and click OK.

2. With the instance of Circle on the Stage, do a motion tween. To keep things from getting too complicated, name this layer Fast (indicating that the circle in this layer will move fast). To name the layer, click once in the Timeline so that it has the focus and then double-click on just the name of the layer (initially Layer 1) and type a new name.

By the Way

Focus Indicating Active

Focus applies to all kinds of computer buttons and fields generally. In an online form, only one field has focus at a time. That is, if you start typing, you'll be typing into whichever field currently has focus. When you tab through a form, the focus moves from one field to the next.

In Flash, several buttons and fields also reflect focus. Even the Stage can have focus (indicated by a subtle highlight at the top of the window). If you click in the Timeline, it will have focus (indicated by a highlight outline). Quite often, it might not be entirely clear which window, panel, or button has the focus, but you should be conscious of which does.

3. Because the Timeline has only one frame so far, position the instance of Circle on the left side of the Stage. Then click the cell in Frame 31 of the Fast layer. Select Insert, Timeline, Keyframe (or press F6).

4. Make sure that the red current-frame marker is on Frame 31 and move the circle all the way to the right side of the Stage.

5. To make a motion tween, either right-click (use Control+click on a Macintosh) on the first keyframe and select Create Motion Tween or select the first keyframe and from the Properties panel select Motion from the Tween drop-down list.

6. Create a new layer by either selecting Insert, Timeline, Layer or clicking the Insert Layer button at the bottom left of the Timeline (see Figure 41.1). Name this new layer Slow, the same way you named the other layer Fast (in step 2).

   From this point forward, you need to be conscious of the layer in which you are currently editing (that is, you need to know where you are). You can only be in one layer at a time, which is indicated by the pencil icon in the layer (see Figure 41.2).

7. Copy an instance of Circle from the Fast layer and paste it in the Slow layer. Click an instance of Circle (to select it) and copy it (by pressing Ctrl+C). By

clicking an object on the Stage from the Fast layer, you cause that layer to become active. Before you paste, make sure you make Slow the active layer by clicking the word Slow and then pasting. Position the copy of Circle you just pasted on the left side of the Stage, but do not cover the other one.

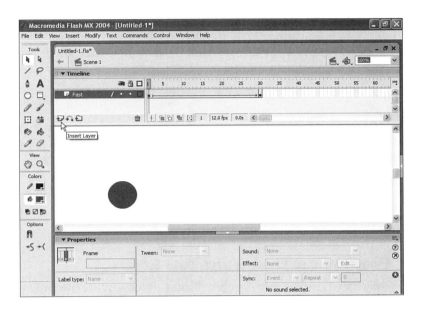

FIGURE 41.1
Using the Insert Layer button at the bottom left of the Timeline is a quick way to insert a new layer (just like selecting Insert, Timeline, Layer).

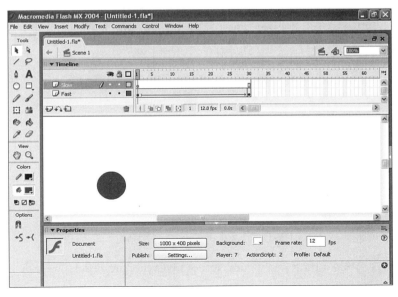

FIGURE 41.2
The pencil icon indicates which layer is currently active (in this case, Slow).

8. To keep things straight, tint the instance of Circle in the Slow layer. Select it and in the Properties panel, select Tint from the Color Styles drop-down list and then select a color that is different from the color of the other circle.

9. In Frame 31 of the Slow layer, select Insert, Keyframe. Move the instance of Circle in Frame 31 over to the right side of the Stage (but not as far to the right as you moved the circle in the Fast layer).

10. Set a motion tween for the first frame of the Slow layer. Test the movie, and you see two circles moving across the screen—two things animating at once!

11. Save this file because you'll use it in the next task.

The discussion so far shouldn't suggest that layers are to be avoided. Just the opposite: You should feel free to use as many layers as you need, even if only for visual layering. Although a Flash file with hundreds of layers might take a long time to open when editing, all those layers are combined upon export (not unlike what happens with Photoshop's Flatten Image command). Although layers are useful for organization and stacking purposes, they're absolutely *necessary* for animation effects.

Layer Properties That Help You Edit

You've already seen how the pencil icon indicates which layer is currently being edited. Other icons in the Timeline indicate layer properties that can be modified. Check out Figure 41.3 for a quick overview of these properties, and then we'll discuss each in detail. (By the way, most of the buttons and features listed have ToolTips.)

FIGURE 41.3
There are several layer types and properties.

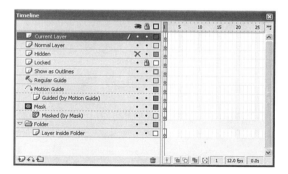

Figure 41.3 shows almost every variation of layer property. Here's a quick introduction to each one:

▶ **Layer Name**—This property lets you give any layer any name you like. You'll stay organized better if you take advantage of this feature and name layers logically.

▶ **Show/Hide Layer**—This property allows you to hide the contents of any individual layer temporarily by clicking the dot beneath the eye. If you click the Eye button on top, you hide or show all layers. Remember that this affects only what is seen while editing because exporting a .swf sets all the layers to Show.

▶ **Lock/Unlock Layer**—This property lets you individually lock or unlock layers selectively (or all at once).

▶ **Show Layer as Outlines**—This property lets you view the contents of a layer as outlines, almost like making the layer contents invisible but not as extreme. Similarly to Show/Hide, this setting affects only how the layer appears to you (the author). The outline color can be changed through the Layer Properties dialog box (available if you double-click the Layer Outlines button or the Layer Type icon, such as the Page Curl on the far left). In addition, if you use Edit, Preferences to open the Preferences dialog box, select the General tab, and select the Highlight color setting Use Layer Color, then the clips selected in this layer will highlight in the same color.

▶ **Normal Layer**—This layer type is the plain page icon with a curl in the bottom-right corner. This is the default type of layer.

▶ **Regular Guide Layer**—This layer type is a special layer into which you can draw anything you want (usually shapes, to help align graphics or notes to other team members). Everything contained in a Guide layer is excluded from export when you create a .swf, so it won't show up in your final file, nor will it add to file size.

▶ **Motion Guide Layer**—This layer type acts like a Regular Guide (they're both guides, after all); however, a Motion Guide layer contains a line to which you associate a motion tween, which is in a Guided layer. This is how you make a motion tween follow a path.

▶ **Guided Layers**—This layer type is available only if the adjacent layer above it is set to Motion Guide. In the Guided layer, you can create a motion tween that follows the path drawn in the Motion Guide layer.

▶ **Mask Layers**—This layer type lets you place any shape or Movie Clip symbol that will define the visible (and nonvisible) portion of the layer below it, which is set to Masked. Just like a mask you put on your face, in a Mask layer you draw where you want holes in the mask.

▶ **Masked Layers**—This layer type is available only when the layer directly above is set to Mask. The contents of a Masked layer will be invisible except in areas where objects are placed in the Mask layer. You won't see this effect until you test the movie or lock both the Mask and Masked layers.

▶ **Folders and Layer Folders**—These settings are very different from the other layer properties because you can't have any content in them. However, after you make a layer folder, you can nest other layers (and even other layer folders) inside it.

Some of the icons indicating layer properties (in Figure 41.3) are easy to access, whereas others involve several steps. We'll look at Guide and Mask layer types later in this chapter. In the following task, you'll begin to work with the easy ones: Show/Hide, Lock/Unlock, Show as Outlines, and Layer Folders:

1. Open the file you created in the previous task and scrub a little to recall how it plays.

2. How do you know which circle is in which layer? If the circles intersect the same area, you'll see one in front of the other. Move the current-frame marker to Frame 1. By just looking, you can't really tell which one is which. You could read the layer name that you wrote—but Fast and Slow aren't very clear and, besides, you could have made a mistake. The fact that the layers contain instances of the same symbol makes it even more difficult to tell. To figure it out, temporarily change the Show/Hide option for one layer at a time. Try clicking the eye at the top of the Timeline. Notice that this hides every layer. Click the eye again, and the layers will all be shown again. To hide just one layer, click the dot under the eye in the layer of your choice. Click the dot in the Fast layer. Not only do you see a red × over the dot (when it's hidden), but everything on the Stage from that layer is hidden (just temporarily). By process of elimination, you can figure out which layer is which by making one invisible.

3. Make all the layers visible again, and you can determine which circle is which another way—by using outlines. Click the square button on the top of the Timeline (see Figure 41.4) to Show All Layers as Outlines. This should make the contents on the Stage appear in outline form. Hopefully, they appear in different colors so that you can tell them apart.

4. If both layers are showing up in the same color, just double-click the Show Layer as Outlines box for one layer. If you click the button once, it toggles between the Outline and Normal views. When you double-click, you're taken to the Layer Properties dialog box, which is similar to that shown in Figure 41.5. Alternatively, you can single-click a layer (to make it active)

and then select Modify, Layer. We'll cover this dialog box more later, but for now, select a different color from the Outline Color swatch and then click OK. The outlines in that layer should have a different color now.

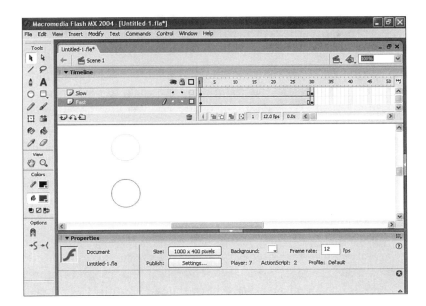

FIGURE 41.4
The contents of layers can be viewed in outline form.

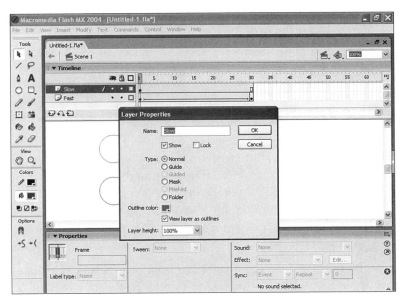

FIGURE 41.5
All layer settings are shown in the Layer Properties dialog box (which is accessible by selecting Modify, Layer or by double-clicking the Page Curl icon or the Show Outlines icon).

Managing Layers

On the surface, layer folders are a pretty straightforward feature. You can nest layers inside folders. This way, if you have 100 layers, they don't need to fill 100 rows. You can create layer folders by clicking the Insert Layer Folder button (near the Insert Layer button) or selecting Insert, Timeline, Layer Folder. Then you can click and drag layers inside folders. You can even drag folders inside folders.

Although layer folders probably don't warrant an entire task, let me point out a couple hidden benefits. Besides just collapsing the Timeline, a folder can be hidden just like a layer can. When you hide or show a layer folder, you automatically hide or show all the nested layers. If hiding layers is a good feature, hiding layer folders is a great one. You can also lock or unlock layer folders. In practice these two subtle features may have greater value than layer folders themselves.

So far this hour, you've learned two things about layers. First, extra layers let you animate more than one thing at a time. Motion tweening in particular can animate only one instance per layer. If you want two items to use motion tweening at once, you must put each animation in a separate layer.

Second, you learned how several layer properties allow you to distinguish and change layers individually. By using Show/Hide, Lock/Unlock, and Outlines, changing them is quick and easy. Remember, though, that the layer properties we've explored so far (including Name and Layer Folders) have no visual impact on what the user sees—changes to these properties are only for you, the author. Even a hidden layer will be visible to the user. There are more properties, which we're about to study, but the ones we've talked about so far can be considered for authortime only.

Using Layer Properties for Visual Effect

The four remaining layer types (Guide, Motion Guide, Mask, and Masked) are very powerful. Unlike the layer properties covered so far in this chapter, these four will have a lasting visual impact on your user. Using these layer properties is more involved than simply clicking an icon in the Timeline. However, when you see what they can do, you'll understand why it's worth the additional effort.

Guide Layers

Guide layers become invisible when you export a movie. (I said we would be covering layer properties that have lasting effects, and the first one we look at is something that becomes invisible.) Guides are very useful and if you use them correctly, they can have a huge impact on what your audience sees, even though they won't be exported with the movie.

Why would you want something you draw to be excluded from export? There are two primary reasons. One reason to use Guide layers is for registration purposes. Into a Guide layer, you can draw lines or shapes to which other objects can snap for consistent positioning. Maybe you want a title to appear in several sections of a movie. If you draw a horizontal line into a Guide layer, all the titles can be snapped to that line. But when the movie is exported, no one will see that line.

Another reason to use Guide layers is that you might have lots of visual content that you keep on the Stage for personal reference or notes to others in your group. If it's all in a Guide layer, you'll see it only while authoring. Similarly, you might have a layer of an animation that you decide at the last minute to remove. Instead of actually removing the entire layer, you can just change it to a Guide layer. It will still be there as a backup if you change your mind later, but otherwise no one will see it. You'll create a guide layer just for alignment in the next task.

Perfect Registration

By the Way

Registration refers to alignment. In commercial printing, registration is critical because each ink color is printed separately. Registration marks are used to line up all the plates precisely. In multimedia, registration serves much the same purpose. For example, if you're looking at several pages of text, if they're all registered the same, you won't see text jumping all over the screen between pages.

Suppose you're building a presentation that includes onscreen text and a graphic frame that provides borders. You would like to position the text onscreen without overlapping the borders. A shape in a Guide layer can serve to define the areas that are safe for text. Just follow these steps:

1. In a new file, first draw a filled box the size of the Stage. (You can use the Info panel to make it the exact size.) Then use the Pencil tool (with the Pencil Mode set to Smooth) to draw an enclosed irregular box within the box you just drew. Select the center shape with the Selection tool and delete, as shown in Figure 41.6. Select the entire shape and convert it to a symbol (called Frame Shape). Name this layer Registration. This will become the Guide layer.

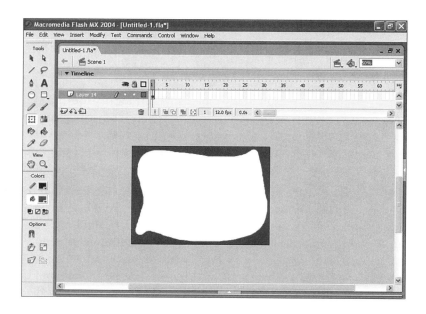

2. Select Insert, Timeline, Layer and name the new layer Interface. On this layer, a copy of the Frame Shape will tween into place late in the Timeline (which will better demonstrate the need for Guide layers). First select the instance of Frame Shape on the Registration layer and copy. Then go to Frame 25 of the Interface layer and select Insert, Timeline, Keyframe (or press F6). Verify that the current layer is Interface (if it is not, click the layer name) and then select Edit, Paste in Place (or press Ctrl+Shift+V) on Frame 25.

3. Click Frame 35 of the Interface layer and select Insert, Timeline, Keyframe (or press F6). Move the current-frame marker to Frame 25 and scale the instance of Frame Shape much larger so that you can't actually see the borders onscreen (as in Figure 41.7). Finally, set motion tweening in the Properties panel when Frame 25 is selected. Scrub to see that the Frame Shape won't appear until Frame 25, when it tweens from outside the Stage.

4. Click in Frame 35 of the Registration layer. Select Insert, Timeline, Frame (or press F5) to make this layer last as long as the Interface layer. Click the Layer Outline button for the Registration layer (so that only this layer shows as an outline). Scrub from the beginning of the movie to the end. Notice that the outlined Registration layer gives a clear idea where Frame Shape will eventually appear, so that you can avoid placing text in that area. However, if you select Control, Test Movie, you'll see that the Registration layer is visible the entire time. Until you change this layer to a Guide layer, it will export with the rest of the movie.

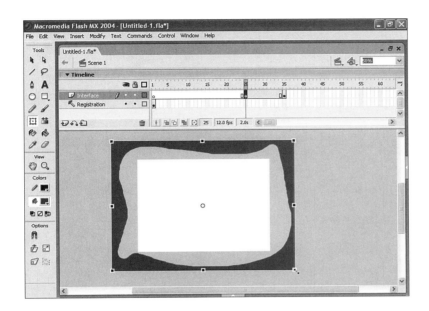

FIGURE 41.7
The first place
Frame Shape
appears is in
Frame 25. Here you
scale it larger than
the Stage so it will
appear to tween
from outside.

5. To make the Registration layer a Guide layer, access the Layer Properties dialog box by either double-clicking the Page Curl icon to the left of the layer name or (with the layer selected) selecting Modify, Timeline, Layer Properties. In the Layer Properties dialog box (refer to Figure 41.5), select the Guide radio button, the Lock check box, and the View Layer as Outlines check box; then click OK.

6. Insert a new layer (by selecting Insert, Timeline, Layer) and name this layer Text. Verify that all the layers are set to Normal except Registration, which should be set to Guide. (If they're not, access each layer's properties individually and set them appropriately.)

7. In Frame 1 of the Text layer, create a block of text with a large font size, such as 40. Type as much text as you can, being careful not to exceed the borders shown in the outline in the Registration layer (see Figure 41.8).

8. Test the movie. You might want to turn off Loop from the Control menu while it's playing.

In the previous example, you created a Guide layer that defined a safe area onscreen for the Frame Shape symbol that hadn't arrived onscreen yet. You might have other shapes that don't appear unless certain conditions are met. For example, if you have buttons that in their Over state expand with large graphics or include a drop-down effect, you might not want other elements on the Stage to be placed where they will be covered up by the button. You could copy the shape of the button when fully expanded and paste it in the Registration layer. If you want to leave reminder notes to other team members or to yourself, you could enter them in a Guide layer as well. The idea is that you can put anything you want into a Guide layer, and it won't export with the movie.

FIGURE 41.8
Using the outlined shape in the Guide layer, you can place the text precisely so that it doesn't interfere with the borders.

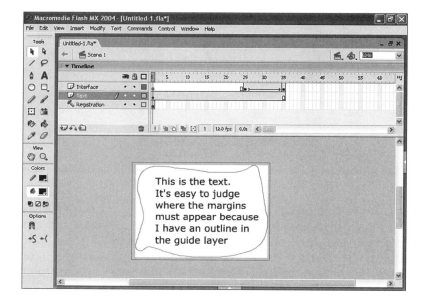

Using a Guide layer for registration, as you just experimented with, is nice because you can use any shape, group, or symbol in the Guide layer. Another feature, called Guides (under the View menu), is confusingly similar: Vertical and horizontal lines are dragged from the rulers on any side of the Stage (View, Rulers must be selected from the menu)—as you did in Chapter 32, "Drawing and Painting Original Art in Flash." Using the Guides feature becomes almost identical to using lines in a Guide layer (provided that you've left the default Snap to Guides setting in the View, Snapping menu).

Motion Guide Layers

If Guide layers are useful, Motion Guide layers are indispensable! A Motion Guide layer is actually a regular Guide layer that happens to have an adjacent layer (below it) set to Guided. The exciting part is that a motion tween in the Guided layer will follow any path drawn in the Motion Guide layer. That means you can draw an S-shaped line in a Motion Guide, and then the Guided layer can include a motion tween that follows the shape. Similar to a regular Guide layer, a Motion Guide layer will be invisible to the user. The thing to remember with Motion Guide layers is that two layers are involved: the Motion Guide layer and the Guided layer. In the next example you'll make a ball in a Guide layer bounce along a line drawn in the Motion Guide layer:

1. In a new file, draw a bouncing line (using the Pencil or Pen tool). This will become the path the ball will follow (see Figure 41.9). It might actually work best if you just draw straight lines and then bend them and snap them together. Regardless of how you draw it, just make sure it's one continuous line that doesn't overlap at all. It doesn't have to be visually interesting because this is only going to be a guide (and thus, invisible).

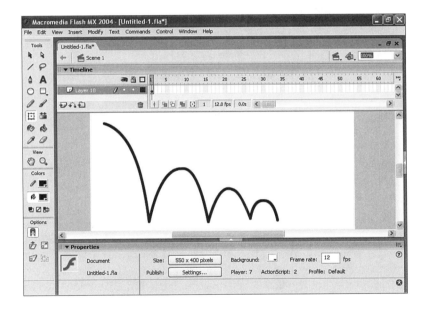

FIGURE 41.9
A pretty simple drawn line will be used as a motion guide (for a tween to follow).

2. Double-click the Page Curl icon to access the Layer Properties dialog box (or select Modify, Timeline, Layer).

3. Name the layer Path, lock it (so you don't mess it up), and change its type to Guide. (Notice that there's no Motion Guide option here.)

4. Insert a new layer by clicking the Insert Layer button at the bottom left of the Timeline or by selecting Insert, Layer. Name this new layer Ball.

5. Most likely the inserted Ball layer will appear above the Path layer. You're going to make this new layer a Guided layer (meaning that it can follow the drawing in the Path layer). Before you can make a layer a Guided layer, it must be directly below the layer that is set to Guide. You can change the layer stacking by dragging layers around. Go ahead and drag the Ball layer down (so it's just below Path).

Notice that not only does this change the layer order, but it also causes the Ball layer to be Guided. You can see this because Path now has a slightly different icon (the arch), Ball is indented, and a dashed line separates the two, as shown in Figure 41.10. This is what you want, but you might not be so lucky to have everything fall into place like this (depending on exactly how you drag around the layers). In addition, when moving layers around, you might not want Flash to change all the layer properties for you. If that's the case, perform an Undo so that you're back to where just the Path layer is a regular Guide layer (with the cross icon) and the Ball layer is above it. You're going to do the same thing again the hard way so that you know how it works.

FIGURE 41.10
The Motion Guide layer (Path) has a special icon, and the Guided layer (Ball) is indented. A dashed line separates the two layers, indicating that they're related.

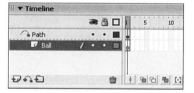

6. Drag the Path layer above the Ball layer. Nothing changes except the layer order. You can't just change the Path Guide layer to a Motion Guide layer (which is what you want in the end). Instead, you can make the Ball layer a Guided layer (now that it's directly under a Guide layer). Access the layer properties for the Ball layer (by double-clicking the Page Curl icon or, with the layer selected, choosing Modify, Timeline, Layer Properties). Notice that the type Guided is available. Only when the layer just above this layer is a Guide layer do you see this option. Click Guided and then click OK.

7. Now you're going to create the animation and snap it to the guide. Into Frame 1 of the Ball layer, draw a circle and make it a symbol (called Picture of Ball). Now, in the Ball layer, click in Frame 50 and insert a keyframe (by pressing F6). Notice that the Path layer doesn't live this long. In the Path layer, click in Frame 50 and insert a frame (not a keyframe) by pressing F5. Go back to Frame 1 of the Ball layer and create a motion tween (by

right-clicking the first keyframe in this layer or selecting the frame and picking Motion from the Tween drop-down list in the Properties panel).

8. Finally, you need to make the ball actually follow the path. This is easiest if you first lock the Guide layer because you're going to snap Picture of Ball to the path, but you don't want to edit the path. Lock the Guide layer by clicking the dot under the padlock in the Path layer. At this point you should find that the Picture of Ball can't be dragged anywhere but onto the line drawn in the Path layer (and you don't disturb the line as it's locked). In Frame 1, make sure Picture of Ball is at the start of the path. Go to Frame 50 and snap the center of the Picture of Ball instance to the end of the path drawn in the Path layer. Test the movie. The ball should follow the path.

What took all the time in the preceding task was learning about changing layer properties and learning some mechanics of how they need to be ordered. All you do is draw a path, make it a Guide layer, make a new layer that's a Guided layer, do a motion tween, and snap the instance in each keyframe to the drawn path. (Sounds pretty easy when I say it like that but, really, that's all you did.)

One little detail that people seem to forget: When you snap a symbol instance to the guide, you must snap the center of the symbol (which is editable by using the Free Transform tool). If you set the motion tween plus the layer types to Guide and Guided first, Flash won't let you snap any point *other* than the center.

Let's quickly explore one other option for motion guides. When you select a keyframe with a motion tween, the Properties panel shows the option Orient to Path. The effect of this option is that the instance being tweened will rotate toward the direction it's traveling. You can see the effect of this option best when the symbol isn't perfectly round. We can change Picture of Ball temporarily to see this effect. From the Library window, you can access the master version of Picture of Ball. In the master version, just draw another little circle next to the circle (don't let it touch because you want to be able to remove it later). Back in your main scene, you can look at the Properties panel for the first frame of the Ball layer; to do this, you make sure that you're in the scene, select the first keyframe, and then bring up the Properties panel. Select the option Orient to Path and then view the results by clicking Play. Turn off Orient to Path (in the first keyframe) to see the difference.

In the previous bouncing ball task, I purposely had you step in every possible pitfall so that you could learn how to recover. However, it happens to be much easier with the Add Guide Layer button. If you've already drawn a ball, you can click the Add Guide Layer button (see Figure 41.11) to automatically add a new layer, make that layer a Guide layer, and make the current layer a Guided layer. This button attempts to do several steps in one move, but it can be difficult to use.

Mask Layers

If Guide layers are useful and Motion Guide layers are indispensable, well, Mask layers are unbelievable! Masking is really a different feature entirely. Mask Layers is similar to Guides and Motion Guides only in that it's a layer property, and you need at least two layers: one for the Mask layer and one for the Masked layer (similar to Guide and Guided). The graphical contents of the Mask layer determine which parts of the Masked layer will show through. It's as if you're drawing the holes to see through in the Mask layer.

The basic orientation of the Mask and Masked layers is similar to the Motion Guide/Guided layer arrangement. For masking, you first specify one layer's Type property as Mask. Then, you'll find the Masked setting available when you access the layer properties for a layer directly below the Mask layer. However, you won't actually see the masking effect unless you test the movie or lock all the layers involved. It will all make more sense when you create a spotlight mask in the next example. Here you'll create a spotlight effect that appears to light up a skyline of buildings:

1. Create the spotlight and its motion. To do so, in a new file, draw a filled circle and convert it into a Movie Clip symbol called Spot.

2. Name the layer in which the Spot instance resides Spot Motion.

3. Insert keyframes in Frames 10, 20, and 30. In Frame 10, move Spot to a new location, and move it again for Frame 20. Frame 30 should match Frame 1.

4. Set up motion tweening in Frames 1 to 10, 10 to 20, and 20 to 30, either with the right-click method or from the Properties panel.

5. Change the Spot Motion layer's Type property to Mask. Double-click the Page Curl icon for this layer to access the Layer Properties dialog box.

6. Notice that the Page Curl icon changes to the Mask icon (see Figure 41.12). Lock the Spot Motion layer so that you don't accidentally change it.

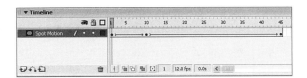

FIGURE 41.12
The Mask layer
(Spot Motion) no
longer has the
Page Curl icon;
after you change its
type to Mask, the
icon looks different.

7. Insert a layer below the Spot Motion layer and change its type to Masked.
Click the Add Layer button (at the bottom left of the Timeline). The new
Layer might appear above the Spot Motion layer; that's fine. Name the new
layer Skyline.

8. In order for Skyline to be a Masked layer, it must be below the other layer,
so click and drag down the Skyline layer. If you get lucky, the Skyline layer
will automatically change to Masked (and you'll see an icon like the one
shown in Figure 41.13). However, it's easy to do by hand, too. If you must,
access Skyline's Layer Properties dialog box and change the type to Masked
(which will be available only if the next layer above it is already set to
Mask). The result should resemble Figure 41.13.

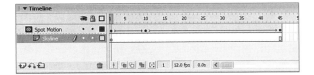

FIGURE 41.13
The Masked layer
Skyline has a spe-
cial icon; it's
indented, and a
dashed line sepa-
rates it from the
Mask layer above.

9. In the Skyline layer, draw lots of boxes in different colors to resemble a city
skyline. You will see the mask effect only if you test the movie or lock all the
layers.

10. Change the background color of the movie to black (by selecting Modify,
Document or clicking the Stage and using the Properties panel).

    As interesting as this looks, there's something missing. This is the way a
    spotlight would look in space, where there's no atmosphere. The black back-
    ground is too dark. You need to make another layer with a dim version of
    the skyline to make this more believable.

11. Select all the boxes you drew in Skyline (you need to make sure that just
this layer is unlocked to select it) and convert the shapes into a Movie Clip
symbol called Building Graphic.

12. To put another instance of Building Graphic into a new layer, create a new layer (by clicking the Add Layer button) and name it Dim Skyline.

13. Analyze the Type property of each layer (which is easy to see by its icon). Chances are that the Dim Skyline layer is also a Masked layer. One Mask layer can have several Masked layers. Set Dim Skyline to Normal, but only after you move it down below Skyline. If Skyline is no longer directly under the shadow of Spot Motion, it will also revert to Normal. Drag the Dim Skyline layer down below Skyline, and then set the Type property for Dim Skyline to Normal.

14. Copy the instance of Building Graphic and paste it in place (by pressing Ctrl+Shift+V) into the Dim Skyline layer. Hide all layers except Dim Skyline (so you're sure which one you're affecting). Then, with the instance of Building Graphic in the Dim Skyline layer selected, access the Properties panel. Set the Color Style to Brightness and set the slider to –40%.

Looks great, eh? You didn't need to create this Dim Skyline layer to learn about masking, but it's a nice touch.

You can do some sophisticated stuff with masking. For example, you could edit the master version of Spot and maybe cut out part of the fill (by using the Lasso tool). The Masked layer will show through only where there's something in the Mask layer. Unfortunately, this is an all-or-nothing situation. That is, the mask is either on or off. You can pull off the effect of a graduated mask by putting the graduation in the Masked layer (because it won't work in the Mask layer). Another idea is to make a duplicate of the Spot symbol—but one with a transparency gradation fill. Then you can make a separate layer where this duplicate follows the same path as the spot.

The preceding task was a case of moving the mask. Quite often, however, you'll find situations in which the Mask layer should remain still and the Masked layer is the one to move. Suppose you're building an animation of someone sitting inside a train, and you want the effect of mountains and clouds passing by the window. If you had a wide picture of mountains and clouds, you could easily do a motion tween to make it pass by. Without masking, you would have to cover up the left side and the right side (surrounding each window) with graphics of the inside of the train. These carefully sliced covers would need to be in a higher layer (to cover up the picture), and it would be more work than it needed to be. With masking, all you need is a Mask layer with the exact shape of the windows and a Masked layer containing the tween of your wide picture. This is a case of the masked part moving and the mask staying still. Just realize that anytime you want to cut out part of another image, you can do it without really cutting any-thing. Masking has amazing potential for visual effects.

Summary

We covered a lot of material for something that appears to be a simple interface component—layers. It's hard to say that layers aren't primarily for visual stacking because that's exactly how they work. Remember that grouping shapes (or, better yet, putting them in the Library) also lets you stack them (within one layer). However, creating separate layers is sometimes more convenient.

Layers are useful for more than creating the layering effect, however. The number-one rule of motion tweens is that only one object (an instance of a sym-bol) be tweened per layer. If you want more things to animate, you have to put each one in its own layer.

The Show Layer as Outlines feature provides a way to view the contents of any layer as an outline. Those properties are accessible right in the Timeline. The Guide Layer property excludes an entire layer from export but keeps it in the source Flash file for any purpose, including registration. Motion Guide layers let us pair up the Guide layer with a motion tween (in the lower layer) to follow a drawn path. Finally, Mask layers (paired with a Masked layer) give us a way to hide all portions (except those we indicate) of another layer.

CHAPTER 42

Animating Using Movie Clip and Graphic Symbols

When you see what Movie Clip symbols can do, you'll be blown away. Inside a movie clip, you can create an animation and then animate an instance of that clip. This means that, for example, you can create a rotating wheel clip and then animate the rotating wheel so that it not only rotates but moves across the screen as well.

This chapter doesn't try to summarize movie clips because there is so much to say that I couldn't cover everything. The biggest goal is for you to understand movie clips and how they compare to plain old Graphic symbols.

Movie Clip Symbol Behavior

Some people wrongly think that Graphic symbols are only for when the symbol contains a single frame and Movie Clip symbols are only for when you have multiple frames. You can work this way, but there's more to it. For example, say you make a Graphic symbol of a wheel (a circle with lines for spokes). You can then use an instance of your Wheel symbol inside a Movie Clip called Rotating Wheel—where the Wheel symbol rotates. Then the movie clip can be used in the creation of a Car symbol (which is a Graphic symbol because the car itself won't need multiple frames). Finally, the Car symbol can be animated across the screen, and both wheels will rotate the whole time. Don't worry if this is confusing; you'll do a example pretty soon to make it clear. Just remember: You can use movie clips even when you don't need multiple frames.

Creating a Movie Clip

Making a movie clip is like making any symbol. In the following example, you'll first create an animation inside a movie clip. Then, when you tween an instance of the clip, it will tween as well as animate. Specifically, you'll make a wheel and then use an instance of that wheel to create a rotating wheel. Finally, you'll use two rotating wheels to create a car symbol. You'll animate the car (and see its wheels rotating, too):

1. Draw a circle with a few lines crossing it. Don't make it perfectly symmetrical—that way you'll be able to see it rotate. Select the entire shape and then select Modify, Convert to Symbol (or press F8). Name the shape Wheel, choose the default Movie Clip behavior type, and then click OK. You're going to make a movie clip of the wheel spinning next, but you need an instance of the plain wheel first; remember that you can't motion tween anything except symbol instances.

2. Select the onscreen instance of the Wheel symbol and convert it to a symbol. Select Modify, Convert to Symbol (or press F8), name it Rotating Wheel, make sure you leave Movie Clip set as the behavior, and then click OK. I know you already had a symbol, but consider what converting to a symbol does: It takes what's selected and puts it into the Library. In step 1 you put a shape in the Library. In this step you took an instance of Wheel and put it in the Rotating Wheel symbol.

3. Go inside the master version of Rotating Wheel by simply double-clicking the instance onscreen. In the edit bar you should see Scene 1: Rotating Wheel. If you now single-click to select the instance (inside Rotating Wheel) you should see "Instance of: Wheel" in the Properties panel (as shown in Figure 42.1). This means that Rotating Wheel contains an instance of Wheel.

FIGURE 42.1
The Properties panel displays a selected symbol's original name.

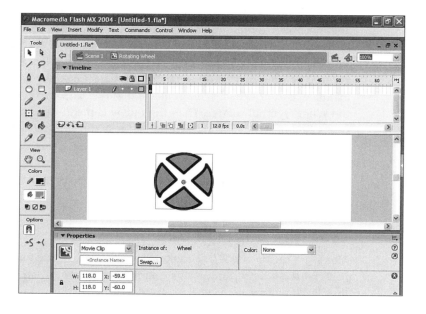

4. Do a simple motion tween inside the master version of Rotating Wheel. To do this, click in Frame 20 and insert a keyframe (by pressing F6). Select the first keyframe and from the Properties panel select Tween Motion, Rotate CW 1 Time.

5. Go back up to the scene. You should see an instance of Rotating Wheel, although now it has a 20-frame rotation you can't see. Use Test Movie to ensure that it rotates.

6. Create another instance of Rotating Wheel by either copying and pasting the instance onscreen or by dragging another instance from the Library. Position the two Rotating Wheel instances side-by-side and then use the Brush tool to draw the car body. Select everything and convert it to a symbol called Car (leave it with the Movie Clip behavior).

7. Insert a keyframe at Frame 30 (in the main Timeline) and then with Frame 1 selected, set the Properties panel to Tween Using Motion. Move the instance of Car in either Frame 1 or Frame 30, and you should be able to see the car move when you scrub (just like any other motion tween). To see the wheels rotate, test the movie. Scrubbing only previews the animation across the Timeline in the current movie clip, not any nested movie clips. (Only Graphic symbols preview when you scrub.)

If you aren't familiar with nesting symbols, the preceding example might have been a little confusing. Here you worked from the specific to the general. You made a Wheel symbol, and you made a Rotating Wheel symbol that contained Wheel because you needed a symbol *inside* Rotating Wheel to do a motion tween. Then you used two instances of Rotating Wheel in the creation of the Car symbol.

Comparing Movie Clip Symbols to Graphic Symbols

It makes no difference whether your master symbol is a graphic or a movie clip. The symbol behavior affects only the default symbol behavior for instances dragged straight from the Library. What matters is the symbol behavior of the instance on the Stage. If you drag a movie clip from the library, it will start with the Movie Clip behavior, but you can change it (for a given instance) to Graphic by using the Properties panel, as shown in Figure 42.2. It's the instance's behavior that matters.

Multiframe instances set to the Graphic behavior have a few unique options. The Properties panel changes to include a few extra options. When you select a symbol with the Graphic behavior, the Properties panel lets you specify which frame (within the symbol) will appear first. In addition, other options from the drop-down list provide a choice between Loop, Play Once, and Single Frame. By combining these settings, you can vary exactly how an instance with the Graphic behavior appears.

FIGURE 42.2
An instance on the Stage (regardless of the master symbol's default behavior) can have any behavior you select from the Properties panel.

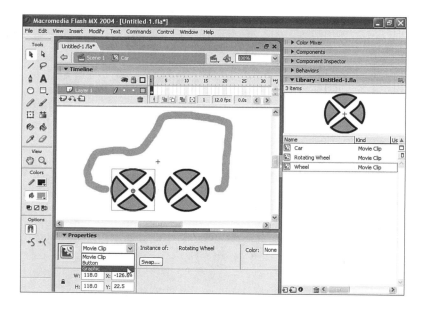

Suppose you have two instances of Rotating Wheel that use 20 frames for one rotation. You could use both instances as graphics and set both to Loop, but on one, you could set the first frame to 10. The two wheels would both rotate continuously, but they would be offset by 180 degrees.

If you compare the options in the Properties panel when a movie clip is selected (compared to a graphic), you'll notice only one seemingly minor field for Instance Name. It really isn't minor at all, as you'll see in the section "Addressable Movie Clip Instances," later in this chapter, and again in Chapter 44, "Using ActionScript and Behaviors to Create Nonlinear Movies." For now, just realize that you can name movie clip instances individually in the Properties panel.

If the only difference was a few settings in the Properties panel, you could do exercises with Loop, Play Once, and Single Frame, and that would be the end of it. However, Graphic symbols differ in another major way. Multiframe Graphic symbols (even when set to Loop) become locked to the Timeline in which you place them. For example, a 10-frame Graphic symbol placed in Frame 1 of a

Timeline will display Frame 1 in Frame 1, Frame 2 in Frame 2, and so on. If you place this Graphic symbol in a Timeline that's only 5 frames long, the instance of the symbol will display Frame 5 when it gets to Frame 5, but it will go no further. It's locked to the Timeline where it's used.

Instances behaving as movie clips are independent. They always play all their frames and loop. Think of a movie clip as marching to the beat of its own drummer. A 10-frame movie clip doesn't care whether it has 10 frames to live, 100 frames, or just 1 frame. It plays all its frames when it can, like Rotating Wheel used in creating the Car in this chapter's first example. (Movie Clip behavior is like sounds with the Sync setting Event.) The next example will drive home the differences between graphic and movie clip instances.

Here you'll see how movie clips loop independently of the Timeline in which they reside:

1. In a new file, select Insert, New Symbol (or press Ctrl+F8), name the new symbol Numbers, select Movie Clip for the behavior, and then click OK. (Notice that this takes you inside the master version of Numbers.)

2. In Frame 1 of Numbers, use the Text tool and type **1** near the center of the screen. Insert a keyframe in Frame 2 and change the onscreen number to **2**. Continue inserting keyframes and changing the contents to match the frame number all the way to Frame 10.

3. Get back to the main scene (make sure you're not still in Numbers) and drag an instance of Numbers onto the Stage from the Library. Select Control, Test Movie (or press Ctrl+Enter)—remember, using Test Movie is the only way to see movie clip animation. All 10 numbers appear in sequence, even though you used only 1 frame of the main Timeline.

4. Back in the scene, insert a frame (not a keyframe) in Frame 5 (click Frame 5 and then select Insert, Timeline, Frame or press F5), which really just extends the life of this Timeline. Use Test Movie again, and you should see no change.

5. Drag another instance of the Numbers movie clip onto the Stage. For just this instance, change the symbol behavior to Graphic by accessing the Properties panel while the instance on the Stage is selected. With the instance still selected, make sure the Options drop-down list is set to Loop. Now test the movie again.

6. If the movie is playing too fast, try a lower frame rate. The result is that only Frames 1 through 5 of the graphic instance are displayed while the movie clip continues to run. Back in the Timeline, try scrubbing back and

forth in the main scene. Although the Graphic symbol shows only the first 5 frames (it has only 5 frames to live), it also gives you a good preview while scrubbing.

7. While you're testing the movie, select Control, Stop. This stops the red current-frame marker from advancing, but notice that the movie clip keeps right on playing. The graphic is locked to the Timeline into which it's placed, whereas the movie clip plays independently.

There are a few additional points to notice in the preceding example. First, movie clips always loop. (There's no "play once" option. In Chapter 44 you'll learn how to create a behavior that says "Stop at the last frame.") But because of this, movie clips are sometimes extra work. Also, it might seem like a drag that only Graphic symbols are previewed when you scrub, but there's good reason for this. Graphics are previewed because they're locked to the Timeline, and therefore Flash knows exactly how they'll play. Movie clips play at their own rate (and can be started or stopped any time through scripting). Therefore, Flash has no idea exactly how they'll play and can't give you a preview. If nothing else, just remember to always use Test Movie if you want to see what the user will see.

When to Use Movie Clips

Generally, you should use movie clips for everything you can, even if it's just a static (single-frame) graphic. You'll see later in this chapter that movie clips can contribute less to the file size than Graphic symbols, so using them is almost a no-brainer. However, there are some reasons to use Graphic symbols instead.

Multiframe Graphic symbols are appropriate any time you really need to preview while you're working. The fact that movie clips don't preview when you're scrubbing can be a real hassle. For example, if you're synchronizing lip movements in a character, you probably want to use multiframe Graphic symbols. Also, a movie clip's automatic looping means that if you don't want it to loop, you need to do more work—you need to put a script into the last frame to make it stop. Also, specifying a first frame by using multiframe Graphic symbols is so easy that it's hard to resist this feature. Using scripting in movie clips to do this is more complicated and slightly more work (though also—ultimately—more powerful, too).

Although the Graphic symbols lock themselves to the Timeline (making synchronization easier), there are difficulties to overcome as well. A common problem arises when the number of frames in the symbol doesn't match (or evenly divide into) the number of frames where you place it. For instance, if you use Graphic symbols for Rotating Wheel in this chapter's example, you have to make sure the Car symbol has exactly 20 frames in order for the wheels to fully rotate. If the car has 1 frame, the wheels won't spin. If the car has 10 frames, you'll see half the rotation, and then it will repeat. A movie clip, in contrast, will continue to play, regardless of how many frames it is given. If your nested animation has a different number of frames than your Timeline, you should either use movie clips or make sure the Graphic symbols have the appropriate number of frames. Using movie clips is usually much easier because they're more flexible than graphics.

This discussion shouldn't distract from the main reason to use either movie clips or graphics, which is that you want to create a motion tween. You can use motion tweening only on an instance of a symbol. If the symbol you're tweening happens to have multiple frames, so be it. By nesting clips inside clips, you can create very complicated effects that would be very difficult to create by hand in one Timeline. So although either a graphic or a movie clip qualifies (as a symbol instance) for motion tweening, the difference is that a movie clip animates on its own time, and it doesn't matter how much space you provide in the Timeline where it is used.

Subtleties of Movie Clips

We've already discussed the biggest difference between Movie Clip symbols and Graphic symbols—a movie clip's Timeline is independent. Obviously, there's more. Movie clips are addressable, in that you can use ActionScript to direct messages to individual instances of a movie clip, such as a Stop command. Also, Movie Clip symbols are usually smaller than Graphic symbols, in that file size is minimized.

Addressable Movie Clip Instances

Remember that the Properties panel provides a place to name a movie clip instance (see Figure 42.3). What's the point of naming an instance if the symbol already has a name in the Library? It provides a way to give each instance on the Stage a unique name. Only then can you address individual movie clips. Think about how you address a person. You first say his name, and then you tell him what you want. If you want him to stop, you say, "Joe, stop." This is the concept of addressing, which we'll talk about more in Chapter 44.

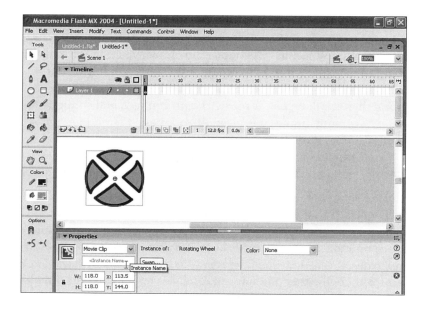

Do you recall how the movie clip kept animating even when you stopped the
Timeline in the last example? Stopping the Timeline is like yelling "Stop!" into a
crowd. Simply saying "stop" isn't enough. You have to say, "Hey, Movie Clip 1,
you stop." But you can't talk to an individual instance unless that instance has a
name. As you'll soon see, you can do much more than tell movie clips to stop.

File Size Savings

Movie clips that contain nested clips tend to be smaller than Graphic symbols.
You only need to do a few tests to prove this. Let's say you have a line and you
make it a movie clip. Use that line to create a square (make the square a movie
clip). Use four instances of the square clip to make another movie clip (called
Four Square). Continue this for several more nestings. Export the movie and note
the file size. Try it again, using plain Graphic symbols. Compare how much bigger the file is using graphics than using movie clips! When I conducted the preceding test between two otherwise identical files, the one using movie clips was
one-tenth the size of the other! This could mean the difference between a site that
downloads in 10 seconds and one that takes nearly 2 minutes.

Flash lets you scrub to preview the effects of a graphic instance, and this is a clue
as to why they're bigger. Scrubbing works because Flash knows exactly how a
graphic instance will behave. With movie clips, Flash doesn't know exactly

because movie clips can be addressed dynamically. You haven't seen this in action yet, but movie clips can start and stop (and more) during runtime. Flash waits until it is playing the movie to decide how the movie clip will perform.

When you export a movie, Flash calculates exactly how the Graphic symbol will act. This is known as *prerendering* the Graphic symbol, and it takes a bit of extra disk space to contain that information. Prerendering means that the file plays a bit more swiftly. But when you have symbols inside symbols inside symbols, all that nested prerendering starts to take up file space. As a result, Graphic symbols are bigger than Movie Clip symbols. If you want to see what makes up a movie's file size, you can select View, Bandwidth Profiler while testing a movie or select File, Publish Settings to open the Publish Settings dialog box and then select Generate Size Report.

The lesson here is that you should almost always opt for movie clips unless you're taking advantage of one of the benefits of graphics.

When Is Runtime?

Runtime refersto the point at which the user is watching your movie (as well as when you're testing the movie). You can do almost anything while authoring, but after you export a movie, you're limited to what's possible at runtime. A lot of things get locked down—for example, you can't change the frame rate at runtime.

By the Way

The way I'm using *render* here refers to the work that the computer must do to draw everything onscreen. Some text and graphics are rendered ahead of time. Prerendering may take a long time, but when you do the work ahead of time, playback speed is quicker. Most digital video is prerendered. In Flash, some graphics get prerendered and others are rendered on-the-fly during runtime. Generally, rendering on-the-fly takes more processor power (although it's seldom enough to overwhelm the user's machine).

Effects on Download Order

All this trash talk about graphics shouldn't scare you off. Besides being totally appropriate for scrubbing, they also have a nice effect on downloads. Specifically, Graphic symbols only need to download one frame at a time—and therefore exhibit a better streaming effect than Movie Clip symbols. That is, a movie can begin to play before it's entirely downloaded. In the case of a frame containing a movie clip, all nested frames need to download before Flash will proceed to the next frame. This isn't a super-critical point because Flash files tend to be very small, and there are other ways to optimize a movie. I just thought it would be worth mentioning at this point how Graphic symbols stream better.

Summary

This chapter didn't contain a lot of new material. You already knew two big concepts: how nesting of symbols works and how symbols can be used for both motion tweens and efficiency. When doing motion tweens, maybe you tried to make a symbol a multiframe symbol. Now you should understand that you can do that and there are options about whether the multiframe symbol you're tweening is behaving like a movie clip or a graphic.

You can't scrub when using movie clips—or at least you won't see them animate until you run Test Movie. This is another reason to avoid using movie clips when you really need the capability to scrub—such as for lip synching. Also, after you do a couple file size tests, you'll remember that movie clips are fundamentally smaller than graphics. Finally, the fact that only movie clips can be given an instance name will prove, in the long run, to be the most significant attribute of movie clips.

CHAPTER 43

Making Interactive Buttons

Now that you've learned how to create basic drawings and simple animations in Flash, we can move on to what's possibly the most compelling attribute of Flash: interactivity. A plain linear animation can be quite powerful on its own. When you add interactivity, though, the users are engaged. They become part of the movie. In this chapter and the next, you'll learn how to add interactivity to movies.

The most straightforward way to add interactivity is by adding buttons. This way, users can click buttons when they feel like interacting—maybe they want to stop and start an animation at will. Or maybe you would like them to be able to skip ahead past an introduction animation.

Flash makes it easy to create very sophisticated buttons using any shape. In addition, it's easy to add visual enhancements, including animation and sound effects. This chapter you'll learn how to create the visual elements of buttons. Then, in subsequent chapters, you'll start making the buttons do things.

Making a Button

Any time you create a new symbol, you must specify the behavior as a Movie Clip, Button, or Graphic. So far you've only chosen Graphic or Movie Clip. Creating a button is actually no more difficult than selecting Button as the behavior. The following example looks at creating a button in more detail:

1. In a new file, draw an oval or a rectangle that will become your button.

2. Use the Selection tool to select the entire shape.

3. Convert the shape to a symbol by selecting Modify, Convert to Symbol (or pressing F8).

4. Name the symbol MyButton, make sure that you select the Button behavior, and then click OK.

5. Test your movie (by using Control, Test Movie or pressing Ctrl+Enter) and notice the way your mouse cursor changes when you place it over the button (as shown in Figure 43.1).

6. Save this file because you'll add to it in the next task.

Did you
Know?

> **Enabling Simple Buttons**
>
> It's actually possible to preview buttons without testing a movie. To do this, you
> select Control, Enable Simple Buttons. However, this feature is more trouble than it's
> worth. You have to turn it off in order to modify your button (if you want to click to
> select it you don't want it behaving like a button). The best way to "see" the button
> is to use Test Movie.

Making a button looks easy, doesn't it? Even though you did make a button in
the preceding task, it probably falls short of your expectations in two general
ways: It doesn't look like a button (with various states) and it doesn't act like a
button. (Currently nothing happens if you click the button while testing the
movie.) We'll address the issue of making the button *do* something in Chapter 44,
"Using ActionScript and Behaviors to Create Nonlinear Movies." For now, though,
you can complete the following example to make the simple button look better
by adding an over state and a down state:

1. In the file that contains the MyButton symbol that you created in the previous task, double-click the instance of the button, and you are taken into the
   master version of the symbol. If you're having trouble clicking the button
   because you keep getting the hand cursor every time you go over the button, select the Control menu and make sure that the menu item Enable
   Simple Buttons does not have a check mark next to it.

   Now that you're in the master version of the MyButton symbol, you should
   notice that this symbol has only four frames—and instead of being numbered, they're named Up, Over, Down, and Hit (see Figure 43.2). They are
   still four frames—they just all have names. Into each frame, you'll draw
   how we want the button to appear for various states. The up state already
   contains how the button looks normally.

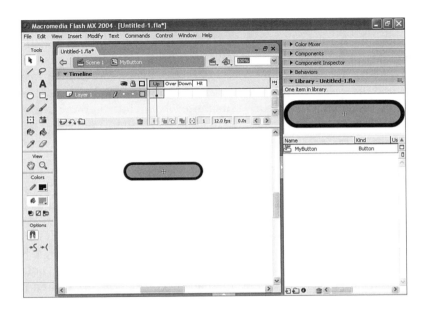

FIGURE 43.2
Inside the button
symbol are four
named frames.

The Four States

The up state contains the visual look of the button in its normal state. Over contains the look for when the user hovers his cursor over the button. Down is when the user clicks. Hit is a special state in which you place a visual representation of what portion of the button you intend to be clickable. This is what the user must "hit" in order to see the over and down states.

By the Way

2. In the Over frame, draw how the button will look when the user's cursor hovers over it. To do this, insert a keyframe into the second frame of the button by clicking in the Timeline under Over and pressing F6 or selecting Insert, Timeline, Keyframe. Select the Paint Bucket tool and a color similar to but slightly lighter than the color currently filling the rectangle shape. Fill the shape in the Over frame with the lighter color.

3. Insert a keyframe in the Down frame by clicking in the Timeline under Down and pressing F6 or selecting Insert, Timeline, Keyframe.

4. Select the entire contents of the Down frame and—using the arrow keys on your keyboard—nudge the shape down and to the right three pixels (click three times with the right arrow and three times with the down arrow).

5. You're done editing the master button, so get back into the main scene (either by clicking Scene 1 at the top left of the Timeline or by pressing Ctrl+E) and test the movie by selecting Control, Test Movie.

This task proves you can create a pretty advanced button with very little effort. The various states contain the graphics for how the button will look in different situations: Up is the button's normal state, over is when the user passes the cursor over the button, and down is when the user presses the button. In the preceding task you had the states change just the color and location of the graphic, but you can put anything you want in each state (and you will later in this chapter).

Defining a Button's Hit State

In the preceding task you saw that there are four states. In addition to up, over, and down, there's one called hit. The hit state is never visibly seen by the user. It defines where the user must position her cursor to show a button's over state or where she must click to see the button's down state. Imagine that you had a doughnut-shaped button. If you didn't set a hit state, the user wouldn't be allowed to click anywhere in the hole (similar to Figure 43.3). However, if you inserted a keyframe and drew a solid circle (no doughnut hole) in the Hit frame, the user could click anywhere within the solid circle. This can also be useful when you want a small button but you don't want to frustrate the user by requiring her to have the precision of a surgeon. I say, "give them a break," and make the hit state big enough to easily click even if that means that it's bigger than the button itself. You can practice this in the following example.

FIGURE 43.3
Changing the shape contents of a button's hit state affects what portion is clickable.

Did you
Know?

Hit State Is Always Present

The first four frames of a button are used, regardless of whether you place keyframes (or even frames) into all four of them. Compare this to a normal Timeline in which you insert only two frames. By the time the playback head reaches Frame 3 or beyond, you don't see anything on the Stage. However, buttons break this fundamental concept by effectively inserting frames (not keyframes) in all four frames—at least that's a good way to think about it. Therefore, if you draw only into Frame 1, that image will remain as the visual element for all four frames (Up, Over, Down, and Hit).

Here you'll create a large hit state so the button is easy to click:

1. In a new file, use the Text tool to draw the word *Home*.

2. Using the Selection tool, select the text block you just created and convert it into a symbol (by pressing F8 or selecting Modify, Convert to Symbol). Name it Home Button, make sure that you select Button behavior, and then click OK.

3. Test the movie (by selecting Control, Test Movie) and notice how the button is sensitive to where you move your cursor. You see the hand cursor only when you're exactly on top of the text. Back in the file, you can fix this by creating a larger hit state for the button.

4. Double-click the button so you can edit the master button. Inside our button, insert a keyframe in the Hit frame by clicking in the Hit frame and pressing F6 or selecting Insert, Timeline, Keyframe. Realize that the Home text in the Hit frame is just a copy of text in the Up frame; inserting a keyframe copies the contents of the other frame.

5. While in the Hit frame, use the Oval tool to draw a filled oval that's slightly larger than the text (turn off Snap to Objects temporarily if you want). When you have your oval, you can delete the text (from only the Hit frame). (After you draw the hit state, you can delete the Home text because the user never actually sees anything that's in the Hit frame.)

6. Test the movie now by selecting Control, Test Movie or pressing Ctrl+Enter, and you see that the button gives the user a break because it's much easier to click.

For the button in the preceding task, you used a hit state to create a larger area for the user to click. Often you can forgo creating a hit state, and the button's solid areas will define the clickable (or "hot") area. Just remember that without a hit state, the closest keyframe to the left of the Hit frame will define what's hot— that is, the graphics in the down state.

Minimizing a Button's Impact on File Size

Regardless of how fast everyone's Internet connections are getting, there's no excuse for a file that's bigger than it has to be. And just because you're creating buttons in this chapter doesn't mean that you can ignore file size considerations. In the previous task, I instructed you to insert three keyframes and use the Paint Bucket to color the shape in each differently. I didn't want to diverge from the main task, but hopefully you were thinking, "Hey, if all we're doing is changing the color or location, we should be using symbols instead of a new shape in each keyframe."

Using Symbols Inside Buttons

Although most people understand why symbols are useful and important, many don't use symbols as much as possible. For example, if a multistate button has three identical keyframes, the contents of each keyframe are duplicated. This isn't a problem if you use instances of a symbol on each frame. People often mistakenly think that because a button is a symbol, editing its contents will take full advantage of symbols. You need to consider using symbols while you're inside symbols. Anytime you copy and paste (which happens when you insert a keyframe), you should consider using symbols, even if you happen to be editing a symbol's contents.

In the following state you can try creating a multistate button again—this time using the symbols in each state instead of new shapes.

Start this example from scratch, by following these steps:

1. In a new file, draw an oval. This will become your button.

2. Use the Selection tool to select the entire oval you just drew. Convert the oval into a symbol by selecting Modify, Convert to Symbol or pressing F8. Name it MyButton, make sure that the behavior is Button, and then click OK.

3. Next, you need to edit the master version of the button you just created. Double-click the instance of the button and you are taken inside the master version. Inside the master button, you should see the oval shape you drew. Notice that it's not a symbol—it's a shape. After all, you just told Flash to convert the shape into a symbol, so inside the symbol you have a shape. This will be an issue if you start adding keyframes inside the button.

4. To be totally efficient, convert the oval shape itself to a symbol before you add any more keyframes. Select the entire shape, select Modify, Convert to Symbol, name the symbol Oval, select the Movie Clip behavior, and then click OK.

5. Now that the first keyframe contains an instance of the Oval movie clip, insert a keyframe in the Over frame. Tint the instance of the Oval symbol by selecting the Oval symbol and from the Properties panel choosing Tint in the Color Styles drop-down list, picking a hue, and setting the amount to 100%. If you want, you can even scale the instance of Oval and make it slightly larger.

6. Insert a keyframe in the Down frame. Flash copies the contents of the previous frame. Nudge the tinted instance of Oval in the Over frame down and to the right. To do this, with the Oval symbol selected, click the down arrow twice and the right arrow twice.

7. Go back to the main scene and test your movie. It should look like Figure 43.4, and the file size should remain small because you did it all with just one shape.

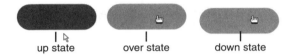

up state   over state   down state

FIGURE 43.4
A visual change occurs in the three states of the button: no effect for the up state, tinting for the over state, and change of position for the down state.

Hopefully, you're beginning to get excited about the power you have to create buttons. Even the quick-and-dirty buttons you're making in this chapter's tasks are looking pretty good. We're *still* going to wait until next chapter to make the buttons do anything when they're pressed. In the meantime, you'll see that there's lots more you can do with buttons.

Advanced Buttons

If you think the buttons you've been making are exciting, just wait. You're about to make some very sophisticated buttons, and you'll have a chance to apply both your new knowledge of basic buttons and a little of what you've learned about animation from previous hours.

Animated Buttons

Creating an animated button in Flash is easier than you might imagine. Do you want a button that is animating at all times or one that just animates when the cursor passes over? How about both? You can do anything you want; as you'll see in the next example, you just put an animated movie clip in the appropriate states of the button. That's it.

In this example you'll create a button that animates when the user rolls over it:

1. In a new file, use the Text tool to type the word **Home** on the Stage (make it fairly large). Select the text with the Selection tool, convert it to a symbol (by selecting Modify, Convert to Symbol), name it Plain Text, select the Movie Clip behavior, and then click OK. You will use this symbol extensively.

2. The text onscreen is an instance of the Plain Text symbol, and now you can create a Movie Clip symbol that animates the Plain Text symbol on the Stage. With the Plain Text symbol selected, select Modify, Convert to Symbol, name the symbol Animating Text, select the Movie Clip behavior, and then click OK.

3. Now you can edit the Animating Text symbol. Access the contents of this symbol by double-clicking. Make sure you're in the Animating Text symbol before you do anything else (look at the edit bar to make sure).

4. Inside the master Animating Text symbol, insert a keyframe at Frame 30 and one at Frame 15. (Create Frame 30 before you change the instance at Frame 15—so it ends in the same location as where it starts.) Scale the Plain Text symbol instance in Frame 15 so that it's noticeably larger. Go back and set tweening in Frame 1 and Frame 15 to Motion (by right-clicking each keyframe, individually, and selecting Create Motion Tween). Scrub the Timeline to get a feel for the animation.

5. Go back to the main scene (by clicking Scene 1 at the top left of the Timeline or pressing Ctrl+E). Delete everything on the Stage (by selecting Edit, Select All, and then selecting Edit, Clear—or better yet, by pressing Ctrl+A and then pressing Delete). You're not deleting any symbols; they're both safe in the Library. Open the Library by selecting Window, Library or pressing Ctrl+L. Drag an instance of the Plain Text symbol onto the Stage.

6. Now you're ready to create your button. Once again, with the Plain Text symbol selected, convert it to a symbol (by selecting Modify, Convert to Symbol), name it Animating Button, select the Button behavior, and then click OK. By converting the existing Plain Text symbol into the Animating Button symbol, you're using an instance of a symbol to create the button.

7. Now you can edit your button and make it animate. Double-click the Animating Button symbol instance on the Stage; you're taken inside the button—which you can confirm already has an instance of the Plain Text symbol in Frame 1.

8. Place an instance of the Animating Text movie clip in the button's over state (Frame 2). You could drag it from the Library and align it to the Plain Text instance in the up state. However, you're going to do it another way

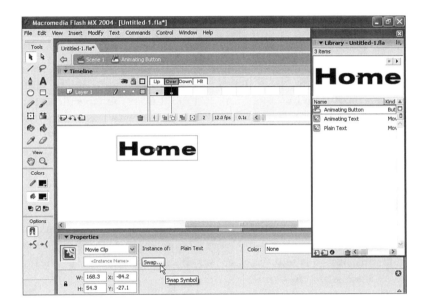

that won't require any manual alignment. Insert a keyframe into the over state (by pressing F6). This copies everything from the Up frame (an instance of the Plain Text symbol).

9. In the Over frame of the button, access the Properties panel and select the Plain Text instance on the Stage). Click the Swap button in the Properties panel, and the Swap Symbol dialog box appears (see Figure 43.5).

FIGURE 43.5
You can swap the symbol to which an instance is linked without changing any other properties (such as position) of the instance.

10. The Swap Symbol dialog box shows all the symbols in your Library and a dot next to the one the current instance is linked to (see Figure 43.6). Click Animating Text and then click OK. You've now swapped the instance (previously Plain Text). You should see that the name of the current symbol listed in the Properties panel (next to Instance of:) has changed.

11. The button is lacking a nice large hit state. It has a hit state, but it's kind of a moving target and difficult to access. In the master version of the button's Hit frame, insert a keyframe and draw an oval that is at least as big as the word *Home*. After you draw the oval, delete the instance of Animating Text that was automatically placed in the Hit frame when you inserted the keyframe; it's not necessary. (Note that you could have used Onion Skin tools to align the oval to the text in the previous frame.)

FIGURE 43.6
In the Swap Symbol
dialog box you can
select a different
symbol.

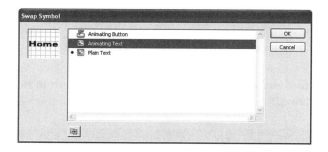

In the preceding task you created a button that uses a movie clip in its over state. However, instead of creating from the "top down" (that is, making the button and then putting a movie clip in the button), you did it from the "specific to the general" (or from "inside out"). First you created a symbol with text (Plain Text). Then you animated Plain Text in the movie clip you named Animating Text. Finally, you created the button and used the Plain Text symbol in the Up frame and the Animating Text symbol in the Over frame.

Button Tracking Options

A button's tracking option is a subtle attribute that gives you additional control over exactly how the button acts. In Figure 43.7 notice that in the Properties panel, while any button is selected, there's a choice between Track As Button (the default) and Track As Menu Item.

FIGURE 43.7
The Properties
panel lets you
specify whether a
button will track as
a button or as a
menu item.

The easiest way to understand tracking is to have more than one button and make sure the buttons have over states that are visually different from their up states. (You could have several instances of the same button.) If you leave them all with the default setting Track As Button, when testing the movie, you can click and hold one of the buttons, and you won't be able to access any other button while you keep the mouse down. Many Flash buttons work this way. For example, if you click a button and keep the mouse pressed while you roll over other buttons, only the one that you clicked initially will be affected. This is the action caused by the default setting Track As Button.

Now, if you set several buttons to Track As Menu Item and test again, you'll see that even if you've started to click one button, if you hold your mouse down and roll over other buttons, they will react (and register if you let go). This is similar to regular menus: When you click and hold and then move up and down, you're able to let go on any item in the menu.

The difference between these options is very subtle, but you should realize that they're available. The Track As Menu Item option can be appropriate when you have many buttons onscreen (like, say, when creating a drop-down menu). Usually the default Track As Button is fine.

Sounds in Buttons

There are several ways to include sounds in buttons. In the simplest form, a sound can be placed in any keyframe. For a sound to occur when the user's cursor goes over a button, just put a sound in the over state. Fancier effects can get more complicated. For example, making a sound loop *while* the user's cursor is over the button takes a few more steps. Ultimately, however, to create complicated sounds and effects, you need to learn about ActionScript, covered in Chapter 44. For now, we'll cover two basic forms of sounds in buttons: simple sound effects in the over state and looping sounds within a button.

First, let's try an example where you'll make a button that plays a sound when the user rolls over it:

1. In a new file, draw a rectangle shape, convert it into a symbol (by selecting Modify, Convert to Symbol or pressing F8), name it Audio Button, select the Button behavior, and click OK.

2. Double-click the instance so you can edit the master button.

3. Inside the master version of the button, you can concern yourself with the over state (where you'll include a sound). Of course you need a new keyframe in the over state because sounds are only placed in keyframes. However, before you insert a keyframe (which, if inserted now, would copy the shape from the Up frame), you need to convert the shape in the Up frame to a movie clip by selecting it all, selecting Modify, Convert to Symbol, naming it Shape of Button, selecting the Movie Clip behavior, and clicking OK.

4. Insert a keyframe in the Over frame. (You can tint Shape of Button or scale it if you want a visual effect when the user rolls over the button.) Then, with the Over frame selected, access the Properties panel. Notice that you don't see any sounds listed in the Sound drop-down list because you haven't imported any (see Chapter 40, "Including Sound in Animations").

5. Instead of importing a sound from a file, use one that comes with Flash. Select Window, Other Panels, Common Libraries, Sounds. Open your file's Library (by selecting Window, Library or pressing Ctrl+L) and drag the Breaker Switch sound item into your Library. Now select the Over frame and use the Properties panel to select Breaker Switch (because it's been imported into your file).

6. Test the movie to see (and hear) whether it works.

7. Save this file because you'll use it in the next task.

That task wasn't so bad. Just put a sound in the keyframe of the over state of a button! In the preceding task you used the Breaker Switch sound in particular for two reasons. First, it saved you the hassle of finding a sound. Also, it is a short sound. Had you chosen a longer sound, such as Beam Scan, you might have noticed that there's enough time to roll over the button, roll off, and roll back on quickly, which causes a layering effect on the sound that is not exactly pleasant. You can fix that by changing the Properties panel's Sync setting to Start.

You'll see how a long sound (or worse, one that loops forever) requires such additional consideration in the next task. Generally, I suggest that incidental sound effects—such as rollover sounds—be very short so that they don't become tiresome for users. A gratuitous sound effect that's cute the first time can become really annoying when it repeats.

Let's try creating a repeating sound effect:

1. Edit the master button you created in the previous task. If you aren't already inside the master button, double-click the instance of the button.

2. Select the keyframe in the over state. Change the Repeat drop-down list to Loop.

3. Test the movie. There are some problems. The sound Breaker Switch doesn't loop well. However, that's the least of the problems—and one that could easily be rectified with an alternative sound. The serious problems that we'll address are (1) the sound will layer on top of itself every time you roll off and then roll back on the button and (2) when the sound starts, it never stops.

4. Three other Sync settings exist besides the default Event. In this case, you want the sound in the over state to start playing only if it isn't already playing. In the master Button symbol, set the Sync setting for the sound in the Over frame of the button to Start (that is, while the frame is selected, use the Properties panel to select Start from the Sync drop-down list). Test the movie

again, and you see that you fixed the problem of the sound starting again after it has already started.

5. The sound still continues forever once started. The opportune time to stop the sound is when the user rolls off the button—the up state. There happens to be an action called Stop All Sounds, but what if you want other sounds to continue playing? You only need the particular sound that's looping to stop. In the up state's keyframe, add the same sound. But this time, select the Stop setting in the Sync drop-down list, to cause only that particular sound to stop. To do this, select the first keyframe (in the up state), and then in the Properties panel, select the same sound you're using in the over state (Breaker Switch) from the drop-down list of sounds available, and set the Sync drop-down list to Stop.

6. Test the movie, and it should work.

Invisible Buttons

Invisible buttons are very useful. They're easy to make, too, as you'll see in the next task. You'll create an invisible button, and Flash will let you (the author) see the invisible button as semitransparent cyan; the user won't see anything.

It might seem useless to make a button the user can't see, but it's actually quite useful. The only trick is that you'll probably want to place the invisible button on top of something visual. For example, what if you had a map on which you wanted the user to be able to click specific areas (maybe cities) and learn more about the one she clicked? All you would need is one big picture of the map and lots of invisible buttons placed in key locations. This would be more practical than cutting the map into little pieces and making buttons out of each piece.

Let's practice creating and using an invisible button:

1. Select Insert, New Symbol, name the symbol Invisible, select the Button behavior, and then click OK. This takes you to the master version of the symbol you're creating. Flash expects you to draw something here in the master version of the Invisible button symbol.

2. Leave all the frames of the button blank, but in the Hit frame insert a keyframe. (Because the previous keyframe is blank, this is the same as inserting a blank keyframe.)

3. Draw a circle around the center (the plus) in the Hit frame. (To center it, you can draw a circle and then cut and paste or use the Info panel to set the center to 0,0.) Your button's Timeline should resemble the one in Figure 43.8.

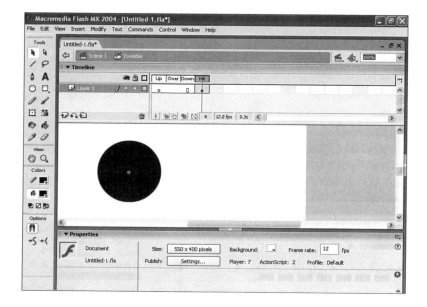

4. Go back to your main scene and drag an instance of this Invisible button from the Library to the Stage. Check it out; it's cyan. Test the movie, and you see nothing (except that your cursor changes when it reaches the button's location).

5. In the main scene, draw a large box and then a few circles in different locations on the box (as shown in Figure 43.9). Imagine that this box is a large map and each circle indicates a city. Then drag an invisible button from the Library for each circle you drew. Line up the buttons and scale them appropriately to cover each circle.

For something you can't even see, invisible buttons are actually quite powerful. It's safe to say I've never done a project without them. Their main advantage is they keep the visual elements separate from the button's functionality. You can place invisible buttons on top of anything to effectively create a button the user can see and click. Realize that invisible buttons (or any buttons, for that matter) don't do anything until you attach behaviors or ActionScript to them.

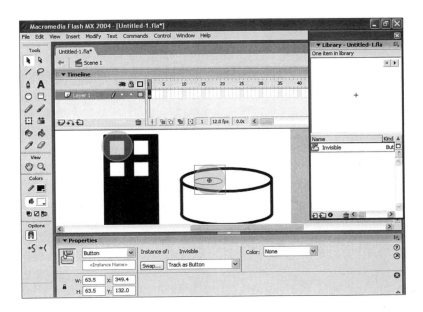

FIGURE 43.9
Invisible buttons can be placed on top of any drawing.

Summary

Now you should understand how to create buttons from any shape in Flash. In this chapter you also learned how to make a button change visually when the user's cursor rolls over or clicks it. You learned how to control exactly what part of the button is clickable (the hit state) as well as how to make an animated button. Not only did you learn visual stuff, but you learned how to put sounds in buttons and even how to make invisible buttons.

You should be able to apply many of your animation skills to make compelling buttons. However, you've only learned the first half—how to make the buttons *look* cool. In the next hour you'll embark on making the buttons function—making them do things by attaching behaviors.

CHAPTER 44

Using ActionScript and Behaviors to Create Nonlinear Movies

Flash's programming language is called **ActionScript**. Like any programming language, ActionScript lets you write instructions that your movie will follow. Without ActionScript, your movie will play the same way every time. If you want the user to be able to stop and start the movie, for example, you need ActionScript. Actually, Flash MX 2004 also includes **behaviors**, which are snippets of ActionScript that you can add without needing to know all the details behind the code. It turns out that even with behaviors, you can do much more if you invest just a little bit of time learning ActionScript. In previous chapters you learned how to create buttons. In this chapter you'll learn how to attach ActionScript to those buttons both manually and with behaviors.

The topic of scripting is very deep. We won't cover it all in this book. Rather, we'll cover the basic concept as well as look at typical applications for scripting. This way, you'll build a good foundation on which to grow at your own pace.

Using ActionScript

Scripting is nothing more than writing instructions. Each instruction tells Flash to do something very specific. For example, "play," "stop," or "set that movie clip's alpha to 50%." By keeping each piece of ActionScript very specific, you can easily piece together more advanced instructions. But at the core, each "sentence" (or line of code) is a single instruction.

All your ActionScript is typed into the Actions panel. Open the Actions panel and follow along as we explore. Select Window, Development Panels, Actions (or press F9). Take a quick look at Figure 44.1, and then we'll cover a few more details before you complete a few examples.

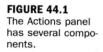

FIGURE 44.1
The Actions panel has several components.

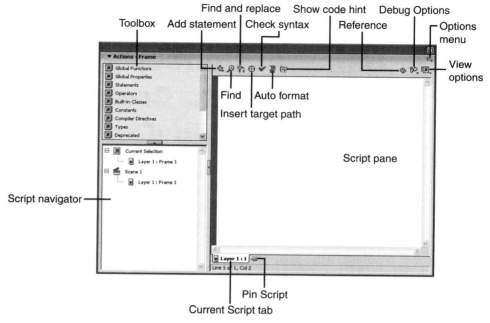

The Actions panel has the following features:

▶ **Toolbox**—The Toolbox list provides access to all installed actions. It is organized like folders.

▶ **Script pane**—In the Script pane, your actions will appear in order of execution.

▶ **Navigator pane**—In the script navigation pane, you can see all the scripts in your movie.

▶ **Current Script tab**—The Current Script tab indicates which script is currently being edited. Figure 44.1 indicates that the script is for Layer 1. Compare this to how the Properties panel shows you the currently selected instance.

▶ **Pin Script**—The Pin Script button adds a tab for a particular script so that you don't have to first select the object or layer into which you want to add a script. Normally, the Actions panel acts like other panels—always reflecting the settings for the currently selected item (in this case, the script for the selected keyframe or object, such as a button).

▶ **Options menu**—The Options menu (as on any panel) contains additional settings. Preferences such as script font typeface are available.

▶ **Reference button**—The Reference button provides online help with any selected piece of ActionScript.

▶ **Options toolbar**—The Options toolbar includes the following buttons:

  ▶ **Add Statement**—This button, which I call the "plus button" throughout the rest of this book, pops up a menu that provides the same script elements found in the Toolbox. The menu also shows the key combination for each script that has one (see the later tip).

  ▶ **Find and Find and Replace**—These buttons let you search scripts as you would in a word processing program.

  ▶ **Insert Target Path**—This button helps you address specific objects, such as particular clips. You'll learn that scripts can apply to individual clips (say you want to play or stop just one clip—you have to target that particular clip). This button helps you specify a target clip.

  ▶ **Check Syntax**—This button ensures that your ActionScript has no errors. (This won't guarantee that the movie will behave as you had in mind—only that you have no show-stopping errors.)

  ▶ **Auto Format**—This button cleans up your code by adding indentation where appropriate. This makes it much easier to read.

  ▶ **Show Code Hint**—This button re-triggers the code-completion helper that appears as a ToolTip to help you complete ActionScript (when Flash knows what you're about to type).

  ▶ **Debug Options**—This button lets you add and remove **breakpoints**. where you purposefully make Flash pause on a specified line of code so that you can investigate how it's playing (or, most likely, not playing the way you expected). You can also add and remove breakpoints by clicking in the gutter to the left of any line of code. You'll see a red dot appear to the left of the line of code.

  ▶ **View Options**—This button gives you a few formatting options related to how scripts will appear, such as displaying line numbers (which I recommend).

Keyboard Shortcuts for Actions

Did you Know?

In the Actions panel under the Add Statement (+) button, you'll find key combinations such as Esc+go. This means the action can be inserted by simply pressing the following keys in sequence (not at the same time): Esc, g, o. If you find yourself inserting the same action repeatedly, you might use this method instead because it's quicker than typing the code manually.

Syntax is unique to each programming language. Every piece of ActionScript has a very specific syntax that must be followed. As an analogy, consider how every email address has to have the form *name@domain.com* or it won't work. Flash has no mercy for invalid syntax—you'll see errors appear in the Output window until you resolve the errors. Even after you perfect the script, the movie may not play exactly as you had in mind. Luckily, there are plenty of ways to ensure that your scripts have perfect syntax.

You can easily add an action from the Toolbox by double-clicking or dragging it to the right side of the Actions panel (the Script pane). You can build a complex set of instructions, one line at a time. A **statement** is a code sentence that uses only words from the ActionScript language.

Again, **actions** are instructions. Flash will follow each line of code in sequence. Some actions are complete pieces of instruction, with no additional modifications on your part. For example, you can add a `stop` action, and when Flash encounters it, the playback head will stop advancing. However, many actions require that you provide additional details (called *parameters*). For example, an action such as `gotoAndPlay` requires that you provide the additional detail about what frame number or frame label you want to go to.

Specifying Actions by Using Parameters

Now you can try out actions and parameters. You'll see that some actions are quite simple. The following example is a quick exercise that uses actions and parameters to make the last few frames of an animation loop. After you complete it, we'll step back to analyze what you did in the example:

1. In a new file, use the Text tool to create a text block containing the word *Welcome*. Make sure the text type is Static. Select the block and convert it to a symbol. Make it a movie clip and name it Welcome Text.

2. Position the movie clip instance in the center of the screen, and insert one keyframe at Frame 20 and another at Frame 30.

3. Move the current-frame marker to Frame 1 and move Welcome Text all the way off the Stage to the left. Set motion tweening for both Frame 1 and Frame 20. In Frame 20, use the Properties panel to make the tween rotate one time clockwise (CW) on its way from Frame 20 to Frame 30. Test the movie. Notice that the whole movie loops over and over. Instead of leaving the animation as is, you're going to make the rotation part (from Frame 20 to Frame 30) loop forever.

4. You can add actions to any keyframe, but instead of mixing scripts with your animation, you can just make a whole new layer exclusively for actions. Name the single layer Animation and then choose Insert, Layer and name the new layer Actions. Make sure the current layer is Actions (you'll see a pencil in the layer). Select Frame 30 in your Actions layer, insert a keyframe (by pressing F6), and then access the Actions panel (by pressing F9). Make sure Frame 30 remains selected when you edit the Actions panel by noting that the tab reads "Actions:30" and has the keyframe icon (as shown in Figure 44.2). You're going to set an action to execute when the playback head reaches Frame 30.

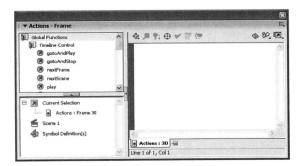

FIGURE 44.2
The Actions panel is opened right after Frame 30 is selected so that you can set an action to execute when the playback head reaches that frame.

5. To insert a `gotoAndPlay` action, select Global Functions, Timeline Control and then double-click `gotoAndPlay`. You should see a `gotoAndPlay` action added to your script in the Script pane on the right (see Figure 44.3). Because this action requires parameters, a code hint will appear to help guide you. If it goes away, just click inside the parentheses following `gotoAndPlay` and press the Show Code Hint button.

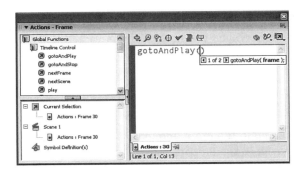

FIGURE 44.3
Right after you insert `gotoAndPlay`, the Actions panel is populated as shown here.

6. You always type parameters inside the parentheses. In this case, type **20** because that's the frame number to which you want to go and play. Therefore, the finished action in the script area should read `gotoAndPlay(20);` (as shown in Figure 44.4).

FIGURE 44.4
This is how the complete code looks. Every time the playback head reaches Frame 30, it goes back to Frame 20 and plays.

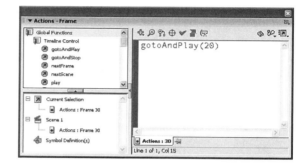

7. Test the movie (don't just play in the authoring environment). It plays once, and then every time it gets to Frame 30, it goes back to Frame 20 and plays again.

As easy as the preceding example was, there is one thing in particular that could make it better. Consider the amount of work involved if you changed the location of the keyframes. For example, what if the second keyframe (Frame 20) had to move to Frame 25? Of course, the initial tween would take longer to play, and the rotation would be quicker, but the loop would also stop working properly. To fix it, you would need to remember to edit the action in Frame 30 so that it read `gotoAndPlay(25);`. You would have to repeat this fix every time you changed the location of the keyframe where the rotation starts.

Naturally, there's a better way. Instead of making the destination of `gotoAndPlay` an explicit frame number, you can change the parameters to make the destination a named frame label, which will be the same for the frame, no matter where it is located in the Timeline. You'll use frame labels in the next exercise.

In these steps, you'll improve the `gotoAndPlay` action by supplying a frame label instead of a frame number. Here are the steps:

1. In the file created in the preceding example, click Frame 20 of the Animation layer. In the Properties panel you should see a place where you can type a frame label. Label this frame Loop Start (see Figure 44.5).

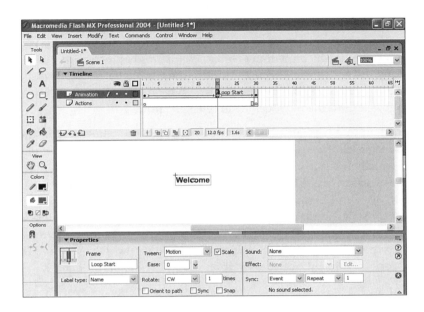

FIGURE 44.5
If you label Frame 20 (via the Properties panel), the destination of the gotoAndPlay action can change from an explicit number (20) to a label name (Loop Start).

2. Click Frame 30 in the Actions layer and open the Actions panel.

3. You're going to modify the gotoAndPlay line in the Actions panel. Change 20 to "Loop Start" (with the quotation marks). The final script should read gotoAndPlay("Loop Start");.

4. Test the movie; it doesn't look any different from the old version to the user. Now go back to the Timeline and click Frame 20, and then click and drag it so Loop Start is now Frame 10.

5. Test the movie again. The animation now loops back to Frame 10, where you moved the Loop Start keyframe. The power of using a label as the destination of the gotoAndPlay action is that it means you can go back and move the location of the Loop Start keyframe to any frame you want, and it still works!

Frame Actions

You just saw how placing one action in a keyframe and changing its parameters makes the playback head jump to a different frame. Step back a second and consider what else you've learned. Actions are instructions that you want Flash to follow. Actions do things. You can modify actions by changing their parameters. This is all good information; however, if actions are instructions, exactly when does Flash *follow* those instructions?

The answer depends on where you put the actions. You can put actions both in keyframes and on any object type, such as button instances, movie clip instances, and components. In the preceding example you placed an action in a keyframe. In that case, the action was executed (that is, the instruction was followed) when the playback head reached that frame. If you put an action in Frame 10, it would not be followed until the playback head reached Frame 10.

With an action in a keyframe, the user doesn't do anything but wait for the playback head to reach the appropriate frame to see the action happen. Although this isn't exactly interactivity, it's quite powerful. For example, often it's useful to place a `stop` action in the first frame so that your movie initially appears paused and won't play until a `play` action is encountered (usually when the user clicks a button). Another example might be when you want to stop in the middle of an animation. All you need is a keyframe and a stop action. There are many more types of keyframe actions, which are good for when you want something to happen at a certain moment in the animation—not just when a user clicks.

Notice that in the previous example you simply used frame actions. The actions were executed when the playback head reached that frame. This is just one of the three places you can put actions; you're about to see the other two—button actions and movie clip actions.

Button Actions

Putting an action in a keyframe causes the action to execute when that frame is reached. However, putting an action on an instance of a button makes the action execute when the user clicks the button. The decision of whether to put an action in a keyframe or a button is simple. If you want an action to occur when a particular frame is reached, put it in a keyframe. If you want an action to occur when the user acts (for example, when he clicks a button), put the action in an instance of the button.

Keyframe actions are pretty straightforward: You just assign them to keyframes. Button actions, however, require that you specify to which *mouse event* you want the action to respond. Do you want the action to respond when the user presses the button or when the user releases the button? Maybe you want the action to execute when the user rolls over the button. This level of detail gives you the power to make an action perform exactly as you want.

Mouse events are specific situations that refer to exactly how the user is interacting with a button. For example, one mouse event is `press` and another is `release`. When you specify to which mouse event you want an action to respond, you are specifying exactly when the action is to execute. Only in actions attached to objects do you need this extra level of specificity because actions in keyframes simply execute when the keyframe is reached. All mouse events include the word on followed by the actual event name in parentheses (for example, on(press)).

The best way to see how mouse events work is to try it out. In the following example you'll add to the preceding example buttons that let the user stop and continue the animation while it plays:

1. Either use the file created in the previous examples or make a new file with a motion tween over several frames (make sure you can see something moving while the animation plays).

2. Insert a new layer for the buttons. You don't want to place buttons in the layer that has the animation; that would affect the tween. Name the new layer Buttons.

3. Into the new Buttons layer, draw a rectangle that will become a button. Select it, and then convert it to a symbol (by pressing F8). Name it MyButton and make sure the behavior is set to Button.

4. You're going to need two buttons, so either copy and paste the instance that is already on the Stage or drag another instance of the MyButton symbol from the Library onto the Stage in the Buttons layer. Apply a Tint color style to each instance—one red (for Stop) and one green (for Play). As you recall, you do so by selecting the button instance on the Stage and using the Properties panel to select Tint from the Color drop-down list and then selecting a color and percentage.

5. Give each button a memorable instance name (say "green" and "red"). Use the Properties panel to set the instance names.

6. Now you need to attach an action to each button individually. Select the red button and access the Actions panel. The tab should read "red" and have an icon of a button. This way you know you're editing the script for that button instance. Click the plus button and select Global Functions, Timeline Control, stop.

7. Unlike a keyframe action, which can appear as a single line of code, a button action requires at least two extra lines of code: one before and one after the main script so that the script is wrapped inside an event. Think of the main script (in this case, stop()) as the meat of a sandwich, but it's not complete without pieces of bread above and below the code. Any code attached to a button has to be surrounded by an on event. Therefore, place your cursor in front of the s in stop and then type the following:

```
on(press){
```

Then press Enter.

8. Click after the last line of code (that is, after `stop()`), press Enter, and type this:

```
}
```

The resulting script looks like this:

```
on(press){
 stop();
}
```

Notice that you should indent the second line for clarity. This is a very good habit to adopt. You can always clean up your code by pressing the Auto Format button in the Actions panel.

9. The preceding steps are painful because they step through every last detail. If you know you're going to be adding code to a button, you can start by defining the event (the bread, if you will) and then come back to insert the meat. For the green button, you'll do just that. Select the green button and open the Actions panel. Confirm that the green button appears in the current script tab at the bottom of the Actions panel. Next find the on action in the Toolbox, under Global Functions, Movie Clip Control, on. Insert it into your code and notice not only that both pieces of bread appear (the on(){ and }), but that a list pops up, from which you can select the press event. Go ahead and double-click press.

10. As for the "meat" of this script, you have to be sure to place it between the two curly braces. Click at the end of Line 1 and press Enter. Now add the play action found under Global Functions, Timeline Control, play.

11. Test the movie, and you'll find that when you press the buttons, the movie will play and stop.

By the Way

No More "Normal" Mode

In previous versions of Flash, you could set the Actions panel to Normal or Expert mode. In some ways, Normal mode was nice because it attempted to ensure that your code syntax was accurate. In other ways, it was more trouble than it was worth. In any event, it's gone now. You won't find it if you're looking. You'll see later in this chapter that providing behaviors is one way Macromedia is making up for removing Normal mode.

It doesn't matter whether you think about the main script (stop or play) first or whether you first think of the event that will trigger it. You'll always need both parts: the event and the actual script. In the case of scripts placed in keyframes, you don't specify any events because keyframe scripts are executed when Flash reaches the correct frames.

Keeping All Code in One Place

By the Way

In many ways, putting code right on buttons (as you did in the preceding example) makes perfect sense. You find the instructions for the actions when you select the buttons, and that gives you a bit of context. However, it can also mean you're running around selecting different instances to reveal their scripts—sort of like the card game Concentration. I have mixed feelings about whether this is the best way to learn. In any event, it's not the ultimate way to program.

Just so you can see what I'd call a better solution, I'm going to show you an alternative to the preceding example. All you do is make sure you give your buttons instance names (as you did in the preceding example: green and red) and type the following code into the first keyframe of the movie:

```
red.onPress=function(){
  stop();
}
green.onPress=function(){
  play();
}
```

Translated, this says that the instance named red shall execute the code stop() when the onPress event occurs. You always leave the word function as is. Notice that onPress in this syntax is equivalent to on(press) when placed right on the button. I'm sure you can guess that the last three lines make the green button trigger the script play() when it gets pressed.

From this point forward, if I say "put an action on a button," I mean you can either use on(press) right *on* the button or .onPress, as shown previously.

A few issues are worth discussing before we conclude with the basics of attaching actions to button instances. First, it's important to remember to put actions on button instances, not on any of the keyframes in the master button. It might seem convenient to include actions as part of the master symbol so that those actions will be included automatically. People often try to do this. It simply won't work. However, you can attach an action to a button instance and then convert that instance to a movie clip (basically, a clip with an instance of a button in it already). You'll see many other such techniques later in this chapter. For now, just remember that actions don't go inside the master symbol of a button.

Movie Clip Actions

You've seen how to place actions in keyframes and on button instances. Most of the actions you'll encounter are likely to fall into one of those two cases. However, there's a third place where you can attach actions: in instances of movie clips. It's a little confusing because, unlike with buttons, you can put actions inside a master movie clip in the Library. However, the rule that you can only put actions in keyframes, button instances, and movie clip instances remains—so if you put any actions *inside* a movie clip, you have to put them in one of those three places (keyframes, nested buttons, or nested clips) inside the clip. We've already discussed putting actions on buttons and in keyframes—and those techniques will work inside master movie clips. But now you're going to see how actions can also be placed on instances of movie clips.

Actions on movie clips are powerful. It would get complicated to fully explore this feature now, but you can do a exercise that gives you a taste. These steps show you how to attach actions right onto clip instances:

1. Create a movie clip that contains several frames and some kind of animation inside the clip (so you can see whether it's playing).

2. Place this movie clip on the Stage and test the movie (to verify that it's animating). Your main Timeline should have only one frame.

3. Back in Flash, select the instance of the movie clip on the Stage and open the Actions panel. (Confirm that you've got the movie clip selected by looking at the current script tab.)

4. In the Toolbox insert onClipEvent, which is listed under Global Functions, Movie Clip Control. The code and code hint will appear as shown in Figure 44.6.

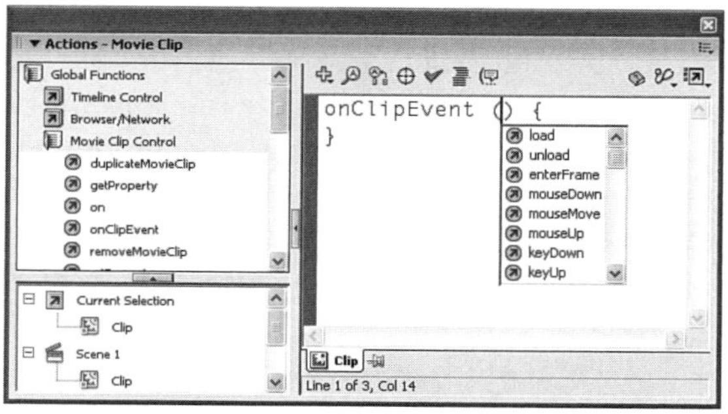

FIGURE 44.6
The skeleton for onClipEvent is similar to that of an on event.

5. Like buttons requiring that you use on events, clips require that you use onClipEvent events. Select or type load. This event will trigger when the clip first loads.

6. Between the two curly braces insert a `stop` action. The resulting code so far should look like this:

```
onClipEvent(load){
  stop();
}
```

Feel free to type it by hand, but be sure to type it *exactly*.

7. You will add two more actions that respond to the `mouseDown` and `mouseUp` events. For this example, when the user clicks `mouseDown`, the movie clip should start to play. When the user stops clicking (that is, when `mouseUp` occurs), the movie clip should stop. You can add all that to the script for the selected clip. The separate events, however, must appear as independent sandwiches (well, starting and ending curly braces). To add the additional actions, click once after the closing curly brace and then press Enter. Either type or use the Toolbox to add two more events so that the entire script now looks like this:

```
onClipEvent(load){
  stop();
}
onClipEvent(mouseDown){
  play();
}
onClipEvent(mouseUp){
  stop();
}
```

8. Test the movie. It's actually pretty sophisticated, despite the simplicity of the script. Go back and reread the script (in the Script area of the Actions panel) attached to the movie clip instance.

There are a few important things to note about the preceding example. First, the movie clip events `mouseDown` and `mouseUp` respond to any mouse click—not just to clicks on the movie clip itself. If you want something that responds to clicks right on a graphic, using a regular button is easier.

Also, the actions you attach to a movie clip instance apply only to that instance. It might be more explicit if you precede `stop()` and `play()` in all cases in the preceding example with `this.`, as in `this.stop()` and `this.play()`. This makes more sense when you think about it because it means just that one movie clip will stop or play. You can prove this to yourself several ways. Drag another instance of your movie clip from the Library (and don't attach any actions to this instance). When you test the movie, the `stop` and `play` actions apply to (that is, "target") only the clip with the actions attached.

Finally, this example shows that you can write code to respond to various events (in this case, load, mouseDown, and mouseUp). For each one, you have the two pieces of bread plus the meat in the middle. What I haven't mentioned yet is that you can stack the sandwich with many layers of meat. That is, for one event, you can trigger several lines of code. For example, when the mouseDown event occurs, you could have a sound start playing in addition to the play() action triggering. As long as you put your code between the two curly braces, one event can trigger as many lines of code as you want. (This is also true with buttons and on events.)

The basic things to remember are that just as with buttons, actions on movie clip instances are wrapped inside events. Buttons respond to the on event, whereas movie clips respond to the onClipEvent. Finally, actions attached to movie clip instances affect only the particular instances to which they're attached.

Using Behaviors

You've got enough of the basics of scripting down to move on to behaviors. I realize that behaviors are intended to make programming easier for novices, but in my opinion, you'll get a lot more out of them if you understand what they're doing. Behaviors simply insert several lines of ActionScript in one swoop. For scripts that require you to specify parameters, the behavior will prompt you for data. Another interesting feature of behaviors is that even after you've inserted a complete script, you can come back and make edits to it without touching the code. That is, you can use the Behaviors panel as your interface to edit the underlying code.

All this can make a programmer very nervous because she can feel out of control. In any event, I do believe it's important to see what's happening. For that reason, during the following discussion and examples, be sure to keep open your Actions panel and watch the changes that occur in the Actions panel when you make changes to the Behaviors panel. Let's first take a tour of the Behaviors panel. Open the Behaviors panel (by pressing Shift+F3 or selecting Window, Development Panels, Behaviors) and take a look at Figure 44.7.

The Behaviors panel has the following features:

- ▶ **Add Behavior**—You always select a behavior to add by clicking the Add Behavior (plus) button. This reveals a hierarchical menu of all installed behaviors.

- ▶ **Delete Behavior**—The Delete Behavior button lets you remove a behavior. Alternatively, you can just select and delete any row containing a behavior that you want to remove.

▶ **Move Up and Move Down**—These buttons let you reorder multiple rows of behaviors (you can add more than one).

▶ **Event**—The Event drop-down list lets you specify a trigger for any added behavior. Remember that when attaching actions to objects, you have to specify events such as press or release.

▶ **Action column**—The Action column simply presents the name of any added behavior. In addition, you can double-click any row in this column to repopulate a behavior after it's added.

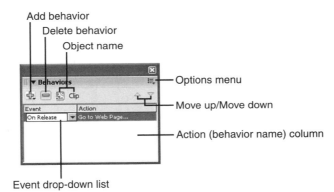

Add behavior
Delete behavior
Object name
Options menu
Move up/Move down
Action (behavior name) column
Event drop-down list

FIGURE 44.7
The Behaviors panel has several components.

The whole idea of the Behaviors panel is that it will insert the ActionScript code for you. Most behaviors prompt you for additional details so that parameters can be set. Also, if you need to re-edit a behavior, you can do it through this panel. Actually, you can tweak any behavior by editing the resulting code by using the Actions panel. If you edit the code through the Actions panel, however, you not only potentially break it, but the Behaviors panel can't access code after you've changed it. (Please don't let this prevent you from trying to learn from mistakes here—it's not like you'll cause some sort of meltdown.)

Using the getURL **Action**

Whereas the gotoAndPlay action jumps the playback head to another frame, getURL jumps the user to another Web page. If you're familiar with how a hyperlink works in HTML, you should know that getURL is the same thing. With gotoAndPlay, you need to specify as a parameter the frame to which you are navigating. With getURL, you need to specify to what URL you want to navigate.

URL stands for *uniform resource locator* and is the address for any Web page. If you want to use the getURL action to jump to my home page, for example, you need to know the URL (which is http://www.phillipkerman.com).

The following example teaches you how both getURL and the Behaviors panel work.

You'll build a hyperlink in this example. Here are the steps:

1. In a new file, create a Button symbol called myButton and place an instance on the Stage. Give this instance the name go.

2. With the button instance selected, open both the Actions panel (by pressing F9) and the Behaviors panel (by pressing Shift+F3). Move the Actions panel to the side because you're only going to use it to watch what's happening behind the scenes.

3. Make sure the button is selected by ensuring that you see myButton, <go> in the Behaviors panel.

4. Click the plus button in the Behaviors panel and select Web, Go to Web Page. Into the URL field that appears in the dialog box, type **http://www.phillipkerman.com**. (Leave the Open In option set to the default, _self.)

5. Test the movie. Or, better yet, select File, Publish Preview, Default or press F12—so you can watch this in a browser. Just click the button in the Flash movie and, if you're connected to the Internet, you'll hyperlink to my home page.

You can see that the ActionScript produced by the preceding example is the same as if you had created it using the steps in one of the earlier examples. That is, you can also select getURL in the Actions panel toolbox under Global Functions, Browser/Network. The getURL action is nearly the same as gotoAndPlay(), except that the parameter needs to be a URL. If you want to change the event that triggers this behavior, click On Release in the Behaviors panel, and you can select from the other events available to buttons, as Figure 44.8 shows.

FIGURE 44.8
The Behaviors panel lets you change the event trigger without affecting the underlying code.

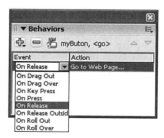

You can also change the destination URL by double-clicking in the Action column in the Behaviors panel. That will redisplay the dialog box that appeared in the first place. You can actually do all these modifications (change the event, change the URL, and even delete the whole behavior) through the Actions panel. You get the same results either way.

You can expand the set of behaviors installed on your machine. Actually, it's not terribly difficult to make your own. A behavior is really just a template of code. It gets a bit more involved when you define the dialog boxes that pop up, but it's all fairly straightforward. My point here is that you might not like the set of behaviors that ships with Flash at this point, but you'll surely see more over time.

Behaviors are simply a tool that guides you through ActionScript. But they can become more trouble than they're worth, especially when you know exactly what you want to do. Sort of like cookie cutters, they're great for holidays, but sometimes you just have to use your fingers and shape the cookie yourself. However, there are some really great benefits to behaviors, too, as discussed in the following sections.

Addressing Movie Clips

The navigation actions you saw in the preceding section are good for jumping around within a Timeline or throughout the Web. However, you know that movie clips have their own Timeline. What happens when you want to jump around within a movie clip? If you put an action inside the movie clip or if you attach an action to the clip, it's pretty straightforward. If you have a `stop` action on a button inside the movie clip, for example, it will cause the movie clip to stop (provided that it has multiple frames). So scripting is easy when you put an action in the master clip or on a clip instance.

Your job gets a little more complicated when you want to send an action to another clip remotely. For example, say you have a movie clip and a button on the Stage (the button is not inside the movie clip). If you put a `stop` action on the button, it will cause only the main Timeline to stop; the movie clip won't stop. To direct an action to a clip, you first address, or "target," that particular instance of the movie clip (remember, you could have several instances on the Stage at once). You can do this in Flash in several ways.

Consider that you have to do two things: address the clip and tell it what to do. Remember that instances of movie clips can be named (via the Properties panel). You can only address named clip instances. So addressing a clip is simply stating its name. If the clip is nested inside another clip, you must address its entire path (or full address). You place the action immediately following the clip's address.

It might be easiest to understand this by using pseudo-code. You can use the programmer's trick of writing scripts in your own words—being as clear as possible—just to get things sorted out. Then you translate to real code. For example, if you wanted a clip instance named ball to stop playing, you might say (in pseudo-code): "ball, you stop." In English, you might say "stop ball," but remember that you have to address the object first and then tell it what code to execute.

The syntax to address an object uses what's called *dot syntax*. For example, this code would actually make a clip instance named ball stop playing:

```
ball.stop();
```

If that sounds simple, then you've got about one-third of ActionScript under your belt. Now let's try addressing out.

In this example you'll address and stop instances of wheels that are inside a clip of a car:

1. You'll need a car with rotating wheels, like the one you made in Chapter 42, "Animating Using Movie Clip and Graphic Symbols." Remember that you achieved this by working from the inside out. First, you made a clip of a wheel called Plain Wheel (a circle with lines that would be noticeable when it rotated). Then you used an instance of Plain Wheel to create another clip called Rotating Wheel. Rotating Wheel contained an instance of Plain Wheel in Frame 1 and one in Frame 20. You set a motion tween to rotate the wheel in the first keyframe of Rotating Wheel. Finally, you used two instances of Rotating Wheel in the creation of the car. At this point, either revisit that example in Chapter 42 or create the Rotating Wheel clip.

2. Drag one instance of Rotating Wheel to the Stage. Test the movie to confirm that the wheel is rotating and take note of the direction in which it's rotating.

3. Drag another instance of Rotating Wheel and place it to the left of the other instance. With the Properties panel, name one of the instances front_wheel and the other back_wheel, as shown in Figure 44.9.

4. Draw a car body (nothing fancy) around the two wheels. Select everything and choose Insert, Convert to Symbol (or press F8). Name this new movie clip Car.

5. On the Stage you have an instance of Car, but it has no instance name yet. Use the Properties panel to name this instance the_car. (Note that a clip instance name should have no spaces and should not begin with a number.)

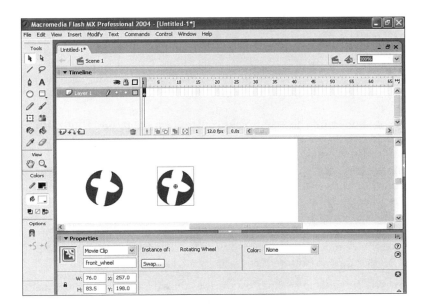

FIGURE 44.9
Using the Properties panel, name each instance of Rotating Wheel so that each can be addressed individually.

6. Insert a keyframe at Frame 40 and move the_car to another place on the Stage. In the first keyframe, set motion tweening.

7. In a new layer, draw a rectangle to be used as a button. Select it and convert it to a symbol called myButton, making sure to set its behavior to Button. Copy and paste this button so that you have two instances. Set the Properties panel's Color drop-down list to Tint and pick a green color for one instance and a red color for the other. Then name the button instances green and red.

8. Select just the red instance of myButton. Open the Actions panel (confirm that the tab name matches the instance name). Type the following code (either by hand or by dragging pieces from the Toolbox):

```
on(press){
  stop();
}
```

9. Test the movie, and you'll see that the stop button stops the car from moving across the screen, but it doesn't stop the wheels from spinning. You need to add additional actions to stop the wheels.

10. Back in Flash, access the actions for the red button and add two additional lines of code. Change the code so that it reads as follows:

```
on(press){
 stop();
 this.the_car.front_wheel.stop();
}
```

Because you want the front_wheel instance to stop, and that instance is inside the instance the_car, you need to include that entire path when you address front_wheel. You'll need a third line of code to stop the back_wheel instance, too, but you can insert it a different way. Click right after the semicolon that ends either stop action and press Enter. In order to address the back_wheel instance, click the Insert a Target Path button (it looks like a crosshairs). The Insert Target Path dialog box pops up, with a hierarchy of the named clip instances in your movie. Next to the_car, click the plus sign to see the named clip instances inside it. Click back_wheel and then click OK. Notice that the address this.the_car.back_wheel appears.

11. Now you have to say what you want to do with the back_wheel instance. The easiest way is to just type .stop(); so that it matches the code that stops the front wheel. The only tricky part is that you must remember to follow stop with parentheses. The finished code appears in Figure 44.10.

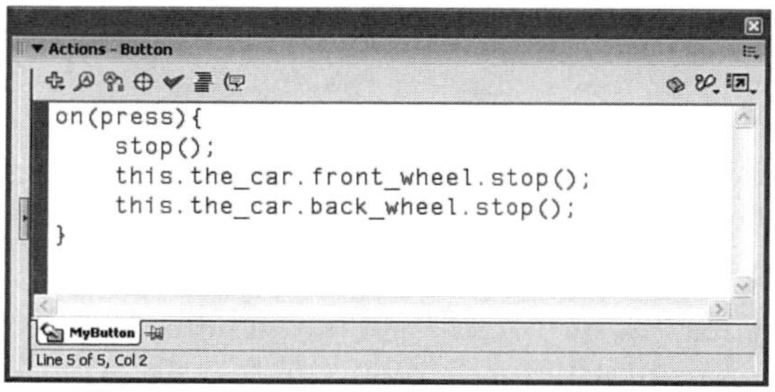

FIGURE 44.10
The code for the stop button includes these three lines of code.

```
on(press){
    stop();
    this.the_car.front_wheel.stop();
    this.the_car.back_wheel.stop();
}
```

12. Test the movie. When you click the red button, the car and both wheels stop. You could repeat this process with the play action (that is, play()) on the green button to allow a user to make the car move again.

Addressing clips is simple, as long as you remember to name your instances. (Just make sure each instance name is just one word and does not begin with a number.) Using the Insert Target Path dialog box is a nice way to learn the syntax for addressing. When you choose the clip from the hierarchy, Flash automatically puts it in the correct syntax. Addressing clips goes from the general to the specific, as in `this.the_car.back_wheel`, but until you know these conventions, it's probably safest to use the Insert Target Path dialog box.

Summary

This chapter touched on the fundamental things you can do with actions. You have learned how an action can be placed in a keyframe to execute when that frame is reached and in instances of buttons to execute when the user clicks. You have learned that the exact mouse event to which you want to respond needs to be specified. You have also learned how actions can be placed inside movie clip events attached to instances of movie clips.

Not only have you learned where actions go, but you have learned that many actions require further specification in the form of parameters. If you understand this simple concept, you'll be able to apply that knowledge to almost any action you encounter because most actions require parameters. This chapter just scratches the surface of how to use actions, but hopefully the concepts covered make sense to you because the same structure and terms apply to all kinds of scripting in Flash.

CHAPTER 45

Publishing Your Movie

The final step in any Flash production is publishing. The Publish feature can do many things. In addition to exporting a .swf file and the corresponding HTML file, you can use Publish to export other media types, such as QuickTime, plus traditional formats, such as GIF and JPG. All these formats will be discussed in this chapter.

How to Publish

Publishing is as easy as selecting File, Publish. In practice, however, you'll want to first save your files in a known folder and then step through all the publishing settings. You might even want to use Publish Preview to both publish and immediately see the results. The following exercise steps you through a scenario using Publish:

1. Either open a movie you've created in the past or create a simple animation. Make sure there's some visual change; for example, a movie clip might tween across the screen.

2. Select File, Save As and save this file in a new folder that contains no other files.

3. Select File, Publish Settings. The Publish Settings dialog box appears. Note that any changes you make in the Publish Settings dialog box will be saved with this file. However, you can save your settings as a profile that becomes available to other files.

4. Select the Formats tab of the Publish Settings dialog box so you can specify which formats will be exported. For every format you select, an additional tab will appear (see Figure 45.1). The options in this dialog box will be covered in depth later in this chapter. For now, select Flash, and HTML. Notice that each file has the same name as your source file (with a different extension). You can override this setting, but leaving it is probably easiest—you can always rename files on your hard drive before you upload them. (Clicking Use Default Names restores any changes you make to the filenames.)

FIGURE 45.1
The Formats tab of the Publish Settings dialog box allows you to specify which file formats you plan to export.

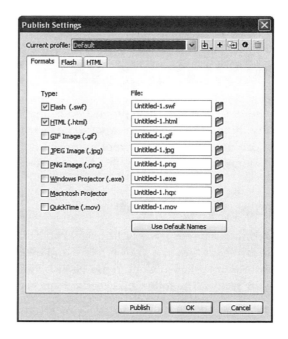

5. Click the Flash tab and take a quick look at the Version option. Determining which setting to choose for this option is subjective. For this exercise, suppose you want your movie to work for users who have the Flash Player 6 plug-in or later. Change the Version drop-down list's setting to Flash Player 6, as shown in Figure 45.2.

By the Way

Using V2 Components

If you're using any of the V2 components, you'll need to publish using Flash version 6 or 7. And if you publish as version 6, you'll also have to select the option ActionScript version 2.0.

6. Click the HTML tab. Here you can make some adjustments to the HTML that Flash will create. From the Template drop-down list, select Flash Only. Next, click the Settings button, and you see that this template will actually produce three HTML documents: the detection file (that is, the default that everyone visits first), the content file (for the users with the Flash Player), and the alternate file (where those without Flash will be directed). The idea is that everyone will first visit the detection file where—if Flash is

detected—the user gets redirected to the content file; otherwise, the user gets directed to the alternate file. You can either keep the alternate file that Macromedia produces (which includes a link to let the user upgrade) or replace it with your own HTML file.

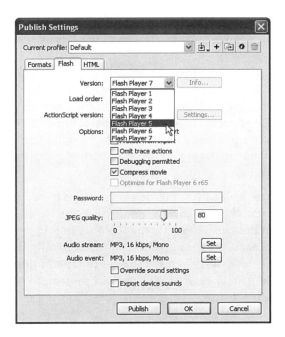

FIGURE 45.2
You can ensure that your movie will work with older versions of the Flash Player by changing the Version setting in the Flash tab.

7. Set the Dimensions option to Percent and then type **100** in both the Width and Height fields so the movie will entirely fill the browser window. You can come back later and make changes to any of these settings. For now, just make sure the check boxes Loop and Display Menu are unchecked. (Unchecking Display Menu prevents users from seeing the extended options when right-clicking your movie.)

8. When you've gone through both tabs (for the two formats you selected), click OK. The publish settings are saved. Select File, Publish. It might not seem like anything happens, but all your files are exported into the folder where the source file resides. Go into that folder and double-click the HTML file that matches your movie's name (that is, the detection file). If you have the Flash 6 plug-in (or later), you'll be redirected to the file that plays your movie. To see what users without Flash will see, launch `alternate.html`.

By the Way

Using Off-Limits Features

If you are using a Flash Player 7–only feature (that is, Flash MX 2004) and you attempt to publish to an earlier version of the Player, you'll see a message explaining the issue when you export the movie. For example, if you plan to export Flash Player 5 movies, remember to always change the publishing settings (under the Flash tab) to Flash 5 before you start. This way, all the newer features that are off limits to the older version are highlighted yellow in the Actions panel, and you'll know which features to avoid.

Compared to using Test Movie, the preceding exercise was a lot of work. Realize, though, that when using the method described in this exercise, you get to step through each detail and decide how it should be published. By the way, selecting File, Publish Preview (or pressing F12) is the same as using File, Publish, except that immediately following the export process your default browser is launched with the HTML file.

The preceding exercise walked you through each tab of the Publish Settings dialog box, and you made changes as you went. This is the typical approach. Although you might not choose exactly the same settings in real life as you did in the exercise, the process is the same. After a few more details about this particular exercise, you'll take a look at the rest of the options later in this chapter. The point is that this was just an exercise. The options chosen are not necessarily the ones you'll always want to use.

By the Way

Testing All Player Versions

In order to see what users with older Flash Player versions will experience, you need to uninstall the Flash Player. Macromedia has two TechNotes that describe the process of uninstalling the player. At www.macromedia.com, simply search for either TechNote article number 12727 or 14157 by typing these numbers into the search field at www.macromedia.com.

There are other templates available in the HTML tab. These correspond to files installed in the HTML folder inside the Configuration folder. You can add to these templates by making your own templates or downloading others. It takes some knowledge of HTML, but instructions are available in the help file "Using Flash," where you'll find "Publishing" and then a subsection titled "Customizing HTML Publishing Templates."

You can make minor adjustments to the built-in templates rather easily, as shown in the following example:

1. Find the First Run folder adjacent to your installed copy of Flash 2004 (in a subfolder called en, for English). Inside the HTML folder you'll find the templates used by the Publish Settings dialog box. The default location in Windows is C:\Program Files\Macromedia\Flash 2004\en\First Run\HTML.

2. Start by creating a movie that includes an animation of a clip instance of a box moving from the top-left corner of the Stage to the bottom-left corner. Use the Align panel's To Stage option or the Info panel to align the box to the edge of the Stage in both keyframes.

3. Select File, Publish Settings and choose both HTML and Flash. From the HTML tab, select the template Flash Only. (Leave Detect Flash Version unchecked.) Click OK.

4. Press F12 to use Publish Preview. Notice that the square doesn't actually reach the left edge of your browser.

5. Close the browser. Save the movie and then close Flash. Find the file called Default.html inside the HTML configuration folder (identified in step 1) and copy and paste it.

6. Rename the copied file myDefault.html and then open it in a text editor such as Notepad.

7. Change the very first line from this:

   ```
   $TTFlash Only (Default)
   ```

   to this:

   ```
   $TTNo Padding
   ```

   This changes the template name to No Padding. You can name it whatever you want; just be sure to retain the first three characters, $TT, when you do the renaming.

8. Change the part in the 12th line from this:

   ```
   <BODY bgcolor="$BG">
   ```

   to this:

   ```
   <BODY bgcolor="$BG" topmargin="0" leftmargin="0"
   marginwidth="0" marginheight="0">
   ```

   This changes all the margins to 0 pixels wide.

9. Save and close this file. Restart Flash and open the movie you created earlier in this exercise.

10. Select File, Publish Settings. From the Template drop-down list on the HTML tab select the template you just created: No Padding. Click OK.

11. Press F12, and you should see a preview—this time, with no padding around the movie.

You can make more significant changes to the templates than shown in the preceding exercise. In addition, there are many other places where Flash allows customization to the Actions panel and pre-installed templates through the First Run configuration folder. It's worth snooping through and reading the help files on this topic.

Using Named Anchor Frames

You can give your users a way to use their browser's back button while viewing your Flash movie using *named anchors*.

Say you place a tag in the middle of a Web page (by using the HTML <a name="midpoint">). You can then provide a link that jumps to that point (scrolls the page) by using the HTML <a href="#midpoint">. Also, you can navigate directly to that midpoint from another page by using the address index.html#midpoint, for example. There's not much more to this HTML feature than to show you how Flash can tap into it. Try the following exercise to make frame labels behave like HTML anchors:

1. In a new file, create keyframes at Frames 5, 10, and 15. Go to Frame 5 and draw a red blob on the Stage. Go to Frame 10 and draw something green. Then in Frame 15 draw something blue. Think of each color as a different section in your movie.

2. Successively select each keyframe and each label by using the Properties panel. Label them red, green, and blue, respectively. After naming each, select Anchor from the Label Type drop-down list.

3. Make a new layer that defaults to 15 frames long. Into the new layer, draw a rectangle that will become a button. Select the shape and convert it to a button symbol. Create two copies of the button instance and place them in the same layer.

4. Select just the first button instance and open the Actions panel. Type this code:

```
on(press){
 gotoAndStop("red");
}
```

5. Repeat step 4 with the other buttons, but change the part that reads "red" in the script to read "green" and "blue", respectively.

6. Select the first keyframe and type the following script:

   ```
   stop();
   ```

   Test the movie to confirm that the three buttons take the user to three different screens.

7. Take advantage of the Named Anchor feature by opening the Publish Settings dialog box and from the HTML tab select the template called Flash with Named Anchors. Use Publish Preview, and you should see that you can click the browser's Back button and even bookmark any colored section. Notice the browser's address bar changing, too.

The Named Anchor feature involves labeling keyframes with the Named Anchor option so that users can either bookmark or click the Back button to return to those keyframes. In your projects, you'll have to determine early on which frames are "anchor-worthy"—that is, which ones break up the content logically or might be worth bookmarking. If you want a more advanced implementation of capturing the browser's Back button, you should read how the LocalConnection object was employed in the Pet Market blueprint application. You can find the article by typing **pet market localConnection** in the search field at www.macromedia.com.

Deciding Which Media Types to Publish

Comparing the different media types available in the Publish Settings dialog box's Formats tab is really a case of comparing apples to oranges. You can export a JPG image or you can export a QuickTime movie. The former is a static image, and the latter is a digital video. This encompasses quite a range of options, making a comparison difficult. The only two media types comparable to GIF are JPG and PNG because they are both static image types. Therefore, instead of comparing the media types, the following sections cover each individually.

Publishing Flash (.swf) Files

.swf is the format you'll likely choose every time. It's the reason you're reading this book—to make scalable vector animations that play well over the Internet. If there's one disadvantage to using this option, it would be the fact that a few potential users don't have the required (but free) Flash Player.

You'll find some interesting options in the Flash tab (see Figure 45.3) of the Publish Settings dialog box:

FIGURE 45.3
The Flash tab of
the Publish
Settings dialog box
contains all the
export settings for
the .swf file you're
publishing.

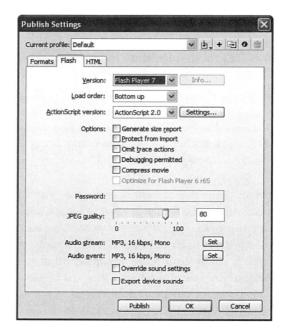

▶ Load Order affects in what order the layers appear as the movie downloads. Bottom Up, for example, causes the lower layers to become visible first. In reality, many users won't notice a difference with different load orders because they affect just the first frame and becomes apparent only on slow connections.

▶ Generate Size Report exports a text file that contains the same information you learn when using the Bandwidth Profiler. When you're testing a movie that includes the Trace action the output window appears with a message parameter that you provide. Omitting Trace actions won't make any difference if you play the movie in a Web browser because Trace has no effect in a browser. The output window will only pop up while you're authoring, so, really, this is more of an authoring preference than a publishing setting.

▶ The Protect from Import option prevents others from importing the .swf file into their own Flash files. Keep in mind that the .swf file you post on your Web site does download to every user's machine (in a folder such as Temporary Internet Files in the Windows folder, for example). In my opinion, the Protect from Import option has limited value. First, when someone imports a `.swf` file, each frame is imported as a separate keyframe. No ActionScript is retained. Second, just because some users import your file doesn't mean they're allowed to use it. Realize, too, that your `.swf` is by no means hack-proof. Sensitive data such as passwords should never reside in a movie.

▶ The Compress Movie option is a no-brainer: You should always leave it checked. This compression/decompression routine was added to Flash to reduce the file size of `.swf` files. It has nothing to do with the quality settings on your raster graphics or sounds. Basically, everything else, including your scripts, can be compressed (and then seamlessly decompressed on the user's machine). The Compress Movie option is available only when you publish as Flash 6 or later because older Flash players can't decompress these movies.

The default compression for the raster graphics and audio can be globally specified in the Flash tab of the Publish Settings dialog box. You can override compression settings made for individual sounds if you check the Override Sound Settings option.

Finally, unlike most publishing settings, which are chosen as the last step, the choice of which version of Flash to export is one you should make early in a project. First of all, you can export Flash version 7, and your movie might play fine in the Flash 6 player; however, any new (previously unsupported) features will fail to execute and lead to unpredictable results. If you're not taking advantage of any Flash 7–only features, your movie will play fine. If you change this setting to, say, Flash 5 and simply use Test Movie, you'll see a report of any unsupported features you've included. This feature is nice because it enables you to fix these problems. However, instead of fixing problems after they're created, you can set the Flash Version option as the first step in a project. This way, as you build, all the unsupported actions will appear in yellow.

Publishing HTML Files

Although the HTML tab of the Publish Settings dialog box has been discussed several times already, there's additional information in it that you'll find valuable (see Figure 45.4). First, realize that every setting in this tab (except for Device Fonts) affects only the HTML file. You can always open the HTML file in a text editor and make edits manually. If nothing else, the Publish Settings dialog box gives you a way to learn all the HTML settings that are available. To learn them, all you need to do is look at the corresponding HTML files created.

FIGURE 45.4
The HTML tab of
the Publish
Settings dialog box
contains a number
of options, includ-
ing which HTML
template you want
to use.

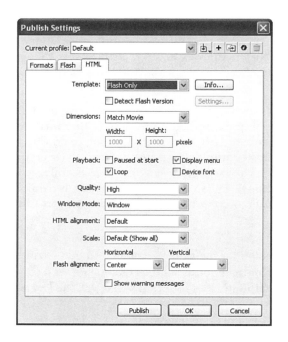

Normally, users can right-click your movie to display a menu like the one shown in Figure 45.5 (on the Macintosh, they would use Control+click). Only a mini-mized version of this menu will appear for users if you deselect Display Menu in the Playback section of the HTML tab. The menu isn't actually removed; it's just a lot shorter than usual. Keep in mind that the Debugger line appears only for users who happen to have Flash installed.

FIGURE 45.5
The menu that
appears when a
user right-clicks
your movie, as
shown on the left,
can be reduced to
the version on the
right.

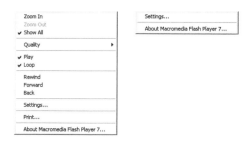

The Windows Mode setting applies only to movies viewed in Windows and through Internet Explorer version 4 or later. Although this applies to a large audience, it is limited. Also, the other settings in this drop-down list—Opaque Windowless and Transparent Windowless—affect only HTML pages that have elements in layers. As if this weren't enough, the performance drops for these options. Feel free to explore these options, but I recommend leaving the default, Window.

Publishing GIF, JPG, and PNG Files

JPG and PNG are both static image formats. GIF has a sister format called *animated GIF* that is, in fact, an animation format. All three of these formats have their own unique attributes. GIF files always have 256 or fewer discrete colors and tend to be most appropriate for geometric images. JPG is best for photographic or continuous-tone images. JPG can also withstand significant compression with acceptable quality loss. PNG is a high-quality image format that allows for additional types of information to be included. For example, a PNG file created in Macromedia Fireworks has additional options, such as layers and shadow effects. Despite some discussion in the past, PNG hasn't become a Web standard. However, when you want to export the best-quality image, PNG is a good choice—just don't expect a small file size.

When it comes to Web delivery, your decision for static images is between JPG and GIF. Realize that the question about which static format to use arises only when you attempt to deliver an alternative image to users who don't have the Flash Player. For example, every Flash project I've worked on has provided no alternative. The users need the Flash Player; otherwise, they can't see the site—it's that simple.

When you want to provide an alternative to users who don't have the Flash Player (as you did in the first exercise), you need to decide between JPG and GIF. This decision is based on the nature of the image. Remember, though, that it's not the whole movie that's used; it's only one frame of the movie that you get to use for such static formats. Flash will, by default, use the first frame of your movie for any static image format. The movie's first frame, though, could be entirely black. In order to specify a different frame, you simply open the Frame panel and create a label in the chosen frame called #static. It's best to insert a new layer and then a keyframe exactly where you want this label, as shown in Figure 45.6, but this is a relatively simple way to tell Flash which frame to export.

After you decide which frame to use, you can decide (based on the contents of that frame) which format to use—GIF or JPG. Remember, photorealistic images are best in JPG format, and geometric shapes are best in GIF format.

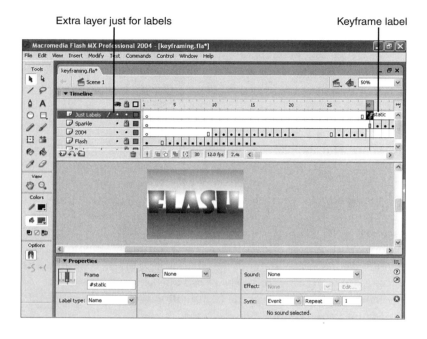

Extra layer just for labels

Keyframe label

FIGURE 45.6
Labeling a frame with #static tells Flash you want this frame to be used (instead of Frame 1) when publishing a static image.

PNG might seem like a useless format because the files are large and browsers don't really support them, but there is some value. Of course PNG is a great image format to import, but here we're talking about exporting. If you want to export the highest quality possible, you should use PNG. There might be several reasons to do this. For instance, even though the options available for exporting a GIF file from Flash are extensive, previewing the effects of every slight change is a tedious process of trial and error. You have to make a change, publish, and then view the results. Frankly, there are better tools for creating GIF files (as well as JPG files, although this is not quite as obvious). Macromedia Fireworks, for example, lets you change all the output options for a GIF file while watching the image quality change (see Figure 45.7). This fact alone might make the extra steps you're about to learn worth the effort. For the most control over the GIF file you're creating, first use Flash to export a 24-bit PNG file (the export options for PNG are shown in Figure 45.8). Then open that PNG file in another image-editing tool (such as Fireworks) and export the GIF file. You can still use Flash's Publish feature to create the GIF and HTML files—but you simply replace the GIF file Flash creates with one you create using a more suitable tool.

Preview of the exported image

JPG compression settings

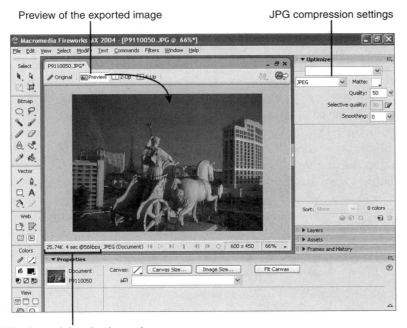

FIGURE 45.7
Fireworks is a much better tool than Flash for creating static graphics (such as GIFs).

File size and download speed

FIGURE 45.8
Exporting a PNG file gives you the best-quality static image.

The choice between JPG and GIF might be moot if you want to supply animation to users who don't have the Flash Player. Only GIF has the Animated Playback option (see Figure 45.9). You have several options when creating an animated GIF. Most are self-explanatory. You won't notice, however, an option to specify the first and last frames—Flash will simply use the first and last frames of your movie. To override this, just label the frame you want to be used first as `#first` and the last frame as `#last`. Also, recall from a previous exercise that you can let Flash create the HTML image map to be used with your static (or animated) GIF. Flash will create that image map (with all the clickable areas) based on all the buttons that happen to be onscreen in the last frame of your movie. However, you might not have any buttons in the last frame. Just as you can specify which frame is used for static images, you can specify for which frame you want the onscreen buttons to be used in the creation of the image map. Simply label the frame `#map`. That's it.

FIGURE 45.9
Of all the traditionally static image formats, only GIF provides the Animated option.

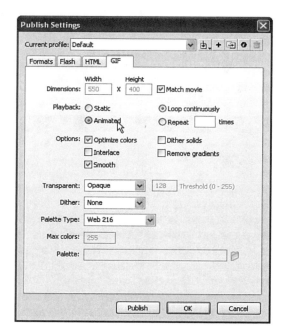

Projectors

If you put your `.swf` file in a Web page, users just need the Flash Player to view it. When you installed Flash, it installed the Flash Player, so you can simply double-click any `.swf` file on your computer and it will run. If you want to send this file to someone (that is, you don't want to publish it in a Web page), you can. The only catch is that the user has to have the Flash Player installed.

Alternatively, you can create a projector, which is a standalone executable. Think of a projector as a modified version of the Flash Player that will play only the .swf file you specify. One way to make a standalone projector is to open a .swf file with the Flash Player (just double-click a .swf file on your computer). Select File, Create a Projector and then name the file you would like to create. That's all there is to it. One catch is that your .swf file grows by nearly 1MB when you convert it to a projector. That's the size of the Flash Player (which you're including in the projector). The other catch is that the projector you just made will run only on the platform you're using (Windows or Macintosh). .swf files work on any platform because the user already has the Flash Player unique to that platform installed. Because projectors have the platform-specific player built in, they can be played only on that platform.

To create a projector for whichever platform you're not using—Windows or Macintosh—you could repeat the steps just listed on a computer using the target platform. However, you don't have to do this. From the Formats tab of the Publish Settings dialog box, you can specify for which platforms you want the projector made (see Figure 45.10). The projector file that Flash creates can be sent to whomever you want. If you're sending a file from Windows to Macintosh, Flash saves the projector in a compressed and "bin-hexed" format. Bin-hexing is necessary to allow you to send the file to a Macintosh computer via email (or another method). The Macintosh user must decode the bin-hexed file by using software such as Aladdin System's freeware StuffIt Expander for Mac (available at www.aladdinsys.com).

Projectors provide a nice way to use Flash for standalone applications. For example, you might be making a presentation to an audience and want to use Flash to create the "slides." Obviously, you can add a lot of spice to your presentations. The action fscommand is designed for this purpose. The parameters for fscommand include fullscreen, quit, and many others. For example, you can put the action fscommand ("fullscreen", "true") in the very first frame to make your projector fill the screen. Then, in the last frame, you can place a button with the action fscommand ("quit") as a way to exit.

The fscommand action includes options to affect standalone projectors.

Although it is more difficult to distribute projectors than simply posting to a Web site, projectors work great for presentations. A lot of people create portfolios of their work that they distribute via CD-ROM. They can include lots of uncompressed audio and high-quality images, for example, and there are no download issues. Just remember that if you use the `fullscreen` option of `fscommand`, you need to give your users an obvious Quit button, too.

FIGURE 45.10
Standalone projectors can be exported when you publish for both Macintosh and Windows.

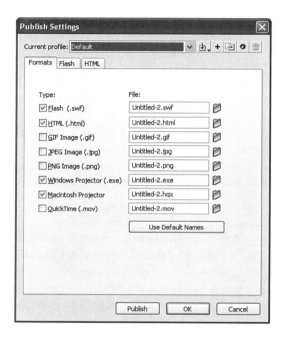

By the Way

Better Projectors

If you're using a lot of projectors or just want some added features, you really ought to check out the various third-party projector-making tools available. You can add really powerful features above what Flash can do by itself.

QuickTime

You can export a QuickTime video that includes Flash. The Publish Settings QuickTime option lets you create a QuickTime video (that requires the QuickTime player).

Although it's kind of cool how you can add a Flash "layer" (including interactivity) to a QuickTime video, the fact is, Flash video has improved so much that there's little reason to do so. In my opinion, the main reason to export a

QuickTime video is when you produce a Flash movie that doesn't perform well on lower-end machines. Exporting a QuickTime video puts your presentation in a form that's more likely to play consistently than a straight .swf.

To create a QuickTime with a Flash layer, all you do is create a linear animation in the main Timeline and then select the QuickTime tab when publishing. There are a few more settings you can specify, as shown in Figure 45.11, but most of them are self-explanatory. Just remember that you're exporting a QuickTime video with a Flash layer, not a Flash movie (as you've done in almost every other exercise in this section).

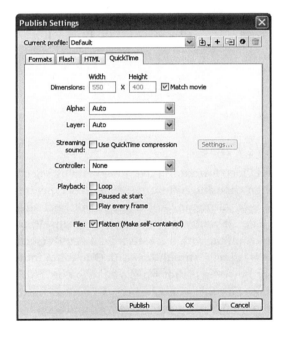

FIGURE 45.11
The QuickTime tab of the Publish Settings dialog box provides many details to control an exported QuickTime video.

Exporting Other Media Types

Believe it or not, Flash can export even more media types than those listed in the Publish Settings dialog box. Just select File, Export, Export Movie, and you'll see a list under the Save as Type drop-down list that's quite long (see Figure 45.12). In addition to the formats listed in the Publish Settings dialog box, you might see others that interest you. The following sections cover two formats you might find particularly useful: AVI and image sequences.

FIGURE 45.12
All the formats
Flash can export
(including those
found in the
Publish Settings
dialog box) are list-
ed in the Export
Movie dialog box.

Publishing AVI Files

AVI is another digital video format. It's available only by selecting File, Export, Export Movie and then choosing AVI from the Save as Type drop-down list in the Export Movie dialog box. Although QuickTime has distinct advantages over AVI (the Flash track, for one), if you want, you can export an AVI file from Flash. To do so, you need to be familiar with a few technical details (such as compression), but the overall process is pretty straightforward. One thing that's important to realize from the start, however, is that when you're exporting an AVI, movie clips won't play. You can use Graphic symbols only. (Of course, buttons and actions don't work either because AVI is a noninteractive animation format.)

Publishing Image Sequences

Image Sequences is another option that is available only in the Export Movie dialog box. A bitmap sequence, for example, will export a static BMP file of each frame in your movie. Several sequence formats are available (refer to Figure 45.12). They're all basically the same—only the file format varies. The process is the same for each format. You select File, Export, Export Movie, select the file format from the Export Movie dialog box, and then name the file. The name you give will be used only as the prefix. For example, if you name the file myMovie, the filename containing Frame 1 will be called myMovie0001.bmp (or whatever file extension matches the type you're exporting). After you name the file and click Save, you'll be shown a dialog box in which you can specify the details for the selected file type. It's sort of a mini version of the Publish tab. For bitmap sequences, you have to specify details for bitmaps, for example.

You might be intending to create an animation in another software package that can import sequences of static images. For example, if you have an animated GIF-creation tool, you could import a sequence of high-quality bitmaps that Flash exported. You could also use the static images from a QuickTime video inside Flash. Because you can't actually use QuickTime video in a .swf file, you could first import a QuickTime video into Flash, export a sequence of high-quality BMP files, and then delete the QuickTime video from your Flash file and import the BMP files into Flash. What's really convenient is that the numbered BMP files that Flash created upon export will be imported sequentially and placed in separate keyframes, thus saving you what would otherwise be a painstaking task of importing many individual frames.

Similarly to exporting AVI files, when you export image sequences, you can't use movie clips (they just don't animate). Obviously, audio won't have any effect either because you're exporting images only. This might seem like the least likely use for Flash; however, you should realize that any time you see something that *looks* like video in Flash, you're probably just watching a sequence of static images.

Summary

This chapter discussed all the common ways to export Flash movies and wrapped up our look at the Macromedia Flash application. Other, less traditional, applications, such as using projectors, static images, QuickTime video, and image sequences, were also discussed.

For the traditional .swf in HTML option, Publish gives you a nice interface to select options; then Flash actually creates the files for you. Templates can include code to optionally supply users with an alternative image. Also, other options in the Publish Settings dialog box let you specify how such an image will be exported.

Less-traditional applications, such as using projectors and QuickTime video, can give your Flash movies a life beyond the normal Web page application. Some of these technologies are on the edge of innovation, and now you have a better idea where you can take Flash!

PART IV
FreeHand

CHAPTER 46

Understanding the FreeHand Interface

Finally, we reach the last application within the Macromedia Studio MX 2004 application suite—FreeHand MX. FreeHand is an illustration tool much like Adobe Illustrator. Unlike the Fireworks and Flash applications you've already seen, FreeHand is a pure illustration tool. Although it can do simple animation and create graphics for the Web, FreeHand MX is the application you should turn to when you simply want to draw—whatever the output medium.

The FreeHand Interface

If you've read the rest of the chapters, you've probably become accustomed to the structure of the information presented about each product—first the interface is presented, followed by a discussion of the basic tools, then coverage of the application use. We'll follow the same pattern here, but with a minor difference—because many of these tools have already been covered in the Flash and Fireworks products, we'll focus mainly on where FreeHand MX differs from the other studio applications. Trying to fit a product suite like Studio 2004 into an 800-page tome is a bit of a feat, so we've tried to keep the redundant information to a minimum. But, I digress—on with the introduction.

The FreeHand interface is divided into five primary areas of interest, as shown in Figure 46.1.

Document—The Document area contains your active drawing. This is where you'll create your masterpieces and do most of your interacting with FreeHand.

Tools—The Tools panel provides access to the tools you'll use to create your images, such as lines, pens, and so on.

Properties Inspector—The Properties Inspector enables you to quickly adjust attributes of a selected object (such as color, pen size, and so on).

Panel Groups—Even though the Properties Inspector and Tools panels are panels, they are not part of the default Panel groups. Many additional tools and settings are located in the Panel Groups on the right side of the display.

Menus—The FreeHand MX menu is an alternative means of accessing most of the same properties as the Properties Inspector.

FIGURE 46.1
The FreeHand interface is divided into five working areas that you should become familiar with—menu, Tools, Document, Properties Inspector, and Panel Groups.

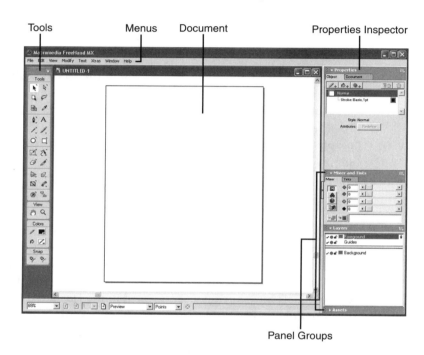

Tools   Menus   Document   Properties Inspector

Panel Groups

If you haven't discovered by now, the Studio 2004 applications provide multiple means of accessing the same features. This is a blessing for the user, who can find the most comfortable techniques for her computing style, but it's a logistics nightmare for those who try to describe the product. We've done the best we can to cover what seems natural to us, but you might find shortcuts that aren't covered here.

The Document Window

The Document window provides your workspace for illustration. To create a new document select File, New. A new window appears, as shown in Figure 46.2.

FIGURE 46.2
An empty
Document window.

Within the Document window is a visual representation of a page. The area out-side the page is called the *pasteboard*. The pasteboard, although saved as part of your document, is not included when you output the file to the printer.

Grids and Rulers

To supplement the Document window, you can add rulers by selecting View, Page Rulers, Show.

To change the units of the ruler use the units pop-up menu at the bottom of the Document window.

Did you Know?

You can also add two types of grids to the window—normal and perspective—by selecting View, Grid, Show and View, Perspective Grid, Show, respectively. Both of these grid types are active in Figure 46.3.

To force objects that you add to the document to snap to the normal grid, select View, Grid, Snap to Grid. This helps you align shapes without having to drag with pixel-point accuracy. If you want additional control over snap-to positions, you can add guides to the window.

You can edit the two types of grids by selecting View, Grid, Edit for normal grids and View, Perspective Grid, Define Grids for perspective grids.

Did you Know?

FIGURE 46.3
Add grids to your
document to aid
your illustration.

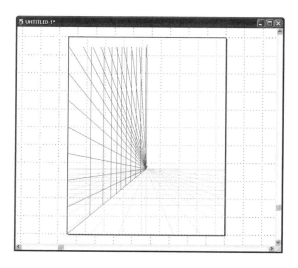

Guides

A *guide* is a user-defined horizontal or vertical line that can be used to help align objects. To add a guide to the Document window, click and drag from inside either the horizontal or vertical rulers. A blue line is added as you draw across the window.

By the Way

> If you don't see the line in the Document window after you release your mouse, be sure that View, Guides, Show is selected in your menus.

Subsequent objects you add to the document (we'll get to actual drawing in the next chapter, don't worry!) snap to the guides if View, Guides, Snap to Guides is selected.

You can drag guides to reposition them or drag them out of the page to remove them completely. If you want to add multiple guides in a grid (or partial grid) style layout, select View, Guides, Edit and then click the Add button and pick how you would like the guides laid out in the document.

Info Toolbar

To aid in your use of the document, you can add the Info toolbar to your work-space. Select Window, Toolbars, Info to add the toolbar shown in Figure 46.4.

FIGURE 46.4
The Info toolbar
helps locate your
position within a
design.

The Info toolbar displays the location of your cursor, the size of an object as you draw it, and the currently selected object, if any.

Window Status Bar Controls

Along the bottom of the Document window are four status bar controls. These can be used to change the following settings:

Magnification—To zoom in and out of the Document window, use the magnification setting at the bottom of the Document window; the magnification option from the View menu; or, finally, the Zoom tool in the Tools panel, which we'll discuss shortly.

Current Page—Jump between the different pages in a document. See Chapter 50, "Advanced Drawing Tools and Techniques," for information on creating multiple pages in FreeHand.

Display Mode—Select between four modes of decreasing detail. The Preview modes come closest to the printed page, whereas the Keyline modes do not show fills, but are much faster. If FreeHand seems sluggish on your system, you might want to adjust these settings.

Units of Measure—Select which unit sizes are displayed in—inches, points, picas, and so on.

Tools

The FreeHand Tool panel, shown in Figure 46.5, is the source for everything you'll be using to create your images. Because you've already seen almost all these tools in Fireworks and Flash, let's just review them quickly—going from left to right, top to bottom:

Pointer—Used to select individual objects or draw a selection rectangle.

Subselect—Selects individual objects in a group or points within a path.

Page—Used to select, move, and resize pages within the pasteboard.

Lasso—Selects non-rectangular areas.

FIGURE 46.5
The FreeHand tools
are similar to those
in Flash and
Fireworks.

Output Area—Defines an area of a page that will be used for printing or exporting.

Eyedropper—Quickly chooses a color by clicking an existing color within the document.

Pen/Bezigon—Both of these tools draw by defining points in a path, although in a slightly different manner.

Text—Adds text to the design.

Line/Spiral/Arc—Simple tools for drawing lines, spirals, and, you guessed it, arcs.

Pencil/Variable Stroke Pen/Calligraphic Pen—Artistic tools for free-style drawing.

Ellipse—Creates ellipses (circles and ovals).

Rectangle/Polygon—Draws simple rectangular shapes and other polygons.

Transform Tools—The transform tool collection is used to scale, rotate, and otherwise alter the appearance of onscreen objects.

Freeform/Roughen/Bend—Used to nudge, jagged-ize, and bend existing paths for special effects.

Eraser—Erases parts of active paths.

Knife—Cuts a single path segment into one or more parts.

Perspective/3D Rotation/Fisheye—Used to modify the perspective grid, perform 3D rotation of a selected object, or create fisheye effects over a region of the page.

Extrude/Smudge/Shadow—The Extrude tool creates a 3D shape by stretching a path. Smudge adds a gradient 3D extrusion effect, whereas Shadow simply creates a drop shadow.

Trace—Traces a bitmap to convert it into a scalable vector path.

Blend/Mirror/Hose/Chart—The blend tool "morphs" one shape into another. Mirror mirrors a selection, and Hose "draws" using a stream of shapes. Finally, Chart is used to create simple pie, bar, line, charts and so on.

Action—Assigns Flash actions to an object.

Connector—Used primarily for creating flowcharts, connector lines "connect" two or more objects and stretch automatically as the objects are repositioned.

Hand—Repositions the viewing area in the Document window.

Zoom—Zooms in on the document. Hold down Alt or Option (Mac) to zoom out.

Stroke Color—Sets the color of the strokes (lines) in a drawing.

Fill Color—Sets the fill color for filled shapes.

Snap to Point—Snaps objects as they are dragged to points in other objects.

Snap to Object—Snaps objects to other objects as they are being dragged.

Panels and Panel Groups

As with the other Studio MX applications, FreeHand provides access to the majority of its features by way of panels that are, by default, located along the right side of the screen in Panel Groups. The default Panel Groups are arranged by function, but you can rearrange panels to your liking using the Panel Group pop-up menu located in the upper right of each Panel Group—see Chapter 1, "Understanding the Dreamweaver and Macromedia Studio Interface," for more information on working with panels within the Dreamweaver MX product.

Properties Panel Group: Object/Document Panels

Unlike the other Studio MX 2004 applications, FreeHand does not have a single Properties panel, but a Properties panel group that includes an Object panel with properties for the current object, such as stroke width, color, fill, effects, and so on. The Object properties panel is shown in Figure 46.6. You'll use the Object panel frequently as you design in FreeHand MX.

FIGURE 46.6
The Object proper-
ties differ slightly
from other Studio
MX applications.

The second panel in the Properties panel group is the Document panel. In this panel, you can alter the print resolution, page layout, and add pages through the panel group pop-up menu.

Other Panels

The Properties panels are used to perform general functions that affect a wide variety of settings. FreeHand contains a number of other action-specific panels that have far more specialized uses. Some you'll use frequently; others you might never touch.

Although we'll be looking closely at the available FreeHand panels throughout the next few chapters, this is a brief summary of which tools are available and their purposes:

Answers—FreeHand MX help. The Answers panel has been removed from the other Studio MX 2004 tools and will probably disappear in future versions of FreeHand.

Layers—Used to manage multiple composition layers in FreeHand. Layers can contain different portions of your designs that you composite over one another—such as foreground over background or even individual objects within the foreground.

Swatches—Color swatches you've saved for future use.

Styles—A collection of graphic styles used in your document. Using the Styles panel, you can create styles that are applied to multiple objects repeatedly in your document.

Library—The Library stores symbols (groups of objects) and master pages for easy reuse throughout a document.

Color Mixer—Simply put, the Color Mixer mixes colors for use when drawing.

Tints—Creates lighter versions of a color based on a percentage of the original color. 100% is the original color, whereas 0% is white.

Halftones—Applies object-specific halftone settings to a document. Normally, a default halftone style is applied to the document when printing to PostScript; the Halftones panel can override this default.

Align—Aligns objects in the design based on their edges, centers, and so on.

Transform—You can easily access the functions for rotating, skewing, scaling, and otherwise altering your design objects.

Navigation—Used to attach URLs to objects. If the design is exported to a Flash, a PDF, or an HTML document, these are automatically converted to links in the output file.

Did you Know?

The Answers panel was deemed redundant and confusing by Macromedia and was removed from all the 2004 MX applications. It is still visible in FreeHand, but your best bet for finding help is the FreeHand MX Help, located under the Help menu.

FreeHand Menus

The FreeHand MX menus are largely self-explanatory. Use the File menu to create new documents, open existing files, and save and export the active document in a variety of formats. The Edit menu is used for the standard cut, copy, paste, duplicate, and find/replace operations. With the Modify menu, you can apply changes to the selected object. The Text menu can help control font and other style information when adding text to a page, and Xtras contains extensions to the FreeHand application that help simplify complex operations. Finally, the Window menu is used to open any of the available panels or toolbars if they are not visible onscreen.

Did you
Know?

Many of the common FreeHand menu functions can be accessed through toolbars that can be added to your workspace. Use Window, Toolbars to add basic file operations (Main), text functions (Text), and so on. Earlier you saw the Info toolbar, which shows simple location information as you use your cursor onscreen.

Summary

The FreeHand MX environment is similar to the rest of the Studio MX 2004 applications. Although FreeHand hasn't yet been updated to a "2004" designation, you can still find your way around the application without any problem. FreeHand's main interface features are the Document window, Tool panel, Properties panel group, and other various action-specific panels. Now that you know the names and basic purposes of the tools, let's put them to use in Chapter 47, "Working with Pages and Basic Objects."

CHAPTER 47

Working with Pages and Basic Objects

Now that you know the basic tools in FreeHand MX, you can start to design your own documents. Similar to Flash and Fireworks, FreeHand's drawing tools are reasonably straightforward. This chapter guides you through the process of opening a new document and working with the basic FreeHand drawing tools so you can get started right away.

Working with Documents

Everything you will do in FreeHand takes place in a single FreeHand file with the extension .fha. FreeHand documents can have multiple pages, but unlike Dreamweaver Web sites, these pages are all stored within the single .fha file. To create a new document, select File, New. FreeHand displays a new document window, as shown in Figure 47.1.

By default, only a single page is created within the document. To add pages or change the size of the page you're on, you need to access the Document panel in the Properties panel group. Figure 47.2 displays the Document panel.

Page Properties

Use the pop-up menu beside the page orientation buttons to select a predefined page size—the default is Letter. Click the orientation buttons to choose between normal (left) and landscape modes. You can also define your own custom page sizes by typing the dimensions in the X and Y fields.

If the unit being used for page size doesn't look familiar, change your units using the pop-up menu at the bottom of your document window.

Did you Know?

FIGURE 47.1
Get started by cre-
ating a new docu-
ment.

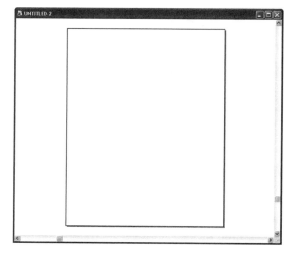

FIGURE 47.2
The Document
panel controls the
size of your page
and layout of multi-
ple pages (if you
have more than
one).

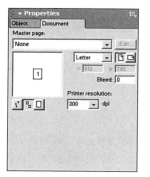

Adding and Working with Additional Pages

On the left side of the Document panel is a square area that represents an
overview of all the pages included in your document. On a single-page document,
you should see a tiny box inside the rectangle—that is your page! You can zoom
in and out of the pane overview using the three icon buttons below it. The button
on the far left zooms out the farthest, whereas the button on the right zooms in.

To add pages, select Add Pages from the panel group pop-up menu. You are
prompted for the number of pages to create and a page width and height. Again,
these can be chosen using a pop-up menu of common sizes or by manually entering a size.

After pages are added, they appear in the overview rectangle and can be dragged to change their positions in the document, as shown in Figure 47.3. Note that pages can be positioned anywhere along the edge of another page, but they cannot overlap. To jump to a page in the overview, double-click it.

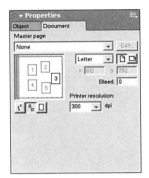

FIGURE 47.3
Additional pages are displayed in the document overview rectangle.

Pages can be removed and duplicated using the Remove and Duplicate options found under the panel group menu.

Using the Page Tool

To work with pages directly within the pasteboard (your workspace), you can use the Page tool (the second tool down on the left of your tool palette). To quickly access the tool, press D. You'll notice you can now click and drag pages directly in your window or click the corners to drag and resize the pages.

Master and Child Pages

As you work with the Document panel, you'll see references to master and child pages. A *master* page is simply a template, and a *child* is a page that inherits the properties of the master. To create a new master page, or convert an existing page into a master page, use the New Master Page or Convert to Master page option from the panel pop-up menu.

After a master is defined, you can use the pop-up menu at the top of the Document panel to choose between the various masters, or you can select None. Click the Edit button to open and edit the master page in a different window.

After a master page is defined, additional pages you create are considered child pages and inherit the objects you've added to the master. If there is a child page that you *don't* want to inherit the master's appearance, select Release Child Page from the panel group menu.

Using the Basic FreeHand Object Tools

With a document layout under control, you're ready to start using the FreeHand drawing tools. Don't worry—if you decide you want to add pages or modify the document layout later, you can access the Document panel at any time.

For most users, especially those familiar with Fireworks or Flash, the basic FreeHand drawing tools are simple to use. For each tool, we'll provide a brief description of its purpose and use. We're not going to spend pages and pages on how to draw a circle; we'll give you just what you need to get the job done.

Basic FreeHand Terminology

Before we get started a few pieces of terminology are important to grasp before moving forward. Many of these you might have seen or heard in other chapters, but if you've started reading here, you're going to be scratching your head.

First, FreeHand is a *vector* drawing program. This means that as you draw, FreeHand doesn't store information about each pixel that appears onscreen; it stores information about the shapes that are drawn on the screen. This enables you to resize images without loss of quality and output them to high-resolution devices (printers and so on) and take advantage of the full resolution of the device.

The objects FreeHand creates are defined by points and paths. A *point* is exactly what it sounds like—a point in the document to which "things" can connect. A *path* is the connection between two or more points. For example, a line is defined by two points with a path between them.

A vector object (such as rectangle) appears on your screen visually as a rectangle when you draw it in FreeHand. What you are seeing, however, are not the points and path: You are seeing a *stroke*. A stroke is like the stroke of a pen along the path that has been defined. Although shapes you draw in FreeHand have a default stroke, you can remove these strokes and have completely invisible objects. Alternatively, you could add multiple different strokes to a single object, which would have the effect of tracing along the paths with different style pens.

If that doesn't make complete sense, don't worry, it will. Just keep in mind that when you draw an object onscreen, you're really adding three things: points, a path, and a stroke.

Selection Tools

The selection tools—the pointer, Subselect, and Lasso—are ones you've seen and used repeatedly throughout the Macromedia suite. These are what you'll use to select objects in the pasteboard. The pointer selects whatever you click or can be used to click and drag a selection rectangle around multiple objects. Subselect is used to select individual points (you'll learn why you'd want to do this a little later), whereas Lasso can be used to draw an arbitrary selector around however many shapes you want to select.

If you've used a program (even the other Macromedia applications) that has a lasso tool, you'll notice a nice feature about the FreeHand Lasso. As you draw with it, it automatically closes itself. The Lasso tool always closes itself when you release the mouse button, but FreeHand shows you *where* it will close itself if you were to release the button at any time.

Lines, Spirals, and Arcs

The Line, Spiral, and Arc tools are accessed by selecting them from the pop-up menu in the Tool panel (the default is the Line tool). To draw with each tool, click and drag and then release the mouse button when the onscreen shape is the right size and in the right place.

The Spiral and Arc tools, besides resizing as you drag, also change their curve directions as you drag around the screen. Play around with these tools to get a feel for how they work. Figure 47.4 shows the Line tool on top, Arc in the middle, and Spiral on the bottom.

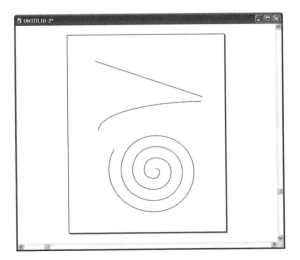

FIGURE 47.4
The Line, Spiral, and Arc tools draw lines, arcs, and spirals.

Hold down Shift to constrain the endpoints of each object to 45° increments.

To adjust a few properties for the Spiral and Arc tools, double-click these tools in the Tool panel. The Arc tool enables you to change whether the arc is open, concave, or convex. The Spiral settings provide more customization, such as the direction of rotation, whether to increment the space between spirals as the shape grows, and so on.

Ellipse

The Ellipse tool, located directly below the Line/Spiral/Arc tool is used to draw circles and ovals (ellipses). To draw one of these shapes, click where you'd like one corner to appear; then drag to size the object. To constrain the image to a perfect circle, click and drag while holding down the Shift key.

Figure 47.5 shows a document with several ellipses added.

FIGURE 47.5
The Ellipse tool in action.

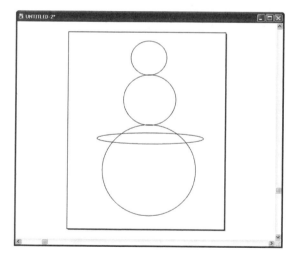

Rectangle/Polygon

Moving on, the Rectangle tool can be used to draw rectangles and squares, and the Polygon tool can draw any regular polygon. Much like the Ellipse tool, you can force the Rectangle tool to draw perfect squares by holding down Shift as you click and draw.

By default, the Polygon tool draws a hexagon. To change the shape, you must change the number of points used in the figure. Do this by adjusting the points value for the path in the Properties Inspector when the object is selected, or double-click the Polygon tool to display the polygon settings, as shown in Figure 47.6.

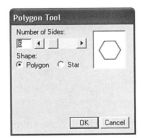

FIGURE 47.6
Alter the type of polygon being drawn.

Change the figure by changing the number of sides or choosing between polygon and star shapes.

Pencil/Variable Stroke Pen/Calligraphic Pen

The Pencil, Variable Stroke Pen, and Calligraphic Pen tools are all used to draw freeform shapes on your pages. The difference between these tools is the types of line they generate.

The Pencil tool draws simple lines, just like a pencil. The Variable Stroke Pen, on the other hand, works with a pressure-sensitive tablet to vary the width of lines as you draw on a page or press your number keys. Finally, the Calligraphic Pen draws using a long, thin pen tip, just like a calligraphic pen.

Each of the tools can be modified by double-clicking its tool panel icons when it's selected. The Pencil tool enables you to choose the precision (how much the line is smoothed as you draw) and whether it should be a dotted line.

The settings for the Variable Stroke Pen determine the minimum and maximum width for the lines that are drawn. Finally, the Calligraphic Pen lets you choose the width and the angle at which the pen is "held." If you set the pen width to Automatic, you can change the width just as you would with the Variable Stroke Pen or use a pressure-sensitive tablet. Figure 47.7 shows the results of using the Calligraphic Pen.

FIGURE 47.7
Use the Calligraphic Pen to create calligraphy-like effects.

Pen/Bezigon

The Pen and Bezigon tools are used to draw curved or straight paths. Unlike the pencil tools, these are not quite "freehand" tools, as you'll discover when you use them. The Pen is good for creating Bézier curve paths, whereas the Bezigon tool is easiest to use for straight line segments.

To use the Pen tool, click once where you'd like to start drawing. Now you can move your mouse to where you'd like the line to end, but here's where it gets tricky. If you want the line to be straight, click once to set a new "straight" point; if, on the other hand, you'd like to create a curved line between the two points, click and drag to set the second point and adjust the curve between your two points. Continue this process to draw your entire figure. Click a point you've already drawn or double-click to end the path.

The Bezigon tool is much easier to use; you just click once to get started and then click wherever you'd like to create a straight segment between two points. Continue using this technique to draw a sequence of straight line segments to draw your figure. Again, end the sequence by double-clicking or clicking an existing point in the figure.

For more information on using the Pen tool and editing Bézier curves, see the section "Editing Bézier Curves" in Chapter 24, "Working with Vector Paths."

Text

To add styled text to your document, click and drag to define a text area. A rectangle appears where you can type your text. Use the ruler to adjust tabs, and use the Text menu to change the attributes of the text you're adding. If you already have styled text in another application, you can simply copy and paste into FreeHand. Figure 47.8 displays the FreeHand text input system.

> If you don't like going to the menu to select text settings, you can access everything (size, justification, style, and so on) from the Object panel while inputting text.

Did you Know?

FIGURE 47.8
Edit text directly in FreeHand.

FreeHand sports many text styling tools along with a standalone editor and spell checker, all of which are accessible from the Text menu.

> For fine-tuning text spacing, kerning, and other attributes, use the Object panel.

Did you Know?

Connector

The final tool we'll look at in this chapter is the Connector. It is used to draw line segments that "connect" other objects. When the objects are moved in the pasteboard, the connectors are redrawn to maintain the connections between objects. This is a great tool for creating flowcharts. To use the Connector, click and drag from one object border to another.

By default, the connectors are drawn centered on any of the sides of an object. To change the connection location, select the Connector and use the offset settings in the Object panel to change the offset from the center.

Bitmaps

FreeHand doesn't really provide the bitmap editing features you've seen in Fireworks. That doesn't mean, however, that you can't add bitmaps to your document. To add a bitmap image, use File, Import to select an existing file, or simply copy and paste from another application. Your cursor appears as an *L* on its side; this marks the upper-left corner of the bitmap. Position your cursor where the image should appear and then click to add it to your design.

Did you Know?

> The Object panel can be used with a bitmap to view the alpha channels/transparency and to transfer the image into Fireworks for optimization.

When you add a bitmap to a FreeHand document, by default it is not stored in the document but is linked into it. This means that, if you remove the original file or need to send the file off for printing, you must include the bitmap source images as well. See Chapter 51, "Preparing for Web or Print," for more information on how FreeHand simplifies this process.

Basic Object Operations

After you've added objects to your document, you'll probably want to rearrange them, even delete or duplicate a few. To work with an object that has been added to your document, first use the selection tools to highlight it in your document.

After an object is selected, you can drag it to reposition it in the document. Use the Edit menu to copy, cut, paste, clear, or duplicate the selection. You can also alter highlighted objects themselves using the adjustment handles that appear when they are selected. Lines, for example, highlight and display adjustment handles on each end. You can click and drag these handles to change the size or position of the line. Remember that, because you're working with vector graphics (unless you happen to have added a bitmap), resizing an object does not decrease the quality.

Object Alignment

To align multiple objects on your page—such as aligning a series of circles you've drawn, one inside of another—you can use the Align panel, shown in Figure 47.9.

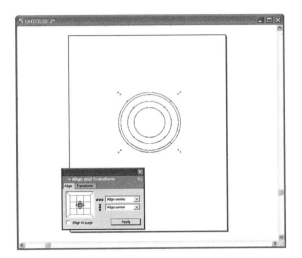

FIGURE 47.9
Use the Align panel to align multiple objects.

To align the objects visually, click inside the square alignment preview area. Alternatively, use the two pop-up menus to choose how the objects will be aligned horizontally and vertically. If you like to distribute your objects across the page, use the Distribute options rather than Align.

Use the Align to Page check box to align/distribute objects with respect to the current page size.

To quickly align to top, left, right, bottom, and so on edges of several objects, use the Modify, Align menu.

Summary

This chapter covered the FreeHand drawing tools you're most likely to use on a regular basis. The page management features enable you to add and rearrange pages in the pasteboard at will. The drawing tools give you the flexibility to create whatever image you can imagine. This chapter touched on basic object settings, but the next chapter takes a more detailed look at how you can change the appearance of the objects you learned about here.

CHAPTER 48

Using Path Tools, Strokes, Fills, and Effects

In the last chapter, you learned about the tools in FreeHand that you can use to create your images. This chapter takes that knowledge further by examining the tools you can use to edit the paths you've drawn; adjust the strokes applied to them; and add fills, colors, and special effects!

Editing Paths

You have paths in your documents created using the basic FreeHand MX tools, but it's unlikely that just putting a few shapes onto a page are going to give you the flexibility you need to create a masterpiece. This chapter reviews the tools available for modifying the paths you've drawn into the paths you *wanted* to draw. Remember, FreeHand MX is a vector graphics program—it isn't quite the same as using a paint program or photo editing suite.

Eraser

The Eraser tool can be used to break apart a path you've drawn. For example, if you draw a line and then use the Eraser tool to "erase" part of the middle, it breaks the line into two pieces, completely removing a portion the same size as the Eraser. (You can set the Eraser size by double-clicking the Tool panel.)

In the case of erasing a portion of a line, the two pieces that are left after using the Eraser are separate objects and can be selected and edited as individual unique objects. Closed objects are a bit different. When you erase a closed object, the object stays closed—it does not simply break and become an open object. If you pull the Eraser entirely through the closed object, *then* it breaks into two pieces, as shown in Figure 48.1.

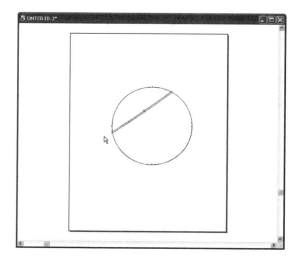

By the Way

An object must be selected to use the Eraser tool.

Knife

If the Eraser doesn't do what you want, the Knife might be the tool you are looking for. The Knife cuts through paths, breaking them into multiple parts. Unlike
the Eraser, the Knife does not remove any of the original path. Also unlike the
Eraser, dragging the Knife across the path of a closed object *does* break the closed
path. Be sure that the object is selected before trying to use the Knife.

Double-clicking the Knife tool enables you to change whether the tool operates in
FreeHand mode (the default) or Straight mode (works on a straight line) as well
as the width.

Freeform/Roughen/Bend

The Freeform, Roughen, and Bend tools, although grouped together in the
FreeHand Tool panel, create very different effects on the objects to which you
apply them. These are great tools, so don't pass them by! Again, be sure you have
an object selected before trying to use any of these tools; otherwise, they'll do a
whole lot of nothing.

Freeform

The Freeform tool works a bit like dragging your finger through wet paint. You can "pull" a portion of a path around the pasteboard as you drag your cursor. Your existing path isn't broken and is extended while you drag. This can be used to stretch out paths that aren't quite right or add subtle adjustments when needed. Double-click the tool to adjust its size and operation.

Roughen

The Roughen tool fractalizes a path. To use this tool, make sure an object is selected and then click and drag anywhere in the pasteboard. As you drag, the edges of your object "roughen" in appearance. This might sound strange, but it's something you just need to try to fully understand it. Figure 48.2 shows the before and after of an object that has been roughened.

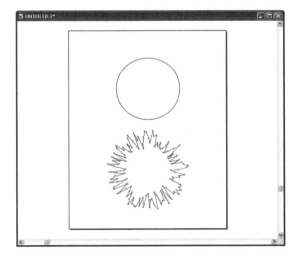

FIGURE 48.2
Roughen...
roughens.

Double-click the Roughen tool to set how rough it will be on your path.

Bend

The Bend tool "bends" the edges of an object. For example, if you "bend" a square, the edges take on a concave or convex appearance, depending on the direction in which you're dragging. Bend applies to an entire object and changes it as you click and drag in the pasteboard. The point at which you click determines where the sides are pulled or pushed from—that is, if you want the bend to be symmetric, click in the center of your object. Figure 48.3 shows a bent square.

FIGURE 48.3
The Bend tool bends the sides of your objects.

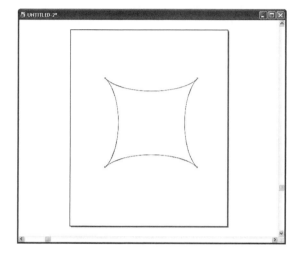

Transform

The transformation tools are used to apply uniform changes to your objects. These should be familiar to you by now from the Fireworks and Flash applications, so we'll just briefly review them here:

> **Scale**—Shrinks or grows an object. Select the object you want to scale, select the Scale tool, and then drag the object handles to increase or decrease its size. Hold down Shift to maintain the same aspect ratio as you drag.
>
> **Rotate**—Rotates the object around a point you select. Select the Rotate tool and then click and drag on the pasteboard at the point you want the object to rotate around. As you drag, the object rotates freely. Release the mouse to finish.
>
> **Skew**—Bends your object like a parallelogram (opposite sides stay parallel, but inside angles change). The effect is that your object slants in a direction. Click and drag with your object selected and it skews as you drag.
>
> **Reflect**—Creates a mirror image of your object about an axis of your choosing. Click anywhere in the pasteboard where you'd like the center of the reflective axis to appear. While holding down the mouse button, drag to rotate the reflection axis and preview the reflected object. Release the mouse button to reflect your object.

To quickly enter a free-transform mode, double-click the object you want to trans-form. A dotted line appears around it. Click and drag on any of the handles to resize the object. Click and drag inside the selection area to move the object. Or, position your cursor near one of the corners to grab and rotate the shape.

Did you Know?

Join and Split

If you have two paths you'd like to make one or want to split an existing path on one or more points (and don't want to use the Knife tool), the Join and Split tools can come in handy.

One or more paths can be joined into a single path by selecting the two paths in the pasteboard and then selecting Modify, Join. Two unclosed, nonintersecting paths automatically are connected.

To split a path apart at a single or multiple points, use the Subselect tool to select one of more points on the object; then select Modify, Split from the menu. The object is split at the selected points.

Combine Tools

The Combine tools (located under the Modify menu) are used to combine multi-ple paths, much like Join. These tools, however, apply special rules when combin-ing. The Union, Crop, Punch, and Intersect methods are discussed fully in the section "Combining Paths" in Chapter 27, "Tools and Techniques for Design and Layout."

Divide

Unique to FreeHand MX is the Divide tool. Similar to the other tools, Divide works on intersecting paths. However, rather than combining them into a single path, it creates multiple separate paths for the areas where the paths overlap. For exam-ple, Figure 48.4 shows two overlapping objects to which the Divide tool has been applied, as well as the individual paths that are created as a result.

Blend

Another interesting Combine tool is Blend. Although you have seen this tool in other applications, it works slightly differently in FreeHand. Blend enables you to morph one object into another. To do this, create the start and end image to use for the blend; then select them both on the pasteboard. Finally, select Modify, Combine, Blend from the menu or use the Blend tool to drag from one shape to another. A sequence of intermediate paths is created to morph from one shape to another. Figure 48.5 shows a square blended into a circle.

FIGURE 48.4
Divide overlapping paths into multiple parts that are delimited by the overlap.

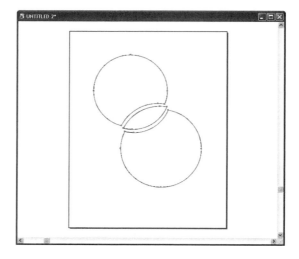

> **By the Way**
>
> To set the number of steps it takes to go from one object to another select the blended object. Then open the Object panel and adjust the Steps attribute. This increases or decreases the number of steps between the blended objects. The default is 25.

FIGURE 48.5
Blend one object into another.

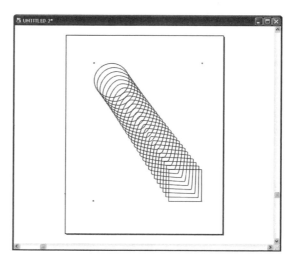

The easiest way to access one of the intermediate shapes is to double-click it with the Subselection tool and then click and drag inside the free-transform box to drag it anywhere in the pasteboard.

An additional Blend feature is the capability to join a blend to a path (select Modify, Combine, Join Blend to Path). With this tool, you can create a blend using the instructions provided here and then draw a new path in the document that you want the blended shapes to follow. Finally, select both the blend object and the path and select Join Blend to Path. The blend is redrawn along the path you selected.

Alter Path Tools

The Alter Path tools, also accessible under the Modify menu, can be used to apply yet more interesting transformations to an existing path. The three tools you'll use when interacting with basic objects are Simplify, Expand Stroke, and Inset Path:

Simplify—Removes points that are not necessary to "definitively" define your selected path. As points are removed, the path looses some detail but becomes smoother. If you draw a shape using a freeform tool, you might want to use this function to remove any jitters that might have occurred while you were drawing. The only option for Simplify is choosing how simplified the result will be.

Expand Stroke—Creates a composite path based on your original path and an expanded version of the same path. If the original path was filled, the fill is removed and placed in the space between the new and original paths. The result, for example, of expanding a filled circle is a donut shape with the same fill as the original circle. The Expand Stroke settings provide control over the styling of the stroke corners.

Inset Path—Creates a larger or smaller version of the selected path and any intermediate versions you'd like. Use the Step setting and a positive Inset value to create one or more smaller copies of the path. Using a negative inset creates larger versions of the path. Adjust the Miter settings to change how corners are drawn on paths. Figure 48.6 shows a multistep inset path applied to a circle.

For more detailed information on how these tools work, see the section "Altering Paths" in Chapter 27.

FIGURE 48.6
The Inset Path tool
can create multiple
larger or smaller
copies of a path.

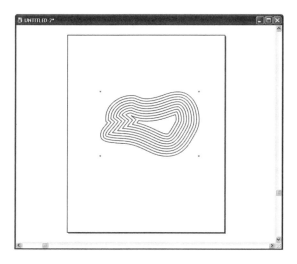

By the Way

> Some tools are missing from the Combine and Alter Paths sections because they do not apply to what we've currently covered in the text. Don't worry—we'll get to them soon.

Different Strokes

We've spent a lot of time looking at the tools that create paths and tools that modify paths, yet to see the results of any of any changes you make, you have to actually see something. What you see onscreen is either a stroke along a path or a fill in a closed path. Up to this point, you haven't seen how either of these visual elements can be edited. Let's fix that by starting with a look at strokes, and how they can be edited, followed by fills.

Changing the Stroke

By default, objects you add to your FreeHand document inherit a basic black 1-point stroke, as seen in the Object panel in Figure 48.7.

To change the properties of a stroke, click the attached stroke in the Object panel. The panel refreshes to show the properties for that stroke, as shown in Figure 48.8.

FIGURE 48.7
By default, objects inherit a 1-point stroke.

FIGURE 48.8
Change the properties for the selected stroke.

The top setting is the style used for the pen creating the stroke. A basic stroke just creates a solid color. Use the other options to create brush-style strokes or make the shape look as if it were drawn with a calligraphy pen (using the calligraphy style).

For whatever style you've selected, there are additional settings that you can adjust. For example, in Figure 48.9, the basic stroke style is selected. For this stroke, you can adjust the color by clicking the color swatch (see the upcoming section "Basic Color Fills" for more information), the width of the stroke, how corners are drawn, and whether to use dashed lines; you can even draw arrowheads, and more!

To familiarize yourself with the stroke options, try each one and adjust the settings to gauge the possible effects. Unfortunately, it is beyond the scope of this book to document every single possibility because there are thousands!

Adding Strokes

A unique feature of FreeHand is that you can add multiple strokes per path. To do this, click the Add Stroke button in the upper-left corner of the Object panel when you have a path selected. Doing so adds a second basic stroke to the object. Although this might seem pointless, what makes it powerful is that the strokes can be selected separately within the Object panel and have entirely different properties assigned.

For example, try drawing a simple shape and using the Stroke tool to adjust the basic stroke so it is 12 points wide. Now, click the Add Stroke button to add a new stroke, and adjust its properties so it is 4 points wide and white. The result of a circle is shown in Figure 48.9.

FIGURE 48.9
Multiple strokes can create layered effects on a single path.

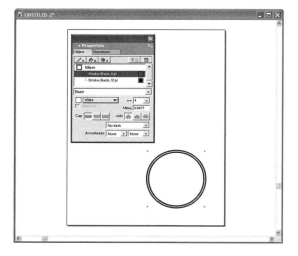

By adding multiple layered strokes, you can create interesting effects with just a single path. This enables you to create visually complex images while keeping the objects as simple as possible.

To remove a stroke, select it in the Object panel and click the trash can icon in the upper-right corner of the panel.

Did you Know?

The ordering in which strokes are added makes a difference. For example, if the white stroke had been added first and then the black stroke, the white stroke would have been completely covered and not visible.

If you find you've added strokes in a different order than what you wanted, you can click and drag them within the Object panel to reorder them.

Fills

Up to this point, you've been working with objects that have no fill. Therefore, if you position one object on top of another, you can see the strokes of another object through it. To add some substance to your artwork, you can fill in closed polygons using color, patterns, or even gradients.

Basic Color Fills

The simplest way to add a basic color fill to an object is to select it in your document and click the color swatch beside the paint bucket in the Tool panel. This displays a small color palette from which you can pick.

Choosing a color immediately fills the shape. To completely remove a color, click the color swatch and select the square with a red line through it—this is a transparent fill.

If you don't like the color options available from the basic palette, you can select the color wheel icon to open your system color chooser, or click the color square on the far left of the palette to switch to an eyedropper tool that lets you sample colors from anywhere in your document.

Another option is to use the Color Mixer panel, shown in Figure 48.10. Accessible from the Window menu, this tool provides a quick means of choosing colors in a variety of color spaces. Use the icons on the left side of the panel to choose your color picker method; then use the controls in the panel to select a color. Finally, drag from the color strip at the bottom into an object, a stroke, or another color swatch to fill using that color.

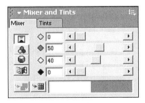

FIGURE 48.10
Select your colors in the Color Mixer panel.

If you want to use a monochromatic scale, open the Tints panel. Shown in Figure 48.11, this panel enables you to choose a color (by clicking the color swatch or using the pop-up menu) and then adjust the slider to select the tint level desired. The swatch below the slider changes to show the selected color.

> **By the Way**
>
> In Chapter 49, "Managing Objects with Grouping, Layers, and Assets," you'll see how colors you've chosen can be stored for future use in the Swatches panel.

FIGURE 48.11
The Tints panel can create a monochromatic scale.

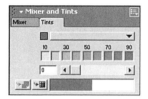

Advanced Color Fills

When you add a color fill using any of the techniques we've already discussed, what you're really doing is automatically adding a new fill attribute to the object. In the Object panel you should see a Basic Fill line appear; you can select this line and edit the fill attributes much as you did with the stroke attributes earlier.

Like strokes, many styles of fills are available, such as simple patterns, textures such as burlap, or smooth gradients. You can add one of these advanced fills by clicking the Add Fill icon (second from the left) at the top of the Object panel or by simply modifying a basic color fill by selecting from the Fill Style pop-up menu. Figure 48.12 shows the Gradient Style panel and a gradient-filled object.

FIGURE 48.12
Select and apply gradient-style fill effects.

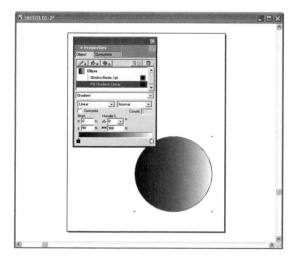

After choosing a style, use the controls in the panel to alter how the fill appears. For gradient fills, for example, controls are available for the start and stop colors and gradient type (radial, linear, and so on). You will also notice controls that appear onscreen in the object itself for some fills. A radial gradient fill, for example, adds handles for choosing the center of the gradient as well as the horizontal and vertical sizes of the gradation.

To remove an advanced or basic fill, select it in the Object panel and then click the trash can icon in the upper-right corner of the panel.

Again, there are so many possible options, you will want to take a few minutes to move from style to style and see what is available and what each of the settings can do.

Like strokes, you can add multiple fills using the Add Fill button in the Object panel. Although adding multiple basic color fills is pretty pointless (they would cover each other up!), you could, for example, add a texture fill and a basic color fill to create a texturized color, and so on.

Did you Know?

Applying Effects

The final attribute that can be applied to an object is an *effect*. An effect is visual magic. It does something that can't (easily) be done with a pen and paper. In other Macromedia applications, you might have noticed that when you fill an object, you can select the opacity/transparency of the object. In FreeHand, the capability to alter transparency is missing from the basic object properties, but it is available as an effect.

The Add Effect button is the third button from the left in the Object panel. Slightly different from the other attributes, effects are added on an existing stroke or fill. Select the stroke or fill that should inherit the effect and then use this button to pick and choose from one of more of these effects:

Bend—Pulls or pushes points away from a point you define. This is the same as the Bend tool discussed previously in this chapter.

Duet—Clones, rotates, and combines an object with copies of itself.

Expand Path—Creates a resized copy of the existing path.

Ragged—Adds a ragged edge to the path without changing the original path.

Sketch—Creates a hand-drawn look to the path without modifying the original path.

Transform—Applies transformations (scaling, rotation, and so on) to the selected path.

Bevel and Emboss—Adds bevel and embossing effects to create a 3D-like appearance.

Blur—Smoothes and removes detail from images by adding a blurring effect.

Shadow and Glow—Adds shadows or glowing effects to the selected path.

Sharpen—Increases the sharpness and contrast of the selected object.

Transparency—Adds a transparency effect to the selection, allowing you to choose the opacity of the object.

Figure 48.13 shows emboss and drop shadow effects applied to an object.

FIGURE 48.13
Use these tools to create dramatic 3D-like effects without altering the original path.

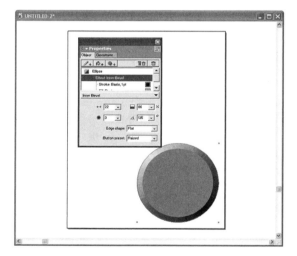

Effects are unique in that they can be nested in other effects or have fills and strokes nested inside of them. If you add a transparency effect, for example, and you want both your fill and stroke to be transparent, you can drag the stroke and fill in the Object panel so that they appear under the effect. This applies the same level of transparency to both the fill and stroke.

If you then subsequently decide you want to apply an additional effect to the fill but not the stroke, you can select the fill and add another effect to it. That effect is nested within the original transparency effect and the fill is nested within that.

Using the concept of nested effects and multiple strokes and fills, you can turn a simple single path into a complex figure that would normally take multiple paths to create.

> To delete a branch of effects/strokes/fills within the Object panel, select the nested group you want to remove and then click the Remove Branch trash can icon (second from the upper-right corner).

Did you Know?

Changing Ordering

A you'll probably want to start applying to paths (especially after you add color and fill effects) is ordering. FreeHand is basically a 2D program, but there is still depth to the display. Just as pieces of paper can lay on top of one another and obscure what is under them, objects in FreeHand can lay on top of each other and hide parts you might want to show.

To change the ordering of an object, select it in the document and then use these selections under Modify, Arrange:

> **Bring to Front**—Moves the object so it lays in front of all other objects. This is like picking up a piece of paper and putting it on the top of a stack.
>
> **Move Forward**—Moves the object forward one level. The object can still be obscured by things that are even further forward than it.
>
> **Move Backward**—Moves the object down one level.
>
> **Sent to Back**—Sends the object to the very bottom of the ordering. All other objects are considered to be on top of that object.

Ordering allows you to selectively layer the parts that make up your document. Without effective management of ordering, you would have to draw all your shapes in exactly the right order to be displayed the way you want!

Summary

This chapter covered a great deal of information. You should now be able to modify paths you've created in FreeHand as well as change strokes, fills, and effects at will. By allowing paths to take on multiple attributes, Macromedia has made FreeHand capable of turning the ordinary into the extraordinary, all the while keeping the number of objects you have to manage in your document at a bare minimum.

CHAPTER 49

Managing Objects with Grouping, Layers, and Assets

Now that you know how to use the drawing tools, edit paths, change strokes, and even apply special effects, it's time to learn the tools available for keeping your document in order. It isn't uncommon for a complete drawing to have hundreds of individual paths making up the image. Trying to manage all the objects individually would be a nightmare. Thankfully, FreeHand MX provides what you need to keep from being overwhelmed by a complex document.

Creating Groups

By default, objects you add to a document are managed individually. Consider Figure 49.1—a simple smiley face consisting of five separate objects (head, eyes (2), nose, and mouth). Even though you could lasso or group select all the objects, wouldn't it be easier if they were all accessible as a single unit?

Grouping objects allows them to moved, resized, and so on as a single object. To group objects together, select them in your document and select Modify, Group. A single selection box appears around the group, which you can use to resize or move everything within the group simultaneously, as shown in Figure 49.2.

To ungroup a set of items, make sure the group is selected and then select Modify, Ungroup.

Previously in the book, you read how the Subselection tool can be used to select individual points in a path. It can also be used to select and manipulate single objects within a group. Rather than ungrouping just to make changes, the Subselection tool can modify the contents of a group while it is still grouped.

Did you Know?

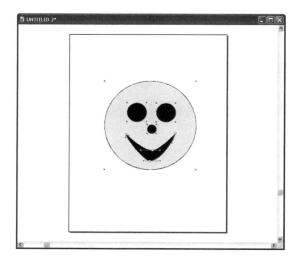

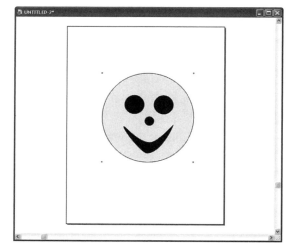

Locking Objects

As you manipulate objects in your document, you'll (hopefully) eventually place something exactly where you want it and won't want it to move again. Unfortunately, it's easy to accidentally select and bump or resize an object. To prevent this, you can use the Lock feature of FreeHand MX to keep any changes from being made.

To lock an object, select it in your design and select Modify, Lock. The object can still be selected as per usual, but it can't be changed until it is unlocked by selecting Modify, Unlock.

Layers

Another way to keep track of your objects is to employ the use of layers. *Layers* provide a means of separating related portions of your design from one another and limiting what can be edited or even seen at a given time.

Traditional animators, for example, did not draw each frame of animation from scratch. They utilized a background layer, on top of which they overlaid mid-ground objects and, finally, foreground objects. When creating a new frame, the background, and often mid-ground, layers could be reused. The animator could simply focus on whichever layer she needed to work on rather than having to work with them all simultaneously.

FreeHand MX works in much the same way. You can draw related portions of your image into one layer and then switch to another layer for other related objects. When working in a layer, you don't have to worry about accidentally altering the contents of other layers. In fact, you can hide layers you are interested in, effectively clearing your workspace to only the objects you are interested in.

To open the Layers panel, select Window, Layers. Figure 49.3 shows the Layers panel with several layers already in place.

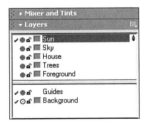

FIGURE 49.3
Use the Layers panel to organize related portions of your document.

Although I've already added some layers in the sample figure, three layers are present by default:

> **Foreground**—The default drawing layer. Everything you've drawn to this point has been added to the foreground layer.

Background—A layer in which the objects you add appear lightened. This layer is primarily used for pasting in original bitmap images you are rebuilding or tracing. The background layer is not included when you print.

Guides—This layer contains all the onscreen guides (grids and so on) that you add to your document workspace.

You can add multiple foreground and background layers to a project. Printing layers are separated from non-printing layers by a divider line in the Layers panel.

Layer Controls

Located near the layer names in the Layers panel are controls for activating, hiding, and performing other actions on layers.

Activating Layers

To draw into a layer, it must be the active layer. Active layers are denoted by the pen icon to the right of the layer name. For example, in Figure 49.3, the Sun layer is active. To activate a layer, click the layer name.

A short click is used to activate a layer (moving the pen icon). A long click selects a layer without changing it to the active layer.

The moral is, if you attempt to activate a layer and only select it, try not holding your mouse button down so long.

Hiding Layers

When you're working on a layer, sometimes it is useful to hide one or more of the other layers that might visually interfere with your design work. To toggle the visibility of the layer, click the check mark column in front of the layer line you want to toggle. The Sky, House, Trees, and Foreground layers are hidden in Figure 49.3.

Did you Know?

To quickly hide or show all the layers, use the All Off and All On options, respectively, in the Layers panel group pop-up menu.

Locking Layers

Much like you can lock objects or groups of objects, you can also lock layers. The objects in a locked layer cannot be moved, removed, or otherwise changed. In the

Fireworks chapters, you learned that hidden locked layers are a good place to store backups of your bitmap images or other parts of your drawings that you don't want to risk accidentally losing.

To lock a layer, click the Lock button in the layer line of your choice. The lock icon toggles between a closed and open image indicating the layer's locked or unlocked status.

Layer Highlight Color

To the immediate left of the layer name is a small square; this is the layer high-light color. Objects within that layer are highlighted using the selected highlight color. To choose a new color, use the Color Mixer panel and drag from the mixer to the layer highlight color square.

> An easy way to set the highlight color is to select a color using the Paint Bucket tool's panel swatch and then drag from the Paint Bucket swatch to the highlight color square.

Did you Know?

Keyline and Preview Modes

The final layer control is the keyline/preview toggle—a small circle beside the check mark column. Clicking this circle toggles between preview and keyline modes. The preview mode displays the layer as it will appear when output. The keyline mode, on the other hand, does not display any of the defined object fills, making it much easier to see the components that make up your image. This is an onscreen change and does not affect the output of the design.

Managing Layers

To add a new layer, select New Layer from the panel group drop-down menu. Alternatively, you can completely duplicate the contents of a layer by selecting it and selecting Duplicate from the panel group menu. Change the name of a layer by double-clicking its label in thelist. Remove layers by selecting them in the Layers panel and selecting the Remove option from the same menu.

Layers, like objects, lay on top of one another and can be dragged in the listing to a new order. Layers at the top of the list are on top of other layers. As mentioned earlier, the divider line separates background from foreground layers. Dragging a foreground layer below the divider line turns it into a background layer, and vice versa.

Although the easiest way to add objects to a layer is to make it active and draw in it, you can add existing objects to a layer by selecting them in the document, selecting the layer you want to move them to, and then selecting Move Objects to Current Layer in the panel group pop-up menu.

You can combine the contents of layers by merging them. To merge all the foreground layers, select Merge Foreground Layers from the pop-up menu. Alternatively, Shift-click to select multiple layers and then select Merge Selected Layers from the menu.

Maintaining Assets

To help you most effectively utilize FreeHand MX and keep from having to perform redundant work, several tools are provided to help manage assets for your documents. The assets panel group consists of three individual panels:

> **Swatches**—Keeps custom color swatches you've defined.
>
> **Styles**—Holds commonly used stroke, fill, and other style combinations for easy reuse.
>
> **Library**—Provides a holding place for symbols, which are simply groups of objects you want to reuse.

Swatches

Consistent use of color is important for creating a visually attractive image. You can use the Eyedropper tool to repeatedly sample colors for reuse, but you can also add colors directly to the Swatches panel, shown in Figure 49.4. Colors are added and labeled with a numerical representation; you can double-click the label to rename them something recognizable.

The easiest way to add a color to the Swatches panel is to select your color using the Color Mixer or Tints panel (see Chapter 48, "Using Path Tools, Strokes, Fills, and Effects," for details); then click the Add to Swatches button, highlighted in Figure 49.5.

Alternatively, click and drag a color from the mixer swatch (or any other swatch) into the empty area at the bottom of the Swatches panel to add a color.

After you've added a color to the Swatches panel, it can be used just like a swatch from the mixer (or any other color selection tool).

FIGURE 49.4
The Swatches panel contains commonly used colors.

FIGURE 49.5
Use the Tints or Mixer panel to quickly add a swatch.

As with most panels, you can drag the elements (in this case the color swatches) to wherever you'd like them in the list.

By the Way

Styles

The Styles panel contains stroke, fill, and text style combinations you can quickly assign to any object or text area. As you've seen, FreeHand provides the ability to create multiple layered stroke and fill effects that can sometimes be quite complicated. Rather than re-creating this each time you add a similar object, you can store the style and apply everything all at once.

The Styles panel is shown in Figure 49.6. By default, styles are shown in Previews Only mode, which displays only a thumbnail preview of what the style looks like. You can also see style names by using the panel group menu to switch to a large or small list view.

Managing Styles

To add a style to the Styles panel, create an object with the style information you want to store, select it, and select New from the panel group pop-up menu. Or, simply drag the object into the Styles panel. To apply a style, select the object you want to apply the style to and then simply single-click the style you want to apply.

FIGURE 49.6
The Styles panel
stores stroke and
fill information.

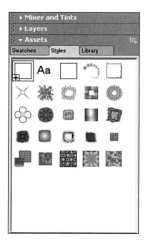

Styles can be removed or redefined using the options of the same name from the panel pop-up menus. To remove all styles that aren't being used, select Remove Unused. When redefining a style, you'll need to know its name, which means that switching to a list view (which includes the name) is probably a good idea.

Inheriting Style Information

Another feature of styles is the capability of a style to inherit information from another style or not pass some of its information on to an object. To set inheritance and what the style affects, select Style Behavior from the panel pop-up menu. The dialog box shown in Figure 49.7 is displayed.

FIGURE 49.7
Select other styles
from which your
style will inherit
and what it will
affect.

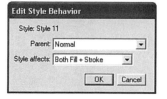

Use the first pop-up menu to select a parent style; this is the style from which your style will inherit properties. Second, set the Affects pop-up menu to the elements you want affected (such as the stroke/fill) when applying the style to an object.

If you select Style Behavior with a text style selected, FreeHand displays a different dialog box with font style-specific settings to choose from.

By the Way

The Library and Symbols

The final Asset group element is the Library. The Library is used to store objects or group of objects called *symbols* for ease of reuse. An extremely nice feature of symbols (and the Library) is that, if you modify a symbol in the Library, it is automatically updated wherever it has been placed in your documents.

Managing Symbols

To create a symbol and add it to your document, select an object or objects and select Modify, Symbol, Convert to Symbol. The created symbol is added to the Library panel, as shown in Figure 49.8. You can also drag the object(s) directly to the Library panel to add the symbol.

FIGURE 49.8
Add symbols to your Library.

After an object is added to the Library, you can drag it out of the Library panel to add a new instance of it to your document.

To edit an existing symbol, double-click it within the Library. A new window opens with *just* the symbol in it. Perform your edits, close the window, and the symbol is updated.

Remove or duplicate existing symbols using the panel group pop-up menus.

> If you'd like to use symbols you've defined in FreeHand in Flash, use the Export Symbols selection under the panel group pop-up menu.

Symbol Groups

If you have a number of symbols and want to organize them into logical groupings, you can create symbol groups by selecting New Group from the panel pop-up menu. This adds a folder to the Library panel. Rename the folder by double-clicking its label; then drag your symbols into the folder.

Master Pages

Master pages are also stored in the Library and can be added, edited, and removed using the panel pop-up menu. For more information on master pages, see Chapter 47, "Working with Pages and Basic Objects."

Summary

This chapter covered the tools that are at your disposal for keeping your drawing objects organized. FreeHand artwork can quickly grow out of control, and an understanding of how to successfully manage projects is of paramount importance. With the help of the Layers panel and Assets panel group, you can keep common elements of your document grouped logically and reuse colors, objects, and styles that would otherwise take time to re-create.

CHAPTER 50

Advanced Drawing Tools and Techniques

You've reached the point in FreeHand MX where you should know most of the available tools and features for manipulating onscreen objects. This chapter covers advanced features that apply to several tools you've already seen as well as the FreeHand MX "Xtras"—plug-in tools that, although included in FreeHand MX, are not part of the core program functionality. Nonetheless, these Xtras provide some of the more interesting and advanced features in FreeHand.

Brushes

In Chapter 48, "Using Path Tools, Strokes, Fills, and Effects," you learned how strokes can be changed to a number of shapes and styles. Plenty of built-in options are available, but you can also create your own brushes using a brush symbol. For example, assume you've created a figure that you want to use as a brush, such as that in Figure 50.1.

Next, select Modify, Brush, Create Brush. Click Copy when prompted to make a new brush. This copies the object(s) to a new symbol, which is subsequently used as a brush.

You are now prompted with the Edit Brush dialog box, shown in Figure 50.2.

Although this might seem a bit confusing, its complexity gives you a lot of complexity in designing your brush. Use these settings to choose your brush behavior:

> **Brush Name**—The name for the customized brush you are creating.
>
> **Include Symbols**—Use the + and - buttons to add or remove additional symbols you want to be a part of the brush. Use the up and down arrows to move the symbols up and down in the drawing order.
>
> **Paint**—Use a set number (default of 1) of copies of the brush to paint the entire shape. The brush is stretched as needed.
>
> **Spray**—Use multiple copies of the brush to paint the shape, maintaining the original shape of the brush.

Count—The number of copies of the brush to use if painting.

Orient on Path—Determines whether the object will curve with the path or maintain its original orientation.

Spacing—The amount of distance between each copy of the brush shape.

Angle—The amount of rotation between each copy of the brush shape.

Offset—The distance offset from the original path.

Scaling—The change in size between each instance of the brush shape.

FIGURE 50.1
To create a brush, first create the image you want to use.

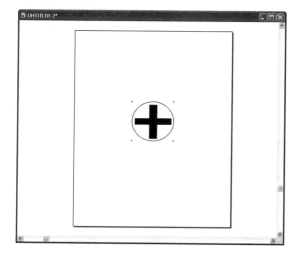

FIGURE 50.2
The Edit Brush window enables you to fine-tune the settings for a brush.

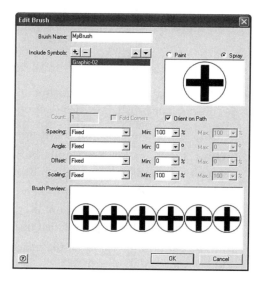

As you change the settings for the brush, the Brush Preview changes to display how the stroke of a line would appear rendered with the brush. Click OK to save the brush.

Many of the brush attributes enable you to select Random as an option. Using random sizing and angles can create an "organic" appearance to the object you're creating.

Did you Know?

To use the customized brush, create your shape and then select the shape's stroke in the Object panel. Select Brush from the stroke pop-up menu; then select the name of the brush from the pop-up menu under that. Your object is re-rendered using your custom stroke, as shown in Figure 50.3.

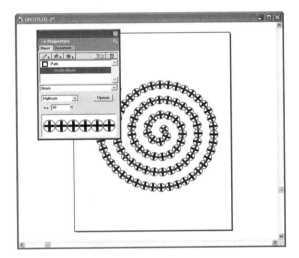

FIGURE 50.3
Apply your custom brush to a stroke.

Hoses

The Hose tool (found in the Xtra Tools toolbar) works like a paint brush that paints with images of varying sizes. To use the hose, you should have several shapes already created. Then, double-click the Hose tool to open the hose definition window, shown in Figure 50.4. Using the pop-up menu at the top of the window, you can select a predefined hose (such as Leaves or Flowers) or New to make your own.

FIGURE 50.4
Define the images
used in your hose.

Assuming you're creating your own hose, select the New option; then provide a name for your new hose. Next, select one of the hose spaces in your FreeHand document, copy it, return to the hose window, and click Paste In. Repeat the process for all the shapes you want to use in the hose.

As you add shapes to the hose, the Contents pop-up menu grows to contain the new shapes. You can select shapes and select Copy Out to copy them or Delete to remove them from the hose.

To adjust the options for the hose you've created, click the Options radio button near the top of the window. The Order pop-up menu can be used to choose in what order the shapes are displayed. The Space, Scale, and Rotate settings determine the spacing, scale, and rotation that are applied between each of the images that is output. Finally, close the hose window to save and activate the hose.

> When you draw with the hose, it's the same as drawing with any of the freeform tools. You aren't, however, creating a path. The tool simply copies into the document individual instances of the images that make up the hose.

Basic 3D Illustration

FreeHand MX is primarily a 2D drawing program, but it offers several tools for creating 3D effects and objects without a need for a separate 3D CAD program.

Even if 3D isn't your thing, the ease of use of the FreeHand tools definitely makes them worth at least a look or two.

Perspective

In Chapter 46, "Understanding the FreeHand Interface," you learned about perspective grids. If you have a perspective grid added to your document, you can attach any of your objects to the grid using the Perspective tool found in the Tools panel. To use the tool, select the object you want to attach to the grid and then drag it on top of the grid—*do not release the mouse button.*

When the object is roughly where you want it, you must press one of your arrow keys to attach it to the grid. For a horizontal grid, press the up or down arrow; for a vertical grid, press the left or right arrow. If you have more than one vanishing point, press the arrow key toward the vanishing point you want to use. After the object is attached, as shown in Figure 50.5, you can drag it anywhere you'd like on the grid using the Perspective tool.

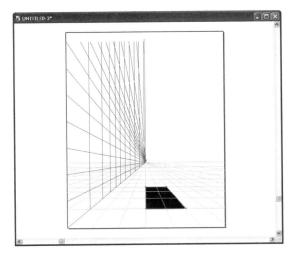

FIGURE 50.5
Attach an object to the perspective grid.

If you attempt to drag a perspective object using the normal selection tool, the object is detached from the perspective grid (retaining its perspective shape) and behaves like any other object.

3D Rotation

The 3D Rotation tool takes a 2D object and rotates it in three dimensions. To use the tool, highlight the object you want to rotate and click and drag from the point you want the object to rotate around. For example, if you want to spin an object in place, click in the middle of the object. To rotate around a vertical axis, drag left and right, and to rotate about a horizontal axis, drag up or down. Release the mouse button to finish the rotation.

To set additional options for the 3D rotation (such as what the object orients around), double-click the 3D Rotation tool in the Tools panel.

Fisheye Lens

The Fisheye Lens creates an effect that appears as if your objects are wrapped around the outside (convex) or inside (concave) of a sphere. To start using the Fisheye Lens, double-click the tool in the panel. FreeHand displays the Fisheye set-up window, shown in Figure 50.6.

FIGURE 50.6
Configure how the fisheye effect appears.

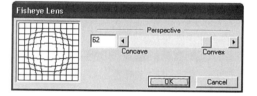

Use the slider to adjust from concave to convex; the grid updates to preview the curve as you drag.

Finally, to apply the effect, make sure the Fisheye tool is selected and then click and drag around the objects to which you want to apply the effect. When you release the mouse button, the objects are warped to the same perspective you con-figured.

Shadow

The Shadow tool creates a "shadow" object that is based on a selected object. By double-clicking the Shadow tool, you can select the size, type, and fill of the shad-ow. To use the tool, highlight the object you want to add a shadow to and click and drag to where you want the shadow to appear.

After releasing the mouse, the object and the shadow behave as a single object (a composite path). If you want to move the shadow, you can use the Subselect tool.

Smudge

The Smudge tool works much like a shadow, but rather than creating a single "shadow" copy of the object, it creates multiple copies of the object that slowly (by default) fade to white. Double-clicking the Smudge tool enables you to set the colors that the stroke and fill fades (or darkens) to.

To create a smudge, select the object to which to apply the effect and then click and drag to set the endpoint for the effect. Figure 50.7 shows the results of a smudge action.

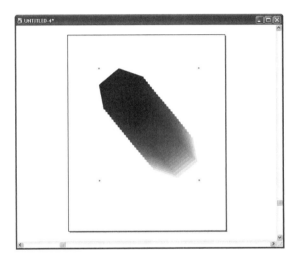

FIGURE 50.7
By default, a smudge is a collection of fading copies of an object.

Extrusion

The Extrude tool is perhaps the most interesting of the FreeHand 3D functions. This tool enables you to easily create simple 3D objects within FreeHand by extruding a shape you create. To understand extrusion, picture a cake decorator. To create fancy frosting effects, he uses a tip with a special shape, such as a star or flower. In FreeHand, that shape is an object you create. The decorator then forces frosting through the shaped tip to add as much depth as he wants. With the Extrude tool, you create the same effect as pushing the frosting through the tip.

To get a feel for the tool, draw a simple shape in your document and select it. Using the Extrude tool, drag away from the shape. As you drag, you are moving the vanishing point for your creation. The shape stretches to become a 3D object. A circle becomes a cylinder and a square becomes a cube, as shown in Figure 50.8.

FIGURE 50.8
Extrude your
shades to add
depth.

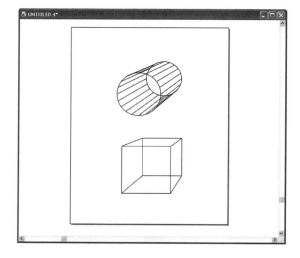

After releasing your mouse button, you'll notice that a small, circular handle appears on the back side of the 3D object. Dragging this handle increases or decreases the length of the object.

To rotate the object in three dimensions, double-click it with the Extrude tool. A circle appears around the object. Drag the triangular handle on the circle to change the z-axis, or drag inside the circle to rotate on the x-axis and y-axis.

Did you Know?

If you create multiple extruded objects, you'll probably want them to appear as if they exist in the same space with one another. To do this, they should share the same vanishing point. To combine the vanishing points of multiple extrusions, select them and then select Modify, Extrude, Share Vanishing Points.

Watch Out!

When rotating your object in 3D, do *not* use the 3D rotation tool—it will skew your image. Instead, use the Extrude tool.

Profiles

After you've created an extrusion, you can make it significantly more detailed by changing the profile. The *profile* sets either a static path for the extrusion (similar to the cake decorator moving the frosting tube as it is applied) or a bevel profile similar to if the tip on the frosting could become larger or smaller at will).

To access the profile for an extrusion, select it and open the Object panel. With the extrusion selected, three buttons are visible on the lower-left side of the panel. The bottom button, shown selected in Figure 50.9, is the profile.

FIGURE 50.9
Set a profile for the extrusion.

To set a profile, you must first make a path that defines the profile. If you simply want the extrusion to follow a path, just draw the path you want it to follow. To use the bevel profile, however, you'll need to imagine what you want the contour of the object to look like. For example, in Figure 50.10, I've created a path that profiles the side of a vase. To apply the profile, copy it and click the Paste In button in the Object panel. After a few seconds, the object takes on the appearance of the profile (see Figure 50.10).

Using the other settings in the profile, you can adjust the "twist" of the profile, the angle of a static profile, and the number of steps (smoothness) taken to build the profile.

All extruded objects actually already have a profile: a straight line that is used as a static profile.

By the Way

Other Extrude Settings

Two other buttons are visible in the Object panel when an extrusion is selected. The first (top) provides access to the numeric values for length, position, and rotation in 3D space. The second button, surface, enables you to apply lighting effects to the object and switch between shaded and wireframe views of the surface. Try experimenting with the surface options; you can create realistic-looking objects using the right settings.

FIGURE 50.10
Profiles can drasti-
cally alter the
appearance of an
object.

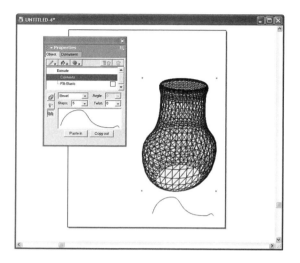

Text Revisited

Earlier, you saw that text is easy to enter into FreeHand MX, either by typing or pasting from another application. You haven't, however, seen any of the effects that can be applied to text to make it more than just some words on your screen. Let's take a look at some of the advanced text features.

Attaching Text to a Path

By default, text follows a straight line. Given the ease with which you can make curves, objects, and so on in FreeHand, it stands to reason that text also can be bent or twisted to follow a path. Attaching text to a path is similar to attaching a blend to a path, which you've already done.

First, create both the text and the path you want the text to follow. Next, select both the text and the path, and select Attach to Path from the Text menu. The text appears wrapped along the path.

In attaching the text to the path, you've created a new Text on a Path object. Selecting this object and viewing the Object panel gives you additional options for orienting the text in different ways. The default method for attaching text to a path is to rotate around the path, which rotates letters so they fit against the path. Another choice is Vertical, which places the text in an upright position and moves the bottom of each letter to follow the path. The other two Skew options stretch the text vertically or horizontally to keep it on the path.

Adding Text Inside or Outside an Object

By default, a text box is rectangular, which doesn't give you much flexibility for adding written content to your design. To place text inside an object (so it follows the sides of the object), select the closed shape to which you want to add text and then select Text, Flow Inside Path. You can then type directly into the object, as shown in Figure 50.11.

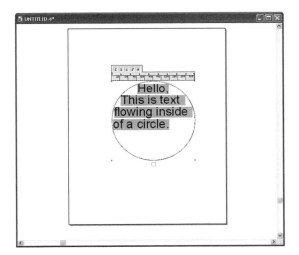

FIGURE 50.11
Use Flow Inside Path to add text to an object.

To perform the opposite effect (keeping text outside an object), first create the text in your document however you would like. Next, create (or select) the object you want the text to flow around and bring it to the front. The object must be arranged in front of the text before continuing.

Finally, select Text, Flow Around Selection. You are prompted by a window with two buttons at the top. The left button cancels any flow-around effect set for an object, whereas the right button sets the effect. Click the right button and enter any right/left/top/bottom padding you'd like. Click OK to flow the text around your object.

Multicolumn Text

Another way to manage your text is by setting the number of rows and columns it occupies using the Object panel. With a text block selected, open the Object panel and click the fourth button down on the lower-left side of the panel. This opens the column display, shown in Figure 50.12.

FIGURE 50.12
Create multicolumn
text with ease.

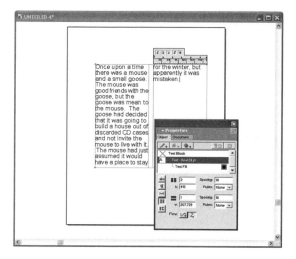

Two sets of options are visible in the panel. The first set controls the number of columns, spacing, and width for the columns. The second controls the number of rows, row spacing, and height of the rows. At the bottom of the panel is a flow control used to set whether text flows left to right across the columns or from top to bottom down the columns. Figure 50.12 demonstrates two-column text.

Linking Text Objects

When you are designing a brochure, you often want text to appear in multiple locations on a page but content often changes over the course of a project, as do the specifications (size, font, and so on) for the text itself. In other applications you have to copy and paste text from one area to another as it grows or shrinks to ensure that it still fits the design. In FreeHand MX, however, you can use text object linking to link multiple areas that hold text. When the text grows too large for one area, it spills into the next, and so on.

To create linked text areas, first draw the text areas and objects you want to contain text in your design. Next, select the first text area and take note of the link handle in the lower-right corner of the text block. Drag from this handle to the next object into which text should flow. A line is drawn linking the two areas, and the second area also shows a link handle. Drag from that handle to the third text area, and so on until all the objects are linked. You can now type in the first area and the text will flow into all the linked objects, as shown in Figure 50.13.

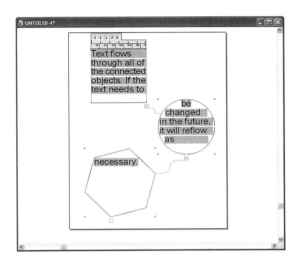

FIGURE 50.13
Linked text areas add to the flexibility of a design.

Converting Text to Paths

As you work with text, you might find that the text tools are flexible but don't give you the same type of control as the object tools. You can't alter the points that make up individual letters to reshape them, and so on.

If you've gotten text as far as you can with the text tools and want to start working with it as a graphic, you can convert it to a graphic by selecting Text, Convert to Paths. Your text becomes objects in the design that you can select and reshape at will. You cannot, however, reedit the actual text.

Other Text Tools

The FreeHand text tools are very robust. As you work with text, keep in mind that FreeHand has included a spelling checker (select Text, Spelling, and check out the Spelling application preferences), a simple text editor (select Text, Editor), and the ability to define commonly used text styles as a FreeHand style (see Chapter 49, "Managing Objects with Grouping, Layers, and Assets," for more information on styles).

Also be aware of the breadth of settings that are accessible within the Object panel for selected text. Almost every attribute of text can be changed, and the Object panel is the easiest place to do it.

Envelopes

The Envelope tool is a bit unusual and is applied in a different manner from the other tools we've discussed. This tool creates the effect of mapping your objects onto another shape, such as a circle or star. Your object is warped to fit the envelope.

The easiest way to get a sense for what the tool does is to use it. Create a composite object (something more than just a simple square or rectangle); then open the Envelope tool by selecting Window, Toolbars, Envelope.

Several predefined envelopes are already included with the tool. You can access these using the pop-up menu in the toolbar. To apply an envelope effect, click the Create Envelope button at the far left of the toolbar. Figure 50.14 shows what was previously a rectangular shape with the Circle envelope applied.

FIGURE 50.14
Apply an envelope
to a shape.

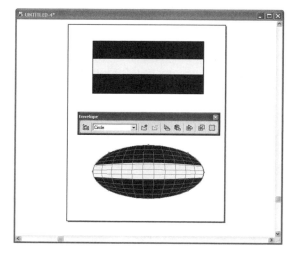

Along the edges of the envelope are handles for shaping the envelope you've applied. As you drag the handles, the contents of the envelope change. Use the preset envelopes to get close to the effect you want; then modify it using the handles. You can save the customized envelope by clicking the button immediately following the envelope presets.

To aid in altering an envelope, click the last button in the envelope toolbar, called Show Map. This displays a grid over the surface of the object, demonstrating how it will be changed.

To remove an envelope entirely (returning your object to its original appearance), click the second button from the right side (Remove Envelope). Alternatively, if you like the effect, click the third button from the right (Release Envelope) to return to a normal editing view with the effects applied to your object.

Trace Tool

Although we can't effectively demonstrate the Trace tool with a screenshot in a book, it is an excellent implementation of a bitmap-to-vector graphics conversion tool. You learned about the Trace tool in Fireworks, but it does not offer the features available in FreeHand's tool—most notably, the ability to find and trace color regions within color images. Within FreeHand, you can convert a full-color bitmapped image into vector graphics art.

To use the Trace tool, first double-click it to configure the basic operation. The trace set-up screen is shown in Figure 50.15.

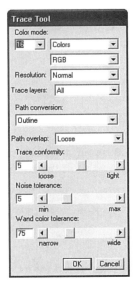

FIGURE 50.15
Configure the Trace tool before using it.

Select the number of colors the final image will have (note that choosing too many colors effectively results in an image in which every pixel is defined as a separate object, eliminating the usefulness of the tool). Select whether to use color or grayscale; the resolution; which layers to trace (foreground and background);

how to convert paths (by outlining them, finding the center line, and so on); as well as the tolerances for tracing, noise, and color. Click OK when you're ready to use the tool.

To apply a trace to a bitmap, select the Trace tool and use it to draw a rectangle around the object you're tracing. Release the mouse and wait. Depending on the complexity of the image, the trace can take quite some time, but eventually you will have a multivector object representation of the original image.

Xtras

FreeHand MX comes with a number of Xtras you can use to perform everything from simple cleanup operations to creating and modifying charts. When you've become familiar with the core FreeHand tools, you might want to check out the options under the Xtras menu:

Animate—Aids in creating simple Flash animations. You'll use this Xtra in Chapter 51, "Preparing for Web or Print."

Chart—Opens a simple spreadsheet and creates basic bar charts from values you provide, as shown in Figure 50.16. Although the Chart tool is available on the standard FreeHand Tools panel, the ability to edit charts is available only as an Xtra.

Cleanup—Removes overlap, simplifies paths, and performs other basic path operations.

Colors—Applies color adjustments to objects. The Colors Xtras can lighten and darken colors or increase and decrease saturation. These Xtras provide more color adjustment features than the core tools.

Create—Used to create blend or emboss effects on a path.

Delete—Removes unused colors or text areas from a document.

Distort—Adds distortion to an object, including the ability to fractilize an object.

Other—Gets and sets metadata stored for a document, such as the Creator, Caption, City, State, and so on.

Path Operations—Perform basic path operations such as cropping, expanding the stroke, inset, and so on.

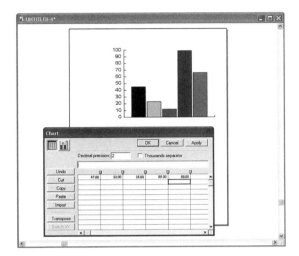

FIGURE 50.16
The Chart tool Xtra
can create and edit
bar charts.

You might notice that there is repetition between the Xtras and the core FreeHand tools. This is an unusual interface decision, but it doesn't matter which route you take to perform an action. Selecting Modify, Alter Path, Inset Path is just as valid as selecting Xtras, Path Operatings, Inset Path.

Summary

This chapter covered several tools and topics for creating advanced 3D designs and using the FreeHand text tools to their fullest. The final chapter discusses the ways in which you can output a document after you've completed the design.

Even though we've covered a great deal of ground in only a few chapters, dozens of settings are available that you should take the time to explore to fully appreciate FreeHand. Each object has settings you can alter using the Object panel or by double-clicking the tool in the Tools panel. Only by exploring the effects of these settings can you truly begin to appreciate the flexibility of FreeHand. We could literally create hundreds of pages of screenshots to show the effects of each and every option, but that is beyond the scope of this book. Explore the tools you have available—you might be surprised at the ways in which they can be used.

CHAPTER 51

Preparing for Web or Print

Although creating in FreeHand for the sake of "doing art" is certainly acceptable (and encouraged), more than likely you're working on a project that is destined for print, the Web, or both. This chapter wraps up our look at FreeHand by examining the special tools provided exclusively for print and Web output. Up until now, the tools have largely been output agnostic—what you'll be seeing here are those tools specialized for certain output methods.

Outputting to HTML

When FreeHand was developed, the focus for the application was still traditional print output. Over the years, features have been added to make FreeHand play nicely with the Web and with Macromedia's other Web-specific applications.

Adding Links to a Design

FreeHand can be used to add links to objects in a page design. You can subsequently export the document to HTML and the links are carried through. However, don't expect to migrate all your Web development to FreeHand, although it does work and is easy to use.

Assume that you've created a multipage document with button objects that you'd like to turn into a Web page, as shown in Figure 51.1.

To attach a link to one of the buttons on a page, select the button and open the Navigation panel, shown in Figure 51.2.

To link the button to a page already in your design, use the URL drop-down menu to choose a named page. For more information on adding pages to a document, see Chapter 47, "Working with Pages and Basic Objects." Alternatively, you can fill in a text URL (such as http://www.shadesofinsanity.com/).

Text Links

Links can also be added to text within a FreeHand page. To add a link to a text string, select the text and then highlight only the word or words you want to be clickable. Next, use the Navigation panel to add a link using the same technique just discussed.

FIGURE 51.1
FreeHand can be used to design and create simple Web pages.

FIGURE 51.2
Use the Navigation panel to attach links to objects.

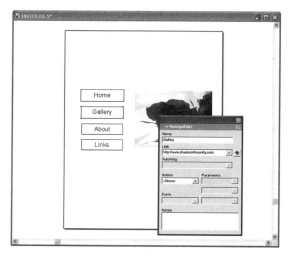

When a text link has been added, you'll notice that the Substring field directly below the URL contains the link text you selected.

Using the File, Export command, you can choose to export your document to the popular PDF format. FreeHand-generated PDFs automatically support the links added via the Navigation panel.

Finding Links

To locate objects linked to a certain page or URL, open the Navigation panel without any objects selected. Type or select a URL in the Link field; then click the icon immediately following the field. This searches your document for any objects with the chosen link and selects them.

Publishing HTML

To output the pages as HTML, select File, Publish As HTML. The screen shown in Figure 51.3 is displayed.

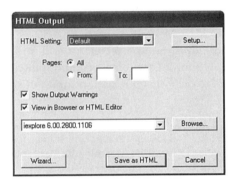

FIGURE 51.3
Output the pages to HTML.

Before going any further, click the Setup button to select the HTML output settings. If you need to maintain compatibility with older browsers, changing these options is very important. Figure 51.4 shows the HTML setup options.

Use the + and - buttons to add or remove setting profiles. By default, there is a single default profile. You don't need to create multiple output profiles unless you are dealing with a wide variety of Web sites.

To prepare for outputting your documents, click the Browse button to select a document root for your pages. This is really just the location where the files will be saved, so don't be confused by the *document root* terminology.

FIGURE 51.4
Select your output options.

Next, use the Layout pop-up menu to choose whether the objects on the page will be laid out with layers or with tables. Table layout is compatible with older browsers but does not support object overlapping. If you require a different text encoding, use the Encoding pop-up menu to change the default.

For the image export standards, use the Vector Art and Images pop-up menus to select an image output standard. For greatest compatibility, use either GIF or JPEG image formats. Click OK to activate your settings and return to the HTML output window.

Note that FreeHand defaults to SWF as the graphics format for vector art; this requires the viewing browser to have the Macromedia Flash plug-in installed.

Finally, back in the HTML output window, select the pages you want to output, whether you want to see any output warnings (problems sometimes arise when converting complex layouts to a Web-ready format), and which (if any) browser or editor should be opened to view the documents.

Finally, click Save As HTML and your Web pages are generated. You can then open the pages in Dreamweaver MX 2004 for refinement, if necessary.

Outputting Flash Animation

This book has a number of chapters dedicated to creating Flash animations directly in Flash MX 2004. With the power of the full Flash authoring environment available, it might not be clear why you'd want to author Flash in FreeHand. The answer is two-fold. First, FreeHand provides an easy introduction to Flash techniques for someone who is experienced with the FreeHand design tools. The second reason is simply because it's there.

Animation Frames

To create a FreeHand animation, you must create a separate layer for each frame of the animation. The bottommost layer (closest to the divider line in the Layers panel) is the first frame, whereas the layer on top of that is the second frame, and so on. To create traditional animation, you develop your design in one layer, duplicate it, make small changes for the objects you want to appear as in motion, and then repeat the process for subsequent frames. Obviously, FreeHand MX is not intended to be a serious animation tool! Nonetheless, you can easily create interesting animated effects with the help of a tool you learned about a few chapters ago—the Blend tool—and an Xtra called Release to Layers.

Release to Layers

The Release to Layers Xtra takes each step of a blend, or each letter in a text string attached to a path, and moves it to its own layer. The result is similar to the tweeking you learned about in Part III, "Flash."

For example, consider the blend that has been created in Figure 51.5.

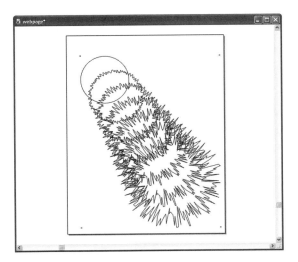

FIGURE 51.5
Create a blend and use it for animation.

Using the Release to Layers tool, you can easily turn this simple morph into an animation. To do this, select the blend and select Xtras, Animate, Release to Layers. You are prompted for a few options, as shown in Figure 51.6.

FIGURE 51.6
Select your
Release to Layers
options.

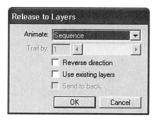

Several options are available for how Release to Layers creates the animation:

Sequence—Moves objects/letters to new layers one after the other—a single object per layer.

Build—Builds on each layer by including the objects that came on the layer before it. This has the effect of the blend or text building as the animation plays.

Drop—Copies all the objects to each of the layers but removes one, starting at the beginning and progressing to the end. This can be considered the inverse of the Sequence option.

Trail—Similar to Build, but it only copies a certain number of previous frames to the current frame (rather than all of them). The effect is like having a trail that lags behind the moving object. If you select Trail, be sure to set the number of frames that will be used to create the trail. The default is one (the active frame and the frame preceding it).

Reverse Direction—Reverses the direction of the animation.

Use Existing Layers—Uses existing layers rather than adding new layers, starting with the first foreground layer.

Send to Back—If the Use Existing Layers option is selected, this option forces the objects being added to the already present layers to be moved behind other objects.

To create a simple moving object, just select Sequence and click OK. You should notice a number of new layers (that correspond to the number of steps in your blend), as shown in Figure 51.7.

The Action Tool

If you want to create an object in the movie that a user can use to jump to another page with a different movie, you can use the Action tool, located above the Hand icon in the Tools panel.

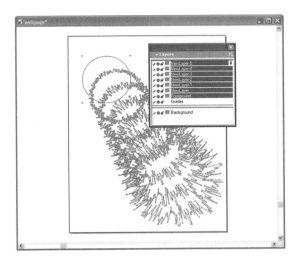

FIGURE 51.7
New layers are created for each frame of the animation.

For example, you might create part one of the animation on page one and part two on page two (see Chapter 47, "Working with Pages and Basic Objects," for information on creating pages). To provide a link to jump to page two of the animation, you add an object (such as a button) to page one that the user will click to move to the page two movie. With that object selected, click and drag from it to the page in the pasteboard to which you want it to jump. As you drag, a line appears, linking the object to the page.

By default, FreeHand adds a Flash action called Go to and Stop for the button you create. If you'd like to go to the page and play the movie on the page, you can adjust these settings in the Navigation panel when the button is selected, as shown in Figure 51.8.

Use the Action pop-up menu to select what the button should do, and use the Event pop-up menu to choose when it should do it. The Parameters pop-up menus are used to select the appropriate settings for the chosen action, such as to which page your are jumping.

Rather than using the Action tool to link a button to a page, you can simply assign the action by selecting the object to use as a button and changing the properties in the Navigation panel.

Did you Know?

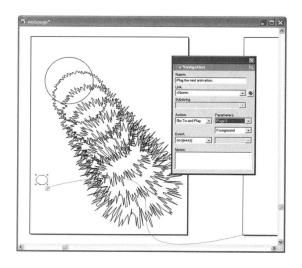

Testing the Movie

To test the animation you've created, select Window, Movie, Test. A Flash preview window appears, as shown in Figure 51.9.

FIGURE 51.9
Preview your new animation.

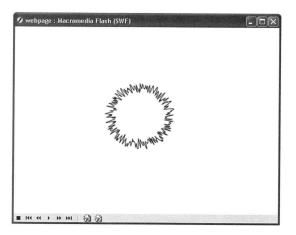

Use the playback controls in the lower-left corner of the window to stop, rewind, step backward, play, step forward, or fast forward. The two icons that follow the playback controls enable you to export the Flash file or configure movie settings.

Exporting a Movie

To export a movie, you should first verify and change the movie settings for FreeHand. These options control how animations on multiple pages are dealt with, whether movies are locked, and so on. To open the settings dialog box, either click the Setting button at the bottom of the movie Test window or select Window, Movie, Settings. The settings window is shown in Figure 51.10.

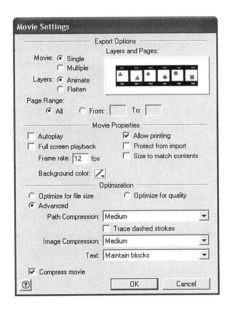

FIGURE 51.10
Select the settings for exporting your finished movie.

The following options are available:

Movie Single—Creates a single movie from all the layers on all the pages.

Movie Multiple—Creates multiple movie files, one for each page.

Layers Animate—Treats each layer on each page as an individual frame.

Layers Flatten—Flattens the layers on a page. You can then use the flattened layer as a single frame in the movie.

Page Range—Selects the pages that should be used when making the movie.

Autoplay—When checked, the movie automatically plays when loaded.

Full Screen Playback—Enters a full-screen mode at playback.

Allow Printing—Allow viewers to print the frames of the movie.

Protect from Import—Does not allow your movie to be imported into other applications (such as Flash). It is effectively locked from editing.

Size to Match Contents—Sizes the movie playback area to fit the objects in the movie.

Frame Rate—The number of frames per second that will be displayed.

Background Color—The color that will appear behind the movie. By default, the movie is transparent, allowing the color of a Web page (if it is played on a Web page) to show through.

Optimization—Select to optimize for size or quality, or use the Advanced radio button to choose your own compression settings.

Click OK to save your settings. Finally, select File, Export and select the SWF (Flash) output format to save the file. You should now have a fully functional Flash file for inclusion on a Web page, CD-ROM, and so on or for opening in Flash MX 2004 itself.

Print Output

The next output style we'll look at is print—you remember that, right? From the olden days, back when we used to put things on paper? This section examines some of the print-oriented features of FreeHand that help you get what you see on your screen onto paper.

Color Matching and Calibration

One of the most difficult aspects of print publishing is color matching. What you see on your screen isn't necessarily what you're going to see when you have a job printed. To standardize the process of color selection, several commercial color matching systems are available. These systems catalog and ID colors. By using one of these known color IDs, you are assured that your output will match the color you want. These matching systems have preprinted color swatches available that you can use for the selecting your colors.

The most prolific of the color matching systems is Pantone. The Pantone colors are included in FreeHand MX and can be accessed through the drop-down panel group menu in the Swatches panel. To use a Pantone color, select the color library from the drop-down menu. A Pantone selection screen appears, as shown in Figure 51.11.

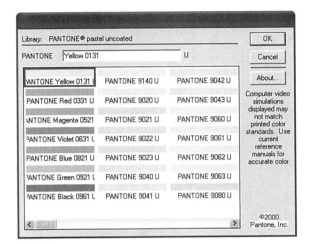

FIGURE 51.11
Select from commercial color matching systems.

After choosing your color, click OK. The color is added to the Swatches panel for ease of access.

You should not assume that the onscreen Pantone colors are a true or accurate representation of the color you're choosing. Although they're close, you should use printed Pantone color swatches to make your matches.

To order Pantone color guides, visit http://www.pantone.com/shop/shop.asp?idArticle=511&.

Did you Know?

Using Pantone colors results in predictable printed output when you use a professional print shop; it does not necessarily mean that your printer will output what you expect.

The process of matching your onscreen colors to your printed colors is called *color calibration*. To calibrate your colors, open the Colors category of the FreeHand preferences. Here you can choose a built-in color management system, such as Apple's ColorSync or Adobe Digital Science (be sure to click Setup to select color profiles for your monitor and printer). Alternatively, you can manually adjust colors by selecting Adjust Display Colors from the Color Management pop-up menu and then click Calibrate. A calibration window, shown in Figure 51.12, appears.

Hold a printed sample by your screen and click one of the colors that should (but doesn't) match. The color selection dialog box is displayed, allowing you to fine-tune the color display so it matches your printed output. When you're finished matching as many colors as possible, click OK.

FIGURE 51.12
Calibrate your
colors visually.

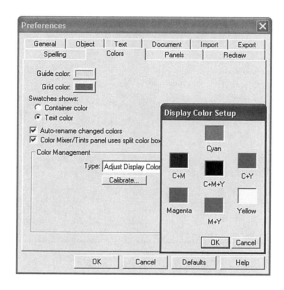

Raster Effects Resolution

If you use the special effects, such as the drop shadow or bevel tools you learned about in Chapter 48, "Using Path Tools, Strokes, Fills, and Effects," you've used raster effects. A raster effect is applied to a vector object, but the effect it creates is a bitmap. For raster effects to output in as high quality as possible, the effect should be rendered in the same resolution as your output device. By default, raster effects are applied at 72 dots per inch (dpi), which is far below standard print resolutions.

To change the raster effects resolution select File, Document Settings, Raster Effects Settings. You are prompted for a ppi value (pixels per inch). Enter the appropriate resolution for your printer, or select from common output resolutions in the drop-down menu. Note that when the Optimal CMYK rendering check box is active, any color management you've applied will be discarded.

Halftone Settings

When printing to a PostScript printer (Macromedia's recommendation for achieving the highest-quality output), you should set custom halftones for the objects you are printing. *Halftones* are the small dots that, when varied in size, produce the print gradations between light and dark. You can access the halftone settings by selecting Window, Halftones at any time.

Output Regions

When printing a page, you might not want to print the entire page to your output device. To limit what is printed, you can use the Output Region tool (third down on the left side of the Tools panel) to select a region of the page that will be printed. To use the tool, simply select it in the Tools panel and then click and drag to select the printable region of your page. Anything outside this selection area will be ignored.

> The objects that aren't selected in the output area are still saved with your document; they just aren't seen during printing.

By the Way

To remove an output region, use the Output Region tool to select the existing region; then press the Delete key.

Sending Files to the Printer

When preparing a file for shipping to a print house, you have three choices: embed all your source images (TIFFs, EPS, and so on) into the FreeHand file itself, collect all the files required into a single location that can be easily sent to the printer, or send a PDF file. FreeHand MX makes doing any of these simple.

Embedding

To automatically embed the source files for any external files you import, you must modify the Import preferences for FreeHand MX. Open the application preferences and click the Import category, shown in Figure 51.13.

If you've already added images to your document, they are not embedded simply by toggling this preference. You need to use the Links dialog box to manually embed your images.

To open the Links dialog box, either select Edit, Links or select an image in your document and click the Links button in the Object panel. The window shown in Figure 51.14 is displayed.

To embed an image, select it in the list and click the Embed button. If the original image file subsequently is changed, you must open this dialog box again and click the Change button to update the embedded image.

Collecting for Output

If you'd rather keep your image files separate from the FreeHand document, you can select File, Collect for Output to pull all your source images and fonts into a single location.

FIGURE 51.13
To turn on embedding, click the option Embed Images and EPS upon Import.

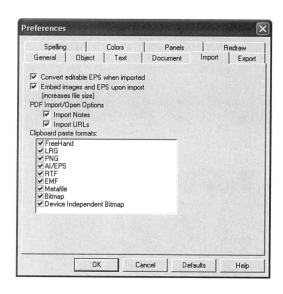

FIGURE 51.14
Manage links to external documents.

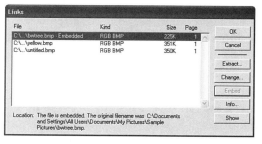

First, you are prompted with a warning about the legality of distributing your font files. Make sure you are allowed to include your fonts with your files before sending them to a printer. Next, FreeHand creates a Document Report that contains information on all the files, fonts, and so on that make up your image. This is useful to the printer for verifying that what they are outputting includes everything you expect it to.

Finally, you are prompted for a location to save all the files. All the imported images and any fonts you used are copied to this directory along with the final FreeHand document. You can now send these to the printer without worrying about not including a file or font.

Outputting to PDF

A popular way of distributing files for output is the PDF format. PDF can embed fonts and high-resolution images in a single file. Better still, PDF does not require that the person or facility working with the file have Macromedia FreeHand installed. Unfortunately, the PDF format does have a few drawbacks—most notably, you cannot use EPS images, Postscript effects, or transparency. If you're unsure whether this will affect you, try outputting your document as a PDF and then viewing it with Adobe's free Acrobat Reader software (http://www.adobe.com/) to verify the output.

To create a PDF, select File, Export and select the PDF format. Next click the Setup button to open a window similar to that shown in Figure 51.15.

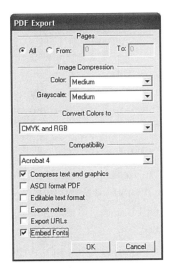

FIGURE 51.15
Export to PDF format.

Use the PDF settings to select the pages you'd like to print, whether images should be compressed (thus loosing quality), a color conversion, and which version of Acrobat you want to be compatible with. You can also choose a few esoteric output settings, such as the ability to output ASCII PDF files (for transmitting to/across legacy systems), as well as the ability to make the PDF text editable and export notes, URLs, and fonts along with the document. Click OK when you're finished with the setup; then click Save to save your PDF file.

Printing

Finally, if you want to print a document on your own output device, you can do so by selecting File, Print. On Mac OS X, your next step is to select FreeHand MX from the Print dialog box's pop-up menu. To access all the features available for FreeHand MX printing, click the Advanced button to open the window shown in Figure 51.16.

FIGURE 51.16
Access the
FreeHand printing
options.

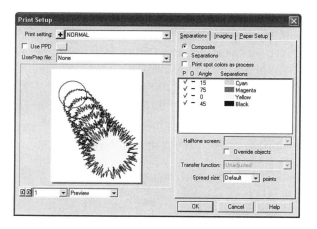

From this screen, you can choose your print quality, PPD (printer description file), as well as view a preview of the output. Using the controls in the lower-left corner of the window, you can move between multiple pages in a multipage document.

To the right of the preview is a pane with three tabs:

Separations—Used for controlling composite (all colors output on a single page) or separation (each color on a separate page) output.

Imaging—Select what will be output to the printer. You can choose to include crop marks and so on.

Paper Setup—Select the paper size and orientation for your output device.

When finished, click OK. Then click Print to print your document.

Summary

This chapter covered the final step in using FreeHand MX—outputting your document. We've attempted to cover FreeHand in as much depth as the scope of this book allows, but we encourage you to continue to explore the application and all the Macromedia Studio applications.

Macromedia has created a rich suite of applications that can be adapted to almost any print or Web publishing workflow. Just because we covered something in the book one way doesn't mean it can't be done another, or that what we described is the best way for your particular needs. Our goal has been to introduce you to the tools you have available, and we hope we have succeeded!

Index

How can we make this index more useful? Email us at indexes@samspublishing.com

How can we make this index more useful? Email us at indexes@samspublishing.com

How can we make this index more useful? Email us at indexes@samspublishing.com

How can we make this index more useful? Email us at indexes@samspublishing.com

How can we make this index more useful? Email us at indexes@samspublishing.com

How can we make this index more useful? Email us at indexes@samspublishing.com

opacity (Fireworks), 343

Open Browser Window behavior, 186, 192-194

Open Browser Window dialog box (Dreamweaver), 193

Open in Frame command (File menu), 152

Open SourceSafe Database dialog box (Dreamweaver), 239

opening
    browser windows, 192-194
    Code Inspector, 76
    Fireworks MX, 261-263
    hyperlinks in new browser window, 106-107
    inspectors, 25
    panels, 25
    Quick Tag Editor, 78

Optimization setting (FreeHand), 718

Optimize command (Dreamweaver), 94

Optimize panel (Fireworks), 277, 377

optimizing images, 93

Optional Region object (Dreamweaver Insert bar), 14

Options menu (Flash Action panel), 600

Options tab (Edit Stroke dialog box), 353

Options toolbar (Flash Action panel), 601

Ordered List object (Dreamweaver Insert bar), 18

ordered lists, 37

orientation of text (Fireworks), 346

origin points (Bézier curves), 334

origin vectors (Bézier curves), 334

Other Characters object (Dreamweaver Insert bar), 19

Outdent button, 38

Outer Bevel command (Effects menu), 312

outlines, displaying Flash layers as, 557

Output Area tool (FreeHand), 648

output regions (FreeHand), 721

Oval Marquee tool
    Fireworks, 267
    FreeHand, 298-299

Oval tool (Flash), 431

ovals, drawing with FreeHand, 658

over state (buttons), 585

Overflow setting (CSS Style Definition dialog box), 177

P

<p> tag, 33

padding (table cells), 125

Padding setting (CSS Style Definition dialog box), 176

Page Break setting (CSS Style Definition dialog box), 177

Page Preferences dialog box (Dreamweaver), 66

Page Properties button (Dreamweaver), 40

Page Properties dialog box (Dreamweaver), 40-43, 142

Page Range setting (FreeHand), 717

Page Rulers command (View menu), 645

page titles, 40-41

Page tool (FreeHand), 647, 655

pages (FreeHand). See also Web pages
    adding, 654-655
    child pages, 655
    duplicating, 655
    master pages, 655-656
    properties, 653
    removing, 655

Paint Bucket tool
    Fireworks, 268
    Flash, 429-430
    FreeHand, 302-303

panning, 411, 542

Pantone colors, 719

paragraph (<p>) tag, 33

Paragraph object (Dreamweaver Insert bar), 17

paragraph settings, 344-345

Param object (Dreamweaver Insert bar), 13

parent directories, 62

_parent targets, 107, 156

parsing forms, 224

Password text fields, 210

Paste command (Edit menu), 308

pasteboard (FreeHand), 645

pasting text into Web pages from files, 38-39

How can we make this index more useful? Email us at indexes@samspublishing.com

How can we make this index more useful? Email us at indexes@sampublishing.com

Tabular Data object (Dreamweaver Insert bar), 16

Tag Chooser object (Dreamweaver Insert bar), 14

tag selector, 23

tags, 5

    <!–, –> (comment), 178

    <alt>, 392

    attributes, 74

    blockquote, 38

, 33

    deprecated tags, 36

    <div>, 160

    <doctype>, 73

    Dreamweaver preferences

        code hints, 83

        code rewriting, 83-84

        color, 81

        format, 82-83

    editing in Dreamweaver

        Code view, 73-77

        Quick Tag Editor, 78-80

    <font>, 36

    highlighted tags, 77

    invalid tags, 77

    <p>, 33

    refining with CSS, 177-178

Target drop-down menu (Properties Inspector), 156

targeting, 156-157

targets, 107, 156-157

Template Properties dialog box (Dreamweaver), 256

templates

    behaviors, 258

    cloaking, 251

    compared to library items, 249

    creating, 249

        from existing Web pages, 251

        from scratch, 252-253

    creating Web pages from, 256

    defined, 249

    downloading from Web, 250

    .dwt file extension, 252

    editable regions, 253-255

    editing, 257

    importing XML into, 254

    placeholder images, 253

    styles, 258

    updating Web pages with, 257

    viewing in Assets panel, 249-250

Templates panel (Dreamweaver Assets panel), 112, 118, 249

Test Movie command (Control menu), 489

Testing Files section (Site Definition wizard), 49

testing movies, 716

text

    aligning images with, 89-91

    alternative text for images, 91-92

    break (<br>) tag, 33

    centering in Web pages, 31

    color picker, 34-36

    copying/pasting into Web pages from files, 38-39

    creating in Flash, 431-433

    CSS (Cascading Style Sheets), 36-37, 174

    drawing with FreeHand, 661

    entering into Web pages, 31

    fill colors, 456-457

    Fireworks text

        attaching to paths, 345-346

        converting to vector paths, 368-369

        creating, 339

        Find and Replace feature, 341

        horizontal scale, 345

        importing, 340-341

        indenting, 345

        kerning, 344

        leading, 345

        orienting along paths, 346

        paragraph settings, 344-345

        properties, 342-343

        selecting, 339-340

        spacing, 345

        spell check, 341

        text blocks, 344

    Flash Text, 96-98, 416

    font smoothing, 381

    form text fields

        attributes, 209-211

        creating, 207-209

        Multi Line fields, 210

        Password fields, 210

        Single Line fields, 210

How can we make this index more useful? Email us at indexes@samspublishing.com